W9-CBT-658

AMERICAN FURNITURE

1620 to the Present

AMERICAN

Elizabeth Bidwell Bates

FURNITURE
1620 to the Present

Jonathan L. Fairbanks

RICHARD MAREK PUBLISHERS
NEW YORK

Designed by Andor Braun

Typography by Fisher Composition, Inc.

LIBRARY OF CONGRESS CATALOGING IN PUBLICATION DATA

Fairbanks, Jonathan L.
American furniture, 1620 to the present.

Bibliography: p.
Includes index.
1. Furniture—United States—History. I. Bates, Elizabeth Bidwell.
II. Title.

NK2405.F34 749.213 81-3706
ISBN 0-399-90096-9 AACR2

Printed in the United States of America

Acknowledgments

MANY TALENTED PEOPLE HAVE contributed generously to this book, which could not have been done without their assistance—supplying insights, information, photographs and talents for design and production.

When research for the book was begun in the early 1970s, the study of American furniture had been enriched by exhibitions which examined with fresh vision aspects of the decorative arts almost entirely ignored by earlier scholars. Such an exhibition was "Nineteenth-Century America" at the Metropolitan Museum of Art (1970). Increasing numbers of revisionist articles in books and antiques journals soon followed. A new breed of scholars was beginning to emerge in the seventies. Drawing conclusions only after the study of primary documents and detailed examination of the furniture itself, they developed new approaches to the understanding of American furniture.

The discoveries of those who are rewriting the history of American decorative arts have contributed indirectly to the book through their articles, books and conversations, and directly, by their reading and critiquing of the manuscript. Special associates must be mentioned, as each has made important contributions in an area of special expertise.

The earliest chapters in the book were given a thorough scrutiny and revision by Robert F. Trent. He also incorporated important insights into the chapter entitled "Away from the Mainstream." Wendy Cooper, Brock Jobe, Anne Farnam and others who worked on the Museum of Fine Art's exhibition, "Paul Revere's Boston, 1738–1810" (1975), supplied information for several examples of Queen Anne, japanned, Chippendale and Federal period furniture illustrated in this book. Michael Brown critiqued and assisted with portions of the Federal chapter. Rob Emlen clarified ideas concerning Shaker furniture. The Frontier chapter evolved from an exhibition sponsored by Philip Morris, Incorporated, and the National Endowment for the Arts which was held at the Museum in 1975 and entitled "Frontier America: The Far West." Elisabeth Sussman, a special assistant for this exhibition, helped interpret and bring together furniture and other works of art from west of the Missouri River. Much information about Frontier furniture derives from lenders to this exhibition.

Jan Seidler made contributions to the Victorian chapter. Wendy Kaplan made significant and generous contributions to many of the periods of study. The contemporary chapter was critiqued by Carol Warner. The manuscript has undergone many revisions. Throughout its development, skillful and thoughtful effort was applied by Joy Cattanach, Beth Carver Wiess, Deborah Emerson, Eleuthera duPont, Deborah Shinn, the late Laurie Crichton, Karol Kaiser, Nancy Webbe, Deborah Gieringer, Margaret Moody, Deborah Hale, Ellen Abernethy, Jody Brooks, Naomi Remes and Mary Quinn. Robert Q. Walker and the late Vincent Cerbone, two furniture restorers, worked with upholsterer Andrew Passeri to restore several examples that are illustrated. Unheralded throughout the book are superb photographs of furniture owned by the Museum of Fine Arts, mostly taken by staff photographers Wayne Lemmon and Imants Ansbergs.

Many articles, books and collections served as invaluable resources for the book. The bibliography lists such materials, as they are too numerous to include here.

Without the dedication of dealers and collectors who discovered, documented and preserved American furniture, no book of this sort would be possible. By publishing many of their choices, the book celebrates their willingness to share. This book also pays tribute to numerous unnamed dealers who helped collectors. Many individuals deserve credit, especially those who made donations of furniture to museums. In order to offer the largest number of illustrations possible, names of donors who gave furniture to the Museum of Fine Arts are not repeated under each Museum picture, but rather are listed in alphabetical sequence together with names of other individuals who contributed to this book in various ways. Some prefer to remain anonymous. Titles and institutional affiliations are omitted.

Richard E. Ahlborn
The American Institute of Interior Designers, New England Chapter
Samuel Putnam Avery Fund
Stephen Baird
William N. Banks
Jerrold and Joni Barnett
Lu Bartlett
Mary W. Bartol, John W. Bartol and Abigail Clark
The Historical Department of the Church of Jesus Christ of Latter-day Saints
James K. Ballinger
Daniel Bazan
Barbara Boylston Bean
George O. Bird
George Nixon Black
Margaret B. Blackman
Miodrag and Elizabeth Blagojevich
David Blaney
Bloomingdale's
Hezekiah E. Bolles Fund
Ronald Bourgeault
John T. Bowen
The late E. Boyd
Mrs. George Brooke
John Burke
Alfred Bush
Faith P. and Charles L. Bybee
Arthur Tracy Cabot Fund
Dr. and Mrs. Benjamin H. Caldwell, Jr.
Eugene J. Canton
Nancy Richards Clark
Landon T. Clay
Robert Coates
Martha C. Codman
Helen and Alice Colburn Fund
Clement E. Conger
Mr. and Mrs. Thomas K. Connor
Georgianna Contiguglia
J. Templeman Coolidge
William J. Cressler
Laurie Crichton Memorial Fund
Carl L. Crossman
Phillip H. Curtis
Gypsy Da Silva
Ellen Paul Denker
Ronald A. DeSilva
Richard Dietrich of the Dietrich Brothers Americana Corporation
Mr. and Mrs. Michael Dingman
Eileen Dubrow
Richard S. du Pont
Mr. and Mrs. H. H. Edes
Richard Edwards
William Voss Elder, III
Nancy Goyne Evans
Dean F. Failey
Avard T. and Maude F. Fairbanks
Doris Fanelli
Dan and Jessie Lie Farber
John Fatula
Catherine Faucon
Wilson H. Faude
Donald Fennimore
Mrs. Stephen S. FitzGerald
Benno M. Forman
Julia Knight Fox Fund
Peter Freed
John Freeman
Hollis French
Donald R. Friary
L. Thomas Frye
Beatrice Garvan
James L. Garvin
Maurice Geeraerts
Mr. and Mrs. Samuel K. George, III
Craig Gilborn
Mr. and Mrs. John Gill
The Gillette Corporation
Phyllis Gilmore
Benjamin Ginsburg
Ludwig Glasser
Joyce Goldberg
Caroline Goldsmith
Anne Golovin
John Gordon
Henry D. Green
Barry A. Greenlaw
Richard N. Greenwood
Constance Greiff
Wallace B. Gusler
Roland B. Hammond
David A. Hanks
Robert B. Hanson
Mr. and Mrs. Maynard L. Harris
Sue Hazlett
Morrison H. Heckscher
Darrell D. Henning
Peter Hill
Henry-Russell Hitchcock
Mrs. Stephen J. Holmes
Graham S. Hood
Frank L. Horton
Charles F. Hummel
Jethro Hurt
Edwin E. Jack Fund
Florence S. Jacobsen
Mr. and Mrs. Timothy Jayne
Donald Jenkins
Brock and Barbara Jobe
Mr. and Mrs. Edward C. Johnson, III
Philip M. Johnston
Patricia E. Kane
Mr. and Mrs. Maxim Karolik Collection
Mr. and Mrs. George Kaufman
Roland Hammond
Myrna Kaye
James E. Kettlewell
John T. Kirk
Arthur Mason Knapp Fund
Jane B. Kolter
Edward F. LaFond, Jr.
Robert Lafond
Lagoon Corporation
Misses Aimée and Rosamond Lamb
Mrs. Horatio A. Lamb
Claire Leary
Bernard and S. Dean Levy
Taylor Lewis
Mr. and Mrs. Bertram K. Little
Margaretta M. Lovell
Randell L. Makinson
Mr. and Mrs. Richard Manney
Cathryn J. McElroy
Mr. and Mrs. Joseph McFalls
Mrs. Mabel H. F. McInnes
Dr. and Mrs. J. W. McMeel
Mr. and Mrs. Robert L. McNeil, Jr.
Christine Meadows
Mr. and Mrs. Matthew Mitchell

Christopher Monkhouse
Mrs. Charles Monstead
The late Charles F. Montgomery
Milo M. Naeve
The National Endowment for the Arts
Marion John Nelson
Dr. and Mrs. Matthew Newman
Edward E. Nickels
The Deborah M. Noonan Foundation
Richard and Jane Nylander
Jacquelyn Oak
Sarah Olson
Mr. and Mrs. Joseph K. Ott
John Page
Robert L. Parker and Margaret S. Parker
Thomas Wendell Parker
Mrs. Jefferson Patterson
J. H. and E. A. Payne Fund
Donald C. Peirce
Muriel N. Peters
Mr. and Mrs. Dudley Leavitt Pickman
Dudley Pickman
Dianne Pilgrim
Warren Platner
Jessie J. Poesch
Gail Prensky
Richard H. Randall, Jr.
Bradford Rauschenberg
Norman S. Rice
Stephen T. Riley
Alexandra West Rollins
Beatrix T. Rumford
Albert Sack
Israel Sack
Francis Gruber Safford
Robert St. George
Gordon K. Saltar
G. W. Samaha
Mr. and Mrs. Peter B. Schiffer
Karol A. Schmiegel
Marvin D. Schwartz
John P. Sedgwick
The Seminarians
Raymond V. Shepherd, Jr.
Hadas Siev
Jane E. Sikes
Stuart Silver
Clement M. Silvestro
Ellen Smith
Miss Laura Huntington Smith
Mary L. Smith Fund
Paul Smith
The Society for the Preservation of New England Antiquities
Frank Sommer
J. Peter Spang, III
Margaret Stearns
Cecilia Steinfeldt
David Stockman
David Stockwell
Mr. and Mrs. Stanley Stone
Donald Lewis Stover
Anthony A. P. Stuempfig
John A. H. Sweeney
Seth K. Sweetser Fund
Ross E. Taggart
Mrs. Pauline Revere Thayer
Robert T. Trump
Charles H. Tyler
Mr. and Mrs. Frederick Vogel, III
Mrs. Jean Frederic Wagniere
Elizabeth Walton
John S. Walton
Barbara and Gerald Ward
William Francis Warden Fund
David B. Warren
Mrs. Northam Warren
Deborah D. Waters
Dr. Katherine J. Watson
Carolyn J. Weekley
George Weissman
Linda Wesselman
Pam Wesson
Christopher Wilk
Elizabeth S. Winton
Gillian Wohlauer
Edwin Wolf, II
Edward J. Wormley
Millicent Worrell
Mr. and Mrs. Eric M. Wunsch
Joanne B. Young
Deborah Zaitchik
Anne Zeller

This list is but a token of appreciation. It is bound to be incomplete, but its length indicates the generosity and interest of those who care about American furniture.

The integrity and enthusiasm of Richard Marek, editor and publisher, made the work of all of us possible. His choice of Andor Braun as designer guaranteed impeccable taste and intellectual challenge. With unmatched dedication, Michele Salcedo has made contributions beyond words of gratitude or description. The extraordinary Dale Jagemann managed the feats of copy editing and production with grace and skill.

Special thanks are due to the families of the authors: Louise Fairbanks, whose patience and encouragement endured; Robert and Elizabeth Zenowich, who give meaning to all things.

Jonathan L. Fairbanks
Elizabeth Bidwell Bates

Contents

Introduction

THE RATE OF SURVIVAL of American furniture exceeds by far that of most other American arts and crafts. Although countless pieces have been lost or destroyed over the years, furniture was the least expendable of decorative art objects; everyone needed it. Furthermore, it was movable, in most cases sturdy and more durable than other art forms, and when of quality, it appreciated in value over the years. It was passed on from generation to generation because it served both utilitarian and aesthetic needs.

The immense quantity of surviving materials for research presents both advantages and disadvantages for the interpreter. When data is numerous, almost any theory can be illustrated through selective sampling. Conversely, this also means that exceptions to theories can be easily discovered and used to disprove a claim. Thus, this book's most important contribution is its detailed factual matter, which offers the beginning student, the serious reader or the connoisseur something more than theoretical musings.

The process of selection for illustrations was difficult. Arguments can always be made why one and not another piece or group of furniture was illustrated. Considering the vast numbers of works available, there are bound to be gaps. However, no other book on the history of American furniture is as inclusive or offers such a wide and varied survey. This book was not meant to supplant the excellent publications concerning specific collections, periods, regions or forms in American furniture. It augments and draws upon such published sources, which are listed in the bibliography; the reader is advised to consult them for more detailed information.

This book was planned to illustrate more than the well-known masterpieces so frequently published from public collections on the Atlantic seaboard. Although a representative sampling of these works is included, many superb examples from private collections are shown as well. In addition, new discoveries of both grand and modest pieces of furniture are shown together with those better known. No reader's eye can be adequately exercised without comparative examination, highlighted by an explanation of not just how one work differs from another, but if possible, why. Selection was partly based upon different regional and cultural traditions in furniture. These "dialects" of style help explicate the story of settlement and growth in America and the development of the American craft-person's skills and imagination.

Another aspect of furniture history emphasized in this book is the significance of the Victorian and post-Victorian cabinetmaker. Excellent craftsmanship did not die with the industrial boom and the advent of power machinery around the year 1840. Much shoddy furniture was made then, but the myth of the death of fine craftsmanship after 1840 was perpetuated largely because of stylistic preferences, rather than by rational analyses of workmanship. Every generation produces excellent craftsmen.

Most of the furniture pieces illustrated have extensive family pedigrees. Such genealogies have sometimes been deleted in order to offer more entries. More important than genealogies and the furniture's association with events or people is its importance in terms of style, design, structure or use of materials. This visual or unwritten history is what most of the best collectors instinctively sense when they judge the formal qualities of a table, chair or case piece.

The authors assert that there are no significant

boundaries separating the realm of fine arts from that of furniture or other crafted arts. Boundaries are only maintained by people who have a vested interest in artistic class distinctions. Such distinctions arose during the Renaissance when painters, sculptors and architects found it useful to present themselves as virtuosi, soaring above "mere" craftsmen. Today it is unproductive to continue such a pretense of hierarchy in the arts. In this book, fine furniture is discussed in terms of its formal artistic qualities of line, color, form, texture and other plastic elements. Furniture is compared with related examples of painting, architecture and sculpture. The reader will find that craftsmen are also referred to as artists. While perhaps novel for some readers, this is already a well-accepted point of view. Perhaps less familiar is the analysis of furniture as an index of social and technological evolution. Furniture styles suggest changing attitudes toward posture, comfort and social hierarchy. Tradition versus change are two threads woven through every chapter of the book. Whether overt or implied, symbolism in ornament and form is another component in understanding American furniture. Clearly the study of furniture offers many more dimensions than simply comprehending its practical uses for sitting, sleeping or storage. Beyond these necessities, furniture involves the shaping of the movable environment. At its best furniture expresses the inner world of the imagination.

Surveying the subject of furniture made and used in America is something like assembling part of this country's man-made landscape. The resultant massive jigsaw puzzle offers an abundance of both missing and extra parts. Despite the complexity of its subject matter, the book is written for the general reader. The format is chronological, but overlapping themes and movements are not always conveniently linked in strict sequence.

A major goal of this book is to encourage a broad public interest in craftsmanship. Nearly every town in this country has more to contribute to the study of historic and contemporary American furniture. We hope that the examination of both representative and unusual forms of American furniture will result in heightened appreciation and new points of departure for further research.

AMERICAN FURNITURE

1620 to the Present

I

The Beginnings

WOOD WAS THE ESSENTIAL MATERIAL out of which the New World was built. Houses were made of it; it burned in fireplaces for cooking, heat and light; buckets, barrels, tools, eating utensils, carts, wagons, ships—all were made partly or wholly of wood. And so was furniture.

Artifacts—plain or intricate, restrained or exuberant—provide some of our best means for understanding the people who settled the North American continent. Like the Indians they encountered when they arrived, the first immigrants relied on oral communication to transmit traditions from generation to generation. Many were yeomen, tillers of the soil, who survived by virtue of their practical skills. Their legacy is not contained in the written word, but in what they made and what they built.

The colonists sought to impose their traditions on the land. They felt threatened by the heavily forested landscape, so unlike the open fields of Europe, and reshaped the land into a pattern that was familiar to them.

At the same time, the New World presented the settlers with a wealth of land and timber they could never have known in their native towns and villages. In America, raw materials were cheap, and skilled labor was at a premium; coopers, joiners, turners and carpenters could revel in the new respect accorded their services as they sawed, planed and carved the timber of the vast forests.

The earliest settlers brought few objects with them on their cramped, uncomfortable voyages, but deeply embedded habits, customs and tastes were cherished. Old forms and the tools needed to make them were reproduced virtually unchanged, and persisted long after they had been abandoned "back home."

Panels
Medfield, Massachusetts. 1655.
Made by John Houghton (1624–1684) of Dedham, Massachusetts.
Oak. H: 12″ W: 8″.
Medfield Historical Society, Medfield, Massachusetts.

The Puritan meetinghouse dominated both the temporal and the spiritual lives of New England settlers. The carved oak panels shown below came from the minister's desk or pulpit of the first meetinghouse of Medfield, Massachusetts. Their maker, John Houghton, was an apprentice of John Thurston of Medfield, whose works are exactly like the joined church paneling and furniture of his native County Suffolk in England. Although New Englanders were determined to found reformed civil and ecclesiastical states, their initial material culture varied little from that of their native England.

RICHARD CHEEK, PHOTOGRAPHER

The four lilies seen on the carving above represent spiritual rebirth—from a lifeless bulb, a flower blooms. To seventeenth-century settlers, the carving represented regeneration.

Most of the Pilgrims were unsophisticated farmers and cloth workers; few were formally educated. Victims of the religious intolerance that plagued England, they sought first to build new lives in Holland, but soon became anxious that their children were not retaining English ways. Although they had struggled to achieve even marginal material security in Holland, they chose to forfeit all their gains and move to the New World.

Many Pilgrims did not survive. Already weakened by conditions aboard ship, they reached the Massachusetts coast in November

1620, to be greeted by a winter far more harsh than any they had known. They buried their dead and persevered.

Although the Pilgrims were not the first Europeans to settle in North America and archeologists have unearthed records of other settlements, Pilgrim furniture is the earliest to have survived with a strong tradition of family ownership. If these traditions can be relied upon, the earliest Pilgrim furniture is almost a generation older than datable works produced in the other colonies.

The most common Pilgrim furniture has not survived. Only objects that were owned by important figures seem to have been treasured and preserved. Our understanding of the Pilgrim world is therefore incomplete, but what survives is suggestive of complex and rich influences of trade and culture of Northern Europe upon these travelers to the New World.

Detail of Headstone
Dorchester, Massachusetts. 1681.
Slate. H: 23" W: 23".
Boston Parks and Recreation Commission.

DAN FARBER, PHOTOGRAPHER

Seventeenth-century carving in America was not limited to wood. This headstone, made for the grave of John Foster (Dorchester printer and mapmaker), was carved in durable, crosscut slate. The subject, Time staying Death's hand from extinguishing the flame of life, derived from an illustration in a book of emblems, but it was simplified and placed in a new context which gave it terrifying power. Representational subjects like this one were far rarer on New England gravestones than the more usual foliate carving. Abstract foliage (as shown on the borders) of a similar design genre is also found painted and carved on American furniture.

Tools
From Mechanick Exercises, or the Doctrine of Handyworks,
Applyed to the Art of House-Carpentry *by Joseph Moxon (London, 1679).*

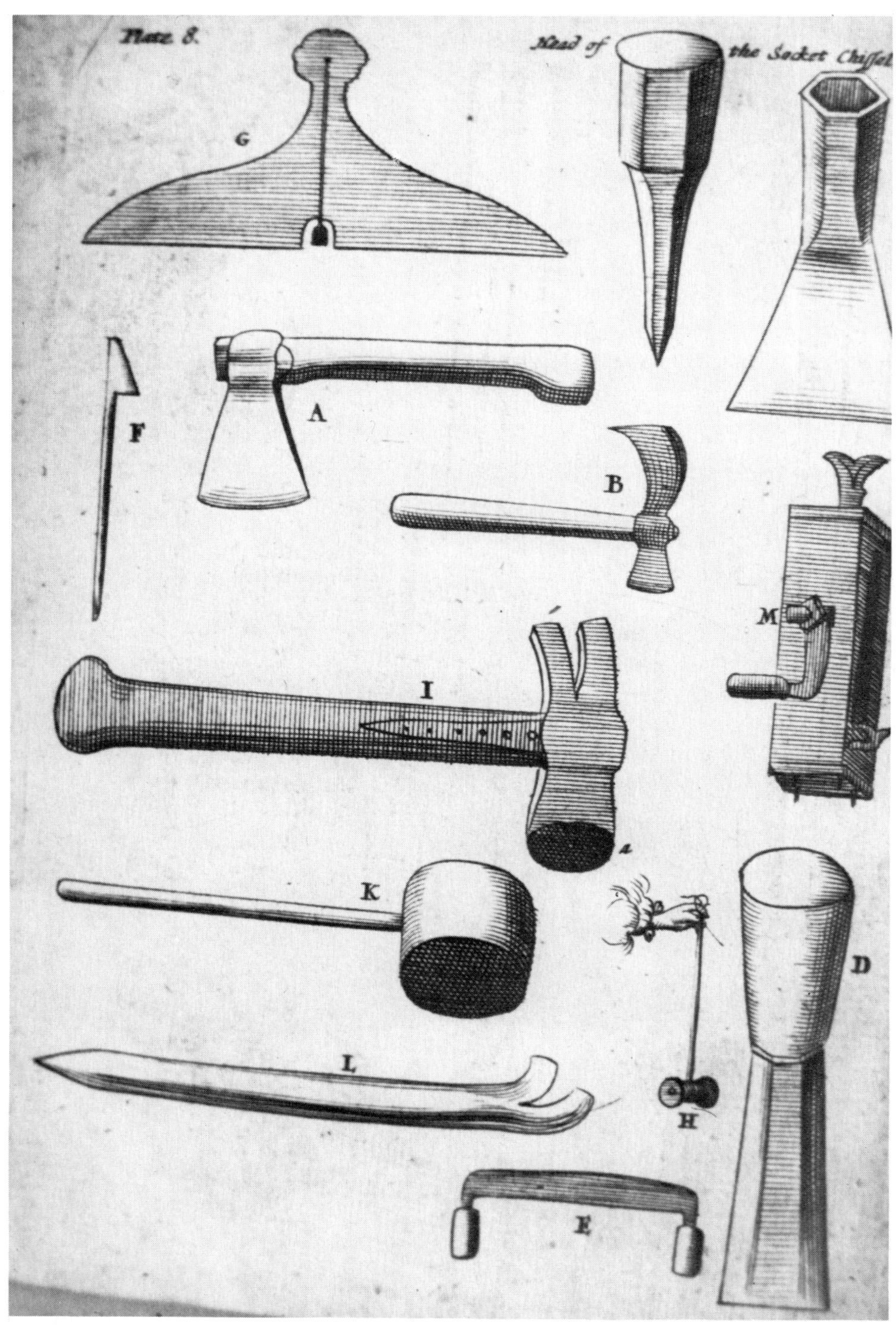

COURTESY OF THE WINTERTHUR MUSEUM LIBRARY.

In the seventeenth century, wooden products were made with fairly simple tools: saws, planes, chisels, hammers, measuring instruments, compasses and turning lathes. Skills were acquired in an apprenticeship system; a boy of thirteen or so worked with a master craftsman who instructed him in the "Art and Mysterie" of his trade. This tradition-bound, authoritarian system accounts in part for the perpetuation of old methods and styles both abroad and in provincial areas.

No period illustrations of seventeenth-century American tools survive. But from those few early tools that survive and fragments excavated from house sites, we know that colonial Americans used tools much like those in Moxon's book.

Cumbersome tools such as these were used by farmers and carpenters as well as by joiners and turners. Some tools had been refined and specialized for the making of furniture: compasses, knives, chisels, and planes with edges shaped to produce moldings. Illustrated here are only a few of the tools made for the splitting and rough-shaping of wood. One can often find the marks of these tools on hidden surfaces of furniture. Exposed surfaces were smoothed with chisels, planes, files and scrapers and sometimes finished with sharkskin and rottenstone.

Mortise and Tenon

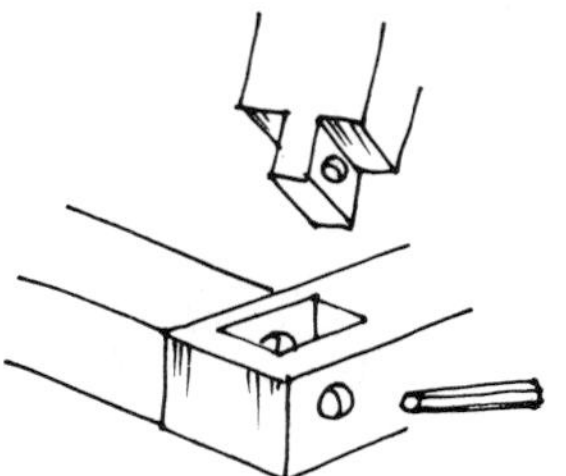

The system of mortise-and-tenon joinery and panel framing is basic to seventeenth-century construction. The mortise hole was chiseled in one piece of wood, and a tenon or tongue was shaped to fit into the space. A second hole was drilled for a whittled peg that secured the joint. Little seasoning of furniture woods was necessary with these joinery methods, which took into account the natural process of shrinking as wood aged.

Pegged Hinge. Trask Chest (page 13).

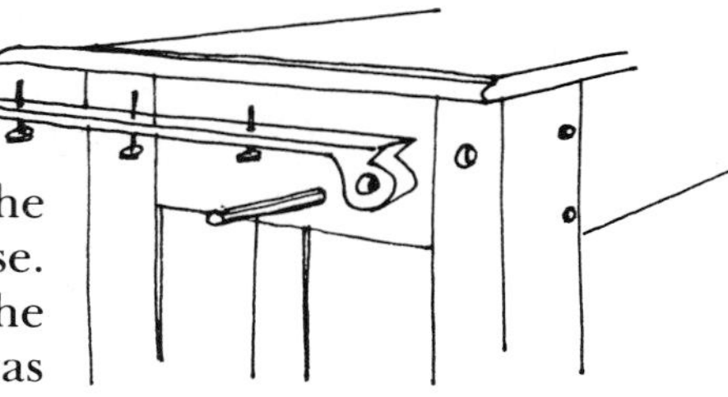

This pegged strap hinge was suitable for a box or a chest lid. The strap is nailed to the bottom of the lid—where it fits outside the case. Holes were drilled through both the strap end and the side of the piece to be hinged. A trunnel, or wooden pin, subsequently was driven through these holes.

Snipe-Bill or Go-Bent Hinge. Connecticut Chest (page 12).

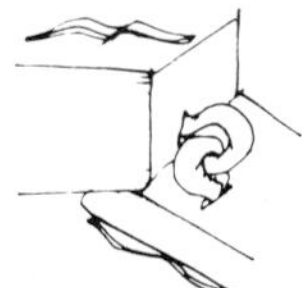

Few pieces of seventeenth-century furniture have survived undamaged after three hundred years of use. Conspicuous gouges and rust and stain marks indicate the original location of the missing parts. It is especially informative to see a piece that still has its original hinges. This hinge looks and functions much like a modern cotter pin. Pieces of heavy, handwrought wire were driven into the wood of both the box and the lid, and each piece then bent over to encircle its mate.

Lock Plate. Dennis/Searle Chest (page 14).
Iron.
Museum of Fine Arts, Boston.

Although iron parts on furniture were as scarce as uses of wood were abundant, some locks, escutcheon plates, nails and hinges were employed. The pointed outline of this escutcheon indicates the design influence of the medieval past.

An escutcheon plate was added to a chest or box to protect the wood against wear from the key. Frequently the plate was imported along with the lock works. However, over the centuries, when a key was lost, boxes and chests were often forced open, loosening the nails of lock and escutcheon plate so that many have been lost.

DRAWINGS BY ALICE WEBBER

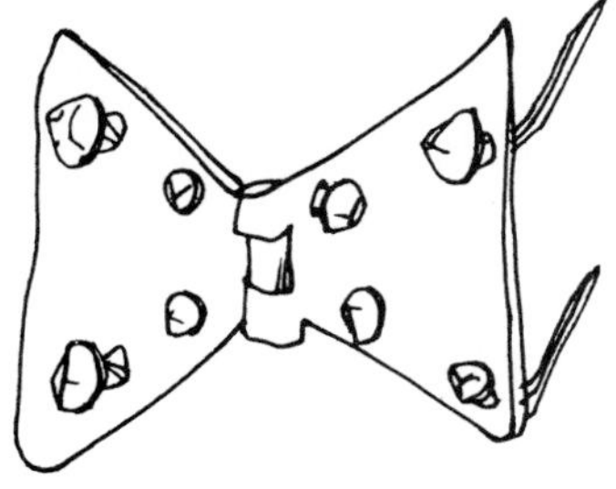

Table Hinge
Museum of Fine Arts, Boston.

The colonists were encouraged to import manufactured goods rather than make their own. Although most metal products were imported, there were blacksmiths in America who made hinges such as this, sometimes in fanciful shapes. The shape of the hinges suggested a butterfly to connoisseurs of a later age.

A space was chiseled to receive the hinge, which was secured with heavy handwrought nails. After the mid-seventeenth century, this variety of hinge was rarely used on furniture of the highest quality.

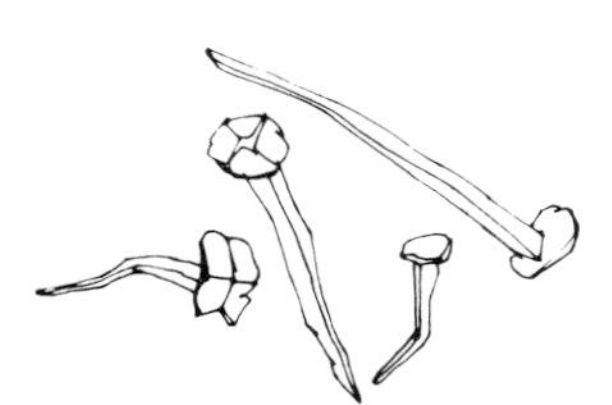

Wrought Nails

Before 1790 all nails were forged by hand. "Rose-headed" nails, commonly seen in seventeenth-century pieces, were tapered on all four sides, and the head was formed into many facets as the end was hammered over with repeated blows to form the top.

Exploded Diagram of Dennis/Searle
Chest Construction

The drawing of the chest on the opposite page gives some indication of the complexity of the joiner's craft. The form of the chest is deceptively simple, but close examination reveals techniques of great skill and craftsmanship.

Each piece was measured with a marking gauge and shaped for its specific function. When disassembled, the chest is a puzzle of carefully notched and fitted parts. The correct assemblage of the parts was indicated by Roman numerals cut with a chisel.

Before the upright stiles and horizontal rails were joined together to form the frame, they were sawn, planed, chiseled and grooved to receive the panels and muntins (vertical supporting pieces) that filled in the walls of the chest. Holes were drilled in all the joints to accommodate whittled pegs that held the chest together. Tenons were cut to fit into chiseled mortise holes. The posts which formed the legs were notched to receive the thin riven boards which were framed by rails and stiles. Bottom boards were simply nailed beneath the lower rails.

Panels, which shrink and swell in response to changes in temperature and humidity, were fitted into the frame in slots, where they could slightly shift. This eliminated stress on the panels and subsequent splitting of the wood held in place by the frames.

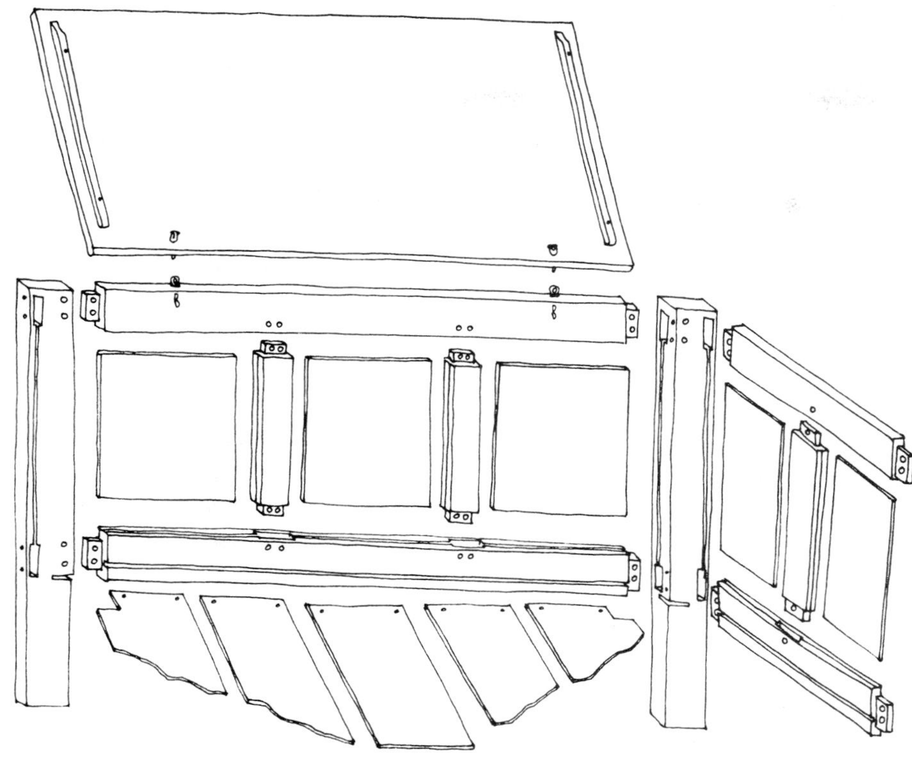

DRAWINGS BY ALICE WEBBER

House Framing
View from Inside Corner Post of the Boardman House, Saugus, Massachusetts. c. 1689.

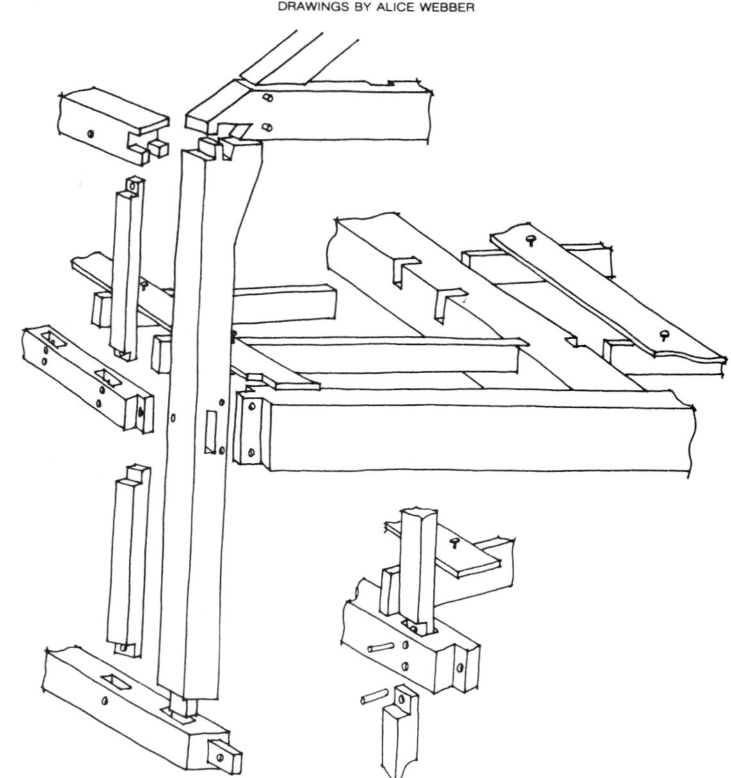

Most joiners trained in rural areas of England could as easily erect a house as make the frame of a chest or chair. Both types of structures were held together by a system of mortise-and-tenon framing—joinery held together with wooden pegs driven into auger-drilled holes.

Balusters and Spindles

Balusters, spindles and bosses were products of the turner's art. The basic lathe-turned forms were simple: the sphere and the tapered spindle, but the complex combinations of these shapes are rich in effect.

The close-grained hardwoods used for nearly all turned parts on seventeenth-century furniture were painted a jet or ebony color. This was intended to simulate the appearance of exotic woods. The results were abundant in contrasts: swells and troughs, smooth ornament against swirling textures, and glowing color against the neutral foil of deep black.

The method of turning applied spindles began with the gluing of two blocks of wood to the sides of a thin board. The composite block was then set in the lathe and turned to the desired shape with chisels and gouges. When completed, the outer pieces were soaked free of the core, producing two identical half-spindles.

Balusters and spindles were fashioned after long-established patterns. But turners developed personal preferences, and many distinct approaches to turning can be found in different areas of seventeenth-century America. The different patterns of turnings often serve to distinguish the work of individual shops.

Newbury, Mass.
1675–1680

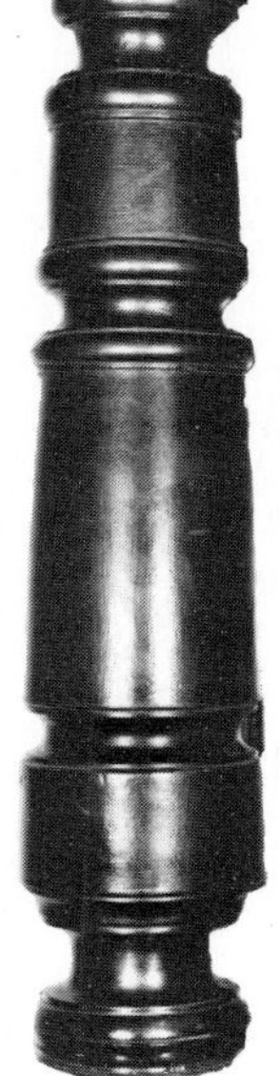

Duxbury, Mass.
1670–1695

Essex County,
Mass.
1675–1695

Wethersfield,
Conn.
1680–1700

Wethersfield,
Conn.
1680–1700

Boston, Mass.
1660–1680

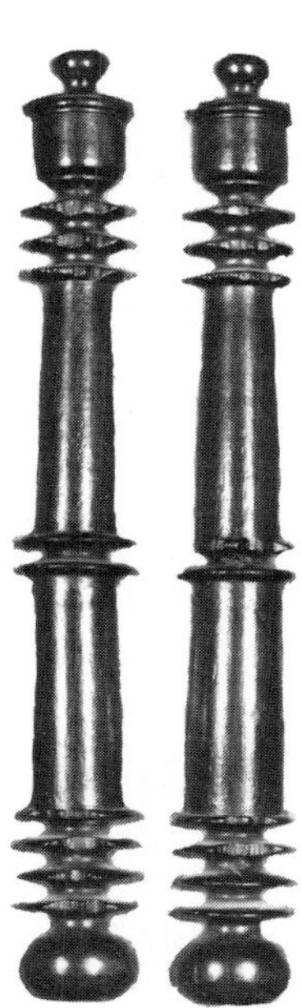

Salem, Mass.
1680–1700

Duxbury, Mass.
1670–1695

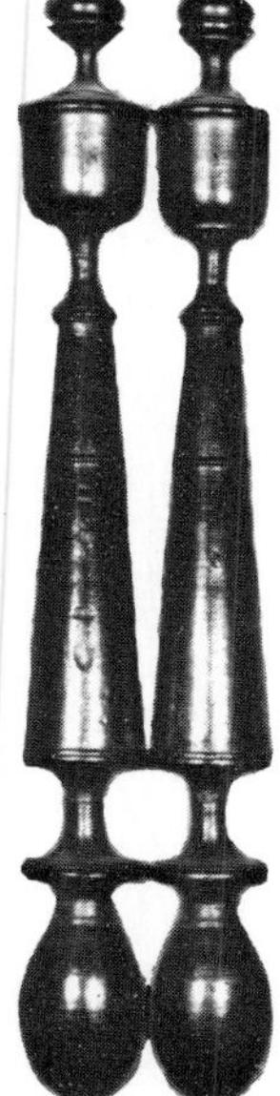

Wethersfield,
Conn.
1680–1700

RICHARD CHEEK, PHOTOGRAPHER

Chest
St. Olave's Parish, Southwark, London, England.
1550–1600. Oak, with holly and walnut veneer.
H: 23¾" W: 45¼" D: 22".
Dedham Historical Society, Dedham, Massachusetts.

Michael Metcalf, a weaver of Norwich, Norfolk, brought this chest with him to New England in 1637, when he settled in Dedham, Massachusetts. Unlike most English furniture of the seventeenth century, the chest is constructed of boards dovetailed together at the corners, and its front surface is decorated with finely made colored veneers. Inlaid work, portraying fantastic architectural scenes, and dovetailed board construction are both techniques brought to England by immigrant craftsmen from the Low Countries and from German cities on the Rhine. Thousands of such craftsmen, who were fleeing religious persecution on the Continent, brought advanced techniques and styles to ports along the English Channel and laid the basis for profound changes in the English furniture-making trades, especially in London, after 1660.

Chest
Dedham, Massachusetts. c. 1650. Attributed to John Houghton (1624–1684). Oak, pine.
H: 26 3/16" W: 41 5/8" D: 18".
Museum of Fine Arts, Boston.

The carved panels of this chest relate directly to the Medfield meetinghouse pulpit panels (page 2) John Houghton made in 1655.

The chest bears traces of its original verdigris (blue-green) paint; verdigris is the most common paint color found on furniture of this period. Traces of joiner's marks on the sides and interior allow us to reconstruct how Houghton designed and built the chest. Compass marks reveal how he laid out the pattern for carving.

PHOTOGRAPH BY WADHAMS/MAHAFFEY

Chest
New England. 1620–1660. Red oak, pine.
H: 33 7/8" W: 48 1/4" D: 23".
Museum of Fine Arts, Boston; Private Loan.

The joined chest illustrated here was believed to have been brought over on the *Mayflower* in 1620 by Edward Winslow, who later served three terms as governor of Plymouth Colony. However, recent wood analysis suggests it was made in New England. The lid and feet have been restored, but the case is substantially original. This object is another illustration of the strong parallels in decorative motif between the furniture of rural England and that made by craftsmen during the first years of settlement in New England. Chests of this type continued to be made in New England until the 1730s, although they were no longer very fashionable in England after 1660.

RICHARD CHEEK, PHOTOGRAPHER

RICHARD CHEEK, PHOTOGRAPHER

Board Chest
Probably Connecticut. 1680–1710.
Pine. H: 24″ W: 55″ D: 18⅛″.
The Mabel Brady Garvan Collection,
Yale University Art Gallery.

Chests constructed of six boards nailed together were an economical alternative to joined chests. The front of this example is enlivened by shadow moldings run with a plane and by ochre graining suggestive of exotic woods. A faint band of red paint around the edges of the front gives much the same emphasis as the frame of a joined chest.

Although wide boards were increasingly scarce in England, the forests of New England provided ample lumber for sawmills which sprang up on the numerous rivers and tidal basins. Board chests became a staple of American household furniture and continue to be made in the twentieth century.

Chest with Drawer
Marshfield, Massachusetts. 1650–1700.
Oak, white pine, cedar, maple.
H: 32″ W: 53½″ D: 20¾″.
Museum of Fine Arts, Boston.

Construction methods had changed little from the Middle Ages. Evolving taste and different places of origin are most readily apparent in the approach to ornament. Comparison of this chest with the Salem area example illustrates how variations on the same basic chest structure permitted diverse design effects.

Many chests and cupboards with panels, turnings and sawtooth detail similar to those on this chest have histories associating them with the Plymouth Colony. The black paint that fills the ground of the panels and the earth-red paint of the moldings is largely original.

Symmetry and division of surface into geometric units were the most frequent design strategies used by furniture makers of the seventeenth century. On this chest, applied spindles, bosses and other rich surface decoration were handled in an architectural manner, breaking up the rigid rectangle of the chest shape into separate compartments. This type of ornament was probably introduced into England by craftsmen who had immigrated from the Low Countries.

Chest with Drawer
Salem, Massachusetts. 1660–1690. Oak, maple.
H: 29¾" W: 47½" D: 21⅜".
New England Historic Genealogical Society, on Loan to the Museum of Fine Arts, Boston.

Most surviving examples of seventeenth-century American furniture have been altered or have lost some of their original parts.

Close inspection of this chest reveals paint in the porous oak, indicating that it was originally painted, as was customary. Ornamental bosses had been fixed to the corners of the rectangular panels, as is shown by the holes from the nails which held the bosses in place.

The chest descended in the Trask family of Salem, and is a key to identifying a Salem style of joinery.

Drawers in the bases of seventeenth-century case pieces were made of inch-thick oak boards—some as wide as fifty inches. Each ponderously heavy drawer was supported by a center runner slotted into a channel.

14

Chest of Drawers
Newbury, Massachusetts.
Carved with "ISM" and "1678." Formerly attributed to Thomas Dennis (working 1663–died 1706) or William Searle (1634–1667). Oak, maple, sycamore, walnut, tulip.
H: 42" W: 44¾" D: 19⅞".
Winterthur Museum.

This chest of drawers is one of the most famous pieces of seventeenth-century New England furniture. The ornament seems almost alive; it includes virtually every device of the joiner's design vocabulary to exercise and delight the eye. The use of elaborate turnings, moldings and carvings contradicts the stereotype of a dour, plain Puritan world.

Dated "1678" and carved with the initials "ISM" (the "I" representing an old-style "J") for John and Mary Staniford, Thomas Dennis's Ipswich neighbors, this object long served as a cornerstone of all attributions made to Dennis.

Chest
Ipswich, Massachusetts. 1670–1700.
Attributed to Thomas Dennis (working 1663–died 1706)
or William Searle (1634–1667).
Oak, pine. H: 30½" W: 44⅜" D: 19".

A carved and painted masterpiece of seventeenth-century New England joinery, this chest has panels decorated with scrolls, palmettes, tulips and leafage reflecting both medieval and Renaissance ornamentation. It is an incomparable record of taste, not only of the maker, but also of the subsequent owners, who did not tamper with it. Though somewhat faded, the original red and blue-black painted decoration remains. Unfortunately, much of the earliest furniture made in America has been denuded, stripped of its original paint. This chest offers us an unaltered glimpse of the American past.

The chest seems at first sight to be a simple example of joinery; yet all its parts are so neatly articulated that the viewer is unaware of the complex framing technique. The panels on the sides and back were left plain. The joiner probably expected the chest to be observed from the front alone.

Chest
Probably Portsmouth, New Hampshire.
Carved with "R S 1685."
Oak, pine. H: 31¾" W: 53¼" D: 20".
Museum of Fine Arts, Boston.

The glowing ochre, vermilion, verdigris and gray decoration of this chest's facade once more suggests the vitality of seventeenth-century taste. "R S" has not been identified as yet, but an identical example in a private collection carved with "J W 1684" possesses a strong history of early ownership in Ipswich, Massachusetts.

The chest also displays an extremely rare combination: a joined front with the back and sides made of plain boards. Little is known about the English precedents for this practice. But shield-shaped reserves, whiplash S-scrolls, whorl rosettes, and quadrilateral buds are all carved motifs found on furniture made in Gloucestershire, in England's West Country.

RICHARD CHEEK, PHOTOGRAPHER

Chest with Two Drawers
Wethersfield, Connecticut. 1675–1700.
Oak, maple, pine.
H: 40 1/16" W: 48" D: 21 5/8".
Museum of Fine Arts, Boston.

Chest with Two Drawers
Upper Connecticut River Valley, Hadley Area.
c. 1700. Carved with "Mary Pease." Oak, pine.
H: 41 1/2" W: 44 7/8" D: 20 1/2".
Museum of Fine Arts, Boston.

It is much easier and less complicated for a furniture maker to adapt new styles of ornament as his expression of individuality than to bring about change in a basic furniture form. So many chests with flat sunflower and tulip carving have been traced to the Hartford-Wethersfield area that they constitute a distinct regional school. There are enough variations in the carved ornament to suggest that this was a popular style to which several carvers contributed their talents and subtle innovations.

The chest from the Hadley area is conceived in a more linear design fashion than the Wethersfield chest. The carving is not contained rigidly within the borders of the panels. Instead, the surface is overrun with decoration. The owner's name, Mary Pease (1668–1746), has been carved on the center rail surrounded with interlaced tulips, pinwheels, compass work, and even stylized faces. The paint, refurbished in the twentieth century, follows seventeenth-century practice.

RICHARD CHEEK, PHOTOGRAPHER

Chest of Drawers
Boston, Massachusetts. 1670–1700. Oak, walnut and pine. H: 34¼" W: 40" D: 22½". Shelburne Museum.

Both the form and the ornament of this chest are typical of what can be considered a Boston area style of seventeenth-century furniture.

Unlike most early case pieces, this object has drawers constructed with heavy crude dovetails holding the drawer sides to the fronts. The use of walnut in fashioning the applied moldings of the drawer fronts is a second technique thought to be typical of Boston workmanship.

Such details reflect the dependence of Boston's craftsmen on London prototypes rather than on provincial English schools of furniture. In addition, many of Boston's joiners emigrated from London or were trained by joiners from London. While most early Boston furniture is not equal in quality to furniture produced by the best London shops, it does reflect refinements in technique and design.

Cupboard
Eastern Virginia. 1640–1660.
Oak, walnut, yellow pine.
H: 49¾" W: 49¾" D: 18⅞".
Museum of Early Southern Decorative Arts, Winston-Salem, North Carolina.

This is probably the earliest extant American cupboard. One of only two that survive from the South, it differs from its New England counterparts in having an open display shelf, panels made of yellow pine, and applied ornaments made of walnut.

The stark outlines of the case are enlivened by crisp, boldly turned pillars, bosses and spindles, which bring to mind the exuberance of the Elizabethan Period from which its design was derived.

Cupboard
Newbury, Massachusetts. 1680–1700.
Oak, pine, maple.
H: 58″ W: 49⅛″ D: 23″.
Gift of Mrs. J.B. Paine to the Massachusetts Historical Society, Boston, Massachusetts.

Cupboards were the most elaborately ornamented furniture of seventeenth-century America. Show pieces, the visible evidence of substance and prosperity, cupboards were owned only by the wealthy. According to contemporary usage, those with enclosed lower sections were called press cupboards and those open below, court cupboards.

Summaries of the artistic aspirations of early American joinery, these pieces present overpowering visual effects. Brilliant ebonized turnings are played off against the undulating grain of the oak. The mass of the balusters contrasts with the flatwork carving and geometric panel construction.

This piece has descended with only minor adjustments—the brass key plate and light-colored knobs have been added, but the original colors of its surfaces have not been tampered with.

Kas or Press
New York City, Kings County or Queens County.
1650–1700. Oak, with walnut inlays.
H: 70⅝" W: 67¼" D: 27⅜".
Winterthur Museum.

This large wardrobe would have satisfied the style preferences of the Low Countries of Europe. The original owner of the object probably was accustomed to heavy raised panels and intricate inlay with tulips, vines, pinwheels and zigzag geometric motifs in contrasting colors set into the oak background of the case. A fondness for inlay prevailed among Dutch furniture craftsmen far into the eighteenth century.

Large storage pieces were extremely useful in houses without closets. Chests or cupboards were considered so indispensable that they were often part of a bride's dowry, especially among families of German background.

Press
Eastern Virginia. 1680–1700. Walnut, yellow pine. H: 61⅝" W: 61¼" D: 20¼".
Museum of Early Southern Decorative Arts, Winston-Salem, North Carolina.

English habits of clothing storage were not very different from those of the Continent during the seventeenth century. Inventories of American colonists who died before 1720 often contain references to "presses," sometimes described as "a press to hang clothes in." Undoubtedly many of these were simple cases built of pine boards nailed together. Others, like this unique survivor from the South, were constructed of oak or walnut.

Architectural grandeur and functional informality are simultaneous here. The doors are of uneven width; behind the narrower door are shelves, and behind the wider one are rows of pegs for hanging clothing.

GEORGE J. EVANS, SR., PHOTOGRAPHER

Kas
Northern New Jersey. 1700–1740.
Tulip, pine of the Taeda group, red gum.
H: 69⅜" W: 62⅝" D: 24⅜".
Monmouth County Historical Association.

The Dutch love of decorative images brings the surface of this *Kas* to life. Swags of voluptuous fruit were painted in gray and white to suggest the deep carving found on high-style European examples.

Unencumbered by the spirit of Puritanic sumptuary laws, Dutch interiors were even more colorful than those of New England—enlivened by bright delft tiles and ceramics, rich textiles, paintings, prints, brass and copper. Such a *Kas* would have been full to bursting with linens and clothing.

Trestle Tables

The earliest settlers were hard pressed to convert standing timber, raw clay or fieldstone into habitable dwellings. Large families in small houses were customary—enclosed space was precious. The principal room of the house was most frequently referred to as the "hall," a verbal throwback to the great medieval hall. The clutter of household effects from the enormous variety of activities that took place in the hall made space-saving a constant problem. Knockdown furniture was one imaginative solution. These simple, practical adaptations of table forms had been in use since the Middle Ages.

The drawing is based on an enormous trestle table at the Metropolitan Museum of Art. It is one of the most monumental tables of its kind to survive from seventeenth-century New England. The board—the top of the table—is not attached, so it was easily removed from the supports, known as the frame. The trestle supports were knocked down by pulling the wooden pins from the stretcher. Turned up, the table occupied very little space and could be stored at the side of the room or in a loft or lean-to.

Trestle Table
Connecticut. 1720–1750.
Oak, maple. H: 29" W: 67⅝" D: 28¼".
Greenfield Village and the Henry Ford Museum, Dearborn, Michigan.

The construction of this table unites simplicity of design with artful joinery. The diagonal braces between the uprights and the stretcher

are later additions and should be disregarded in imagining the table's original appearance.

Despite the medieval character of its form, the table was made during the first half of the eighteenth century and served as the communion table for the Congregational Church of Lebanon, Connecticut.

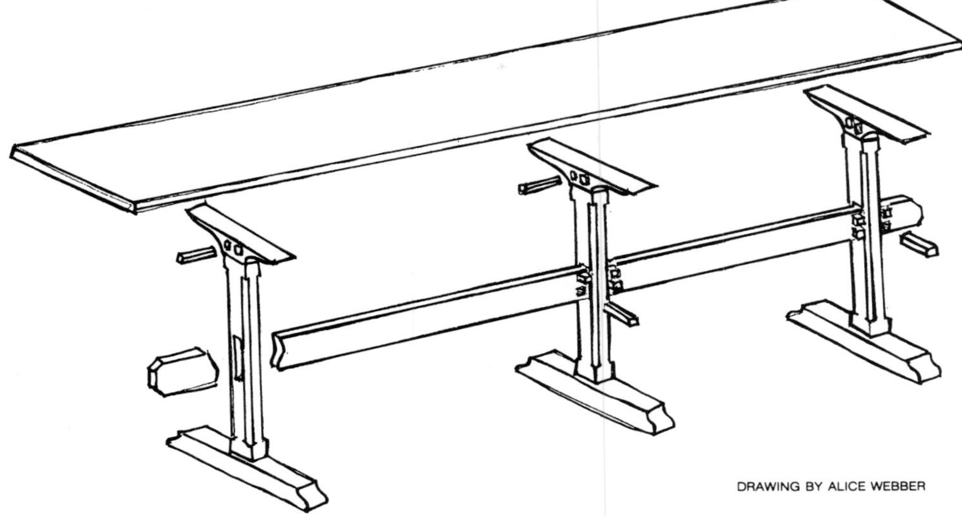

DRAWING BY ALICE WEBBER

Trestle Table
Possibly Virginia. 1700–1750.
Walnut. H: 26½" W: 47" D: 22".
Colonial Williamsburg, Williamsburg, Virginia.

A variant of the trestle table form, braced or sawbuck tables are a triumph of structural simplicity and strength. Like their trestle-based counterparts, sawbucks are easily knocked down by lifting off the table-board and removing the wedges that hold the cross-rail of the frame in place.

This example, a rare survival from the South, has the refinement of chamfered legs and rails, and its profile has been softened by centuries of heavy use.

Chamber Table
Salem, Massachusetts. Carved with "PB 1690."
Oak, maple. H: 34⅞" W: 37¼" D: 17⅞".
Winterthur Museum.

Chamber tables are one of the surprisingly refined forms to survive in some numbers from seventeenth-century Massachusetts. The case, which is ornamented with stopped panels and applied bosses, was intended to hold jewelry, combs, and other grooming paraphernalia; its interior is divided into compartments by many small partitions, as is the drawer. The reel turnings of the frame upon which the case is set are often found on case pieces made in Salem.

25

Folding Table
Essex County, Massachusetts. 1660–1690.
Oak, maple. H: 26½" Diameter of top: 36".
The Metropolitan Museum of Art,
Gift of Mrs. J. Insley Blair, 1951.

After generations of use, this unique folding table has an integrity all its own. Eighteenth-century red-and-black feather painting on the base, gray-and-white marbleizing on the top, and black coloring on the feet and balusters perfectly complement the noble form.

The table is powerful in its sculptured composition and solidity of form. The leaf and gate which allow the table to be opened up into a round surface were not, in this case, designed explicitly to conserve space. As the baluster turnings suggest, this table relates directly to the great cupboards of the period and was probably a luxury form. It would have been seen standing in the middle of a formal parlor, accompanied by large case pieces and a set of upholstered chairs. When used for dining, the table would have been draped with a white linen cloth which had been folded and pressed to produce a pattern of many small, sharply creased squares.

Draw Table
Windsor, Connecticut. 1640–1660.
White oak. H: 33⅜" L: 72⅛" D: 35⅜".
The Connecticut Historical Society.

Sturdily constructed of oak, with heavy turned balusters and an architectural flourish of triglyphs applied to the frieze, this monumental draw table is the only surviving American example of its form. It originally stood about forty inches high on turned feet. A clever mechanism once permitted flat leaves to be drawn from under the top at either end; when the leaves were fully extended, the table would have been some eleven feet in length!

The foursquare, rigid dignity of such tables might suggest that they were intended for use in meetinghouses or other public buildings, but inventories indicate that they often stood in the houses of wealthy magistrates and merchants.

Table with Leaf
Pennsylvania. 1700–1740.
Black walnut.
H: 31 5/16" W: (open) 60 1/2" D: 47 3/8".
Winterthur Museum.

The monumental proportions of this table make it seem deceptively early. It was probably made in Pennsylvania by a first-generation German craftsman, during the first half of the eighteenth century. The form is related to the great *Schranks* and dower chests produced by those of German descent until the mid-nineteenth century.

Chair-Table
Marshfield, Massachusetts. 1650–1690.
Oak, pine, white cedar; vermilion paint traces.
H: 56" Diameter of top: 47 3/4".
Collections of Greenfield Village and the Henry Ford Museum, Dearborn, Michigan.

Seventeenth-century Americans were versatile and stylish in their approach to practical problems. The generous tabletop of this chair fended off drafts when it was tipped up, and the drawer beneath the seat provided convenient extra storage space.

Basically, the object is a simple framed oak stool. The seat rail is decorated with interlaced arches, and the most elementary sort of carving enriches the wide stretchers.

As most of the furnishings and objects necessary to day-to-day living were kept in one main room, furniture was expected to perform several functions. The colonists performed the tasks upon which life was dependent in the small space of the early hall. Activities took place as close as possible to the limited warmth and light of the fireplace. We know from inventories that one could find beds, barrels, iron pots, small animals, and even lumber in the dimly lit main room of the first settlers.

DAN FARBER, PHOTOGRAPHER

Cradle
Leyden, Holland. 1610–1620.
Wicker, deal, leather.
H: 27" L: 36" W: 16".
Pilgrim Hall, Plymouth, Massachusetts.

Before hazarding the experiences of the New World, the Pilgrims spent several years in Leyden, a Dutch city. Among the furniture they brought with them to Plymouth was this Dutch wicker cradle. According to tradition, Peregrine White, the first child born in Plymouth Colony, was rocked in it aboard the *Mayflower* while the first shelters were being constructed.

The cradle has survived in an excellent state of preservation, testimony to the veneration with which this object was invested by Peregrine White's descendants. The rockers were probably replaced at a later date.

Trundle Bedstead
New England. 1720–1800.
Oak, pine. H: 19½" W: 47½" L: 62".
Museum of Fine Arts, Boston.

Turned Bedstead
Eastern Massachusetts. 1690–1730.
Black ash. H: 49½" W: 51" L: 81".
Museum of Fine Arts, Boston.

The principal knowledge we have of seventeenth-century American beds is derived from probate inventories and from European prints. Three main types of beds were used: heavy joined bedsteads with paneled headboards and turned front posts; lighter, simple bedsteads designed to be entirely covered with textile hangings, called "French" beds; and finally, turned bedsteads related in form and decoration to turned chairs. A variation on the joined bedstead was the trundle bedstead, a low, paneled frame set on wheels, intended to be stored under a larger bed during the day.

In seventeenth-century parlance, a bed was the mattress and its stuffing, rather than the frame upon which it was placed. Mattress stuffings ranged from expensive down, to less expensive flocks or chopped wool, to lowly rush, grass or straw.

In addition to the mattress, beds were customarily furnished with a heavy bolster—a round pillow set on the upper portion of the mattress. People often slept sitting up because of chronic pulmonary complaints, so the bolster would have been supplemented by one or more pillows.

The range of rich decorative hangings for bedsteads was surprisingly broad. Highpost beds could be furnished with valances hung from the tester at the top, four curtains, a headcloth, and bases suspended from the rails. Some beds were trimmed with extravagant fringes, lace, plumed finials, and fancy ribbons and tapes. Given the high price of textiles during the period, a highpost bed with its hangings was often the single most expensive piece of furniture in a household.

The turned bedstead above seems to be the only surviving seventeenth-century American example. The turnings of its posts are strongly reminiscent of table legs and newel posts from late seventeenth-century staircases. The spindles of the head and foot are very similar to those seen on turned chairs. The bedstead originally had only one turning at each foot. The lower turnings at the feet are nineteenth-century additions.

The trundle bedstead is typical of many examples which survive; they are extremely difficult to date with any certainty and probably were made virtually unchanged from 1680 to 1820.

Slat-Back Armchair
Plymouth County, Massachusetts. 1690–1720.
White oak, maple. H: 36¾" W: 20½" D: 17¼".
Museum of Fine Arts, Boston.

Hewn chairs, stools and benches were staples of European folk furniture from the Medieval Period until the late nineteenth century. This chair is in this tradition and should not be interpreted as evidence of a "frontier" aesthetic. Although any settler with basic woodworking skills could have made this chair, it is probable that such furniture was a regular product of joiners and carpenters.

The oak splats were riven from a log with a froe, and the square posts and round stretchers were worked with a draw-shave. Traces of the original Spanish brown paint remain in the grain of the wood and in crevices; the splint seat, referred to as "bast" or "plaited," is made of oak or ash strips and is old, if not original.

Turned Armchair
Perhaps England. 1600–1620.
Probably European ash; leather seat not original.
H: 47" W: 25" D: 16".
Pilgrim Hall, Plymouth, Massachusetts.

A battered relic of the first days at Plymouth, this chair is a prototype for many New England examples. According to tradition, it was owned by Governor John Carver, and such is its fame that any similar early turned chair which does not have spindles under the arms or below the seat is traditionally called a "Carver."

It was long thought that the chair was made in Massachusetts soon after the Pilgrims arrived; however, wood analysis suggests that it may be made of European ash. Since Carver in fact died only four months after he arrived at Plymouth, it seems likely that this chair is one of the few things that can be claimed to have come over on the *Mayflower*. Almost identical chairs and turnings were made in the New England colonies.

Governor William Bradford's Turned Armchair
Massachusetts. 1629–1657.
Red ash.
H: 45″ W: 24½″ D: 18½″.
Pilgrim Hall, Plymouth, Massachusetts.

One of the most elaborately turned great chairs made in America, this extraordinary survivor has physically fared better than its counterpart, the Brewster chair. Both were probably made by the same chairmaker–turner; their form, construction and dimensions seem to come from the same pattern. The Bradford chair has a history of ownership traceable to one of the most important figures of the Plymouth Colony. It is from Governor William Bradford's *History Of Plimmoth Plantation* that we have a firsthand account of the trials and aspirations of the colonists.

Wear on the lower extremities of the chair has reduced the lower stretchers to half their original size. The seat frame is mortised and tenoned through the sturdy uprights of the posts, leaving the ends of the tenons exposed. The seat is original. Upper ends of the front legs probably terminated in turned spheres, now worn away.

Turned Armchair
Plymouth County, Massachusetts. 1620–1630.
Ash (by microanalysis).
H: 45″ W: 24″ D: 18″.
Pilgrim Hall, Plymouth, Massachusetts.

Chairs of this design are frequently called "Brewster" chairs—after the original owner, William Brewster. The use of the same pattern or template indicates that pieces were made by the same person: the choice of ornament is the signature. The turnings show a high degree of skill. The repetition of the same shape in rhythmic patterns makes this the most advanced of American turned chairs.

The stature of this chair—even in its worn and incomplete state—captures the imagination. Wear, scars and missing parts all heighten one's sense of history.

Wainscot Armchair
Ipswich, Massachusetts. 1663–1667.
Attributed to William Searle (1634–1667).
Oak. H: 48½" W: 25½" D: 18".
Bowdoin College Art Museum, Brunswick, Maine.

The greatest of all known seventeenth-century American joined armchairs, this example was made by William Searle, a joiner of Ipswich who came to New England from Ottery-St.-Mary, Devonshire, where he had been trained by his father. Thomas Dennis (working 1663–died 1706), who married Searle's widow, made a nearly identical chair, which is now in the collection of the Essex Institute, Salem, Massachusetts. Dennis was probably from the same English town as Searle, since his works are in the same style, though not as accomplished.

The urn and flowers, strapwork, S-scrolls, grotesque brackets and urn finials of the chair are carved with a subtlety and finesse rarely seen in the best English work. Furniture and interior woodwork from or near Searle's native town prove this distinctive vocabulary of ornament to have been widespread in the West County of England in the last half of the seventeenth century.

Joined Armchair
Plymouth County, Massachusetts. 1620–1646.
Red oak. H: 42" W: 24" D: 17".
Pilgrim Hall, Plymouth, Massachusetts.

According to long-standing tradition, this chair belonged to Governor Edward Winslow of the Plymouth Colony. A false legend claimed that the chair was brought to Plymouth on the *Mayflower;* however, recent microanalysis of the wood shows it to be red oak, which was not planted in England until the 1690s. The existence of a number of chairs with similar detail and form suggests there was a talented joiner working in the Plymouth Colony between 1620 and 1646.

The wainscot back and strong arms set upon sturdy posts present an imposing appearance, fit for a patriarch—most suitable for the progenitor of a family that rose to enormous wealth and power in Massachusetts Bay.

The rigid profile of the chair is relieved only by a few curves on the crest and seat-rail. Some marks of a molding plane add to the decoration of the crest and soften the edges of the rails and stiles. Despite this ornament, the effect of the chair remains solid and strong. Console brackets or ears once completed the chair's crest.

Wainscot Armchair
Essex County, Massachusetts. 1670–1700.
Oak. H: 40¾" W: 23¾" D: 16½".
Museum of Fine Arts, Boston.

One of a group of six nearly identical chairs from Essex County, this chair illustrates one common form of square, wrought column used extensively during the period. The top panel of the back is ornamented with floral rosettes set within a guilloche, or never-ending spiral, but on the other chairs of the group the back panel is filled with intersecting arches or S-scrolls. The seventeenth-century attitude toward ornament was a flexible one; a variety of stock motifs could be manipulated within a single format.

The lower panel of the back probably was left blank because the seat would have been furnished with a sumptuous down cushion.

Wainscot Armchair
Freehold, New Jersey. Carved with "RIR 1695." White oak, pine of the Taeda group. H: 42¾" W: 25¾" D: 27¾".
Monmouth County Historical Association.

It is not usual for a "great chair" to have an association with a woman, yet the initials (the "I" an old-style "J") carved on the back panel of this chair stand for Robert and Janet Rhea of Freehold, New Jersey. Rhea was a Scottish joiner and carpenter who worked in the Freehold area between 1685 and 1720.

The tall, narrow back, broad seat and outward flaring arms are typical of Scottish wainscot chairs of this period. The carved grooves and chevrons of the back recall medieval "linen-fold" paneling, and the central thistle is the Scottish national emblem.

Turned Armchair
Suffolk, Virginia. 1680–1700.
Ash, white oak, juniper.
H: 38¾" W: 20" D: 17½".
Colonial Williamsburg, Williamsburg, Virginia.

Southern turned chairs differ from their New England counterparts in numerous ways. They often display many finely turned spindles and a form of turned or cut-out arm which protrudes over the tops of the front posts. This may be the result of the English regional origins of Southern craftsmen. Compare it to the Brewster chair (page 31).

The basic heavy mass of the chair is enlivened by many subtleties which are not at first apparent. The four posts gently taper from the bottom to the top, and they are set at a slight cant which lends the overall form a racy stance.

Chair
New York City. 1640–1660. Cedrela (Spanish cedar).
H: 36½" W: 15¾" D: 15".
Museum of the City of New York.

This rugged chair was once owned by Sara Rapalje, considered the first European child born in New Netherlands. The sturdy triangular blocks pegged in at the joints permitted the chair to withstand heavy abuse. The leather of the seat is neatly shaped around the rear posts. The rear posts are subtly shaped to accommodate the chair's occupant, in a way which might not at first be apparent. Similar chairs appear in many seventeenth-century Dutch genre paintings.

Slat-back Armchair
Eastern Long Island, New York. 1680–1720.
Maple, ash, hickory.
H: 46″ W: 26⅜″ D: 21¼″.
Winterthur Museum.

The complex turnings and shaped back slats of this magnificent chair relate directly to Dutch prototypes. Joiners and turners trained in Dutch woodworking traditions continued to work in the New York area after the conquest of New Netherlands in 1664. Although this example shows the Dutch tradition at its peak of vigor, some chairs made in New York and New Jersey as late as 1850 display mixtures of Dutch and English design elements in their composition.

Leather Armchair
Boston, Massachusetts. 1660–1670.
Oak, maple.
H: 38″ W: 23⅝″ D: 16⅜″.
Museum of Fine Arts, Boston.

An impressive, throne-like chair, which belonged originally to Dr. Zerrubabel Endicott (1637–1683-4) of Salem, Massachusetts, this is the sole surviving upholstered New England armchair from the seventeenth century.

The frame, which bears economical ball turnings, is punctuated by rows of bright brass nails which emphasize the upright contour of the object. The cushion on the seat, covered in wine-colored velvet and tassels, is a reproduction based on those seen in many prints and paintings of seventeenth-century interiors. It allowed the chair's occupant to adjust his position in relation to the back and epitomizes the near-Oriental texture and color with which people were fascinated during this period.

PHOTOGRAPH BY WADHAMS/MAHAFFEY

RICHARD CHEEK, PHOTOGRAPHER

Joint Stool
Plymouth County, Massachusetts. 1670–1690.
Oak, pine.
H: 19¼" W: 13½" D: 12¼".
Museum of Fine Arts, Boston; Private Loan.

The stout construction of seventeenth-century frames is apparent in this simple joint stool. A necessary part of most interiors, stools were used as tables as well as for seating.

Centuries of use of this rugged frame have worn down the feet. The pine top is a replacement; originally a thick oak plank with a molded edge was pinned to the frame.

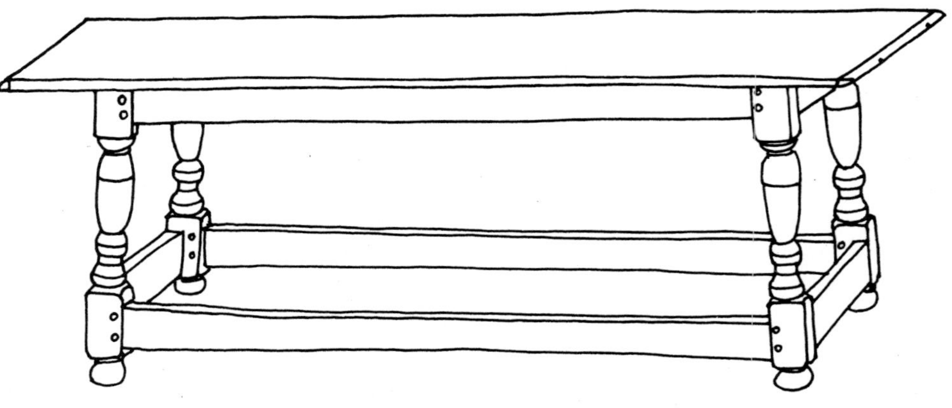

DRAWING BY ALICE WEBBER

Form

A form was essentially an extended version of a joint stool. Forms were used in conjunction with long joined or trestle tables. The strong communal associations of two or three people sitting on a single bench hark back to the great central halls of medieval houses; these same associations stand in marked contrast to the use of individual chairs, which became widespread in the eighteenth century.

Leather Chair
Boston, Massachusetts. 1675–1695.
Oak, maple.
H: 32 3/8" W: 17 7/8" D: 15 1/8".
Museum of Fine Arts, Boston.

GEORGE FISTROVICH, PHOTOGRAPHER

Thousands of leather, turkey-work and cloth-upholstered chairs like the one shown here were made in Boston for local use as well as for export to the other English colonies of the North American mainland and the Caribbean. They were sold in sets of six, twelve—even eighteen. Most New England examples are virtually identical to the London-made chairs after which they were modeled, save that they are fashioned of native maple and oak rather than the European beech used by English chairmakers.

The chair is shown prior to restoration. The leather back is shattered, and a trim strip around the seat is missing, as are the turned feet. The back and seat are stuffed with twisted grass and lined with canvas.

Chair
Philadelphia, Pennsylvania. 1680–1704.
Walnut. H: 39 1/4" W: 18 7/8" D: 19 5/16".
Winterthur Museum.

The type of ornament seen on this chair—elaborate twists of wood producing ripples of light and shadows, and known during the period as "twist turn'd"—came into fashion at Charles II's court in the mid-1660s. It quickly entered into the ornamental vocabulary of London craftsmen and was brought to Philadelphia in the 1680s.

Some turners possessed the lathe attachments which permitted them to produce twist ornament by machine, but most chairmakers resorted to skillful use of a round rasp to make it.

This is a surprisingly fashionable object to have been made and used in Philadelphia a few short years after the town was established. It would have been used with a heavy down cushion, which filled the visual gap between the seat and the back.

Oil on Canvas
"Mrs. Elizabeth Freake and Baby Mary."
Boston, Massachusetts. 1674.
H: 42½" W: 36¾".
Worcester Art Museum, Worcester, Massachusetts,
Gift of Mr. and Mrs. Albert W. Rice.

This sensitive masterpiece of early New England portraiture shows every detail of finery in dress, jewelry and furniture that a delicate hand could convey. The painter had little feeling for light and shadow, but he was a master of line and color.

The faithful rendering of what the painter saw adds dimension to our awareness of seventeenth-century Boston's taste. The fondness for complex, ornamental patterns, like those shown on Mrs. Freake's lace, relates directly to the design sensibility which delighted in strapwork carving. The deep colors are glowing, much like those of the Dennis chest of drawers (see page 14).

The inventory of Mrs. Freake's husband, John, proves that the Freake household actually contained turkey-work chairs like the one in which Mrs. Freake is seated, resplendent with fringes and tassels.

Turkey-Work Couch
Boston, Massachusetts. c. *1698. Maple, oak. H: 46½" L: 60" D: 21".*
Essex Institute, Salem, Massachusetts.

Even in its worn and faded state this turkey-work couch evokes a colorful image of luxury.

One of two upholstered New England couches to survive from the seventeenth century, it has the added distinction of retaining its original brilliantly colored upholstery. The covering, called "turkey work" during the period, was a woven, knotted pile fabric imitating textiles from the Middle East; it was manufactured in England and was used as upholstery material for seating furniture and cushions, and for table carpets and bed hangings.

The upholstery shows the geometric pattern of the colored portions of the pile. The coarse hemp ground that is exposed was originally filled with black wool pile, which has disintegrated.

The couch belonged originally to John Leverett (1662–1724), president of Harvard College from 1707 until his death.

It was accompanied by a dozen turkey-work chairs during its use in the Leverett household.

II

1690–1725

The William & Mary Period

Age of Cabinetmaking

BY THE 1660S, fundamental changes were taking place in England which resulted in the Anglicization of the American seaboard. When Charles II ascended the throne in 1660, new design ideas and a mixture of stylistic crosscurrents were brought to England from the Continent. While in exile (1645–1660), Prince Charles and his courtiers were exposed to art in Holland and France when these countries were in their golden age as centers of brilliant and revolutionary thought. A passion developed for reasoned understanding based on observed experience, as opposed to earlier traditions of absolute or divine law. The study of nature and perception of light offered challenges to the intellect and visual pleasure to the observer. Great minds in both science and the arts became excited over optics and the observation of nature, which resulted in the establishment of such institutions as the Royal Observatory at Greenwich for the scrutiny of the heavens and for the perfection of navigation.

The science of optics in turn contributed to new adventures with the effects of light and shadow in painting, architecture and the decorative arts.

Fresh ideas were expressed in furniture design by discarding the old system of construction. The traditional method of joining and pegging oak panels within frames had been standard English practice since the Middle Ages. But after hundreds of years, this system was replaced by a new method which employed exotic-looking burled veneer glued onto pine plank backing boards. With this new system it was no longer necessary to nail or butt heavy oak drawer sides to even heavier fronts. Instead, finely cut dovetails made it possible to frame drawers and chests made of thinly sawed pine. This lighter construction encouraged greater height and more freedom of design than had before been possible. A new term, "cabinetmaker," came into use in order to distinguish the craftsman practicing this new system from the old-fashioned joiner of wooden panels.

Carved and turned ornament in furniture reflected the ornateness of the current fashions, even to the multitude of curls found on fashionable men's wigs. While courtly manners and tastes were not immediately adopted in America, there were more than a few individuals able to afford the latest mode. The kind of ornament which was to become fashionable in American furniture included sculptural foliate detail and elongated cone-shaped turnings as the major ornamental devices of what is somewhat inaccurately called the William and Mary style. William of Orange and Mary Stuart unquestionably had a profound impact upon the arts after the Glorious Revolution of 1688, for they reinforced the influence of Dutch craftsmen and designers in England. But attempts to explain style change closely through political reigns invariably oversimplify the story.

Charles II and his followers brought to the English court not only design influences from Holland and France but more widespread foreign influences as well. Through his marriage with the Portuguese princess, Catherine of Braganza, new elegance and taste were introduced to English society, which in many ways had remained backward-looking for centuries. Development of world trade and taste for Eastern exoticism was encouraged by Catherine and her entourage. The Portuguese trade brought tea, porcelain, spices and lacquer from the Far East. Competing nations, eager to capture the Eastern market, granted generous concessions to their own companies: The East India Companies of Holland, France, England and Denmark. Independent of government control, these companies sent ships around the Cape of Good Hope to Batavia and India for cotton, opium and raw silk. From Ceylon came cinnamon, coffee and ivory. From Sumatra came pepper and spices, exotic woods, lacquer and silk. Tea and porcelain came through trade with the Philippines, Korea and China.

At first the impact of Eastern trade goods on European arts was felt only in court circles where great wealth was essential to command these precious treasures from afar. But as a rising class of merchants accumulated sizable fortunes, court fashions were imitated both abroad and in the provinces. The furniture in America which most closely followed the extravagances of court ornamental carving has often had its arched and pierced stretchers termed "Portuguese" in recognition of the influence that Catherine of Braganza had in shaping English fashion. Carved tassel or paintbrush-like feet on furniture of this period have also been attributed to Portuguese influence, although they are more often referred to as "Spanish feet." Whatever the stylistic sources for early eighteenth-century furniture in America, its energetic forms followed a vigorous period of international exchange. The merchant class acquired newly imported goods from London whenever possible. American furniture was made to look as if "lately from London." By the end of the seventeenth century the merchant's power even exceeded that of the clergy. The trade situation became so favorable to colonial merchants that the English Board of Trade recommended overhauling the entire system. But then, as now, no set of governmental rules could prove truly effective in controlling the force of new ideas and opportunities in the marketplace and the arts.

As social roles became more structured, the individual began to exercise greater effort to control his place in society, his piece of land and his profession. He was keenly aware that the design of his home and furniture gave clear messages of his status to his neighbors. By the early 1700s, well-to-do colonists were no longer satisfied to merely add a room or wing onto their homes as the demands of growth dictated. Formal order and symmetry became design imperatives, expressive of the rational, logical world of eighteenth-century thought. Symmetry and order demanded not only a balanced facade and central entry hall to a building, but also dictated symmetrically divided rooms with specialized functions. Furniture was made to be placed in balanced arrangements, a further way of expressing rational thought. A natural result was the development of new specialized forms of furniture: the daybed or long bench with a backed end usually made to tilt; dressing table; high chest or chest on frame; easy chair; compartmentalized desk; high-backed chair; tea table; spice chest;

japanned high and low chests on turned frames. For the most part the construction of these pieces was light and they often seemed almost to float in defiance of gravity. Their proportions were compressed vertically like the tall sash windows of the early eighteenth-century American home. The design of furniture reflected the early eighteenth-century sense of scale and proportion, which moved away from the seventeenth-century horizontal to the eighteenth-century vertical axis.

The taste for the tall shapes of furniture of this period has also been identified with the attenuations of the Mannerist style, which was transmitted from sixteenth-century Italy to the Low countries and from there to England by the seventeenth century.

The ornament of William and Mary furniture is stylistically more advanced than the furniture's overall form. Instead of being Mannerist, the ornament is Baroque in style. Its richly inlaid surfaces, bold C-scroll carving and deep turning are alive with movement within the confined border of symmetrical frameworks. With its energetic spirit, play of light and shadow and optical richness, the ornament of William and Mary furniture in Colonial America owes its aesthetic forms and design techniques to the seventeenth-century art of Northern Europe, especially to the gifted Huguenot designers and craftsmen who left France with the revocation of the Edict of Nantes, and migrated to Holland, England and America.

The William and Mary style dominated furniture design only briefly in this country. Its relative rarity and close approximation to English furniture of the late seventeenth century make this period of American furniture little studied, seldom collected, and much misunderstood. William and Mary furniture is exciting, for it forms an important point of transition from the late-medieval to the modern world, is completely expressive of its time, and provides much visual pleasure.

Comparison: Drawer Sides, 17th- versus 18th-Century Construction

RICHARD CHEEK, PHOTOGRAPHER

Drawer
Massachusetts. c. 1680.
Oak and pine.
H: 5¾″ D: 20″.

Drawer
Massachusetts. 1700–1730.
Walnut and pine.
H: 5½″ D: 18¼″.

Two basically different approaches to the design and construction of early furniture are illustrated by contrasting the sides of these two drawers. In the seventeenth-century drawers thick planks of oak have a slot running lengthwise. A wooden runner projecting from the frame of the drawer opening fits into this slot. The sides of the drawer were butted and nailed, and the bottom was a simple pine slab nailed into place. Rudimentary dovetail construction was introduced in the last quarter of the seventeenth century. By the turn of the century those who used dovetail construction began to call themselves cabinetmakers rather than joiners. The bottom drawer, from an early eighteenth-century chest, shows the refined use of dovetails. This allowed the craftsman to use thin board construction together with elaborately veneered front surfaces.

Brass handles or drawer-pulls were introduced on American furniture early in the eighteenth century at the same time as dovetail construction and lightweight drawer fabrication made them practical. The visual variety that brasses added to a piece of furniture was important. They punctuated the surface of a design with glitter and lively movement in much the same way as burled veneer, japanning or painted ornament did.

Six-Board Chest
New England. Dated 1715.
Marked "I S." White pine. H: 27½" W: 48" D: 20".
Wadsworth Atheneum, Hartford, Connecticut.

Six boards are butted, lapped, nailed and hinged together to form this chest. Simplicity and the sensible use of material insured the survival of this form from the Middle Ages through the nineteenth century in both America and in Europe.

The chest appeals through the directness of its construction. However, the desire of its builder to make something more than an ordinary box elevates this chest from the class of a merely useful object to an imaginative and compelling piece. Much of its charm, of course, comes not only from the directness of workmanship but the effort of its maker to scribe and punch a decorative message on the otherwise plain face. Hearts, tulips and the unidentified owner's initials "I S," together with the date "1715," are punched in expressive starlike patterns in an arrangement reminiscent of a plan for a formal garden.

In the early years of the eighteenth century, furniture evolved from heavyset chests with a low center of gravity toward more elevated, lighter case pieces supported on turned frames. These illustrations summarize the evolutionary trend, but the choice of examples used is purely arbitrary. There are no real connections of direct descent between any of the pieces compared; the evolutionary idea is implied rather than real. While change did take place over time, the introduction of a new form like a desk on frame did not necessarily eliminate the need for chests.

Chest with Drawer
Guilford-Saybrook Area, Connecticut. 1700–1720.
Pine top, oak framing, tulip and chestnut panels.
H: 34½" W: 48" D: 20¼".
Collections of Greenfield Village and the Henry Ford Museum, Deerborn, Michigan.

This is an excellent example of a type of decorated chest produced along the Connecticut shore of Long Island Sound from Guilford a few miles east to the mouth of the Connecticut River at Saybrook. The initials "A S" painted at the center of the upper panel are those of the original owner who is as yet unidentified.

The maker of this chest was conservative, for in the shape and framing of its panels, seventeenth-century traditional construction methods remain unchanged. Yet there is a gesture toward vertical movement with the addition of a drawer at the base. This chest represents an intermediary step from a lidded box form to a chest of drawers. In more sophisticated towns, elaborately supported chests of drawers on turned frames were being made while this form of chest, made in a country village, changed very slowly.

The painted decoration shows the ornamentor's creativity. The profuse, crewel-like painted design covers the surface and obscures the somewhat old-fashioned character of the chest's joinery. On a blackish-green ground, the painter filled the spaces with yellow, red and green vines, flowers, and abstract dots and scrolls. Hardly an inch is left undecorated. Even the side panels show exotic-looking birds with long, prehistoric-looking necks and bumblebee bodies, soaring with wings outstretched.

Chest with Drawer on Frame
Eastern Massachusetts. 1700–1720.
Oak, pine. H: 35" W: 30¼".
Collection of the Brooklyn Museum.

Once owned by the Hancock family, this chest represented a new development in furniture. Its open stretcher base with turned members supporting the case illustrates the vertical proportions in furniture that became pronounced after 1700. This was the essential first step toward the introduction of large cases of drawers on elaborately turned bases now known as "highboys."

The chest's most remarkable feature is its rich original painted surface. The front panels are vermilion-colored with arching trees painted in deep brown and muted white. Ebonized moldings surround the panels and provide a contrast to the lively exotic graining painted on the rest of the chest.

Chest of Drawers
Perhaps Philadelphia Area. c. 1700.
Walnut; drawer linings: chestnut.
H: 38½" W: 45½" D: 23".
Philadelphia Museum of Art.

Furniture of this early style is not often found in eastern Pennsylvania. The facade of the chest with its geometric molded panels suggests seventeenth- rather than eighteenth-century style. But large dovetail construction of the drawer sides indicates that it is the work of an eighteenth-century cabinetmaker rather than a joiner. Removal of later additions of bracket feet revealed the original ones shown in this picture, formed by an extension of the chest's framing to the floor. The brasses are not original.

Chest of Drawers
Philadelphia. Signed and dated "William Beakes 1711."
Walnut; secondary wood: long-leaf pine.
H: 40¼" (top) D: 22" (top).
A Chester County Collection.

Documented early eighteenth-century furniture from Philadelphia is rare, but even scarcer are signed and dated pieces with their original finishes. This chest of drawers is an important document of Middle Colonies' taste.

Its maker, William Beakes, was apprenticed to William Till of Philadelphia in 1694. Beakes came to Philadelphia from Bucks County, near "Pennsbury," where his father had purchased a thousand acres of land from William Penn. The chest descended in the family of Samuel J. England of Oxford, Chester County.

The chest, "of the best sort, but plain," is beautifully made and designed, with handsome graduated drawers bearing their original escutcheon plates. As with the 1707 Edward Evans scrutoire, the design emphasis is suave, bold molding. The feet are a massive 6¾ inches high and 5 inches in diameter. They are shaped like small urns and greatly contribute to the piece's successful design. On top of the chest are a pair of early eighteenth-century imported brass candlesticks and a two-handled English delft posset pot of comparable date. Posset pots were used to serve a spiced hot alcoholic beverage ceremonially, each person in turn sucking the hot milk, curdled with ale, through the spout.

GEORGE FISTROVICH, PHOTOGRAPHER

RICHARD CHEEK, PHOTOGRAPHER

Chest of Drawers
Chester County, Pennsylvania. 1720–1760.
Walnut; secondary wood: tulip.
H: 40" W: 43½" D: 22".
Collection of Mrs. Charles L. Bybee.

This type of vine-and-berry inlaid tulip motif is characteristic of Chester County cabinet-making. However, examples of work of this monumental size and ornateness are scarce, and seem to represent a fairly conservative tradition of inlay work which persisted in the Delaware Valley and moved southward into Virginia and western Pennsylvania with the migration of craftsmen late in the eighteenth century.

Opinions differ concerning the date when this inlay work was most popular. There are some dated works surviving from the 1730s, and these design motifs persisted through the eighteenth century.

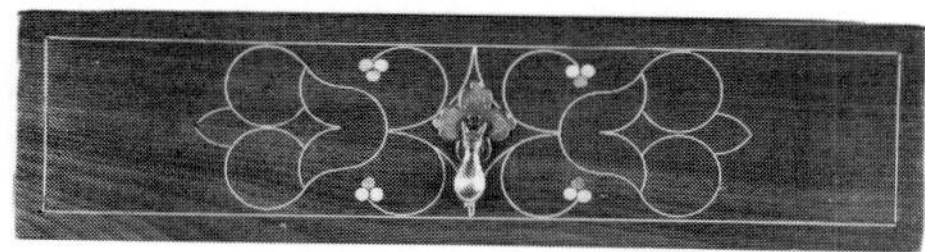

Chest of Drawers
Eastern Massachusetts. 1710–1720.
Painted pine.
H: 43″ W: 38½″ D: 20¾″.
Collection of Mrs. William Clay Ford.

Problems engendered by the new dovetail drawer construction had been resolved by the time this chest of drawers was made. Even so, the joinery of the front of the drawers with its sides is fairly crudely done—simply butted and joined with a single giant dovetail nailed to the facing plank of the drawer for greater security. The sides of the chest are great pine slabs held together at the bottom with sturdy cross members. Despite the fairly crude construction, the chest itself, with its painted surface, has a delicate appearance.

A number of similar painted chests survive and have been called "Harvard chests." However, the brick buildings pictured on the drawer have no connection with any actual structure built at Harvard College.

The painted design of white and red lines on a black ground simulates the effect of japanning, or imitation lacquerwork, in paint. This design is a spirited example of early New England folk or provincial art which has parallels in needlework designs, engraving on silver, and tombstone ornament of the period.

Chest with Drawers
Coastal Connecticut. Dated 1724.
Tulipwood.
H: 47¼" W: 42½" D: 20".
Winterthur Museum.

The new emphasis on vertical proportions was made possible by the introduction of dovetail construction, which allowed for the stacking of banks of lightweight drawers.

In this example, the new verticality is expressed through the two sets of drawers which are framed below a lidded chest. Earlier chests customarily had a single set of drawers and a lower center of gravity.

The chest's painted ornament commands admiration. The surface is covered with cream and black vine and tulip motifs firmly outlined and balanced around a central axis. A small central panel depicting architectural forms is a vestige of wooden inlay decoration featured on sixteenth-century nonesuch chests from London (see Metcalf chest, Chapter I, page 10).

ROBERT ST. GEORGE, PHOTOGRAPHER

Chest-on-Frame
Signed by Edmund Titcomb, d. 1723,
Newbury, Massachusetts.
c. 1700. Case, drawers: white pine; feet, scrolled legs: maple. H: 51 1/8" W: 42" D: 21 1/4".
Collection of Historic Winslow House Association, Marshfield, Massachusetts.

As recently as 1969, the location of this key specimen of the cabinetmaker's art in New England was not known to furniture historians. It was recognized as one of the rare signed and documented examples of the second major style of furniture making in this country. The chest's design shows a dramatic movement toward vertical composition. It is lifted off the ground with a curvilinear stand that reflects the energy of Baroque art. The flat S-scrolls of its base suggest that the maker, Edmund Titcomb, must have been well aware of fashionable London design, which by the 1660s had been strongly influenced by immigrant designers and craftsmen from the Low Countries. The Anglo-Flemish traditions reflected in this piece are remarkably sophisticated, considering that the town in which it was made was a very modest rural village well into the eighteenth century.

While the overall form of the chest and its moldings and brasses are sophisticated, the finish and construction is simple and coarse. It is stained or painted a simple dark-brown color. The maker economized by not using expensive veneers. The chest's strong silhouette and dramatic base make the work successful.

Oil Painting
"Pieter Schuyler, New York." 1700–1710.
The Mayor's Office, Albany, New York.

This portrait of Pieter Schuyler (1657–1724), mayor of Albany and commander of its fort, epitomizes the style that dominated all the arts in early eighteenth-century America.

The portrait presents an imposing, vigorous image. Schuyler's stance is formal, stiff and authoritarian. His wig is formally parted in the middle, his figure ornately clothed, his feet firmly positioned. Furniture of the period had a similar stance. The ornate crestings of chairs and cornice moldings of case pieces correspond to the elaborate wig worn by Schuyler. His massive body is comparable to the case of a chest of drawers. In both painting and furniture ornamental surface is emphasized and symmetry maintained. Long rows of buttons punctuate Schuyler's coat in almost the same way that rows of brasses arrest attention on high chests. The lower edges of Schuyler's coat and britches form a stylized arch as delightful as the arched skirts of William and Mary high chests. Schuyler's legs seem turned of wood rather than formed of flesh. His polished black shoes seem to parallel the ebonized ball feet frequently found beneath the stretchers of chests on frames. The horizontal element of the stretchers may correspond to the fringe at the bottom edge of the table in the painting. Such comparisons may seem fanciful, yet they indicate a design preference shared by both the fine and decorative arts during this period.

Turned Leg on High Chest of Drawers
Massachusetts. 1700–1720. Maple.
Collection of the Museum of Fine Arts, Boston.

Superb turning is the earmark of quality in early eighteenth-century furniture. In order to communicate variations of turnings, descriptive terms are used today which were not used in the eighteenth century. Cup-turned, bowl-turned, trumpet-turned and serpentine and scroll legs are the most popular terms for the different supporting members of high chests. This leg is cup-turned. It tapers smartly toward its lower end with an inverted baluster terminating the leg at the stretcher. The stretcher is lap-jointed at the corner, drilled at this point, and a dowel or wooden pin joins the leg to the turned foot. The construction system is quite fragile; thus relatively few high chests of this style survive.

High Chest of Drawers
New York City, Kings County or Queens County.
c. 1700. Gumwood, tulip, pine and oak.
H: 58" W: 45" D: 24½".
Metropolitan Museum of Art, New York.

Early settlers of New York, Long Island and New Jersey brought with them strong Dutch and Flemish traditions of furniture design, influenced by French Huguenot immigrants to the Low Countries. Baroque spiral twisted legs such as these are rarely found in American furniture. The chest's flat top, shallow cornice and simple arched moldings suggest the piece was made very early in the eighteenth if not late seventeenth century.

High Chest of Drawers
New England, Probably Massachusetts. 1700–1720.
White pine frame, burled maple veneer,
walnut borders; legs have been altered.
H: 58" W: 40½" D: 23".
Winterthur Museum.

Although this veneered New England high chest and the chest from New York share almost identical organization of parts, the visual effects they convey are strikingly different. Both chests have the early feature of a single, arched molding separating the drawers. Both have the early and rare form of a single horizontal drawer just below the separation between the upper and lower cases. Such a division was necessary to make it possible to move the chest without damage to the legs and feet. Furniture of this period was designed with mobility in mind.

In contrast to the plain skirt of the New York high chest, this one has a set of three arches, providing a graceful transition from the vertical element of the legs to the broad horizontals of the case. This gives the composition a vertical lift, which creates the impression that the drawers sit lightly on the turned base. The cabinetmaker of this piece took full advantage of the veneer's lively pattern and manipulated it to accent the drawer-pulls and escutcheons. The surface of the veneer has depth and shimmer reminiscent of seaweed in deep water or the translucent qualities of tortoiseshell. Since veneering the turned legs would have been impractical, the legs were painted to simulate burl, giving the chest a unified aesthetic.

Comparison: Two High Chests on Turned Frames

These chests on turned frames illustrate the contrasts between those made in New York and Massachusetts. While the general design of both pieces is similar, the differences in specific details, construction techniques and woods used indicate regional preferences. The New York chest has more flaring and sharp-edged turnings than the New England example and is made of red gum, ash and elm. These woods are not commonly used in New England chests, which are usually made of pine and maple.

The high chest was a new form in American furniture introduced early in the eighteenth century. It demanded the mastery of turning, dovetailing, veneer and inlay work, and the specialized knowledge of finishing the surface with shellac.

When edging the curved bottom of the skirt, it was customary to nail a beading or thin band of wood around its border. This not only gave definition and smoothness to the sawn arches of the skirt, but

High Chest of Drawers
Probably Massachusetts. 1700–1725.
Pine frame; sides and structural parts maple, maple with walnut and maple curled veneer.
H: 63⅜" W: 40" D: 21⅜".
Collection of the Museum of Fine Arts, Boston.

There are both design parallels and differences between this Massachusetts piece and the one opposite made in Flushing, New York. Most striking is the contrast between the surfaces, for the New England facade expresses movement and pattern, while the New York example is rigidly organized and plain. Yet the organization of both pieces seems to have evolved from similar design sources. Even the arches of the skirts and the double molding detail around the chests' borders reflect a consistency in style.

the top plinth of each leg to form a unified line across the front. The detail is best appreciated by touch. Instead of finishing nails, large rose-headed ones were customarily used to fasten down the beading.

The stretchers almost always repeat the shape of the skirt in high chests of this period. This repetition and counterpoint of patterns reflects an interest in movement that was most effectively expressed in the arts of seventeenth-century Baroque Europe.

High Chest of Drawers
Flushing, New York.
Inscribed on back of case, lower center drawer: "This was made in ye Year 1726 by me Samuel Clement of Flushing June 8." Red gum, ash, elm.
H: 72" W: 43¼" D: 24½".
Winterthur Museum.

Samuel Clement, who made this chest, inscribed his name and the date. Most craftsmen did not sign their works, but relied on word of mouth or newspapers for advertisement. In small towns with populations concentrated near the marketplace, this means of advertising was adequate. Anyone capable of making a work as complex as this chest would certainly have been well known in a community numbering only a few thousand.

Despite the curves of the skirt and stretchers, the design is geometric and symmetrical. The upper drawers are divided by bands of inlay that span their borders. This design almost persuades the eye that each drawer is really two. The dominant central axis is further heightened with a set of brass keyhole escutcheon plates formally balanced with teardrop pull-brasses on either side.

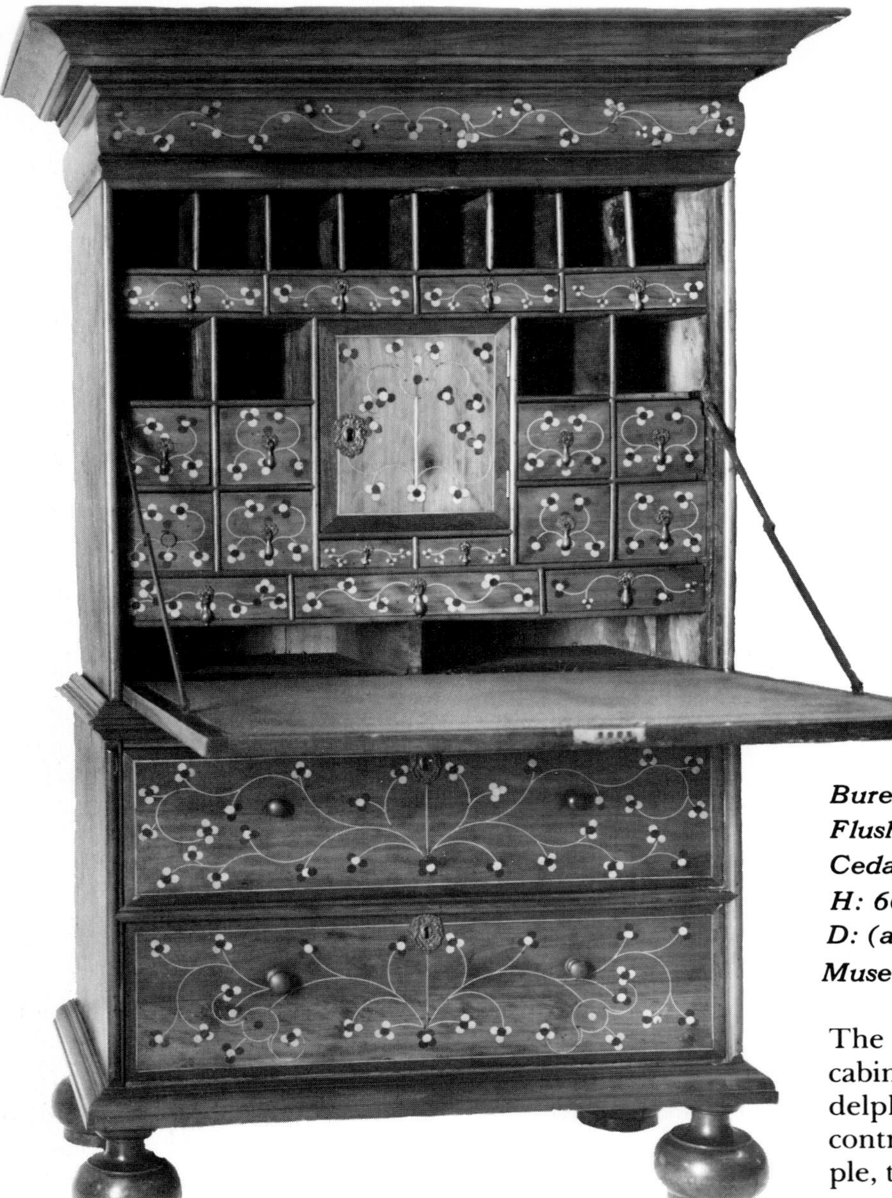

Bureau-Cabinet
Flushing, New York. 1690–1720.
Cedar, cherry, mahogany.
H: 66¾″ W: 34″ D: 17¼″ W: (at cornice) 42″
D: (at cornice) 22″.
Museum of the City of New York.

The dimensions and design of this powerful cabinet and desk are similar to the Philadelphia piece marked by Edward Evans. In contrast to the simplicity of the Evans example, the ornamental inlay on this cabinet fairly overwhelms the surface with stylized tulip and vine floral motifs. This profuse detail reflects the Dutch aesthetic for ornate surfaces. The piece was owned by descendants of Joris Dirchsen Brinckerhoff who immigrated from Dreuth County, Holland, in 1636. It was probably made for his grandchildren—either Joris (1664–1729) or Derick (1667–1778), both successful farmers in Flushing.

Bureau-Cabinet
Philadelphia. Stamped "Edward Evans 1707."
Black walnut; secondary wood: pine; brasses not original.
H: 66½" W: 44" D: 19¼" (at center molding).
Colonial Williamsburg, Williamsburg, Virginia.

This signed and dated Philadelphia bureau-cabinet is among the earliest and most important examples of eighteenth-century American furniture. Although the rarity of this form's survival makes comparison with other Philadelphia pieces difficult, the cabinet is a sophisticated product of an urban craftsman.

The piece is boldly simple with its plain sculptural cornice, waist and foot moldings. The many drawers and chambers for business papers emphasize the practical nature of the cabinet's design.

Although the style of ornament changed, the basic form of these writing cabinets persisted in America until the Federal Period. The only additional desk form developed was the mid-eighteenth-century library or writing table—essentially two boxes with a flat top.

Desk and Bookcase
Philadelphia, Pennsylvania. 1700–1715.
Walnut veneer on pine; secondary wood: chestnut. H: 81" W: 40" D: 25".
The Library Company of Philadelphia.

This monumental example of William-and-Mary style cabinetwork possesses a fairly dependable history of having once belonged to William Penn, proprietor of Pennsylvania. Originally it sported looking glasses in the doors of the upper section and "teardrop" brasses with rounded back plates. The molding around the base and the present turned feet are old replacements. However, the desk is substantially unaltered, and demonstrates that Philadelphia's earliest cabinetmakers, many of whom were trained in London, were capable of producing extremely refined case pieces. Like the best London furniture in this style, this desk relies on carefully calculated proportions rather than ornamentation for its effect. The walnut veneer originally possessed a brilliant surface sheen from a varnish. The customary polish or varnish was shellac, imported from India, which greatly enhanced the optical richness of the matched symmetrical grain of the wood surface.

Chest of Drawers and Desk
Boston Area. 1710–1730.
Burled walnut veneer on white pine.
H: 39½" W: 34" D: 19½".
Collection of Mrs. Charles L. Bybee.

The earliest desks in America were simply slant-top portable boxes placed on dressing stands, tables or chests. By the early eighteenth century the writing portion of the desk and its base support became unified. Some cabinets with drop lids were made with open stands and were called scriptors or scrutoires, bastardized from the French term *escritoire.* Cabinetmakers in Boston are known to have shipped such scrutoires to Virginia in 1729. Yet the better-known desks to survive from the period are like this example—a slant-top desk combined with a chest of drawers. Its richly figured veneer surfaces simulate tortoiseshell work, demonstrating the strong appeal that the appearance of exotic materials held for Boston's mercantile class.

Several similar examples of furniture made in the Boston area suggest the presence of a strong regional school of cabinetmakers who worked in this manner. The eight-pointed star or compass inlay in the center of a lid or door was a favorite device of the Boston-area school. On top of the desk are two English or Dutch brass candlesticks, made about 1700, and a three-part fuddling cup of blue-and-white English delft.

EDWARD A. BORDONE, PHOTOGRAPHER

Tall Clock
New Jersey. 1723.
Dial Face Inscribed: "ISA. Pearson, Burlington."
Walnut case; backboards hard and soft pine.
H: 80⅛" W: 17⅛" D: 9½".
Winterthur Museum.

During the early years of American settement most timepieces were imported. American-made examples as early as this one are rare. The case's flat top and the simple circular dial and bull's-eye peephole are distinctively early eighteenth-century features for clocks made in this country.

An inscription inside the door confirms the early date: "Made for Elisha Laurence 1723." The maker, Isaac Pearson (b. 1685), was a Quaker and a proprietor of the ironworks at Mt. Holly, New Jersey, between 1730 and 1749. Although his name is engraved on the brass clock face, this is no assurance that he also made the case. As was customary with most clockmakers, Pearson probably hired a nearby cabinetmaker for the case while he fabricated the works.

The only relationships to the William and Mary style are the tall proportions of the clock case and the ornamental, Baroque foliate detail cast in brass and applied to the four corners of the dial face. The form of this clock case is stripped to its barest essentials. This is achieved without loss of graceful lines or proportions. The plainness may reflect Quaker rejection of nonessential ornament or preference for function above ostentation. The same preference for simplicity is found in later eighteenth-century Pennsylvania clocks as well, notably some made by David Ritterhouse of Norristown.

Table with Drawer
Possibly South Carolina. 1690–1730.
Walnut, hard yellow pine and poplar.
H: 28⅛" W: 33" D: 23¾".
Collection of Colonial Williamsburg, Williamsburg, Virginia.

Table with Drawer
Virginia or North Carolina. 1690–1730.
Walnut, hard yellow pine and poplar.
H: 28" W: 31$\frac{5}{16}$" D: 20⅞".
Collection of the Museum of Early Southern Decorative Arts, Winston-Salem, North Carolina.

Southern William-and-Mary style furniture rarely survives, and these two examples give only a glimpse of what must have been a complex stylistic development, largely independent of Middle Colonies' or New England work.

The South Carolina table is light and airy. Its frame and top are distinguished by many fine details, such as the molded edges of the drawer and top, and the applied beading around the skirt. The Virginia or North Carolina example possesses robust turnings, which blend well with the rounded edges of the sinuous cross stretchers, a detail not often seen in surviving Southern work.

MIODRAG BLAGOJEVICH, PHOTOGRAPHER

Tea Table
Virginia, Possibly Williamsburg. c. 1710.
Walnut. H: 27½" W: 26½" D: 21½".
Collection of the Colonial Williamsburg Foundation, Gift of Col. and Mrs. Miodrag Blagojevich.

A great rarity of Virginia furniture, this table is an early example of a new form—a table made for the special purpose of serving tea. Its columnar turned legs with rings at their base and capitals are very close to those beneath the arms of the Speaker's Chair of the Virginia House of Burgesses. For that reason it is felt that the table might have been made in Williamsburg. Additional evidence for this theory is provided by the double molding that is glued and nailed around the border of the top of this table. This treatment is found on another table made in Colonial Williamsburg (compare with the tea table, Chapter III, page 126).

Comparison: Two Small Tables

These two tables illustrate an important trend in furniture evolution over the first quarter of the eighteenth century. The example from New York is stylistically the earliest. It is stoutly framed with legs and stretchers composing a rigid, cubelike space. By contrast, the more advanced New England table creates a sense of movement with its splayed legs, arched skirt and oval top. Its turnings undulate and are less crisply defined than in the example from New York. The fluid composition of the New England table reflects the development of motion in design that gained momentum as the century progressed.

Chamber Table
New York. 1690–1720.
Walnut.
H: 23¾" W: (of frame) 25" D: (of frame) 19¾".
A Chester County Collection.

Discovered in Flushing, this diminutive table is one of five or six pieces of New York furniture with distinctive ball-, urn- and baluster-turned ornaments. It is an excellent illustration of how heavier, seventeenth-century furniture forms could be adapted to the lighter weight and new functions of the William and Mary style. While not a true chamber table, such as might have accompanied a high chest of drawers, the table probably functioned as a dressing stand. Although little is known of early New York furniture as yet, this is clearly one of the major pieces.

GEORGE FISTROVICH, PHOTOGRAPHER

Table
Coastal New England. 1700–1740.
H: 25¼" W: 32½" D: 22½".
Winterthur Museum.

This is the supreme example of one of the most collectible forms in early American furniture—the tavern table. The dynamic splay to the legs, the well-formed turnings, boldly carved Spanish feet and vigorously shaped arch are all features which give this table a special stance and beauty.

The term "tavern table" is often a misnomer. It identifies a wide variety of small, low, stretcher-based tables that served many domestic purposes, including tea service. These tables were easily portable and by no means exclusively used in taverns.

RICHARD CHEEK, PHOTOGRAPHER

Slate-Top Table
Base and Turned Frame, Boston; top, Switzerland. 1700–1720.
Base: maple, white pine and walnut; top: varied woods.
H: 30⅛" W: 44⅛" D: 30¼".
Collection of the Dietrich Brothers Americana Corporation.

The Boston craftsman who made this table joined a traditional dressing-table base to an imported Swiss top. Normally a dressing table would have had a rectangular wooden top with simple molded edges rather than the eight-sided top of this example. Its slate center suggests that the table was meant for mixing and serving drinks.

Despite the eighteenth-century "marriage" of the Boston-made base with the imported Swiss top, the effect is harmonious. The craftsman in Boston used elaborately burled veneer on the front apron and drawers to complement the figured marquetry border which surrounds the slate.

RICHARD CHEEK, PHOTOGRAPHER

Comparison: Two Tables

Controlled movement was a major aesthetic objective in American arts in the early years of the eighteenth century. These two tables illustrate different ways in which the illusion of movement was achieved. The design of the dressing table's S-scroll legs is repeated in the stretchers. In the gateleg table, motion is suggested by the multiple turnings on the legs and stretchers.

Gateleg Table
New England, Probably Massachusetts. c. 1700. Maple frame; mahogany top; secondary wood: pine. H: 28" L: (opened) 48". Collection of Mrs. Charles L. Bybee.

This table represents a form which remained popular from the late seventeenth century through the first quarter of the eighteenth. Practical in design, it could occupy a narrow space when closed and easily be placed against the wall. The table was also aesthetically appealing with its contrasts of plain, broad surfaces against ornate turnings. The mahogany top is an index of the new proclivity for imported tropical woods—a taste which became increasingly important as a design factor through the eighteenth century.

The design of this table is animated, the ball feet supporting the stretchers adding to the spirited appearance. The top appears to hover above the drawer. The V-shaped carving at the corner of each leg provides a fine transition between the drawer and frame.

The Baroque-style scrolled legs joined near the floor with crossed serpentine stretchers, an unusual form in American furniture, are not unique, for a few related tables have been found in New England. Examples seen in seventeenth-century Dutch genre paintings suggest the design influence of Holland and the Low Countries.

Dressing Table
New York or New Jersey. c. 1700. Walnut. H: 21" W: 36½" D: 28⅜". The Brooklyn Museum.

Tables As Space-Savers

These tables present two different solutions to space-saving in early eighteenth-century furniture. One has a swing leg with a tilting top, the other, drop leaves supported on movable wing brackets. New England houses, built small to conserve heat, required practical, space-conserving furniture.

Folding Table
New England. 1710–1740.
White pine top; birch base.
H: 23¾" W: 34" D: 23⅔".
Collection of the Museum of Fine Arts, Boston.

The swing legs rotate around wooden washers on a pin held steady by the fixed pair of legs. The stretchers of both sets of legs are notched to close the legs into a compact, flat space over which the top folds. Because it is easy to store, this piece is popularly known as a "tuckaway" table.

Although utilitarian in design, the table is not devoid of style. The legs are smoothly shaped with baluster and ring turnings. It has a simple grace which would have been lost in the hands of a less sensitive craftsman.

Butterfly Table
New England. 1710–1760.
Maple top; maple legs and stretchers; pine frame and drawer linings.
H: 26" W: (leaves up) 50"
W: (leaves down) 16" L: 37½".
The Wadsworth Atheneum, Hartford, Connecticut.

Many small New England homes only had a main multipurpose chamber used for cooking, eating, entertaining and sleeping. For such a room a drop-leaf table was desirable.

This table is beautiful as well as practical. The sweeping winglike brackets supporting the table's hinged leaves are its outstanding features. Although drop-leaf tables with wing supports are not exclusively an American invention, this particular design, combined with the generous use of maple, is unique to this country. Ample supplies of maple in North America enabled local craftsmen to freely span broad surfaces with this handsome and enduring material. Maple was also an excellent wood for turning legs and shaping stretchers. White pine was only used on the table's supporting box and drawer. The overall form of this table is merely an enlarged joint stool with hinged leaves and butterfly bracket supports added.

Great Cane Chair
London. 1700–1710. Walnut. H: 52⅞" W: 24⅜" D: 25¼".
Collection of the Museum of Fine Arts, Boston.

Indicative of the most advanced design known in early eighteenth-century America, this chair, one of a set, was made in London and imported to Connecticut for Hezekiah Willys (1672–1741) of Hartford. The chair represents the outstanding level of craftsmanship that could be achieved in London at a time when the trade was highly specialized. Several different artisans were involved in making such a chair, including turners, joiners and carvers, who were frequently hired from shop to shop on a piecework basis.

The chair's sophisticated moldings embody mature English Baroque design. They reflect an understanding and integration of the angular profiles introduced into England through Daniel Marot, French architect and furniture designer. Marot's fully developed Baroque designs had a profound influence on English domestic arts and consequently, those of America. The chair's history of ownership in America demonstrates one way in which furniture style and design migrated to the colonies.

Caned-Back Armchair
Boston Area. 1710–1730. Maple, painted black; later addition of rockers, now removed and restored to original design.
H: 49½" W: 23¼" D: 16½".
A Milwaukee Collection.

Caning is rarely found in American-made furniture of the early eighteenth century. This specimen is related to a small group of pieces that are marked with a double "E" monogram. All have similar carved leafage in their crests and seem to be stylistically and structurally related. The monogram poses an unsolved riddle of identification. The enigmatic mark may represent a craftsman, journeyman, owner or merchant.

Compared with that imported for Hezekiah Willys in Connecticut, this chair is simpler in its form and ornament, for it was probably produced by less specialized workers. Although less complex, the chair is sculpturally strong, representing provincial aspirations for the vigorous movement, scrolled ornament and turned elements of London chairs. With simplification of form, American chairmakers arrived at distinctive and compelling solutions, related, but not identical, to English counterparts.

P. RICHARD EELLS, PHOTOGRAPHER

The arched cresting and molded banisters of the backs of these two chairs represent an important design preference in the coastal Delaware–middle New Jersey region. A careful study of turnings on similar chairs from this region would reveal local schools of craftsmen not yet identified.

Banister-Back Side Chair
Probably Philadelphia, Pennsylvania. 1700–1725.
Maple, pine. H: 49½" W: 19½" D: 17¼".
The Newark Museum, Newark, New Jersey.

This side chair belonged to a set of six or twelve chairs originally owned by John Gill I, a founder of the town of Haddonfield, a New Jersey community near Philadelphia. Gill came from England around 1702. Unlike most New England banister-backs, Philadelphia chairs of this kind have crests set on top of the posts and wide, reeded banisters. The conical turnings seen in the front stretchers are a regional characteristic, as is the star punchwork. The exact precedent for this design is not yet known but the chair probably reflects a provincial interpretation of cane chairs made in London.

Great Armchair
Pennsylvania–Delaware Valley, Probably Vicinity of Chester, Pennsylvania. 1720–1750.
Maple and tulip painted black; rush seat. H: 48" W: 21½" D: 18".
Mrs. Herbert F. Schiffer.

This represents the Pennsylvania chairmaker's answer to the more elaborately carved New England banister-back chairs. Its lack of carved ornament reflects a rather conservative, practical approach. Although the chair was made in a region settled by a mixture of Swedes, Dutch, German and Scotch/Irish, the dominant culture was provincial English.

Though the chair is sturdy and practical, it also has several flourishes of the turner's art, demonstrating the maker's excellent craftsmanship.

Comparison: Boston Chairs

Although one of these two Boston side chairs has caning for its seat and back and the other has leather, their shapes are basically the same. Clearly, they are both meant to be viewed from the front, as most of the ornamental detail is found there. When not in use they were probably placed against a wall, lined up with other members of their sets. Such sets were ordinarily made to complement the room's architectural scheme.

Side Chair
Probably Boston Area. 1700–1730.
Maple, painted black; probably the original cane seat and back.
H: 49¼" W: 18⅛" D: 15".
A Milwaukee Collection.

The delicately shaped scroll and arched details of this chair were derived from the England of Charles II and William of Orange, who imported Portuguese artisans to England and encouraged Flemish designers and craftsmen to settle in London. English cane-back chairs with Flemish scroll backs and Portuguese feet were imported to America in the late seventeenth century. The elaborate scrolls and cutwork of these English chairs were imitated in local New England woods by newly arrived craftsmen. The results were quite similar. Therefore, it is somewhat difficult to distinguish those chairs made abroad and imported here from those made in this country. For reasons characteristic of provincial societies, such as the higher cost of labor and lesser availability of specialized craftsmen, chairmakers in America tended to simplify the forms known abroad. The surfaces of such chairs became more broadly treated, open, and generous of materials, the result of economic conditions where labor is dear and materials plentiful.

Side Chair
Boston Area. 1720–1750.
Maple. Frame painted black; recent leather upholstery, dark green.
H: 45″ W: 17⅝″ D: 14½″.
Museum of Fine Arts, Boston.

This chair represents a popular type commonly exported from Boston and sold throughout the other colonies. Its reproduction leather upholstery with spaced brass-headed nails approximates the appearance of the few examples which survive with their original covering.

Responding to the competition which Boston chairmakers were giving craftsmen in Pennsylvania, Plunket Fleeson, a Philadelphia upholsterer, advertised in a 1742 newspaper that he was selling chairs "cheaper than any made here or imported from Boston." Two years later he advertised again and disparaged Philadelphians for encouraging "the Importation of Boston Chairs." His protests against their importation suggest that the Boston chair was a popular item of colonial trade. Recent research shows that fully half of the furniture imported to Virginia between 1729 and 1760 came from New England, mostly from Boston. Chairs formed the largest single group of furniture imports. Thus this chair is a material example of the growing mercantile economy before the Revolution.

Armchair (Elbow Chair)
(With Five-Banister Back)
Coastal New England, Probably Massachusetts.
Maple with ash turnings, painted black to simulate ebony; rush seat.
H: 47½" W: 23" D: 18".
Museum of Fine Arts, Boston.

Called "elbow chairs" in eighteenth-century America, armchairs with banister backs were produced along the Northeast coast in New Hampshire, Connecticut, Massachusetts and New York. The Gaines family of Ipswich, Massachusetts, and Portsmouth, New Hampshire, were among the craftsmen who made chairs of this sort.

The carving at the crest of the chair is its most complex and interesting feature. A person seated in the chair gained importance and stature from the crown behind the head. The deeply cut C-scrolls and foliate ornament burst with energy. This carving manifests a provincial understanding of English Baroque design.

Side Chair
Probably Boston Area. 1700–1730.
Maple, painted black over light blue. H: 48" W: 19" D: 14¾".
A Milwaukee Collection.

Because of its great sweeping crest, dramatically supported by turned posts with their silhouettes repeated in the three split banisters of the back, this chair is an exciting work of art. The baluster turnings between the blocks of the legs and on the back are vigorous. Repeating the shape of the crest, the front stretcher completes the composition. Carving similar to the foliage motifs below the front stretcher is found on other furniture of this period, documented to the Boston area.

RICHARD EELLS, PHOTOGRAPHER

Settle
Probably Pennsylvania or New Jersey.
1700–1780. Pine, originally stained red-brown. H: $52\frac{1}{2}$" W: 74" D: 22".
Museum of Fine Arts, Boston.

The settle form evolved from built-in furniture of the late Middle Ages. A functional object, the settle both protected the body from the drafts of great halls and by its placement before or beside a fireplace, served to contain the heat. Often it was used in conjunction with a crane to support blankets to form a small chamber of comfort before the fire. The hood and the deep skirt of this settle were evidently designed to aid its conservation of heat.

Cushions, pillows and blankets were used to make the settle comfortable. Although the settle is an interesting object with strong, formal artistic qualities, it loses a certain amount of meaning seen in a museum gallery away from its domestic context.

These two settles demonstrate the endurance of commonplace furniture in America. The panel and frame joinery of their workmanship has roots in longstanding north European woodworking traditions.

Settle
Probably Pennsylvania.
1700–1750.
Walnut; leather.
H: $48\frac{13}{16}$" W: 72" D: 29".
Winterthur Museum.

Tradition-bound Americans maintained a continuity of furniture forms which were little affected by rapid changes in urban fashion. The persistence of the settle form from the late seventeenth to the nineteenth centuries indicates that Americans found this particular article of furniture highly useful and attractive.

This settle was probably made in eastern Pennsylvania, where the tradition of panel and frame joinery persisted for over two hundred years without substantial stylistic changes. Elaborate veneering, turning or carving was simply not in the vocabulary of the joiner's trade, and such specialized work had no market in this area. This massive piece must have been an important architectural element in its original setting. Remarkably, it has survived at least two centuries of use with its original leather back and seat. The stretching of the leather over a frame serves to uphold the body in much the same way as webbing functions in upholstery. It is the countryman's answer to urban upholstery. For added comfort it must have once had some bolsters or pillows.

These examples of upholstered seating furniture are part of a large, interrelated group of chairs made in Boston and New York between about 1695 and 1720. Their strong affinity stems both from a common origin in Anglo-Flemish Baroque design and a sharp competition between Boston and New York craftsmen. Future researchers will undoubtedly discover new specimens and documentary research about such chairs, but the four illustrated here are key examples and extraordinarily beautiful objects.

PHOTOGRAPH BY WADHAMS/MAHAFFEY

Leather Great Chair

New York City. 1710–1730. Maple, oak. H: 47¼" W: 23½" D: 22⅜".

Museum of Fine Arts, Boston.

The only surviving armchair of an important school of New York chairmaking, this example gains additional importance through the preservation of its original upholstery foundation, leather covering, brass nailing and ebonized finish. The heavy rolled arms, accented with naturalistic acanthus-leaf carving, relate directly to French precedents and may represent the work of a Huguenot craftsman working in New York.

Small urn-shaped feet are missing from the frame, and the iron tie-rods bracing the arms are nineteenth-century additions.

Elbow Leather Chair
New York. 1700–1720.
Maple and oak; leather upholstery.
H: 52″ W: 24½″ D: 22″.
Greenfield Village and the Henry Ford Museum, Dearborn, Michigan.

This chair was once owned by Colonel Pieter Schuyler (1657–1724), the first mayor of Albany, New York. It bears its original dark-brown leather covering, which is crosshatched or diced. The original gilt-brass nails are spaced about three-fourths of an inch apart and run around the seat and back in two parallel rows, the same "double nail'd" treatment seen on the Winterthur example. The rear of the back panel is not covered in leather; the original sackcloth which forms the foundation for grass stuffing is left exposed.

The relationship between this chair and the following example is to be seen in the central element of the carved crest and stretcher: a rather spiky pair of C-scrolls. In most other details, the chair resembles its Boston counterpart quite closely.

Leather Armchair
Boston, Massachusetts. 1710–1725.
Maple, red oak.
H: 35⅛″ W: 24″ D: 27½″.
Winterthur Museum.

This exact form of chair is listed in the early eighteenth-century accounts of Thomas Fitch (1669–1736), Boston's most successful upholsterer of that period, as a "carv'd Russia leather Elbow chair." The diamond crackle of the original Russian leather of this example is the result of the curing process, when the hides were hammered in two directions. Fitch's accounts occasionally note another detail seen here, double nailing, or the use of two rows of brass upholstery nails.

The C-scrolls and leafage of the carved crest and front stretcher; the urns, bases and columns of the turned posts and stretchers; and the swept, rolled arms are all refined details that prove that Boston's upholstered chair industry produced furniture of the best quality.

Great Armchair (Elbow Chair)
New York. c. 1700.
Maple and red oak; upholstery modern.
H: 54" W: 22½" D: 16¾".
Collection of Mrs. Charles L. Bybee.

The splendid Flemish-style scroll-carved ornament of this chair prompted an antiquarian in 1906 to conclude that it was Dutch, rather than American, in origin. Recent microscopic analysis of its woods proves that it was made in this country. It is one of the finest and most vigorously carved works in a small group made in New York, which closely approximate their Anglo-Flemish antecedents. Tragically, it was irreparably charred in a recent fire.

EDWARD A. BOURDON, PHOTOGRAPHER

Easy Chairs

The comfortable easy chair as we now know it was an important innovation from abroad that arrived in this country late in the seventeenth and became popular in the early eighteenth century. Before that time comfort in seating was largely achieved through the use of fully stuffed down pillows.

Seventeenth-century upholsterers in England developed their art through the stretching of webbing and soft cushioning materials across frames of furniture to uphold the sitters. Therefore, the guild of this specialized craft was first known as "upholders." In eighteenth-century America upholstery became a dominant profession in the furniture trade, for it involved not only the padding and covering of furniture but included the entire gamut of textile furnishings as well. Window hangings, bedstead coverings, curtains and bedding—all sorts of textile coverings were part of the upholsterer's business. As the coordinator of increasingly lavish room appointments, the upholsterer of the eighteenth century was both a decorator and a furniture and furnishings entrepreneur.

These New England examples all were reupholstered in fairly recent years. However, only the Franklin family chair (see page 79) represents a serious and rigorous reconstruction of its original form and fabric.

Easy Chair
New England. 1710–1725.
Maple; secondary woods: pine and oak.
H: 50⅞" W: 32⅛" D: 21¼".
Winterthur Museum.

The straight, upright thrust of the chair back is artfully contrasted with sweeping wings and broadly scrolled arms. The skirt and crest profiles are distinctive features of Baroque design that clearly separate the chair from an earlier generation of taste in this country.

Easy chairs were frequently made for the comfort of the aged, ill or infirm. In eighteenth-century inventories, they are most frequently located in bedrooms and not, as we use them today, in the more public areas of the house.

Easy Chair
Boston, Massachusetts. 1710–1725.
Maple and pine.
H: 48¾" W: 29⅛" D: 20½".
Museum of Fine Arts, Boston.

This example, one of the earliest American easy chairs, once belonged to Samuel Franklin (b. 1684) of Boston, a cousin of Benjamin Franklin. The chair is historically interesting, and has undergone accurate reconstruction of its original upholstery.

The choice of coarse, blue-green twilled or worsted wool fabric was based upon fragments discovered underneath the earliest eighteenth-century tacks found on the chair's frame. The

down-filled cushion is based upon prototypes in the Victoria and Albert Museum. The shapes of the arms and wings were reconstructed from surviving documents—original pieces of padding from another New England wing chair of the same period.

Aspects of this chair's design relate it to other chairs of the period and region. The multiple turnings, double-rolled arms, scalloped front skirt and strongly raked back have counterparts in New England leather-, cane- and banister-back chairs.

Easy Chair
Massachusetts. 1715–1730. Maple. H: 48¼" W: 33¼".
Museum of Fine Arts, Houston; The Bayou Bend Collection.

It had been customary to reupholster easy chairs in velvet keeping the lines of the wings, back and seat cushion fairly trim. This easy chair represents twentieth-century restoration practice. Eighteenth-century upholsterers more likely used twilled or patterned wool fabric and almost always generously stuffed a seat cushion with fluffy down. Wings and arms had similarly full profiles.

Daybed
London, England. 1680–1700.
Maple painted dark brown;
cushion modern. H: 40" W: 21⅛" L: 64".
Pilgrim Hall, Plymouth, Massachusetts.

A member of the Winslow family of Plymouth supposedly brought this daybed from England to America. Its carving and turning includes the basic vocabulary of ornament produced by the furniture makers of the Boston area.

In England such a piece was known as a daybed, and in this country, a couch. Couches with a single back at one end and a long bed in front supported by legs came into general use in America in the early years of the eighteenth century.

The famous Boston diarist Judge Samuel Sewall in 1719 requested that his daughter's furniture be ordered in England: "A duzen of good black Walnut chairs, fine Cane, with a Couch." This couch may be just the sort Sewall had in mind.

Comparison: Three Couches

Daybeds are descendants of the seventeenth-century couch. Elaborate Baroque decoration is applied to a modified form: the stance is lowered, the back and one arm omitted, the other arm hinged.

Couch
Boston Area. 1710–1730.
Walnut; cushion modern.
H: 40" W: 21½" L: 61½".
Museum of Fine Arts, Boston.

Comparisons between American and English provincial styles may be made by studying this New England couch in relation to the imported Winslow family daybed. The New England example is clearly much simpler. It is closely related to regional canted-back chairs with carved crowns, leafage and bold turnings. The strong turnings on the stretchers and the block-and-turned legs of this couch are features favored by New England craftsmen. The turnings offered a highly ornamental effect without reliance upon richly carved ornament. Only the barest sprouts of leafage were carved in the crest.

The crest is a vigorously abstracted arch. It crowns a frame which reclines through the release of a chain at the top corners, swinging on pin hinges that connect to the bottom stretcher bar of the back frame.

Couch
Virginia or North Carolina. 1710–1720.
Soft maple and oak, originally painted black.
H: 34¼" W: 21¼" L: 62½".
Museum of Early Southern Decorative Arts, Winston-Salem, North Carolina.

This couch, like its New England counterpart, has a hinged back. But instead of a fixed seat frame, it has a separate frame worked in cane. Exceptionally sturdy in construction, it is mortised together with square joints at each juncture of leg and stretcher. This construction detail is apparently characteristic of much Southern furniture.

New England Furniture. 1700–1760.
Museum of Fine Arts, Boston.

American furniture forms, details and cabinetmaking traditions persisted long after the period in which they were first developed had passed. Few people threw away the old to embrace completely the new. Within a home, styles were commonly intermixed; even individual pieces of furniture frequently mixed stylistic features. The past should be viewed through complex layers of overlapping and interpenetrating styles, national and regional preferences, differences of economic position, diverse personalities, and the willingness to change or cling to old attitudes. In this vein, an evolutionary analysis of artistic currents in the American colonies seems forced or somewhat arbitrary as is even the assembling of a group of objects such as this.

The setting is a room with woodwork taken from a number of different Essex County, Massachusetts, houses and reassembled at the Boston Museum of Fine Arts to suggest a "best chamber" from a moderately well-to-do New Englander's home, c. 1700–1730. White pine sheathing panels the walls of the room and broad white pine boards form the floor. This kind of early American setting had an enormous vogue in museum installations in the late 1920s and 1930s. This room offered the warm color of well-seasoned wood, suggesting that furnishing materials were supplied from the vast resources of pine, oak, maple and other native woods. The message of the room is one of mood, not fact. Yet it clearly speaks of an age when wood was the primary material for bettering the conditions of life.

The most ornate object is quite logically an imported piece, an English looking glass. The other hanging framed objects are called quillwork sconces. A popular exercise for young ladies in New England to demonstrate taste and skills, these sconces were made from seaweed, rocks, shells, mica flowers, wirework, and wax figures of dolls, lamb and fruit—all coated with mica to shimmer in the light of candles.

The sconces' intense surface movement is echoed in the painted, vinelike details which decorate the front of the oak-and-pine two-drawer chest. Its center panel bears the unidentified initials "ES" and the date "1704," surrounded by a painted circle of herringbone details and tulip and floral scrollwork. The chest was probably made in Wethersfield, Connecticut. It illustrates in painted form the persistence of a decorative type of chest that had been made in the Connecticut River Valley since the late seventeenth century.

Near the chest is a Connecticut turned armchair, probably made in the Guilford area between 1700 and 1720. Made of ash and maple with a rush seat, it was once painted green and later a deep red-brown color. The pattern of the chair recalls the famous armchair belonging to John Carver in Plymouth (see Chapter 1, page 30), and hence it is called a Carver-type armchair. This Connecticut chair represents a continuation of the Carver archetype perhaps a century after the first documented appearance of the form in New England. The turnings of the Connecticut chair are not as bold or as deeply sculptural in profile as the turnings on the Carver prototype, but the basic form persists.

Next to the chair is an iron and brass candlestand with cross arms designed with a spring clamp that raises or lowers the candles on the straight, tapering shaft. This type of candlestand is a delightful invention of the American blacksmith, quite unlike anything made abroad. The candlestand bears the name "B Garrish" and the date "1736" engraved on the shaft.

DAN FARBER, PHOTOGRAPHER

A black painted armchair with its original leather seat and back is in the foreground. Although this armchair was recently found at an auction in Ohio, it is of a type that was made in the New York area between 1710 and 1725. Despite the fact that the chair derives its basic form from English furniture of the 1670s, this American example was probably made in the eighteenth century. Such turned furniture—with emphasis on fat urn shapes and balusters, blockings, ball-and-ring ornament for feet, finials and stretchers—continued to be made in America throughout much of the Georgian Period. This furniture had a strong influence on the taste of a vast number of Americans long after the time when similar styles had passed out of fashion abroad.

III

1725–1760

Queen Anne & Early Georgian

THE TASTE FOR TALL, ornamental, unstable-looking furniture popular in the first quarter of the eighteenth century gave way to furniture that was quiet in design, compressed to lower proportions, and subtly curved. The new style emphasized ornament selectively placed on broad surfaces, focusing attention upon the refined carving and the natural beauty of richly colored woods.

The American colonist embraced the principles of strength, order, balance and reason associated with Classical civilization. This ethos formed his attitude toward life and was manifested in his buildings and furnishings. The philosophy of reason found creative expression in other art forms of the eighteenth century, dominating music, poetry and literature, as well as material culture. Furniture of this period is carefully designed, skillfully perfected, gracefully adapted to suit the needs, scale and comfort of the human body. Its form shows thoughtful balance of voids to solids, of plain surfaces to ornament, and of curved to straight lines. Mahogany and walnut were the primary woods; pine, tulip, ash, chestnut and maple usually the secondary woods.

Both maker and buyer of the eighteenth century were quick to perceive subtle variations in form and pattern. To appreciate the aesthetics of the period, the viewer must sharpen his faculties to distinguish among the many variations of pattern in chair backs, crestings, carved ornament, legs, feet, shells, pediments, volutes, finials and pilasters. Broad surfaces with textural contrasts of materials such as gold leaf and polished brasses heightened the richness of the visual effect. The practiced eye or hand should glide across polished or shellacked surfaces, sensitive to areas of ornamentation that arrest attention at important points of transition. This movement within a defined boundary is the essence of Baroque design.

The sensibility of the eighteenth century is illustrated in the ideas of the English painter and satirical artist William Hogarth (1697–1764), who explained in his *Analysis of Beauty* (London, 1753) that waving or serpentine lines pleased the eye. Intricate form and infinite variety, Hogarth felt, could be achieved with contrasting curves intertwined in opposite directions. Such S-shaped lines suggested motion, which as Hogarth observed, "leads the eye a wanton kind of chase, and from the pleasure that gives the mind, entitles it to the name of beautiful."

Hogarth was not the first person to observe and write about the artistic merits of S-shaped or undulating lines; he articulated and added to ideas that had long been known among artists and designers, acknowledging previous writings on the subject. By the early eighteenth century these ideas had become a pervasive system of vision and design. Hogarth illustrated pictures of cabriole legs of chairs and other forms which demonstrated the importance of what was then called the "precise line." By the late 1720s the bold double-C scroll and heavy S-shaped swelling of Baroque art in the seventeenth century began to yield to a refined S-shaped line in both ornament and form. With this came the second phase of the Baroque style to fashionable centers in America. Form and order became integrated, rational and balanced.

This new style, with its assured grace, balance and emphasis on refinement, is commonly known today as "Queen Anne," although in its day there was no special name for what was simply up-to-date and in good taste. Queen Anne (James II's younger daughter) succeeded her sister Mary, reigning from 1702 to 1714, long before the style which bears her name became widespread in England or known in America. The style persisted both here and in England during the reigns of Kings George I and II (1714–1760). In the American colonies it continued as a vital force until well after the Revolution, and it might better be identified with the architectural design of the Georgian Period. Both furniture and architectural styles from 1725 through the 1760s relate to the Italianate influence of Andrea Palladio, whose sixteenth-century buildings and books revived interest in ancient Roman architecture and subsequently provided further inspiration for British designers and their colonial counterparts.

RESTRAINED OPULENCE

High Chest of Drawers (Detail)
Charlestown, Massachusetts. 1739.
Ebenezer Hartshern (Hartshorne) (1690–1781).
Walnut and pine. H: 90″ W: 41½″ D: 21½″.
Museum of Fine Arts, Boston.

Contrasts among the varied materials of this high chest are visually exciting. The high chest has motion, but its composition is strongly unified and self-contained. Balance between activity and structured calm characterized the tastes of fashionable Americans in port towns of the Eastern seaboard during the second quarter of the eighteenth century. This sense of design was so logical and appealing that it persisted in many towns and villages throughout most of the eighteenth century.

The sides of the high chest are made of solid walnut. The pine drawers have their fronts veneered with figured walnut cut from the crotch of the tree. The veneer is matched at the center of the drawers to emphasize the overall symmetry of the chest. Birch and sycamore inlay stringing outlines the borders of the drawers and pediment. The most dramatic visual focus is the deeply carved and gilded shell of the upper center drawer. Compass star inlay, characteristic of the Boston area, flanks the center shell.

The Charlestown, Massachusetts, joiner, Ebenezer Hartshern, inscribed his name and the date 1739 on the back of the lower half of this high chest, and while he took credit for making it, there were several other people involved in its creation. The person who commissioned the chest, though unknown, must have played a significant role in its production, because while several strikingly similar pieces are known, all have variations in their design. No two purchasers were likely to order exactly the same combination of features in such a major piece of furniture, and rarely have the names of these patrons survived.

The variety of woods, nails, hardware, glues, veneers and shellacs that were used to fabricate this piece suggests that Hartshern had a network of suppliers or tradesmen in the Boston area. If he did not have specialists in his own shop or did not personally possess a wide range of skills and tools, he probably relied upon a turner to supply pendant drops and turned finials. It was customary to enlist the talents of inlay and veneer makers, who specialized in supplying finely cut and patterned woods. Japanners in Boston often executed the carving and gilding necessary to bring the work to its ultimate richness. Perhaps as many as a half dozen different suppliers and artisans played important roles in the creation of this high chest.

Despite the several skills represented, the organization of the piece is unified and harmonious. Its surface design complements the form. A perfect balance exists between the skillfully crafted ornament and the sensuous quality of brilliantly figured wood.

One recent discovery mars this masterpiece of Massachusetts furniture: Its legs are recent additions, with their joints cleverly concealed beneath the veneer on the facade. The legs are such faithful replicas of those that once graced this piece, that they had been assumed to be the originals until X-ray investigation revealed modern dowel joinery within the body of the piece.

The following chairs exhibit transitional stylistic characteristics. They show a conservative adherence to the turned, vertical William and Mary style and incorporate the curves of the Early Georgian Period.

Side Chair
New York, Probably Hudson Valley. c. 1750.
Maple, oak, cherry, rush.
H: 39⅝" W: 22⅝" D: 20⅛".
Winterthur Museum.

Chairs of this type, usually painted black or rich blue-green, were made along the colonial seaboard. They are sometimes called Dutch chairs, as they are frequently found in New York State. The chairmaker adapted a turner's tradition of the earlier William and Mary Period to the style popular after the first quarter of the eighteenth century. The most up-to-date feature of the chair is its vase or fiddlebacked splat. The heart motif cut out of the center of the splat suggests the persistence of a folk tradition.

DOUGLAS ARMSDEN, PHOTOGRAPHER

Side Chair (One of a Set of Four)
Portsmouth, New Hampshire. 1725–1740.
Maple. H: 40½" W: 18" D: 18".
The MacPheadris-Warner House, Portsmouth, New Hampshire, on Loan from Reverend Charles T. Brewster.

This chair's harmonious blend of turned, carved elements and shaped skirt are associated with the William and Mary style. However, the vase-shaped splat suggests that the chair was probably made after the first quarter of the eighteenth century. As a statement of provincial taste, the mixture of styles indicates stylistic transition and a maker with a partial understanding of fashions from abroad. While attempting to keep up to date, he remained loyal to the tradition of carving and turning in which he was trained. The rush seat was probably added sometime in the nineteenth century. There is evidence that a frame fitted into the seat at one time.

The chair's turned and deeply carved front legs and feet handsomely combine rugged simplicity and elegance; the scrolled and cusped crest provides a graceful terminus. Richness is achieved with painted ochre- and umber-colored graining, which, if not original, is of an early date. The graining was done before many minor changes were later made on the chair, and so deserves acceptance as part of the character and integrity of the piece. This chair possesses a robust quality which has great appeal to the sensitive collector today.

Armchair
Probably Boston Area. 1715–1740.
Maple. H: 44¾" W: 23" D: 18¾".
Museum of Fine Arts, Boston.

This armchair is a rarity, as few American-made caned chairs have survived from the eighteenth century. Although the presence of caning usually suggests foreign origin, the woods in this chair, tested by microanalysis, indicate it was made in America.

The sculptured abstract character of the chair's moldings and the simple but strong profile of its crest are visually appealing. Straight lines, in contrast to the curves of arms, legs and crest, demonstrate the chairmaker's awareness of the changing fashion, which demanded the incorporation of the S shape. In overall form, however, the vertical shape of the chair places it within the design approach of the William and Mary Period.

Armchair
New England. c. 1725–1760.
Maple. H: 44⅛" W: 25½" D: 16½".
Museum of Fine Arts, Boston.

This type of chair was commonly made in coastal New England. It combines features of the earlier William and Mary Period with the S-shaped additions of the more up-to-date Queen Anne style. The carved crest and Spanish feet, the turnings and shaped terminals of the arms are the backward-looking features. The vase or fiddle-shaped splat is the most advanced stylistic note. Combining styles of both periods, the chair has an additional quirk: arms supported on cantilevered brackets. No one seems to know the purpose of this peculiar design, although there are several other chairs with similar treatment. One can speculate that the arm supports were swept backward to allow room for the dress of the sitter.

Armchair
Philadelphia. 1740–1780.
Maple (original red-brown stain or paint removed); secondary wood (rear seat frame block, right): white cedar; rush seat.
H: 41¾" W: 27½" D: 16½".
Collection of Mrs. Charles L. Bybee.

Joiner and cabinetmaker William Savery (1721–1788), who kept a shop in Philadelphia at the Sign of the Chair below Market on Second Street, made and labeled similar chairs for Philadelphians who had a taste for practical furniture. The sturdy form of the chair, its stout cabriole legs and turned stretcher parallel the form of the transitional armchair made in New England (see top of page 90). The strong front stretcher in both chairs suggests that preference for the turner's art was not forsaken by either maker or buyer when a practical chair was needed.

The frequent survival of armchairs like this is a tribute to sturdy construction, and suggests that such chairs were extremely popular and produced in quantity over a long period. Since the basic shape of this chair is also found combined with a later Chippendale-style back, there is no doubt that this chair type was made in and around Philadelphia well after the American Revolution.

REGIONAL VARIATIONS IN SIDE CHAIRS

As cabinet- and chairmaking centers became well established in the early years of the eighteenth century, regional preferences for certain designs and construction techniques became pronounced in each area. The following are broad guidelines to these regional characteristics, to which, of course, there are always exceptions.

New England side chairs are usually tall and have legs framed by turned and joined stretchers. Carving on New England chairs is thin and crisp except in Newport, where it is both sharply defined and robust. New York side chairs are lower and broader in profile than their New England counterparts. The carving, though deep, may appear lifeless and flat. Philadelphia chairs are sculptural in form, generous in proportion, and seldom have stretchers. Their carving is vigorous, lifelike, and well integrated into the overall design.

Back-splat design, use of woods and local construction methods are additional means by which side chairs can be regionally differentiated.

RICHARD CHEEK, PHOTOGRAPHER

Side Chair
Philadelphia. 1730–1760.
Walnut. H: 40" W: 20⅜" D: 16½".
Museum of Fine Arts, Boston.

When a new style of flowing S-shaped lines was introduced into American furniture the nomenclature describing these curves was probably far less complicated than it is today. Current descriptive terms—horseshoe-shaped seat, serpentine stretchers, hooped back, spooned splat, lambrequin carved knees, slipper feet, fiddle-shaped splat—are useful for helping the novice to see specific details but tend to encourage piecemeal viewing, which misses the point of such furniture. For in this period American wood craftsmen achieved a harmony in their work that merits viewing in its own terms. The total composition of such furniture is more impressive than the sum of its parts. While this side chair is one of the least ornamented in high-style Philadelphia chairmaking, its simplicity is deceptive. There is a flowing grace and rhythmic balance to the motion of the chair which conforms to the precise line of beauty that Hogarth explained was the basis of aesthetic perfection.

In stance and overall appearance this chair seems to be free-flowing, avoiding any graceless right angles in the juncture of members. Even where the seat rail joins the rear leg, shaped bracket blocks were included to soften the transition. Yet by contrast to the chair's freedom of design, the actual construction of the seat frame is heavily braced. It is made of slabs of walnut securely joined at right angles and doweled into the front legs. The rim, or lip, of the seat frame, which contains the slip-seat, is a separate piece, glued to the upper edge. The refined grace of the chair is almost anthropomorphic in its effect.

HELGA PHOTO STUDIO, INC.

Side Chair
Newport, Rhode Island. 1725–1760.
Mahogany, veneered maple splat.
H: 41" W: 21¼".
Preservation Society of Newport County.

The tall, sleek, Oriental-looking splat of this side chair recalls the Far Eastern imports that captivated the imagination of wealthy people both here and abroad in the eighteenth century. The shape of the back perfectly conforms to the lumbar region of the human spine. The simplicity of this form is gracefully counterpointed by the rippling effect of the skirt and sculptured inner edges of the front legs. Elegance of design is achieved through the elimination of the usual medial stretcher.

Side Chair
Boston, Massachusetts. 1730–1760. American black walnut, soft maple; slip-seat. H: 39 11/16" W: 20 13/16" D: 16 7/8".
The Mabel Brady Garvan Collection, Yale University Art Gallery.

This side chair is a classic of its era—one of the most popular chair forms throughout New England, it is handsome, yet practical and durable. Although the legs are quite sturdy, there was no chance taken that they would become loose: stoutly joined with turned-and-blocked stretchers, they were pinned at the ankles for added security. In his account books from the 1730s, Boston upholsterer Samuel Grant records the use of the compass seat and horseshoe feet in such chairs.

This particular chair is presumed to be part of a set made for Reverend Edward Holyoke, president of Harvard College (1737–1769).

Side Chair
Newport, Rhode Island. 1750–1770.
Mahogany. H: 39" W: 21" D: 18".
Museum of Fine Arts, Boston.

The precise outline and harmonious proportions of this Newport side chair make it a type eagerly sought by collectors. Popular in its day, this form enjoyed a long period of production.

Some chairs of this type had turned stretchers; others had none. Some were made with pad, or "colt," feet, as they were called in the eighteenth century. The claw-and-ball foot was a more expensive feature than the pad foot, not necessarily an index to a later date. The choice between pad or claw feet seemed to depend upon the buyer's taste and the amount he was willing to pay.

Side Chair
New York. 1740–1760.
Walnut; secondary woods: pine and maple.
H: 38½" W: 22" D: 18⅜".
Private Collection.

The basic form of this chair parallels others made in Newport, Rhode Island, although some proportions and details differ. Inter-coastal trade between Boston, Newport, Connecticut, eastern Long Island and New York City was well established in the eighteenth century. Comparisons among chairs from these regions demonstrate the effects of coastal trade upon stylistic preferences. Since furniture as well as craftsmen and craft practices migrated with coastal trade, it is instructive to compare this New York chair with one made in Newport.

This chair has a brilliantly figured walnut-veneer back and an undercut shell at the crest with foliate streamers trailing on either side. The breadth and gentle curve of the compass seat, the large, simple knee brackets and the shaped rear feet are all features found in New York chairs of the period. However, they are not necessarily exclusive characteristics of New York chairmaking.

Side Chair
New York. 1742–1770.
***Mahogany with ash, pine and maple.** H: 41¾" W: 22½" D: 18".*
Museum of Fine Arts, Houston, The Bayou Bend Collection.

Although found on English examples, the cypher back splats on this set of chairs are unique in America. Cypher initials were more often engraved on eighteenth-century silver. The letters *R, M* and *L* worked into the back of the side chair shown are believed to be the initials of the owners, Robert and Margaret (Beekman) Livingston, who were married in 1742. It would seem likely that this chair and the others of the set were made at the time of the marriage to symbolize, with intertwining initials, the joining of two eminent New York families. Despite the likelihood of the chair's first owners, it is also possible that their son Robert, who married Mary Stevens in 1770, could have had the chair made at that later date. If so, the chair would have been stylistically quite late for its time and place.

The breadth of this chair's seat and the low profile of its back are features often found in New York seating. The rear legs with shaped feet, while not a uniquely New York characteristic, are frequently found in chairs from the area.

Side Chairs (Pair)
Boston Area. 1730–1750.
Walnut. H: 43½" W: 21" D: 19¾".
Museum of Fine Arts, Boston.

The tall spoon-shaped backs and elongated legs of these side chairs suggest that they are among the earliest examples of the Queen Anne style produced in coastal New England. Their form is severely restrained but elegant in the subtlety of the curves.

Although the seats have been recently reupholstered with a blue wool moire fabric commonly used in the early eighteenth century, the tacking pattern of the brightly polished brass-headed nails follows exactly the original pattern that studded the borders of the seat in the eighteenth century.

PHOTOGRAPH BY WADHAMS/MAHAFFEY

Watercolor Drawing
"Peter Manigault and His Friends," By George Roupell.
Charleston, South Carolina. c. 1754.
Winterthur Museum.

This rare interior view of an eighteenth-century American home records sparse furnishings—no curtains, table linen, carpet or elegant upholstered furniture. The spareness of the room may well have been the way the room was regularly furnished or an adaptation during the heat of Southern summers.

Eight fairly conservative-looking chairs surround a large table, their pierced backs the only ornamentation. The most elaborate and up-to-date furnishings are the rococo candlesticks on the table.

Much of the surviving eighteenth-century furnishings made in the South seems either to be extremely elaborate and high-style or fairly simple, like the furniture in this room. Large quantities of New England furniture were imported to the South and a considerable amount of furniture came directly from abroad.

The drawing of Peter Manigault and his friends stands testament to the life-style of the mid-eighteenth century. The party is convivial, but not rowdy. Though at ease, the sitters maintain a certain formality. The furnishings of the room, simple yet appropriate for their purposes, are a portrait of an eighteenth-century gentleman's entertainment, drawn from memory by one who was there.

Details of Shell Carving from a Philadelphia Chair Compared with Those from a Newport Chair

The ornamental devices of shell and volute signal a change in style that took place in American furniture about 1730. These ornaments were well adapted to the streamlining and simplification which changed furniture and the other arts with the waning of the William and Mary style. Artisans from each region carved these motifs in different ways, but all followed the same basic scheme. Such carved detail was subordinate to the whole, and was judiciously reserved for accent at knees, crests, and other areas critical to symmetry and balance.

Carved Shell Detail from Crest of Philadelphia Armchair, c. 1760.

This naturalistic representation of a scallop shell was a favorite among Philadelphia carvers, whose shell carvings ranged from the elaborate to the relatively simple, as shown here. In such a shell stood Venus, the goddess of beauty, as portrayed by Sandro Botticelli. The shell has served as an emblem of generation and beauty ever since.

Carved Shell Detail from Crest of Side Chair
Newport. 1740–1790.
Museum of Fine Arts, Boston.

Newport shell carving has a unique character: simple and deeply carved, with generous volutes terminating at the lower edges. The form so satisfied both Newport furniture makers and clients that it persisted long after popularity of the shell motif waned in other American towns.

RICHARD CHEEK, PHOTOGRAPHER

Armchair
Philadelphia. 1730–1760.
Walnut. H: 41½" W: 32¼" D: 18¾".
Private Collection.

A superb sense of abstract design combined with flawless craftsmanship make this work a masterpiece. It is of a type made by William Savery (1721–1788), Quaker cabinetmaker of Philadelphia.

Crisp, sharp edges on this chair blend into rounded contours, offering pleasing contrasts. The leitmotif of the design is the abstracted yoke, most prominent at the center of the crest rail but repeated throughout the chair. The design of the foot, today referred to as drake or trifid, was popular with many Philadephia and New Jersey chairmakers before the American Revolution.

Armchair
Newport, Rhode Island. 1730–1760.
Walnut, cherry seat rails affixed; original cowhide upholstery with brass nails. H: 35" W: 22½" D: 19½".
Winterthur Museum.

The reverse scroll arms of this chair are almost identical to those in the portrait of Abraham Redwood, founder of the Redwood Library in Newport. Arms of this form are rare in American-made furniture; they are more commonly found in English furniture of the early eighteenth century.

Oil Painting
"Abraham Redwood,"
By Samuel King (1748/9–1819). Newport. c. 1760.
The Redwood Library and Athenaeum.

The painting's high degree of finish and compactness of composition express a taste which was paralleled in American furniture in the first half of the eighteenth century. Newport furniture especially carries the mastery of control, polish and symmetrical composition to its highest level of achievement in this country.

The S-shaped line dominating furniture of this period is also found by tracing the shape of Mr. Redwood's wigline, curve of collar, waistcoat opening, and profile of the armchair. The controlled, finely shaped double curve permeated all the arts; it was the line of grace and cultivation, a signal of taste or learning.

Pair of Side Chairs
New York. c. 1750.
Burled walnut veneer on walnut; seat frame white pine and maple.
H: 38½" W: 22" D: 18⅜".
Museum of Fine Arts, Boston.

Dressing Table
Northeastern Massachusetts (Probably Boston), or New Hampshire. c. 1740.
Walnut veneer on pine. H: 29 1/16" W: 33 13/16" D: 21 9/16".
Museum of Fine Arts, Boston.

Broad low seats and tapered rear legs with shaped feet are characteristic of chairs produced in New York. A cupid's bow at the base of the splat and back stiles which repeat the profile of the splat are other New York regional features. However, the chairs have a long history of ownership in Boston.

The needlework on the slip-seats of these chairs was made by Margaret Fayerweather Bromfield, whose portrait was painted circa 1750 by John Greenwood.

Early ownership of this table in Portsmouth suggests that it could have been made in that area, but it shares features with dressing tables made in Boston. Intercoastal trade between these two major seaport towns assured a common sphere of influence in the arts well into the nineteenth century.

Needlework Slip-Seat
Boston. c. 1750.
By Margaret Fayerweather Bromfield.
Wool on linen.
Museum of Fine Arts, Boston.

Bold floral needlework in brilliant and rich hues almost seems to overshadow the refined detail of carving on the chairs for which the needlework was made. There was nothing precious or timid about eighteenth-century taste, though it may seem that the refined lines of the chair would be discordant with the scale of the needlework. Yet they work well together. Strong movement and depth in the needlework is echoed by the sculptural quality of the chair.

Variations in the shapes of chair backs made during the second half of the eighteenth century offer a means of identifying schools or workshops of craftsmen from different regions. Voids between the splats and the side rails sometimes suggest profiles of fantastic animal or bird heads. Since chairmakers used rigid templates sawn from thin boards to serve as tracing guides or patterns (like the pattern of a tailor), the shape of each back helps identify the shop which produced the chair.

Side Chair
Massachusetts Bay,
Northeastern Massachusetts.

A sedate, round-headed bird head with a small pointed bill is the most commonplace silhouette found on chairs from the Massachusetts Bay to Connecticut and New Hampshire.

Newport, Rhode Island.

A "classic" back from a Newport chair outlines a sharp-billed bird of prey.

Portsmouth, New Hampshire Area

Eccentric silhouettes are found on rural provincial furniture like this chair from the Portsmouth area. The chairmaker failed to realize a careful balance between solids and voids—a mistake not generally made by more sophisticated craftsmen.

New York

The voids and solids of this chair back are harmoniously balanced with the silhouette of this bird.

Side Chair
Philadelphia. c. 1750.
Walnut.
H: 40" W: 20" D: 19¾".
Museum of Fine Arts, Boston.

Few American chairs more successfully communicate a sense of complete mastery of line than this Philadelphia example. At first glance the chair seems simple in design; further examination illuminates a complex and sculptural profile. The anonymous chairmaker achieved the epitome of quiet grace. A knot in the back of the splat may have been consciously selected in order to highlight the figured or grained surface. Several similar chairs from Philadelphia have such knots, indicating that the choice was intentional.

RICHARD CHEEK. PHOTOGRAPHER

Seat-Frame Construction—c. 1750 Rhode Island Chair Compared with an Example from Philadelphia

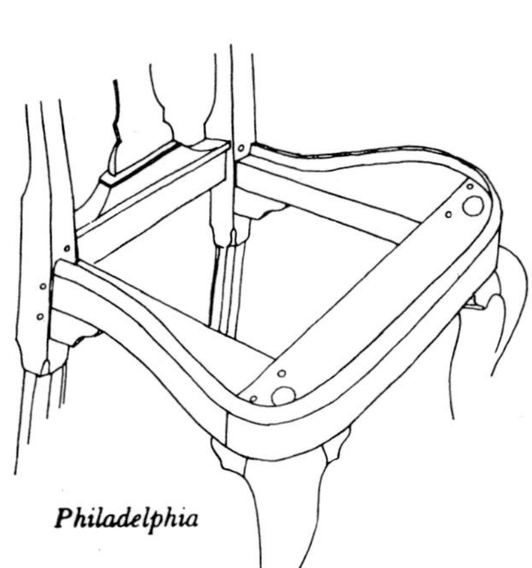

Philadelphia

The seat frame of the Philadelphia chair is made from three solid walnut slabs. Above these slabs a molding is glued to form the rim of the seat, into which the slip-seat fits. The front legs are fastened into the seat frame with a large hand-cut dowel which is continuous with the front leg. It penetrates the front slab of the seat frame at each corner. Tenons from the sides are pinned through the top of the front seat rail on either side of the leg dowel.

The chair made in Rhode Island has its front leg secured through the front corner of the seat frame. The rounded corner of the leg is pinned through tenons which are mortised into the leg at the front and sides. The legs are further strengthened inside the seat frame with vertical glue-blocks. The rim of the seat is an integral part of the seat frame.

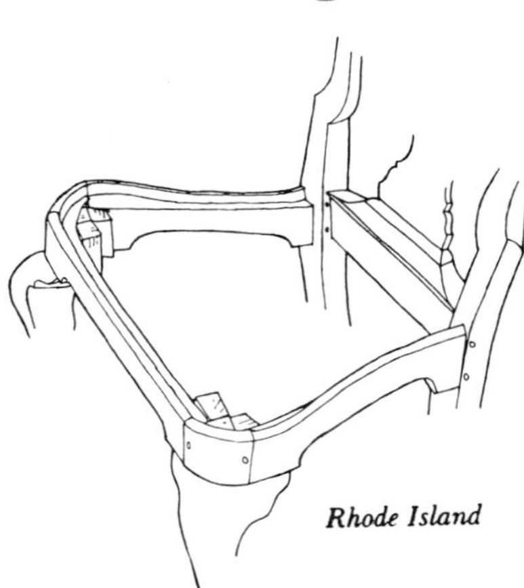

Rhode Island

Comparison: Philadelphia and Rhode Island Side Chairs

Certain construction features differentiate New England side chairs from those made in Philadelphia. The characteristics are most clearly revealed by comparing the backs of two chairs. The example from Rhode Island has square rear legs joined together and to the front legs with stretchers. The Philadelphia chair has no stretchers and the rear legs are shaped or rounded. The joinery of the seat frame is also different. While the seat frame on the Rhode Island chair is mortised, tenoned and pegged together, the tenon is not exposed through the rear legs as it is on the Philadelphia chair. The drake or trifid foot is found frequently on furniture made in Philadelphia and the Delaware Valley. The birdlike claw-and-ball foot is characteristic of mid-eighteenth-century New England high-style furniture.

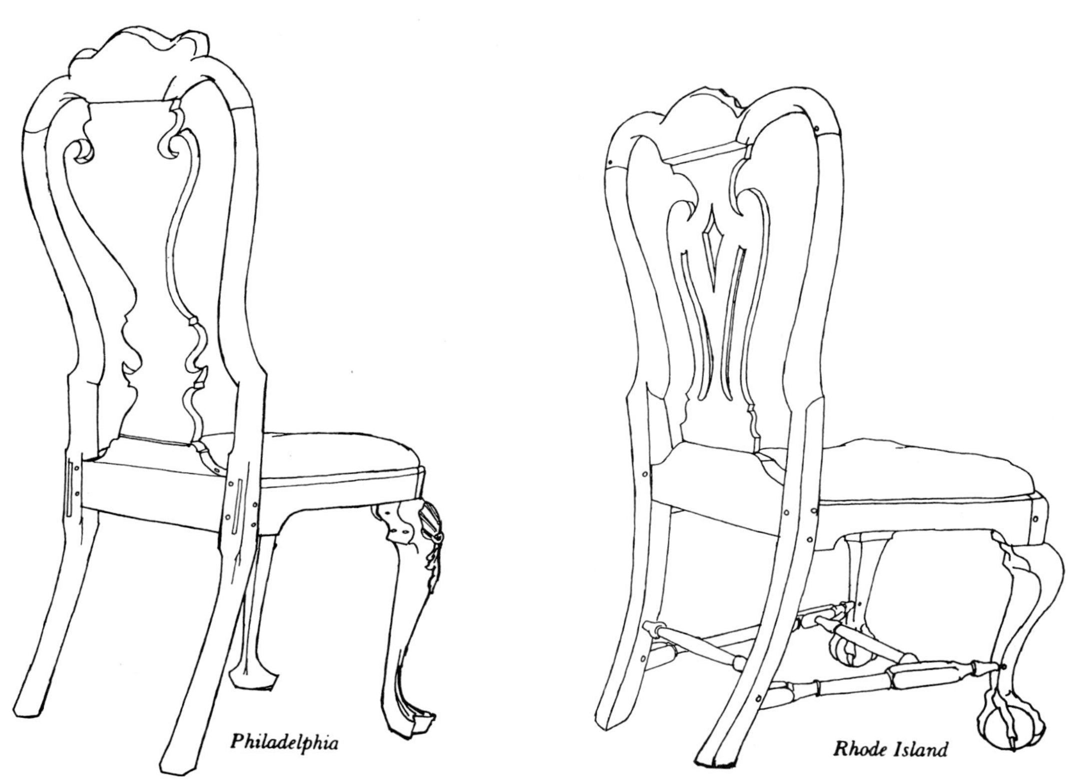

DRAWINGS BY ALICE WEBBER

Side Chair
Pennsylvania. 1720–1740.
Walnut. H: 43" W: 22½" D: 15¼".
Winterthur Museum.

This chair's severity of line and utter simplicity of form are in perfect harmony with the restraint and geometrical precision of the best building practices of the second quarter of the eighteenth century.

Low-seated but high-backed, such chairs are now called "slipper chairs," and are assumed to have been made for women of small stature. Period dresses demonstrate that early eighteenth-century women were generally smaller than women are today.

DELMORE WENZEL, PHOTOGRAPHER

Upholstered Stool
Newport, Rhode Island. 1730–1760.
Walnut. H: 17½" W: 20" D: 16".
Collection of Mr. and Mrs. Stanley Stone.

Few American-made stools are more graceful or striking in design than this example. Beautifully carved shells on all four legs imply that the stool was intended to be seen from all directions.

Slipper Chair or Back Stool
Newport. 1730–1760.
Walnut.
H: 42½" W: 22½" D: 22".
Collection of Mrs. Charles L. Bybee.

Elegant simplicity of line distinguishes this slipper chair. The carved shells at the knees add just the necessary ornament to satisfy a sense of luxury without distracting from the unity of form. The chair is an elegant example of understatement and great beauty. Not only a rare form, the chair represents the highest quality of workmanship in the Newport colony.

RICHARD CHEEK, PHOTOGRAPHER

Easy Chair with Original Wool Upholstery
Boston Area. 1740–1760.
Walnut, white pine.
H: 48" W: 35¼" D: 34".
Collection of the Brooklyn Museum.

The original salmon-colored damask-patterned wool fabric covers this easy chair. The figure was made by watering the cloth and pressing it with a hot plate for the floral and the moreen (zigzag) patterns. Such figured worsted fabrics were used not only for furniture upholstery but also for curtains and bed hangings.

Fabrics listed in early accounts as cheney and harrateen were the most commonly imported textiles used for home furnishings in eighteenth-century America.

Upholstered Easy Chairs

The development of the upholstered easy chair is a great artistic triumph of eighteenth-century furniture design. The brilliant pattern of this example with original needlework is striking, the overall lines of the piece crisply defined. A sense of arrested motion is implicit in this splendid work.

Easy or wing chairs were made for the comfort of the ill, aged or infirm; thus few eighteenth-century portraits show youthful sitters in such chairs. The chairs were most frequently used in the bedroom or room of retirement, not in the parlor or front room. However, there must have been exceptions, for it is hard to imagine an easy chair covered with as much elaborate needlework as this not to have been on show in the best room.

Easy Chair
Newport, Rhode Island.
"Gardiner Jun[r] New Port 1758."
With original flame-stitch covering.
H: 46¾" W: 31½".
The Metropolitan Museum of Art, New York.

The best-documented easy chair to survive from the eighteenth century bears its original needlework upholstery, as do only a few other examples. Most upholstered chairs were not covered with needlework, but with brightly colored woolen fabrics in basic primary hues.

Easy Chair
Philadelphia, Pennsylvania. 1740–1760.
Mahogany with pine frame.
H: 47½" W: 38" D: 26".
Private Collection.

Engineered for the ultimate in visual pleasure and human comfort, this easy chair reflects the achievements of Philadelphia furniture craftsmanship as the town entered into an exciting period of growth and commercial prosperity. The great flair of its arms and wings begins at the C-scroll cutaway that joins the armrests and vertical roll to the seat frame. Moving upward and outward like a cresting wave, the wings of this chair carry the line to a gentle, rounded top. The vigor of outline is best seen without upholstery. A side view of the chair "undressed" shows the bold shape of the armrest sawn and rasped into shape and organized into a complex and sturdy framework. The cabinetmaker made allowance in building the frame for the upholsterer's webbing and rolls of sweet grass that were to be attached along the edges where the human body would exert pressure. Large open spaces were left in the framing at the seat and back for horsehair, linen lining and down cushions. This arrangement permitted a gentle suspension of the sitter in a firm but flexible sling within a frame filled with the softest natural products available. The whole was covered with sensuous fabrics such as silk damask, wool moreen or with rich needlework to create an effect of dazzling richness and extraordinary comfort. The chair is upholstered in a pale-yellow damask outlined with blue-green galloon, contemporary with, but not original to, the frame.

Sofa
Philadelphia, Pennsylvania. 1730–1770.
Walnut; secondary woods: ash and hard pine.
H: 36" L: 84" D: 26".
Winterthur Museum.

Elegant simplicity distinguishes this sofa. Its sweeping crest and graceful arms flow smoothly together in complete harmony with the cabriole legs and carved stocking feet. Straight arrow-shaped stretchers connecting front and rear legs are uncommon in Philadelphia furniture. Sofas, as a genre, were very rare in this period. The simplicity of this sofa offers a monumental effect that is as satisfying as abstract sculpture.

Crewel Bed Hangings
York, Maine. c. 1745. Made by Mary Bulman.
Worsted (loosely twisted) wool needlework on linen.
Old Gaol Museum, York, Maine.

This is the handsomest and most famous set of American bed hangings that survive as a complete unit.

Bedsteads were often merely frames made to support richly figured textiles in homes of the well-to-do. The bedstead, with its fittings and hangings, was often the most expensive and elaborate piece of furniture in the home. Such hangings were complicated affairs, meant to enclose the bed entirely. The tester, or top, with its canopy was a frame that supported valances on the sides and a headcloth that hung behind the pillows. Curtains at four corners were suspended behind the tester and were meant to be drawn closed at night. A counterpane (coverlet) covered the bed. Sometimes an extra set of hangings was suspended around the base of the bed at the sides and end. With such an elaborate enclosure there was little chance for night drafts after the evening fires burned out.

The housewife or schoolgirl who wished to demonstrate her needlework skills usually purchased her ground cloth, called fustian, from abroad, with a design already traced onto its surface. Mary Bulman probably obtained her patterns from Boston, as the work resembles embroidery designs from that area. The patterns derived from a long tradition of English work. The boldly designed foliate and vine motifs of this example suggests a preference for the exotic; they are related to "India work" printed and embroidered silks. Utilitarian objects were often given special needlework: petticoats, pocketbooks, seat covers and fire screens were among the most popular forms that were decorated.

The Flat Top

Flat-top design is one index of early form. Flat-top tankards, high chests and clocks reflect a design preference which persisted from the seventeenth century. This series of four examples shows how flat-top arches found in the aprons were replaced by deep round arches as changing aesthetics encouraged motion in composition.

High Chest of Drawers
Massachusetts or Portsmouth, New Hampshire. 1725–1750.
Walnut veneer on pine.
H: 71" W: 41½" D: 22½".
Museum of Fine Arts, Boston.

Brilliant veneer and an unusual arrangement of the grain on the facade of this piece are its most arresting features. The flat top and hidden drawer in the cornice suggest a fairly early date in the second quarter of the eighteenth century. Each drawer is smartly bordered with veneered bands, stressing the piece's bilateral symmetry.

High Chest of Drawers
Newport, Rhode Island. 1730–1760.
Maple and chestnut, painted brown.
H: 64⅞" W: 39" D: 21".
Collection of Mrs. Charles L. Bybee.

This chest, with its original brasses, stands daintily upon broad legs that taper smartly to fine slipper-shaped feet. To give this composition lift, a deeply arched skirt undulates from the legs to the central pendant-drop. The dark-brown, semitransparent glazed pigment that covers the piece may have been what eighteenth-century inventories termed "Spanish brown." This coloring was probably meant to simulate the rich effect of mahogany.

High Chest of Drawers
Maidenhead (now Lawrenceville), New Jersey. c. 1740.
Walnut, pine and holly; original engraved brasses.
H: 69½" W: 43¾" D: 22".
The Newark Museum.

Carved ornament, moldings and fluted columns are not smoothly articulated on this example. Its maker seemed to be copying case furniture produced in nearby New York City which, while not the epitome of grace, was more smoothly organized. (The mahogany high chest, also shown here, is a slightly later example of the New York style.)

The moldings of this case piece have an angularity and projection which are echoed in the flat-top arches of the skirt. Carving at the knees continues the column's design of fluting, but without successfully terminating it. Despite these flaws, the piece has a pleasing sense of order and is well proportioned. Its drawers are thoughtfully graduated in depth. The chest was made for Joshua Smith as a gift for his daughter, Catherine Smith Stevens.

ARMEN PHOTOGRAPHERS

COURTESY OF BERNARD AND S. DEAN LEVY, INC.

High Chest
New York. c. 1750.
Signed in Chalk on the Bottom of the Lower Central Drawer and on the Bottom Board of the Upper Portion "R. Carter."
Mahogany; secondary wood: poplar. H: 73½" W: 41½".

Robert Carter was a partner of Thomas Burling, the famous New York City cabinetmaker, in 1783. Judging from his known work and bills of sale, Carter had an extensive clientele in New York and Albany. This highboy, which is stylistically earlier in date than other works attributed to this maker, was therefore probably repaired by him.

The highboy possesses a possibly unique detail in the applied carved shells above the fluted chamfered sides. In addition, the removable cabriole legs, like those of Rhode Island highboys, are found on only one other New York example, a highboy made for Philip Van Rensselaer, now in the Albany Institute of History and Art.

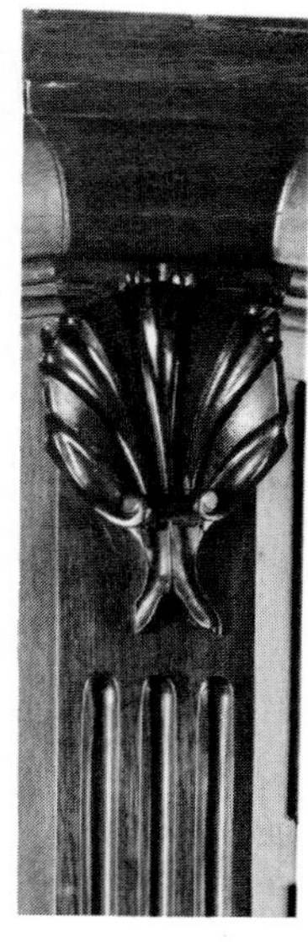

RICHARD CHEEK, PHOTOGRAPHER

Inlaid Star Detail from Dressing Table
Boston Area. c. 1730–1750.
Private Collection.

Inlaid compass or star details were favorite decorative motifs of early eighteenth-century Boston cabinetmakers, and were derived directly from London craftsmen. Compass inlay was most frequently set in the center of large wooden expanses such as desk lids and tabletops—presumably to embellish otherwise plain surfaces or to conceal edges where veneer fletches were joined together.

Acorn-shaped pendant-drops originally completed the dressing table's bilaterally symmetrical composition. Secured only with central dowels, pendants and finials are the details most frequently lost over time. However, the monetary value of the furniture they once ornamented is little affected by their absence, so rare is the furniture they grace.

Dressing Table
Boston Area. c. 1720–1740.
Walnut; secondary wood: white pine.
H: 75" W: 95" D: 57".
Private Collection.

This example illustrates the beginnings of blocked furniture in New England. One senses the difficulty that the craftsmen had with integrating a new design concept within the traditional form of a dressing table. The ornamental effect of the blocking is dramatic and appealing in both this and the Joseph Davis dressing table (page 115), but in neither case is it completely harmonized with the design of the whole as in the desk and bookcase made by Job Coit, Jr. (page 118).

RICHARD CHEEK, PHOTOGRAPHER

Blocking in New England Furniture

Blocking in furniture refers to the raised and depressed profile of panels on the facade of case pieces. The panels are not applied, but in most cases cut out from the solid wood of the drawer fronts. A considerable expenditure of effort and material by the craftsman is required to achieve the desired results. Blocked furniture was produced almost exclusively in New England, and reached the highest artistic level in Boston and Newport. It reflects design theories transmitted to Colonial Americans through the works, immigration or training of Continental and English craftsmen. The idea of blocking was not generated in this country but it survived here long after the taste for block-fronted furniture declined abroad. The blocking design was developed and perfected over several generations in Boston and Newport in a way unknown abroad.

Dressing Table
Boston. c. 1730.
Made by Joseph Davis (Working 1726–1732).
H: 30½" W: 36½" D: 23½".
Walnut and white pine.
The Dietrich Brothers Americana Corporation.

This dressing table represents an attempt at unity of form and ornament. A chalk inscription on the bottom of a drawer identifies it as the work of Joseph Davis who served his apprenticeship to Job Coit in Boston, circa 1725–1726. Since Coit is the earliest cabinet-maker identified with the block-front design, one might assume that Davis learned the blocking technique from him.

Although the design of this table is similar to the preceding example, it is simplified. The feet are no longer strangely carved animal paws but are smoothly shaped hoofs or slippers on a pad. The shell is not as striking as the previous example but it flows smoothly within the whole composition. Still, abrupt junctures of fluted pilasters and blocking details persist. While Davis may have learned blocking technique from Coit, his design was not as successful, for the facade of this dressing table is a composition of arresting parts rather than an integrated whole.

Both the domed top of the Bagnall clock and the bonnet top of the Wade highboy (page 117) demonstrate the makers' interest in crowning their works with an arresting architectonic feature, using curved forms to achieve this end. In the process the old-fashioned flat-top design, which had been popular for generations, was replaced by curvilinear forms.

Tall Clock
Boston. c. 1715–1730.
Movement by Benjamin Bagnall (1689–1773).
Walnut and white pine. H: 92" W: 21" D: 10".
Collection of Mrs. Charles L. Bybee.

This domed-top tall clock is a most imposing example, with works by Boston's first authenticated clockmaker. The surfaces of the clock are beautifully figured in a deep honey-colored walnut. Contrasting with the walnut is the brilliant brass of the clock face and the richly gessoed and gold-leafed surfaces of the column capitals and the gilt-ball finials. "Pillars and balls" were the eighteenth-century terms used to describe these features.

RICHARD CHEEK, PHOTOGRAPHER

RICHARD CHEEK, PHOTOGRAPHER

High Chest
Ipswich, Massachusetts. 1740–1760.
Descended in the family of Colonel Nathaniel Wade.
Walnut veneer on white pine and maple, hickory.
H: 82″ W: 40½″ D: 23″.
Collection of Mrs. Charles L. Bybee.

This high chest is one of the most handsome examples of those made north of Boston, possessing a beautifully figured walnut front and maple sides. Although the pattern of graining is lively, it does not distract from the whole design. Two monumental and deeply carved shells dominate the composition.

This chest displays a sharply contoured profile within its low-arched pediment. Such features are characteristic of the high chests made in the Ipswich-Salem area.

Desk and Bookcase
Boston. Signed and Dated: "Job Coit Jr / 1738."
Black walnut and white pine.
H: 99½" W: 39½" D: 24⅜".
Winterthur Museum.

This is the earliest known example of American block-front furniture that is dated. It shows a thorough integration of overall form and blocking, rather than the blocking serving merely as applied ornamental detail.

The maker of this piece, Job Coit, sold it to Nathaniel Henchman, the father-in-law of Thomas Hancock, founder of the Hancock fortune. It is likely that the piece once stood in the great Hancock mansion on Beacon Hill until about 1793.

Desk and Bookcase
Boston. 1730–1750.
Walnut, white pine, maple.
H: 88½" W: 29⅝" D: 29½".
Museum of Fine Arts, Boston.

Prim and vertical in its proportions, this desk and bookcase is rich in ornamental detail. On the exterior, boldly patterned inlaid compass stars enhance lid, doors and crest. Within, two deeply carved shells above the bookcase and shapely drawers add sculptural dimension. The piece is, perhaps, the finest and earliest example of its type made in America. It follows English models closely, and sets a high standard for the Boston furniture industry which developed most fully the blocked-shell design in desk interiors.

Side Table
Massachusetts. 1740–1760. Mahogany; walnut and marble top.
H: 30¼" W: 47⅞" D: 22¹⁄₁₆".
Museum of Fine Arts, Boston.

RICHARD CHEEK, PHOTOGRAPHER

The great sweeping line to the top of this table is emphasized by the deep overhang of the marble. The cabriole legs' smoothly rounded knees taper to fine angles and generous pad feet, features found on the best Massachusetts furniture. The shape of the apron expresses vitality, its alternating rhythms contrasting with the severe simplicity of the rest of the table. In considering regional preferences for side or serving tables it is instructive to compare this one with the table that John Goddard made for Anthony Low of Newport in 1755, shown below.

*

This side table is documented by a bill from John Goddard to Captain Anthony Low, dated September 15, 1755, mailed in receipt of thirty pounds for its manufacture. It is the earliest documented piece of furniture by John Goddard, and it is among the most unusual. Goddard was one of the Townsend-Goddard family of craftsmen who produced masterpieces of conservative elegance for almost two centuries (Job Townsend, 1699–1765; Edmund Townsend, 1736–1811; John Goddard II, 1789–1843).

The severely bold, plain lines of the table's serpentine front, rounded corners and massive skirt are powerful. The strong and slender cabriole legs, with sharply edged pad feet and crisply formed angles on the sides and front edges, are characteristics of Newport craftsmanship. The figured gray-and-white marble is original. The harmony of all parts, the generous sweep of the top, and the stance of the table as a whole are magnificent. The table's rounded corners suggest the influence of French taste.

Side Table
Newport, Rhode Island. 1755.
Made by John Goddard.
Mahogany frame; chestnut blocks and maple back rail. H: 26¾" W: 45½" D: 21⅞".
Collection of Mr. and Mrs. Joseph K. Ott.

HELGA PHOTO STUDIO, INC.

COURTESY OF ISRAEL SACK, INC.

Dressing Table
Philadelphia, Pennsylvania. 1730–1760.
Walnut. H: 28¾" W: 34¼" D: 20⅜".
Private Collection.

The deeply arched apron of this table has an unusual profile and vigor of line. Its reverse scroll silhouette moves with graceful transition into the three-dimensional volume of the legs. The scroll on each side of the knee carries the curve of the apron into the long curve of the leg just where knee blocks are joined with nails and glue to brace the legs.

A severely plain piece of thin walnut tops this case with ease and generous span. The brasses are massive in scale for the dimensions of the drawer fronts. None of the ornament is fussy or small in scale; the piece is ample, robust and handsome, and artfully combines sensitive design with sound structure.

Dressing Table
Southern. c. 1750.
Walnut, pine. H: 29½" W: 33½" D: 19".
Colonial Williamsburg, Williamsburg, Virginia.

Much Southern furniture is simple. The legs of this piece barely curve with a slight bow formed by the turner when the legs were on the lathe. The apron of the table has a similar muted quality. The inlay of the top introduces a note of elegance with its broad band of herringbone forming a rectangle.

RICHARD CHEEK, PHOTOGRAPHER

Card Table
Boston. 1730–1760.
Walnut, tulip, ash.
H: 28″ W: 28¾″ D: 17⅜″.
Museum of Fine Arts, Boston.

Lt. Governor William Dummer of Massachusetts (1678–1761) is thought to have owned this table, which bears its original needlework. Despite the familiarity with English examples of this form, it is unusual for an American card table of this period to have an oval-shaped top. The support system for the folding top is also English in character. The rear or center leg pulls out of a mortised slot in the frame rather than swinging out, the common design for Massachusetts card tables. The cabinetmaker might well have been an English immigrant or, as the furniture crafts in Boston depended on successful competition with imported goods, the maker may have used an actual English example as a prototype.

Card Table with Needlework Top
1730–1760. Mahogany, pine.
H: 27" W: 35⅝" D: 35⅛".
Museum of Fine Arts, Boston.

Less than a half dozen American Queen Anne-style tables survive with their original needlework tops. Few are more dramatic than this one which has no recorded history of ownership before 1928. Typical of card-table construction, the lid folds to close the needlework from sight, thereby preserving it from fading by overexposure to light. The far legs, instead of swinging, are hinged to fold like an accordion.

Bold, spare lines and rounded edges characterize the shape of this piece. Its turret-like corners are dished to provide space for candlesticks. Smoothly scooped pockets for mother-of-pearl counters alternate on all four sides of the border. A checkered string inlay defines the edges.

The needlework, tacked into a shallow setting, pictures a shepherdess asleep, reclining against a tree. Around her swirl other elements—floral details of carnations, tulips, leaves, birds, a male figure and a town on a hill. It is a dream-like composition in wool-and-silk tent stitches that echoes details from English pastoral prints and Indian printed cotton and silk embroideries. The composition is similar to several other needlework pictures made in the Boston area. Oil paintings by John Singleton Copley and Joseph Blackburn portraying Boston ladies posed as shepherdesses demonstrate that idyllic pastoral fantasies captured the imaginations of eighteenth-century Bostonians.

RICHARD CHEEK, PHOTOGRAPHER

Construction Details Under Boston Tea Table

The underside of furniture reveals clues to age not visible from the top. One important indication is the mellow color acquired by oxidized raw wood through exposure to the atmosphere over time. Note the light image of the stretcher bar on the center of the drawer bottom where the bar protected the wood from exposure.

Wood shrinks with age, often cracking when it has been tightly held in place with nails, glue, glue-blocks, screws or other fastening devices. The crack on the top of this tea table is the result of such shrinkage, though it would not trouble even a fastidious collector who would consider it an important sign of age.

Rough-hewn chisel marks that shape the apron of this table show the hand workmanship customary in eighteenth-century American furniture. Mechanical band-saw or power-tool marks (not found on this table) would suggest modern workmanship—either fakery, honest repairs or reproduction of an early piece.

Tea Table
Boston Area. 1730–1760.
Unidentified Chalk Initials "AO" Under Drawer Bottom.
Mahogany, pine.
H: 27½" W: 19½" D: 31¾".
Private Collection.

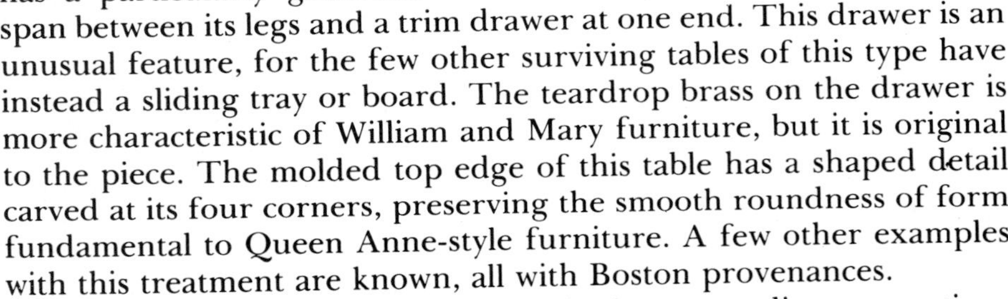

COURTESY OF ISRAEL SACK, INC.

The popular eighteenth-century pastime of tea drinking brought with it elaborate equipage requiring special tables for the service. Some of the most beautiful tables made in America resulted from this fashion. This one has a particularly generous span between its legs and a trim drawer at one end. This drawer is an unusual feature, for the few other surviving tables of this type have instead a sliding tray or board. The teardrop brass on the drawer is more characteristic of William and Mary furniture, but it is original to the piece. The molded top edge of this table has a shaped detail carved at its four corners, preserving the smooth roundness of form fundamental to Queen Anne-style furniture. A few other examples with this treatment are known, all with Boston provenances.

The table is extraordinary not only for its outstanding proportions and unique drawer, but also for the splendid sweep connecting the finely tapered legs with the scrolled apron.

Tea Table
Boston Area. 1720–1750.
Walnut, white pine.
H: 28½" W: 25¾" D: 17½".
Museum of Fine Arts, Boston.

This tea table, unusually small in size, combines beauty with utility, for it is both elegant in design and easy to move around. Its flexibility reflects early eighteenth-century habits of dining or taking tea in any number of different rooms.

The tabletop, broad but thin, seems to float easily over the robustly arched skirt. Supporting the mass are especially long and finely tapered legs ending in sturdy pad feet of a typical Massachusetts form. The thinness of the ankles is a highly desirable feature found on the best early Georgian furniture. The table's surface finish is original; the warps, dents, scratches and marks on the piece are telltale signs of age. The table exhibits rare form and subtle beauty.

Mixing Table
Boston Area. 1730–1750.
Maple, painted black; delft tile top.
H: 26⅜" W: 29" D: 24¼".
Collections of Greenfield Village and the Henry Ford Museum, Dearborn, Michigan.

This New England mixing table exhibits the slender, tapered and gracefully curved legs found in stylish furniture of the "best sort." Its top is inset with twenty delft tiles with biblical scenes painted and glazed on the surface. Such a stain-resistant surface was a practical solution to possible damage to the finish caused by spilled alcoholic beverages. Several similar examples with ceramic inset tops survive from Massachusetts and Connecticut.

This table demonstrates freedom from turned stretchers, elaborate inlay, shaped apron and pendant turnings characteristic of an earlier style. Its simplicity, openness of composition and unity of design command admiration.

Folding Tea Table
New Hampshire, Probably Portsmouth.
1740–1760. Cherry and birch.
H: 25" Diameter of top: 26".
Museum of Fine Arts, Boston.

Although at first glance this table seems like a handsome, small, yet otherwise unexceptional piece, its design is special. The legs swing and the hinged top tilts to fold away into a remarkably small space only four inches deep. In the antique furniture trade this type is known as a "tuckaway" table. It was a popular form in New England where many fine homes were constructed small to conserve heat, making space a premium. This table was found in Portsmouth, New Hampshire, and is thought to have been made there. The shape of the feet, with the generous pad beneath the club, is found throughout New England, and is especially prevalent in coastal Massachusetts furniture.

DAN FARBER, PHOTOGRAPHER

Tea Table
Williamsburg, Virginia. c. 1735.
Mahogany; secondary woods: yellow pine, oak.
H: 26¾" W: 29½" D: 17⅜".
Colonial Williamsburg, Williamsburg, Virginia.

Recent research has shown that artistically advanced furniture was made in the Southern colonies. Much of it was extremely complex and stylistically sophisticated. This table, which descended in the Galt family of Williamsburg, is spare, suave and elegant. It is related to a group of pieces which seem to be connected with the maker of the famous tall-backed Speaker's Chair of the Virginia House of Burgesses. The most obvious feature shared by this group is the bulbous-shaped club foot. The craftsman who made this table and related examples must have been among the finest workmen in Williamsburg in the 1730s. He was fully aware of advanced London taste and in many respects ahead of his counterparts in the Northern seaport towns.

Drop-leaf Table
New England. 1750–1790.
Maple. H: 27⅛" W: 14½" D: 45⅛".
Collection of Mrs. Charles L. Bybee.

This table is simple, sturdy and practical. Its hinged leaves are supported by swing legs smartly turned and shaped in a gentle cabriole form. Generous extra platforms of wood support the club-shaped feet like shoes or soles, a characteristic often found on New England Queen Anne furniture. The apron of the table is straight, and aside from the shape of the leaves and the interlocking molding at the hinge of the lid, the table is unadorned and totally functional in design. It probably represents the least expensive production of a first-class cabinet shop rather than the work of a country craftsman. Over the years the table has accumulated a number of layers of paint which have become worn and muted with age.

Dining Table
New Jersey. 1740–1780.
Walnut, with pine brace.
H: 29" L: 48" W: 19¼" (with leaves down).
Collection of Mrs. Charles L. Bybee.

The simplicity of this table may in part be due to a Quaker aesthetic or merely the solution to functional needs. The trifid foot with its shaped center rib shows a relationship to Philadelphia practices, but its depth and simply cut shape is a provincialization of the more polished Philadelphia manner. A deep arch to the end of the table skirt unites the shape of the legs when the wings are down. An early book on New Jersey furniture claims that the table was made circa 1740, from a tree which grew near Colestown, New Jersey.

DAN FARBER, PHOTOGRAPHER

Corner Table
Virginia. c. 1730.
Walnut. H: 28¼" W: 44½" D: 21¾".
Museum of Early Southern Decorative Arts, Winston-Salem, North Carolina.

Drop-leaf tables were space-saving pieces of furniture popular throughout the American colonies. This example, with its straight tapering legs, has New England counterparts with similarly turned legs and simply shaped feet above a pad. Turned legs for tables were the simple alternative to the shaped cabriole legs of more costly furniture. It took less work for the craftsman to turn a leg of this sort than to shape a cabriole leg through offset turning and hand-shaping. Thus this type of leg was economically expedient to make and was enormously popular.

The ring turning at the top of each leg, together with the block above it, recalls the design tradition of William-and-Mary-style furniture of the previous generation. This holdover shows that the maker of this table combined old with new features in his work.

Interior View of the Queen Anne Dining Room at The Winterthur Museum

The Queen Anne Dining Room is a classic museum installation. It was personally shaped and used by the foremost collector of American decorative arts, Henry Francis du Pont. Its richness of objects, colors and texture probably surpasses what any early American home contained. As such, it presents an ideal—an image of the past which reveals the taste of twentieth-century connoisseurs even more than those of the eighteenth century.

Paneled woodwork in the room comes from a home in Derry, New Hampshire. The set of upholstered New York armchairs are covered with blue resist-dyed slipcovers in a bold floral pattern, setting a major color chord for the room. The blue and white theme is repeated in the imported delftware which is dominated by a monumental Bristol punch bowl on the center of the table (marked "George Skinner, Boston, 1732"). A rich collection of American silver locked in a cupboard adds further luster to the setting.

No amount of archaeological correctness in reconstructing the furnishings of a period room has matched the artistic mood presented here. Despite its historical flaws, the Queen Anne Dining Room remains one of the most visually exciting and appealing room installations in any American museum, as it represents the mature taste of a great collector.

IV

1710–1820

Japanned Furniture

"JAPAN ALONE HAS exceeded in beauty and magnificence all the pride of the Vatican at this time, and the Pantheon heretofore . . ." So wrote John Stalker and George Parker in the first and most famous book on the art of japanning: *A Treatise of Japanning and Varnishing* (Oxford, England, 1688). Although they claimed that their engraved plates were exact imitations of works by the inhabitants of Japan, Stalker and Parker also admitted having "helpt them a little in their proportions, where they were lame or defective, and made them more pleasant yet altogether as Antick." But they assured their readers that their objective was to represent "true genuine Indian work." Westerners made no fine distinctions between the cultures of China, India and Japan. Their imaginations stirred by exotic imported luxury goods and tales of Eastern splendor, Europeans and Americans accepted free interpretations of or substitutions for genuine Oriental art.

The most impressive group of eighteenth-century American japanned furniture to survive was made in Boston where more than a dozen japanners were active. High chests, three dressing tables, a stand, clock cases and smaller objects are known.

Why Boston should have been the most important center for japanning may be explained in part by its impressive commercial growth late in the seventeenth century at a time when there was a vogue in London for the imitation of things Oriental, called "chinoiserie." The Bostonians who could afford japanned furniture were the successful merchants who copied London fashions. Merchants like Thomas Hancock and Charles Apthorp, for example, were constantly importing manufactured goods for sale to American colonists.

The art of japanning was also connected to trades other than furniture decorating. Perhaps the most skilled japanner in town was Thomas Johnston, Sr. (born in England in 1708, active in Boston, 1732–1767), who not only ornamented furniture, but also engraved copper plates for prints, painted coats of arms, built organs, and sold looking glasses. His elaborate trade card, which he engraved himself, claimed that he sold "Chests of Drawers, Chamber and Dressing Tables, Tea Tables, Writing Desks, Book-Cases, Clock-Cases, & c." Japanning was hardly a step away from portrait painting or limning likenesses. Thomas Johnston's son, John (active 1773–1789), was a japanner as well as a portrait painter, and his other sons, Thomas, Jr., and Benjamin, were also japanners.

William Randall or Randle (active 1715–1739) is one of the earliest japanners whose identified works survive from Boston. He was also a cabinetmaker and dealer in domestic goods. The Town House, or Old State House, which was near Randall's shop, faced the town house of Charles Apthorp, one of the wealthiest merchants of Boston. He had formed a company with Captain Mark Trecothick, who shipped looking glasses for sale to coastal port towns. Apthorp supplied the money for the business, Randall and his partner, Robert Davis, performed the work of making the glasses and their frames, and Trecothick did the shipping. The business was apparently successful. When Randall went into the business of tavern-keeping, Davis acquired the family shop and married his master's daughter. An inventory of the estate of Robert Davis, taken shortly after his death in 1793, lists the tools and supplies necessary for decorating furniture and looking glasses. His japanning materials included smalt, lampblack and designs or cartoons for his japanned work.

Most japanned furniture in America is unsigned and undated. The form and decoration of an object were determined by the customer and cabinetmaker. The goal of the japanner was to cover the piece with paint and varnish to simulate the work of Oriental lacquer. An inability to obtain the proper materials or techniques of true Oriental lacquerwork did not dissuade the American japanner. He smoothed the maple or pine surface before tracing his designs. He modeled figures and landscape ornament such as trees, rocks and flora in shallow relief directly onto the wood with gesso—a mixture of gum arabic, glue, whiting and other powders. When this was dry the surface was smoothed with sharkskin and a red-brown stain was applied. Over this ground color, lampblack powder in oil resin was dashed broadly with a brush to simulate the effects of tortoiseshell and lacquer. Sizing was brushed onto the raised gesso area and silver or gold leaf and silver or gold powder were applied. After this layer was dry, details were drawn with a fine brush dipped in lampblack. This step gave the work its distinctive Oriental character. Other layers of varnish were then applied, and finally the whole was polished with a complex organic varnish mixture known as "white varnish" and/or a spirit varnish made of seed-lac (shellac). This final varnish was made from the resinous deposits of an insect, *Coccus lacca,* left on the branches of trees in India, which was dissolved in alcohol. The shellac varnish gave the surface a brilliant luster and optical depth which simulated effectively the surface of Oriental lacquer. The composition of the imitation lacquer did not ensure the longevity of the ornamentation. The different rates of shrinkage which characterize wood, gesso, paint and shellac have combined to make these pieces the most vulnerable and fragile pieces of art in American collections. Nevertheless, they are some of the most stunning examples of Colonial taste. The classic Baroque proportions of the furniture contrast dramatically with a whimsical disregard for Western tradition in the ornament. In spite of seemingly opposed stylistic views, East and West are harmoniously blended with a bold freedom that documents an age of enterprising mercantile and artistic adventures.

High Chest (page 132) and Dressing Table
Boston Area. c. 1710–1715.
Maple and white pine.
Chest—H: 64¼" W: 40¾" D: 22½".
Table—H: 30½" W: 34" D: 21½".
Private Collection.

These are the most important recent discoveries of early eighteenth-century japanned furniture made in Boston. Originally they were owned by members of the Cogswell family of Massachusetts, descending in the same family for generations until coming onto the market. The

name "Scottow" is inscribed on the back of the drawers throughout the high chest. The Scottows were a family of Massachusetts joiners or furniture makers who practiced in Boston in the late seventeenth and early eighteenth centuries.

The faceted legs on the high chest are unusual features in American furniture. Also unique to American furniture is the dressing table with a japanned top. It pictures a fantastic landscape filled with restless movement. The legs and stretchers carry through the idea of excited movement both in their form and in the japanned ornament which covers their surfaces.

High Chest of Drawers
Boston, Massachusetts. 1725–1739.
Japanned by Robert Davis.
Maple and white pine.
H: 68⅞" W: 41¾" D: 22⅞".
The Baltimore Museum of Art.

In addition to the signature of the japanner, Robert Davis, this chest bears the initials "WR," which probably stand for his father-in-law, William Randall, who was both a cabinetmaker and a japanner. The chest may represent a collaborative effort made sometime before Randall turned over the family business to Davis and occupied himself with tavern-keeping.

Since the chest is one of the rare signed pieces, it is an important document. Over the years it has lost much of its ornamentation, but the conserved parts which remain suggest that Davis had a broad compositional instinct, relishing large-scale figures and an informal arrangement of loosely balanced parts. This piece, while only a glimmer of its former glory, does yield clues to the earliest manner of Boston japanning.

Dressing Table
Boston, Massachusetts. 1730–1750.
Maple and white pine. H: 30½" W: 34". D: 21".
The Metropolitan Museum of Art, New York.

The gold-leafed shell of this table forms a central ornament around which the rest of the japanning is symmetrically organized. A pair of columns flanking the shell and the formal organization of the brasses further heighten the symmetry of the piece. Yet within this formal structure, the play of ornament manages to avoid rigid balance. The top of the table is where the greatest freedom is expressed—with complete asymmetry of design.

High Chest of Drawers
Windsor Area, Connecticut. 1736.
Maple and pine of the Taeda group.
H: 61⅛" W: 41⅜" D: 22".
Winterthur Museum.

This chest with its nonacademic proportions and unusual treatment of the cabriole leg has captured the fancy of furniture students since it was first shown in the Connecticut Tercentenary Exhibition of 1935. The piece reflects a rural vision of what was going on in Boston—remembered impressions of what was fashionable. In the process of transferring the idea to the Windsor area something quite new, remarkable and exciting took place. This country cousin of the sleek japanned high chests of Boston is remarkably alive and vital. The piece seems almost ready to walk away, so insistent are the curves of its legs and skirt. Other related pieces from the Windsor area suggest it was an active center for this type of japanning from the 1720s on.

The decoration simulates japanning simply. The red ground over which a black pigment is painted follows the Boston tradition of tortoiseshell japanning. But here similarities cease. Decorative figures are not built up with gesso (chalk and glue), but are merely painted on in a cream oil paint. The variety of figures is splendid. The crowned lion is not an unexpected subject. But what enigmatic meanings are implicit in the giraffes, deer, gazelles, exotic flowers and birds? Three of the most remarkable images are an imaginary sea horse with coiled tail, an Indian with bow and arrow shooting a bird, and a kneeling, knightlike figure (perhaps a falconer) holding a bird of prey. These images are not articulated in any particular arrangement. They float in undefined space as pure fantasy or dream-world imaginings.

High Chest of Drawers
Boston, Massachusetts. 1725–1740.
Maple and white pine.
H: 71¾" W: 42⅞" D: 24¾".
Museum of Fine Arts, Boston.

This flat-top high chest is one of the most splendidly preserved examples of early Boston japanning. The glistening ornamental detail is a radiant example of the magnificence of mercantile Boston at the time when old-style Puritanism was on the wane.

In many ways, this high chest relates directly to the piece signed by Robert Davis, now at the Baltimore Museum of Art. But the ornament here is more precisely articulated. Perhaps this articulation can be explained by the fact that this piece has not suffered the surface losses of its Baltimore cousin. In any case, it seems to fall in the early group of japanning made before mid-century and is related to the Davis-Randall school.

High Chest of Drawers
Boston, Massachusetts. 1740–1750.
Case Made by John Pimm; Japanner Unknown.
Maple and white pine. H: 95¾" W: 42" D: 24½".
Winterthur Museum.

The most famous example of Boston japanning is the "Pimm Highboy," so called because of chalk inscriptions of the word "Pimm" on its drawers. This gives us the name of the cabinetmaker, John Pimm, who constructed the case. Unfortunately, the name of the japanner is unknown, although there has been a fairly consistent attribution of the work to Thomas Johnston, which cannot be supported by documentation. It would be splendid to know who did ornament this piece, for there are a number of japanned pedimented high chests which are related stylistically. According to family tradition, this example belonged to Joshua Loring (1716–1781) of Jamaica Plain and Boston.

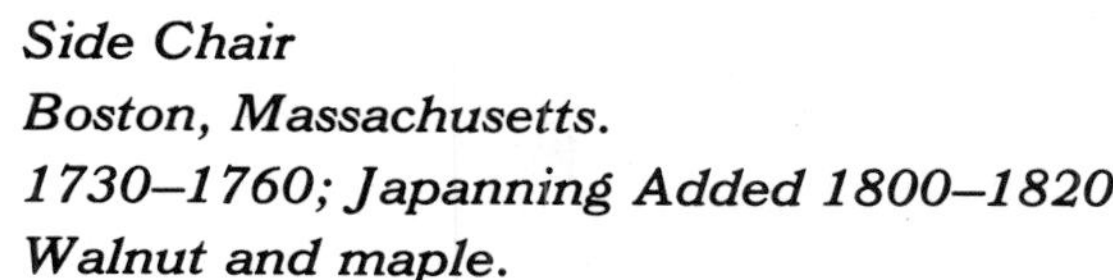

Side Chair
Boston, Massachusetts.
1730–1760; Japanning Added 1800–1820.
Walnut and maple.
H: 40″ W: 20¼″ D: 14″.
Collection of Mrs. Charles L. Bybee.

Although this chair was made in Boston well before the American Revolution, the japanning was not applied until the Federal Period. The small scale of the ornament and the tight detail of classical leafage suggest the later neoclassical taste of a japanner of the early years of the nineteenth century.

This side chair is part of a set or sets now in different collections, and was owned by the Winthrop-Blanchard and Gardner families of Boston. For a long time it was claimed that the chairs were sent to China for their ornament, but the workmanship is not Oriental; it is nineteenth-century chinoiserie.

RICHARD CHEEK, PHOTOGRAPHER

Tall Clock
Boston, Massachusetts. c. 1749.
Works by Gawen Brown; Japanning
Attributed to Thomas Johnston.
White pine. H: 94½" W: 22¼" D: 10¾".
Winterthur Museum.

Gawen Brown, who made the works of the clock on the right, came to Boston from England as a mature craftsman. An advertisement makes a connection between Brown and Thomas Johnston, suggesting that Johnston must have japanned this clock case. It represents a more developed phase of japanning in Boston than that of the earlier and simpler ornament of Randall and Davis. The ornamental detail is more richly developed, with a greater sense of three-dimensional plasticity, and the organization of the composition is more compact.

Tall Case Clock
New York City. c. 1755.
Works Made by Bartholomew Barwell (w. 1749–1760).
Oak, japanned. H: 96 ".
The Brooklyn Museum.

Freely handled splotches of paint were dashed onto the background of the clock case to simulate the appearance of tortoiseshell. The pattern of these random patches enhances the overall complexity of detail of the japanning.

Craftsmen who japanned furniture in New York were either few in number or not prone to give public notice of their trade. Only the names of Gerardus Duyckinck, Sr. and Jr. are known by advertisements. Yet several handsome examples of what must be New York japanning survive on clocks marked by New York makers.

In order to fill the tall case door with an effective design the motif of an Oriental-style bridge was used, together with figures, flowers, trees and rocks. Although the bridge motif was a traditional means by which the japanner could carry the eye upward in zigzag fashion, no two clocks have the same patterns. Japanners recombined detail to offer a variety of pictorial patterns.

RICHARD CHEEK, PHOTOGRAPHER

V

1750–1780

The Chippendale Period

TWO OPPOSING STATES of mind conditioned attitudes toward design in eighteenth-century American furniture. The older and traditional point of view produced works that were restrained in form and ornament. Furniture and architecture were composed within ordered boundaries of well-defined and balanced parts; a sense of order and symmetry persisted, despite changing fashions, throughout the eighteenth century. In the form and ornament of early Georgian architecture and Queen Anne furniture (both of which persisted long beyond the period outlined by Chapter III), symmetry, smooth surfaces and restrained ornamental detail controlled much furniture design.

However, a new rococo impulse fostered a freer approach to design. By mid-century the inverted pear shape began to replace the sphere as the ideal basic form. This resulted in greater freedom of movement and instability of composition. The new style introduced only a few new types of furniture for popular use, yet the variations on traditional pieces became numerous and complex. A new piece of furniture, the fire screen, was used to shield the sitter from heat and sparks from the fire, as well as serving to display the needlework of the lady of the house. Elaborately fretted or galleried tea tables, richly carved stands for china jars, and girandoles were other newcomers. Bureau tables and large-scale library furniture also made their debut as rooms in homes became more specialized. Despite these introductions, most of the change in furniture came simply through modification or addition to those forms which had been made before.

The new style introduced a fresh interest in brilliantly carved and figured surfaces. The preferred woods were West Indian or Central American mahogany. The grain of the wood selected gained special emphasis because its pattern sometimes violated the boundaries of the strict bilateral symmetry vigorously maintained throughout the first half of the century. Carved ornament in the new style became much lighter and more spirited than before. S-shape scrolls evolved into swirls and naturalistic foliage expressive of movement and vitality. The light and shadow, which previously had been bold and solid, dissolved into shimmering patterns that caught small flickers of light on facets and hatching, artwork detail and foliate carving. The luster of this new furniture and its dazzling effects of carving were heightened with the use of brilliant French shellac polish which revealed the full optical depth and color of the wood. Furniture of this period needs to be considered in the context of a culture that savored lush figured silks and damasks, polished leather, elegant crystal, and elaborate ruffles and lace worn by both men and women.

The use of rich materials offered the well-to-do a symbol of station; they were well aware of the textural contrasts offered by combining polished brass nails and silk upholstery on mahogany furniture. In the eighteenth century people took note of variations of patterns cut into the splats of chairs and were alert to the quality and character of carving on the legs and feet of furniture. Details such as shells, pediments, finials and other features which required carving added to the cost of making furniture. A considerable investment of a craftsman's time and talent could be involved in refining features which were above and beyond mere utility. Such costly embellishments were perceived instinctively as good. The twentieth-century student imbued with ideas of severe functionalism does not naturally come to this same conclusion.

The new style in eighteenth-century furniture is identified in both England and America with the name of the famous London entrepreneur and craftsman Thomas Chippendale (1718–1779). In 1754 he published a handsome and large volume of furniture designs entitled *The Gentleman and Cabinet-Maker's Director.* The *Director* was so popular that it was republished in 1755 and again with additional plates in 1762. All three editions were owned and used in eighteenth-century America. Although the *Director* was not the only book of furniture designs known here, it was certainly the standard work of its day and it exceeded all others in terms of ambitiousness of designs and lavishness of engraved plates. The third edition offered some two hundred prints of magnificently engraved furniture designs. In his preface, Chippendale explained that the *Director* was meant to assist the gentleman in his choice of designs and the cabinetmaker in the execution of his works. A great variety of details were illustrated; an almost infinite variety of combinations could be employed.

Three basic styles were offered by the *Director:* Chinese, Gothic and Modern (or French taste). The Chinese and Gothic designs were hardly literal in their rendering of ancient or foreign works. Instead they were fantastic, imaginative evocations of cultures which were strange and wonderful to the eighteenth-century mind. So distorted from their sources were the Chinese and Gothic plates in the *Director* that they are now better understood as aspects of what Chippendale identified as the "modern taste." Today this "modern taste" is called the rococo style. The word rococo came into use during the nineteenth century, used first in derision of the style which at that time had fallen out of popular favor. It derived from the French word *rocaille,* referring to the rock work, shell and naturalistic grotto ornament which played such an important part in the evolution and artistic development of the style which started late in the seventeenth century in the court of Louis XIV under the brilliant leadership of designers Jean Bérain and Pierre Lepautre. By the 1730s the principle of asymmetry had been introduced and a second phase developed through designers Nicholas Pineau and Juste Aurèle Meissonnier, who also worked for the French court.

Adoption of the rococo in England came about slowly. Accepting the delicate and excited lines of rococo ornament, the English designers and craftsmen fused the new style with old familiar forms. For England and her colonies, the rococo was essentially an ornamental addition which did not change the basic proportions of furniture or architecture profoundly. The most outlandish flights of rococo fancy were left behind in France and on the Continent.

French rococo ornament did find its way into English architectural design books which were popular in the American colonies. Abraham Swan's *The British Architect* (London, 1745), and *A Collection of Designs in Architecture* (London, 1757) illustrated foliate ornament for houses which were just as useful to carvers of furniture as they were to architectural craftsmen, for the aesthetics which controlled proportions of furniture and rooms were the same. It is significant that Chippendale's *Director* introduced his work with seven plates devoted to ancient classical architectural orders and rules for proportions and drawing. He begins the preface as follows: "Of all the Arts which are either improved or ornamented by Architecture, that of CABINET-MAKING is not only the most useful and ornamental, but capable of receiving as great Assistance from it as any whatever." Order was the essence of eighteenth-century thought. It was the substratum of attitude which conditioned all the arts.

In part because of a quest for intellectual order and symmetry in the Age of Reason, forces were unleashed which led toward freedom of thought and action in this country. But those who would search American furniture for signs of cultural revolution will be disappointed. The stylistic lead of the mother country was clearly the main force which conditioned the form and ornament of furniture, architecture and the other arts.

Americans built their civilization upon what they remembered, brought with them, imported or learned through illustrated books from abroad. The hope of English merchants and craftsmen—indeed, the basis of mercantile trade theory—was that the colonies would become suppliers of cheap raw goods to Britain and consumers of expensive imported finished products. But instead, the colonials asserted what they felt were their basic rights as free Englishmen. Restrictions on manufacturing in the colonies failed to discourage craftsmen who vigorously entered the marketplace as unfettered competitors with their English counterparts. As shops opened in the colonies the need for imported furniture declined. A rise in furniture production in major seaport towns grew to meet the requirements of an expanding population. By mid-century, furniture making was a major urban industry. Craftsmen in this country competed successfully with imported products and in some cases even bettered these models. It was the issue of freedom to make and sell goods rather than the style or form of the products which helped to generate unrest and dissent in the colonies. Nonimportation agreements in 1765 were signed eagerly. It was good business for the local furniture makers to require American customers to buy homemade products.

The dynamics of the urban marketplace in colonial centers brought about a period that is recognized as one of the greatest ages of craftsmanship. Workers of all sorts were involved: cabinet- and chairmakers, upholsterers, carvers, Windsor chairmakers, turners, artisans and merchants who supplied specialized goods such as gilding, japanning, fastening devices, hardware, glass, moldings, veneer and inlay work, brass and wood. The freedom of work offered in America came about through the lack of a guild or formal regulatory system. This helped the furniture industry to grow and develop.

Despite the opportunities offered in this country to bypass strict regulations, each town was dominated by practicing artisans whose work served as a standard of excellence. It was not possible for a craftsman to take shortcuts in workmanship and still compete successfully for the patronage of persons who were able to buy both locally made and imported furniture. The novice craftsman began to learn his trade around the age of ten or thirteen through an apprenticeship of seven years living and working with a master. Some people were able to learn so quickly that they could purchase a few of their remaining years from their master to become journeymen before the full apprenticeship term was completed. The journeyman continued to perfect his art by journeying from shop to shop as a piece worker until he had saved enough money to establish his own shop as a master craftsman. This method of training accounts for the high level of workmanship maintained in much eighteenth-century furniture. A craftsman who learned his art by this system knew the whole business. The system insured the transmission of traditions of construction techniques and preferences for certain design features. This led to the growth of recognizable traits in furniture which can be identified with furniture made in specific regions.

Infused into this matrix of tradition, the immigrant craftsman brought up-to-date carving styles, construction features and designs from Dublin, Liverpool and London. Immigrant craftsmen were prone to boast in ads that their workmanship was the best because it was based upon a regular apprenticeship in one of the most important shops in London (by inference, not one of the irregular apprenticeships in lesser shops in America). The aspirations of buyers and sellers are reflected in advertisements with such phrases as "choice household furniture . . . all of the best workmanship" and assurances that the craftsman "endeavours to please his customers by the goodness of his work and the moderation of his prices."

Economic mobility of the craftsman—the freedom to change vocational directions as opportunities presented themselves—is an important part of the story. The Philadelphia furniture maker Benjamin Randolph (w. 1762–1785), who was a dispatch carrier for General Washington, sold his city real estate and cabinetmaker's tools by the time of the Revolution to move to New Jersey to produce pig iron at the Speedwell Furnace in the middle of the Pine Barrens. This represents a fairly characteristic instance of upward economic mobility among craftsmen. Freedom of choice offered the craftsman a chance to succeed in business, rising from craftsman to gentleman, from shop to country estate. It was the pattern of success in the career of Paul Revere, which was repeated many times over for other craftsmen. History is reflected in almost every cabinetmaker's biography: Benjamin Frothingham (1734–1809) of Charlestown, Massachusetts, is well known. More than seventeen pieces of furniture made by him are recorded today by his label or signature. They range from relatively plain pieces to more elaborately carved examples in both the Chippendale and the Federal styles. Frothingham's father was a joiner with a shop on Milk Street, in what is now the heart of Boston's financial district. The young Frothingham set up an independent shop in Charlestown by 1754, in what was a vital furniture-making district in greater Boston. His shop was burned by the British military force, together with some twenty-nine other cabinetmakers' homes and shops on June 17, 1775, at the time of the Battle of Bunker or Breed's Hill.

Frothingham was a man of action. Like Revere he had tasted military service early in his life. At twenty, he had served in Captain Richard Gridley's military and artillery company and was part of the expedition to Quebec during the French and Indian War. Seasoned with such experience he probably shared a common feeling that the recovery of England's war losses was unjustly sought through taxing colonials who had so valiantly served their mother country.

With the opening of the Revolution, he was commissioned a first lieutenant in 1775. Wounded at Bethlehem, Pennsylvania, and serving valiantly later, he rose to the rank of Major by the end of the war. In 1789, when Washington came to New England on his triumphal tour as the new President of the United States, he called upon Major Benjamin Frothingham in Charlestown to honor one who had served his country well and who was a member of the Society of the Cincinnati, one of Washington's distinguished officers. After the war Frothingham returned to cabinetmaking and adapted well to the changing styles of the new Federal Period.

Not all craftsmen were successful during the late eighteenth century. The Revolution was a disruptive force, and many suffered for years afterward from slow economic growth. Changing styles made elaborately carved or ornamented furniture outmoded. But the foundation of the craft which had been well established by mid-century served as a springboard for new developments in furniture craftsmanship after 1800.

Oil Painting
of Jeremiah Platt (1744–1811).
New York. 1767.
By John Mare (1739?–1802).
Signed: "Jno Mare, Pinx^t. 1767."
H: 48½" W: 38½".
The Metropolitan Museum of Art, New York.

The salient aesthetic features of this painting are asymmetry of composition and the optical effect of shimmering textures of varied materials (for example, silk, lace, skin, hair, carved wood and brass). Asymmetry and movement form the basis of rococo taste which, by the mid-eighteenth century, was accepted and applied to furniture and other arts by fashion-conscious Americans.

Although the artist, John Mare, signed and dated the canvas, it took fifteen years of detective work to identify the subject: Jeremiah Platt, a prosperous New York merchant.

During the Revolution, Platt was in partnership with his brother-in-law, Samuel Broome, and together they were involved with the equipping of vessels as privateers. While Platt died insolvent, the inventory of his house shows that he was a person of substantial means, and that his home was handsomely furnished. His 1811 inventory lists one large framed picture valued at $1.00 (which may be this one). The inventory also lists three red window curtains, red cord and tassels. It is only speculation that these were the curtains and tassel pictured here, for painting background drapery was a convention of portraiture of the time. Of special interest is the side chair of Chippendale design on which Platt rests his hand. The carved detail and shape of its splat are so specific that the artist must have used an actual chair for its model. It is possible that the chair was made in England, but perhaps it represents one made in New York City.

Comparison: Regional Preferences

RICHARD MERRILL, PHOTOGRAPHER

High Chest
Newport. 1750–1785.
Goddard-Townsend Shop.
Mahogany with mahogany veneers; secondary wood: white pine.
Height (upper case from finial to top of mid-molding): 56".
Width at pediment: 46½". Depth: 25½".
Museum of Fine Arts, Boston.

High Chest
Philadelphia. 1760–1785.
Mahogany with mahogany veneers; secondary woods: tulip (drawer sides), pine (drawer bottoms).
Height (upper case from bottom of mid-molding to top of finial): 51½".
Width at pediment: 39½". Depth: 20¾".
Museum of Fine Arts, Boston.

The upper halves of two high chests are compared here to illustrate the differences of stylistic preference that two different Quaker communities had for similar forms at about the same time. The Newport high chest is conservatively simple in its outline, ornament and surface. The grain of the veneer of the drawer fronts on this piece is carefully selected to hold the viewer's eye within the compositional boundaries of the facade. Finials, moldings, brasses and panels are tightly organized and compact. The case is severely symmetrical and serenely quiet. Although made in the Chippendale Period, it is, essentially, Queen Anne design. By contrast, the high chest from Philadelphia is alive with ornament, richly figured mahogany and pierced brasses. The visual effect of this piece is explosive. At its summit is a cartouche which soars out of the pediment with a carefree asymmetry echoed by the lively mahogany veneer patterns of the drawer fronts.

We may never be able to explain why such regional preferences developed—why Newport craftsmen held fast to a design established by the 1750s or why Philadelphia craftsmen continued to develop more elaborate high chests long after that form was out of style in London. But clues to regional preferences may be found in the character of the closed or open crafts communities of Newport or Philadelphia, respectively.

Detail, Shell-Carved Drawer Front, Dressing Table
Philadelphia. 1760–1780.
Mahogany; secondary woods: pine and poplar.
H: 31" W: 33¾" D: 30".
Museum of Fine Arts, Boston.

Carving such as this demonstrates that craftsmen in America were able to compete with English products imported to the American colonies. Although Philadelphia was but a small town by today's standards, it sustained a remarkable community of craftsmen, artisans and artists at the time when this carving was done.

The ruffle of the shell, diapered and punched background and freely looped overlapping leafage were characteristic features of Philadelphia carving before the Revolution when Benjamin Randolph, Thomas Affleck, Thomas Tufft and others produced their finest work.

Foliate carving in Philadelphia during the Chippendale Period surpassed the work of other regions of America in both amount and quality of workmanship. These two examples demonstrate graceful movement and lifelike naturalism.

The shell carving represents greater restraint in design. Its composition is almost perfectly symmetrical. The swan carving, however, moves with greater freedom; it is much lighter in effect.

The swan of the drawer panel on the right swims serenely in a shimmering field of delicately carved wood. The S-shaped neck of

DAN FARBER, PHOTOGRAPHER

Carved Detail,
Lower Center Drawer Panel,
Low Chest of Drawers.
Philadelphia. c. 1770. Mahogany.
H: 31⅞" W: 32⅜" D: 36¼".
Museum of Fine Arts, Boston.

the bird is emblematic of the eighteenth-century idea of beauty, and as such the bird is a symbol of grace. Other meanings may be associated with this subject as well. Figural carving of this sort was popular in pre-Revolutionary Philadelphia. Some were adapted from illustrations of the popular *Aesop's Fables*. Others were copied from such sources as Thomas Johnson's *A New Book of Ornaments* (London, 1762). It is possible that the swan of this drawer was adapted from a detail in an engraving of a sideboard table that appeared in another London publication: *Household Furniture in Genteel Taste for the Year 1760 by a Society of Upholsterers, Cabinet-Makers & c.* But if this design source was used by the Philadelphia carver, he merely found it a convenient inspiration upon which he built a world of fantasy and curves. The columns at either end of the drawer seem distorted by a peculiar system of viewing—a kind of perspective parallax that had intrigued the great French designer Jean Pillement. Such columns found their way into the English decorative vocabulary through the *rocaille* designs for chimney pieces and looking glasses of Thomas Johnson. In turn, Philadelphia carvers seem to have especially favored these singularly strange and angular forms that never offered any real architectural support.

Two Side Chairs

Schematic Drawings Representing Typical Features Found in High-Style Chairs Made in Massachusetts and Philadelphia in the Chippendale Period.

Features that are commonly used to identify chairs from two different regions are characterized in these drawings. The Massachusetts chair has back posts below the seat that are square in section. The rear and side rails have concealed mortise-and-tenon joints fastened with pegs where they join the back posts. The front legs have sharp knees and terminate in birdlike claw-and-ball feet with raked-back talons. The side and front rails of the seat frame are tenoned into the upper section of the front legs. Squared seat frames have simple triangular corner blocks of horizontal grain glued and nailed into place.

The Philadelphia chair has rounded back posts or stump legs. Tenons of the side seat rails are mortised through the rear legs and exposed at the back of the chair. Carving is richly fluid and deep, and the foliate detail seems natural and alive. Sinuous claw-and-ball feet are usually smoothly rounded at the knuckles and sinewy in carving. Within the squared seat frame vertically grained corner blocks of quarter-round shape are glued around the inside of the legs.

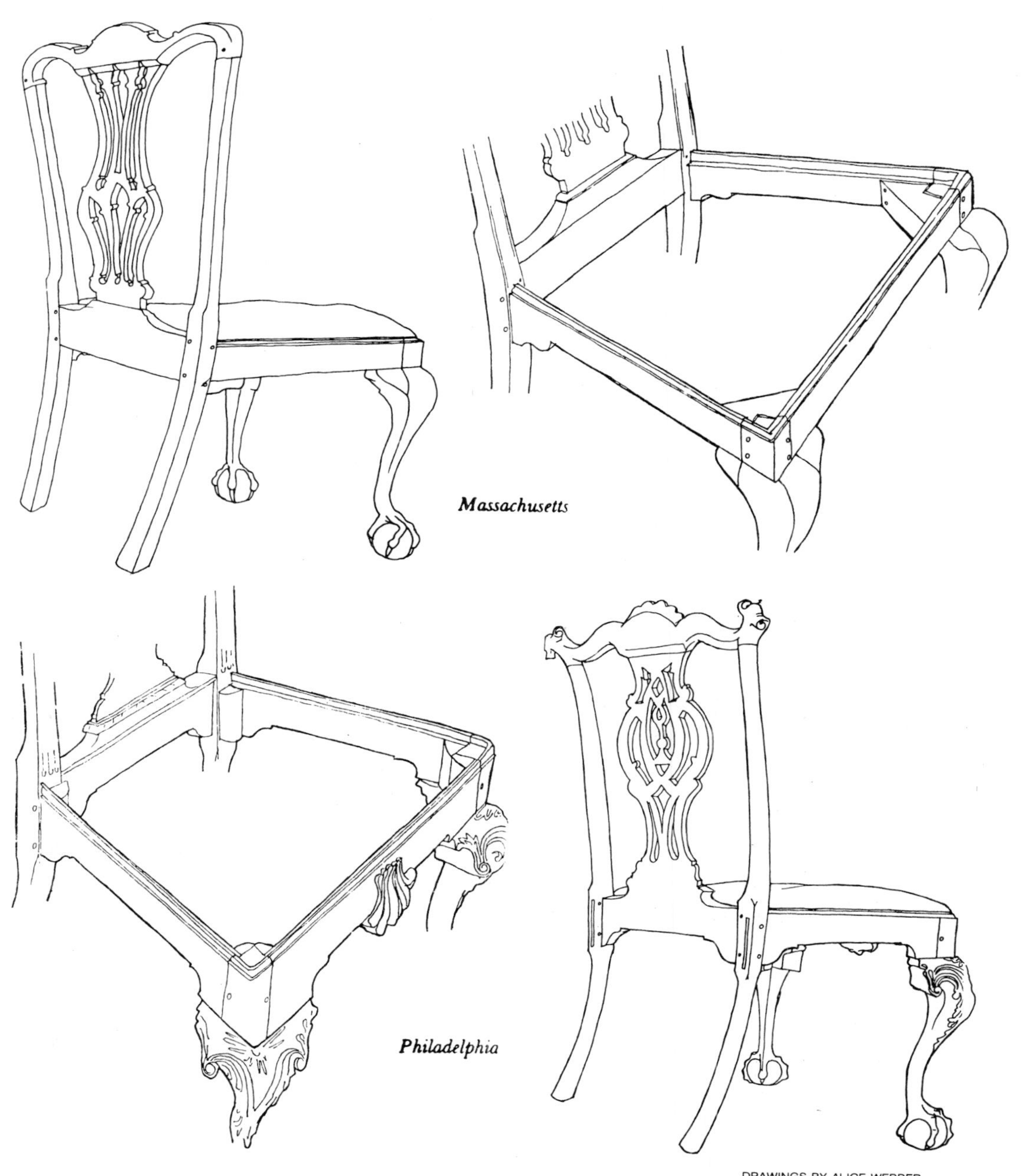

DRAWINGS BY ALICE WEBBER

Side Chair
Boston or Salem. 1765–1780.
Mahogany, maple and white pine. H: 38¼" D: 17¾" W: 23⅝".
Massachusetts Historical Society on Loan to the Museum of Fine Arts, Boston.

RICHARD CHEEK, PHOTOGRAPHER

While this side chair reproduces the back shape of a parlor chair which the English designer Robert Manwaring published in 1765, the overall treatment was executed in a recognizably Massachusetts manner. The stiles of the back are shaped more finely than those suggested by Manwaring. The legs and eagle claw feet are completely New England in character—they could not be mistaken for English.

This chair has its original eighteenth-century linen case lining covering its hair-and-grass-stuffed seat. The slightly shaped back feet are unusual for Massachusetts Chippendale furniture, and are more common to New York chairs.

Simpler versions of this chair also exist. They have the same basic shape and silhouette to their backs but have no ornamental carving. These were probably made in the shop of the same chairmaker, but for a reduced cost to the buyers.

Side Chair
Philadelphia. 1760–1780.
Mahogany; secondary wood: pine.
H: 40" W: 23" D: 16".
Anonymous Gift to the Department of State, Diplomatic Reception Rooms, Washington, D.C.

Vigorous carving marks this chair as an outstanding piece of Philadelphia craftsmanship. The detail flows, as in the S-formed leafage of the crest which blends into the bold sweep of the ears. The tapered stop fluting on the back posts is masterly in its handling.

This chair resembles an armchair which has a tradition of having been made by the Philadelphia craftsman Jonathan Shoemaker (1726–1793, working in Philadelphia, 1757–1793).

Side Chair

Newport, Rhode Island. 1780–1790.

Townsend-Goddard School. Walnut; 19th-century needlepoint seat.

H: 37" W: 20⅞" D: 19½".

Greenfield Village and the Henry Ford Museum, Dearborn, Michigan.

Crisp, logical lines define the back of this chair. A handsome balance of spaces—voids to solids—distinguishes its shape. Stop-fluted front legs, typical of many fine examples of Newport furniture, are soundly joined together with stretchers which were a feature of New England eighteenth-century chairs. The legs are pinned into tenons at the front seat rail.

Carved detail is executed delicately, in the same shallow manner as engraved Federal silver. For this reason, it would seem probable that this chair was not made before the Revolution. Such delicate ornament reflects neoclassical taste, first introduced into the arts of this country at about the time of the Revolution and growing more popular thereafter.

The overall form of the chair, especially the interlaced shape of its back, is reminiscent of the earlier mid-eighteenth-century designs of Robert Manwaring. The chair pictured here represents the third or fourth modification of the original design, which probably came to Newport via sea trade connections between Providence and Philadelphia. The choice of claw-and-ball feet or pad feet on cabriole legs, or straight or "Marlborough" legs, possibly embellished by stop fluting or molding, was a matter of personal preference on the part of the maker or the purchaser.

Side Chair
New York. 1756.
Mahogany; secondary woods: American beech and hard pine.
H: 38¾" W: 22¾" D: 21".
Winterthur Museum.

This chair may not be the most exciting example of its type, time and place, but it was the first to draw the attention of connoisseurs to New York craftsmanship.

The diamond motif of the back splat set behind large scroll loops is a design that was preferred in the New York area. It also was utilized on chairs from Massachusetts and sometimes in Connecticut. Worth special note is the relatively flat carving of the leafage at the knee of this chair. At the uppermost corner of the leaf, near the corner of the seat frame, is a small diamond-shaped area that is cross-hatched. Such cross-hatching, together with the flat leafage, is characteristic of New York carved ornament.

Side Chair (One of a Pair)
New Jersey. c. 1770–1780.
Mahogany; secondary wood: yellow pine.
H: 39½" W: 22" D: 20".
The Newark Museum.

Henry Lupp, a silversmith from New Brunswick, New Jersey, owned this chair, part of a set probably made by a local craftsman. Living somewhat closer to New York than Philadelphia, the chairmaker produced a specimen which, with its diamond and scroll splat, reflects more of New York taste than of Philadelphia. The feet are, however, of the Philadelphia school. A relatively simple and in some ways awkward chair, it tries to imitate the graces of Philadelphia and New York chairmakers but falls short, lacking the charm found in the work of country chairmakers and the elegance found in cosmopolitan centers. Yet it is sturdy and sound, decorated with ornament that does not seem to overreach the skill of its maker. It is a good example of furniture of middling quality made in a town under the influence of a major urban center.

ARMEN PHOTOGRAPHERS

The splat patterns of these four chairs suggest the variety of possibilities derived from rococo Gothic motifs of the Chippendale Period. Details from each can be found in Chippendale's Director, *but each represents taste popular in a specific region.*

Side Chair
Boston Area. 1770–1795.
Mahogany; secondary woods: maple and white pine.
H: 37" W: 21⅜" D: 17⅝".
Museum of Fine Arts, Boston.

The interlaced "Gothic" splat of this chair was adapted from Plate XVI in Chippendale's *Director*. The pattern remained popular in the Boston area long after the American Revolution.

There was a strong tendency in New England to perpetuate rococo designs and details of carving in the Federal Period furniture and in architecture, which architectural historians call Late Colonialism. The slow economic recovery of the region after the Revolution and the basic conservatism among New Englanders caused the retention of earlier forms.

The carving of this chair, typical of the coastal Massachusetts school, is well executed but is quite restrained and low in relief. The flat leafage does not disguise the sharp corners of the knees of the chair. This treatment represents a type of easily identified Massachusetts carving. The addition of turned stretchers, even when the construction does not warrant this reinforcement, is another characteristic of New England chairs.

Side Chair (One of a Pair)
Philadelphia. 1760–1780.
Labeled by Thomas Tufft (c. 1738–1788).
Mahogany; secondary wood: white cedar.
H: 38⅞" W: 23¾" D: 21⅜".
Winterthur Museum.

This is one of the most beautiful examples of Philadelphia chairs, its lines flowing and graceful. Although solidly built, its components are deftly handled. The transition between the legs and front skirt is smoothly designed: a C-scroll edging carries the arch of the cabriole leg to the center carved pendant or cartouche. The tracery of the back Gothic arches was designed with some improvements on the lines of Plate XVI of Chippendale's 1762 *Director*. According to its label, the chair was made and sold by Tufft.

The pattern of this Gothic tracery chair was a favorite among Philadelphia craftsmen and their clients before the Revolution. In addition to Tufft, Benjamin Randolph used the design. But Randolph's labeled Gothic splat chair in the Garvan Collection at Yale University has straight legs, no carved ornament, and has a far less graceful back splat than does that of Tufft.

HELGA PHOTO STUDIO, INC.

Side Chair
Probably Baltimore. c. 1775.
Mahogany with pine corner blocks.
H: 39″ W: 23″ D: 18″.
Department of State, Diplomatic Reception Rooms, Washington, D.C.

This is one of a set of Chippendale-style chairs once owned by Francis Scott Key (1779–1843). The diffusion of design influences from Philadelphia to Maryland is suggested when one compares it with a Philadelphia side chair.

Baltimore and the Eastern shore areas were developed with superb houses, but it was not until the growth of the seaports during the Federal Period that the products of local furniture craftsmen matched the wealth of the area. During the Chippendale Period, the most elegant was imported.

The design elements of the Key chairs are not as smoothly integrated as they are in high-style Philadelphia examples. The carved ornament seems rather abruptly located on the Key chairs, and lacks the graceful transitions characteristic of Philadelphia furniture.

Nevertheless, the Key chairs have energy. Note the vigorous C-scrolled Gothic tracery back, the boldly flared ears of the crest, and the deep carving of the shell and knees heightened with punchwork background. Diamond-patterned carved lines and punched ornament offer textural contrast underneath the ruffled carved crest. The color or patina of the chairs is superb.

Side Chair (One of a Set of Twelve)
New York. 1762–1790.
Mahogany with pine corner blocks. H: 38″ W: 23″ D: 20″.
Collection of Mrs. George Maurice Morris.

The back of this chair is a variant on a "Gothic" theme, as seen in Plate XII in Chippendale's 1762 *Director.* It is a design that was popular among New York families.

Despite the similarity of the chair back with the plate in the *Director,* it is probable that the chairmaker took his template not from the print source but rather from an imported English chair. Possibly he brought his template directly from England.

The wavy gadrooned lower edge of the front seat rail is a feature of chairs made in New York. Blocky claw-and-ball feet and back posts with squared feet are other earmarks of New York taste.

RICHARD CHEEK, PHOTOGRAPHER

Side Chair
Philadelphia. 1770–1772.
Made by Benjamin Randolph (1721–1791).
Mahogany; secondary wood: white cedar.
H: 36$\frac{7}{8}$" W: 23$\frac{3}{4}$" D: 23$\frac{1}{2}$".
Winterthur Museum.

One of the most exciting discoveries in recent years was a group of five chairs from this set of what originally may have numbered thirteen, made for General John Cadwalader of Philadelphia. Before the discovery, only this single chair of the set, owned by Winterthur, was known. It was considered one of Benjamin Randolph's six sample chairs purported to have been made as samples of his mastery of the art of chairmaking. However, because the chair was so elaborate, and so closely followed English practices of chairmaking and carving, some critics felt that it was an imported high-style English specimen assembled in Philadelphia rather than made there.

Recent study suggests otherwise. The secondary woods of the newly discovered chairs confirm that they were made in America. Research also proves that Randolph's shop had carvers sufficiently acquainted with the most fashionable English practices to be able to produce such furniture. Whether the work was done by John Pollard (1740–1787) or by Hercules Courtenay (1744?–1784) under the supervision of Benjamin Randolph is not especially important, for both probably had sufficient skill for this work.

The most elaborate Chippendale side chairs of Boston, Philadelphia and Charleston, South Carolina, are compared here to demonstrate regional preferences for ornamental design and construction features inherent in both high-style and provincial products of the colonies. However, the task of separating colonial products from those made for exportation in England, Ireland and other regions of the British empire is far from complete.

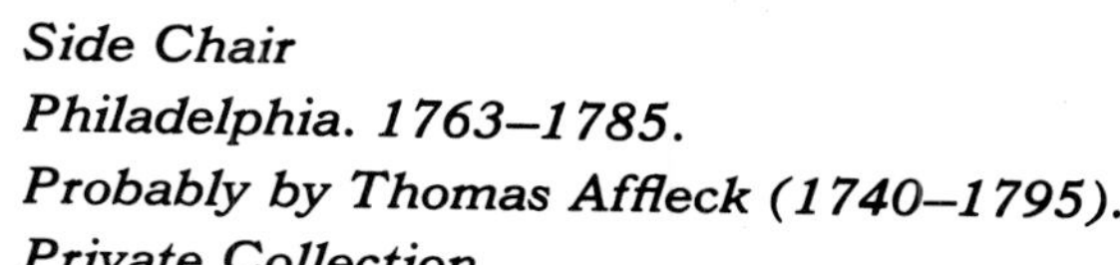
Side Chair
Philadelphia. 1763–1785.
Probably by Thomas Affleck (1740–1795).
Private Collection.

This is the most elegant side chair made in eighteenth-century Philadelphia. Thomas Affleck, to whom it is attributed, made similar chairs for the Fisher family of Wakefield, Quakers who helped to establish his career in Philadelphia.

It is not surprising that the back of this chair follows every detail of a chair-back design shown in Chippendale's 1762 edition of the *Director* almost line for line—Affleck owned his own copy. Despite the closeness with which the design of the back follows the plate, and Affleck's training in Edinburgh, Scotland, and London, the front legs of the chair are not at all like those shown in the *Director*. They follow leg patterns popular in Philadelphia.

Armchair
Probably Boston. c. 1765–1785.
Mahogany; secondary woods: soft maple and birch.
H: 37¾" W: 24¾" D: 19⅝".
Yale University Art Gallery.

JOSEPH SZASZFAI, PHOTOGRAPHER

The splat of this chair, one of a set of twelve, almost exactly matches that of an English chair that was brought to Boston around 1750 and was owned by William Phillips. Perhaps influenced by the Phillips' chair, a Boston chairmaker developed his own version.

The asymmetrical carved leafage at the knee of this chair derived from English models. It is characteristic of a small group of Boston-made furniture, including card tables, a settee and other chairs.

Side Chair
Charleston, South Carolina. 1760–1780.
Mahogany.
H: 40" W: 24" D: 20".
Greenfield Village and the Henry Ford Museum, Dearborn, Michigan.

This side chair is one from a set made for Drayton Hall, an elegant eighteenth-century mansion on the Ashley River near Charleston, South Carolina. Identification of wood in some of the chairs of this set suggests that instead of being imported, they were more likely made in America, probably Charleston. The deep and lively ornamental carving on this chair suggests a maker familiar with high-style English Chippendale furniture. The projecting scroll at the knee is an ambitious feature seldom found in American furniture.

Each element of carved ornament is well executed but the carving somewhat overwhelms the unity of the whole. The additive assembly of the components by the craftsman reveals his somewhat provincial eye and his inability to orchestrate parts into a truly organic composition.

Thomas Chippendale anticipated the furniture craftsman's need to accommodate local taste in design by simplification or elaboration. Plate XV of the 1762 edition of his Director, *"Ribband Back Chairs," is the prototype for the "ruffle and tassel" type of chair. In the commentary for the plate Chippendale allowed that, "If any of the small ornaments should be thought superfluous, they may be left out, without spoiling the Design." New York and Philadelphia craftsmen modified the basic motif of console scrolls, tassel and swag to suit regional preferences in design.*

HELGA PHOTO STUDIO, INC.

Side Chair (One of a Set of Six)
Philadelphia. c. 1760–1770.
Mahogany with pine corner blocks.
Seat frame marked "No. VI."
H: 40" D: 16¾" W: 22".
Diplomatic Reception Rooms, Department of State, Washington, D.C.

One of a set of six carved tassel-back side chairs which exhibits unusually rich carving, this chair has what appears to be its original finish.

Elements from English prototypes were grafted onto what was traditional in Philadelphia chairmaking in an independent, creative way. Philadelphians had a preference for sinuous claw-and-ball feet and broad plain aprons relieved only by a central carved shell. The shells carved on the ears and the center of the crest are ornaments found on a group of similar pieces made in Philadelphia.

Side Chair
New York.
Mahogany; tulip slip-seat frame.
"No. VII" chiseled on rear slip-seat rail;
"No. III" chiseled on rear of seat rail.
H: 39" W: 25¼" D: 24".
Museum of Fine Arts, Boston.

The broadly scrolled back with tassel, pendant ruffle and flat-carved leafage are features of this chair and were preferred in the New York area. A gadrooned skirt and severe blocky character to the claw-and-ball feet are other features that characterize its New York origin.

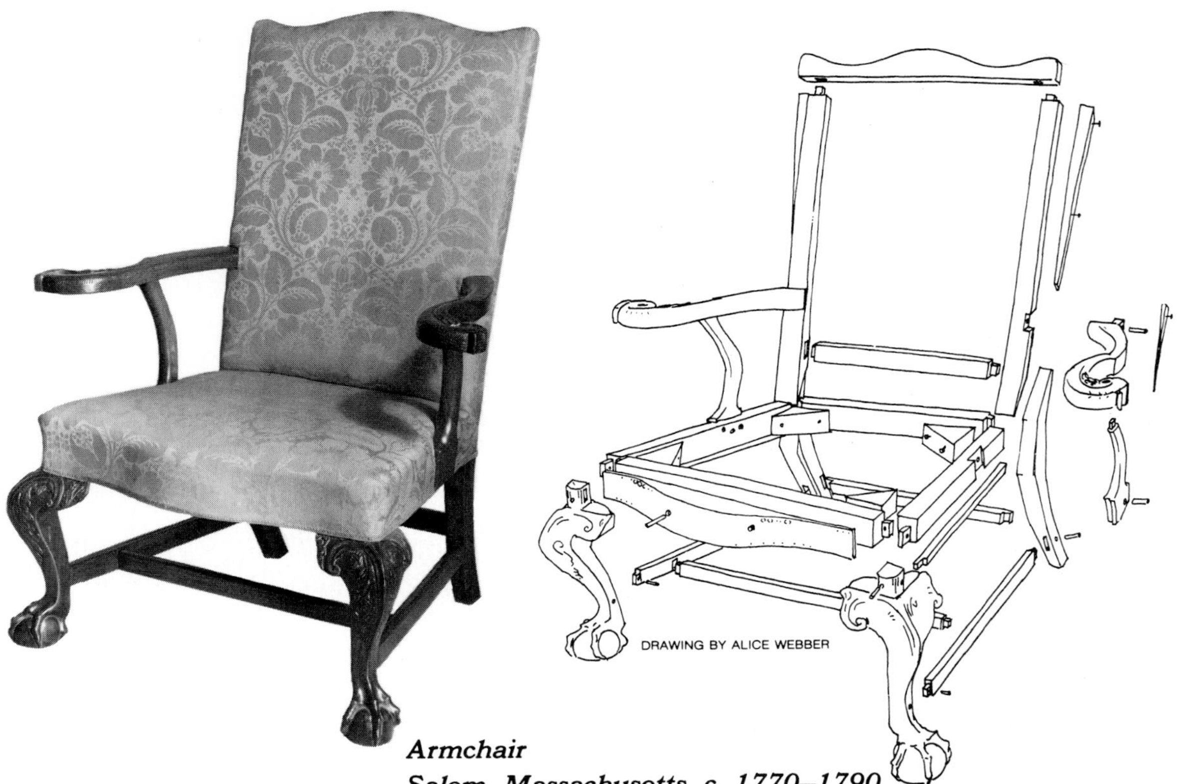

Armchair
Salem, Massachusetts. c. 1770–1790.
Mahogany seat and frame, with pine, maple and oak.
H: 41" W: 31½" D: 25½".
Museum of Fine Arts, Boston.

The disarticulated chair was sketched to show the construction system of an important New England armchair. Its frame is structurally well joined and braced; the joinery consists of a complex of intricate parts. Different woods were used to obtain the best advantage for meeting the stress which is placed upon chairs. As was customary, the seat frame was made of mahogany, as was the back brace, and the blocks were of pine and the supporting structure of maple and oak.

The armchair descended from the prominent Salem merchant Elias Hasket Derby, perhaps the wealthiest New Englander of his day. According to tradition, the chair was lent to Federal Hall in Salem for use by George Washington during his triumphal tour of America in 1789.

Only rarely are such important pieces of upholstered furniture stripped of their fabric for reupholstery. Each time a new set of upholstery tacks is nailed into the tacking edge, the frame is splintered and weakened. If it is possible to trace the original tack holes the alert upholsterer can frequently recreate the tacking pattern appropriate to the period, which makes possible the accurate restoration of a handsome line of brass-headed ornamental tacks.

Masonic Master's Chair
Stamped Signature of Benjamin Bucktrout, Williamsburg. 1767–1770.
Mahogany; secondary wood: walnut; original black leather upholstery.
H: 65½" W: 31¼" D: 29½".
The Unanimity Lodge No. 7, Edenton, North Carolina.

This chair was produced in the Anthony Hay cabinetmaking shop in Colonial Williamsburg, which was owned by Benjamin Bucktrout between 1767 and 1770. It is one of the most ambitious works of its time and demonstrates the high degree of design excellence and superb carving achieved by Virginia craftsmen. The dolphin legs of this chair are literally copied from Plate XXI in Chippendale's *Director* (third edition, 1762). The portrait bust beneath the arch represents Matthew Prior (1664–1721), an English poet, diplomat and a Tory. Perhaps his poem "Solomon" is what commended him to the Masonic position of honor.

The special features of this well-documented chair make it a key specimen for understanding other related examples of Virginia chairmaking and carving styles. It was intended to create an impressive setting, incorporating symbolic motifs.

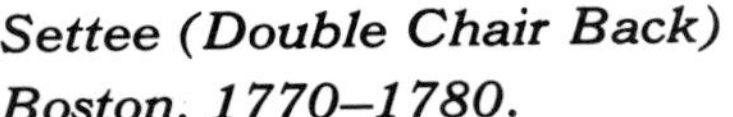
Settee (Double Chair Back)
Boston. 1770–1780.
Mahogany; secondary woods: maple and white pine. H: 37½" W: 73" D: 21¾".
Museum of Fine Arts, Boston.

Only half a dozen Massachusetts double chair-back settees are known today, although they must have been a popular form of furniture in their day. This one is especially fine in its generous proportions and ample, open carving. The crest is sharply defined with precisely carved center shells and finely molded ears. The scrolled arms and leafy carved knees show the detail preferred in Massachusetts furniture. The sharply cornered knees have leafage that is flat but enhanced with punchwork background. Raked-back talons to the claw-and-ball feet are a Massachusetts earmark. The serpentine front seat rail is a special feature that helps compose the whole.

Two settees made in the Boston area are compared here to suggest the choices available in the eighteenth century. Furniture of this quality was not generally "ready-made," but instead was commissioned or "bespoke" directly by client of craftsman.

Upholstered Settee
Boston Area. 1760–1780.
Mahogany; secondary woods: maple, cedar, birch. H: 36" L: 57" D: 24".
Winterthur Museum.

The wings and back of this splendid little settee are refined emblems of formal, elegant posture. The entire effect is graceful to the extent of being almost fragile looking. The back and the arms were originally better padded for greater visual pleasure and physical comfort. The sweep of the arms of the settee seems perfectly suited for the lace that cascaded from the lower-arm sleeves of well-dressed ladies of the period.

The words "settee" and "sofa" seem indistinguishable according to the definitions of a popular early nineteenth-century dictionary published in Massachusetts and sold throughout New England. The term settee described "a long seat with a back." A sofa was "a splendid seat covered with carpets." Both terms were probably used interchangeably in describing this small masterpiece of eighteenth-century New England craftsmanship. Precisely shaped legs which end in claw-and-ball feet are a type preferred in the Massachusetts Bay area. The carving is related to several well-documented Boston area chairs with C-scroll carving spanning the knees.

RICHARD CHEEK, PHOTOGRAPHER

Sofa
Philadelphia. 1770–1790.
Mahogany; silk damask covering.
H: 42" L: 92" D: 38".
Collection of
Mrs. George Maurice Morris.

The greatest contribution of eighteenth-century crafts to the history of furniture was the development of elegant and comfortable seating. Even in the eighteenth century the sofa was recognized as the summit of accomplishments. Many splendid examples of eighteenth-century American sofas survive to prove that colonists appreciated the comforts and sensuous lines of this graceful form. The most impressive sofas of the period came from Philadelphia. The frame and overall dimensions of this sofa look solid, but the great sweep of the arms and peaked serpentine back emphasize the sense of motion. Sofas of this sort usually had a number of loose pillows filled with goose down for added comfort.

Coordination of many different craft skills was involved in making a majestic sofa. The eighteenth-century upholsterer or "upholder" was an enterprising businessman and consultant in matters of good taste and fashion trends. He performed a variety of services very much like those offered by the interior decorator today. In addition to coordinating fabrics and colors and doing the shaping, stuffing and finishing of upholstered furniture, he also supplied the fabrics, engaged in paper hanging and provided window blinds and curtains. The upholstery business also included contracting for chair and sofa frame-making and other joiner's work.

DELMORE WENZEL, PHOTOGRAPHER

Stool
New York. c. 1760.
Mahogany.
H: 17½" L: 25" D: 18".
Mr. and Mrs. Stanley Stone.

American stools of the eighteenth century are rare. Indeed, it is tempting to call this handsome example with its oval seat unique. It has an appearance of solidity and strength that is fitting to its use. The legs have a splendid, generous curve which tapers to square claw-and-ball feet, and are handsomely carved with a cross-hatched V-shaped area between the acanthus leafage, a feature often found on furniture made in New York City. These are unusually well modeled for workmanship of the New York area.

Easy Chair
Philadelphia. 1770–1772.
Attributed to Benjamin Randolph and Hercules Courtenay.
Mahogany; secondary wood: white oak.
H: 45¼" W: 24⅜" D: 27$^{15}/_{16}$".
Philadelphia Museum of Art.

This is a supreme expression of curves, ornament and comfort in eighteenth-century American furniture. It is atypical—only one other closely related example with exposed mahogany scroll arms is known. In contrast to the delicate carving, the joinery is ruggedly done—rudely rasped into shape and doweled with heavy framing in quartered white oak much like the workmanship of Philadelphia Queen Anne Period furniture. The original upholstery was apparently a loose cover not tacked as was the usual custom. Descended from Benjamin Randolph's second wife, Mary W. (Fennimore) Randolph, the chair is alleged to have come from his shop. Several individuals had a hand in completing it—likely the carver who worked for Randolph, Hercules Courtenay (1744?–1784), and an upholsterer of the best sort like Plunket Fleeson.

Easy Chair
Massachusetts. 1760–1780.
Mahogany, maple; wool on linen.
H: 45½" W: 32" D: 32¼".
The Bayou Bend Collection, Museum of Fine Arts, Houston.

Primary colors of red, yellow and blue, eighteenth-century favorites, were combined in arresting patterns to form the original bargello or flame-stitch needlework that covers this easy chair. Hundreds of hours were required to produce such a vivid showpiece. It is not known how many chairs were upholstered in this manner in eighteenth-century America, but only three easy chairs survive today in public collections, bearing their original needlework.

Natural wear and fading have diminished the color of this chair today. Yet despite its age it is remarkably brilliant. The original shape of the upholstery of this chair is of paramount importance as a guide to the proper upholstery for historic furniture of the period.

ALLEN MEWBOURN, PHOTOGRAPHER

Bedstead
Philadelphia. 1780–1790.
Mahogany.
H: 94⅛" W: 75½" L: 90⅝".
Winterthur Museum.

Square legs, called Marlborough legs, were popular in eighteenth-century American bedsteads. They offered sturdy pedestals to the pillars which are the uprights of the bed. This example from Philadelphia with its carved and reeded posts represents a late phase of Chippendale taste; its pillars are similar to those illustrated in the London publication of George Hepplewhite's *The Cabinet-Maker and Upholsterer's Guide* of 1788.

The hangings of this Philadelphia bed are of antique green silk taffeta and are based on a plate in Chippendale's *Director.* Original wooden pulleys in the cornice suggest a design of drapery that would totally enclose the bed.

In the eighteenth century the bed was a most significant piece of furniture. It functioned not only as a small room when closed, but as a costly festooned showpiece when opened. A full range of artistic concerns with order, proportions, divisions of parts, volume, color, texture and ornamental detail were brought together by the upholsterer who coordinated the whole. The bed was composed of a wooden frame with upright pillars, feet or pedestals, headboard, headcloth, footboard or rail, and frame or lath at the top to sustain the tester, valance, cornice and curtains. The rope, canvas ticking, sacking, covering, counterpane, skirt or base valance, fringe and tassels were additional components. Chippendale observed that the ingenious artist could display the full scope of his capacity in a bedstead of magnificence, proportion and harmony.

The textile hangings of a bed were usually the most expensive items. The frame, legs and pillars were merely the means of support for the textiles, although sometimes they were meant to show.

Bedstead Pillar, Frame and Leg
Philadelphia. c. 1770.
Mahogany.
H: 8′ L: (side rail) 73⅝″ D: 53⅓″.
Collection of Mrs. Charles L. Bybee.

DAN FARBER, PHOTOGRAPHER

This is an excellent and rare specimen of Philadelphia craftsmanship. It is spare of ornament and gains its strength from its sculptural form. The leg is as powerful as such a supporting member ought to be. The talons are vigorous and of a form popular in Philadelphia.

Claw-and-ball feet are not common on American bedsteads for the Chippendale Period, but they do survive from most major centers of furniture production. Their form generally follows the pattern found in claw-and-ball feet on seating furniture. This representative example from Philadelphia shows the way in which the rails, legs, posts and pillars are conjoined. The brass which conceals the bed bolt is late in style and is not original.

Pier Glass and Table

Chippendale's *Director* of 1762 contains this image of an exuberant Pier Glass and Table. Probably no American owned anything so extravagant. The closest to it is a Philadelphia side table at the Metropolitan Museum made for John Cadwalader by Benjamin Randolph in 1769, in the "new or French taste." In his commentary on the plate, Chippendale remarked that "A skilful Carver may, in the Execution of this . . . give full Scope to his Capacity." What Randolph or the carver in his shop did was to eliminate the stretchers and trumpeting putto, streamline Chippendale's ragged profile of the legs, and move the figure from the center bottom of the pier glass, adding clothing and a bird, to the central pendant of the table.

Marble-Topped Side Table
Philadelphia. 1769. Made by Benjamin Randolph (1721–1791).
Mahogany; secondary woods: yellow pine (back apron), black walnut (corner braces).
H: 32¾″ W: 48¼″ D: 23⅛″.
The Metropolitan Museum of Art, New York.

This table is the most elaborate of a small group of lavishly carved pieces of Philadelphia rococo furniture, and represents the most advanced form of English-style carving in the colonies. The carving was probably done either by Hercules Courtenay, carver and gilder from London, or John Pollard (1740–1787), who emigrated from London and joined the cabinet shop of Benjamin Randolph just four years before he received payment for the table. It was purchased in 1769 for £94.15—a sum which then had the purchasing power equal to about a seventh of the cost of an elegant house and town property.

The gentleman who made this extravagant purchase could well afford it. He was General John Cadwalader who married a lady of great wealth, Elizabeth Lloyd of Wye House, Easton, Maryland. By the time their home was completed in 1771 he had spent more than £3,600 to refine and furnish it on the west side of Second Street, Philadelphia. The house no longer stands, but much of the art and the furniture made for it exists together with carefully documented records of costs and commissioned craftsmen.

The records afford rare insights into one of the most lavishly appointed houses of Colonial America. Washington and other important visitors to the Cadwalader mansion noted the splendor of the house and its furnishings. John Adams visited Cadwalader and was impressed, "a Gentleman of large Fortune, a grand and elegant House and Furniture."

The plate in Chippendale's *Director* seems to have served as the inspiration for this table, demonstrating the efforts of fashionable Philadelphians to imitate the latest London styles.

Looking Glass and Frame
Philadelphia. 1770–1771.
Made by James Reynolds (1739–1794).
White and yellow pine and tulip; gilt rubbed with white pigment.
H: 55½" W: 28".
Winterthur Museum.

This piece represents the epitome of delicate carving in eighteenth-century American looking glasses. Its attribution to the carver James Reynolds is based on a bill to John Cadwalader which gives its size and a brief description of its frame. It was only part gilt, or gold and white. The looking glass was intended for the master bedroom of General John Cadwalader's town house.

Side Table with Marble Top
Philadelphia. 1760–1790.
Mahogany; secondary woods: oak, tulip, pine; original black-and-white marble top.
H: 29" W: 49¾" D: 22½".
The Bayou Bend Collection, Museum of Fine Arts, Houston.

This half-round serpentine side table is one of the finest works of Philadelphia furniture of the eighteenth century. The carving on its front is shallow but vigorous and exciting. It enhances the strong, sculptural quality of the table's form. The carving on this table's mate, which is in the Pendleton Collection, Rhode Island School of Design, is reversed. This suggests that the pair was designed to make a balanced composition within the same room.

Comparison: Two Drop-leaf Tables

Two drop-leaf tables are compared here to show regional variations on a standard theme. Design and construction conventions as practiced in New York and New England are applied to the essential form of the square-leafed table. Often used for dining, these expandable tables, when not in use, could be closed for unobtrusive placement against a wall. The hinged-leaf table is another example of the multiple-purpose furniture of the eighteenth century.

Dining Table
Charlestown, Massachusetts. 1755–1790.
Labeled by Benjamin Frothingham.
Mahogany; secondary woods: maple and white pine.
H: 28⅛" W: 59" (open) D: 60⅛".
Winterthur Museum.

Simple and practical with a heavy boarded but light-colored top, this table is an archetype of Boston area craftsmanship, probably made about the time of the American Revolution. The maker, Benjamin Frothingham, perhaps not the most gifted craftsman of his time and place, is however the one best understood today because he labeled so many examples of his work.

Dining Table
New York City. 1755–1780.
Walnut; secondary woods: oak, cherry.
H: 29" W: 38¼" L: 50⅜".
Winterthur Museum.

This square table with swing legs and drop leaves is a handsome work, both functional and beautiful. The raised claw-and-ball feet are crisply carved and, like the leafage carving at the knees, are characteristic of the New York school. It is instructive to compare this with the same form from Massachusetts. The New York table is most sturdy looking, with a generous slab of wood on the top and with spare lines and smartly shaped legs.

Comparison: Pedestal-Base Tables

A pedestal-base table from New Jersey is compared with one from Philadelphia to demonstrate their similarity of overall form with differences in execution of details, such as carving. While the Philadelphia tea table is a particularly splendid example of its type, it represents a far more common form than the rare draftsman's table from New Jersey with its adjustable top.

COURTESY OF ISRAEL SACK, INC.

Tea Table
Philadelphia. 1760–1780. Mahogany. H: 28" D: 35".
Privately owned.

Circular tea tables of the eighteenth century were made in seemingly endless variety; some were plain, others elaborately carved. This one strikes a good balance between ornament and form. Philadelphians seem to have enjoyed this kind of table—a type that has a "birdcage" support under the top which allows for both rotating and tilting.

Collectors today eagerly seek tables with a "piecrust" or scalloped edge, one which recalls the shape of silver salvers and trays of the eighteenth century. Below the top, a central support is tapered and fluted in the shape of a Doric column set upon a ball or flattened sphere. The turner's art is displayed here with rings and smartly executed shapes. Overlaying the turning is the carving. The sweep of the legs, the grasp of the claws, the fluidity of the leafage all relate perfectly. The carving enhances the form. The most unusual feature is the paired flowers carved at the peaks of the scalloped-edge top.

DAN FARBER, PHOTOGRAPHER

Draftsman's Table
New Jersey. 1760–1775.
Mahogany; secondary wood: tulip.
H: 29¾" W: 26⅛" D: 26⅛".
Museum of Fine Arts, Boston.

The shape of the pedestal base and column of this table is similar to Philadelphia tripod tea tables with circular tops. But here the top, unlike pedestal tea tables with "bird-cage" mechanisms, does not turn. It consists of a box with a drawer and an adjustable top firmly fastened to the top of the column. Its distinctive character derives from its carving which is more stylized and less deeply sculptured than that made in Philadelphia.

The carving on the feet suggests a highly schematic dolphin head rendered in leafage.

Comparison: Tea Tables

Two tea tables with splendidly shaped rectangular tops are compared to display regional differences of taste in Massachusetts and Philadelphia.

Tea Table
Philadelphia. 1740–1770.
Mahogany. H: 26½" W: 30½" D: 20½".
The Historical Society of Pennsylvania.

The curvaceous tray-like top and sculptured sides of this tea table represent the Philadelphia craftsman's solution to this elegant furniture form. A multitude of teacups, saucers and a tea service could be displayed. This splendid table is expressive of the utmost refinement and sense of grace that captivated the minds of eighteenth-century gentlefolk.

Although the table displays a formal organization of form and spareness of detail that relates to the Queen Anne taste, it was most likely made sometime after the 1760s. One misfortune mars its almost perfect poise. Its feet have been worn or cut in half, therefore failing to give the proper sense of finish and fullness to the design.

Tea Table
Boston. 1750–1775.
Mahogany; secondary wood: maple.
H: 27" W: 32" D: 23½".
Museum of Fine Arts, Boston.

Places for fourteen cups and saucers are provided on the top of this energetic table. The profile of the apron is turreted, echoing the shape of teacups and saucers. The border of the top has an applied molded lip which is shaped to conform to the turrets below. The mass and strength of the design are offset by the elegantly tapered tall legs that terminate in beautifully carved claw-and-ball feet. Graceful leaf carving accents the juncture of the knees at each of the four corners. The form of this table carries the Queen Anne taste for sculptural surfaces well into the Chippendale Period. Not only is this table one of the most striking examples of Baroque design in American furniture, it is also one of the rarest.

Card Table
Charlestown, Massachusetts. 1755–1790.
Made by Benjamin Frothingham (1734–1809).
Engraved by Nathaniel Hurd.
Paper label on card table reads: "Benjn. Frothingham Cabbinet Maker in Charlestown N.E."
Mahogany, white pine and maple. H: 28" W: 34⅛" D: 16¾".
Winterthur Museum.

One of the sleekest claw-and-ball-foot tables from the greater Boston area is this card table by Benjamin Frothingham. The surfaces depend upon form rather than ornament for their aesthetic impact. The smartly tapered shape of the leg with its fine ankle eloquently merges into a birdlike claw-and-ball foot with the raked-back talon so characteristic of the Boston area. The blocking of the apron nicely emphasizes the shape of the candle pockets above. A simple card drawer with a single brass plate and handle accents the spare lines.

Card Table
Philadelphia. 1760–1770.
Mahogany with pine drawer linings.
H: 29½" L: 35½" D: 16¼".
Lent by the Dietrich Brothers Americana Corporation to the Department of State, Diplomatic Reception Rooms, Washington, D.C.

A gadrooned skirt is uncommon on furniture made in Philadelphia; it is more frequently found on furniture from New York City. Exceptional also is the simplicity that marks its character.

The patina of the table is superb. The boldly rounded turret ends, carved acanthus knees, and legs ending in handsomely carved feet characteristic of Philadelphia are all enrichments within the boundaries of Quaker taste "of the best sort but plain." The table is hardly "plain," but by comparison with contemporary card tables made in New York City it is a statement of restraint. This table is one of the most important examples of Philadelphia Chippendale furniture of its type to have appeared on the market in recent years.

HELGA PHOTO STUDIO, INC.

Comparison: Square-Legged Rectangular Tables

Square-legged rectangular tables used for tea serving and china display are compared to suggest the variety of forms available in stretcher-based table design. Both make use of Chinese fretwork for arresting ornamental details. One table was made in Newport, the other probably in Portsmouth, New Hampshire.

RICHARD CHEEK, PHOTOGRAPHER

Tea or Silver Table
Probably Portsmouth, New Hampshire. 1765–1785.
Paper label underneath reads: "Table belongs to Mary Anderson Poore of Greenwood, Maine."
Mahogany; secondary wood: white pine; glue blocks.
H: 27½" L: 32¼" D: 22½".
Department of State, Diplomatic Reception Rooms, Washington, D.C.

Only about a half dozen tables of this extraordinary design are known to exist. While there are differences between these tables, they share an exceptional lightness and vigor of line in the double-scroll arched or saltire stretcher and pierced finial of the crossing. The saw work in the gallery is so lacy in its effect that the craftsman found it necessary to laminate the wood in order to strengthen it.

Undoubtedly the table was a conversation piece in its day. Even now it cannot help but attract admiration and attention. In spite of the obvious relish that the craftsman took in the elaborate detail and complex lines, it is a functional piece. It suits the needs of serving tea well: the pierced gallery protects silver and china from slipping off the edge, and arched stretchers provide comfortable foot room for the server at the table. Ornament and utility are so well integrated that this piece is a joy to study.

Pembroke or Breakfast Table
Label of John Townsend, Newport, Rhode Island. 1760–1800.
Mahogany; secondary woods: maple and ash.
H: 26¼" W: (with leaves down) 20¾" D: 33½".
Winterthur Museum.

A bill dated June 2, 1798, from John Townsend to Walter Channing for one Pembroke table at $14 suggests that tables like this may have been made well into the Federal Period even though it was a form suggested by Thomas Chippendale's *Director* of 1762 (Plate No. LIII). But a much simpler version with drop leaves, bearing Townsend's label, now in the collections of the Colonial Society of Massachusetts, is probably the actual one referred to by the bill.

This table does make use of some of the ideas suggested by Chippendale's breakfast table. Although Chippendale suggested an elaborate Chinese fret below the table apron, Townsend had the good sense to simplify the design and carry out the fret detail in a more modest way with pierced stretchers. The straight Marlborough legs of Chippendale's design are given more elegance by Townsend with stop fluting and a pierced bracket to assist the visual transition between the horizontal line of the apron and the vertical line of the leg. Subtle enrichment below the drawer is achieved through an incised diaper pattern along the apron.

The Pembroke or breakfast table is a lightweight, movable piece of furniture popular in both the Chippendale and Federal periods. It was used for table games and to serve food and tea.

Card Table
New York. 1760–1780.
Mahogany; secondary woods: oak and tulip.
H: 27⅜" W: 34" D: 16⅝".
Museum of Fine Arts, Boston.

More than twenty-five card tables of this serpentine form are known to have come from wealthy eighteenth-century New York families. This is a classic example and represents the finest artistic solution to the form in American furniture design. Its angular, rugged claw-and-ball feet are characteristic of New York-made furniture. The straight vertical line which defines the rear talons is a distinguishing regional hallmark. The green baize top, although worn, is original.

The fifth leg that swings to support the folding top is a feature common to card tables from the New York area. When the leg is out and the leaf is opened, a secret drawer is revealed in the back side of the frame under the tabletop.

Chests, dressing tables, bureaus, desks and bookcases were all terms used to identify special functions of cabinets and chests. These forms of furniture in New England were often shaped with concave and convex panel fronts—blocking—or were serpentine in form.

Blocked furniture usually had a concave center flanked by raised side panels. This scheme suggests that the original purpose of blocking was to provide space in the center for the knees of the sitter. A plate in Chippendale's Director *of 1762 illustrates such concave centers for "buroe dressing tables."*

The Newport example with its kneehole center was obviously used as a dressing chest or bureau-dresser. By contrast, the chest from Boston has no kneehole and its blocking is too shallow to provide the sitter with adequate knee space. The shaped facade is merely a vestige of what was once a practical function. Its craftsman has thoughtfully carried the handsome shape of the blocking through to the border of the top and to the base.

Bureau-Table
Newport, Rhode Island. 1765–1780.
Labeled "Edmund Townsend."
Mahogany with tulip drawer sides; chestnut drawer bottoms.
H: 33½" L: 36½" D: 20⅜".
Museum of Fine Arts, Boston.

The visual effect of this bureau is one of massiveness and strength. Its top is a full three-fourths of an inch thick, but within the chest the drawers are remarkably thin and lightweight in construction. Ultra-fine dovetails join the sides of the drawers together.

From the magnificent workmanship of the case and the splendor of its perfect balance of carving, brasses and pattern of its grain, it is reasonable to assert that Edmund Townsend was a great craftsman who worked in a style that maintained a strong conservative taste for Queen Anne forms throughout the Chippendale Period.

RICHARD CHEEK, PHOTOGRAPHER

Chest of Drawers
Boston. 1760–1790.
Mahogany and white pine.
H: 30¼" W: 36" D: 21¼".
Museum of Fine Arts, Boston.

The shape of the front of this chest moves in a very gentle way from convex on the side panels to concave in the center. At the transition point between, a splendid swirl of wood, like the movement of a wave, carries the eye vertically to where the movement is reflected in the shape of both the top and the base. The design is magnificently executed and is emphasized by beading around the edges of the drawers. All brasses and keyhole plates are original.

Block-fronted furniture was popular in Boston, Salem, Newport and Connecticut. It is seldom found from urban New York and rarely, if ever, does it seem to have been made further south in the eighteenth century. While other examples of blocked furniture are more robust and visually arresting, few are as sophisticated and subtle as this one. Perhaps it represents a late manifestation of the Boston block-front style.

Chest of Drawers
Boston. c. 1760–1790.
Mahogany; secondary wood: white pine.
H: 33⅞" W: 40⅞" D: 21⅜".
Museum of Fine Arts, Boston.

This is one of the most handsome and substantial serpentine chests of drawers produced in eighteenth-century New England. The carved detail on its feet is very closely related to carving on a chest signed and dated 1782 by the Boston cabinetmaker John Cogswell (1738–1818). However, it is not possible to claim that Cogswell actually made this chest of drawers. Boston did have a handful of carvers who presumably ornamented a variety of works including frames, architectural woodwork, ships and furniture.

New England cabinetmakers produced more serpentine chests in the eighteenth century than those known from the other colonies. This one, among Boston's best, is worthy of comparison with those made by Jonathan Gostelowe in Philadelphia at about the same time, and one recently discovered, probably made in Salem, Massachusetts, bearing the date 1783 and the initials "TN," which could stand for Thomas Needham (1755–1787).

Serpentine Chest of Drawers with Writing Top
Philadelphia. c. 1770–1790.
Mahogany, pine.
H: 33" W: 46" D: 23".

Philadelphia chests of this bold sculptural form with canted feet of ogee profile are usually attributed to the hand of Jonathan Gostelowe (1744–1795), who had a shop in Church Alley between Market and Arch streets in Philadelphia. Other related Philadelphia serpentine chests with massive bracket feet like this one, and with solid construction and numerous glue bracing blocks on drawer bottoms, are in the collections of the Winterthur Museum, the Chew Mansion and the Garvan Collection, Yale University.

COURTESY OF BERNARD & S. DEAN LEVY, INC.

DAN FARBER, PHOTOGRAPHER

Chest of Drawers
Newport, Rhode Island. c. 1770.
Goddard-Townsend School.
Mahogany; secondary woods: pine and chestnut.
H: 35¼" W: 51½" D: 27¼".
Anonymous Loan to the
Museum of Fine Arts, Boston.

A French sea captain who Americanized his name to Peter Simon commissioned a Newport cabinetmaker to make this chest of drawers. The unusual rounded corners and curved apron suggest that the captain wanted a French-style commode-bureau with swelled drawers. It would be reasonable to assume that this is the simplified Newport version of such a French design. It is not the most artistically successful piece of Newport cabinetmaking, but it is among the most interesting in terms of American response to French taste. The surfaces are lavished with a majestic sweep of figured mahogany, quite stunning in effect. Talons of the feet are smartly carved on all sides, and are typically "Newport" in their open claws.

RICHARD CHEEK, PHOTOGRAPHER

Chest of Drawers
Boston. c. 1765.
Mahogany; secondary wood: white pine.
H: 30" W: 36" D: 20".
Gift of the Honorable C. Douglas Dillon and Mrs. Dillon to the Department of State, Diplomatic Reception Rooms, Washington, D.C.

This bombé or kettle-shaped chest is the best example of its type produced in eighteenth-century Boston. It was originally owned by Ebenezer Storer II and bears witness to the elegance of taste which characterized the life-style of elite society in eighteenth-century Boston.

The bombé or swelled shape was a form much admired by Boston furniture craftsmen and their clients, and was a hallmark of style in that town. First appearing in Boston in the 1750s, the bombé shape continued in demand through the period of the Revolution and into the 1780s, long after it had passed out of fashion abroad. The excellence of the overall proportions of this chest and the subtle form of its serpentine front are noteworthy. The shape of the case is paralleled by the profile of the drawer sides. Lively graining of the mahogany on all exposed surfaces is selected to reflect the great swelling curves of the form itself. As a special complement to the piece, imported cast ormolu or fire-gilt rococo brasses of the highest quality embellish the front. The C-scroll and floral ornament of the brasses intertwine with a phoenix in the crest. To sharpen the detail of the casting, the background of much of each brass was chased with a toothed chisel which left finely textured marks.

Pier Table or Console Table
Boston. c. 1740–1770.
Mahogany and white pine;
black-and-gold marble top.
H: 29" W: 28½" D: 17⅛".
Museum of Fine Arts, Boston.

RICHARD CHEEK, PHOTOGRAPHER

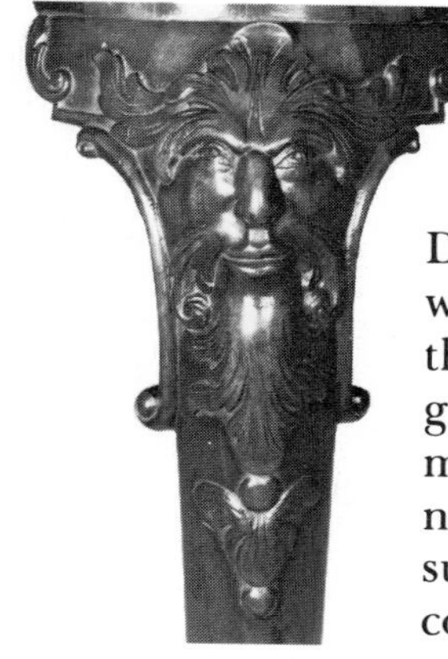

Descended in the Fayerweather family of Boston, this table is related to a small group of furniture with masked carving that seems not to have been made or survived elsewhere in the colonies.

Writing Table
Boston. c. 1740–1760.
Mahogany, white pine, tulip, maple.
H: 42⅛" W: 35¾" D: 22⅞".
Museum of Fine Arts, Boston.

This is one of the most unusual pieces of Boston furniture of the eighteenth century. We call it a writing table because that is the closest form to it identified in Chippendale's *Director* of 1762. No other eighteenth-century towns in America are known to have produced pieces quite like this example with its carved human faces

on the knees of the legs. Fantastic heads in architectural carving exist on Philadelphia buildings such as Independence Hall and Christ Church, but not on furniture.

The idea for carved masks seems to derive from ideas generated by the English designer-painter-architect William Kent (1685–1748), who studied in Italy. He carried back to England a profound admiration for the work of Andrea Palladio and became a prominent advocate of Palladian design.

While the knees are ornate, the rest of the piece is quite simple. Such an odd combination has caused some question as to whether or not the piece has had significant changes over the years. Close study of the structure proves that no major changes have taken place.

Desk
Salem Area. c. 1760–1790.
Mahogany; secondary wood: white pine.
H: 43½″ W: 43⅞″ D: 20⅞″.
Museum of Fine Arts, Boston.

This desk is a perfected example of a small group of bombé-shaped pieces that are attributed to cabinetmakers working in Salem, Massachusetts, in the manner of the Boston school. Recent study suggests that it was probably made in or near Salem by a cabinetmaker who was taken with the swelled base or bombé form that so captivated the imagination of eighteenth-century Boston cabinetmakers. Despite apparent influences of the Boston school in the form of this piece, construction details are more closely related to Newport cabinetmaking traditions.

Features which relate this desk to Salem include a crisply carved claw-and-ball foot, and a bracket to the leg which has a shape closely related to those on a block-fronted desk signed by Henry Rust, a cabinetmaker active in eighteenth-century Salem. At least two other bombé desks survive with family histories that tie them to Salem, both of which are closely related to this one. Of the three, this desk is artistically the most successful. The sweeping lines of its sides are particularly graceful.

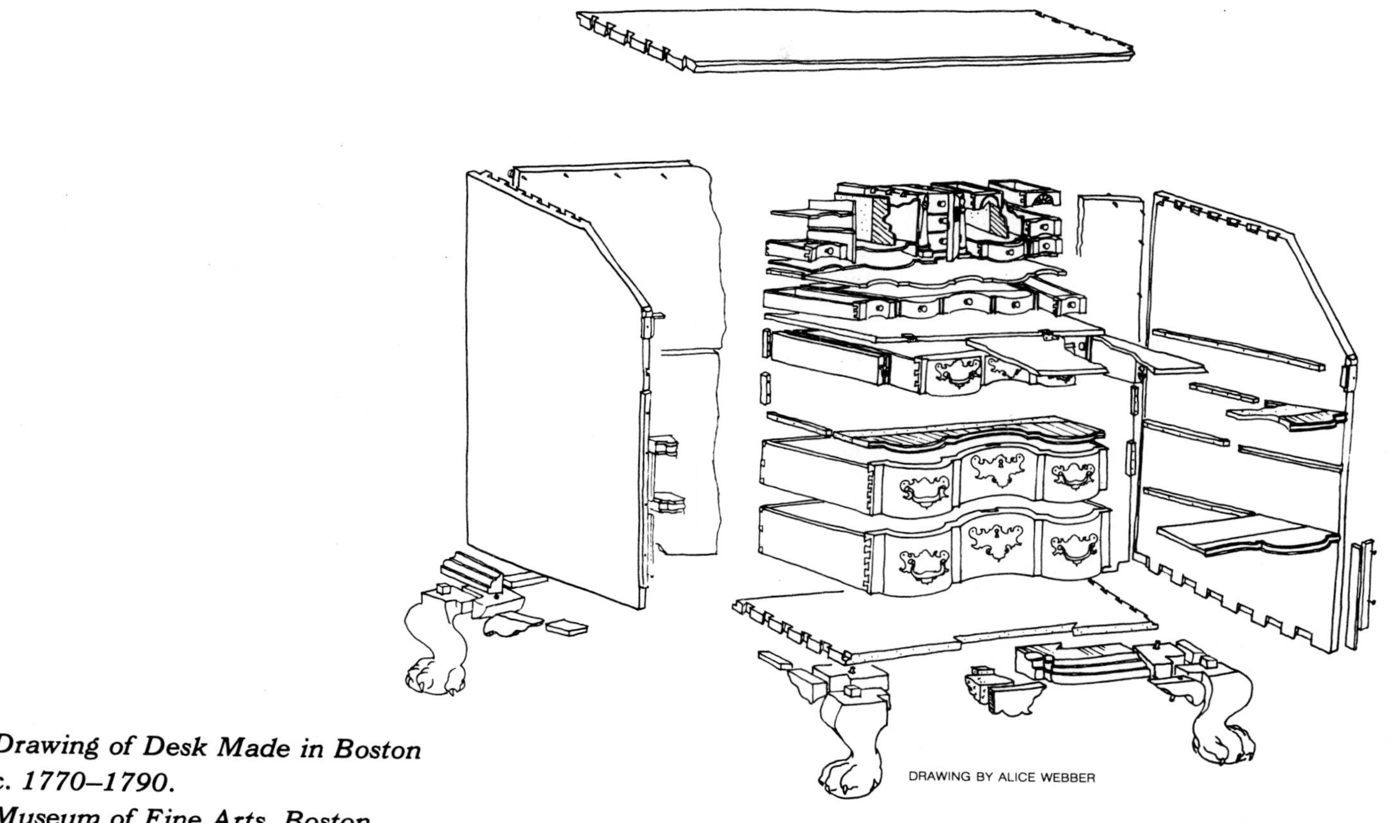

Drawing of Desk Made in Boston
c. 1770–1790.
Museum of Fine Arts, Boston.

Eighteenth-century desks and other cabinets are sleek but not simple. A cutaway view of an example from Boston shows intricate complexity of structure and superb workmanship. Construction details of case furniture differ in other regions of the colonies. This drawing, therefore, merely hints at the type of visual dissection necessary to make meaningful comparisons between furniture from different colonies. The giant dovetail which joins the bottom board to the front rail of this desk seems to be an indication of Boston craftsmanship. It is not a feature generally found in cabinets made in other areas.

Comparison: Case Furniture

Two masterpieces of Boston case furniture reveal two different American solutions to English Baroque design that remained popular in the Boston area through most of the eighteenth century. The bombé form of chest (kettle-shaped base) was simply a manifestation of graceful movement in the contours of furniture. The same movement was expressed somewhat differently in blocking—panels which alternated between forward and backward thrusting from the vertical surface of the chest.

RICHARD CHEEK, PHOTOGRAPHER

Desk and Bookcase
Charlestown, Massachusetts. 1753.
Made by Benjamin Frothingham, Sr. (1708–1765) or Jr. (1734–1809).
Mahogany; secondary woods: red cedar, white pine.
H: 97⅜" W: 44½" D: 24⅝".
Diplomatic Reception Rooms, the Department of State, Washington, D.C.

Magnificently patterned mahogany, superb architectural detailing and proportions, and flawless workmanship make this Boston desk and bookcase a masterpiece. Signed and dated in 1753 by Benjamin Frothingham and an unidentified "Do Sprage," this desk and bookcase is the earliest dated bombé piece known to have been made in America. Three generations of Frothinghams worked as cabinetmakers in Boston and Charlestown, and this signature may be either that of Benjamin Sr. or of Benjamin Jr. The desk, capped by a typical New England swan's neck pediment, displays the same monumentality and straight-sided drawers of an English linen press imported to Boston. Frothingham also applied a beaded molding, now missing, around the upper drawer of the desk section. This was a feature commonly found in English cabinetwork. The bombé base and foot of Frothingham's piece are closely related to designs in the 1754 edition of Chippendale's *Director*. Taken together, these factors imply that Frothingham's bookcase was well within the mainstream of London furniture design.

Desk and Bookcase
Boston. c. 1778.
Mahogany; secondary woods: red cedar and white pine.
H: 96⅜" W: 43" D: 23".
Winterthur Museum.

An inscription in the desk's secret compartment records that it was purchased in 1778 by Josiah Quincy (1710–1784) of Braintree, Massachusetts. In many respects it is the finest example of block-front furniture made in the Boston area. Certainly, it is among the most richly ornamented, with fluted Corinthian columns and pilasters on lower and upper sections. The carving on the bracket feet, pierced brasses, shell and floral ornament is brilliantly distributed across the surface with sufficient unadorned space between. The drawers represent the triumph of quality and design in block-front furniture, a form which originated in Boston and then became popular both in Salem and Newport.

Comparison: Desk and Bookcases

New York and Philadelphia desk and bookcases of the highest quality are compared here. Both are architectonic in design. Both offer an overall commanding presence which hearkens backward through generations of English taste. In detail, however, both pieces display flourishes of rococo carving characteristic of workmanship in their respective towns.

Desk and Bookcase
New York. c. 1770.
Mahogany with tulip drawer linings.
H: 98½" W: 44" D: 22".
Gift of Mrs. Richard Rhodebeck to the Department of State, Diplomatic Reception Rooms, Washington, D.C.

This desk and bookcase is the finest of its class to survive from pre-Revolutionary New York. Precisely chiseled details at the cornice, around borders of the door panels and at the feet, enclose broad expanses of magnificently figured mahogany surfaces which create a simple yet powerful desk form. The detail is so arranged as to arrest the eye at the perimeter of the piece, and to draw attention to the grandeur of the wooden surface contained within. The interior is fitted with serpentine drawers and three deeply carved shells.

Taste for broad expanses of highly figured wood persisted in New York through the Federal Period. Similar design arrangements and feet are found on furniture labeled and attributed to Samuel Prince.

COURTESY OF BERNARD & S. DEAN LEVY, INC.

Desk and Bookcase
Philadelphia. 1755–1775.
Mahogany, white oak and long-grained pine.
H: (desk) 43½"; (to bust) 107"; W: 47½" D: 24½".
Private Collection.

This is the most ambitious desk and bookcase made in eighteenth-century America. The upper section represents a serious study of Neo-Palladian architectural orders; the lower section was copied almost line for line from Plate LXXVIII in Chippendale's *Director* of 1754. The effect of the piece with its beautifully organized parts is majestic. Each inch of carving commands careful study. The ornament is equal to any carving on the furniture made for General Cadwalader in Philadelphia (for example, see page 153).

An image of a similar desk and bookcase appears at the bottom center of Benjamin Randolph's trade card. It is tempting to speculate that this great case piece was therefore produced in Randolph's shop.

In 1973 the antiques world was stunned by the discovery of this great work, which ranks at the top of all work produced in eighteenth-century Philadelphia. It is a central piece in understanding the extent to which Philadelphia craftsmen could follow the precepts of Chippendale.

Comparison: High Chests and Chests-on-Chests

During this period the upper classes required large-scale case furniture for storage. Such furniture was an obvious demonstration of wealth and at the same time provided practical storage since built-in closets were not common in the eighteenth century.

Two of Philadelphia's grandest high chests are compared to suggest the vigor of workmanship and variety of shapes available. They were all designed upon a basic form of two stacked cases of drawers with a separation somewhat below the center. For the sake of mobility, it was customary to attach large brass handles on the sides to assist in separating and carrying the upper and lower sections.

High Chest of Drawers
Philadelphia. 1765–1775.
Mahogany; secondary woods: cedar and tulip.
H: 91½" W: 46¾" D: 24¼".
The Metropolitan Museum of Art, New York.

The most impressive high chest of drawers made in America is illustrated here.

The color of the mahogany is unusually light and has handsomely patterned grain. "Horseflesh" mahogany is the current term for this type of graining. The form of the piece, while majestic, is not unusual in itself. The scrolled pediment, the skirt and the lower center drawer especially have vitality and motion in the carving. The *rocaille* ornament plays such an important role that despite the plain-faced drawers the entire outline of the piece seems alive.

Thomas Chippendale's *Director* served as a source for the original urn finials on the cornices. The elaborate asymmetrical carving of the lower center drawer is based on a plate for a chimney piece from Thomas Johnson's *A New Book of Ornaments* (London, 1762).

The great case furniture made in Philadelphia on the eve of the American Revolution is monumental. But viewed in the proper architectural setting, it does not look ponderous. It is divided into harmonic proportions with drawers graduating in size from top to bottom. Such pieces were made as a part of the architectural expression of Georgian homes in and near Philadelphia, and thus demanded a particular quality and volume of architectural space.

High Chest of Drawers
Philadelphia. 1765–1780.
Mahogany; secondary woods: tulip, white cedar, oak and yellow pine. H: 7′6″ W: 42¾″ D: 23⅛″.
Winterthur Museum.

John Fanning Watson, Philadelphia's nineteenth-century antiquarian, recorded that in the eighteenth century it was the custom to display an ample chest of drawers in the parlor or sitting room. It was not thought unusual to rummage for clothing even before company.

The wood pattern on the drawer fronts of this piece is somewhat distracting in this photograph, but not when the piece is actually seen. The carving arrests the viewer's attention. The upper section within the pediment is especially rich. It is a pure fantasy of C-scroll carving, columnar devices and swags of flowers.

Comparison: Desk and Bookcases

Newport and Philadelphia desk and bookcases are compared to show how differently these regions handled identical furniture designs. The desk and bookcase forms from both regions are masterpieces.

Desk and Bookcase
Philadelphia. c. 1770.
Mahogany, cedar; tulip drawer linings.
Inscribed in pencil, left envelope drawer: "C Wistar 1791."
H: (to cornice) 89¼"; (to top) 109¾". W: 42" D: 22¾".
Philadelphia Museum of Art.

The most elegant articulation of detail and proportions in Philadelphia furniture are arrestingly combined in this work which resembles pieces documented to the hand of Thomas Affleck. Despite its monumental size, it is visually light instead of ponderous, unlike so many case pieces of the period. The lightness is achieved partly through a delicate balance of proportions and the use of tall, vertical and richly grained but otherwise plain panels of the upper doors of the bookcase. The wood of the lower drawers contrasts brilliantly with the richly pierced brasses. These brasses move the eye of the observer upward to the midpoint of arresting beauty—the sculptured interior of the desk.

An unusual feature of this desk is its use of two small drawers as lid supports instead of the usual vertical sliding boards. Delicately carved moldings which surround the upper door panels emphasize the importance of the doors to the overall composition. The burst of carving in and above the crest is brilliantly shaped around the double arches of the doors. The central *rocaille* shell is so deeply and richly carved that its ribs are completely pierced for three-dimensional effect. The shell is applied rather than carved out of the solid panel.

While the actual structure of this desk and bookcase is substantial, and the wooden members are thick-bodied, the visual effect of the whole seems almost to be dancing to eighteenth-century music. The impression is one of an evanescent experience so light and delicate that it seems almost to transcend the material world. The experience derives, in part, from the freedom of carving in the asymmetry of the cartouche above the volutes of the crest. The lively organization of carved leafage around the shimmering edges of the central shell also add to this experience. Yet most of the impact of the visual experience is dependent upon the organization of the piece, which has a carefully calculated development of parts based on a harmonic system of proportions.

Desk and Bookcase
Newport, Rhode Island. 1760–1785.
Townsend-Goddard School.
Mahogany; secondary woods: pine, cherry, chestnut.
H: 95¼" W: 39⅞" D: 23⅝".
Museum of Fine Arts, Boston.

To own a six-shell block-fronted desk and bookcase from Newport represents the summit of many collectors' ambitions. The sculptural quality of the convex and concave carving and blocked facade offers enormous appeal.

These Newport pieces represented a conservative tradition in American design in the eighteenth century. Over several generations, a local school of cabinetmakers linked by marriage, taste and economics perfected, refined and reinterpreted the Baroque style with satisfaction, while the rococo style advanced in Boston, New York and Philadelphia.

Styles in Newport changed slowly. When John Folwell of Philadelphia solicited subscriptions for an edition of Chippendale's *Director,* every port city except Newport responded.

Chest-on-Chest
Boston. 1782.
Signed "John Cogswell,
Middle Street, Boston, 1782."
Mahogany and white pine.
H: 97" W: 94¼" D: 23½".
Museum of Fine Arts, Boston.

RICHARD MERRILL, PHOTOGRAPHER

This case piece represents the culmination of the development of the bombé form, or kettle-shaped base, in Boston furniture. Dutch, French and English cabinetmakers had played with the form in the seventeenth and early eighteenth centuries. By the time the idea reached Boston, the popularity of the form had begun to wane abroad. In 1782, when this chest was made, the bombé form had become quite special and peculiar to this region.

Some changes on this piece have taken place over the years: brasses were changed sometime in the nineteenth or early twentieth century; the original eagle finial is mounted on what may be a remodeled urn or pedestal. Despite the changes, the piece remains a major document of Boston workmanship.

Library Bookcase or China Cabinet
Charleston, South Carolina. 1755–1775.
Mahogany, mahogany veneers.
H: 105¾" W: 92" D: 27½".
Museum of Early Southern Decorative Arts, Winston-Salem, North Carolina.

One of the most magnificent pieces of furniture made in pre-Revolutionary America, this large case piece is based on Plate 93 of the 1754 edition of Thomas Chippendale's *The Gentleman and Cabinet-Maker's Director.* The applied fretwork of the midsection and cornice once was thought to be a signature of the shop of Thomas Elfe, an English cabinetmaker working in Charleston between 1747 and 1775, but is now believed to be a hallmark of Charleston shops in general. Chippendale's *Director* was rarely followed so precisely.

Tall Clock
Williamsburg, Virginia. c. 1770.
Movement by Thomas Walker of Fredericksburg, Virginia.
Mahogany and mahogany veneer; secondary woods: yellow pine, tulip, cherry and oak.
H: 106" W: 14⅜" D: 6⅞".
Museum of Fine Arts, Boston.

Although the brass face of this clock was engraved by Thomas Walker of Fredericksburg, Virginia, for many years its case was assumed to have been made in Philadelphia. Recent research has rejected this notion. By detailed comparison with structural features found in furniture of the Anthony Hay shop, the case is now believed to have been made in Williamsburg, Virginia. Despite the fact that it is missing its original pierced fretwork from the pediment and a band of fretwork above its door, it is the most splendid example of its form from Eastern Virginia.

Pole Screen
Boston. 1760–1790.
Mahogany; secondary wood: pine; embroidered panel with wool and silk yarns and paint on linen.
H: 64½" H: (screen) 27¾" W: 22½".
Museum of Fine Arts, Boston.

This fire screen descended in the Revere family. The style of framework of the screen with its tripod base spans the dates of Paul Revere's first and second marriages. It seems most likely that Sarah Orne Revere, whom the patriot silversmith married in 1757, produced the needlework displayed on the screen. The screen could be raised or lowered, and was used to shield the face from the open fire when seated near the hearth. Its major function, however, was to display the handiwork of the mistress of the house. The tripod stand is elegantly carved with sweeping arched legs terminating in elongate claw-and-ball feet. Its plain pole is surmounted with a neatly carved finial. The frame surrounding the needlework is held fast on the pole by a simple iron strap bent to yield a friction grip. The importance of ladies' handiwork is symbolized by this screen—an archetype of civilized living among the eighteenth-century genteel class.

RICHARD CHEEK, PHOTOGRAPHER

Oil Painting
"Mr. and Mrs. Thomas Mifflin," By John Singleton Copley.
H: 61½" W: 48".
The Historical Society of Pennsylvania.

Mrs. Mifflin sits in a high-backed chair working at a tape loom used for weaving tapes and fringes, a polite and useful pastime for ladies in the eighteenth century. The tape loom rests on a spider gateleg table that was used as a studio prop by Copley in other portraits. It was a means for Copley to "confuse the eye" of the viewer where the complexity of spatial problems and foreshortening of many legs gave him a compositional dilemma. It focused attention on the faces and hands of the sitters. His intricate arrangement of hands in this case was made possible through Mr. Mifflin's casual use of a Boston side chair back as an armrest.

Copley's composition was arranged in his studio when this prominent Philadelphia Quaker couple came to Boston. It is an ingenious cluster of furniture which compresses the sitters in space. This picture is one of Copley's greatest double portraits executed before the Revolution, done shortly before his departure for the Continent and England. The spider gateleg table was probably English, although a few seem to have been made in this country.

Tape Loom
Probably American. 1750–1780.
Mahogany. H: 12¼" L: 14⅝" W: 7½".
Winterthur Museum.

Similar to the tape loom in the Copley portrait of Mr. and Mrs. Mifflin, this tabletop loom is of a type commonly used by eighteenth-century gentlewomen. Tapes had a variety of functions and were most often used to trim upholstery, drapery and clothing.

VI

1780–1835

Neoclassicism

The Federal Period 1780–1810

IT WAS CLEAR TO the leaders who shaped the new American nation that contemporary parallels could be drawn from the heroic deeds of men of antiquity. American leaders sought appropriate emblems for the aspirations of their new nation, yet they did so in a traditional way, applying new meanings to familiar symbols. The glory of Rome, in particular, served as an archetype for Americans. It seemed fitting, therefore, that the Great Seal of the United States should incorporate a native species, the eagle—a symbol of Roman power. The American eagle captured the imagination of American craftsmen and their patrons. Eagles were inlaid on furniture; they were carved, painted, etched, hammered and cast to decorate every sort of object from ships to sewing boxes. The ubiquitous eagle found its way into almost every form of the arts and crafts of Federal America in spite of Franklin's famous objection that the eagle was a cowardly bird: he preferred the turkey.

Beginnings of the neoclassical style in America were evident in 1774 during the Continental Congress. Benjamin Randolph, a master of the Philadelphia school of rococo Chippendale style, produced a writing box for Thomas Jefferson, upon which, according to tradition, Jefferson drafted the Declaration of Independence. The "Independence Desk" was not made in the rococo style: it is a simple, practical box appropriate to its time and function. Its only significant ornament is a string inlay, which sounded one new stylistic note of the neoclassical taste—delicate, light ornament.

The taste of Washington and Jefferson was more advanced than that of most of their countrymen. They were acutely aware that their houses, furnishings and decorations would influence the new order. Gouverneur Morris of New York advised President Washington that it was important "to fix the taste of our country properly . . . your example will go very far. . . ."

Even after the Revolutionary War, neoclassical taste knew no political bounds. The exportation of furniture from England to the United States increased during the Federal Period. Washington followed British inspiration for his additions at Mt. Vernon. His great banquet hall—"The New Room"—was brought to completion in 1786. The ceiling and pilasters of the room were adorned with stucco festoons of bellflowers or husks in low relief; in the cove joining the walls and ceilings, the festoons were caught at their crests with ribbons tied in bowknots; semicircular paterae, cameo-like plaques, punctuated the intervals of the swags; the color of the ornament was off-white, painted to contrast with the gray-green background. The grand banquet room at Mt. Vernon represents one of the first major architectural expressions of Robert Adam's influence in this country.

Inspired by Roman ruins during his travels, British architect and furniture designer Adam collaborated with his brother James to produce rooms embodying their reinterpretations of the neoclassical style—the results were airy, light in color and effect. Their vision of neoclassicism became the vogue in England in the 1760s as high-style Britons turned their backs on Baroque forms and rococo ornament. For most Americans, the taste of neoclassicism grew gradually during the period after the signing of the Treaty of Paris in 1783. This new style entered the mainstream of American design in different ways: the importation of exemplary foreign furniture, emigration of cabinetmakers, and the importation of design books. George Hepplewhite's *The Cabinet-Maker and Upholsterer's Guide* was published after his death by his wife, Alice, in 1788. Thomas Sheraton's *The Cabinet-Maker and Upholsterer's Drawing Book* (1791–1793) was a handsomely illustrated two-volume work that promulgated Adamesque-neoclassical designs at the popular and practical level. Most American cabinetmakers combined details from both Hepplewhite's and Sheraton's books without fine distinctions. But Sheraton believed he was introducing new designs and wrote that Hepplewhite's *Guide* represented the nadir of old-style taste. The basic differences between Hepplewhite's designs and Sheraton's are that Hepplewhite showed furniture with more curvilinear features and carved ornament while Sheraton favored a fiercely rectilinear silhouette, tight in profile and given to painted surface or inlay.

Sheraton and Hepplewhite were not the only source books for furniture designers and cabinetmakers of the Federal Period. Thomas Shearer published an illustrated book entitled *The Cabinet-Maker's London Book of Prices* in 1788. Stylistically this book falls between the work of Hepplewhite and Sheraton. Its plates, whose designs were drawn from others such as Hepplewhite, show furniture of relatively conservative character. It was meant to set prices rather than fashion and was probably conservative to avoid going out of date too quickly.

Cabinetmakers emigrating to America brought with them firsthand knowledge of current styles and practices. Skilled cabinetmakers from England like John and Thomas Seymour, father and son, came first to Portland, Maine, in 1784, and moved to Boston in 1794. Within two years John was listed in the Boston directories as a cabinetmaker. The Seymours prospered as did many craftsmen who made furniture in advanced foreign styles.

Political and cultural ties between France and America strengthened during the Federal Period. Philadelphia was especially receptive to French *émigré* craftsmen and intellectuals: John James Audubon, Alexandre Lesueur, Pierre Charles L'Enfant and Joseph Bonaparte were part of the artistic and cultural life of that city. While the influence of French taste was promoted by the presence of the *émigrés,* the vogue for gilt and painted furniture in the style of Louis XVI was further stimulated by the importation of royal furniture after the collapse of the *Ancien Régime.* Gouverneur Morris and James Swan of Boston were both in Paris at an advantageous moment to make purchases of royal furniture when the crown property was dispersed in 1794. James Swan, a well-connected merchant in Paris, built a lucrative trade importing to France the grain and other raw goods which were in desperate demand after the French Revolution. He exchanged these goods for superb furnishings from noble households that had been confiscated by the New Republic. Swan shipped his treasures to America for sale in New York, Philadelphia and Baltimore, saving some of the best furniture for his family's use in Massachusetts. Today, much of the furniture is at the Museum of Fine Arts in Boston.

John Adams, Benjamin Franklin, Thomas Jefferson, George Washington, James Madison and James Monroe are all known to have imported or purchased neoclassical French furniture. Jefferson shipped eighty-six crates of effects from Paris when he returned to America in 1789. Much of his furniture was sold after his death, so we can only imagine the extent and quality of the furniture he collected, but a few pieces survive at Monticello—a pair of Louis XVI looking glasses and some relatively simple *fauteuils* or upholstered easy chairs.

American master craftsmen who had to compete with emigrant craftsmen and imported furniture were quick to adapt. Before the start of the nineteenth century, neoclassical taste had become the reigning fashion of the new American Democracy. Americans had seen, and in some cases owned, superb furniture—furniture whose production demanded the most exacting skills performed by many different specialists: cabinetmakers, inlay artisans, carvers, gilders, painters and upholsterers. Although there were large American shops that employed carvers, gilders and upholsterers and some special artisans who moved from shop to shop, most furniture production could not be so highly specialized. Americans were in a hurry. Population was growing; frontiers were being settled rapidly. As a result, most of the work produced here was much simpler, less highly ornamented than that abroad.

The Federal government encouraged home industry, and helped the growth of domestic manufacturing. The furniture business grew. Maritime prosperity in Salem, Baltimore and Providence opened new markets with more jobs for craftsmen. New kinds of specialized furniture came into being; secretary-desks, worktables, basin stands, night tables, sideboards with enclosed cupboards and drawers, cellarettes, knife boxes and pianoforte cases are some of the new forms which required a diversity of skills. There was a need for inlay makers and craftsmen who could supply thin veneer sheets to be sold by the yard. Inlay makers produced stringing, banding, pictorial and figured inlay which so dominated the area of sales that it is often possible to identify the probable place of origin of a piece of Federal furniture on the basis of the inlay work. Like the flat carving, painted ornamental gilding required specialists whose work can sometimes be recognized. Metal hardware, brass or enamel fittings, exotic woods and other accoutrements are less useful in making regional analyses, as they were often imported.

Master cabinetmakers prospered, and commission furniture warehouses which also sold furniture by other craftsmen developed as populations increased in the nineteenth century.This growth took the furniture business beyond that of the small craft shop where the patron had played an important role in the design process. Instead, the customer saw and purchased what was already finished. Custom-made furniture was still available, "bespoke" or on order. But for impatient Americans, the new trend of warehousing furniture caught on, moving the craftsmen away from commission work toward stockpiling, speculation and large shops. Standardization of popular forms became a necessity with the rapid growth of furniture warehousing and the increased use of machines in furniture production. Work on broader, simpler surfaces, keeping handwork at a minimum, well suited the neoclassical styles.

With the growth of the furniture industry and the opportunity to make fortunes by careful business practices, frictions between journeymen and masters grew. In 1794 and 1795, when Philadelphia was the center of contention in the furniture business, the journeymen published their own price book, *The Journeymen Cabinet and Chair-Makers Philadelphia Book of Prices.* They announced that members of the Journeymen's Society would refuse to work in the shops of any master who would not pay the fixed wages. By 1796, the Philadelphia journeymen won their demands. As a result they worked a six-day week and an eleven-hour day, and averaged one dollar per day. New York craftsmen followed suit in 1802 and 1803, patterning their published appeal on the Declaration of Independence.

The end of the Federal Period brought with it a decline of respect for those values expressed by Lord Chesterfield in *Principles of Politeness and of Knowing the World* (Carlisle, Pennsylvania, 1809). Lord Chesterfield explained that a gentleman should never be in a rush. He must be polite in every posture, expression and gesture, command respect, but not demand attention. Boorish manners were to be avoided at all cost. Dress and taste should be simple yet within the rules of common sense and current practice. A gentleman should be elegant in his disposition and carriage. Chesterfield admonished: "Now to acquire a graceful air you must attend to your dancing."

The furniture of the Federal Period fairly dances in its adherence to a vision of lightly poised neoclassical style. To be understood, furniture of this era needs to be viewed through the looking glass of its own time when tightly fitting clothes, tall hats, high waists and slim skirts, long trousers and tight-fitting sleeves, elongation of all silhouettes were the taste in dress. Such refined and smartly organized patterns of behavior and taste were part of the precise, tidy, well-proportioned and severely restrained order of the Federal Period. Perfection of furniture parts—neat inlay and polished surfaces—are but facets of this order. The character of the Federal Period was summed up by William Bentley, the Salem diarist; after visiting the residence of Oak Hill, furnished by Elizabeth Derby West, he recorded that she "never violates the chastity of correct taste."

Chest-on-Chest
Salem, Massachusetts. 1796.
Traditionally Attributed to William Lemon.
Probably carved by Samuel McIntire. Mahogany and pine.
H: 102½" W: 46¾" D: 23".
Museum of Fine Arts, Boston.

Tradition and change are combined in this great case piece made for Elizabeth Derby West of Salem. It marks a watershed of style in American furniture, incorporating the end of an era and the start of a new one. The form of the cabinet, its Georgian-style architectural massiveness, serpentine lower drawers and ogee bracket feet look backward stylistically to the earlier Chippendale Period. By contrast, the ornamentation shows a fresh, vigorous interest in neoclassicism. The urns, swags, baskets filled with fruit and the beautifully carved female figure all show a precision with the chisel and a knowledge of classical antique ornamental design inspired by a generation of discoveries of ancient art made abroad. The design incorporates garlands, grapes and a symbolic figure, suggesting the growth of the new republic of the United States. The choice of such symbols was especially meaningful to members of the Derby family whose great wealth and power were intimately connected with the free enterprise and economic destiny of the country.

Complex ideas implied by McIntire's choice of ornament were brilliantly expressed. Typical of most transitional or innovative works, the ornamentation was stylistically in advance of the form of the piece; the exquisite McIntire carving seems "stuck on" rather than integrated with the whole.

Chest-on-Chest
Made by Stephen Badlam, Lower Dorchester Mills, Massachusetts.
Mahogany and pine. H: 101½" W: 51½" D: 23⅜".
Pediment Figure of Liberty and Fame
Carved by John and/or Simeon Skillin, Boston, Massachusetts. 1791.
The Mabel Brady Garvan Collection, Yale University Art Gallery.

When Stephen Badlam made this monumental work for Elias Hasket Derby of Salem, the craftsman was conscious that he was constructing a piece of furniture of exceptional quality and importance. Members of Boston's best-known ship carving family (John and Simeon Skillin) were called upon to make allegorical figures on the pitched pediment. The central figure bears symbolic attributes of Virtue, represented by a wreath; Truth, suggested by the gilded sun; and a Phrygian cap on the tip of a pike representing Liberty. When the Skillins carved this figure they were also at work on a ship for Derby, carving a masthead, brackets, trailboards, quarter-pieces, stern rails, badges and festoons. On May 10, 1791, for all this work they charged £31.15.0 with a ten percent reduction to £28.11.6 for prompt payment of their bill.

Cabinetmaker Stephen Badlam charged Elias Hasket Derby £19 for the "Case of draws exclusive of [excluding] the carving." Badlam was proud of his achievement. He wrote a note to future owners and attached the note to this piece. The note stated that the chest is a work of consequence that should be well cared for and kept out of sunshine. This is a rare record of pride that an American craftsman took in his work.

Oil Painting on Wood Panel
"The Washington Family." 1789–1790.
By Edward Savage (1761–1817).
H: 18⅛" W: 24⅛".
Winterthur Museum.

This oil sketch by the New England artist Edward Savage is a compelling and instructive ideal image of the first family of Federal America. Savage painted several versions in different sizes; this picture was probably the original sketch made directly from life and upon which the others were based.

George Washington and his wife are shown with Martha's children from her first marriage. Standing behind Martha is a servant, Billy Lee. Major Pierre Charles L'Enfant's plan of the Federal City is spread on the table showing the projection of a national capital which Washington did not live to see completed.

The most popular American print of its time was based on this painting. Numerous impressions were issued to satisfy the insatiable public demand for an image of the first family. The composition proved so satisfactory that presidential family portraits for several generations followed the same arrangement. By the middle of the nineteenth century, faces and clothing were changed for Lincoln and Grant family portraits, and the servant was not included.

The furniture in the Washington family painting is not distinguished for advanced style. Washington sits on a chair in the French taste with gracefully curved cabriole legs. Martha's dress obscures almost all but the tall back of a chair upholstered in red figured damask. The chair back is studded with brass-headed nails. The draped column and the globe beside Washington are artistic conventions meant to convey the idea of classical learning and a world view.

MARLER, PHOTOGRAPHER

Mt. Vernon Banquet Hall (1776–c. 1785)
The Mt. Vernon Ladies' Association of the Union, Mt. Vernon, Virginia.

George Washington was among the first to introduce into America in a grand way the architectural neoclassical style of English architect Robert Adam. Washington wedded the new style to an older tradition as he finished his Banquet Hall at Mt. Vernon. Although the Hall was built in 1776, it was not finished with mantel, stucco ornament and paint until after 1785 in the manner described by Washington as follows:

> I have a room 32 by 24 feet, and 16 feet pitch, which I want to finish in stucco; it is my intention to do it in a plain neat style; which, independently of its being the present taste, (as I am informed), is my choice.

Elegant ornamental swags, garlands and oval paterae lace the stucco detail of the ceiling, cove and entablature of the room. The old-style Palladian window, or "Venetian window" as Washington called it, was similarly ornamented with neoclassical detail on its borders. Throughout the room the shallow relief detail was emphasized by contrasting cream color paint against shades of green—creating an effect of carved antique bas-relief sculpture like that simulated by Wedgwood pottery.

Sheraton-style chairs, which Washington bought in 1797 from cabinetmaker John Aitken of Philadelphia, are lined up against the wall. Originally there were twenty-four such chairs from Aitken's shop, arranged in a manner following Thomas Sheraton's illustrations of great formal rooms.

Secretary-Bookcase
Philadelphia, Pennsylvania. c. 1797.
Made by John Aitken.
Mahogany, white pine, yellow poplar. H: 95¾" W: 38" D: 28".
The Mt. Vernon Ladies' Association of the Union,
Mt. Vernon, Virginia.

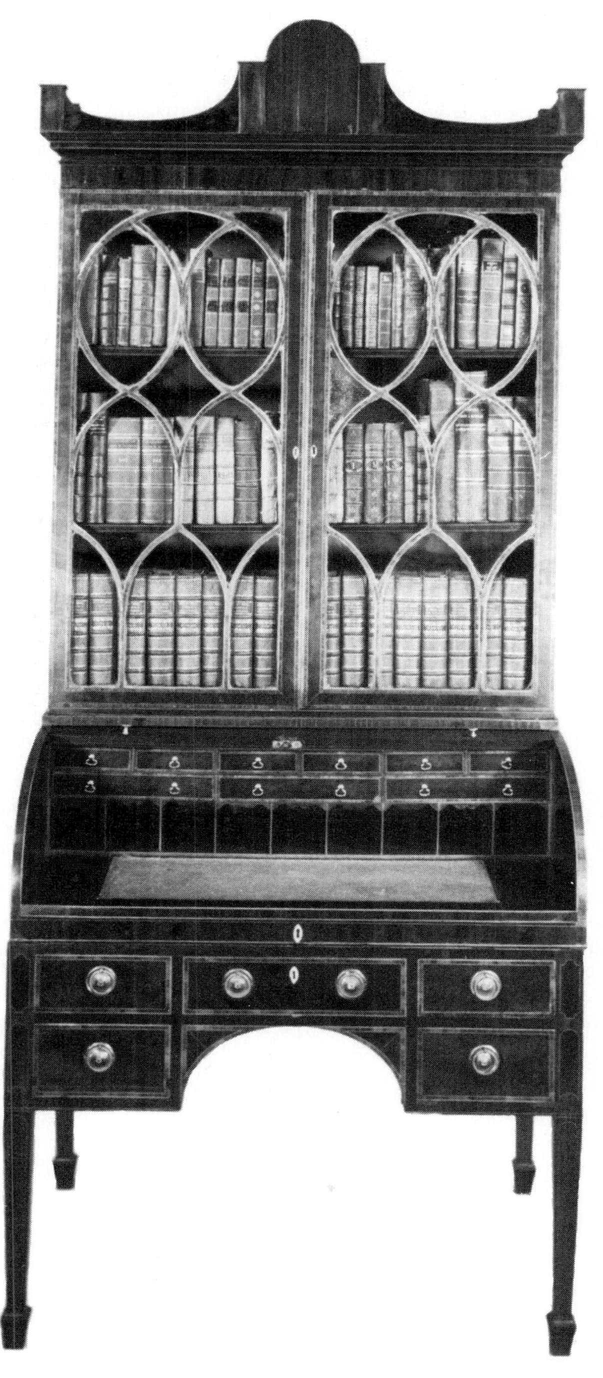

While the Federal City was being designed and built beside the Potomac River, the United States capital was located in Philadelphia. Washington lived there during his two terms as President, from 1790 to 1797. Before leaving Philadelphia, he purchased a number of pieces of furniture from local craftsmen. Perhaps the finest piece and certainly the best-documented example which Washington took to Mt. Vernon is this "tambour Secretary & book case" for which he paid the cabinetmaker John Aitken $145. The "tambour" reference of Washington's accounts was a term commonly meaning a rolling door made of many wooden slats of wood glued to a canvas backing. For this secretary-bookcase it formed a "rollaway" concealed in the desk top, hidden from view when the desk was ready for use (as pictured here).

Portable Writing Desk
Philadelphia, Pennsylvania. c. 1775–1776.
Made by Benjamin Randolph for Thomas Jefferson.
Mahogany with green baize-lined writing board.
H: 3½" W: 9¾" L: 14⅜".
Smithsonian Institution, The National Museum of American History, Washington, D.C.

Few pieces of American furniture have such rich associations as this simple desk. It was made by cabinetmaker Benjamin Randolph of Philadelphia for Thomas Jefferson when he was in that town attending meetings of the Continental Congress. During both the first and second meetings of the Congress Jefferson stayed with Benjamin Randolph. According to Jefferson's written account, this desk was used by him when he drafted the Declaration of Independence.

Although a simple piece of furniture, the desk is ornamented with a band of string inlay—a harbinger of neoclassical taste more than a decade in advance of the popular use of stringing in Federal American furniture. This piece symbolizes not only a historic moment for the birth of the Nation but also, in a modest way, the beginnings of a new style and taste; a new approach to design in this country.

Armchair
Philadelphia, Pennsylvania. 1791–1793.
Made by Thomas Affleck.
Mahogany and white oak. H: 36¼" W: 24" D: 22".
Independence Hall National Historical Park.

Thirty of these chairs now in the National Park Service Collection at Independence Hall offer visitors to Congress Hall an authentic image of the seating made by Thomas Affleck between 1791 and 1793 for the House of Representatives and the Senate when the United States Capitol was located in Philadelphia.

While these chairs retain the basic organization of French armchairs, they are far simpler and lighter in their overall form and detail. This simplicity derives not only from a need for economy but also from a new sense of style.

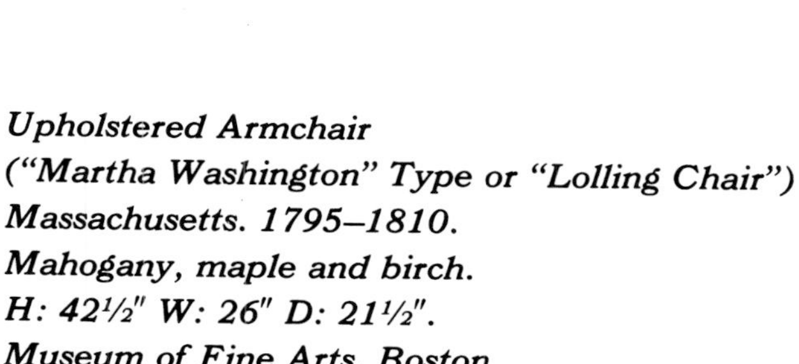

Watercolor
"The Morse Family."
Charlestown, Massachusetts. 1811.
By Samuel F. B. Morse (1791–1872).
H: 12" L: 15".
Smithsonian Institution,
The National Museum of American History, Washington, D.C.

Rare interior views of the Federal Period sometimes reveal the persistence of old-fashioned furniture and architecture in the homes of notable Americans. This watercolor shows that the handsome Chippendale style and a new carpet were in use in an important room in 1811, when the painter, Samuel F. B. Morse, did this charming family portrait. Morse, who later became an eminent artist and inventor, was only twenty at the time.

The painting shows his father, the Reverend Jedidiah Morse, standing at the center of the table examining a globe together with his sons and wife. The globe represents the elder Morse's extensive knowledge of geography.

Upholstered Armchair
("Martha Washington" Type or "Lolling Chair")
Massachusetts. 1795–1810.
Mahogany, maple and birch.
H: 42½" W: 26" D: 21½".
Museum of Fine Arts, Boston.

At the time when tall-backed, upholstered open armchairs of the Federal Period were being made in New England, they were called "lolling chairs." In 1778 an Englishman who complained about the advances of luxury in the *Gentleman's Magazine* (XLVIII, p. 587) described in scornful terms the "two armed machine adapted to the indulgent purpose of lolling, and so unwieldy as only to be conveyed, to the great endangerment of the carpet, from one part of the room to the other, upon wheels."

The term "lolling chair" is often found in eighteenth- and early nineteenth-century inventories and bills of sale. The term is suggestive of a physical attitude—a stance of grace and ease consistent with the genteel posture often pictured in period portraits. Such graceful mien seems embodied in tall-backed New England armchairs with their delicately shaped wooden arms and trim legs.

Chairs of this general form had been made in France and England during the early to mid-eighteenth century. By the 1760s popularity of the form waned abroad, but grew in this country. The design idea survived in America and developed its own peculiar characteristics. Tall backs and slim, tapering arms and legs were emphasized. The New England craftsman played upon the basic form and in the process developed a distinctively "American" chair type. New England, and especially Massachusetts, was the main center of its development. Documented examples outside of the New England region are rare. This one has an especially fine shape to its molded arms, and a smartly shaped crest.

Upholstered Armchair
("Martha Washington" or "Lolling Chair")
Lower Dorchester Mills, Massachusetts. c. 1795.
Stamped "S. Badlam" for Stephen Badlam (1751–1815).
Mahogany with hard maple, birch, white pine.
H: 41" W: 25½" D: 21".
Winterthur Museum.

The noted cabinetmaker Stephen Badlam, whose name is stamped on this chair, employed various craftsmen for specialized work. Most notable was the carving done for him by John and Simeon Skillin of Boston for the great chest-on-chest made for Elias Hasket Derby and now in the Garvan Collection at Yale University (see page 200). In addition to Badlam's name the initials "S.F." are stamped on this chair. These may represent the name of a journeyman who was working in Badlam's shop. Samuel Fisk (d. 1797) is a likely supposition. The same initials are stamped on a pair of Chippendale-style armchairs from Boston.

Not many chairs of this form are marked with the names of the makers. And very few bear carved ornament. The ornament on the front legs of this chair is closely related to other furniture bearing Badlam's stamp. The motif is fairly consistent: a daisy surmounting pendant husks or bellflowers, above stop fluting. The form of the chair is strong and the effect is solid rather than highly stylish. There are more visually arresting chairs of this type, but few are more competently handled either in overall design or in complex detail.

Armchair
Boston, Massachusetts. 1797.
Made by George Bright (1727–1805).
Mahogany with original leather upholstery.
H: 34" W: 22" D: 24".
The Society for the Preservation of
New England Antiquities, Boston.

This armchair, part of a set of thirty, was made for Boston's new State House, which was designed by Charles Bulfinch and finished by 1797. The maker of these chairs, George Bright, was paid $240 for the set. One of Boston's most eminent cabinetmakers, Bright descended from three generations of craftsmen who had worked in the furniture and upholstery trades.

RICHARD CHEEK, PHOTOGRAPHER

Oil on Canvas
"The Sargent Family."
Massachusetts. c. 1800. Artist Unknown.
L: 50¼" H: 38".
The National Gallery of Art,
Washington, D.C.

The tapered feet on many Federal chairs characterizes the preference for precision in form and stance. The prim effect of the side chairs, upholstered in black horsehair (haircloth) and finished with brass tacks, is repeated in gesture with the pointed toes of the man's shoes. Symmetry is emphasized at the window with a birdcage on either side, balancing the two chairs below. The parents are linked together in the composition with what seems to be two sets of twin children. Charming in gesture and sentiment, the painting was apparently meant to please with a visual alliteration on the theme of symmetry—paired cages, side chairs and look-alike children. A brightly painted floor covering (perhaps an oil-painted canvas) and a strongly patterned wallpaper show that chaste plainness of taste was not in fact an overriding principle with the Sargent family.

Early Federal Side Chairs

A revolution in seating design took place in the United States during the late eighteenth century. The solid, heavy construction of the earlier Queen Anne and Chippendale styles gave way to the introduction of fragile, light and delicate chairs which were easy to move about. This was not simply a change in appearance but a whole new approach to design that swept the country, giving new attention to veneers, inlay, low relief and small-scale carving. The great variety of lightweight side chairs that survive from Federal America is an index of their popularity. Rooms became specialized with different functions demanding a diversity of new chair and other furniture forms.

Choices of detail were based on what the maker could sell the customer. Each extra feature—bit of carving, inlay or fancywork—increased the unit cost because it took extra time and talent to finish.

The following is a sampling of side chairs made in different regions of post-Revolutionary America. They are divided into three major groups—shield-back, square-back and oval-back chairs. Even within such narrow design limits the variety is astounding and regional features can be distinguished.

Side Chair
Lower Dorchester Mills, Massachusetts. 1790–1800.
Stamped on Rear Seat Rail: "S. Badlam"
for Stephen Badlam (1751–1815).
Mahogany, maple, ash. H: 38" W: 21" D: 18".
Winterthur Museum.

Slightly heavier than many later Federal chairs, this chair shows a blend of Chippendale and Hepplewhite influences. The heavy stop-fluted legs are its earliest stylistic features, and owe their form to Chippendale sources. The pendant bellflower carving on the legs and the sheaf-of-wheat shield back are stylistically more advanced, making a transition from Chippendale to Hepplewhite.

Inside the seat rail a stamped "SF" suggests the possibility that a journeyman of those initials was working for Badlam. The chair is also marked "S. Badlam," which identifies it with that well-known cabinetmaker who had a shop in Lower Dorchester Mills, not far from Boston.

Side Chair
Charlestown, Massachusetts. c. 1790–1800.
Labeled by Jacob Forster (1764–1838).
Mahogany; satinwood inlay and birch.
H: 37½" D: 20¾".
Private Collection.

This chair is simply composed but attractive. Jacob Forster called attention to the sharp character of the back by outlining it with fine-line inlaid stringing. Similar chairs were produced by other Boston area chairmakers, such as Samuel Stone and William Alexander.

COURTESY OF ISRAEL SACK, INC.

Side Chair
Salem, Massachusetts. c. 1795. Carving Attributed to Samuel McIntire.
Mahogany, pine.
H: 39⅜" W: 18½" D: 21¾".
Museum of Fine Arts, Boston.

This most elegant Federal side chair from Salem was made for Elias Hasket Derby. Its maker based his design on Plate 2 of George Hepplewhite's *The Cabinet-Maker and Upholsterer's Guide* (London, 1788). Yet some modifications and improvements were made in the process; this chair is no mere copy but a highly personal and delightful work.

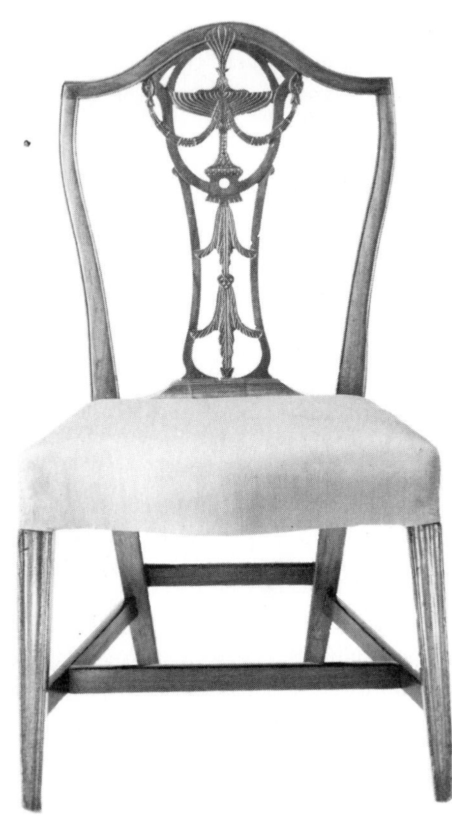

Side Chair
Rhode Island. c. 1800.
Mahogany, birch and red oak. H: 39¾" W: 19¾" D: 17¾".
Winterthur Museum.

The cylix motif which Samuel McIntire sketched for Salem chair backs may have been inspired by the back of a Rhode Island chair like this one. The design of the back seems almost scratched or engraved rather than carved. The effect is quite linear. Such attention to line is characteristic of provincial workmanship not only in furniture, but also in painting and architecture. It is the draftsman's solution to design rather than developing the full plasticity of the material. The overscaled pendant bellflowers of the back are so intensely textured that they dominate the design.

Side Chair
New York. c. 1800.
Mahogany, red gum and white pine.
H: 39½" W: 21⅛" D: 16".
Winterthur Museum.

Of all Federal chairs this is among the most beautiful because of its molded frame, crispness of carving, and restraint in the design movement of the back splat. The swags of the back are gracefully and naturally suspended to fall around the framework of the central oval. At the lower point of the shield the carved leafage is sharp and precisely defined in a manner not found outside of the New York school.

The major weakness in this design is its rather dull front feet. Had the original buyer been willing to pay for the extra cost of spade feet, the overall stance of the piece would have been improved.

Side Chair
Baltimore, Maryland. c. 1790.
Mahogany.
H: 36⅞" W: 20⅞" D: 18⅝".
The Baltimore Museum of Art.

This side chair was part of a set of furniture made for Charles Carroll of Carrollton (1737–1832), a signer of the Declaration of Independence and an influential figure in Maryland. The design is adapted from Plate 28 of Sheraton's *The Cabinet-Maker and Upholsterer's Drawing Book.* The carving of the Prince of Wales feather in the back, the swags below and the leafage carving at the base are magnificently executed. The pendant bellflower carving on the legs shows design motifs that were soon adapted to shaded inlay ornament furniture from the Baltimore-Annapolis region.

Side Chair
Annapolis, Maryland. 1790–c. 1797.
Labeled by John Shaw (working 1773–c. 1828).
Mahogany with tulip and white oak.
H: 37½" W: 20⅝" D: 21⅛".
Winterthur Museum.

The most idiosyncratic side chair of its time and place, the splat of this chair seems to wriggle with energy. At the top the splat design merges into a pair of eagle heads conjoined by a sunburst glory—a sign of nationalistic pride. The chair is believed to have been owned by Robert Bowie, who was elected Governor of Maryland in 1803.

The charm of the chair is its naive and original treatment of the splat. There is an awkwardness of scale and integration of parts that reveals that its designer did not fully understand principles of neoclassical reserve and proportions.

Side Chair
Boston, Massachusetts. c. 1800.
Mahogany, birch and maple.
H: 36" W: 18" D: 21¾".
Museum of Fine Arts, Boston.

This chair is part of a set owned by Elizabeth Derby West and used in her house, Oak Hill. The simplicity of the shape of the chair represents Boston's counterpart to the urn- and square-back chairs made in New York City at about the same time.

The reeding on the legs is finely tapered. The only design flaw of the back is its fragility, but the space is interestingly divided.

Armchair (One of a Set)
Salem, Massachusetts. c. 1802.
Carving Probably by Samuel McIntire.
Mahogany. H: 20⅞" W: 34⅜" D: 19⅝".
Winterthur Museum.

This armchair is one of a set made for the parlor of the Pierce-Nichols house, Salem Street, Salem. The design is based on Plate 33 of Sheraton's *The Cabinet-Maker and Upholsterer's Drawing Book* (London, 1792). Punchwork background and bellflower carving of the type seen here is normally attributed to the school of Samuel McIntire of Salem.

Side Chair (One of a Set of Six)
Hartford, Connecticut.
Made by Samuel Kneeland (1755–1828) and Lemuel Adams (dates unknown), Partnership: September 10, 1792–March 9, 1795.
Cherry with white pine blocks. H: 38¾" W: 21½" D: 20".
Winterthur Museum.

This is one of a remarkably preserved set of six side chairs that have retained their original canvas seats (painted to simulate leather) with swag-studded brass nails.

Kneeland and Adams, whose bill of sale for the chairs was dated 1793, are most famous for having made the furniture which still stands in the Old State House in Hartford. Their furniture is light, graceful, and displays a distinctive sense of pattern and precise carving and inlay. They employed workmen from both New York and Boston and advertised that they made all kinds of "Cabinet Work of Mahogany, and Cherrytree, in the newest fashions." The back splats of these chairs, while seemingly related to the urn shapes of Salem-made furniture, are distinctive and eloquently delicate.

Side Chair
New York. 1800–1810.
Possibly by Slover and Taylor (working 1802–1805).
Mahogany, oak. H: 36⅝" W: 21¼" D: 17½".
Museum of Fine Arts, Boston.

Square reeded legs, finely tapered, complement the reeding of the elegantly shaped columns of the back of this side chair. Its design and character are very similar to a chair with a partial label of Slover and Taylor reproduced in *Antiques* in November 1923.

Several similar examples are known with slight variations in details. This one is among the most nicely detailed; the carving is exceptional. The tapered columns descend to remarkably fine bases. The pattern for this chair was described in *The New-York Book of Prices for Cabinet & Chair Work* . . . , 1802, and hence it was a form which a number of New York craftsmen probably made, not just the firm of Slover and Taylor.

Side Chair
Baltimore or Annapolis, Maryland. c. 1800.
Mahogany. H: 36½" W: 20⅞" D: 20⅜".
Winterthur Museum.

The balloon shape in this chair back is distinctive. The idea comes from a plate in Sheraton's *The Cabinet-Maker and Upholsterer's Drawing Book* (Plate 28), and while it seems to have been a favorite among Maryland chairmakers, it was uncommon in the Northern States. The splay to the back, tapering downward, is unusual and graceful; the gentle sweep of the crest of the chair is elegant. The half-upholstered seat rail as well as the stringing inlay on the lower edge of the seat frame are keys in identifying Maryland-made Federal furniture. The stringing inlay is composed of a central hairline joining a series of squares or circles like pearls spaced along a string.

RICHARD CHEEK, PHOTOGRAPHER

Side Chair
New York, New York. c. 1800.
Mahogany; rails ash and birch.
H: 35 15/16" W: 21½" D: 17⅞".
Museum of Fine Arts, Boston.

This side chair represents one of the most popular types made in New York—a square-back design copied almost literally from a plate in Sheraton's *The Cabinet-Maker and Upholsterer's Drawing Book* of 1793.

A detailed photograph shows the shallow depth of carving needed to produce a glittering effect in the bright light made possible by the new Argand lamps. The light admitted into spacious and large-windowed rooms of the period also allowed for close-range appreciation of small-scale detail.

Upholstery of Federal Furniture

American neoclassical furniture had smartly tailored upholstery. Springs were not used at the time and therefore the shape of the upholstery followed the frame. Federal upholstery was tightly organized and boxlike. Precise edges at the borders were made by tightly sewing the horsehair foundation into what was termed a "French edge." Comfort came from down-filled pillows and bolsters.

Sharp definition in reeding and bas-relief demanded precise, spare upholstery which would not compete for visual attention. When carved ornament became bolder during the 1840s, upholstery began to gain enough mass and volume to dominate the shape of the furniture.

Easy Chair
New England. c. 1800.
Mahogany, maple and white pine; yellow wool upholstery.
H: 48" W: 28" D: 25" (at seat).
Collection of Mrs. Charles L. Bybee.

The late Chippendale style, persistent in New England well into the Federal Period, was refined and modified in all furniture forms. The lines of this easy chair suggest a late date. While the crest of the piece is boldly flared, the wings and the straight rolled arms are delicately shaped with a precision and thinness of form characteristic of the late eighteenth century.

RICHARD CHEEK, PHOTOGRAPHER

Armchair (One of a Pair)
Boston, Massachusetts. c. 1800–1810.
Mahogany, maple. H: 38" W: 20⅛" D: 19¼".
Museum of Fine Arts, Boston.

Subtle relationships exist in the proportions of the sides of the open arm supports, the legs and the dimensions of the rest of this handsome upholstered armchair. The quality of these proportions gives the piece a stately calm that is seldom found in better harmony in American furniture of the Federal Period. In addition to the overall effect, the details are superb. The arm supports are not merely inverted legs scaled down. There is an effect of visual interchange, but the arm supports have a character and shape of their own. Emphasis on the upward thrust is achieved by their more pronounced tapering. Even the carving is somewhat varied from the leafage on the legs. The organization of design of the carved blocks which join the arm posts to the legs is elaborate and brilliantly made. The chairs descended in the Derby-West family.

Circular Easy Chair
Philadelphia, Pennsylvania. 1805–1815.
Mahogany with cherry, American ash and pine.
H: 46" W: 33½" D: 24½".
Winterthur Museum.

The upholstered scrolled arms of the previous generation of easy chairs is here continued and combined with a lower, rounded back, upholstered in vertical rolls. The turned and reeded legs with bulbous feet and carving help to date the chair. Carving above the reeding is similar to that found on Stephen Girard's set made in 1807 by the shop of Ephraim Haines of Philadelphia.

The front seat rail is elliptical in shape and made of cherry. This is a feature found on other Philadelphia circular chairs.

The problem of keeping a deeply padded chair trim-looking is nicely solved in this design. Here, comfort does not dominate aesthetics. The chair is delicate and trim; much of this effect depends upon the skill of the upholsterer and upon the choice of fabric.

Sofa
Salem, Massachusetts. c. 1800.
Mahogany and birch.
H: 40½" L: 80½" D: 28".
Museum of Fine Arts, Boston.

Perfection in sofas of the Federal Period was achieved by the maker and carver of this piece made for the Derby family. The quality of the carving is like the best of work by Samuel McIntire. The mahogany border at the crest is carved with rosettes and glyphs similar in pattern to that in the cornice from the parlor of Elizabeth Derby West's house in Peabody, Massachusetts, three rooms of which are installed at the Museum of Fine Arts, Boston.

The design of the sofa's sweeping back and scrolled arms was probably derived from a plate of a simpler sofa in George Hepplewhite's *The Cabinet-Maker and Upholsterer's Guide* of 1788. But despite some similarities, the maker of this sofa improved on the Hepplewhite design by giving the crest a gentle swell to its back—repeating the lines of the seat. In addition, a delightful bowknot and cornucopias were carved at the crest to arrest the eye and create a visual climax to the piece. The legs were further enriched with carving on the front with grapes and grape leaves—motifs which Elizabeth Derby West also had cut on her English glassware and painted on her Chinese export porcelain.

Sofa
Salem, Massachusetts. 1800–1810.
Carved in the manner of Samuel McIntire.
Mahogany with ash. H: 38½" L: 75" D: 23½".
Museum of Fine Arts, Boston.

Both Hepplewhite and Sheraton illustrated the square sofa, but it was the innovation of the exposed turned front arms which captured the fancy of American furniture makers and made it one of the most popular sofa forms in Federal America. The general outline of this sofa is derived from Sheraton's *The Cabinet-Maker and Upholsterer's Drawing*

Book of 1793, but the particular combination of details is distinctively of Salem where snowflake punchwork background carvings are commonly attributed to the hand of Samuel McIntire.

Sofa and Matching Armchair
Philadelphia, Pennsylvania. 1790–1810.
Black ash with paint, gilt; 20th-century silk damask upholstery.
Sofa—L: 73½" H: 37" D: 26".
Armchair—H: 35¼" W: 24¼" D: 22½".
Philadelphia Museum of Art.

In 1921 the American Art Galleries of New York sold this large sofa and its twelve matching armchairs as French furniture whereupon they were sent to France. The Beauvais tapestry upholstery which originally covered this set was removed abroad, and the pieces were then felt to be American, not French. So the set was returned to this country (minus the tapestry covering) and was auctioned in New York City. Ever since its return to America, the set has puzzled collectors and students. It follows the lines of Louis XVI designs so closely, that if it is indeed the work of an unknown Philadelphia craftsman, it reflects an advanced taste for French decorative arts surpassed only by that of Jefferson, Monroe, Adams, Gouverneur Morris and James Swan. It is not surprising that the original ownership of this set is documented to Philadelphia where French connections were strong.

Provenance for the set rests on its American wood and on the history of its ownership. The set descended from Eliza and Edward Shippen Burd. Other pieces of Louis XVI-style furniture from Philadelphia with raised gilt decoration offset by gray-white backgrounds exist at Winterthur and in private collections, but none are more visually arresting.

A. J. WYATT, PHOTOGRAPHER

Cabriole Sofa
Baltimore, Maryland. 1790–1800.
Mahogany, oak, tulipwood.
H: 38¼" W: 77" D: 26".
Winterthur Museum.

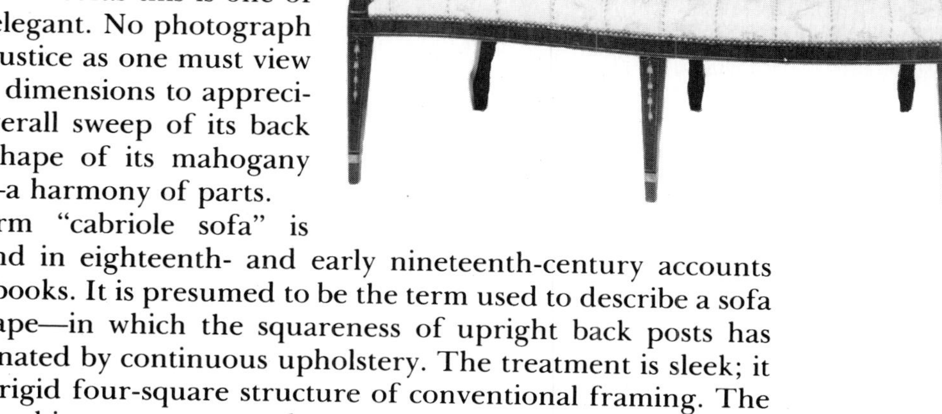

Of all Federal sofas this is one of the most elegant. No photograph can do it justice as one must view it in three dimensions to appreciate the overall sweep of its back and the shape of its mahogany crest rail—a harmony of parts.

The term "cabriole sofa" is often found in eighteenth- and early nineteenth-century accounts and price books. It is presumed to be the term used to describe a sofa of this shape—in which the squareness of upright back posts has been eliminated by continuous upholstery. The treatment is sleek; it defies the rigid four-square structure of conventional framing. The rear legs on this one are unusual. Instead of being finished with legs that splay backward, the feet are made to carry the support inward to conserve space. A somewhat awkward-looking result seems apparent in this photograph, but in reality the shape given to the rear feet is visually harmonious with the whole.

✶

The remarkable settee on the following page with its scroll back and sabre-shaped legs is part of a suite of furniture with matching side chairs and a double chair-back settee with scrolled arms. It is among the most sophisticated works of its time in American furniture. Its structural integration is complex and its contrast of shimmering inlaid tablets of birch veneer is brilliant. Reeding plays only a minor role in design at the upper ends of the arm and back supports. The major design effect is accomplished by its vigorous silhouette.

The sabre legs reflect a knowledge of ancient classical or Grecian furniture in a direct, simple way. Increasing emphasis on sharp silhouette and sabre legs were to become the hallmarks of the next generation in furniture design.

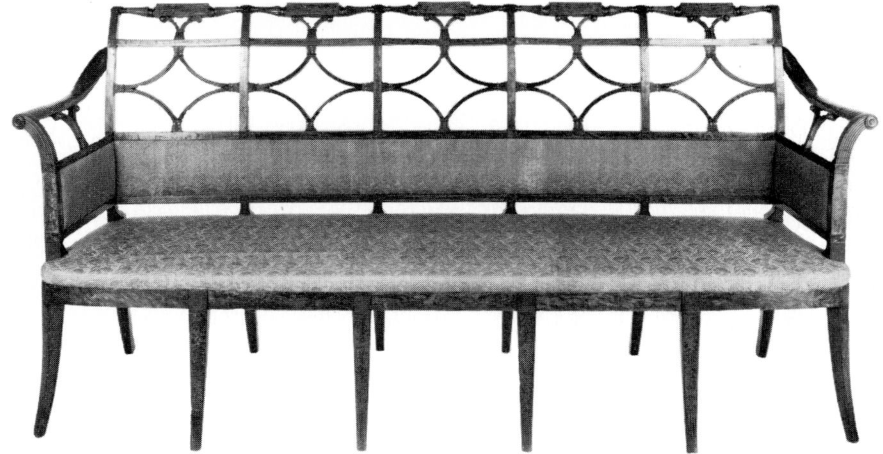

Five-Chair-Back Settee
Boston, Massachusetts. 1805–1810.
Attributed to the Shop of John and/or Thomas Seymour. Mahogany with figured birch inlay, soft maple and birch. H: 42 1/4" W: 81" D: 22 1/4".
Winterthur Museum.

Settee
New York or Albany, New York. 1800–1810.
Birch and cherry painted white with gold.
H: 36" W: 75" D: 19".
Winterthur Museum.

Not all Federal seating was upholstered. This settee was caned. It is part of a rare set of painted furniture (bedstead and chairs) owned by Governor and Mrs. Yates of Albany, New York. Although painted furniture has a low survival rate, it was extremely popular in the early nineteenth century. Attractive and fresh, such furniture was termed "fancy."

The Gothic arches of this chair-back settee have more to do with whimsy than the revival of a medieval style. With Gothic tracery freely interpreted, the designer of this settee played with classical forms in a way not strictly in accord with ancient art. For that reason this settee has an imaginative lightness and dainty quality that appeals strongly today.

Oil on Canvas
"Portrait of Frederick Augustus Muhlenberg" (1750–1801).
New York, New York. 1790.
By Joseph Wright (1756–1793). H: 47" W: 37".
Lent to the National Portrait Gallery by Mrs. George Brooke III.

Washington probably sat in the upholstered chair illustrated in this painting during his Presidential Inauguration ceremony at Federal Hall, New York City. The chair pictured here still exists in the Governor's Room of the New York City Hall, but has now been changed from its original upholstery, which was neatly boxed with gimp or tape borders outlining the handsome mahogany crest.

Below Mr. Muhlenberg's papers is a desk, part of the furniture which is believed to have been designed by Major Pierre Charles L'Enfant, c. 1789, when he remodeled and enlarged the City's old Hall to become Federal Hall, where Washington was inaugurated. In this furniture L'Enfant introduced reeded legs into American furniture and in a simple but effective way added other neoclassical elements such as oval paterae and circular brasses.

Armchair
Coastal Massachusetts. c. 1810.
Maple, painted white with gilt and painted ornamental detail; original rush seat. H: 33½" W: 20" D: 17¾".
Museum of Fine Arts, Boston.

Delicate turned parts are complemented with fine-line freehand painting characteristic of coastal New England artistry. Despite the elegance of pattern formed by interestingly varied parts, the structure of the chair is solid rather than flimsy. The joinery is well structured to brace at every point of stress. A low rate of survival exists for painted "fancy" furniture, as this type was popularly called. Because they were commonly used on porches, in gardens and for parties, most examples have lost much of their original paint. This example has been treated with unusual care, as its painted surface is in remarkably fine condition.

Side Chair (One of a Set of Four)
Boston, Massachusetts.
Probably prior to 1808.
Attributed to Samuel Gragg.
White oak and maple. H: 32" W: 16" D: 14¼".
Gift of Mrs. Ralph Lowell in Memory of Mrs. Arthur L. Williston, Museum of Fine Arts, Boston.

This chair, one of a set of four, is a forerunner of the "elastic chair." While the oak back and seat slats of this chair are bent (using heat, water and molds), the legs and stretchers are the ordinary turned and painted maple common to most fancy furniture of the late eighteenth and early nineteenth century. In addition to the delicacy of line and color which this chair presents, it offers potential insight into technological and artistic transitions.

Side Chair
Boston, Massachusetts. 1808–1815.
Made by Samuel Gragg (1772–1855).
Branded: "S. Gragg/Boston/Patent."
Ash and hickory, painted.
H: 34⅛" W: 18" D: 20".
Charles Hitchcock Tyler Residuary Fund.

Gragg progressed toward a more advanced application of the bentwood technique. The elastic chair was patented in 1808, the first piece of American furniture to use bentwood as a primary structural element.

The chair is a simple but sleek interpretation of the ancient Greek klismos chair, a design for which appeared in Thomas Hope's *Household Furniture and Interior Decoration* (London, 1807). Hope's klismos chair featured a continuous member curving from the top back rail to the front seat rail. Gragg's chair carries the bentwood concept even further using a single wooden member in a continuous sweep from the stile to the side seat rail and down through the front leg to the foot. The painted peacock feathers, also found on other New England pieces, were probably inspired by a wall decoration illustrated in Hope's *Household Furniture* in which large, radiating peacock feathers were central to the design.

Oval-Back Side Chair (One of a Set)
Eastern Massachusetts. 1790–1800. Made for Elias Hasket Derby.
Soft maple, white pine. H: 38⅜" W: 21½" D: 18½".
Museum of Fine Arts, Boston.

Painted furniture was not considered second-class work in the Federal Period; such furniture was ordered by the most fashionable and wealthy persons desiring elegance. Hepplewhite reported that painted chairs "or japanned work . . . gives . . . a rich and splendid appearance." Certainly this set of chairs are the best of their type in Federal America.

The history of these chairs is complex and riddled with problems. The chairs were once thought to relate to a bill which Joseph Anthony and Company of Philadelphia sent to Elias Hasket Derby—for "24 Oval Back, Stuff'd Seats covered with Hair Cloth, 2 Rows Brass Nails . . ."; however, it is not known that the bill actually described a set of upholstered Windsor chairs.

Several copies of these painted side chairs have been made in the twentieth century, so the reader is forewarned to be cautious in buying an expensive "discovery" of this sort without direct comparison to the ones at Winterthur, the Metropolitan Museum or the Museum of Fine Arts, Boston.

DAN FARBER, PHOTOGRAPHER

Card Table (One of a Pair)
Baltimore, Maryland. 1790–1810.
Mahogany, maple, rosewood and other exotic woods, on resinous pine.
H: 29⅝" D: 17¼" (closed) L: 35¼".
Museum of Fine Arts, Boston.

The brilliantly striped banding which surrounds the center panel of this card table is a signal of the inlay artistry of Maryland, probably the work of a Baltimore area craftsman. The central panel with its urn image in veneer is the most arresting feature. But the bellflower or husk pendants and unusual flower-and-vase inlays above the legs are not to be overlooked. They form a simple but elegant frame to the whole frontal view of the tables—which are among the most handsome of the period.

Card Table
Baltimore, Maryland. c. 1800.
Mahogany with white pine and varied exotic wood veneers. H: 28¾" Diameter: 35½".
Museum of Fine Arts, Boston.

As Baltimore grew between 1790 and 1810 to become a major seaport town rivaling the ports of Philadelphia and New York, cabinetmakers of great skill emigrated from England to supply the needs of its prospering townsfolk. Rich decoration with graceful inlay such as that seen in the detail shown here of a stylized leafy flower was the characteristic result.

Brilliant fire or striping in the veneered ovals of this table suggests that Baltimore was its place of manufacture. The use of a stylized tassel motif inlaid down the leg of the table is a feature which was also popular in the area.

Card Table (One of a Pair)
Salem, Massachusetts. 1790–1800.
Mahogany with white pine.
H: 30" D: (top closed) 24⅜" L: 49".
Museum of Fine Arts, Boston.

Made to match the Derby sofa (see page 217) and form a suite of furniture, these tables achieved the highest standards for quality of workmanship and design. The bas-relief carving was probably made by Samuel McIntire (1757–1811), who also worked on Elizabeth Derby West's house, Oak Hill. It is not surprising, therefore, that several design motifs are repeated both in the furniture and the architecture. The spade feet are faced with ebony veneer for a superb and simple accent at the floor.

Desk and Bookcase
Probably Hartford, Connecticut Area. 1790–1810.
Cherry with mahogany; inlaid woods and white pine.
H: 92½" W: 41¼" D: 20½".
Winterthur Museum.

Few Federal pieces excel this outstanding work from Connecticut. It is elaborately inlaid and has pediment tracery so finely sawn that it creates the effect of lace. But despite these ornamental attempts to be fashionable, the form of the desk is rather old-fashioned. It is basically a Chippendale piece overlaid with a profusion of delightfully playful ornaments. The cabinetmaker has elevated an otherwise pleasant, but not unusual, form to a visually exciting experience with inlay, carving and fretwork. Assertive chevron-like stringing around the borders of drawers and doors and inverted icicle-like inlay on the sides stimulate the eye to explore the main pictorial inlay. Vine and floral designs are secondary to the boldly figured eagles on the doors.

Carving similar to that of the urn within the pediment is on a set of chairs made in 1796 for the Hartford State House by Kneeland and Adams. Other pieces with similar inlay from the Hartford area suggest that this example represents a keynote of style for that region.

Chest of Drawers
Hartford, Connecticut Area. c. 1800.
Cherry with pine and chestnut; brasses not original, but of the period.
H: 36⅜" L: (top) 45" D: 22½".
Collection of Mrs. Charles L. Bybee.

RICHARD CHEEK, PHOTOGRAPHER

Chests with brilliant veneer, strongly patterned inlay and sleek lines seem to have been made in the area of Hartford, Connecticut. Although the form of this piece recalls the basic shape of earlier Chippendale case furniture, the chest was made in the Federal Period. The attention given to matching veneer and startling inlay are signs of its later date. The sweep of its boldly curved front is the chest's most distinguished feature. So dramatic is the shape that the drawer fronts bow four inches from peak to valley. Vertical striping in the veneer helps balance the horizontal thrust of the drawer outline. While the visual effect is striking, the physical tensions produced by the different rates of shrinkage of the support wood and veneer over the years have caused difficulties in keeping the veneer from splitting.

Desk
Philadelphia, Pennsylvania. 1800–1810.
Mahogany; satinwood inlay. H: 53" W: 51" D: 23".
Philadelphia Museum of Art.

This piece is a disturbing work on first encounter. It seems too modern for its time. But severely ordered simplicity is seen on other Philadelphia pieces of the period; perhaps it may represent a regional preference for rational form not realized elsewhere in Federal America.

Made for the wife of Dr. Benjamin Rush (1745–1813), signer of the Declaration of Independence and Surgeon General of the Army, this fall-front desk is highly geometric. The precise organization and symmetry of the piece is emphasized by the hairline inlay around its borders. The effect is taut and firm. With dark mahogany, square-faced on the outside, it opens to a surprise of curved satinwood within.

Cylinder-Fall Desk and Bookcase
Probably Maryland. 1800–1810.
Mahogany, satinwood, zebrawood,
tulipwood, hard pine and oak.
H: 102″ W: 42½″ D: 23″.
Metropolitan Museum, New York.

This beautifully proportioned example stands among the finest of all Federal desks. Its subtle combination of curved and straight lines and pattern of brightly banded veneers attest to the quality and provenance of the piece. Brilliantly figured pictorial and oval veneers and flamelike cross-banded borders are most often found on furniture made in or near Baltimore. The eagle, which is original to the piece, is more spirited than most; the Gothic-style tracery is delightfully spare and ingeniously divided. On the front of the cylinder-fall the eagle motif of the crest is repeated in inlay.

DAN FARBER, PHOTOGRAPHER

Cylinder Bookcase

Thomas Sheraton's *The Cabinet Dictionary* provided a Maryland cabinetmaker or his client with an image that inspired an extraordinary counterpart. The side view shown in a plate from the book not only reveals the interior circular layout of the cylinder, but it also illustrates the brass arc hinging mechanism for the writing leaf. The use of this mechanism allowed the cabinetmaker to make the desk portion slide forward of the case. It is this combination of parts that makes the bookcase a true "secretary."

Lady's Cabinet and Writing Table
Baltimore, Maryland. 1795–1810.
Mahogany, satinwood, red cedar.
H: 62⅛" W: 30⅞" D: 22¼".
Winterthur Museum.

At the moment of Baltimore's Federal boom period, this special form of writing furniture became popular in the area. It is now one of three survivors based on Plate 50 of Sheraton's *Drawing Book* (1793), but the basic form was embellished with ornament favored in Baltimore. The pronounced use of satinwood-banding inlay as seen around the circular mirror is a feature common to Baltimore furniture. The *églomisé* reverse and gilded glass paintings handled in the manner shown here are characteristic of the best and most expensive of Baltimore furniture.

Cylinder Bookcase
Baltimore, Maryland. 1811.
Pencil Inscription: "M. Oliver Married the 5 October 1811, Baltimore."
Mahogany, satinwood, maple veneers; cedar and tulip poplar.
H: 91" W: 72" D: 19½".
Metropolitan Museum, New York, Gift of Mrs. Russell Sage and other donors.

Secretary and Bookcase
Salem, Massachusetts. c. 1800.
Perhaps by Mark Pitman (1779–1829).
Mahogany veneer on white pine.
H: 69" W: 37¾" D: 19".
Museum of Fine Arts, Boston.

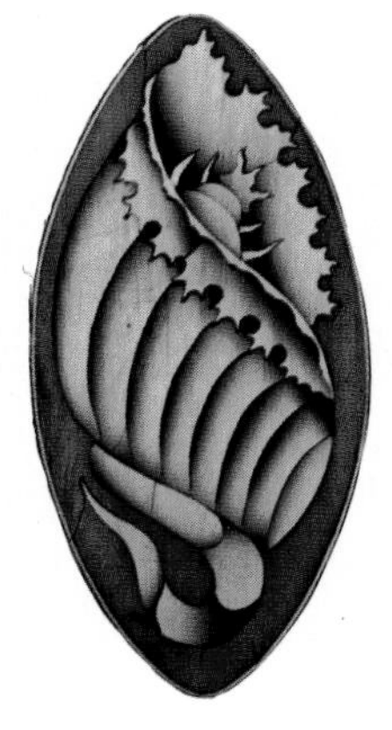

Although small and plain, this secretary is an appealing piece. Its small scale suggests that it was probably a lady's desk. It is a typical specimen of Salem workmanship and could have been made by any one of several early nineteenth-century Salem craftsmen. Although it owes its general form to the English designer George Hepplewhite, in the American antique furniture trade such a piece is known as a "Salem desk." Its pleated silk curtains are new but are correct for pieces of the Federal Period.

During restoration of the desk, a chalk inscription was found on the bottom of the upper section ("Derby/$150") which connects the desk with the wealthiest family in Salem. Another inscription on the bottom of a drawer confirms this provenance: "Vaskell/Salem, Mass."

The only ornamental detail of consequence is an inlaid panel in the pediment showing a beetle crawling out of a shell. This motif occurs on several examples of Massachusetts furniture—on looking glasses, card tables, and other forms as well. It might be assumed that an inlay specialist in the region was producing this inlay for sale to cabinetmakers from Boston to Newburyport.

In the final analysis, the appeal of this piece lies in its proportions, delicacy of scale, and simplicity of design. Handsomely matched mahogany veneer on the front of the drawers adds much visual pleasure and a rich background for the brasses. The brasses are not original but are of the Federal Period and are appropriate.

Pedimented Tambour Desk
Boston, Massachusetts. 1790–1810.
Attributed to Thomas Seymour (1771–1848). Mahogany, mahogany veneer, satinwood, white pine.
H: 65½" W: 36" D: 18¼".
Private Collection.

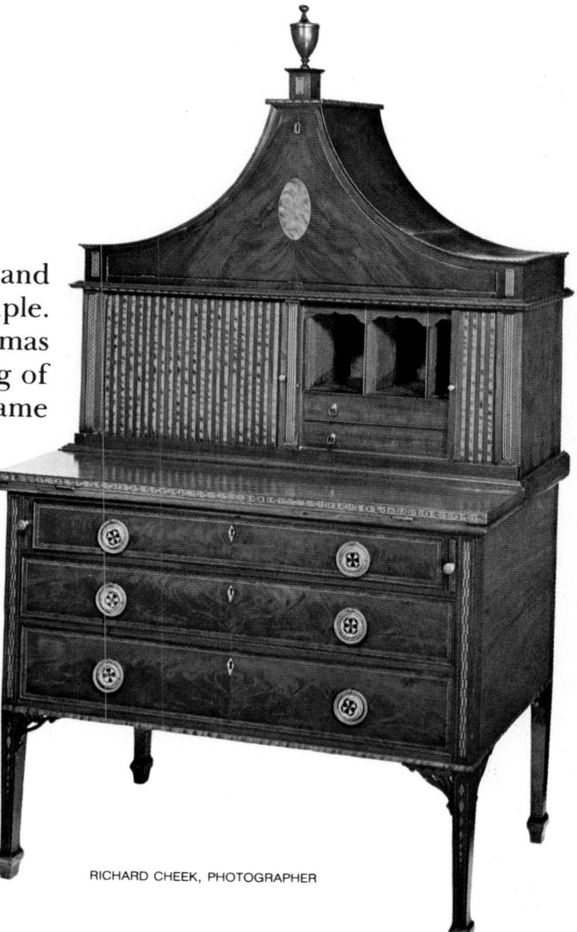

RICHARD CHEEK, PHOTOGRAPHER

Only a handful of tambour desks in the Seymour manner exist and of them only three have pedimented tops. This is the finest example. It was owned by Eliza and Benjamin Proctor. Proctor and Thomas Seymour were partners in the purchase of land from Diana Ring of Boston in 1799, so it seems reasonable to assume that this work came from Seymour's shop.

Extremely fine inlay, patterned to make the eye see movement, characterizes the work of the Seymour school. Contrasting narrow stringing of light and dark lines and minute, tightly constructed, complex bands of inlay along the horizontal edges of the front of the desk are made with a skill and precision not known elsewhere in American furniture of the Federal Period. Letter compartments within the desk are characteristically painted a robin's-egg blue, although this is not necessarily a sign of Seymour's work. A related tambour desk at Winterthur bears the label: "John Seymour & Son, Cabinet Makers, Creek Square." Many of its features are so similar to this one that attribution of this to the Seymour cabinet shop is without question.

This desk, or writing table as it was probably called, represents the summit of skill and quality of workmanship achieved in Federal New England.

Secretary-Bookcase
Philadelphia, Pennsylvania. 1805–1810.
Made by John Davey
and John Davey, Jr. (active 1797–1822).
Mahogany, mahogany veneers, satinwood and mirror glass.
H: 94 11/16" W: 45" D: 22 3/8".
The Metropolitan Museum of Art, New York.

The inlaid ovals and severe lines of this case piece arrest the eye with their geometric shapes. The bookcase has a fall-front drawer that pulls out—the "secretary drawer" first illustrated in George Hepplewhite's 1788 *Guide.* The best architecture in the United States in the early nineteenth century emphasized abstract forms and spaces in much the same way the cubic volume and inlay work are expressed in this splendid piece. The names of cabinetmakers John Davey and John Davey, Jr., are signed in pencil in ten different places on the secretary-bookcase—on the backs of drawers, doors and elsewhere. This may reflect their special pride in the work or may mean that they considered the secretary to be a good example—perhaps a "sample" piece. The boldness with which the veneer is figured and the bright "fire" of some of the banding suggests that the Daveys were familiar with furniture made in Maryland, where brilliant inlay was especially favored.

Specialized Furniture Forms

As the use of different rooms in the home became more specialized in the late eighteenth and early nineteenth centuries, a class of furniture forms developed that had been uncommon or unknown in most houses a generation before. Cellarettes, or wine coolers, for example, were used as special complements for rooms set aside for dining or entertaining guests.

Lined with sheet lead, banded with brass and with lion-mask ring pulls, the cooler or cistern on the left below was to be filled with ice and bottles of wine and placed beside an elegant table. It once belonged to the Derby family of Salem, Massachusetts. Turned circular and tapered legs are reeded along their length and carved at the top, above which are ring turnings.

Wine Cooler or Cellarette
Boston, Massachusetts. 1805–1810.
Mahogany and birch veneer on pine.
H: 22¾" W: 19¼" D: 26".
Museum of Fine Arts, Boston.

Wine Cooler or Cellarette
Southern. c. 1790.
Walnut and maple with brass, copper, and mahogany veneer.
H: 26⅞" W: 26½" D: 21½".
Winterthur Museum.

Wine coolers or cisterns of this sort are normally lined with copper or lead to hold ice and ice water for chilling the bottles. The one on the above right, fitted with a lock, seems also to have been planned for wine storage. The form evokes a familiar image of hospitality and festive good taste at the tableside.

Wine Cooler or Cellarette
Probably Charleston, South Carolina. 1790–1805. Mahogany, bald cypress, pine, tulipwood. H: 40⅜" W: 19⅞" D: 15⅞".
Winterthur Museum.

The presence of bald cypress as a secondary wood in the slide or mixing board together with the embellishment of three unconventional inlaid figured ovals suggests the unidentified hand of an accomplished Southern craftsman from a major center such as Charleston. But such attribution is guesswork. Systematic fieldwork is now being conducted in Charleston which will reveal a more complete history of cabinetmaking in that region.

Worktable
Philadelphia, Pennsylvania. 1805–1810.
Satinwood and mahogany, rosewood, ebony, white pine, tulip.
H: 28⅝" W: 26" D: 13¼".
Winterthur Museum.

This is the most splendid worktable for its place and time known in American furniture. The ornamental detail is superb; the overall effect is rich and powerful. Carving and reeding are subordinated and reserved within the total compositional design. By comparison with the carved detail of the Haines furniture made for Stephen Girard in 1807 (see page 242) it is possible to place this table precisely in a context of workmanship of the highest order. The inlay stringing which rings the lower edge of the kidney-shaped worktable is of a most unusual pattern—almost Egyptian in character.

Sideboard
Baltimore, Maryland. c. 1800.
Mahogany with white pine, maple, satinwood, oak, poplar and ebony veneers.
H: 65½" L: 89" D: 31".
The Metropolitan Museum of Art, New York.

The effect of this sideboard is visual bombast. It was made for David Van Ness who had a house in Dutchess County, New York. Sheffield-plate (silvered) mounts together with brilliant satinwood inlay attract the eye with a splendor of mixed materials. Added to this is ebony veneer and reverse painted-glass panels for an extravagant effect. Within the center arch are griffins holding swags, and a figure of the goddess Minerva on a pedestal. The design for this pictorial inlay comes from Sheraton's *Drawing Book,* the plate of which is identified as an "Ornament for Frieze or Tablet." The spandrels above the arch are magnificently shaded leaf forms with oak branches and acorns. On either side of the top drawers are small inset panels varied in motifs, and therefore not symmetrically balanced.

The entire effect is extraordinary. Certain details relate the piece to Baltimore workmanship; the boldly contrasting geometry of the panels and the brightly striped inlaid bands which border the edges of the piece are unlike inlay found elsewhere along the Eastern coast. Although reverse painting with a white background has been found on Salem and Boston furniture, the colored-glass panels illustrated here are characteristically from Baltimore. Craftsmen from no other region treated pictorial and floral inlays with the same degree of shading and contrasting colored backgrounds.

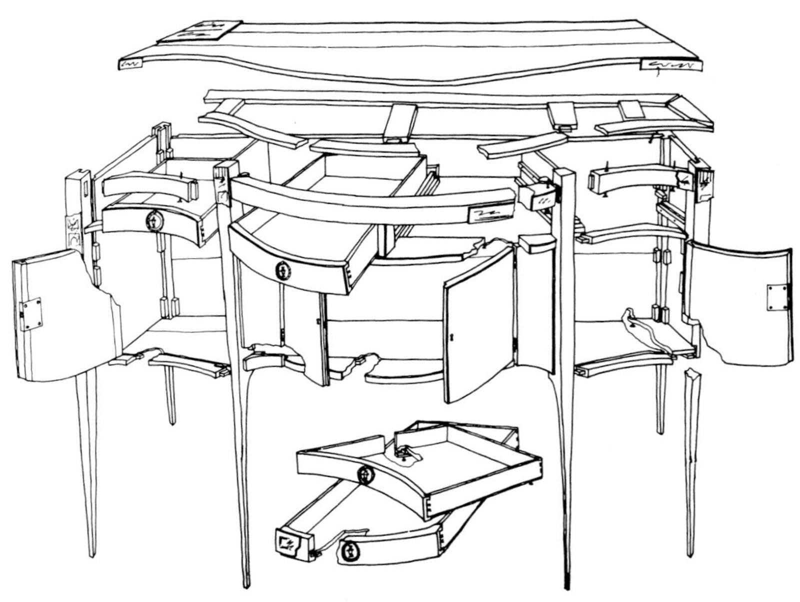

DRAWING BY ALICE WEBBER

Disarticulated Sideboard
New York. 1790–1810.
Museum of Fine Arts, Boston.

Simplicity of outline suggests that Federal furniture is constructed simply. But as this drawing shows, nothing is further from the truth. Joinery and fittings of Federal furniture are precise and complex. The sideboard form was the most important innovation in American furniture of the Federal Period, its great size and sweeping shape made possible by refinements in sawing technology. Extensive development and use of joined glued sandwiches of many different types of wood permitted a freedom of geometry, form and ornament not previously possible.

Major technological advances in the period affected all decorative arts. The use of machines to manufacture precision-cut small square nails, for example, freed cabinetmakers from more crudely fashioned hand-wrought nails from the blacksmith's forge. Thin layering of decorative and exotic woods with figure banding upon a supporting soft pine or tulipwood substructure became the common cabinetmaking practice of urban Federal craftsmen.

This approach to design was parallel to the other arts. For example, in the field of silversmithing the application of silver plate to a copper base (Sheffield) and the use of rolled sheets of such a metallic sandwich, cut with brilliant, tightly organized bands of ornament, came into popular use in America at about the same moment as the similarly veneered Federal furniture.

Sideboard
Boston, Massachusetts. c. 1800.
Mahogany veneer on pine, curly maple, cherry, rosewood and satinwood.
H: 43⅛" L: 65⅞" D: 33¾".
Museum of Fine Arts, Boston.

Trim and square with brilliant patterns of stripes on the three tambour doors, superbly detailed carving and flame-patterned inlay distinguish this piece as made in Boston, probably by the Seymour firm, early in the nineteenth century. It descended in the Lowell, Lyman and Cabot families.

The carving at the four corners below the top and on the legs is sharp and richly done in shallow relief, characteristic of the Boston manner. The carving was probably not done by Seymour; it was most likely the work of a specialist.

Sideboard
New York, New York. 1793–1794.
Made and labeled by William Mills and Simeon Deming.
Mahogany, pine, satinwood.
H: 48¾" W: 74¾" D: 32¼".
Private Collection.

COURTESY OF ISRAEL SACK, INC.

This sideboard was made for Oliver Wolcott, first governor of the State of Connecticut and a signer of the Declaration of Independence. It bears the label of "Mills & Deming." This is one of the most dazzling sideboards of the Federal Period. Its boldly figured mahogany veneer is punctuated by contrasting patterns of light-colored woods in the shapes of paterae, fans, swags and pendant husks. Both large-scale and small intricate inlay ornaments this work. The legs are smartly canted to follow the profile of the cabinet in a manner characteristic of the best of New York work.

This sideboard generally follows the form published in George Hepplewhite's *Guide* published in London in 1788, in which he explained that sideboards, which were then a relatively new form of furniture, were so well received and useful that a dining room was considered incomplete without one.

Huntboard
Maryland. c. 1790.
Mahogany and mahogany veneer.
H: 31⅛" W: 68½" D: 23¾".
The Baltimore Museum of Art.

Tall tables of shallow depth and Southern origin are customarily called "huntboards." In basic form the huntboard was simply a board or frame from which a large group could be served during the festivities after the hunt. The hall or even the porch was the normal place for this activity which was so much a part of Southern tradition. The huntboard was, therefore, a serving table, and functioned in much the same way as a sideboard—but without the need for storage drawers or cabinets. In the Northern states, where serving tables for mixing drinks were made, the huntboard was not a necessary piece of household furniture. Huntboards were positioned just as this one, against the wall.

Elegant with a subtle curve to its top and remarkably contemporary in its understated simplicity, this huntboard appeals through sheer mastery of spanning space with accent notes of ornament at just a few telling spots. Six ovals inlaid with eagles decorate the corners of the table, bellflowers and fine line inlay descend the legs—all integrated at the lower border of the table frame with a spare chevron inlay. The chevron inlay is strung through the center with a minute hairline inlay—a characteristic of Maryland furniture.

Late Neoclassicism 1800–1820

Fluting versus Reeding

The shift from the use of fluting to reeding for ornament marks a style change that took place in America at the start of the nineteenth century. Eighteenth-century cabinetmakers used fluting or concave multiple grooves or moldings to ornament posts, legs, columns and rails of furniture. By contrast, the nineteenth-century cabinetmaker favored the reverse: convex reeding, to ornament the same members of furniture.

By 1810 emphasis was on convex rather than on concave columnar forms. The ornament of circular legs in American furniture was almost exclusively reeded or rope-turned. Earlier use of precisely shaped reeding on the furniture made for Louis XVI and the French Court had a profound impact on both British and American designs. Thomas Sheraton had popularized the manner in the 1790s with his London designs. Duncan Phyfe is the best-known practitioner of this phase of neoclassicism—the English Regency style.

In America a few persons of advanced taste owned reeded furniture in the classical manner by the 1790s. But most American cabinetmakers adopted this significant shift in ornament a decade later. By 1810 the reeded manner was the common vocabulary of nearly every fashionable major cabinetmaker, whether in Boston, New York, Philadelphia or elsewhere. Shapes of legs on furniture from this period vary from straight or tapered or square reeded examples to turned round or even sabre-shaped legs. But the signal decorative element from the antique past is the fine multiple molded reeds that recall the idea of ancient Roman fasces—the bundle of rods surrounding an axe which was traditionally borne in front of the Roman magistrates as an emblem of authority.

The following examples are selected to illustrate parallels of style among the master craftsmen working in the manner of Nehemiah Adams or William Hook of Salem, Thomas Seymour of Boston, Duncan Phyfe or Charles-Honoré Lannuier of New York and Ephraim Haines of Philadelphia.

Details: Carved and Reeded Legs
Salem, Massachusetts. c. 1800.
Mahogany on pine.
Museum of Fine Arts, Boston.

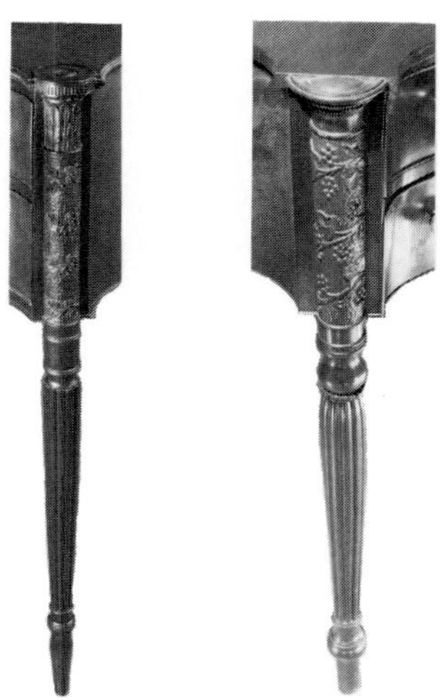

Tapered reeding on turned legs of furniture became fashionable in America around 1800 and dominated the decorative scheme of ornament within a decade. These legs represent two basic types common to New England furniture—straight tapering with a slight swell (or "entasis" as it is technically called) and a more pronounced swell on the tapered leg. The basic scheme of turning with ball, rings, vase or baluster with a simple tapered foot is a common vocabulary of classical form that spans centuries of earlier time and finds expression even in more crudely turned furniture made throughout the mid-nineteenth century.

Armchair
New York, New York.
1810–1820. Mahogany.
H: 32¼″ W: 17¾″ D: 20¾″.
Museum of Fine Arts, Boston.

Side Chair
New York, New York.
1805–1815. Mahogany, maple, ash.
H: 33″ W: 19″ D: 16½″.
Museum of Fine Arts, Boston.

In New York City, the appeal of finely reeded furniture affected every cabinet shop of note. Most prominent of these was the establishment of Duncan Phyfe. Phyfe was born in Scotland and came to this country with his parents in 1783–1784. Within a decade he established his own shop and was still in business in 1840 when the firm was changed to D. Phyfe and Son. His standards of quality were high; they must have affected other furniture shops that were in competition. Although Phyfe's name is almost synonymous with the reeded style, furniture by Michael Allison (1800–1845), George Woodruff (working 1808–1816), and many others is hard, if not impossible, to distinguish from the work of Phyfe. They all worked in the reeded manner and probably the same journeymen moved among different shops, carrying the so-called "Phyfe style" in a wide network throughout New York City and elsewhere.

COURTESY OF ISRAEL SACK, INC.

Side Chair and Settee
Philadelphia, Pennsylvania. 1800–1810.
Mahogany with black ash.
Side chair—H: 36″ W: 18¼″ D: 17″.
Private Collection.
Settee—H: 36½″ W: 75″ D: 23½″.
White House Collection.

These pieces represent the most excellent order of workmanship and design of their time and place.

The gently swelled shape at the tops of the legs and the base of the back supports is carved with leafage in a manner characteristic of Philadelphia workmanship. The carving is low in relief and smooth or gentle in its edges. Unlike New York carving of the same period which is crisp, or Boston carving which is quite sharp, this carving is gentle and undulating. Also noteworthy is the unusual inlay detail of vase and flower in the center of the back splat. Shadow detail in the inlay is suggested by the technique of burning the edges of parts of the veneer in hot sand. The oval shape to the back splat is a neoclassical convention which cabinetmakers sometimes filled with upholstery rather than carving.

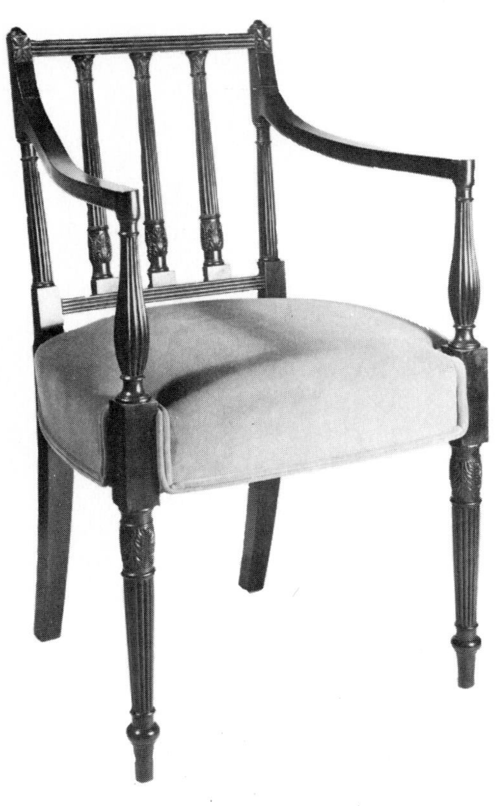

Armchair and Settee (From a Set of Ten)
Philadelphia, Pennsylvania. 1807. Ephraim Haines (1755–1837).
Ebony, ash, white pine.
Armchair—H: 35¼" W: 20⅜" D: 18".
Setee—H: 36" W: 72" D: 25½".
Courtesy, Girard College, Philadelphia, Pennsylvania,
Stephen Girard Collection.

Ephraim Haines was a Quaker who apprenticed in Philadelphia to the cabinetmaker Daniel Trotter in 1791. As was the good fortune of some apprentices, Haines married his master's daughter and inherited the business after the death of Trotter in 1800.

Along with the shop, Haines inherited Trotter's customers; one of the most important was the successful Quaker merchant Stephen Girard. Girard supplied the lumber for this ebony parlor furniture, which was part of a total set of nineteen pieces. The specialized craftsmen who made these works were supervised by Haines, who did not actually make the pieces himself. Like Phyfe and Seymour, Haines was cabinetmaker turned entrepreneur—a manager of business affairs and master of an extensive establishment. After his shop made this parlor set, Haines seems to have specialized successfully in selling lumber—rare and valuable exotic woods which were in demand by cabinetmakers throughout the city.

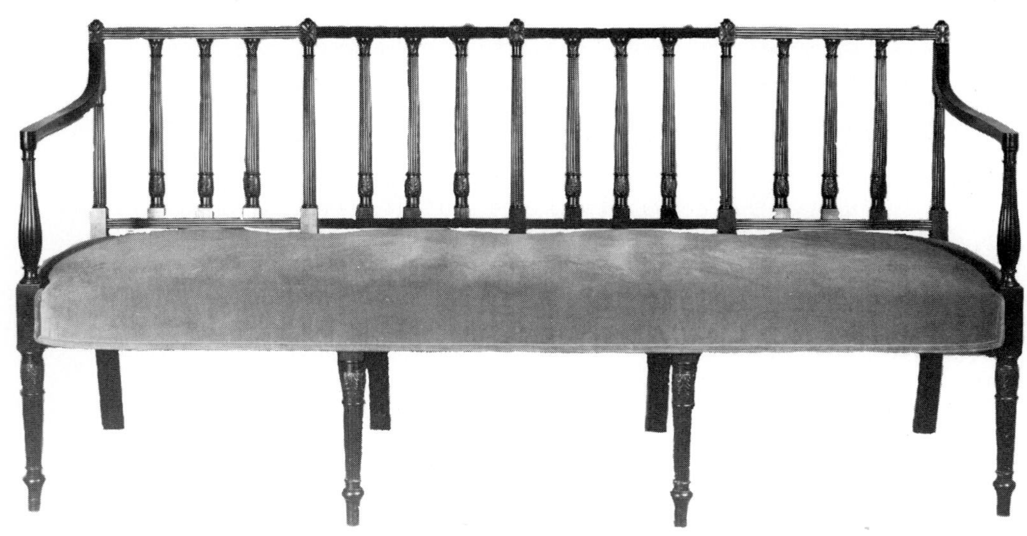

COURTESY OF BERNARD & S. DEAN LEVY, INC.

Side Chair and Armchair (Two of a Set of Twelve)
Boston, Massachusetts. c. 1810.
Mahogany and maple.
Side chair—H: 33″ W: 19¼″ D: 17″.
Armchair—H: 33″ W: 20″ D: 18¼″.
Private Collection.

The original red-leather covering on these chairs is a rare survival that documents the brilliant color and firm, boxlike upholstery of neoclassical furniture. The precise, sharp carving of leafage is smartly executed. The chair backs are supported with three columns which repeat the same crisp reeding of the tapered legs.

It is likely that this furniture came from the Seymour establishment of Boston. In many respects these chairs are comparable to the justly famous ebony furniture made by Ephraim Haines.

While the general form of both Philadelphia and Boston chairs is the same, the handling of carving is distinctly different. The turnings on the feet also differ. The Boston chairs are more advanced stylistically as they have a heavier, more academically correct classical crest or back rail. This suggests that they were probably made sometime shortly after 1810.

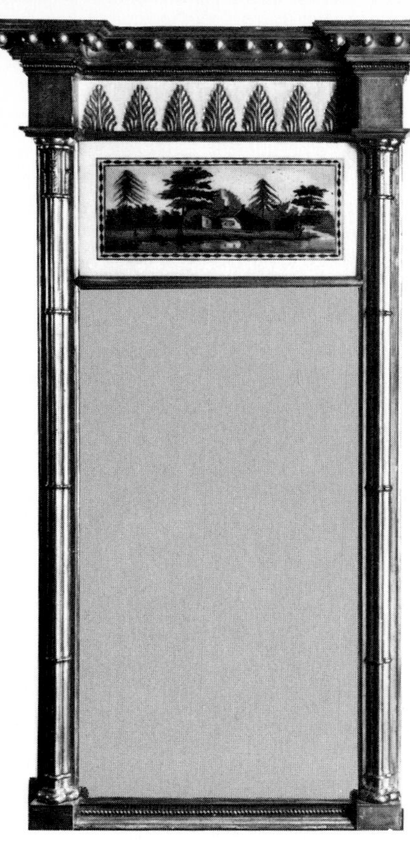

Looking Glass (One of a Pair)
Roxbury, Massachusetts. 1800–1810.
Labeled by John Doggett (1780–1857).
Carved pine; gilt and painted. H: 57" W: 25".
Collection of Mrs. Charles L. Bybee.

Reeding was not confined to chairs, sofas and table legs alone. Although of somewhat different form, the columns of this looking glass consist of a bundle of rods which are basic to the classical idea behind the ornamental device.

The paper label on the back of this looking glass was engraved by painter John Ritto Penniman for John Doggett, who kept a record in account books which are now preserved in the library of the Winterthur Museum. Doggett carried on an extensive import trade in mirror glass, sold hardware goods, made and sold gilt picture frames and lightning rods, and engaged a number of craftsmen to fashion furniture and parts of furniture for sale. It is likely that he hired a decorative artist such as John Ritto Penniman to paint the landscape on the reverse of the glass tablet above the mirror.

RICHARD CHEEK, PHOTOGRAPHER

Cheval Glass
New York. c. 1815.
Mahogany. H: 75" W: 44⅞" D: 27¾".
The Metropolitan Museum of Art, New York.

Both reeding and fluting are used on the pillar posts of this frame-stand and large tilting looking glass. The term "horse" or "cheval" was used by Sheraton in his *Cabinet Dictionary* to describe "a kind of tall dressing-glass suspended by two pillars and claws, and may, when hung by two center screws, be turned back or forward to suit the person who dresses at them." Another term used in the nineteenth century for this form was a "screen dressing glass."

The workmanship of this piece is richly and skillfully articulated. It relates to the documented pieces by both Phyfe and Lannuier. Lannuier's label shows a similar cheval glass with pillars, legs, feet and related crest. Simpler dressing glasses on tilting frames were made in America before this one, but this example developed the basic concept most fully with enrichments of carving, addition of gilt-brass candle arms and movable side trays or "swingers" used to hold various articles necessary for dressing.

Girandole Looking Glass
Boston–Roxbury,
Massachusetts. c. 1810–1825.
Attributed to John Doggett
(1780–1857).
White pine with gold leaf over gesso.
Frame liner ebonized; cut-class pendants, brass bobeches and candle sockets.
Diameter of frame: 29½″.
Museum of Fine Arts, Boston.

Circular looking glasses with convex mirrors were popular in America from about 1805 through the 1850s. They provided a fish-eye reflection of room interiors while distorting the viewer's image. The novelty of such mirrors did not originate in the nineteenth century. As an earlier

example, in the sixteenth century the famous painting of Arnolfini and his wife by Jan van Eyck showed a bull's-eye glass in the background. It is probably not a coincidence that artists of both periods were fascinated with the study of optical illusion and anamorphic or distorted images. An engraved label the Roxbury craftsman John Doggett pasted on the back of other looking glasses shows a girandole glass with many features that correspond to this one. They both include the eagle with spread wings holding festoons of gilt balls in his beak. Dolphins intertwine at the base of Doggett's label. On this example they balance on either side of the crest. Surrounding the mirror glass is a ring of gilt spheres, which also appears on Doggett's label. Doggett sold such balls to other craftsmen; they were a popular ornamental feature of Federal Period looking glasses, frames and cornices.

Looking Glass
Boston–Roxbury, Massachusetts. 1800–1814.
Probably by John Doggett (1780–1857).
White pine with gold leaf over gesso. H: 84".
Museum of Fine Arts, Boston.

This is probably the oval looking glass listed in the 1814 inventory of the estate of Elizabeth Derby of Salem. It came to the Museum of Fine Arts from a Derby descendant, Martha C. Codman Karolik. Carving of the highest order ornaments this work. It probably does not represent Doggett's own carving skills, but rather the work of a specialist hired for the commission. While seeming to be a perfectly balanced composition, close inspection reveals otherwise. A subtle play of shapes is shown in the turn of the eagle's head, asymmetry of leafage and grapes and a subtle intertwining of billing doves at the base. These features give the frame an unusual quality of movement and vitality.

Girandole Clock
Concord, Massachusetts. c. 1816.
Made by Lemuel Curtis (1790–1857). H: 46″ W: 15″ D: 5″.
Museum of Fine Arts, Boston.

Before Lemuel Curtis moved to Burlington, Vermont, in 1821 he produced in Concord, Massachusetts, a clock of this type which today is rare and eminently collectible. The name "girandole" derives from circular convex mirrors popular in the Federal and Empire periods. The shape of the mirrors was carried through in the convex face of this clock and the convex glass face of the pendulum chamber. The interior has splendidly machined brass gears and other parts for an eight-day movement like that of a banjo clock. The true glory of the piece is its vigorously ornamented exterior, so thoroughly in keeping with the spirit of romantic classicism and Empire taste. Carved gold-leaf foliate ornament at the base offers a visually convincing support bracket for the pendulum chamber, which has a ring of gold-leaf balls around a reverse-painted convex glass. Aurora, the Dawn, is pictured with her two-horse carriage symbolizing fleeting time. An enriched gilt-and-polychrome glass panel connects the base with the upper circle that encloses the clock face. Smaller balls surround this face over which hovers a carved and gilt eagle.

The brass scrolls on both sides of the clock recall the so-called banjo clock for which Simon Willard was so famous. Curtis had been an apprentice to Aaron Willard.

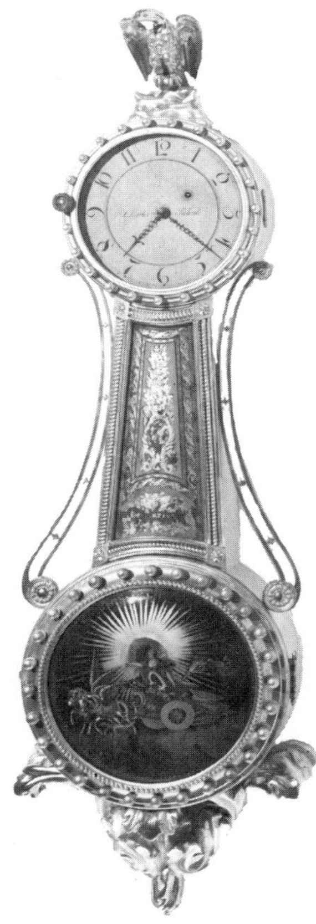

DAN FARBER, PHOTOGRAPHER

Shelf Clock
Boston, Massachusetts. 1817. Aaron Willard (1757–1844).
Mahogany and white pine; brass feet and painted glass.
H: 36″ W: 13½″ D: 5⅞″.
Museum of Fine Arts, Boston.

This is among the finest of the popular shelf clocks produced in quantity in nineteenth-century New England. The cabinetwork on the piece is simple yet beautifully done, reserving almost all ornament to the painted glass panels.

The maker, Aaron Willard, was the youngest of four clockmaking brothers. It is possible that he or his son Aaron, Jr., did the reverse painting on the glass of this clock, yet it also seems likely that John Ritto Penniman, an ornamentalist who specialized in such painted work on furniture, could have been involved. Most delightful is the image of the seated lady with infant on a yellow klismos-type classical chair. The borders of the glass are black and gold and "Aaron Willard/Boston" is highlighted in scarlet.

COURTESY OF ISRAEL SACK, INC.

Worktable
Boston, Massachusetts. c. 1795–1805.
Satinwood with rosewood and mahogany;
burled veneer top; inlaid lunette. H: 29¼" W: 21¼" D: 17".

In the Federal Period ladies' worktables became objects of visual pleasure and an expression of women's leisure and refined needleworking skills. This elegant table has the additional feature of an adjustable writing board covered with green baize. Finished on all four sides and brilliantly ornamented with figured veneer and brass mounts, the table was meant to attract notice and to be seen freestanding prominently in an important room. Its design is unmistakably derived from current English fashion handled in the manner of Thomas Seymour or of the Seymour school. It is the epitome of great craftsmanship—with a variety of contrasting ornament and lavish use of rich materials that enhance rather than interfere with its functional aspects. The drawer on the right side pulls out as a frame. Normally such a frame was fitted with a loose silk bag to hold needlework or sewing materials. This view shows the frame prior to restoration of the bag.

RICHARD CHEEK, PHOTOGRAPHER

Gaming Table
Boston, Massachusetts. 1790–1810.
Mahogany with birch veneers. H: 30" W: 20" D: 30".
Private Collection.

In Federal Boston the diversions of elegant living included theater, music and games. Charles Bulfinch was building splendid homes and public edifices and the cabinetmakers John and Thomas Seymour were fulfilling the newest desires of the elite with magnificent works like this movable gaming table. It is an exceedingly fine object, with precisely reeded and tapered legs and elegant inlay.

English cabinetmaker Thomas Sheraton identified such a table in his *Cabinet Dictionary* as an "Occasional." Like Plate 59 of his *Dictionary,* this table also has a reversible top which slides out and turns over to reveal a chessboard on top or a backgammon board inside the gaming well. Drawers on either end of the table swing out to hold playing pieces. While Sheraton advised in his *Dictionary* that all designs were capable of being finished exactly as illustrated, in this instance the Boston cabinetmakers developed an original design of extraordinary beauty.

DAN FARBER, PHOTOGRAPHER

Pier Table (One of a Pair)
Boston Area. c. 1810.
Mahogany, cherry, pine and mixed inlays.
H: 35¼" W: 55¾" D: 23¾".
Museum of Fine Arts, Boston.

Descending in the family of Elizabeth Derby West, this table and its mate are recent discoveries. Before 1972, when the tables were given to the Museum of Fine Arts, this form had not been known to have been made in Federal America. This pier table matches almost line for line a plate in Thomas Sheraton's *The Cabinet Dictionary*. The main differences are in details. The carved ornament of the table was adapted by its maker to match features carried out in the interior architecture and other pieces of furniture in Mrs. West's home.

Pier Table from
***Thomas Sheraton's* The Cabinet Dictionary**

Thomas Sheraton's Dictionary *identified this Plate, number 63, as a Pier Table, made to fit between the architraves of the windows, and to be raised above the surbase. While adaptations have taken place in the pier table made in Boston, enough similarities with the English prototype exist to identify this plate as the design source. Sheraton's suggestion that the tables be used between windows was probably followed by Elizabeth Derby West, to whom the pair of Boston tables once belonged.*

Sideboard
Salem, Massachusetts. 1808–1809.
Made by William Hook.
Mahogany, figured birch and rosewood veneers on pine. H: 42¾" W: 48" D: 23⅞".
Museum of Fine Arts, Boston.

William Hook (1777–1867) made this small sideboard as a wedding gift to his sister Hannah, who married Peter Folsom in 1809. The lively use of burled light birch veneer on the face of this piece and the rosewood veneer above the fan catch the eye. The fan inlay that boldly spans the upper half of the front of the piece conceals two hinged doors which provide additional storage at a convenient height.

Commode
Boston, Massachusetts. 1809.
Made by Thomas Seymour (1771–1848).
Painted by John Ritto Penniman (1783–1837).
Probably Carved by Thomas Whitman.
Mahogany and mahogany veneer; maple and satinwood veneer on pine, maple and chestnut. H: 41½" W: 50" D: 24⅝".
Museum of Fine Arts, Boston.

One of the finest pieces of Boston furniture of the early nineteenth century, this commode is not only a magnificent work of art, it is also well documented. In 1809, Thomas Seymour billed Madame Elizabeth Derby, daughter of Salem merchant Elias Hasket Derby, eighty dollars for making a "Large Mahogany Commode" and ten dollars for having "Paid Mr. Penniman's Bill, for Painting Shels on Top of D°." Three years later, in 1812, Thomas Seymour noted that the bill together with expenses for several other items was paid in full.

The Boston furniture-making business by the early years of the nineteenth century was large in scale and complex in operation. For important furniture, several different craftsmen were normally engaged to do special tasks. In other words, Seymour not only produced the cabinetwork in his shop, but he also coordinated the work of painters, finishers, other artisans, carvers and inlay workers. Brasses and locking hardware were normally ordered from manufacturing centers abroad—from Birmingham and Sheffield, England, and from France. The cast brass feet and lion's-head pulls are superbly finished or chased; side drawers swing out on custom-made hinges.

The shop that could produce a work of this magnitude was of necessity not only a production center, but also a resource and influence in the furniture trade. It is difficult to prove today who did what in Seymour's shop because he supplied and bought from smaller shops and commissioned individual craftsmen for special work.

Certainly the precision and quality of Penniman's painting implies personal attention of the highest order. The shells painted in the lunette can be identified as follows: from clockwise, a panther cowrie, moon shell, Murex, common wentletrap (scalaria), Bursa rana, and in the center, a harp shell. The fidelity with which this painting is executed is equal to that of a miniature portrait painting. Such splendid furniture demands examination at close range.

Dressing Chest
Boston, Massachusetts. c. 1800.
Mahogany, maple, pine.
H: 74½" W: 40½" D: 22¼".
Museum of Fine Arts, Boston.

The standard form for dressing chests in New England seems to have been established early in the nineteenth century. This example is archetypal—a circular or oval glass suspended on brackets, supported over small drawers upon a chest of drawers. The variations seem infinite and they range in quality from excellent to poor over the half century from 1800 to 1850. This example from Oak Hill is of the highest order in cabinetmaking skills.

DAN FARBER, PHOTOGRAPHER

Dressing Chest with Work Bag
Boston, Massachusetts. 1810–1820.
Mahogany; mahogany veneer on white pine.
H: 71" W: 38" D: 20½".
The Newark Museum.

Almost exactly the same form for this dressing chest existed in Boston a decade earlier, but here the more massive quality of design, heavier use of mahogany veneer and strongly reeded legs demonstrate the design direction that furniture took in the late Federal Period.

The foliate scroll supports on both sides of the looking glass are handsomely gilded and painted to give the illusion of carved and gilded ornament. Most unusual is the sliding drawer at the base of the chest to provide a bag for needlework and other paraphernalia of ladies' work.

ARMEN PHOTOGRAPHERS

Greco-Roman Revival 1815–1835

AMERICA WRESTLED for a second time with the power of Great Britain in the War of 1812, yet the leaders of American taste did not innovate an independent national style. Instead, they continued to shape their ideas and art forms according to the mainstream of European neoclassical thought: an archaeologically accurate revival of the ancient past. American taste moved away from the earlier, delicate Sheraton and Hepplewhite interpretations of neoclassical design after the first decade of the nineteenth century.

The most gifted designer to herald the revived forms of classical antiquity with a sense of archaeological correctness was the architect Benjamin Henry Latrobe (1764–1820). The first fully trained architect-engineer to make a career of his field in America, he made the designing of buildings a profession rather than a gentlemanly pursuit.

In 1809, at the request of President James and Dolley Madison, Latrobe designed the furniture and setting for the Oval Room of the White House. The furniture which Latrobe designed was lost in the Washington fire set by the British in the War of 1812. But Latrobe's drawings and some of his correspondence survive as testimony to the stunning effect of the room: the Oval Drawing Room was draped in red silk velvet and furnished with elegant painted chairs and sofas, artfully positioned.

The drawings of antique classical furniture which Latrobe made for the White House were influenced by Englishman Thomas Hope's *Household Furniture and Interior Decoration,* published in London in 1807. Hope, an avid collector of antiquities and an obsessive traveler, was influenced by his friends, the French designers for Napoleon Bonaparte, Charles Percier and Pierre Fontaine. These designers accompanied Napoleon's armies to make scale drawings of ancient Egyptian and Roman furniture upon which they based their designs and formed the official style of the French Empire. They published their work in the illustrated volume *Recueil des décorations intérieures* (1801, 1812). But these designs were much too extravagant for most Americans. Even George Smith's book, *A Collection of Designs for Household Furniture and Interior Decoration,* London, 1808, illustrated furniture far richer in ornamental pomposity than most Americans desired or could have had made.

Monumental, enduring, solid-looking furniture increasingly became the mode for fashionable American design from about 1815 through the rest of the nineteenth century. Adapted from French design and the English Regency style, furniture progressively became more heavily sculptured and more deeply carved. Classically inspired chair forms became popular—the klismos or Grecian style with sabre-shaped legs and simple curved back and the Roman curule chair with X-shaped legs were two of the most clearly "archaeologically correct" revived forms of the period. Other signals of the new mode were pillars with brass capitals, brass animal paw feet with casters, ornate brass mounts, reeding and "waterleaf" carving. Such ornament enriched many of the early pieces produced by Duncan Phyfe and other furniture craftsmen who worked within the pale of the English Regency style. French Empire taste is represented by caryatid figures, dolphins, monumental animal legs and feet, fire-gilt brass mounts, wreaths, swans and Egyptian details.

American painted and gilded furniture was elegantly executed—with distinctive regional centers producing charming and original works. Gold-leaf decoration in many cases served as a substitute for the rich fire-gilt brass mounts familiar to French furniture. The techniques developed for this decorative work involved stenciling and brush and quill inkwork, covered or polished with clear varnish. Surfaces were sometimes painted to simulate marble, ebony or antique bronze or grained to approximate rosewood.

The effect is serious and sedate. In most cases it has a scholarly or academic character that closely follows the canons of neoclassical beauty. All parts of the furniture were worked smoothly and were neatly finished so that nothing angular or irregular interrupts the graceful but sometimes ponderous flow of line.

Classical expression pervaded the American arts. It embraced architecture, painting, sculpture, government, and even the study of ancient languages. Ladies who lolled artfully on neoclassical furniture were garbed in high-waisted dresses, a romantic allusion to the chiton dress of ancient Greece. White houses, miniature versions of Greek temples, cropped up on every hill, dale and hamlet. There is little wonder, then, that by the 1830s both Philadelphia and Boston were proclaimed by their citizens to be the Athens of the New World. It is not possible to overstress how all-pervasive the Greco-Roman movement in the American arts was. The national style revived the past and discovered new applications of classical antiquity to fulfill part of Americans' search for an imagined world of ideal harmony.

Oil Painting: "The Tea Party."
Boston, Massachusetts. c. 1821–1825.
By Henry Sargent (1770–1845).
H: 64¼" W: 52¼".
Museum of Fine Arts, Boston.

According to tradition this interior view of the artist's home represents how the painter in the early 1820s remembered a party of 1798. Still, the furniture and the draped windows reflect a style current in the 1820s when classicism of the academically correct sort was beginning to be strongly felt in the American arts. Some of the furniture and furnishings pictured here were probably imported from France, including the stylish armchairs with gilt-eagle sides. The three-columned center table in the middle of this painting is a Boston-made piece.

This painting and its companion, "The Dinner Party," were well known and popularly admired in nineteenth-century Boston. Sargent's remarkable achievement of interior perspective, dramatic light and shadow and complex composition owes inspiration to a painting by the French artist François Granet, "The Capuchin Chapel." But more important than the source of inspiration is the remarkably rich decorative detail that offers an insight into the furnishing ideals of early romantic classical America.

This painting shows that by the 1820s it was no longer fashionable to own light, sleek and highly polished mahogany veneered furniture ornamented with delicate inlay. More massive visual effects were desired. Detail was bolder and designers modeled their efforts after works discovered from ancient classical sites in Greece and Rome. Anthemion ornament and acanthus leaves replaced the delicate reeding and minute inlay lavished on furniture of an earlier generation. Columnar forms, instead of being small reeded posts, gained weight and mass and were capped with brass ormolu mounts or gold leaf.

Center Table
Boston, Massachusetts. c. 1820.
Mahogany with mahogany veneer and white marble top. H: 30" Diameter of top: 38".
The Walters Art Gallery, Baltimore, Maryland.

This table was made for the artist Henry Sargent. The table and painting are remarkable and rare documents of American taste circa 1820. They illustrate how shapes and details inspired by the classical past were used to evoke a romantic connection between antiquity and the modern world.

Card Table
Boston, Massachusetts. c. 1818.
Mahogany on pine and oak.
H: 28¾" W: 35¾" D: 17½".
Museum of Fine Arts, Boston.

This table represents a phase of Regency neoclassicism in Boston cabinetmaking which parallels the much better-known work of Duncan Phyfe in New York City. By comparison with New York cabinetmaking, this table is compositionally flimsy in design, poor in construction and not nearly as robust in ornament. Despite these faults, it has an awkward grace that is attractive in its own way.

DAN FARBER, PHOTOGRAPHER

Armchair (One of a Set of Four)
Boston, Massachusetts. 1815–1830. Mahogany, birch; stained mahogany veneer inlay. H: 35" W: 21" D: 21".
Museum of Fine Arts, Boston.

Made en suite with two lyre-based card tables exhibiting the same darkly dyed mahogany inlay, this handsome armchair descended in the family of Colonel James Swan of Boston and Dorchester, Massachusetts. During the French Revolution Swan expanded his business to include exportation of fine furnishings confiscated from the French nobility to purchasers in New York, Philadelphia and Baltimore. He brought an elegant suite of Louis XVI furniture to Boston.

The chair represents a later development in Swan family taste, exhibiting the Grecian influence which typified the most fashionable furniture produced during the Empire Period. Broad slat backs combined with sabre-shaped front and rear legs comprised a chair form commonly known as "klismos" and was based on ancient prototypes.

Side Chair (One of a Set of Twelve)
Baltimore, Maryland. 1820–1830.
Painted cherry. H: 31⅝" W: 18½" D: 22⅛".
Museum of Fine Arts, Boston.

DAN FARBER, PHOTOGRAPHER

This is one of a set of twelve side chairs owned by the Alexander Brown family of Baltimore, possibly from his Greek revival-style house "Mondawmin." The chairs are among the most handsomely designed and painted classical furniture from Baltimore. A rich combination of colors enhances the stately form. A deep Naples yellow or ochre background with Pompeiian red panels is highlighted with gilt, green and black details. The color choices, skillful painting and splendid form of the chair all blend harmoniously. The design of the turned and tapered front legs finds its roots in ancient Rome, but the painted design of the back was inspired by Plate 56 in Thomas Sheraton's *The Cabinet-Maker and Upholsterer's Drawing Book.*

Side Chair
Philadelphia or Baltimore. c. 1830–1840.
White pine, ash, white oak.
H: 32" H: (seat) 17¾" D: (seat) 15¾".
Winterthur Museum.

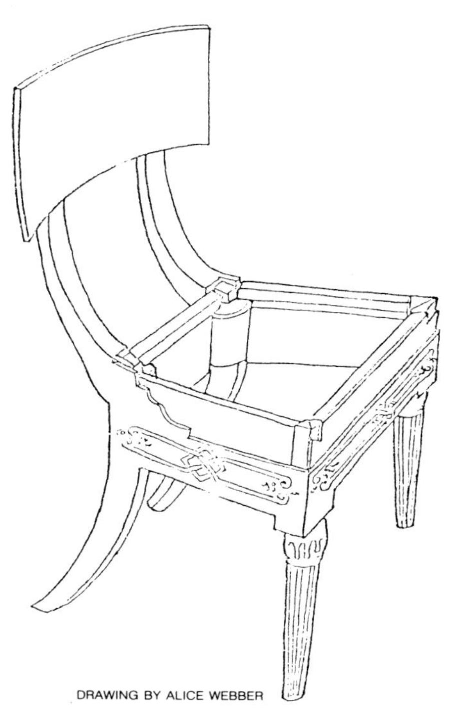

DRAWING BY ALICE WEBBER

Solid and stylish, this chair presents grace of stance together with a ruggedly joined seat frame capable of enduring use. The joinery of the front legs with the seat frame is especially interesting as the legs carry through to the top of the seat frame and are braced well into the structure with a rudimentary dovetail. The upper edges of the seat frame are chamfered toward the center of the seat. The back legs are given extra strength with semicircular blocks, glued into the corners in a manner found in eighteenth-century chairs made in Philadelphia.

Ochre-colored paint covers the overall surface of this chair, and provides a golden tone. Ornamental details are further highlighted with gold leaf. Illusionistic glazed shading is painted in darker tones. The visual effect of the chair is rich and restrained. It is an appearance in harmony with classical sculpture, which was imitated by American sculptors in Italy for use in American homes and public institutions in the 1830s and 1840s.

Side Chair (One of a Pair)
New York. c. 1830.
Rosewood graining over mahogany veneer on ash; upholstered in reproduction silk lampas. H: 31¾″ W: 19″ D: 17½″.
The Newark Museum.

This side chair is an American adaptation of the French Restoration style. The most attractive features of the chair are its swept-back rails echoed in the sabre shape of all four legs.

Rosewood, which was becoming fashionable in America as an exotic import, was simulated with paint covering a mahogany veneer. Rosewood, a harder and more strongly patterned wood than mahogany, was occasionally used in expensive furniture in America in the first decade of the nineteenth century. By the middle of the century its popularity and use was well established.

Armchair
New York, New York. 1815–1825.
Maple, grained to simulate rosewood.
H: 42″ W: 23″ D: 23¼″.
Collection of Mrs. Charles L. Bybee.

Recently restored, this armchair shimmers with a festive style and quality related to other well-documented New York City fancy or painted furniture of the Empire Period. Rosewood-painted background color forms an effective contrast to the applied gilt and goldleaf decoration. Anthemion and other classical devices ornament critical focal points at the crest, on the front seat stretcher, and arms and legs. The caned back and seat carry out an exotic Oriental theme also suggested by the "japanning" or "fancywork" as it was called.

DAN FARBER, PHOTOGRAPHER

Side Chair
New York. c. 1815.
Mahogany; mahogany veneer on front and back-seat stretchers, which are chestnut.
H: 32¾" W: 19¾" D: 23¼".
Collection of William N. Banks.

This Empire-style side chair has exceptionally refined carved detail and a well-designed overall form. The lines flow gracefully together; the carved and gilded front feet add an extra note of elegance below the rich waterleaf carving of the sabre-shaped legs.

Side Chair
Boston, Massachusetts. 1818–1830.
Mahogany painted to simulate rosewood, with brass inlay.
H: 40¼" W: 21¾" D: 19⅜".
Museum of Fine Arts, Boston.

This is one of three visually stunning, matching Grecian-style chairs. The craftsmanship of the chairs is complex. The brass inlay in the back splats is intricately sawn with a fine jeweler's saw and let into the wood with great precision. The bellflower and rosewood inlay of the legs and sides consists of a thin layer of brass rolled over a lead core. The design is imprinted into the brass through the use of a heavy steel rolling die that makes it possible to retain a continuous band of metal, while the lead core allows the strip to be shaped in conformity with the curves of the chair. The inlay strip is then set into a grooved channel and secured with tiny brass pins.

Normally, a cushion with ties and large tassels would cover the caned seat. The mahogany frame of the chair is painted to simulate the effect of rosewood.

Sling-Seated Armchair
New York, New York. 1810–1820.
Mahogany, tulip and hard pine.
H: 40½" W: 21⅝" D: 29½".
Winterthur Museum.

Finely reeded surfaces of this chair relate it to the late Federal furniture made in New York City where the curule form of ancient Roman magistrates' chairs was a favorite design. The base of this chair is a modification of the curule chair shape. The sweeping upper part of the chair is related to the so-called "campeachy chairs," a pair of which were given to Thomas Jefferson in 1819. This chair form had its antecedents in Spanish furniture of the sixteenth century, and chairs with such form were called "Spanish." The manufacturers Joseph Bradley and Company of 317 Pearl Street, New York City, received a diploma in 1839 for their production of "Spanish Chairs"; the award was issued by the American Institute of New York.

PHOTOGRAPH BY WADHAMS/MAHAFFEY

Side Chair
Baltimore, Maryland. 1830–1840.
Painted birch or maple, with original resist-dyed fabric on seat and back panel. H: 33⅜" W: 17¾" D: 19¼".
Museum of Fine Arts, Boston.

A set of six of these chairs was recently discovered in a summer house in Newport, Rhode Island.

The handsome ochre base paint of the chair is heightened with freely painted illusionistic classical ornament. Complementing this is the richly colored resist-dyed cotton upholstery made especially to carry through the classical theme.

Prototype designs for the chairs are found in the *Collection des meubles et objets de goût* by Pierre de la Mésangère (Paris, 1802–1835), and in *An Encyclopaedia of Cottage, Farm, and Villa Architecture and Furniture* by John Claudius Loudon (London, 1833). Loudon's was an especially popular source book in this country.

BEDSTEADS

RUDOLPH ROBINSON, PHOTOGRAPHER

Bedstead and Cornice
Boston, Massachusetts. c. 1808.
Cornice Attributed to William Lemon, Salem;
Gilded by John Doggett, Boston.
Mahogany, oak, pine.
H: 87⅜" W: 67½" D: 81¾".
Museum of Fine Arts, Boston.

This bed remained in Elizabeth Derby's house until it was acquired by the Museum of Fine Arts. The strong reeded and tapered posts and legs place this bed well within the context of neoclassicism that spanned the second decade of the nineteenth century.

For its period, this is one of the finest beds in American furniture history. Its posts are deeply and crisply carved in a style distinctive to Boston (see detail).

The cornice of this bed is attributed to William Lemon of Salem, who billed Elizabeth Derby for his work on the "Bows Darts Quivers Arrows." These emblems of love had little effect on her marriage to Captain Nathaniel West, for the marriage was disastrous, and ended in divorce. Despite the failings of love, the Derby-West household was not deficient in taste. It contained some of the finest furniture of the Federal Period.

*

Bedstead
New York. c. 1812.
Mahogany, poplar and ash.
H: 42¼″ L: 80″ D: 63½″.
Collection of William N. Banks.

In 1813 Montgomery Livingston was billed by the Phyfe cabinet shop for services and several articles of furniture, including this bedstead (shown at left). From 1792 until his retirement fifty-five years later in 1847, Duncan Phyfe operated a cabinet shop in New York City which was considered "the largest and most fashionable establishment in the country." Surprisingly, today fewer than twenty different pieces of furniture survive with Phyfe's label or some other satisfactory documentation.

The itemized charges on the Livingston bill suggest the diversity of activities for which the cabinetmaker could be called upon in addition to the production of furniture, such as assembly or moving, or adding casters. Other surviving bills from the Phyfe shop record charges for reconditioning and upholstering.

To produce this bed Phyfe probably met with Mr. Livingston and, using a cabinetmaker's price book, determined what elements would be employed and the charges for each additional feature. The brass mounts, which make such a stunning contrast to the rich mahogany, were usually imported from France. To complete the bed, mattresses and bolsters could have been acquired from Phyfe or an upholsterer.

Pier Table and Cabinet
Possibly Philadelphia, Pennsylvania. 1810–1820.
Mahogany, satinwood veneer, tulip and white pine.
H: 39" W: 49" D: 27".
Winterthur Museum.

Probably made for official or public use, this table with its compartmentalized top seems too imposing in scale for use in a private home unless the home was of the grandest order. The top bears a mirror within and a rich fan of satinwood rays inlaid on the exterior.

It was probably made in Philadelphia; the carved acanthus-leaf capitals are related to ornament on other pieces from that city. But no other furniture made in America has carved eagles of such quality and ambitious scale. The monopodia which end in lion's feet were devices favored by Joseph B. Barry, one of the finest cabinetmakers of Philadelphia in the heyday of classicism.

RICHARD CHEEK, PHOTOGRAPHER

Drum Table
New York. c. 1818–1830.
Mahogany and mahogany veneer on tulipwood.
H: 28½" Diameter of top: 21½".
Collection of Mrs. Charles L. Bybee.

Compact and movable, rich in its use of highly figured mahogany, this drum table is a very satisfying piece of furniture. Unlike the brass animal paw feet so often found on New York furniture, these feet were carved from the same wood as the four legs.

Since the table is small and easily moved, its adaptability lends itself to a small tea service or a stand for a lamp. Inscribed on the bottom of one of two concealed drawers in the table's apron is the unidentified name "Mendell EM."

Sofa Table
Philadelphia, Pennsylvania. c. 1820.
Mahogany on pine.
H: 27⅝" L: (closed) 37"; (open) 60½" D: 26¼".
Collection of William N. Banks.

The lyre, a classical decorative motif which intrigued Americans throughout most of the nineteenth century, was ingeniously used here in a double crossing to form a pedestal-base support. Winged legs with cast brass animal paw feet support the pedestal and make it movable with brass casters. Touches of carving at various junctures throughout the base of this piece form a handsome contrast with the geometric lines of the top. The construction detail is beautifully crafted and the dovetailing of the drawers neatly done; it must have come from the shop of a master like Anthony Quervelle.

HELGA PHOTO STUDIO, INC.

Card Table (One of a Pair)
New York. c. 1810.
Satinwood, mahogany, pine, brass.
H: 28¾" D: 17¾" (closed) W: 35⅞".
Museum of Fine Arts, Boston.

This is an unusual and beautiful table of blond-colored wood and brilliant, although flat, carving. When the table's top is rotated to open the leaf, one of the legs pivots at the same time to offer better balance. When the top is rotated to close, the leg automatically returns to place and the table can be placed flat against a wall.

Card Table (One of a Pair)
New York. c. 1815.
H: 29½" W: 36" D: 19" (closed).
Mahogany with pine rails. Museum of Fine Arts, Boston.

Of all American card tables of the early nineteenth century, this one (and its mate in the Garvan Collection at Yale University) is most expressive of the resurgent American nationalistic pride that followed the War of 1812. With outspread wings, the eagle stands atop a globe or sphere which represents the world. Supporting the globe is a stand of four smartly tapered legs with acanthus-leaf carving on their tops. The legs terminate in lion-paw feet which harmonize with the lion's mask at the juncture of the legs. The whole is an excellent work of sculpture that functions as serviceable furniture and at the same time merits credit to the carver.

The sweep of the legs of the table blends nicely at the base to carry upward with ease to the dramatic spread of the eagle's wings. Despite the complexity of the forms involved, no single part seems irrelevant or dominates the composition. Beautiful contrasts are maintained between smooth polished surfaces and the textured areas of feathers or foliage. The detailed photograph of the eagle, taken from an unnatural angle for viewing, distorts the visual effect intended by the carver, but the photograph does reveal the magnificence of skillful carving rendered to every feather.

Card Table
New York, New York. c. 1815.
Labeled by Joseph Brauwers (active 1800–1820).
Mahogany. H: 29" L: 36" D: 18" (closed).
Winterthur Museum.

Compositionally, this table is among the most successful of its time and place. There is a handsome balance between severity or simplicity of line and opulence of ornamental detail. The upper and lower parts of the table are solidly and handsomely joined together by a cluster of four columns, their caps and bases accented by ormolu mountings imported from France. Additional mounts are placed just above and below the columns, which emphasizes the centrality of the design. The use of curved lines in the legs contrasts with and softens the severe angularity of the upper section.

Cabinetmaker Brauwers advertised himself on his label as an "ebenist, from Paris." His table represents a manner of workmanship characteristic of the best furniture made in New York City in the French style.

Card Table
New York. c. 1815.
Attributed to Charles-Honoré Lannuier.
Rosewood veneer on white pine; maple border inlay. H: 29⅝" L: 35⅞" D: 18⅛".
Collection of William N. Banks.

This table is much more delicate and smaller in size than the picture might suggest. Perhaps the illusion of mass is created by the monumental quality of the caryatid winged figure supporting the tabletop. Its design is an ingenious solution to a tripod arrangement of support above a four-footed base. Elements of the design seem to have been adapted from Pierre de la Mésangère's *Collection des Meubles et Objets de Goût,* but the handling of overall design is distinctively the work of the French *émigré* cabinetmaker/*ébéniste* Charles-Honoré Lannuier. Three pairs of similar tables are labeled or firmly documented to this master craftsman. This table was owned originally in Charleston, South Carolina, and remains in the South today. Brass inlaid borders on the edges of the top carry the rich contrast of gold against rosewood throughout this piece. The classical animal paw feet with hooked legs are painted a dark green (antique vert). The bases of the caryatid and column supports are similarly toned. The top is banded with a brilliant curly maple border inlay. The original green felt on the playing surface is exposed when the table is opened. Marbleized paper lines the table well. Imported French ormolu mounts above and below the caryatid figure accent the symmetry of this work in a graceful manner characteristic of the best French taste of the period.

Pier Table
***New York, New York.** c. 1815–1820.*
***Mahogany veneer on pine; white marble columns and pilasters.** H: 38⅞" W: 54⅞" D: 21½".*
Collection of Mrs. Charles L. Bybee.

A rich combination of materials distinguishes this generously proportioned pier table. Details of marble, ormolu brass and stenciled borders finished in gold leaf are boldly accented by the deeply colored mahogany background. The carved feet are painted in deep green-black and highlighted with gold powder to simulate antique bronze. The carving above the feet is enriched with gold leaf.

RICHARD CHEEK, PHOTOGRAPHER

Sideboard and Knife Boxes
Philadelphia, Pennsylvania. c. 1825.
Mahogany, ebony, brass.
Sideboard—H: 50″ L: 91″ D: 27″.
Knifeboxes—H: 21⅝″ W: 13½″ D: 14½″.
Philadelphia Museum of Art.

One of the most richly ornamented pieces of American classical furniture, this sideboard is a triumph of workmanship. The matching pair of knife boxes shown on its top, along with a mahogany cellarette (not illustrated), were made en suite for the Gratz family. The figured mahogany veneered surfaces of the sideboard are not glued onto a common wood as was the custom at this period; instead, they were glued onto solid mahogany. Magnificently figured brass inlay is set into ebony panels, accenting the symmetry of the doors and drawers. A backboard, carved in low relief, carries classical detail of foliate ornament with a springing lion in its center.

This unusual sideboard was probably made by Joseph Barry (1757–1839) in the mid to late 1820s. Barry was the only craftsman in Philadelphia to advertise that he made "burl work" or brass inlay. However, a search of the Gratz family papers has failed to document the name of this furniture's maker.

Pier Table
Boston, Massachusetts.
By George Archibald and Thomas Emmons (working 1813–1824).
Mahogany veneer on chestnut; marble top.
H: 33″ (not including top) L: 43¼″ D: 19½″.
Museum of Fine Arts, Boston.

This brilliantly figured table shows the ultimate manipulation of crotch mahogany veneer in the most restrained way. The feet are ebonized and inlaid with an ormolu band. The columns, which are

also veneered, are elegantly tall and have a slight swell or entasis to their profile.

The stencil label of Emmons and Archibald at No. 39 Orange Street, Boston, places the making of the piece between 1813, when the partnership was located at that address, and 1824, when Orange Street's name was changed to Washington Street.

Business was apparently good, for the inventory of Emmons's household belongings suggests that he lived very comfortably. The inventory of Emmons's portion of the workshop stock includes quantities of mahogany, rosewood, kingwood, whitewood, bay, chestnut, birch, ash, and more than four hundred feet of veneer; embossed velvet, haircloth, French lace, yellow plush, and moquette for upholstery; and a large amount of hardware. Notice of the sale of cabinet stock in the *Independent Chronicle* and the *Boston Patriot,* June 1, 1825, mentions "a variety of elegant French Caps and Bases, Rings, Knobs, and other Ornaments." This is evidence that the ormolu used on such pieces as the Museum's pier tables may very well have been imported from France.

Pier Table
Philadelphia, Pennsylvania. c. 1830.
Mahogany and marble.
H: 36⅛" W: 40¾" D: 18⅜".
Collection of Mrs. Charles L. Bybee.

The rich contrasting textures of this pier table's surfaces are gloriously harmonized with the deeply sculptured profile of the wooden base and top. The table is quite small for such a "muscular" shape. Lavish ornament and brightly colored marble columns and piers enrich the stance. Gesso and gold leafage over the feet balance the radiant gold ornament on the shelf. The total effect is grand and impressive.

RICHARD CHEEK, PHOTOGRAPHER

RICHARD CHEEK, PHOTOGRAPHER

Card Table
Baltimore, Maryland. 1820–1830.
Pine grained with paint to simulate rosewood; brass mounts and casters. H: 29⅛″ W: 36″ D: 18″.
Collection of Mrs. Charles L. Bybee.

This center pedestal table is the most arresting of American examples because of its simple angularity of line and brilliance of contrasting painted and gold-leaf ornament. Many classical Baltimore card tables are more elaborately ornamented, but none are as sleek or as trim as this one. Most have their basic structural design concealed under decorative additions that delight the eye but do not enhance the unusual design solution.

A common design problem of the X-frame pedestal base is how to resolve the abrupt transition between the center column and the horizontal stretchers. On this table the problem is solved by the use of Grecian scrolls or volutes decorated with anthemion leaves in paint, gilt and applied brass rosettes. Freely adapting details of foliage and rosettes from the 1812 Parisian edition of Charles Percier and Pierre Fontaine, decorative painters in Baltimore developed an ornamental repertoire instantly recognizable.

To prepare the table for card playing, the top is rotated to allow the hinged leaf to rest on one half of the table frame. Rotating the top exposes a well in the table, which is lined with its original red-woolen figured fabric.

Side Table with Marble Top (One of a Pair)
New York. c. 1820.
Top: Rosewood veneer on pine.
Base: Mahogany veneer on pine.
H: 33⅜" W: 41¾" D: 18 13/16".
Museum of Fine Arts, Boston.

Working in the manner of Charles-Honoré Lannuier, but probably not the product of the *émigré* master's shop, the maker of this table was inspired by the French fashions of Pierre de la Mésangère's *Collection des Meubles et Objets de Goût* and English interpretations of French taste in George Smith's *Cabinet-Maker and Upholsterer's Guide.* The elaborate gold-leaf ornamental detail of the tabletop was stenciled and then quilled in ink, a technique characteristic of New York craftsmanship. This was the local solution to achieving the visual effect of ormolu metallic mounts without going to the expense of actually importing them from France.

When this pair of tables was purchased at auction in 1975, only the gold-leaf stencil decoration on the sides of the top suggested the quality of the gold-leaf work that lay beneath an overall covering of paint on the base and eagles. Sometime in the mid- to late-nineteenth century, when bright effects were considered undesirable, the tables had been painted and/or grained to simulate rosewood. Removal of the later paint revealed stunning qualities of burnished gold leaf. Contrasting with the gilt, dark-green paint or "antique vert" was uncovered on the lionlike bodies of the eagles. Antique vert simulated the appearance of ancient bronze and was highlighted in powdered gold to enhance the effect of burnishing.

HELGA PHOTO STUDIO, INC.

Wardrobe
New York. c. 1815.
Mahogany, white pine, tulip and birch.
H: 96″ (to top of pediment) W: 55½″ D: 20½″.
Collection of William N. Banks.

A similar wardrobe in the New-York Historical Society bears the inscription "H. Lannuier/New York." Had it not been for the chance discovery of this signature in 1963, this work probably would have been routinely attributed to the workshop of Duncan Phyfe or other craftsmen practicing in the Phyfe manner. As more becomes known about New York furniture of the first quarter of the nineteenth century, it becomes apparent that both native and immigrant craftsmen willingly adapted to what was a New York taste in furniture. The styles of Phyfe, Lannuier and other contemporaries do not seem as distinctively different as was once believed.

This wardrobe enclosed neatly fitted compartments—three upper and three lower sliding trays and two banks of five drawers. Its design is a model of convenience and functional utility made in an era when closets (as we know them today) were not ordinarily built into living quarters. The wardrobe was once owned by a member of the Livingston family on the Hudson River.

Boldly figured mahogany panels bordered with broad mahogany bands grace the front of this masterwork. Such highly figured mahogany panels were preferred by wealthy New Yorkers even during the late eighteenth century.

Secretary-Bookcase
New York. c. 1825.
Possibly Made by Joseph Meeks & Sons.
H: 101" W: 55¾" D: 28⅛".
The Metropolitan Museum of Art, New York.

Monumental in form, overwhelming in its dazzling ornament, this secretary-bookcase expresses the material abundance of classical America. Gilding, painting, stenciling and carving are offset by rich mahogany ground, inlaid brass and pleated silk curtains.

Despite the secretary's impressive size and ornamental effect, its decorative painting is executed mechanically. It is similar to the stencil work on Hitchcock chairs. An instructive contrast may be made between it and the freehand brushwork of furniture painters in Baltimore.

Desk
Philadelphia, Pennsylvania. 1815–1820.
Mahogany, bird's-eye maple, American tulip, cherry, pine, padouk inlay, brass. H: 62⅞" W: 35⅝" D: 21⅛".
Collection of Mrs. Charles L. Bybee.

The quintessence of the French taste in American furniture is expressed in this desk made at the time when French culture dominated intellectual life in Philadelphia. The exterior of the desk is severely restrained with the mahogany veneer formally patterned in matching halves to emphasize the precise symmetrical placement of ormolu mounts and chased brasses. By contrast, the interior of the desk is aglow with a brilliantly figured veneer of curled maple. The element of surprise upon opening the desk is in keeping with the aesthetic system of restraint which pervades neoclassical art—a cultivated taste is necessary for appreciation of it. For many viewers the effects are "precious," too subtle, and to others too dull.

To enjoy the excellence of a piece of furniture of this sort one must be prepared to spend time examining its geometry, refinement and the precision of its construction. The vocabulary of ornament, while derived from ancient sources, is in no way a routine copying of classical antiquity.

COURTESY OF THE BAYOU BEND COLLECTION, THE MUSEUM OF FINE ARTS, HOUSTON

Chamber Organ
Salem, Massachusetts. 1827.
George G. Hook (1805–1881).
Rosewood, rosewood veneer, bird's-eye maple and gilded white pine.
H: 106" W: 57½" D: 27".
Essex Institute, Salem, Massachusetts.

There are design parallels between this splendid case piece and the Philadelphia desk for which Anthony G. Quervelle won an award from the Franklin Institute. Made at the same time, both are Greek revival- (Empire) style masterpieces. Both make excellent use of classical columns at their corners. Foliate carving on both is deep and rich. Precise carving on the cornices of both emphasize this prominent architectonic feature.

Throughout the Eastern seaboard, the best cabinets, like this, were monumentally solid and reflected antique classical taste. Clear and handsome solutions to geometric problems were made for both furniture and architecture in the Greek Revival style. Rich touches of ornamental detail were used at transition points in order to enhance the monumentality of geometric form in both buildings and furniture.

As in the past, one is still enchanted with the rich textural surfaces of this piece. Its gold leaf, wood grain and carving are completely harmonious. Of surpassing importance is the imposing overall volume; its formal stately arrangement of parts builds its composition to an impressive unity of design.

George Hook was known only for making organ works, so it is not clear who actually made the case. Since George was the son of the well-established Salem cabinetmaker William Hook, it seems reasonable to presume that the case was constructed under the father's supervision. This piece was the first of some six hundred or more organs made by George and his brother Elias.

Comparison: Cellarettes

Two classical cellarettes are compared here—one made in Boston and the other from New York City. They illustrate how freely cabinetmakers from each area adapted antique models to meet new needs.

Cellarette
Probably Made in Boston, Massachusetts. c. 1815.
Mahogany with brass inlay.
H: 26" W: 36" D: 30".
Museum of Fine Arts, Boston.

The severity of line and geometric form of this lead-lined chest on platform is in keeping with the affinities that early nineteenth-century New Englanders felt for classical antiquity. Because no comparable cellarettes were known from ancient times, the design of this small masterpiece had to be contrived from other classical forms. Did the maker enjoy the irony of selecting as a model an ancient sarcophagus to contain and chill wine bottles beside a Federal Period dinner table?

Cellarette
New York, New York. 1815–1819.
Mahogany and rosewood veneer; black, gilt and brass fretwork ornament attributed to Charles-Honoré Lannuier.
H: 29¾" W: 27¾" D: 22⅜".
The Mabel Brady Garvan Collection, Yale University Art Gallery.

The intriguing suggestion of death and immortality offered by the sarcophagus form and Egyptoid sphinxes with female heads could not have been overlooked by the owner of this cellarette, Stephen Ball Munnox of New York. Complex meanings and symbolism were a vital part of nineteenth-century life, both in this country and abroad. Veneration of age and bygone civilizations and the use of ancient artistic motifs to suggest new associations with the past were implicit in this era of Romantic classicism.

Despite its solemn appearance and sepulchral associations, this cellarette is one of the most handsome works of sculpture produced in early nineteenth-century America. Yet because it is a useful object, its formal qualities as sculpture might be overlooked.

JOSEPH SZASZFAI, PHOTOGRAPHER

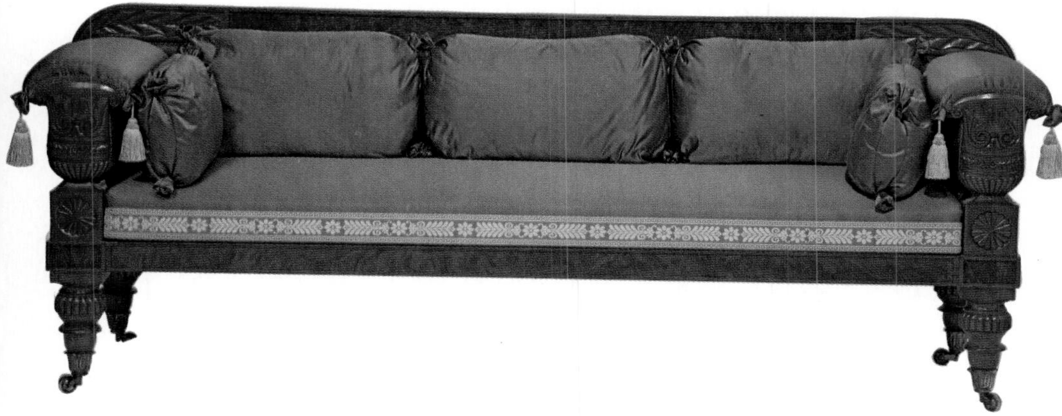

American cabinetmakers had little exact knowledge of the seating, couches and beds used by ancient Greeks and Romans. Ideas came from abroad in the form of fashionable designs—in pattern books and periodicals of taste. This sofa was copied quite closely after a plate in a popular London periodical, Ackermann's *Repository of Arts, Literature, Fashions, etc.* (1821). The illustration is a hand-colored aquatint and engraving which shows an apple-green-colored silk covering to the sofa, with soft pillows probably filled with down. "A Dress Sofa" is its title, meaning a formal, elegant work suitable for the parlor.

Rarely is there such an exact representation of the upholstery of a nineteenth-century sofa upon which to base reupholstery.

Sofa
Boston, Massachusetts.
c. 1821–1830.
Mahogany, pine.
H: 34" W: 88" D: 23¼".
Museum of Fine Arts, Boston.

Couch (One of a Pair)
Baltimore, Maryland. c. 1820–1830.
Tulipwood with brass feet.
H: 16½" W: 45½" D: 14".
Winterthur Museum.

Painted and gilt furniture from cities such as Philadelphia, New York and Boston do not have the abundant, foliate ornamental painting characteristic of Baltimore furniture of the Classical Period. Acanthus ornament on this couch is made of gold leaf with illusionistic shadowing painted upon it. Simulated rosewood graining forms the background painted underneath the gold leaf. The skillful freehand painting, gilding and shading is so remarkably deft and compelling, that no question remains that the unknown decorator was indeed an artist.

Only two can sit on the couch at once. But despite its dainty size and relatively simple basic shape, it has a vigor of design that carries power. The strong contrast of rich coloring and the flowing boldness of design surpass the original intent of the decorator merely to simulate the effects of imported French ormolu or fire-gilt mounts.

This piece was made in Baltimore at a time when that city was an important center of furniture production for homes and public buildings in the Greek revival style.

Couch (One of a Pair)
Boston, Massachusetts. 1818–1830.
Rosewood and rosewood graining on
birch and maple; inlaid brass;
silk upholstery. H: 34⅞" W: 23¾" L: 70¼".
Museum of Fine Arts, Boston.

Nathan Appleton, a wealthy merchant, banker and congressman, acquired four couches of this form for his elegant new classical townhouse on Beacon Street. Several photographs of the interior of the Appleton house survive to record these couches in the parlor at a time when the home was owned by Nathan's grandson, William Sumner Appleton. The last private owner of the couches, an Appleton descendant, called them "napping couches." This may reflect a period term—although the more common early description

was "Grecian couches." Two of the couches are large and the smaller pair, of which this is one, are quite dainty—"ladies' Grecian couches."

It is the finest work of its time from Boston. The flat but textural richness of exotic woods with inlaid brass is unsurpassed. Shallow relief carved in the severely flat woodwork is enhanced through ormolu mounts and finely beaded brass stringing. Some of this stringing (which was missing) has been restored in exactly its original manner. To make the stringing, a thin sheet of brass is rolled over a lead core. The lead allows the stringing to be freely bent to follow the contour of the back where it is nailed into place with brass pins. The new silk upholstery on the couch precisely follows the form and pattern of the original cushion, bolster and back, which had survived under layers of later upholstery.

This couch is a sleek and almost frivolous work; it is a masterpiece. Caning gives it an appearance of lightness and suggests a festive quality that can be termed "fancy." Upon a frame of curly maple, paint simulates grained rosewood. The graining serves as a lively and deeply colored background for the tightly controlled gold-leaf decoration applied to the front-seat rail. Black line shading on the gold leaf ornament is made with ink from a quill. The winged legs are also leafed and the feet are painted a dark bronze-green or "antique vert."

Caned Grecian Couch
New York, New York. c. 1815–1830.
Curly maple, rosewood grained.
H: 30" W: 84" D: 24".
Museum of Fine Arts, Boston.

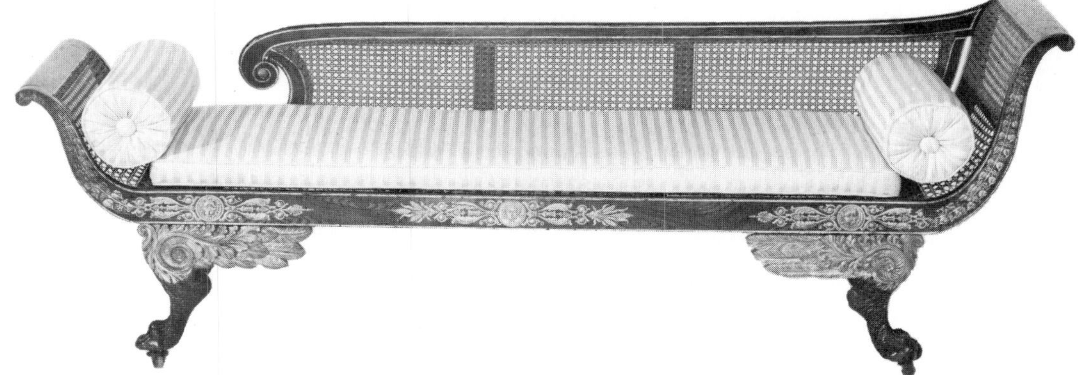

COURTESY OF THE NEW YORK HISTORICAL SOCIETY

Watercolor
"Study for Greek Revival Double Parlor."
New York. c. 1845(?).
Not signed or dated.
H: 13¼" L: 18⅛".
The New York Historical Society.

The Stevens "palace" in New York was completed in 1845 on Murray Street and has long been considered one of the finest examples of Greek revival design in American architecture. This drawing has long been associated with Alexander Jackson Davis (1803–1892) and the Stevens palace, but it may actually represent rooms which were designed for another house.

No matter whether the watercolor represents an actual or an imagined room design, it is a revealing and beautiful work. It records the continuation of purity of classical design well into the mid-Victorian Period, by a major American architect.

The watercolor is illustrated here together with furniture a generation earlier in date because it shows the persistence of the same ideals in their most monumental domestic form. The arrangement and details are severe, uncluttered, spacious and scholarly. The parlor has an archaeological authority from the past.

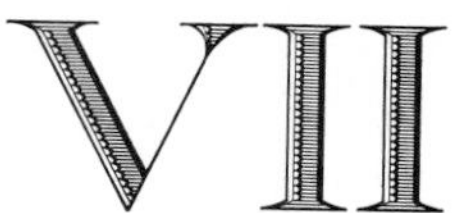

Away from the Mainstream

Furniture Of and For the People

By the nineteenth century most Americans were descended from European ancestors, but the generations which separated them had effected a cultural drift away from European taste. Much American furniture reflected this drift—an unconscious "backwardness" in fashion.

Some culturally restrictive communities, such as those established by German immigrants in Pennsylvania, were extremely slow to change. By the nineteenth century they were two and a half centuries out of phase with current European styles. For them, change did not have a positive connotation. They maintained their old-world values, language and traditions as a part of an isolated social system and adapted very slowly to current fashions. In other communities, where isolation was a matter more of geography than of religious or social outlook, changing urban fashions were misperceived by both craftsmen and clients. Abstractions of the urban sources were blended with accepted local traditional forms to yield new and surprising results.

Other craftsmen, both urban and rural, made plain furniture that was well constructed and nicely proportioned, but severely simple. Reasons for simplicity were varied, usually involving economy, practicality or religion. This chapter samples a wide variety of American furniture made by craftsmen who for one reason or another misunderstood or rejected fashionable urban styles. Their works are quite different from what was being made abroad. Works by people who emigrated from different parts of Northern Europe are compared, not because any real relation existed between them, but because there seems to be a virtual kinship between the works of non-high-style artisans. Their furniture represents the taste of ordinary people—a common denominator that today is recognized by the term "folk art." Unfortunately this term has been misused to embrace all works ranging from rural, popular, vernacular, and provincial to peasant, folk, primitive, ethnic, naive and plain. In plain furniture, for example, such different works as those made by Shakers, Quakers and Windsor artisans can be grouped. None of these were strictly folk artists.

It is difficult to categorize the work not made by high-style artisans into well-defined groups. With the freedom that is characteristic of most of their art, the kinship patterns of furniture made for the common American shade into each other with great subtlety. Yet folk art and popular art seem most clearly at opposite ends of the spectrum. The folk artist-craftsman was conservative and tradition-bound. His approach to his craft was basically anti-progressive and involved handwork that gave individuality to each piece produced. His sphere of travel and distribution of goods was local. By contrast, the popular artisan tended to produce works that appealed to a broader public and followed fashion in a more normal, up-to-date manner. His production technology was more machine oriented and therefore his work was more uniform—not one of a kind. His market was broader than the folk artisan's. The popular artisan tended to export products once he had satisfied local needs.

Overlying both the folk and popular arts was an English-speaking culture which by the eighteenth century dominated the Eastern seaboard. Yet in 1790 only about sixty percent of the population of this country was of English descent. The tastes of non-English cultural groups were quickly assimilated in all areas where settlement came into contact with the predominant English culture. But even if the melting pot metaphor is accepted—that America became a nation blended of nations—there are bold exceptions to homogeneous language, culture and furniture.

The blend was as complex as the many rivers which flowed to the coast along the Eastern seaboard. These waterways offered asylum to a large number of non-English settlements inland, and gave access to the hinterland to settlers who could shelter and maintain non-English, nonurban tastes in their attitudes, styles—and furniture.

WINDSORS

The origins of Windsor chairs in this country are clouded by their very commonplace nature, nor are their antecedents in English Windsor chairs fully clear. While the English versions are distinctly different in appearance, there is no doubt that American Windsors have roots in a long, indeterminate evolution in Northern European folk craft practices. The evolution of Windsors from simple stick furniture to a highly skilled and specialized craft within the furniture-making business is still to be fully explored.

Prior to eighteenth-century industrialization, artists apparently thought the ordinary furniture of the humble peasant or farmer not worthy of notation and, therefore, images of common stick furniture are rarely seen in early genre paintings or interior scenes. Any person who works the land by hand is familiar with the yearly practice of cutting back the woodland edge to prevent encroachment upon the planting fields. This process yields an abundance of small flexible branches well suited to wickerwork, fence or wall construction (wattle to support mud daub clay walls), or fashioning stick furniture. The bending and shaping of green wood most certainly led to specializations that, in time, yielded finely shaped Windsor chairs with turned legs and semiflexible spindle backs.

Because this highly utilitarian furniture form was made originally out of surplus material easily obtained in a woodland and farming culture, Windsor chairs were traditionally inexpensive. Likewise, in eighteenth-century America they could be obtained for only a matter of shillings, despite the complexity of design and engineering involved in their construction. A great deal of their popularity in the early twentieth century can be credited to Wallace Nutting's *A Windsor Handbook,* published in 1917, which called attention to their artistic merits and attempted to categorize them by form and to sort American Windsor chairs according to quality and rarity of design.

In order to fully appreciate Windsor chairs, their construction should be studied. The continuous border of a sack- or hoop-back Windsor was made of a single piece of pliable wood such as hickory, oak or ash. If not green, the wood was soaked or steamed in order to give it flexibility to bend into the shape of the back. The long "stick" that formed the back was first pulled through a shaping die equipped with sharp edges that cut a molded profile, and then fitted into a frame. Left to dry, the arc of the back was fixed in the "memory" of the wood. The completed back arch was then fitted into drilled sockets of the shaped plank seat and, at the same time, the hickory spindles of the back were set into its drilled border. Lathe-turned stretchers and legs were then driven into sockets drilled through the bottom of the seat. With the exception of painting or staining, the job was then complete. An experienced Windsor chairmaker made numerous parts at one time, assembling them as needed. Some of this work was seasonal and kept apprentices busy at times when custom jobs were not in progress.

Because Windsors were usually made of a mixture of woods—hickory for spindles, tulip or pine for the seat, maple for legs, and oak or ash for the bow of the back—they were rarely, probably never, left unpainted in the eighteenth and early nineteenth centuries. Typically, an undercoat or ground, consisting of a pink or light-colored wash, was applied and then covered with the final coat of dark green, black, mahogany, red, brown, yellow or stone color. The chairs were sometimes varnished.

The earliest discovered sale of Windsors in this country dates to September 14, 1754, when John Reynell, a Philadelphia merchant, became indebted to the Windsor chair- and cabinetmaker Jedediah Snowden for "2 Double Windsor Chairs with 6 Legs." A "double Windsor chair" probably meant "Windsor settee," which is another term found in eighteenth-century documents. Countless other period terms testify to the wide variety of combinations of forms available to the inventive Windsor chairmaker. There were high-back, comb-, sack-back and round-top Windsors in addition to low-back, brace-back and children's Windsors.

Philadelphia seems to have been the center where Windsor chairmaking started in this country. Ex portation of chairs from the Quaker City and emigration of craftsmen soon carried the Windsor chair craft throughout the colonies. Connecticut, Rhode Island and Massachusetts craftsmen were quick to adapt the making of Windsor chairs to local tastes and craft skills with distinctive results.

Print After Oil Painting "The Congress Voting Independence, July 4, 1776." Begun by Robert Edge Pine and Completed by Edward Savage. 1788 or Later. Historical Society of Philadelphia, Pennsylvania.

The sack-back Windsor chairs in the foreground of this painting are occupied by Robert Morris (left), Benjamin Franklin (center), and Charles Carroll (right). In all probability these chairs represent some of the 114 Windsors that Francis Trumble supplied the State House (Independence Hall) between 1776 and 1778.

Comb-Back Windsor Armchairs
Philadelphia, Pennsylvania. c. 1726–1756.
Stamped "T. Gilpin" for Thomas Gilpin (1700–1766).
Hickory, ash and tulip.
The Independence National Historical Park, Philadelphia.

These chairs represent the archetypal form associated with the Philadelphia and Pennsylvania Windsor chairmaking tradition in the eighteenth century. The maker, Thomas Gilpin, was born in 1700 in Birmingham Township, Chester County, Pennsylvania, where he worked from 1721 until 1726; he was located in Philadelphia between 1727 and 1756.

The blunt arrow feet on these chairs are typical features of the eighteenth-century Pennsylvania Windsors. What may be peculiar to Gilpin is the elongated decorative turning and chisel scoring on the arm posts and upper legs of the chairs.

Nineteenth-century iron braces are seen between the legs of one of these chairs, once a commode chair (its seat has been filled). Both chairs have lost their original paint.

Comb-Back Windsor Armchair
Pennsylvania. 1750–1780.
Maple, poplar, ash.
H: 40⅜" W: 26".
The Art Institute of Chicago.

This is one of the more exciting variations in American Windsor chairmaking. The visual complexity and vigor of the form derives from the contrast between the small oval seat and the strongly flaring legs and back. The attached arms are let into the fine columnar turnings of the rear posts. This example also possesses two secondary back braces which are set into a coffin-shaped extension at the rear of the seat, a rare and desirable feature.

Writing Armchair
Lisbon, Connecticut. Late 18th–Early 19th Century.
Made by Ebenezer Tracy (1744–1803).
Branded "E B Tracy" on underside of seat.
Soft maple (arm, crest and legs); tulipwood (drawer fronts); white oak (stretchers and spindles).
Traces of red and green paint remaining on refinished surface. H: 43" W: 27" D: 18½".
The Mabel Brady Garvan Collection,
Yale University Art Gallery.

The most popular image of Windsor chairs is the writing armchair. Its design is a monument to Yankee ingenuity and prefigures the functional school chair of the nineteenth and twentieth centuries. This chair includes a shallow box drawer underneath the writing arm plus a candleslide. Under the seat, suspended on runners, is a deep drawer for books and papers. The chair combines the basic low-back Windsor armchair with an offset comb-back crest.

At Ebenezer Tracy's death in Lisbon, Connecticut, in 1803, his shop contained 6,400 "chair rounds" and 277 "chair bottoms"—an inventory which probably accounts for only a small fraction of his annual output. This suggests that the Windsor chairmaking business was a very large-scale enterprise in eighteenth-century America. A successful shop was a highly organized undertaking that supplied an expanding market, and was an important part of the Industrial Revolution of the eighteenth century. Its methods of operation bordered upon the factory system of manufacturing with developed capital, specialized labor and a broad trade network. Large-scale Windsor chairmaking required parts which were standardized and interchangeable, shaping attitudes toward rapid manufacturing techniques that prefigured the assembly-line production methods of early clock and gun factories in Connecticut.

Despite Tracy's well-developed Windsor business, he was not just a specialist in that trade. He also made the usual finished furniture expected of cabinetmakers. Left finished at his death were a clock case, two Pembroke tables and two low bureaus, among other items.

Slat-Back Windsor Armchair
Philadelphia, Pennsylvania. c. 1775.
Stamped "I. Henzey" for Joseph Henzey of Philadelphia; unidentified name painted on underside of seat: "Dallam."
Various woods, painted green. H: 37¾" W: 26¼" D: (seat) 15½".
The Independence National Historical Park, Philadelphia.

COURTESY OF THE WINTERTHUR MUSEUM LIBRARIES

Windsor chairmaking was a vigorous industry in eighteenth-century Philadelphia. Few regions exported more Windsor chairs to a broader network of trade. The products of Philadelphia chairmakers reached south to the Barbados Islands, St. Croix and Jamaica, as well as to many of America's coastal ports.

The popularity of the practical and sturdy Windsors in Philadelphia is well documented. (Note chairs in painting, page 284.)

Modern restorations have been made to this chair: the hand grips have been repaired or replaced, both front feet have been renewed, and part of the turning of the left rear leg is also replaced. The original paint was stripped away some time ago and the chair now bears a dark-green paint, appropriate to its period. Therefore, as a collector's specimen, this piece has shortcomings. But because it bears the mark of its maker, it is an important index to Philadelphia workmanship. The maker, Joseph Henzey, is listed in the Philadelphia City Directories as a Windsor chairmaker from 1802 through 1807. Actually he was making Windsors as early as 1772, and this chair seems to fall into that early period of his career.

The arm posts have nicely shaped vase and baluster turnings, the design of which is echoed in the legs. The tapering feet with straight sides were once thought to be characteristic of New England chairs, but are no longer believed to be a reliable index of New England provenance. Similar chairs were made by a number of other Philadelphia craftsmen, including John Wire and Francis Trumble.

Low-Back Windsor Chair
Philadelphia or New York City. 1765–1780.
Branded "PVR" under seat.
Tulip, maple, red oak. H: 28½" W: 27⅛" D: 20¾".
Colonial Williamsburg, Williamsburg, Virginia.

The broad seat, blunt "arrow" feet and crisp bulbous turnings of the legs, stretchers and arm supports of this chair are all characteristic of Philadelphia work, but Philadelphia chairs were widely copied after 1750 and there is no assurance that this might not be the work of a New York City craftsman.

Armchair
Philadelphia, Pennsylvania. 1785–1796.
Branded underside of seat: "W. Cox." (Working 1767–1796.)
Various woods painted a cream color originally.
H: 37" W: 24⅛" W: (seat) 20".
The Independence National Historical Park, Philadelphia.

The bamboo-turned spindles of the back and legs catered to the popularity of Oriental influences that had filtered into America in the eighteenth century, increasing during the Federal Period through direct trade with China and the Orient.

The lines of this chair and its original light cream-colored paint show the delicacy of taste that became pervasive in the last quarter of the eighteenth century. The strong baluster turnings that were popular with Windsor chairmakers a generation earlier are echoed in the side stretchers that swell in their centers to accommodate the medial stretcher. The swelling is scribed with a line simulating bamboo in an effort to update the old-fashioned feature.

The legs have been shortened slightly and the seat no longer bears its original upholstery, which was tacked over the edge.

Windsor Armchair and Side Chair
(From a Set of Six)
New England. 1780–1810. Stamped "H. Bacon"; chalk inscription: "Cory."
Pine, maple and other woods painted dark green. H: 37½" W: 16" D: 16⅞".
Museum of Fine Arts, Boston.

"Braced bow-back Windsor" is a term used today to describe the form of this set of chairs. Wallace Nutting observed that the weakest part of the Windsor chair was at the point where the back and seat joined together. By adding braces to an extension of the back of the seat this structural weakness was overcome. Braces allowed the resilient spring of the back to function while preventing the spindles from working loose or cracking under strain.

These chairs are especially handsome in the boldness of their tapered, shapely turned legs, the dramatic splay to the legs and the generous overhang or cantilever effect of the back of the seat. They bear several layers of old paint, the most recent of which is a muted dark-green color.

Windsor Settee
Philadelphia, Pennsylvania. 1785–1807.
Branded under seat: "I. Letchworth."
(Working 1785–1809).
Hickory, maple, mahogany and other woods.
H: 36¾" W: 39¾" D: (at seat) 16¾".
The Independence National Historical Park, Philadelphia.

The mahogany armrests that contrast beautifully with the painted surface of the rest of this piece are features found on other Windsors made by John Letchworth. This handsome settee is one of a pair that was repainted a dark green enamel over traces of black and still earlier white paint.

The graceful S-shape of the arms, with the curled handrests, is, in part, carried down to the seat in the curved arm support. The simulation of bamboo on the nineteen hickory spindles of the back is also repeated in the turning of the legs and stretchers. The design of this settee is well integrated and reflects the interest in fine detail and contrasting finish that characterized fashionable taste in the Federal Period.

FANCY FORMS

On-the-spot observation is suggested by a detail from a tiny sketch made by the Baroness Hyde de Neuville (page 290). The view is of the porch of "Morice Ville," owned by Mr. and Mrs. Moreau, exiles from Bonaparte's France. On either side of the doorway are Windsor settees. The picture is a rare record of the way Windsor settees were used in early nineteenth-century America. They were probably left in this position during seasonable weather and moved indoors during winter months. The slab wooden benches visible at the corners of the porch were, on the other hand, probably left outdoors year-round.

The settees in this drawing are more simple than the example

DAN FARBER, PHOTOGRAPHER

Sepia Wash on Pencil
Detail: "The Moreau House."
By Baroness Hyde de Neuville
(c. 1779–1849), near
New Brunswick, New Jersey,
July 2, 1809. Inscribed
"Morice Ville/2 Juillet 1809."
H: 7″ L: 12¾″.
Museum of Fine Arts, Boston.

made by Letchworth, which is now owned by Independence National Historical Park. Yet because almost all Windsors are lightweight and easily moved, it is reasonable to suppose that the Letchworth settee could have been used indoors as well as on a porch, as shown in this drawing.

Windsors are known to have served many different uses. Sometimes they served in formal rooms together with elegant mahogany furniture. At other times they were moved to secondary chambers or used in kitchens or as lawn or garden furniture. The easy mobility of Windsors ensured that they were subject to any informal arrangement that the moment demanded.

Pair Windsor Armchairs
Philadelphia, Pennsylvania. c. 1800.
Signed: "I. B. Ackley" for John B. Ackley, Philadelphia Chairmaker.
Various woods painted black.
H: 38¾" W: 17" D: 19½".
The Independence National Historical Park, Philadelphia.

The maker of this pair of unusual chairs with Gothic-arched backs was established as early as 1790 on Front Street, next to the Delaware River in Philadelphia. The chairs show the maker's adaptability to changing fashions as the emphasis is upon linear movement of Federal taste rather than upon the tradition of boldly turned spindles and stretchers that had so long been a part of Windsor chairmaking through the eighteenth century.

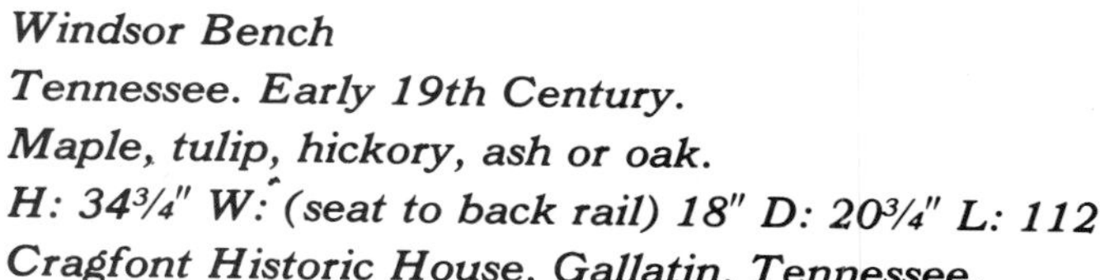

Windsor Bench
Tennessee. Early 19th Century.
Maple, tulip, hickory, ash or oak.
H: 34¾" W: (seat to back rail) 18" D: 20¾" L: 112".
Cragfont Historic House, Gallatin, Tennessee.

This ten-legged arrow-back Windsor bench was owned by General James Winchester of Cragfont in Gallatin, Tennessee. It is a popular Windsor type made in the early years of the nineteenth century—being essentially an elongated group of arrow-back Windsor chairs joined together and terminated at each end with arms. The arrow-back Windsor was easy to construct and simple to transport. Interchangeable parts could be mass produced and compactly packaged for long-distance shipping and easy assembly. For this reason, it is difficult to judge the origins of such a piece based on its place of original ownership.

JACK N. SHWAB, PHOTOGRAPHER

Windsor Settee
Delaware Valley, Philadelphia-Wilmington Area. c. *1800–1820.*
Tulip, hickory, maple.
H: 33⅝" L: 109" D: 20⅜".
Winterthur Museum.

The delicate, almost fragile-looking character of this settee reflects the Windsor chairmaker's consciousness of the Federal taste. Instead of robust, vase-shaped turnings, the legs, stretchers and back spindles are gently undulating in form and are scored to simulate bamboo. The visual effect corresponds perfectly with the lacelike plaster and composition ornament that decorated the architecture of stylish homes in the Adamesque or neoclassical taste. The settee was originally painted a medium blue-green color.

This bench has a history of ownership in Wilmington, Delaware, where it was treasured in the late nineteenth century by a local artist named Robert Shaw (1859–1912). It is the type of practical, yet smart-looking furniture which has endured as artistic furniture from the nineteenth century to the present. But when it was first made, such a bench held popular appeal as useful furniture for all Americans—urban or country, wealthy or of modest means. Its large size, capable of seating as many as five people, suggests that it was probably made on special order for a public building, possibly a meetinghouse.

GILBERT ASK, PHOTOGRAPHER

JACK N. SHWAB, PHOTOGRAPHER

Desk Chair
Southern. c. 1830.
Various woods: maple, tulip, hickory, ash or oak, painted black and stenciled (not original). H: 36" W: 18" D: 20" H: (seat) 21".
Traveller's Rest Museum House, Nashville, Tennessee.

The wear of the lowest front stretcher indicates that this chair has long served people whose habits were to keep their feet on the lowest rung. The chair seat is high, and therefore it would be logical to assert that this chair was used at a desk on a frame, elevating the sitter almost to a standing height. The chair is a type found throughout many of the Southern states where tall writing desks are also frequently found—particularly in North Carolina, Tennessee and Kentucky.

The design is a variant of the arrow-back Windsor. Its tapered and turned "Fancy Sheraton" legs are a sort produced in quantity in furniture factories from Maine to Georgia, the archetype factory of which was the Hitchcock establishment in Connecticut.

Writing Windsor Armchair
Tennessee. Early 19th Century.
Maple, tulip and other woods.
H: 40" W: (seat in front) 20½" W: (across back) 21½" W: (across top board) 21" D: (seat) 17" D: 27".
Cragfont Historic House, Gallatin, Tennessee.

Short arrow-backs on Windsors of this type were popular in Tennessee furniture of the early nineteenth century. This example was owned by the James Winchester family of Cragfont. In many ways the design of this piece is related to the shape of Cragfont's Windsor bench. Tack holes on the seat of the chair suggest that it was once covered and padded, as was often customary with Windsors.

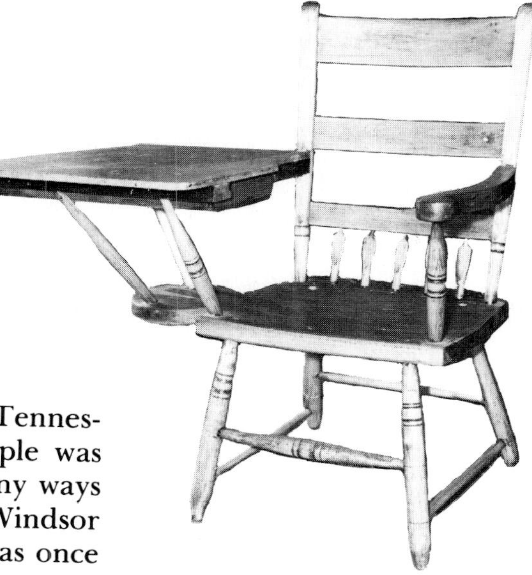

JACK N. SHWAB, PHOTOGRAPHER

Windsor Settee
Massachusetts. c. 1805–1820.
Maple, ash and other woods, painted black with gilt detail.
H: 33¾" L: 72⅛" D: 22⅝".
Given in Memory of Mary McKinley Southwell by Mrs. Frederic H. Sturdy, The Los Angeles County Museum of Art.

Thomas Sheraton's design influence can be seen in this painted or "fancy" Windsor from New England. The conjoined chair-back posts are made of bentwood. Like the arms they add a note of grace and comfort to the spare rectangular composition. The original rush seat is painted, as was the early custom. The front rail of the seat is slightly bowed forward at its center.

The split image of the three posts that are paired in the center of the settee is carried through to the seat only. Small buttonlike turnings that end the tops of each post suggest that the maker did not wish to waste any effort on extra detail. The sturdy bracing of the stretchers connecting the legs together has an effect almost like that of a cat's cradle.

All these elements result in a charmingly awkward grace of unusual appeal.

Arrow-Back Settee
Pennsylvania. c. 1820–1830.
Pine. H: 35" L: 84".
William Penn Memorial Museum, Harrisburg, Pennsylvania.

The lines of this settee translate an earlier fancy Sheraton style into the popular vocabulary of early nineteenth-century turned and painted softwood furniture. This type of furniture was made in small

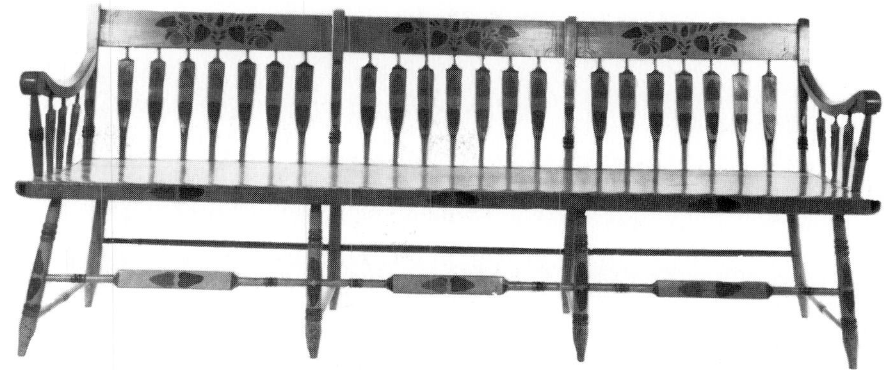

JACK N. SHWAB, PHOTOGRAPHER

shops, painted or decorated by local talent (sometimes with the use of stencils), and was easily transported by wagon. Western Pennsylvania produced much furniture of this variety. By the 1830s the style had traveled with people who moved westward into Ohio and Illinois, where many from Pennsylvania found fertile farmland and good trade along major waterways.

A favorite yellow color was used for the overall hue of this piece. Flat red and black leaves were painted on the twenty-one arrow-shaped flat braces of the back, spindles under each arm and on the legs and stretchers. Pinstriping accents the borders. The broad plank seat contrasts with the light bracing and turning of the other members. Strong, colorful and practical, this settee is visually expressive of the taste shared by well-to-do farm and small-town folk.

COASTAL NEW ENGLAND

Towns and small villages along the New England coast shared a special relationship with major urban centers due to the widespread trade network which brought country produce to the urban markets and, in turn, finished goods to the country. The trade network united Portsmouth, New Hampshire; Plymouth, Massachusetts; New London, Connecticut; and the minor ports of Long Island into a secondary level of urban centers which shared a certain value system and familiarity with new modes. Since many of these ports were located at the mouths of major rivers, they functioned as the transmitters of urban tastes to the hinterlands. In addition to the interpretations of urban furniture forms which they produced, such centers were also the focus of the sale of new designs which were manufactured in urban centers specifically for them. These secondary centers also attracted newly arrived provincial English craftsmen who introduced stylistic variants into the local idiom which were completely unrelated to what was going on in Boston, Newport or New York.

Mixing Table
New England, Coastal Massachusetts. 1740–1780.
Maple and other woods; painted top, marbelized gray-green.
H: 26½" W: 23½" L: 30".
Side Chairs
Newburyport, Massachusetts Area. c. 1770.
Maple, painted mahogany graining. H: 39½" W: 20" D: 19".
Collection of Mr. and Mrs. Bertram K. Little.

The free combination of contrasting elements seen in the table, such as the stiffly contoured legs and dainty but elegant turnings, joined with a hearty top displaying a playful use of paint simulating marble, is characteristic of the best work by country or provincial craftsmen in America.

The side chairs represent the work of a local craftsman whose work is quite distinctive in its assertive linear qualities. Like New England provincial paintings of the time, the chairs show some knowledge of fashionable style with their dynamic "Chippendale ears," but the retention of turned elements and overall stiffness of posture are provincialities that show an unwillingness to leave behind earlier traditions.

Tea Table
Boston, Massachusetts. c. 1770.
Mahogany and white pine.
H: 27¾" W: 32¼" D: 31⅜".
Museum of Fine Arts, Boston.

Armchair
Boston, Massachusetts. 1760–1780.
Mahogany, maple.
H: 41¼" W: 24½" D: 19".
Museum of Fine Arts, Boston.

Side Chair
Boston or Salem, Massachusetts. 1760–1780.
Mahogany, maple, white pine.
H: 37⅝" W: 22" D: 17¾".
Museum of Fine Arts, Boston.

The sculptural qualities of this mahogany furniture made in the Massachusetts Bay area represent the most sophisticated taste of pre-Revolutionary New England.

Two arrangements around tables emphasize the basic differences between country and urban furniture in America about the time of the American Revolution.

The mahogany turret-top tea table, side chair and upholstered armchair are from Boston and Salem. Their surfaces are unpainted and rely on the rich gleam of carved mahogany detail contrasted against imported damask cloth. The effect is sculptural and glittering. By contrast, the country group (a mixing table and pair of side chairs) are grained with paint to simulate richer materials than they were made with. The sharp silhouettes of the chair and table attract attention through their distinctive, crisp edges. Line and color are emphasized by the country furniture in the same way as provincial portrait painters limned faces; the important effects were gained by line and color.

YANKEE BACKCOUNTRY

In eighteenth- and early nineteenth-century America, most New England towns were small enough to walk through within a few minutes—bringing the traveler to the country. Merchants and shopkeepers were aware of the special tastes of country customers, and they advertised goods which would appeal because of their color or usefulness. The easy exchange that existed between country and town before the age of industrialization makes defining "urban" as opposed to "rural" furniture production difficult. The intricate interdependence of goods from both regions meant that town craftsmen produced for a country market. Conversely, rural craftsmen brought their wares to town. So "country" was more a state of mind than a place of production.

The country taste took pleasure in bright, contrasting colors, flat patterns, emphatic ornament and strong silhouettes. By contrast, sculptural form and restrained, controlled ornament pleased the sophisticated urban eye with its less flamboyant effects.

Crown Armchair
Milford, Connecticut. 1742.
Made by David Sanford (1709–1751).
Paper label under stay rail reads: "Made by David Sa . . . Milford, X' 1742." Maple, ash. H: 44¼" W: 23" D: 15½" H: (seat) 16½".
Museum of Fine Arts, Boston.

Banister-back chairs were made in every English colony of the North American mainland and the Caribbean throughout much of the eighteenth century. Many permutations of form and decoration were possible within this restricted format.

This Milford crown chair, so named for its pediment-like crest with heart-shaped cutout, is restrained and classical. In its judicious use of well-turned urns, vases and reels, it possesses large areas which are left plain, the better to set off the ornament which is present. The black-and-gold decoration dates from the mid-nineteenth century and betrays the influence of the Hitchcock chair style. The turned feet are missing.

The chair's maker, David Sandford, was the first apprentice of Andrew Durand (1701–1791), the founder of the Milford crown chairmaking tradition, a highly successful, well-equipped craftsman by country standards.

Crown Great Chair
Perhaps Milford, Connecticut. 1745–1755.
Attributed to John Miles (1708–1755).
Maple, ash.
H: 49⅜" W: 24¾" D: 16½".
Stratford Historical Society.

The streamlined, racy silhouette of this example shows the provincial chairmaker at his best. The complex, fussy carving and turned ornament of London cane chairs are here reduced to an economical formula which is nevertheless compelling. The upward sweep of the shaped arms and the calculated balance of the pediment-like crest with heart cutout are skillful passages of design.

Stand
Newport, Rhode Island. 1760–1780.
Cherry. H: 26" W: 14".
A Chester County Collection.

GEORGE FISTROVICH, PHOTOGRAPHER

Sinuous, snakelike feet and a crisply turned urn set low in the shaft's center of gravity are features characteristic of Newport work. While not the most sophisticated of eighteenth-century Rhode Island designs, the stand has a sturdy quality that is most appealing. The entasis of the column on the shaft and the sprightly lift of the legs suggest that the stand's maker was well versed in the rules of classical architecture. Small stands with circular or polygonal tops are one of the more fascinating forms of eighteenth- and nineteenth-century furniture; they were made over a wide area and often display as much regional diversification as chair forms.

High Chest
Probably Coastal Massachusetts or Connecticut. 1738.
Signed "RLC" and dated 1738.
Pine, oak, maple.
H: 65" W: 47½" D: 24".
Shelburne Museum, Shelburne, Vermont.

Paralleling the styles set in major seaport towns, craftsmen in smaller settlements caught the basic ideas of their urban counterparts and then developed their furniture in a way which pleased their own less sophisticated eyes.

In its form, this painted high chest or chest on frame was inspired by the William and Mary style popular during the first quarter of the eighteenth century. But it is dated and initialed "RLC 1738." This probably represents the date it was made, not a later date of painting as has been supposed. Its rich ochre background color is handsomely figured with pinwheels, vines and tulips.

Kitchen Dresser
New England. 18th Century.
Chestnut and pine with wrought-iron hinges.
H: 73" W: 31" D: 18½".
Old Sturbridge Village, Sturbridge, Massachusetts.

This free-standing kitchen dresser has a handsome shape to its front and a generous overhanging hood at its top. It is an eloquently simple piece of furniture made out of broad sawn boards, shaped and nailed together. The plank door has wrought-iron hinges with spearhead ends.

Chest with Drawer
Massachusetts. c. 1800.
Inscribed "Jabez Bigelow Suth Groton."
Pine, painted with broad graining. H: 31¾" W: 36¼" D: 18".
Gift of Jean Lipman, Phoenix Art Museum.

Dramatic patterns of brown paint on this chest transcend a mere imitation of exotic woods. Among the country painters and stainers who practiced this vigorous sort of work, satisfaction seems to have come in the manipulation of paint for its own sake rather than for the imitation of grain. The patterns are large and applied directly, almost like finger paint. Such work has strong appeal today to those who perceive the vigor of the abstract expressionism of country graining.

KOPPES, PHOTOGRAPHER

Chamber or Necessary Armchair
Connecticut, Perhaps Hartford Area. 1800–1820.
Cherry. H: 41¾" W: 23¾" D: 18¼".
Museum of Fine Arts, Boston.

A provocative design, this chair demonstrates how cumulative stylistic statements evolved in rural areas where local joiners were loath to discard an accepted formula. The rounded contour of the rear posts and crest rail evokes the Queen Anne style, updated with Chippendale ears. The tapered legs and delicate splat with carved details are Federal features; this form of back was especially popular in Hartford and Providence.

The deep skirt, embellished with a carved shell, relates the chair's functions; a chamber pot, generally a pewter one, would have been kept in a frame underneath the slip-seat.

High Chest
Probably New Hampshire. 1760–1790.
Maple, white pine. H: 89¼" W: 40⅜" D: 19⅛".
The Bayou Bend Collection,
The Museum of Fine Arts, Houston.

The striped graining of maple wood was selected for its decorative effect by the maker of the later bonneted high chest of drawers. Not content with the busy pattern of the graining, its maker further enriched the surface with carved pinwheels and fans. The unusually active profile of the skirt adds to the visual excitement. There is a logic to the design of the piece, but not the logic of an urban craftsman who would have been content with a single center shell and a much simpler profile of the skirt. For the country craftsman, proliferation of ornament meant improvement of style.

Desk and Bookcase on Frame
Connecticut. 1750–1800.
Cherry, pine. H: 82¾" W: 35½" D: 19¾".
Greenfield Village and the Henry Ford Museum, Dearborn, Michigan.

Rural New England joiners often built low case pieces (see Dunlap chest-on-chest, page 305). As a result, they devised many forms of short "crooked" or cabriole legs to fit the frame's low format. This fairly straightforward version of a high-style urban desk is embellished with carved details characteristic of the Connecticut River Valley: pinwheels, hexfoils and abstract plant stalks crowned with miniature pediment volutes. Many of these same ornaments are to be seen on "frontispieces," or doorways on houses built between Hartford, Connecticut, and Deerfield, Massachusetts.

RURAL NEW HAMPSHIRE DUNLAP FURNITURE

Furniture made by members of the Dunlap family of rural New Hampshire is unmistakable in design. The vocabulary of ornament includes deeply carved shells, *S*-shaped scrolls for the skirts of case pieces, interlaced basket-weave cornices and unusual bead and dog-tooth classical detail on moldings.

Major John Dunlap (1746–1792) was the central figure in the family. He worked in Goffstown and later Bedford, New Hampshire, just west of Manchester. His brother, Samuel Dunlap (1752–1820), worked with him at carpentry and cabinetmaking, and his four sons were also woodworkers. Although the Dunlaps were located in small towns which had no more than two hundred houses, they worked at a time when the country economy was expanding and woodworking skills were needed. Over the years, a total of fifty-two men were employed by the Dunlaps in various capacities.

Although they lived not far from the Merrimack River, the Dunlaps took little advantage of this transportation resource. Their work was not connected to mercantile trade, which would have exposed them to a broader knowledge of urban styles. Their operation was local, land-locked and tradition-based. Their work included the making of chairs, carved cabinetwork, carpentry and finished woodwork for room interiors. The paneled interiors they made, done at a time when paneled walls were out of fashion in metropolitan centers, often matched the detail of their furniture.

Local woods were used—maple, pine, birch and sometimes cherry—and were originally painted and grained to imitate more expensive woods. Spanish brown, mahogany color and green and orange stains are mixtures recorded in Dunlap family accounts.

DELMORE WENZEL, PHOTOGRAPHER

Side Chair
New Hampshire. 1770–1790.
By Major John Dunlap (1746–1792).
Cherry. H: 44" W: 22" D: 15".
Collection of Mr. and Mrs. Stanley Stone.

Rarely does a country chair survive with its original needlework slipseat. This example also bears its original dark-green paint, which emphasizes its powerful silhouette. The carved shell motif, which was used on chairs made in Boston, Newport and Philadelphia, is exaggerated in scale on the skirt and crest rail in a way consistent with other pieces of furniture made by the Dunlap school of craftsmen. Evincing a knowledge of the Chippendale style, Dunlap also exaggerated the ears of the chair, attaching them to the large crest with a thin connection. The vase-shaped splat of the back is opened with sharply cut flourishes like the *S*-shaped holes on the face of a violin.

Despite the carving and the planed molding on the legs, stretchers and back stiles, the power of the chair comes from its striking silhouette. Its arresting presence is essentially linear in effect.

Chest-on-Chest
Found in Bedford, New Hampshire. c. 1780.
By Major John Dunlap (1746–1792).
Maple. H: 83½" W: 40½" D: 20".
New Hampshire Historical Society, Concord, New Hampshire.

A consistency of style in the design of this case piece and the side chair suggests the same hand at work. Both pieces have flaring ears. The shells on chair and chest are carved in the same way. There is a handsome linearity to both works that is distinctive of the Dunlap school and characteristic of country artisans' work in general.

Major Dunlap understood the importance of finishing the terminal ends of furniture—top and bottom—with ornament to catch the eye.

Chest of Drawers
New Hampshire. 1780–1800.
Attributed to the Dunlaps.
Birch and maple. H: 34½" W: 38¾" D: 23½".
The Currier Gallery of Art, Manchester, New Hampshire.

This four-drawer chest bears the distinctive tooth and bead detail on its skirt molding that is the sign of Dunlap style. In Major John Dunlap's cyphering book there are a number of diamondlike designs that are related to the detail shown here. Diamondlike designs were found not only on furniture but on architectural interiors as well.

Watercolor
By Joseph Warren Leavitt.
Loudon, New Hampshire. 1825.
Watercolor on paper. H: 7″ W: 9″.
Collection of Nina Fletcher Little.

The picture is a summary of naive or provincial tastes—brightly colored and strongly patterned, with a considerable misunderstanding of academic rules of proportions, perspective and color harmony. These violations of academic rules add much to the appeal of the picture. Made to commemorate Lafayette's visit to America, the overscaled figure on the right is presumably he. Sally Emery Morse sits beside the fireplace and Moses Morse is seen in the background in what is supposed to be their farmhouse.

While the figures are not in scale with the setting, the interior is believable. Dramatic contrasts of brilliant color have a logic of their own. The checkerboard floor carries out the affection for pattern that is emphasized by the stenciled wall and freehand painted overmantle. The bright red outline of woodwork is picked up in the color of the unusual low desk and bookcase behind Mr. Lafayette.

The painting suggests that color in the hands of a naive designer was not simply a matter of whimsy, but rather part of a total scheme which we fail fully to understand today because of the separation of furniture and furnishings from their original environment. The Morse home in New Hampshire has not been located. The picture came to the present owner from the great-granddaughter of Moses Morse, having never been out of the family.

Desk and Bookcase
New England. 1760–1810.
Mahogany, white pine. H: 60⅞" W: 41¼" (at cornice) D: 20¼" (at feet).
Colonial Williamsburg, Williamsburg, Virginia.

The short rectangular bookcase section of this desk with its wavy paneled doors is almost identical in form to the painted desk pictured in the watercolor of the interior of the Moses Morse House. Its short upper section is uncommon and suggests that the maker adapted a tall-desk design to a low-ceilinged room.

By changing conventional proportions to fulfill practical needs, American cabinetmakers drifted stylistically from English and European fashions. This piece, made of mahogany, was probably never painted the bright red color shown in the Moses Morse interior. Yet it is but a step away from suiting the interior of a highly patterned and colorful country home.

JOSEPH ADAMS, PHOTOGRAPHER

Armchair
East Hampton, Long Island, New York. 1790–1820.
Nathaniel Dominy V (1770–1852).
Maple, painted or stained dark brown to simulate mahogany.
H: 44" W: 26" D: 20".
Mr. and Mrs. Morgan MacWhinnie;
Society for the Preservation of Long Island Antiquities.

Lively movement in all parts accounts for this chair's striking linearity. Commonly identified as a "fiddleback," the splat derived its basic silhouette from Chippendale-style designs, which had opened or pierced backs instead.

The bow-shaped crest was also inspired by Chippendale furniture, but in this rural piece the crest was not integrated in a sophisticated urban manner. Instead, it rests on the top of the chair like a bird that has just landed. This treatment is naive. But for the rural Dominy craftsman (and his client) the arrangement of parts seemed completely logical. With each new wave of style change the rural craftsman simply adapted the most salient new features to update his basic traditional model for a chair which had been handed down to him by previous generations of craftsmen. By the time this chair was made, the Federal Period (with its emphasis upon lightness of structure and ornament) prompted Nathaniel Dominy V to make the parts of the chair sprightly and thin. It is this slimness combined with the curved elements of splat and crest that make the chair an unusually beautiful example of rural craftsmanship.

Tall Case Clock
East Hampton, Long Island, New York. 1779.
By Nathaniel Dominy IV (1737–1812).
Walnut, pine; pewter dial. H: 87⅜" W: 17½" D: 8⅝".
The Weir Collection.

COURTESY OF THE SOCIETY FOR THE PRESERVATION OF LONG ISLAND ANTIQUITIES

The tall, spare design of this clock case is characteristic of the simple functionalism of a rural cabinetmaker's work. Enrichments to the surface are few. Its simplicity is its beauty. Many other clocks made by Dominy family members were even more elongate and severely plain.

A few simple moldings, some arches and a handsome silhouette constitute the means by which the linearity of the clock is enhanced. Crowning its top is a hint of a double scroll or swan-neck broken pediment—a mere gesture of familiarity with urban style.

This is the earliest and one of the most elaborate tall case clocks of its type made by Nathaniel Dominy IV. He was a major figure in a family of talented craftsmen living on the eastern end of Long Island at East Hampton. The Dominy family supplied the local village needs for cabinetwork and other services, but also delivered their goods across Long Island Sound by boat to New Haven, Old Saybrook and Stonington, and up the Connecticut River. In addition to cabinetmaking, the Dominy family earned a living by farming, carting goods, raising sheep, clock and watch repairing, and other trades in a barter economy. This clock was made for Nathaniel Seaman of Jerusalem, Long Island. Its eight-day movement keeps accurate time and powers a day-of-the-month indicator and a day-of-the-week hand on the dial face.

Shops for clockmaking and woodworking, which served three generations of the Dominy family, survived with accumulated goods and tools attached to the family house in East Hampton. In 1957 negotiations were opened for removal of the tools, materials and shops to the Winterthur Museum in Delaware where they now present the most accurate and complete picture of rural American workshops in any institution.

Chest with Drawer
Oyster Bay or Hempstead, Long Island, New York. 1710–1750.
Pine. H: 38½" W: 41" D: 19".
Society for the Preservation of Long Island Antiquities.

This double-paneled chest with its lift top and single drawer derives not from Dutch taste, but from English traditions on Long Island. Over thirty-five chests of this form are known with histories from the area. None from the Hudson River Valley or other areas of heavy Dutch settlement have been found. This chest form remained popular on Long Island for about a hundred years, starting around 1710. Chests of this type were almost always painted—usually red, blue or green.

THE CONTINENTAL TRADITION

On Long Island, New York, and in New Jersey and Delaware Dutch immigrants found a coastal countryside very much like the low countries of their homelands. They settled there early and resisted change over many generations. This wardrobe or *Kas (Kasten)* is the most characteristic piece of Dutch furniture from the New Jersey area. It could have been made in any of the Dutch settlements of the East coast. It is the low countries' equivalent of the French *armoire* and serves as a place to store linens and clothing, folded on shelves.

The large-scale cornice that overhangs the top of this impressive piece reflects the Baroque style of seventeenth-century Dutch art.

Wardrobe
New Jersey. c. 1750.
Pine.
H: 78" W: 76" D: 28½".
The Newark Museum.

Side Chair
Pennsylvania or Maryland. 1750–1775.
Walnut.
H: 40¼" W: (seat at front) 19½" W: (seat at rear) 15¾"
D: 13" H: (seat) 17¼".
A Chester County Collection.

Although made with neatly molded stiles and rails and a fielded panel, this side chair harks back to seventeenth-century Farthingale chairs, which were either turned and upholstered or joined and carved with elaborate designs. This particular version of the general type probably had its origins in plainer chairs made in the north and west counties of England, where many of Pennsylvania's early settlers originally came from. As is often the case with survivals of earlier designs, this chair's compositional integrity is dependent on carefully calculated proportions rather than on surface decoration.

Slat-Back Armchair
Delaware River Valley. 1750–1850.
Maple.
H: 46$\frac{1}{16}$" W: 22⅞" D: 17".
Museum of Fine Arts, Boston.

Slat-back chairs were the single most characteristic form of seating furniture used in southern New Jersey, Pennsylvania and Delaware during the entire eighteenth century and the first half of the nineteenth century. The type was first introduced by German settlers about 1700, but apprentices soon spread the design to English makers. The form quickly spread from urban shops in Philadelphia to many makers in outlying regions.

A number of index features can be noted: extremely lean components; flattened, rolled arms with a distinctive, squared-off undercutting; arched slats; and oversize ball feet and stretchers. The sharp taper of the rear legs at their bottoms is an early feature which generally did not appear in most other turned chair forms until the Federal Period.

The form was remarkable for its longevity in a relatively unchanged state. Some were being made by hand as late as the 1920s.

Slat-Back Side Chair
Delaware River Valley. 1750–1850.
Maple. H: 47½″ W: 18½″ D: 14⅝″.
Museum of Fine Arts, Boston.

Five-Stretcher Table or Desk
New Jersey. c. 1750.
Walnut. H: 29¾″ W: 42″ D: 23½″.
Collection of Mrs. Charles L. Bybee.

Conservative in design for its time, this table is an excellent example of a type popular in the Delaware Valley throughout much of the eighteenth century. Rarely is any historical information known about such a piece, but in this instance, pencil inscriptions within the drawer give a clue to its original owner, brother of the famous Quaker diarist, John Woolman:

> this desk belonged to
> asher woolman in about
> the year of 1750
> and has always been in this house (except a few yrs that his father had it at his home in the village) was purchased . . . Mother in the yr of 1879 . . . Mary . . . (if no heirs) . . . . go to Gertrude to have it . . . to the Woolman who would prize it . . .
>
> G.W. LEEDS
>
> At Gertrude's death to go to Mary if no heirs then to some one of the Woolman.
>
> G. W. LEEDS

The form of the table suggests slow-to-change tastes of the mid-eighteenth century. The table bears its original finish and wrought-iron arrow keyhole escutcheon. At one time the drawer may have had two teardrop brass pulls instead of the present wooden knobs.

RICHARD CHEEK, PHOTOGRAPHER

THE DELAWARE VALLEY

Non-Germanic settlers in the Delaware Valley maintained woodworking traditions of framing and turning that were familiar to English Quakers from the North Country, Wales and Ireland. Ease of trade and transport by water facilitated the spread of new styles into the countryside—a craftsman or merchant from Wilmington, Delaware, could sail by boat to Philadelphia and back on the same day. Despite this direct connection with the major center of trade and culture in the area, craftsmen in small towns tended to remain conservative in their styles of joinery and chairmaking.

GEORGE FISTROVICH, PHOTOGRAPHER

Inlaid Box
Chester County, Pennsylvania.
Dated 1740.
Walnut with tulip bottom; brass escutcheon plate.
H: 7½" W: 13¼" D: 9".
Harold Chalfond Collection.

With an unusual enthusiasm for light-colored wood inlay, the maker of this box covered its surfaces with whimsical designs laid out with small arcs of the compass. For each arc a corresponding center punchmark was left by the opposite end of the dividers. This accounts for many small black dots across the surface of the box. Clearly visible in this photograph are the dots in the center of the letter *C,* and within the two circles that form the letter *S.* Tulips and stars, pendant buds and treelike fronds are arranged in a profuse, abstracted line across the sides and top. Such copious ornament must have had special meaning since the initials and numbers suggest an important date and an owner. The lock indicates it held valuable contents. The box was, perhaps, a small treasury for personal and valued articles, such as deeds, wills and other private papers, and could have contained money as well as other small valuables. The box is a rare and splendid work, unusually ornate and wonderfully solid. It almost looks like the sturdy stone and brick houses that grace the Chester County countryside.

Armchair
Philadelphia or Chester County, Pennsylvania. 1690–1710.
Walnut, tulip, poplar. H: 47½" W: 23".
A Chester County Collection.

This chair once stood in "Primitive Hall," ancestral seat of the Pennock family. The chair is representative of late seventeenth- and early eighteenth-century rural Quaker taste, and of Welsh joinery traditions transmitted to Pennsylvania in the 1680s.

GEORGE FISTROVICH, PHOTOGRAPHER

Armchair
Pennsylvania. 1700–1730.
Walnut.
H: 44" W: (seat) 21¾" D: (seat) 15½" H: (seat) 17½".
A Chester County Collection.

The space defined by the scroll and cusp contour of the crest rail and original arch cut out of the back panel give this chair a sense of great verve. The rich variety of turned ornament on the lower sections of the frame carry through the active movement and unify the composition.

GEORGE FISTROVICH, PHOTOGRAPHER

Walnut Wainscot Armchair
Delaware Valley. c. 1750.
Walnut. H: 59" W: (seat front) 21" D: 20¼" H: (seat) 16".
A Chester County Collection.

GEORGE FISTROVICH, PHOTOGRAPHER

This armchair traditionally has been known as "the signer's chair," because according to an old hand-written label once attached to the rear of its crest rail it was owned by Caesar Rodney, a Delaware signer of the Declaration of Independence. Much of Rodney's personal furniture was in the Chippendale style, following the mode of current Philadelphia fashions, so why Rodney might have used this chair is a mystery. This sort of chair was popular in Chester County where the Quakers settled early in the eighteenth century. The crown and inverted ears of the crest are characteristic of Chester County chairs made throughout the first half of the eighteenth century.

Wainscot chairs of this sort had been produced in England a full two centuries before "the signer's chair" was made. The conservative nature of Quaker life tended to preserve old-world taste and habits, especially in rural areas, long after the popularity of a form had died out abroad or in more fashion-conscious towns such as Philadelphia, New York or Boston. The framed back and seat display sturdy skills of the joiner, and the lathe-turned members, the skills of the turner. With the exception of the front stretcher, which has been restored, the chair is in its original condition.

Side Chair
1730–1760.
Signed "IN" on both seat boards and on left rear leg.
Red oak. H: 39½" W: (seat front) 18" D: 13" H: (seat) 17¾".
A Chester County Collection.

GEORGE FISTROVICH, PHOTOGRAPHER

This is an exceptionally rare instance of the use of oak in early furniture from Pennsylvania. It differs from its Chester County counterparts in the use of a gently curved, yoke crest rail and wide, urn-shaped splat. Another rare feature is the use of a shoe into which the splat is toed.

GEORGE FISTROVICH, PHOTOGRAPHER

Armchair
Perhaps Lancaster County, Pennsylvania. 1740–1760.
Cherry. H: 41½" W: (front) 22¼" W: (rear of seat) 19¼"
D: 17¼" H: (seat) 17".
A Chester County Collection.

Few chairs have greater charm than examples showing the cumulative influence of two or more successive styles. The framed and turned elements of this one recall the William and Mary style, while the rounded crest rail, shaped splat and outswept arms with handsome incised scrolls are derived from the Queen Anne. Although made in a rural center, the chair displays a number of "advanced" joinery techniques, notably tenons which penetrate through the side seat rails where they join the rear stiles.

GEORGE FISTROVICH, PHOTOGRAPHER

Side Chair
Chester County, Pennsylvania. 1710–1740.
Walnut. H: (back) 42¾" W: (front of seat) 19"
D: 13" H: (seat) 17½".
A Chester County Collection.

Another variation of the Chester County joined chair, this example displays the influence of the William and Mary style in its slats, which function in the same way as split banisters. It was probably intended to be provided with a stuffed cushion for the seat. Such a cushion would alter the chair's proportions considerably, masking the lower horizontal opening of the back and uniting the base with the back. The subtle cant of the back was achieved through a significant cutting away of the plank from which the rear stiles were sawn.

Corner Cupboard
Hackensack, New Jersey. c. 1800–1815.
Pine. H: 90" W: 64" D: 34¼".
The Newark Museum.

Exhibiting the fervor for small-scale shallow detail in Federal America, this corner cupboard seems stylistically allied to the bright-cut silver of that era. Its overembellished, eye-dazzling richness betrays the design sense of a country workman's enthusiastic adaptation and misunderstanding of architectural effects of urban design.

JOHN GILL, PHOTOGRAPHER

Desk and Bookcase
New Jersey. 1750–1760.
Walnut. H: 93" W: 41" D: 24".
Gloucester County Historical Society, Woodbury, New Jersey.

The maker of this piece probably lived in west New Jersey, a step away from Philadelphia, the center of style. He kept his work simple and direct. He worked in walnut, a reasonable substitute for mahogany, and picked his woods in such a way as to show maximum effect of the grain on the bookcase doors and drawer fronts.

All parts of this cabinetwork are relatively plain but in the best taste and show a masterful hand. The desk interior reveals the secret joy of the piece when the lid is opened to display the row of five handsome carved shells, a pair of fluted pilasters and a row of shaped drawers. It is not an unusual arrangement. Similar works are found throughout the colonies.

Ratchet Candlestand
Delaware Valley. 1710–1740.
Walnut.
H: 26". Diameter across grain: 14¼". Diameter with grain: 14½".
A Chester County Collection.

GEORGE FISTROVICH, PHOTOGRAPHER

This candlestand with trestle base and ratchet mechanism superbly performs its intended function of raising or lowering a support for a candle. The design of the candlestand makes it a satisfying work of art in the abstract sense: its various parts are interestingly divided and balanced. The heavy, nicely shaped base leaves no question that the piece is stable. The top is sufficiently broad to catch the unavoidable spatter of wax characteristic of eighteenth-century tallow candles. It is hard to say whether this is a town or country piece; it could well have been used in either place. The temptation today is to think of such pieces as suitable to pine-paneled rooms of rural character, but this notion is probably one derived from collectors' decorating impulses of the 1930s rather than from the actual practice of the 1730s.

Child's Chest
Lebanon County, Pennsylvania.
1840–1850.
Pine. H: 13" W: 19¼" D: 11".

Child's Rocking Chair
Lebanon County, Pennsylvania.
1825–1835.
Pine. H: 22¾" W: 12¼" D: 11½".

William Penn Memorial Museum, Harrisburg, Pennsylvania.

Painted furniture of the "common sort" made in rural Pennsylvania is handsomely represented by these two grained pieces. The turnings of both examples show an awareness of neoclassical form, though surely not a thorough understanding of late Sheraton vocabulary.

Such commonplace vernacular furniture permeated much of the farmland and backcountry of rural America through most of the nineteenth century and much of the twentieth.

"Palatines" was the name they were referred to on ship lists when coming to this country. More recently they have been incorrectly called the "Pennsylvania Dutch" *(Pennsylfawnisch Deitsch*—the peasant version of Pennsylvania *Deutsch).* The flood of newcomers to southeastern Pennsylvania from the Palatinate by the mid-eighteenth century was enormous. The newcomers emigrated from Frankfurt and Strassburg, from Bonn and Mainz, throughout the Rhine Valley, bringing with them memories of homeland and traditional ways of making furniture that were preserved in the New World for generations.

The tulip motif was a favorite ornamental device. It had been introduced in Augsburg in the sixteenth century and, like the heart motif, became internationally favored as an ornamental device by the following century.

The Pennsylvania Germans have preserved their traditions intact to the present day. Their furniture, like their architecture, is massive and richly ornamented with folk motifs. Hardwood furniture of oak, walnut and cherry was usually paneled and inlaid and unadorned with paint. Softwood furniture was usually painted with bright polychromed decoration. Carnations, hearts, birds, tulips, stars and geometric signs were favorite devices—symbols of love, prosperity, fertility and regeneration.

Schrank
Lancaster County, Pennsylvania.
Dated 1766.
Made by D. I Mertz.
Walnut, poplar.
H: 89" W: 84" D: 30".
William Penn Memorial Museum,
Harrisburg, Pennsylvania.

This monumental *Schrank* or wardrobe belonged to a seventeenth-century tradition of unpainted walnut furniture which was brought to Pennsylvania by Germanic settlers after 1720. In addition to elaborate moldings, panels and carved detail, this example sports inlaid work of sulfur mixed in wax or putty. The inlay identifies the original owners and the maker, "D. I. Mertz."

Schrank
Lancaster County, Pennsylvania.
Dated February 17, 1768.
Walnut.
H: 89½" W: 85¾" D: 30⅝".
Winterthur Museum.

A second Mertz product, made for Emanuel Herr and his wife, this *Schrank* demonstrates the consistency of these designs and the formality of the tradition of *Wachseinlegen* (literally "wax inlay"). Monumental storage furniture played an important part in marriage rituals, as the inscriptions of the sulfur inlay make apparent. These forms are perhaps the purest expressions of the Continental Baroque design tradition, which, in the case of English interpretations, was generally watered down in terms of both scale and absolute size. The space they occupy is enormous, and their projecting moldings make them appear even more massive than they in fact are.

Dower Chest with Two Drawers
Berks County, Pennsylvania. 1780–1800.
Pine and tulip poplar.
H: 28⅝" W: 52½" D: 23".
Metropolitan Museum of Art, New York.

The best-known products of the Pennsylvania German *Schreinerei* or joiners' shops were painted dower chests. The intricate decoration of their facades, sides and lids is directly related to the tradition of *Fraktur* or manuscript illumination.

Although certain features of this example, such as the "willow" brasses and the exact form of the unicorns, are derived from English sources, the conceptual framework of the chest is strictly Germanic. What could be more fitting for a dower chest than two unicorns, guardians of maidenhood, which stand watch over the very keyhole and the attendant lily of virtue?

Dower Chest
Rural Pennsylvania. c. 1800.
Attributed to the Rank family.
Pine and tulip.
H: 23½" W: 52" D: 22¾".
William Penn Memorial Museum, Harrisburg, Pennsylvania.

Pennsylvania Germans were fond of imagery. The tulip growing out of a vase has been a popular symbol of the resurrection and regeneration ever since the late Middle Ages in Northern Europe. In this instance the two painted panels surrounded by simulated graining are not identical. A contrast is drawn between open and closed flowers. This interchange is a fitting expression of virginity and marriage, just as the chest itself in its open or closed state was a similar emblem.

A chest of this sort was normally made for a girl at age eight or ten. Her handiwork, personal belongings, blankets and linen were stored in the chest in anticipation of marriage. At the time of marriage the chest and contents were loaded on the bridegroom's wagon as the couple moved to their own home and lands.

The chest was an important means of perpetuating traditions. It was a central artifact of a marriage. It contained not only material goods but record and filial memories. *Fraktur* wedding certificates, house blessings, baptismal records and other colorful paper and personal documents were frequently pasted underneath the lid.

Dower Chest
Lebanon County, Pennsylvania.
Inscribed "Christian Selser [Seltzer] 1775" on the right urn.
Pine. H: 23" W: 52" D: 23".
William Penn Memorial Museum, Harrisburg, Pennsylvania.

Jonestown, a village in Lebanon County, Pennsylvania, about twenty-three miles east of Harrisburg, is identified as the center of a school of ornamental painting represented by the decoration on this chest. However, the artist who did this work, Christian Seltzer, traveled freely about the Pennsylvania countryside, and his work, like pieces by other artists of the Jonestown school, is thus widely scattered.

Characteristic of Seltzer's work is the vase of flowers within a painted panel with foliate border. When the paint was still wet he scratched his name and date through the paint—probably with the sharpened end of the handle of a brush—to reveal the color of the ground below. A similar technique of scratch ornamentation, or *sgraffito,* was practiced by Pennsylvania German potters.

Dower Chest
Rural Pennsylvania. c. 1800.
Tulipwood. H: 29" W: 52" D: 25".
William Penn Memorial Museum,
Harrisburg, Pennsylvania.

The unusual geometry of the painted decoration results from a playful and imaginative use of the compass. Scribed arcs and segments of arcs are disguised in developing the patterns taken by the ornamental painting. Green, red, black and white—basic colors formed of earth pigments—create the rich effect of the facade.

Of all the pieces of Pennsylvania folk furniture, the dower chest is the most significant and the best known. Plain chests were made, but not for the young girl's dowry. Among Pennsylvania German folk, decorated chests were almost always a part of the material goods taken with a girl into marriage.

The Pennsylvania Germans called the dower chest an *ausschteier kischt.* They were popular in this country from the 1770s, or shortly before the American Revolution, to about 1815.

A linsey-woolsey coverlet conceals much of the frame of this daybed. Long after the daybed had passed out of fashion in urban centers, it persisted in Pennsylvania's farming communities. The heart-shaped cutout of the crest is an emblem that has been popular among European folk cultures since the Middle Ages.

Couch or Daybed
Pennsylvania. 1725–1800.
Tulip poplar, painted gray.
H: 35½" L: 75¼" D: 30".
Winterthur Museum.

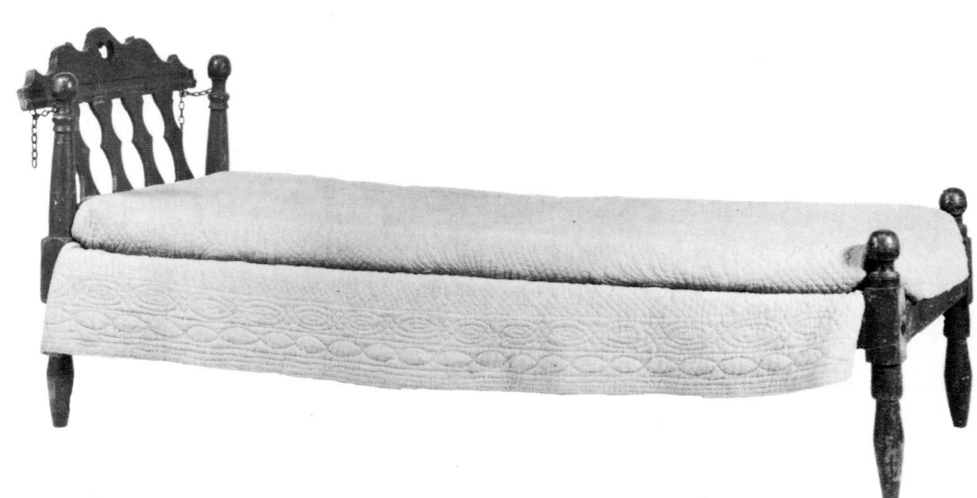

Schrank or Wardrobe
Berks County, Pennsylvania. 1780–1800.
Pine. H: 83" W: 75" D: 27".
William Penn Memorial Museum, Harrisburg, Pennsylvania.

Massive pine case pieces with bright green-, white- and red-painted decor were popular in Berks County. The panels of this *Schrank* were painted with a crumpled rag repeatedly pressed onto the surface to create a stippled effect.

Like most large case pieces in the Germanic tradition, this example can be knocked down in order to move it. Since few rooms had built-in closets for storing clothes or linens, wardrobes of this size were an essential fixture of a prosperous household.

Slant-Top Desk
Mahantango Valley, Schuylkill County, Pennsylvania. Dated 1834.
Painted pine and tulip.
H: 49⅛" W: 39" D: 19¾".
Winterthur Museum.

Flowers, stars, hearts, fans, birds and horses are painted in bright oranges, yellow and red on the dark-green background of this desk. These designs were applied freehand or with a stencil by the artist. Mahantango Valley furniture is frequently dated; the owner's name appears less often. No examples signed by the artist have been found.

This desk was owned by Jacob Maser (1812–1895), who was a furniture maker himself. On the basis of Maser's name, students have attributed related decorated furniture to his school; however, recent research suggests that these objects were not painted by Maser.

Typical of the workmanship of these and other pieces is the modification of Federal motifs and patterns and their incorporation with more traditional devices, such as tulips and hearts.

THE OLD SOUTH AND THE OLD SOUTHWEST

European settlers of the Southern colonies, which became the Old South, represented many cultural backgrounds. The Chesapeake Bay area, devoted to tobacco growing, was based on plantation living. The Carolina Low Country, the center of rice and indigo growing, acquired a seasonal rhythm, with wealthy planter families escaping from their malaria-infested plantations to Charleston, South Carolina, each summer, while slaves and hired workers tended the crops. Charleston had the most cosmopolitan society of the South, dominated by an elite even more Anglophile than that of Chesapeake Bay.

The Piedmont, or Back Country, ran along the Appalachian foothills from Pennsylvania to Georgia and was culturally heterogeneous with a strong middle class, to which German, Scots-Irish and Welsh ways all contributed.

After 1800, the European settlers began to push over the Appalachian Mountains into the Mississippi and Ohio River basins. The mixture of people from the three great cultural regions of the Old South, as well as from the Middle colonies, encouraged a broad proliferation of furniture styles, especially a Federal taste which came to be emblematic of life in the newly settled lands. Furniture made in Kentucky, Tennessee and Ohio often does not reflect a "frontier" aesthetic. Many of the cabinetmakers had served their apprenticeships in the East.

Table
Ebenezer, Georgia. 1735–1745.
Sweetgum, poplar, yellow pine.
H: 26" W: 32" D: 27".
Museum of Early Southern Decorative Arts, Winston-Salem, North Carolina.

This extremely important example of the earliest Germanic craftsmanship in the South was made by a member of the Salzburgers, a religious group led by the Reverend John Martin Bozius, who settled in Georgia in 1733. The four raked, ball-turned legs, joined by flat stretchers, relate directly to German design precedents in the South and also to similar tables fashioned by Germans working a few decades later in Pennsylvania. A distinction must be drawn between relatively direct German influence on the culture of the Piedmont Region and influences stemming from later migration of Germanic peoples down the Appalachian spine.

Side Table
Northeastern North Carolina. 1780–1800.
Walnut, yellow pine.
H: 29″ W: 37¼″ D: 27″.
Museum of Early Southern Decorative Arts, Winston-Salem, North Carolina.

Part of a large group of case pieces and tables by an as yet unidentified cabinetmaker working in the Halifax-Northampton-Bertie County area of North Carolina, this side table is constructed with elaborate joinery. The sides and drawer front are made up of many small, vertical blocks glued together and held with wooden pins. At the junction of the arched stretchers, a small ivory escutcheon or pin is set into the joint, another fine and curious detail found on examples by this maker. Also prominent are the unusual, heavy moldings used to demarcate the top and bottom of the apron. Why the maker chose to fashion such a diminutive object with such massive construction techniques is a mystery.

Country Cupboards and Dresers

Part of house construction, and usually incorporated in the finish work of framed and joined paneling, cupboards and dressers were not generally meant to be movable pieces of furniture. Many, especially corner cupboards, were built in. They were part of an entire furnishing scheme of architecturally finished rooms. But movable furniture they have become, as buildings have been demolished and collectible parts saved.

Corner Cupboard
"Wachovia" (now Winston-Salem, North Carolina). 1750–1770.
Probably Made by the Moravian Brethren's Workshops.
Pine. H: 83" W: 29" D: 34½".
Wachovia Historical Society, Winston-Salem, North Carolina.

Heavy fielded panels, heavy window muntins and wrought-iron rat-tail hinges are features associated with Germanic craftsmanship.

Beaufait or Corner Cupboard
Davidson County, North Carolina. 1818–1830.
Attributed to John Swisegood (1796–1874).
Walnut, hard yellow pine. H: 95½" W: 36½".
Collection of Miss Elizabeth Motsinger.

This subdued cupboard epitomizes Federal taste in the South. Made of carefully selected walnut lumber, it is ornamented with incised moldings and parti-colored stringing. The delicate, arched profile of the broken pediment is a common feature on Federal furniture made in rural America throughout the first half of the nineteenth century.

The cupboard's maker, John Swisegood, completed his apprenticeship in North Carolina about 1817, and in 1848 he moved to Illinois; his master, Mordica Collins, had moved to Indiana in about 1817. The migration of these craftsmen explains why there is such a strong affinity between the furniture of the South and the Midwest.

Slant-Top Desk on Frame
Tennessee. Early 19th Century.
Tulip stenciled and grained to look like mahogany.
H: 47¼" W: 34½" D: 27½".
Dr. and Mrs. Benjamin H. Caldwell, Jr.

A tall desk of a type identified with schoolmasters, this piece is distinguished by tall tapering legs framed with cross stretchers. While this example is simple enough to qualify as Federal vernacular furniture, its form belongs to a tradition well established for tall desks in eighteenth-century America. The ruled lines were used on this piece to achieve a visual effect that stringing would give on a more elaborate desk.

JACK N. SHWAB, PHOTOGRAPHER

Slant-Top Desk
Clarksville, Tennessee Area. c. 1800.
Walnut; secondary wood: tulip. H: 40½" W: 39" D: 21"
Dr. and Mrs. Benjamin H. Caldwell, Jr.,
on loan to the Traveller's Rest Museum House,
Nashville, Tennessee.

Three similar desks are known to have been made in or near Clarksville, Tennessee. With slim, tapering legs and a board framed for a hinged lid, this desk is severe on the outside, reserving its ornament within. Extremely popular in the Southern frontiers and found as far west as Texas, this form had a broad writing surface and a utilitarian arrangement of parts. Multiple reeding on the vestiges of letter drawers and document boxes and a gently scalloped board above the center drawer recalled the stagelike center ornament of high-style Eastern furniture of the mid-eighteenth century.

JACK N. SHWAB, PHOTOGRAPHER

Fall-Front Plantation Desk
"Maple Shade," Gallatin, Tennessee. 1840–1860.
Walnut. H: 57" W: 36" D: 21½".
Mr. and Mrs. Thomas K. Conner.

A box with a hinged fall-front upon a table are the elements that make up the design of this piece. The interior of the box is compartmented to accommodate the many ledger books, papers and accounts that were necessary in managing either a business or plantation. The turned legs are late Sheraton in style and are of the sort that were popular for business, farm and country furniture—in America as well as in England. John C. Loudon illustrated furniture related to this direct and practical work in his well-known book: *An Encyclopaedia of Cottage, Farm, and Villa Architecture and Furniture* (London, 1833). His plates were copied in mid-nineteenth-century America in the popular periodical *The Horticulturist.*

The hinged lid is cleverly elevated a few inches above the tabletop to provide support for the slanting top when open. This design eliminated the need for the pair of wooden slide supports or "lopers" which had been traditional for desk design throughout most of the eighteenth century and much of the early nineteenth century.

Cellarette
Athens, Georgia. 1790–1810.
Mahogany, hard yellow pine.
H: 33½" W: 24" D: 19¾".
Collection of Henry D. Green.

The severe, carefully proportioned cases of much Federal furniture from the South are ornamented solely with abstract vine and floral inlays. Perhaps the most handsome example of its form, this cellarette or bottle cabinet is equal in quality to equivalent forms made in major seaports. The inlays of furniture from the Georgia Piedmont are made of maple, holly or dogwood. Unlike much of the stringing and pictorial inlays used by urban cabinetmakers, these varieties appear to have been made by the local cabinetmaker himself, not by an inlay specialist.

VIC CURTIS STUDIO

JACK N. SHWAB, PHOTOGRAPHER

Fall-Front Desk
Sumner County, Tennessee. c. 1800.
Cherry and tulip.
H: 42½" W: 41" D: 20½".
Cragfont Historic House, Gallatin, Tennessee.

This desk originally belonged to General James Winchester who owned a massive stone house in Sumner County, named "Cragfont." Similarities between this desk and another with a Sumner County provenance suggest that they were probably both made locally by the same as yet unidentified cabinetmaker.

The form of the desk derives from Federal-Hepplewhite traditions which had been popular in cities on the East coast since the late eighteenth century. It was a style that depended for its effect more upon overall form than upon elaborate ornament. For this reason, the desk is an effective design, even though its ornament is restricted to its shaped skirt, french feet, scalloped pigeonholes and improved brass pulls and hardware.

Desk and Bookcase
Kentucky. c. 1800.
Mahogany and tulip.
H: 82½" W: 39" (at desk) D: 20½".
Cragfont Historic House,
Gallatin, Tennessee.

JACK N. SHWAB, PHOTOGRAPHER

This slant-front desk with its brilliantly figured mahogany front is an accomplished piece of cabinetwork. It was found near Lexington, Kentucky, and is presumed to be from that area. While ornamentation is restrained, there is a sure understanding of proportions and dramatic contrasts of materials.

The maker of this piece must have apprenticed in a shop on the East coast from which his craftsmanship and sense of design are surely derived. The muntin patterns in the glazed doors are similar to those illustrated in Hepplewhite's *Guide* of 1788.

Sugar Chest
Tennessee or Kentucky. Early 19th Century.
Cherry with tulip.
H: 39¾" W: 25¼" D: 19¼".
Dr. and Mrs. Benjamin H. Caldwell, Jr.

Sugar chests were a popular form of specialized furniture in the South. They frequently feature a hinged lid on top covering a large storage chamber divided within for brown and white sugar. Beyond these basic requirements, each chest has individual refinements. This example is supported on framed legs with a shallow drawer on the front. It is neatly constructed with fine dovetails and fitted with smartly shaped inlay around the keyholes.

✶

The serpentine shape of this sideboard, its handsomely figured mahogany veneer, delicate line inlay and smartly ornamented legs would make it a good match for furniture made on the Eastern seaboard during the Federal Period. Cabinetmaking skills at this time were so well developed in America, and movement of well-trained craftsmen was so commonplace as the country expanded, that the identification of local regional practices that clearly differentiate craftsmen of one center from another remains a problem.

Sideboard
Tennessee. Early 19th Century.
Mahogany and walnut with tulip.
H: 40¾" W: 65" D: 22½".
Dr. and Mrs. Benjamin F. Byrd, Jr.

JACK N. SHWAB, PHOTOGRAPHER

Clothes Press
Piedmont Area of North or South Carolina
(Found in Columbia, S.C.). Early 19th Century.
Mahogany with tulip. H: 60⅝" W: 48¾" D: 22".
Traveller's Rest Museum House, Nashville, Tennessee.

A neatly made piece of furniture of small proportions and precisely balanced symmetry, this press suggests more than a passing knowledge of the fashionable Federal design of New York City. The reeded edges of the top and front posts are echoed in the fine ring turnings of the delicate legs. Fine line edging surrounding the drawers and the brass lining of keyholes show the sense of finish that carries through the whole piece. Handsomely figured door panels open to reveal sliding shelves of a sort found in the best New York furniture. The brass knob pulls are original.

Desk and Bookcase
Knox County, Tennessee. c. 1800.
Walnut; secondary wood: tulip.
H: 94" W: 42" D: 21½".
Dr. and Mrs. Benjamin H. Caldwell, Jr.

Federal furniture made in Tennessee during the early years of the nineteenth century is sophisticated, well proportioned and refined. Connections with the Eastern seaboard remained important to cabinetmakers of consequence, for as cabinetmaker James G. Hicks of Nashville stated in his newspaper advertisement of 1812, his correspondence with Baltimore and Philadelphia assured customers of the newest fashions. He also added that his furniture was made in the neatest and best manner.

Such terms could be well applied to this piece. It is restrained, graceful, elegant and well constructed. Chamfered corners and a deeply shaped skirt are features of the object that harmonize with the curves of the "French" feet. Its overall effect is one of elegant practicality—a quiet beauty that grows upon, rather than overwhelms, the viewer.

JACK N. SHWAB, PHOTOGRAPHER

JACK N. SHWAB, PHOTOGRAPHER

Sideboard
Nashville, Tennessee Area.
Made by Captain James Hicks, 1815.
Mahogany and mahogany veneer;
secondary wood: tulip.
H: 49" W: 74" D: 24".
Mrs. William H. Wemyss; Loan
to "Fairview," Gallatin, Tennessee.

An ink inscription on a drawer bottom of this sideboard records: "January 24th 1815, Bought this Side Board of/ Capt James Hicks, price $129." Captain Hicks advertised as a cabinetmaker in the Nashville area from 1812 to 1815. In 1816 he moved to Kentucky.

The sideboard reveals that Hicks was quite familiar with the reeded and veneered furniture designs popular on the East coast from around 1810 through the teens. He had a sure sense of design—using the bowed pattern of the front of the sideboard as a device to echo the arch of the backboard above and the apron in the center below. It would seem perfectly reasonable to suggest that Hicks may have obtained his skills and training in Philadelphia, where similar furniture was being produced in quantity.

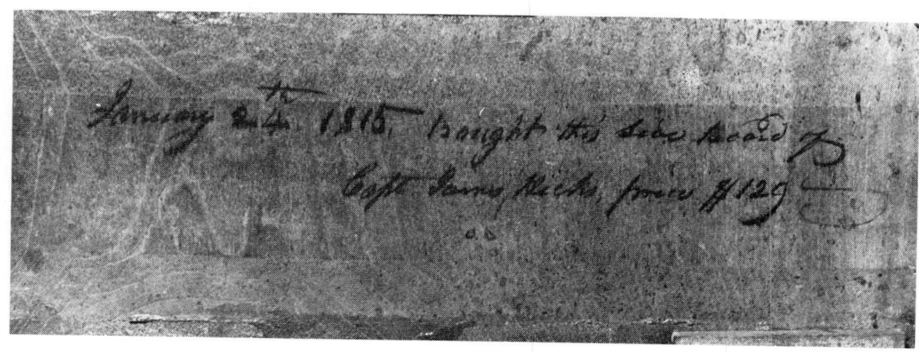
January 24th 1815, Bought this Side Board of
Capt James Hicks, price $129

Catawba Dining Room
Welling (Western), North Carolina.
Early 19th Century.
Museum of Early Southern Decorative Arts, Winston-Salem, North Carolina.

Backcountry taste of the Piedmont South is magnificently represented in this reconstructed interior from a two-storey brick house built for the Perkins family on the Catawba River in western North Carolina. An inscription dates the house as built in 1811. The paint is original and is signed by M. J. Cocker. The marbelized chimney breast and painted woodwork show how a country housewright interpreted the neoclassical style which had been developed by the Adam brothers in England more than fifty years before.

Simple furniture complements the rural character of this room. The dropleaf table from Piedmont, North Carolina, circa 1800, is walnut with a large maple inlay in the shape of a fan. The Windsor chairs bear the label of William Pointer, Richmond, Virginia, circa 1800. The desk-and-bookcase from the Lincoln-Gaston County area of Piedmont, North Carolina, was made of cherry and yellow pine with walnut inlay in the last decade of the eighteenth century. The Windsor bench, circa 1790–1795, was made in Virginia and descended in the Tarry family of Mecklenburg County.

Under the window is a handsome walnut and tulip chest from southeastern Tennessee, circa 1820–1830. Its framed panel construction recalls old-fashioned joinery traditions characteristic of furniture made in the Southern mountains.

FRENCH AND CREOLE FURNITURE OF THE MISSISSIPPI RIVER VALLEY

More than a century of French settlement in the Mississippi River Valley preceded the purchase of the Louisiana Territory by the United States in 1803. Exploration by the Spanish began in 1541 when the river was first seen by Hernando de Soto and continued in 1699, when Pierre LeMoyne, Sieur d'Iberville, entered the East Pass of the Birdfoot Sub-delta. It is, however, to the eighteenth and nineteenth centuries that one must turn to find surviving pieces of furniture made by French settlers or their descendants.

With an early nineteenth-century population of about 8,000, New Orleans, established in 1718, dominated the culture and commerce of the Lower Mississippi River and Delta region. St. Louis commanded the upper Mississippi, at its juncture with the Missouri River. This town, founded in 1764, was the center of the Western fur trade. Its resident population at the time of its transfer to the United States probably did not exceed one thousand people.

Evidence of well-established French and Creole cultures in the Mississippi Valley can still be seen in the typical architecture of the region. High pitched gables and dynamic sweeping roofs with a break high in the roofline are characteristic French features. Houses of stone *(maisons de pierre),* houses of posts mortised into a wooden sill *(maisons de poteaux sur sole),* and houses of posts in ground *(maisons de poteaux en terre)* are found throughout the region, with white plaster walls that contrast with exposed timbers. Despite the abundant architectural evidence of French culture, remarkably few pieces of locally made French-style furniture are known.

The most distinctive form of French cabinetmaking of the area is the large and handsome *armoire* form. Because of high costs of shipping, most pieces of such bulk were made locally rather than imported. Walnut and cherry were favorite woods for these pieces and their doors were usually fitted with elongated imported brass hinges. *Fauteuils* (graceful French-style armchairs), *buffets* and *bureaux* were other forms owned by French traders and plantation owners. According to inventories, plain drop-leaf tables, painted chairs, dining tables, commodes and slat-back chairs were commonplace furniture for the kitchens of the wealthy and for ordinary Creole homes. As a distinctive reminder of pre-Anglo settlement, the Creole patois survives in speech patterns, but most of the commonplace furniture does not—having been discarded with the coming of nineteenth-century prosperity.

Names of some of the joiners who worked in St. Louis are known: Jacques Denis (working 1765–1777), Pierre Lupien *dit* Baron (active 1768–1775), and Jean Baptiste Ortes, who had a partnership with Jean B. Cambus in 1767. Both Ortes and Cambus had been born in France and, like many settlers, brought with them a knowledge of French styles to the New World. Provincial French furniture of the Louis XV and XVI style sports rounded corners, cabriole legs and scalloped skirts, and turned and tapering posts and legs as does much of the furniture of the Mississippi Valley. The ability of the Creole culture to incorporate elements of design from the Eastern United States is evidenced by inlay work found on some of the furniture of the Lower Mississippi; an example is the use of French form with the eagle inlay like that of New England. The various mixtures and blends of traditions and skills from people of differing languages and cultural backgrounds in the Mississippi Valley is still a rich area for research, waiting further analysis.

Buffet
St. Genevieve, Missouri. c. 1805.
Cherry with pine.
Dimensions unknown.
Present location unknown,
formerly Missouri Historical Society.

Side Chair
St. Charles, Missouri. c. 1800.
Cypress with hickory stretchers.
Dimensions unknown.
Missouri Historical Society.

According to French usage a *buffet* was a cupboard or a sideboard table. The shaped skirt and short cabriole legs of this example suggest its French provincial background as vestigial reminders of Louis XV-style furniture. By contrast, the fluted columns inset into the corners and the diamond design of the panels on the doors show the influence that Anglo-American furniture had in the design.

The side chair with its three-slat back and hewn square legs and posts is an example of commonplace simple furniture of the area. It is difficult to identify with a particular national group, but it was a type popular with the Missouri Creoles. Continental North-European furniture of this type is known in prints, drawings and paintings dating well before the seventeenth century.

Simple molded corners on the legs and posts, a slight taper to the splay of the back posts and yoke, and shaved stretchers constitute the frame of the chair. The stretchers penetrate the legs and are exposed at their ends. The seat is made of woven white oak bark. While this chair is a rare example of furniture from the Upper Mississippi, it is by no means unique.

Armoire
Indiana/Missouri. c. 1804–1805.
Cherry with poplar and walnut.
H: 92½" W: 56" D: 20½".
Missouri Historical Society.

According to family tradition, this outstanding case piece was made in Vincennes, Indiana, for Colonel François Vigo who gave it to Jean Pierre Chouteau, brother of René Auguste who, in 1764, at age fourteen, landed with a group of thirty men on the western bank of the Missouri River and directed the beginnings of the building of a trading town that became St. Louis. While Jean Pierre did not become as wealthy a man as his brother, he was a highly respected member of the founding family. When his house burned in January of 1805, his loss was estimated at $30,000.

Although frontier conditions existed at the time of the founding of St. Louis, they did not last long. By the time of the death of René Auguste Chouteau in 1829, his magnificent square stone house contained many mirrors, forty-six "painted and common chairs," ten bedsteads and forty-two pounds of sterling silver plate. An armoire like this clearly indicates an established and comfortable French style of life in the middle of the continent by the early nineteenth century. A culture from France had been recreated by the French settlers of means who made their fortunes in the fur and land trade and other commerce near the great juncture of the Missouri and Mississippi rivers.

Armoire
St. Louis, Missouri. c. 1780.
Walnut. H: 98" W: 64" D: 25".
Missouri Historical Society.

This armoire is said to have been made from a log taken from the first home of Pierre Chouteau, Sr.—an unlikely and romantic notion. It is, however, most certainly a French-style piece of excellent workmanship and design. The sides of the armoire are slightly swelled and the corners are rounded enough to carry through the subtle undulating qualities of rococo design. The cornice, restored in 1949, is not original.

SHAKERS

The styles of country and provincial furniture in America were not completely determined by the background from which a maker came or by the region of his settlement. Sometimes a craftsman's own beliefs or mental "set" had a profound effect on the creation of his furniture. This was especially true of those craftsmen who were members of the United Society of Believers in Christ's Second Appearing, or, as they were popularly known, the Shakers.

Mother Ann Lee, the founder of the group who believed she was an instrument of Christ's second coming, formed a Society of Believers at Watervliet, New York, in the spring of 1776. Removing themselves from the imperfect world, her followers developed a communal sharing of property and sought social and spiritual order. Their aim was to pursue a perfect kingdom of simplicity, purity and integrity—or heaven on earth.

The Shaker way of life was established in a score of communities by the end of the eighteenth century. By 1980, there were only two surviving Shaker communities: at Sabbathday Lake, Maine, and at Canterbury, New Hampshire. In the middle of the nineteenth century, however, there were nineteen villages ranging from Maine to southern Kentucky, with a membership which at its peak numbered over 6,000. Shaker villages were located in rural agricultural areas, where the Believers could lead a secluded life without interference from the world. Most heavily settled were New York and the New England states, with communities in all but Rhode Island and Vermont. A second wave of settlement added "Western" communities in Ohio, Kentucky and Indiana.

The beliefs which shaped the lives of the Shakers had a profound impact upon the design, function and finish of their furniture. Although Mother Ann did not live to see her precepts evolve into a network of villages, each producing its own furniture, her influence remained a strong guide: "Do all your work as though you had a thousand years to live, and as if you knew you would die tomorrow."

Furniture forms that were popular in eighteenth- and early nineteenth-century America underwent purification and simplification as Shaker craftsmen developed a stylistic sense drawn from the geographical areas from which they had come. Although the basic forms of furniture—chairs, chests and tables—derived from popular models known to American cabinetmakers, Shaker craftsmen transmuted these forms by stripping away unnecessary or worldly ornament. Quality of workmanship, sound materials, smooth finish and specific colors became the classic elements of Shaker design. Mother Ann advised that things be made "plain and simple . . . unembellished by any superfluities which add nothing to its goodness or durability," and her teachings were taken to heart. Furniture was developed by the Shakers to serve sensible purposes for the pure and pietistic life. They did not strive to create beauty, but to create practical pieces. Yet when they clarified their design to its purest and most essential form they made remarkably graceful furniture.

By 1789 Shakers were successfully producing chairs for community use and for sale to the world. This industry developed into the chair factory which produced the well-known chairs bearing the Mt. Lebanon stencil. The Mt. Lebanon "sale" chairs are the best-known Shaker chairs; no other communities mass-produced furniture for sale, and this industry was a highly successful enterprise. Furniture from the other Shaker communities, though less abundant, shows a consistency of simplicity. This was the result of pragmatic solutions to ideals.

Not all Shaker-made furniture is distinctively different from the commonplace country furniture of rural America. Interchange between the world at large and the Shaker communities was part of the Shaker life. Shakerism grew through conversion—marriage was not permitted and, with a few rare exceptions, no one was ever born a Shaker. Craftsmen who joined the Society brought with them developed woodworking skills, together with a sense of style which had its impact upon Shaker-made furniture. Despite their intentions to remain separate from the world, the Shakers and their furniture did accommodate to changing styles. New research in the field has revealed a richness of furniture produced by the Shakers which had been drawn from stylistic influences throughout the eighteenth and nineteenth centuries. Although the furniture produced in the second quarter of the nineteenth century is thought of as "classic," it is representative of only a part of their long history.

Shaker Retiring Room
Winterthur Museum.

With woodwork removed from the 1831 dairy and laundry building at Enfield, New Hampshire, this period room represents an idealized Shaker interior with spare furniture and furnishings. The harmony in detail of the built-in cupboards and drawers and the furnishings of the room are clearly in the tradition of simple, functional understatement. Under these circumstances, proportions, line and color play a dominant role in the artistic success of the work. Though Shaker retiring rooms were once furnished with numerous beds, many have since disappeared; the rarest piece of furniture in the room is the cot on wooden rollers.

Dining Table
Harvard, Massachusetts. Second Quarter, 19th Century.
Pine and cherry. H: 28¾″ W: 34″ L: 61½″.
Dr. J. J. G. McCue Collection.

A study in structural and design simplicity, this table from the Shaker community of Harvard, Massachusetts, consists of a simple broad pine top supported on two pedestals. Instead of being joined with a stretcher at the base in the traditional way, the pedestals are braced with diagonal iron struts beneath the top, allowing for unencumbered leg room. The design is a successful alternative to similar trestle tables prepared by the Shakers' contemporaries.

DAN FARBER, PHOTOGRAPHER

Sewing Stand
Hancock, Massachusetts. c. 1830.
Pine, maple, ash. H: 25″ W: 20¼″ D: 19″.
Dr. J. J. G. McCue Collection.

This small sewing stand is one of the great beauties of classic Shaker simplicity. It is perfectly balanced in design, and is constructed of striped ash and maple; the figuring shows through a red stain. The form of the table base derives from a traditional eighteenth-century tea table or candlestand. The top, however, illustrates Shaker design ingenuity. Beneath the simple top with its quartered corners, two drawers are suspended, sliding in and out at either end, perhaps for use by people seated at either side. The design is completely utilitarian and at the same time eloquently graceful. The subtle swelling and tapering of the central column continues the movement of the legs gracefully up to the working top.

DAN FARBER, PHOTOGRAPHER

Tilting Side Chair
New Lebanon, New York. Mid-19th Century.
Maple painted yellow, with original wool tape seat.
H: 37⅛" W: 18½" D: 13½".
Dr. J. J. G. McCue Collection.

This simple three-slat side chair is a classic Shaker specimen. Made in New Lebanon, New York, in the mid-nineteenth century, it was probably a forerunner of the chairs which that community produced commercially. The upright posts are gently tapered and canted inward toward the top to give the chair optical and actual stability. Ball-and-socket feet terminate the back posts at the floor, and allow the chair to be tilted backward without straining its frame. The ball-and-socket feet were fashioned to fit like ball bearings, and were held with a leather thong through their centers so they would not separate from the chair when it was lifted. This design—later patented by the Shakers—is the prototype of the ball-and-socket foot found on contemporary furniture, most notably the chairs of Charles Eames.

Rocking Chair
New Lebanon, New York. 1874–1900.
Ash and maple.
H: 37 1/16" W: 20⅜" D: 27¾".
Museum of Fine Arts, Boston.

For the Philadelphia Centennial in 1876, Gabriel Hawkins of the New Lebanon, New York, Shaker community made and displayed chairs of this type for sale to the world. This chair form was patented in 1874 and shows a definite response to the bentwood Austrian furniture which was popular in America and which was on competitive display at the Centennial at the same time.

Not only were the wood pieces of the frame bent, they were also shaped to taper from thick to thin for ease in bending and for variety to please the eye. Most noticeable is the flattening at the bend of the crest and the arms.

Red and buff listing or woven worsted wool tapes give the seat and back of this chair a checkerboard pattern that is very appealing in its textural contrast with the curved lines of the frame. Not all chairs of this type were actually made by Shakers—some were made outside the Shaker communities by the Seymour Company, a commercial concern with close ties to the New Lebanon Shakers.

Rocking Chair
Enfield, New Hampshire.
Mid-19th Century.
Birch with rattan cane seat.
H: 46" W: 18" D: 20⅜".
Museum of Fine Arts, Boston.

At one time this chair was a simple tall-backed side chair with tilting devices on its rear legs. The rockers were added by the Shakers, after the thin sockets split under the pressure of long use. The elongated flame-shaped finials are characteristic of the turned tops of Enfield chairs which were made for community use and not for sale. This elegant example, lean, spare and tall, is the only Enfield side chair known to have four splats. The caned seat is typical on chairs made at Enfield after the 1840s.

Candlestand
Probably New Lebanon, New York. 1820–1830.
Cherry.
H: 26⅝" Diameter of top: 19⅞".
Dr. J. J. G. McCue Collection.

For utter simplicity and completely harmonious design this candlestand has no peers. The spread of the legs balances the diameter of the top. However, not all of its success can be completely credited to Shaker design ingenuity as many early nineteenth-century New England candlestands are eloquently simple and perfectly balanced.

The gently swelled turning of the center post is quite different from candlestands designed in neoclassical taste. It has a distinctive shape easily recognizable in Shaker furniture. The Shakers took the tripod table form and refined and adapted it in the relative isolation of their community. It survived in use there in just this graceful form long after it had fallen out of fashion elsewhere.

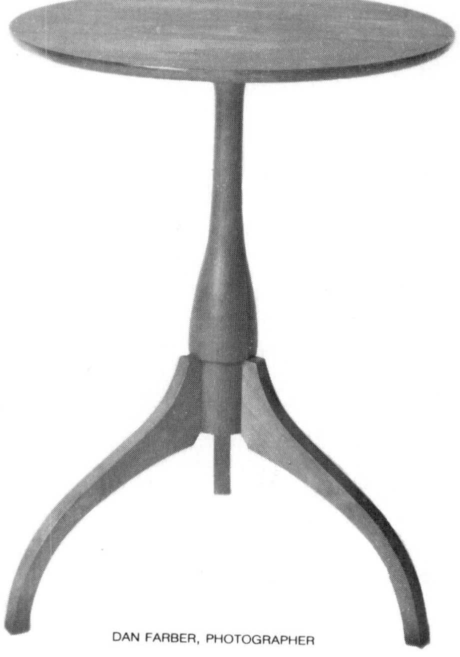

DAN FARBER, PHOTOGRAPHER

CREIGHTON-BRANDFONBRENER, PHOTOGRAPHER

Sewing Desk
Enfield, New Hampshire. c. 1880.
Birch, maple, cherry, walnut, poplar.
H: 39½" W: 33¼" D: 24¼".
Greenwillow Farm Shaker Gallery.

In interpreting Victorian furniture, Shaker cabinetmakers tended to amplify and update the forms with which they were already familiar. This veneered sewing desk has many antecedents in plainer versions of the same piece, and its form is easily recognizable. But the handsome contrast of its light and dark hardwoods, complemented by its original brass-and-porcelain pulls, reveals the strong influence of a Victorian sensibility.

Cabinet on Chest of Drawers
Pleasant Hill, Kentucky, Shaker Community. c. 1820–1855.
Cherry; secondary wood: tulip.
Cabinet—H: 57" W: 41" D: 11".
Chest—H: 42½" W: 46½" D: 22".
Shakertown at Pleasant Hill, Kentucky.

This cabinet, composed of a bookshelf set onto a chest of drawers, is reported to have been used by Mary Settler, the last surviving sister at Pleasant Hill, until her death in 1923. It has a clear finish which has allowed its natural wood surface to mellow with age.

The general design is spare and tall. Ornament is restricted to its turned feet and typical Shaker drawer-pulls. Its flared cornice, however, derives its form from the Empire or Classical style which was commonplace in the showy veneered furniture popular in the first half of the nineteenth century. This cornice indicates that the Shaker craftsman who made this piece was at least passingly familiar with cabinetmaking practices in the world beyond his village.

ZOAR, OHIO

The settlements of Zoar, Ohio, are related to the development of utopian ideals of communal socialism, which formed part of the American social experiment. From earliest settlement, immigrants came to this country with hopes of establishing social perfection. William Penn's policies of toleration encouraged many pietistic communities in Pennsylvania, such as the cloistered village of the Seventh-Day Baptists of Ephrata. Many utopian societies attempted to establish the perfect world. Not all left furniture as distinctive as that of the settlements of Zoar.

Members of The Society of Separatists of Zoar settled in Lawrence Township, Ohio, in 1817. Most of them came from Württemberg, Germany, with their leader, Joseph Bimeler. They owned property and land in common and were sectarian rather than evangelistic in their plan.

Chair or Brettstuhl
Zoar, Ohio. 1850–1875.
Oak and pine.
H: 38" W: 18" D: 19½".

Chair
Zoar, Ohio. 1850–1875.
Walnut.
H: 34" W: 16⅞" D: 16½".

Chair or Brettstuhl
Zoar, Ohio. 1850–1875.
Oak and pine.
H: 38" W: 18" D: 18".

Greenfield Village and the Henry Ford Museum, Dearborn, Michigan.

These chairs from the Zoar settlement might pass for German, were they not made of American woods. Two are made in the *Brettstuhl* or "board chair" tradition of Northern Europe; the center chair closely follows the "Biedermeier" style of middle-class German Empire furniture. The basic form of these chairs differs little from that of chairs made at the same time by German immigrants in Texas.

NORWEGIAN-AMERICAN FURNITURE

In the upper Midwestern United States furniture artisans persist in producing works that reflect their Norwegian heritage. Wisconsin, Minnesota, Iowa and North Dakota are states in which settlers from Norway found land to their liking from the time of their arrival in 1826 on through the nineteenth century and to the present day.

The amazing endurance of their culture in this widespread region might be explained in a number of ways. Prairie isolation may be one factor, but it is probably not the most important. More significant, perhaps, is the natural survival and/or revival of folk and popular art in settlements where family ties are strong and in which the crafts produced have few direct ties to the economic base of daily existence. Through church, family and village associations the remembrance of or longing for Old World traditions remains strong.

Traditional Norwegian carving with its deeply sculptured foliate ornament is frequently blended with motifs adopted from the New World. The American eagle, flag and other national symbols are favorite devices incorporated. Instead of using pine, birch and other woods common to Norway, many of the carvers here use oak and walnut, woods which were readily available. Another departure from Norwegian tradition is that most American-Norwegian craftsmen do not paint their works but leave the grain exposed.

Most of the samples illustrated here are selected from old and new works from the Norwegian-American Museum, Decorah, Iowa. Many of these examples were made by carvers or craftsmen who did not earn the majority of their livelihood by their craft. Their work was undertaken for personal pleasure and made to adorn homes or churches or to be shared with friends. In some cases, these works represent a survival of genuine folk and/or popular traditions despite the cultural homogenization of American life elsewhere in the States.

Chest or Trunk
Made in Norway, brought to Nebraska. c. 1800.
Pine and iron, painted. H: 31" W: 44¾" D: 23½".
Stuhr Museum of the Prairie Pioneer, Grand Island, Nebraska.

RICHARD CHEEK, PHOTOGRAPHER

Made in Norway and transported to Grand Island, Nebraska, in 1864, this chest or trunk has been in the family of Oscar Funru, an early pioneer. A painted inscription on the front reads, "Kari Helleksdatter/Makt 1800/Tvetten 1864." On the back is carved, "Kari Hellekson Sloen/Newman Grove P.O./Madison Co. Neb./Nort Amerika." The chest bears its original vivid floral decoration. It is an example of the many pieces brought by the Scandinavian immigrants in the nineteenth century.

WADHAMS/MAHAFFEY, PHOTOGRAPHERS

Chest
Norway. 1800–1840.
Pine, painted. H: 23" W: 41¼" D: 19¾".
Museum of Fine Arts, Boston.

This example of Norwegian folk art was transported to America in the second half of the nineteenth century and is a superb document of the design preferences of the first-generation Norwegian immigrants in America. The manner in which the painted decoration is applied is known as rose painting ("rosemaling"); this technique flourished in Norway and throughout much of Northern Europe from approximately 1750 to 1850. The inscription reads: "Aanund Haupanger/ Hillsboro Trail Co./ Dakota T./ North Amerika."

While the chest was made early in the nineteenth century, the inscription indicates that it was brought to this country some time after 1880. The town of Hillsboro in Trail County, North Dakota, was platted or mapped out in September 1880, when the railroad first came through that part of the country. The town was named for James Jerome Hill (1838–1916), the empire builder from St. Paul, Minnesota, who founded the Great Northern Railway.

Cradle
Mid-19th-Century Style.
Walnut. H: 20½" W: 21¼" L: 35¼".
From the Olge Eggen Collection,
Vesterheim, Norwegian-American Museum, Decorah, Iowa.

The pegged construction and mortise-and-tenon joinery of this cradle hearkens backward in tradition to the earliest period of woodworking in northern Europe. The cradle shape has remained fairly standard at the folk and popular levels from the seventeenth century to the present day. Variations in ornament and detail are the main clues to dating. In this case the upper ends of the square hewn posts signify nineteenth-century taste.

Bowfront Corner Cupboard
Benson, Iowa. c. 1880.
Made by Lars Christenson (1839–1910).
Pine and other woods. H: 84″ W: 36½″ D: 29″.
Vesterheim, Norwegian-American Museum,
Decorah, Iowa.

Few pieces of recently made furniture bear such assertive peasant motifs as this example. The rich carving is related to northern European decorative arts of the seventeenth century.

This piece represents both a survival and partially a revival of Old World traditions. The maker, Lars Christenson, was born in 1839 in Sogndal, Sogn, Norway, and died in 1910 in Benson, Minnesota. He was a community leader, housebuilder, farmer and butcher. This man of many talents made and carved much furniture and is reputed to have known blacksmithing and carpentry work before immigrating. A great deal of his furniture was made for family members. He was an ingenious and versatile craftsman—one who engaged in the woodworking business on a part-time basis.

Cupboard
Minneapolis, Minnesota.
Made by Leif Melgaard (b. 1899).
Signed and Dated 1971.
Walnut. H: 41" W: 23" D: 12¾".
Vesterheim, Norwegian-American Museum, Decorah, Iowa.

A triumph of virtuosity with the chisel and a superb choice of figured woods distinguishes this cupboard from many others made by Norwegian-American carvers. Its maker was born in Sor-Fron, Gudbrandsdalen, Norway, and trained in wood carving in the Craft School of the Museum of Industrial Art which was then located in Dakka. Leif Melgaard emigrated to this country in 1920 and after brief work as a farmer became employed in the cabinet department of the Lake Street Sash and Door Company, Minneapolis. Norwegian Baroque carving is his particular gift. His craftsmanship is highly professional, as he has devoted a lifetime to a thorough mastery of his art.

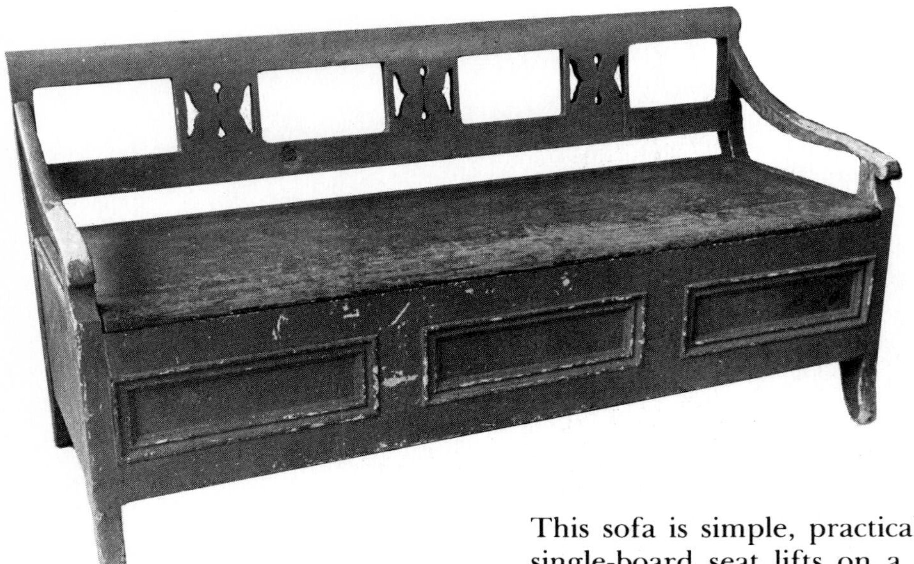

Sofa
Minnesota. 1850–1900.
Pine and walnut, painted gray-blue, stained brown beneath.
H: 37" W: 84" D: 27".
Vesterheim, Norwegian-American Museum, Decorah, Iowa.

This sofa is simple, practical, and yet not devoid of ornament. Its single-board seat lifts on a hinge so the interior can be used for storage. The three ornamental splats in the backrest are carried through in the design of three panels on the front seat frame. Legs and arms are gracefully shaped in a manner that gently echoes the classical lines of Empire furniture.

It would appear to be a pioneer piece made at a time when Norwegian settlement was rapidly developing in the Minnesota area.

Kubbestol (Log Chair)
Highland Prairie, Minnesota. 1925.
Made by Tarkjil Halvorson Landsverk (1859–1948).
Oak. H: 32½" W: 19" D: 21".
Vesterheim, Norwegian-American Museum, Decorah, Iowa.

Chopped from a log and decorated with the traditional foliate ornament admired by Norwegians, this *Kubbestol* is the work of Tarkjil Landsverk who was born in 1859 in Seljord, Telemark, Norway. He died in 1948 in Highland Prairie near Whalan, Minnesota.

After immigrating to the United States in 1884, Tarkjil spent the remainder of his life in Highland Prairie where he farmed, taught school, wrote poetry and turned his hand to a number of crafts. His son, Halvor, continues the popular family craft of making log chairs to the present day.

This particular chair has an unusual sweep to its full back. Its finely curved edge peaks smartly at the top. The ornament is shallow so as not to distract from the movement of the back.

Furniture Group
Norwegian-American. 19th Century.

Kubbestol (Log Chair)
Wisconsin, Iowa or Minnesota.
c. 1862. Painted pine.
H: 31⅜" W: 17¼" D: 14¼".

Backless Stool
Coon Valley, Wisconsin.
19th Century.
Made by Norwegian Pioneers.
Oak, originally painted red.
H: 19" Diameter of top: 11½".

Table
Grand Meadow, Minnesota
(from the first rural school there).
Painted pine, one walnut leg
(recent gray paint).
H: 29½" W: 35½" D: 28".

Side Chair
Probably Minnesota. 19th Century.
Red-stained pine (perhaps elm).
H: 30¾" W: 14" D: 15¼".

Vesterheim, Norwegian-American Museum, Decorah, Iowa.

Some forms of Norwegian-American furniture are quite plain. Without provenance they might be difficult to distinguish from other country furniture. The *Kubbestol* in this group is distinctively Norwegian. It was made prior to 1869 out of a hewn log with a seat plank plugged into its central hole. The backless stool is another compelling example of Norwegian-American design. Chopped out of a simple log, this stool reflects a long-standing tradition of peasant wood craftsmanship from Northern Europe. The side chair and table are conventionally constructed and are good examples of simple home production. They might easily be mistaken for rural non-Norwegian workmanship.

AMERICAN INDIAN

Indians, the first American inhabitants, had seating, storage and sleeping accommodations that were unlike those traditional in Western European culture. Rather than joined woodwork, rigidly framed, the Indians used baskets, woven blankets, reed and fiber matting, bark containers, skin or animal hides stretched or lashed to poles or frames, or bent wood boxes which were sewn, lashed or pegged together. Large earthenware pots helped to meet the storage needs served by the framed wooden boxes of European immigrants. The furniture of most Indian nations was designed to be easily disassembled and light to carry. Most permanent forms had special functions. The earthen lodge of the Mandan Indians had built-in platforms for storage and sleeping.

The Southwest, the area occupied by the great Pueblo civilization, had its most developed period between 1050 and 1400 A.D. Communal buildings were so large that a single building of the Pueblo Bonito may have sheltered as many as 1200 people—the largest dwelling or apartment house in the world before New York apartment housing passed this number in the 1880s. Despite such dense population, the Indians did not use furniture in the joined sense of frame, tenon and mortise: sitting and sleeping platforms were usually integral parts of the architecture.

Perhaps the closest parallel between Indian craftsmanship and furniture in the European tradition is to be found in the highly ornamented carved and painted boxes made by the Indians of the Pacific Northwest coast. But these boxes only seem related to boxes of other civilizations. Instead of being framed, they were actually constructed by bending—a process more closely related to bark craftsmanship than to plank framing.

The varied cultures of the Indian nations suggest the effects that barriers of vastly different terrains, language and distance had upon distinctly different groups. Means of subsistence ranged from elementary foraging to communal agriculture and irrigation. Indians seldom singled out the maker of art works; the work of American Indian craftsmen is usually anonymous.

Storage Chest with Cover
Pacific Northwest. Tsimshian Tribe.
Probably 19th Century.
Yellow cedar sides; red cedar bottom and top. Painted red, black and green. H: 18⅛" W: 36⅞" D: 20⅞".
Portland Museum of Art.

Although this chest is said to have been made by the Tsimshian, it was acquired from the Tlingit tribe. It is a superb example of the carved and painted storage boxes of the Native Americans of the region, which were also used in burial rituals. The figure is GonakAde't, a monster of the headwaters of the Nass River. The face and body of the creature are depicted in an abstract style, with the eyes, nose and mouth in the upper panel and the paws carved and outlined in black paint below.

Although Indian boxes made in the Northwest superficially resemble European joined furniture, they are constructed in a totally different fashion. The sides of these boxes were hand-adzed out of cedar planks until they were extremely thin. They were then grooved, steamed and bent to form the four sides. Where the bent sides butted together at one corner, they were joined together with wooden pegs. A heavy plank was pegged to the bottom and a corresponding top fitted for the lid. The steaming process employed to form the chest sides was allied to the Indian tradition of fabricating objects from bark, and was undoubtedly a technique used only by highly trained professional workmen.

Haida Couch
Queen Charlotte Islands, British Columbia. c. 1880.
Made by Charles Edenshaw (1839–1920).
Red cedar. L: 73½".
Museum of the American Indian, New York.

This handsome couch was made by a Haida Indian chief as a gift to his wife, Isabella. Charles Edenshaw descended from a family of carvers, starting his carving career at the age of fourteen. His reputation as a carver was well established long before white missionaries came to the area in 1878.

Made for use in a European-style house, the couch is longer than usual for a chief's bench and its legs and general form show European influence. But the carving of Isabella Edenshaw's "crests" or family signs is traditional. The carving represents her lineage or descent group: a grizzly bear in the medallion and bear tracks across the top of the back, a dogfish shark on the back and a killer whale on the inside of the arms.

Side Chair
Northwest Coast. Late 19th Century.
Probably Haida Tribe.
Cedar.
H: 33" W: (seat) 17¼" D: (seat) 17¾" W: (crest rail) 20".
Collection of Ralph T. Coe.

The Northwest coast Indians often adapted their traditional arts to the forms and ideas of the European settlers. The form of this chair is adopted from factory-produced furniture; the carving, however, is distinctive to the Haida culture. The cosmology of animal guardian forces in relation to man's world is implied by the beaver that spans the seat. Its tail forms the splat of the chair and its incisors lap over the front edge of the seat. This carving transforms the chair into a work invested with spiritual and vitalistic power.

INDIVIDUALISTIC FURNITURE

Furniture which eludes identification with a major body of similar works is often sought after now because it seems to be expressive of individualistic personalities. But even the most eccentric works are part of a larger cultural context. The unusual ornamental schemes which are pointed to as truly individualistic were often evolved for religious or fraternal groups. In this sense, then, individualistic pieces of furniture are vehicles for group ideals—messages for a select few—which serve a ritual function. Why furniture of this sort today may seem naive, bizarre or otherwise appealing is simply because its meaning and function have become obscured with time.

Chest with Drawers
Hardy County, Virginia. Dated March 1, 1801.
Made for Jacob Wilkin by Godfrey Wilkin.
Walnut, pine; putty inlay. H: 34½" W: 54¾" D: 26½".
Greenfield Village and the
Henry Ford Museum, Dearborn, Michigan.

Few pieces of furniture so clearly reveal a sense of humor and satisfaction with workmanship as does this chest. The intarsia or putty inlay, which records basic data of ownership in evenly spaced lettering, is quoted here with spacing for better readability:

> MARCH 1 JACOB WILKIN HIS CHEAST A D 1801
> GODFREY WILKIN HARDY COUNTY AND STATE OF VIRGINIA

To entertain the viewer, Godfrey Wilkin lettered two stiles which framed the panels with the delightful messages: "READ THES UP/ AND

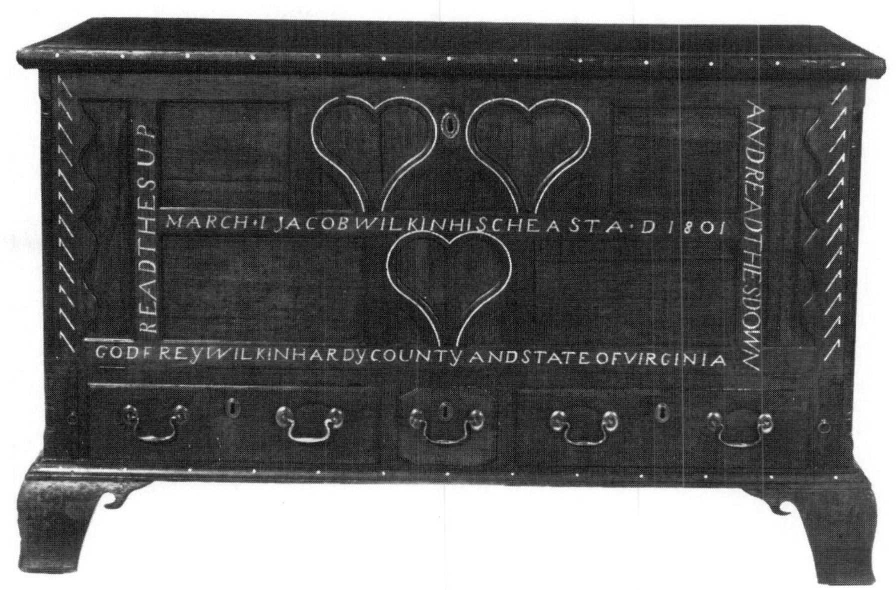

READ THES DOWN." The unusual spelling not only heightens the wit of the message; it also probably reflects the phonetic equivalent of how Wilkin spoke. Both sides of the chest are marked in letters "WEL DON," which records the satisfaction the maker had with his work.

Highly unusual is the false front of the chest. It is hinged just above the lower drawers to permit a fall-front supported on slides like that of a desk. Behind the fall-front are seven small drawers. By any standard this chest is a personal and imaginative work. Its basic form is derived from fairly standard eighteenth-century cabinetmaking practices from Pennsylvania, but through ingenuity and whimsy, its maker has transformed an otherwise ordinary design into something unique and personal.

Couch
Medina, Ohio.
Signed: "W. Granville, January 1853."
Walnut with tulip.
H: 29" (at ends)
32" (at top of back)
L: 78" D: 21".
G.W. Samaha.

This couch was either made for or by the rector of St. Paul's Episcopal Church in Medina, Ohio. Although some of its crest has been trimmed off, the couch retains enough of its naive carving to convey its religious message. The central diapered figure stands in place of the word "Child" in the surrounding words: "A Little [Child] Shall Lead Them." This quotation from the Old Testament (Isaiah 11:6) predicts that the wolf shall dwell in peace with the lamb. Two verses later, Isaiah states that the weaned child shall put his hand in the adder's den without harm. These remarkable events, together with others, were to be signs of the gathering of the outcasts of Israel and the dispersed peoples of Judah from the four corners of the earth. The carver of the couch interpreted Isaiah by showing a child holding a snake and standing beside a wolf with two lambs.

Worshipful Master's Chair
Vinton County, Ohio. c. 1870.
Made by John Luker.
Pine and maple. H: 72" W: 29¼" D: 30".
Courtesy of Mr. and Mrs. Charles V. Hagler.
The Museum of Our National Heritage,
Lexington, Massachusetts.

This Masonic Master's chair is a remarkable hybrid of stylistic motifs painted on a framework that adapts Empire furniture forms in a unique way. The base reflects the superimposed double arcs of the legs found on Duncan Phyfe's curule chairs, fashionable in New York City fifty years before this Master's chair was made. Phyfe's form was itself inspired by ancient Roman magistrate chairs, so the significance of this classical form seems not to have been entirely forgotten in rural Ohio. The splat of the back, together with the shaped plank seat and scrolled arms, recall the form of a Boston rocker. Such rockers were simplified in provincial imitations throughout rural Ohio and Pennsylvania from the 1830s to the early years of the twentieth century.

The crest of the chair, like most official seats, is crowned with appropriate emblems that could be seen and understood by the audience. Dividers and squares were basic measuring tools of masonry and therefore serve as a fitting framing device for the letter "G," which represents "Geometry of God."

This remarkable chair is inscribed with "Manufact'd by John Luker" and "J. H. M. Houston." The chair originally stood in the Swan Lodge, No. 358, in Swan, Vinton County, Ohio, where Houston was the Worshipful Master. The Lodge obtained its charter in 1866 and Houston became the Worshipful Master a year later. He held this post until 1873, so it is logical to assume that the chair was made some time before that date. A new framed and clapboard lodge building was dedicated in 1871; it seems probable that the chair was made at that time.

Sacred Throne
Victoria, Texas. 1880–1920(?).
Perhaps beech or maple. H: 36½″.
Collection of James M. Aldrich.

Found discarded behind a Presbyterian church in Victoria, Texas, this throne displays a complex blend of African and European forms and iconography. Nearly identical ceremonial thrones are in use among the Kom-Tikar of the Cameroons, for whom they embody the order of the universe and provide a context in which leaders may sit in absolute repose and authority.

This African meaning is transformed into a powerful system of Christian doctrine. The slumbering lions, elephant, lamb and bear of the base immediately recall the same Biblical text employed on the Medina couch (page 360), where all wild animals shall dwell in peace with domestic animals and with man.

The front and rear surfaces of the backrest are arranged in a system of types and antitypes. The rear surface gives the Old Testament authority system. Solomon is seated on his throne within the temple of Jerusalem, flanked by the sacred pillars, Jachin and Boaz, guardians of the Ark of the Covenant and symbols of Adam and Eve. Ambiguous in meaning are the two nude figures of women, but the roses are undoubtedly allusions to the Rose of Sharon. The tooled metal disc underneath the throne bears a striking resemblance to Ashanti soul disks, one of whose meanings was that there must be followers in order for a king to exist.

The front surface of the backrest gives the New Testament authority system, under the New Dispensation. Christ is enthroned in glory, resting atop the Church Triumphant. The roses recall the Rose of Sharon. A tall, clothed figure of a woman may represent Mary. Other seated figures may allude to the actual ministers of the Presbyterian church.

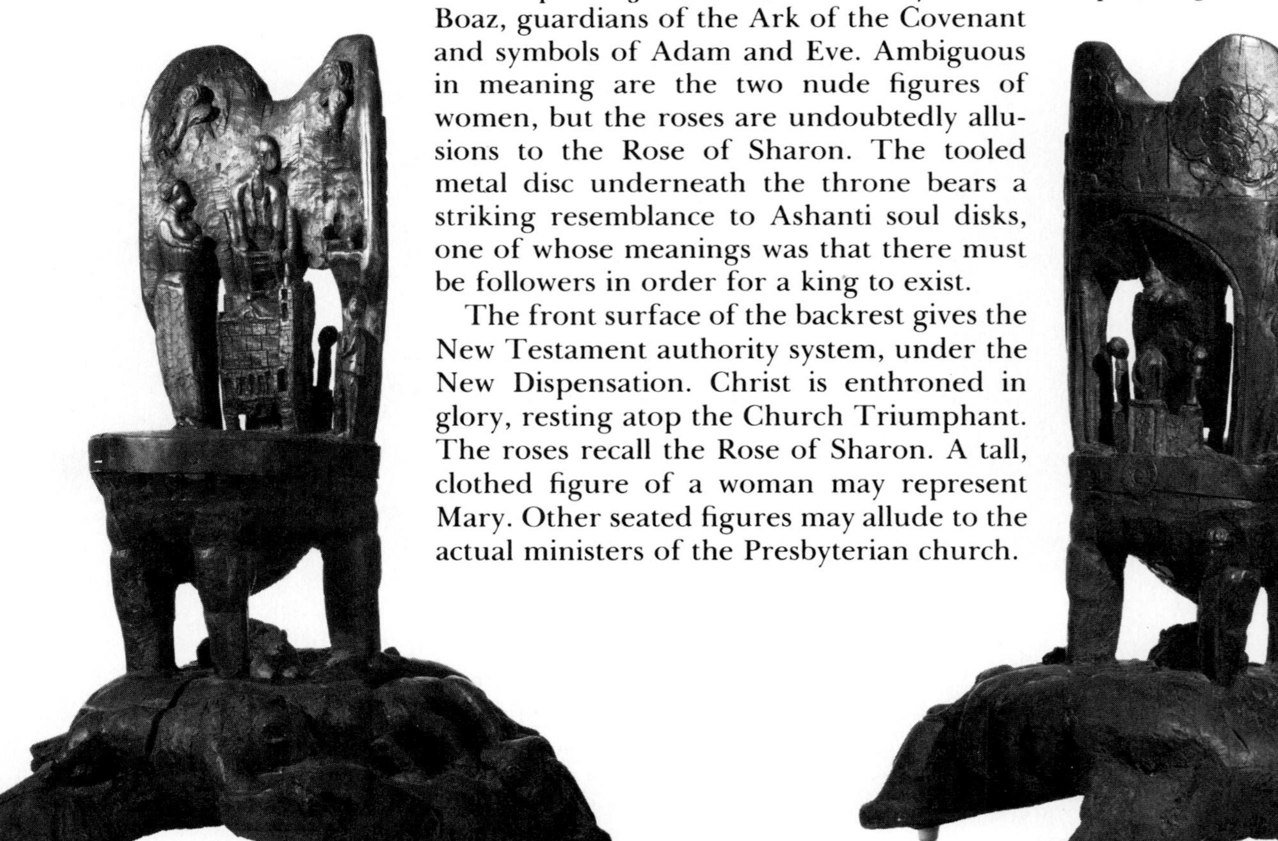

VIII

1830–1900

Victorian America

Queen Victoria reigned longer than any other English monarch—from 1837 to 1901. Her reign spanned the succession of American presidents from Andrew Jackson to Theodore Roosevelt. Therefore, the term "Victorian" implies a long continuity in the development of values and concepts stretching over most of the nineteenth century. During this period there was an enormous growth of empire and national pride, development of vast public enterprises and building of huge private fortunes through exploitation of resources both in England and America. Despite continuity, three discrete phases of the Victorian Period are apparent in American furniture:

Early Victorian (1830–1850), Mid-Victorian (1850–1870), and Late Victorian (1870–1900).

The various styles that evolved were more complex, but their uses were distinctively expressed in each of these phases. Late Victorians generated so many different trends that the most advanced furniture of the period is treated in a later chapter on Reform.

Early Victorian 1830–1850

Nineteenth-century romantics were attracted to artistic styles from distant, remote lands and cultures. By the 1830s they realized that the use of a specific style from the past should not be merely imitative, but should be symbolically evocative. Artists and designers felt that it was their mission to make use of the artistic heritage of past civilizations, and to recast the ideal of ancient art into new molds and models.

The Greek or Classical revival versus the Gothic or Medieval revival were at seemingly opposite poles. Composition of the Gothic revival style involved vertical lines—lines of spiritual aspiration; the Classic stressed horizontal lines. Christian values and pagan ideals seemed in conflict. But both styles shared a common aesthetic quest—to revive past styles for expressive moods.

The famous English designer, architect and ecclesiologist Augustus Welby Northmore Pugin noted differences between Classic and Gothic styles in his controversial, brilliant book, *Contrasts* (London, 1836). He stressed the virtue of Gothic design for Christians and the inappropriateness of pagan classicism in a Christian world. Such differences only highlighted the fact that both Classic and Medieval revivals were inspired by common romantic impulses. Polarities or oppositions were an important element of nineteenth-century romantic aesthetics. Classic and Medieval styles co-existed in Early Victorian America at both the elite and popular levels.

Ancient Greek and Roman forms in furniture had been accurately and beautifully revived in America before the Victorian Period. The persistence and popularization of these forms was the main thrust of the 1830s and 1840s. The Greek revival style was the most popular style in this country at the time when America was expanding westward. Grecian chairs, couches and tables gained a mixture of styles from other lands and times. Gothic details and rococo elements or details were fused with ancient Classical forms to create something new. Late Classical furniture in the Early Victorian Period was anything but archaeologically correct in form or detail. A blend of styles suited the desire for picturesque homes.

New leisure for the American merchant and middle class was expressed in the setting of the Early Victorian parlor. Different styles of classicism suggested different uses. The Doric order was considered serious and masculine—most suitable for important public monuments or housing for powerful steam machinery. The Ionic order, richly fluted, ornamental and slender, was less solemn and considered an excellent choice for domestic architecture and furniture. Temples dedicated to goddesses were associated with the Ionic order. The lavish Corinthian order seemed best adapted for theaters and other places of "festive conviviality." Middle-class Americans most favored the serious and sensible Doric order. It was the least expensive as it had few costly ornamental embellishments.

Parlor furniture emphasized the symmetrical placement of a single center table often with a Doric central pedestal. It was usually draped with a cloth and on its center stood a whale oil or "solar" lamp for reading or needlework. As the most imposing piece of furniture in the parlor, the center table came to symbolize cultivation on the part of its owners.

Early Victorian aesthetics contrasted hard, powerful and overwhelming masculine objects with small, soft, delicate and feminine objects. The Early Victorians emphasized sexual distinctions. It is nonsense to perpetuate a twentieth-century myth that the Victorian bourgeoisie repressed eroticism. Masculine and feminine symbolism was perceived in everyday objects, including furniture.

The late Classical revival style of Early Victorian America adapted to the new technology of steam-powered machine sawing. Broad sheets of elaborately figured mahogany veneers were quickly sawn or planed to cover a supporting structure of less expensive soft woods of white pine or tulip poplar. Major furniture craftsmen quickly discovered the advantages of adopting the new style, including Duncan Phyfe of New York City. In the hands of a skillful designer the furniture of this style could evoke a feeling of the massive simplicity of Egyptian architecture as well as incorporate some Gothic details. At the same time, it retained a basic Classical orientation in its proportions and ornament. In Baltimore, where Classical revival architecture and furniture were produced in quantities (as the prosperity of the city boomed), there was an immense output of veneered Classical furniture in the Restoration style.

The Restoration style has also been called the pillar and scroll style. Furniture made in this style was especially available for the upwardly mobile middle class. It was fairly inexpensive in its simplest forms. Elaborately ornamented and expensive pieces in this style were available to those who could afford them.

The Gothic revival style in Early Victorian furniture in America required an acquired taste and substantial means. Gothic furniture was elaborate and therefore tended to be individually designed and custom made. The supreme American examples of Early Victorian Gothic furniture are the entrance hallway chairs and table made for William and Philip Paulding's Gothic revival villa, "Lyndhurst," on the Hudson River (page 387). The rose-window-backed side chairs and pedestal table were designed in 1841 by architect Alexander Jackson Davis who had designed the mansion three years before.

Mid-Victorian 1850–1870

The rococo revival was the dominant furniture style of the Mid-Victorian Period. A typical room is illustrated in the woodcut of a New York parlor (page 388). Firms that introduced rococo revival furniture continued to make late Classical furniture as well, which was especially suitable for state or official furniture.

As the rococo revival invaded the parlor, Americans were becoming aware of their natural wilderness. Wonder about the virgin land and nature worship popularized naturalistic ornament. Rococo revival carving reproduced birds, fruit, leaves and vines with convincing realism; furniture, paintings and other works of art of the mid-century were drenched with religious overtones as well. This convergence suggests that the rococo revival was involved with something more than a mere reflection of past styles. It seems to have represented a search for the origins of creative power.

The most graceful and elaborate works of Mid-Victorian furniture seem to have been done by the New York master craftsman Alexander Roux, who made the splendid étagère and side table shown on page 392. Equally skillful and in some ways more sophisticated is the work of Charles A. Baudouine. These pieces are compared because they represent the best American workmanship and design in the rococo revival style.

John Henry Belter (1804–1861) is the craftsman with whom the rococo revival style of Victorian America is most popularly associated today. He came to New York from Württemburg, Germany, in 1844, and soon became a leading craftsman. Using iron cauls or molds and steam, Belter developed a way to bend and laminate rosewood. The strength of the laminated wood permitted intricate piercing and carving of leaves, grapes, interlaced vines and floral bouquets. Belter had many imitators even though he made an effort to protect his laminating and bending process with patents issued in 1847 and 1858. Since journeymen carvers and craftsmen moved freely from shop to shop, working in the same manner as in Belter's shop, it is not possible now to distinguish the work of Belter from that of a competitor, unless a label or stamp is affixed to the piece of furniture in question.

The large number of outstanding examples of Belter-like furniture attests to the importance of his shop. It is also supported by the fact that 3,103 furniture craftsmen of German extraction were practicing their trade in New York City by 1860.

Belter employed many German carvers who came to America in the same 1840s migration that prompted his own arrival. They brought remarkable skills in naturalistic carving. Yet some of the ornament of design seems unrelated to nature or even antique rococo styles. The basic skeleton beneath the ornament in many of the chair backs is abstractly conceived as shifting planes, sweeping lines and intertwined motifs that suggest muscular tensions. The strivings and exuberant curves of Belter's furniture indicate an interest in provoking in the mind of the viewer sensations beyond mere naturalism.

Implicit in the curved form and ornament of Belter's furniture was the sensuousness of the S-shaped line of comfort and pleasure. Coiled-spring supports for the seats, horsehair padding and tufted silk upholstery made physical comfort for the sitter a reality.

The few known bedsteads that bear Belter's mark are triumphs of skill and artistic composition. For an age immersed in elaborate ornament, Belter's bedsteads are surprisingly simple and abstract. The S-curve is thoroughly integrated into the form of the bedstead; carved and applied ornament are almost superfluous.

Simple lines in the rococo revival style can be found in some of the least expensive models of middle-class furniture. The lady's chair (page 402) provides a good example. The silhouette of this type of chair almost duplicates the tightly boned corset waist and bulging bustle of the mid-Victorian female figure. The joinery of the chair is of dowel-and-glue construction; the seat is coil-spring supported. This offers a maximum visual effect at the minimum of labor and cost. It is an essay in sleek simplicity made during an age when buyers preferred overstuffing and overornamentation.

Mid-century Boston was not as conservative and backward-looking a city as writers have asserted. An appetite was there for the same deeply sculptured ornament of the rococo revival that pervaded other major American cities in the Mid-Victorian Period. The looking-glass frames illustrated on page 404 were made in Boston by skillful ornamentalists and gilders to dress the Mid-Victorian parlor with elaborate pier and girandole glasses, essential for a successful businessman's home.

Near sources of timber, water and rail transportation, furniture factories in the Midwestern states of Indiana, Illinois and Ohio became part of an important mid-century industry that competed successfully with the trade in the Eastern states. In Samuel Sloan's *Homestead Architecture* (Philadelphia, 1861), works by the Philadelphia cabinetmaker George J. Henkels (1819–1883) are illustrated, accompanied by complaints against the cheap, showy furniture from Western and Southern states. The firm of Mitchell and Rammelsberg (1848–1880) of Cincinnati, noted for inexpensive furniture, was a major source of the competition with Eastern manufacturers. In Chicago, where there was a good supply of timber available and excellent transportation systems, some eighteen furniture factories were in operation by 1860.

The most popular tastemaker of mid-nineteenth-century America was Andrew Jackson Downing, who championed the free diffusion of knowledge among all men. He advised the working class to furnish their homes with simple, inexpensive and nicely painted "cottage furniture." This furniture was made cheaply in factories and then painted quickly by specialists who perfected freehand brushwork and stencil work to a routine. The effect of the cottage furniture was refreshing artistically.

Even the wealthy found cottage furniture appealing. They ordered custom-made suites that were carefully painted by accomplished artists. The illusion of three-dimensional carved detail was often the desired effect achieved by painted cottage furniture. Flowers, birds, vines, fruit and touches of gilding enriched the surfaces of this furniture favored by both the working and elite classes.

Late Victorian 1870–1900

"WHAT WILL BE SEEN TO-DAY?" asked a writer for the *New York Tribune* of May 10, 1876. The question was followed with a three-page description of the most exciting public event in America for a decade: the opening of the New World's Fair, better known as the Centennial Exposition, held in Philadelphia to commemorate the hundredth anniversary of American independence. The writer continued: "Neither of the great World's Fairs held in past years in Europe has equaled it in extent or surpassed it in variety or general interest. At Paris, in 1867, there was a more compact and systematic, and perhaps a more brilliant display, and at Vienna, in 1873, the Oriental nations were more fully represented; but the American Fair possesses many points of superiority over those exhibitions. It shows the natural products, the industries, the inventions, and the arts of the Western Hemisphere as they were never shown before, and brings them for the first time in their fullness and perfection in contrast with those of the Old World. In the Department of Machinery it is incomparably superior to all its predecessors; and in that of farm implements and products it has never been equaled."

Pride in the exposition was well deserved. A nation rent by civil war and floundering in financial depression needed to convince itself of its unity and prosperity. The exhibition was a confirmation of America's well-being, and provided an opportunity to celebrate the enormous industrial energy that had been heightened by the war. The sheer size of the event was characteristically American. Sprawled over two hundred and thirty-six acres of Fairmount Park on the west side of the Schuylkill River, the fair occupied one hundred and ninety-four buildings. No previous exhibition had enjoyed such space. And no previous fair had developed such elaborate transportation to handle its visitors. Claim was made that just one of three steam railways dispatched two hundred and forty trains from its chief terminal daily, epitomizing the energetic motion of an age which felt confident that problems of all degrees could be solved.

Visitors to the Fair found bewildering mazes of technological and industrial exhibits and inventions such as the telephone, the carpet sweeper, the typewriter and the elevator. The celebrated Corliss engine was the display that excited the most universal admiration and wonder. It was the image of power, the physical icon of force. For the age of energy, no other symbol could have been more appropriate.

What did this synthesis of human skill and mechanical energy signify? And how did it affect or reflect the aesthetics of furniture of the day? The writer for the *Tribune* observed that the furniture in the exposition was artistic, if somewhat lacking in originality of design:

> The makers have put forth praiseworthy efforts to give their wares an attractive setting, and have built a series of small rooms, handsomely carpeted and papered, and in some cases having mantels, pictures, and chandeliers. . . . With these home-like surroundings the furniture naturally shows to much better advantage than when set out upon a bare floor in cabinet ware-room style. Some of the heavy walnut work is exceedingly good, and there are a few cabinets and sideboards in light woods that are quite artistic. The West competes with the East in walnut bedroom suites—one of the finest coming from Columbus, Ohio. As a rule the upholstering is not in the best taste. Another fair criticism is lack of originality of design in the most costly and pretentious articles.

By originality of design the writer probably meant style. But artistic style was only one aspect of the business which interested nineteenth-century furniture makers. In terms of priorities, multiplication of product rather than style was a foremost consideration. For with new and improved machine tools, unit costs of furniture could be lowered through production on a large scale. Ornament could be multiplied as well. These innovations expressed important aspects of late nineteenth-century taste: abundant energy, infatuation with machinery, and a sense of self-sufficiency.

Critics of late nineteenth-century American art have lamented the decline of furniture craftsmanship, which they felt was caused by the rise of the profession of architecture, the development and exploitation of the machine and the increasing separation of art from industry. Throughout their first century of independence, Americans had developed design skills to meet the needs of their new country. By the opening years of the nineteenth century, architects like Latrobe and A. J. Davis were designing furniture for commissioned buildings. As the architect gained greater recognition in the role of furniture designer, the furniture craftsman lost his dominance as a creative designer and instead became a businessman or maker of products. The names of the many craftsmen who made furniture after the designs of prominent architects were overshadowed by the reputations of the architects. With the loss of personal contact between the designers and makers of furniture, the craftsman's intuitive knowledge of the limits of his materials was sacrificed.

The gap between designer and producer was aggravated further by the widening gap between producer and retailer. Due to the changing nature of mercantile activity in the nineteenth century, the furniture manufacturer yielded direct contact with customers to the retailer of furniture; the so-called "middleman." The manufacturer issued anonymous catalogs of the products in his "cabinet warehouse" to furniture dealers. Enterprising shopkeepers were much more interested in selling furniture than in celebrating the talents of its producers, and in many cases, they pretended that the wares in their showrooms were of their own make.

As factory assembly lines became more the rule than the exception in furniture production, the furniture craftsman lost his acquaintance with the entire craft and instead became specialized in performing discrete tasks in the assembly process. The result was psychological disaster for the obsolete artisan, whose sense of self-sufficiency and self-importance plunged with his status in the labor force. As the nineteenth century progressed, the furniture industry increasingly employed itinerant workers whose skills and contributions remain largely unknown.

With art and industry separated, furniture makers turned their attention to efficiency of production. Creative design skills were poured into the development of machine tools for processing wood. Although it has been claimed that by 1830 all the basic tools of mechanized society had been invented, the combinations and applications of the basic tools toward a fully mechanized and modern age of iron was just beginning. Within the following quarter century, American technology advanced from the use of wood as the fundamental substance for shelter, heat, furniture and shipbuilding to the exploitation of coal, steam, gas and cast iron for these same ends.

During this age when wood crafts and cast-iron machinery intersected, the inventions which were produced reflected the confident mood in man's ability to shape and master his physical world. The furniture that has been identified with the Baroque and rococo revivals were not simply inferior imitations of the original styles. These pieces were expressions of highly charged emotion and energy, and exuded a sense of joy in the nineteenth century's ability to manipulate novel materials into imposing forms. The compositional devices employed to arouse the viewer's attention included eye-catching patterns, textural contrasts, shifting planes and picturesque massings. The expressive drama and brilliant imagery which were at the center of all the American arts just prior to the Civil War suggested the waning of a "sacred" world view or cosmology and a shift toward a more profane view. With science and machinery as resources and guides it was no longer necessary to look heavenward for artistic inspiration. Darwin's theory of evolution of 1859 and the shattering experience of the Civil War could not have helped but startle and change Americans' fundamental assumptions about their country and world. Neither the universe nor the nation could be explained by simple faith in some preconceived and divine destiny; people turned to technology and science to create order.

The yards upon yards of ornamental detail which were produced so cheaply by machines offered much visual pleasure. Excitement was stirred by the machine's possibilities; there were scrapers, molders, band and scroll saws, wood-polishing machines, planers, carvers, grinders, benders and wood-engraving machines. The European critic de Tocqueville once observed that Americans loved comforts and conveniences. He felt that they confused contraptions with civilization. But America's obvious delight in gadgetry was more complex. In the late nineteenth century, the proliferation of "gadget" furniture was in part influenced by (and a response to) the rise of domestic science. As American cities became more crowded and urban living quarters more cramped, achieving a "modicum of comfort in a minimum of space" was the ambition of many conscientious housewives. Furniture companies that stressed the household convenience and practicality of their goods were justifiably popular. Customers were urged to consider the convenience of patented lounge beds, which converted from sofas to beds, and offered space for bed clothing and reversible hair mattresses as well. Also popular were reclining chairs, which differ little in mechanical detail from the lounging chairs used in American family rooms today, and which reflected the late nineteenth century's growing interest in the importance of both posture and relaxation.

The idea of mobility, which was integral to the machine and to mass production, had profound impact on American thought and action. Speed, convenience, flexibility and adaptability were all factors of nineteenth-century thought which continue as important strains in the twentieth century. The subject has been well explored by Siegfried Giedion's pioneering study, *Mechanization Takes Command* (1948), and in other contexts by Howard Mumford Jones in *The Age of Energy*. As Jones ably argues, the idea of mobility was an absolute virtue in an industrial democracy—a mark of a progressive Western society. Those who did not get on, move and improve, were obviously failures by American definitions of success. The popular character of the arts in Victorian America cannot be stressed enough. Although modern taste tends to condemn the period for its shoddy craftsmanship and seeming excesses, it is important to remember that Victorian technology vastly improved the lives of most people. Although machine production of furniture did serve to mask poor quality beneath surface decoration, it also made the products accessible to those who existed on small incomes. Factory-produced inexpensive furniture, as well as mass-produced textiles, ceramics and wallpaper, helped to create the illusion of material well-being for thousands of American families, and more significantly, brought the decorative arts within reach of all.

Center Table
Philadelphia. 1825–1835.
Probably by Anthony G. Quervelle (1789–1856).
Mahogany, walnut and chestnut. H: 28″ Diameter of top: 43″.
William N. Banks Collection.

A dominant presence in almost any household would be established with this massive but elegant table. The table is not only heavily constructed to support a massive marble top, it is also opulently carved, gilded and painted. The marble of the top has a brilliant surface of black and rose colors veined with gray. It establishes the mood of the piece—rich and exotic. Surrounding the marble is a frame of lunette-shaped inlay made of curled maple. A deeply gadrooned edge completes the top. The original gold-leaf stencil and freehand-painted ornament is handsomely executed on the pedestal and base. The feet are painted a dark-green color and are highlighted with bronze-gold powder on the raised portions of the carving in order to simulate the effect of antique bronze.

Three similar center tables were made for the East Room of the White House in 1829 by Anthony G. Quervelle. Another example of this type, with a mosaic marble top, is in the collections of the Metropolitan Museum in New York.

Pencil Drawing
Coastal Massachusetts. c. 1830.
By Sarah Ellen Derby (1805–1877),
of parents John and Eleanor Coffin Derby.
Privately Owned.

This drawing shows how furniture was placed in the late Classical Period in New England. A prominent central-column center table bisects the room to repeat the symmetry of the fire-place, lamps and swagged windows. A fringed center carpet completes the system. The concept of symmetry in nineteenth-century New England houses was soon forgotten. The New England house developed as needs demanded and tastes changed, altering the arrangement of furniture.

Japanned Octagonal Pedestal Table
Albany, New York. 1830. Painted by Elisa Anthony (Signed and Dated). Pine, cherry, maple.
H: 29" Diameter of top: 32½".
Collection of Mrs. Charles L. Bybee.

The classical form of this table is ornamented in simulated Oriental lacquerwork. Such mixtures of Eastern and Western art demonstrate the fact that romantic taste in the Early Victorian Period eagerly embraced unusual style combinations. All cultures were acceptable sources, but places and people distant in time or space held special appeal.

A Chinese pagoda placed upon a Greek temple form was as common an architectural practice as the use of japanning on a pedestal table of classical form. To the taste of the Early Victorian, the classical acanthus carving and animal feet of the table were entirely suited to the painted Chinese figures and landscape.

The decorative energy of this piece places it in a class out of the ordinary. It is a work of art highly expressive of its time—for in the 1830s great fortunes were being made in the China trade. The table is a remarkable document of Early Victorian taste in America.

RICHARD CHEEK, PHOTOGRAPHER

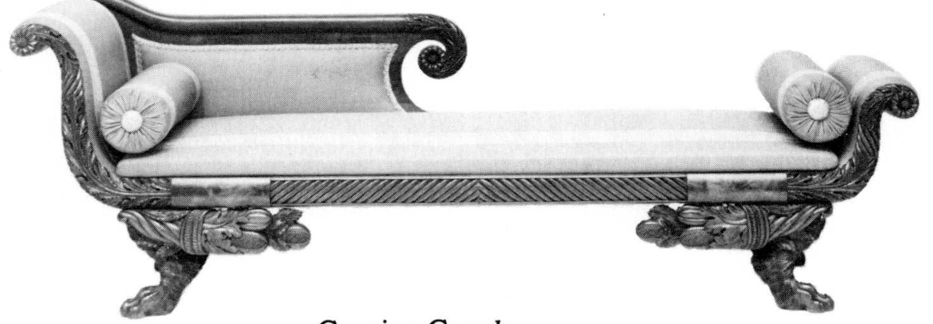

Grecian Couch
Probably New York State. c. 1825–1840.
Branded "Roch" and Signed "R. Rosch CR."
Mahogany, mahogany veneer, tulip and white pine.
H: 27½" W: 80" D: 25½".
Winterthur Museum.

A drawing made before reupholstery shows the basic construction that made this couch both sleek in appearance and solid in structure. The large slip-seat or frame which forms the seat is unusual for a sofa of this period. But the three cross braces that span the seat frame are typical of New York woodworking traditions. The shallow U shape to the cross braces on their upper sides is frequently seen in New York furniture of the Federal and Empire periods. This shape to the cross brace added some clearance from the upholstered seat to help the sitter avoid an unexpected hard spot.

The upholstery was trim, tightly constructed to emphasize the dynamic lines of the couch. No springs were used during this period; only webbing, grass or hair stuffing, and a canvas covering overlaid with the finished silk lampas upholstery fabric. To accent borders and emphasize compositional order, it was customary to use woven cloth tapes of classical design for the margins and ends of the upholstery.

Cornucopias replace the customary wings of the animal-paw feet. Richly carved acanthus-leaf and rosette details enhance the scrolled head and foot of the couch.

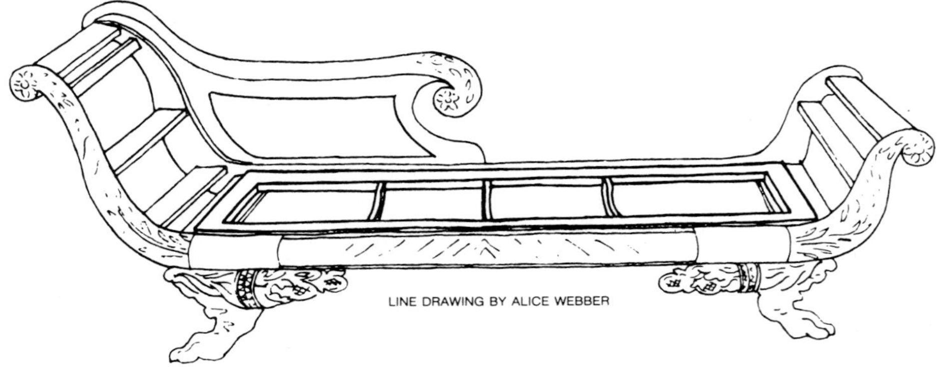

LINE DRAWING BY ALICE WEBBER

Grecian Couch
New York. 1820–1840.
Mahogany and pine veneer.
Collection of Mrs. Charles L. Bybee.

A "Grecian couch" as it was called in Early Victorian America, this seven-foot-long composition of curves and severe straight lines was characteristic of fashionable parlor seating for well-to-do merchants' homes at a moment of high national optimism and extensive commercial growth. The carved cornucopias surmounting the four legs and deeply sculptured foliate detail are adapted from ancient classical sources. Besides reflecting classical culture, they also suggest the expected abundance of a burgeoning new nation.

Horsehair upholstery covers the couch and brilliantly figured mahogany veneer emphasizes the pleasure in optical richness desired by Early Victorian taste both in America and abroad.

Armchair
Massachusetts. Probably c. 1825.
Mahogany front and back; seat rails ash.
H: 39″ W: 23½″ D: 19″.
The Newark Museum.

Part of a set of ten side chairs and two armchairs, this example illustrates the extent to which classical motifs were sometimes adapted in an additive way without great regard for the integration of parts. Each element taken by itself is well executed and appealing. The favorite classical motif of a dolphin on the arms of the chair is even carried through on the crest. But each part seems to have been planned separately without much regard for the adjoining element. Perhaps this disharmony reflects piecework by several different craftsmen, otherwise it could simply indicate that the designer did not have an eye for overall form.

Side Chair Backs—Early Victorian Classical
Coastal United States. 1830–1850.

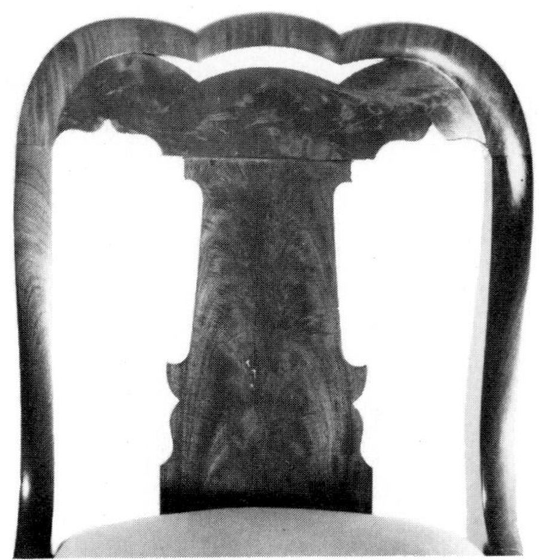

Side Chair Back
Massachusetts. 1830–1850.
Mahogany.
Private Collection.

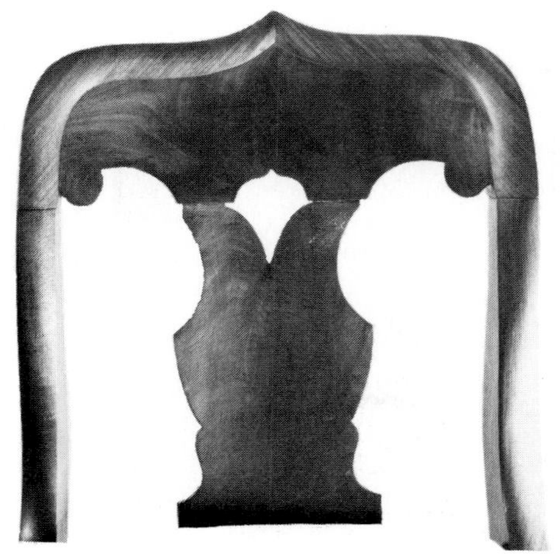

Side Chair Back
Probably New Jersey or New York. c. 1830–1850.
Mahogany.
Private Collection.

Side Chair Back
Massachusetts. c. 1830–1850.
Mahogany.
Private Collection.

Side Chair Back
Probably Philadelphia.
c. 1830–1840.
Maple, painted and gilt.
Private Collection.

Variations on Grecian chair backs are as diverse in form as the Greek revival homes for which they were made. Whether they were factory made or the product of small specialty shops, they all had in common a sleekness of design and a quality of elegant restraint and refinement that reflected an era during which self-improvement societies, lyceums and classical academies were popular.

Detail—Oil Painting on Canvas of Unknown Young Male Springfield, Massachusetts. c. 1840. Possibly by Joseph W. Stock (1815–1855). H: 54" W: 40". Courtesy of James Abbe, Jr.

Broad expanses of mahogany veneer furniture of the 1840s were parallel with the preference for black clothing popular at the same moment. Both furniture and clothing rely for their visual impact upon their silhouette or strong outline and upon the unity achieved through an even balance of parts. Small pattern, detail or intricate workmanship was subdued in all the arts in order to achieve serene, powerful and unified composition. The principle of unity was espoused not only in furniture and clothing design but also in architecture and sculpture. Even in geometrical studies, beauty was considered in terms of classical balance or symmetry. All beautiful objects in nature and art were believed to be composed of identical halves around a medial line or axis. The Greek temple, human face and classical couch were all composed in an arrangement identified as the "symmetry of the first degree."

Watercolor and Gouache
Anonymous American Interiors
Said to Be Portraits of Mr. and Mrs. Wing, c. 1840.
H: 17" W: 14½".
Museum of Fine Arts, Boston.

DAN FARBER, PHOTOGRAPHER

Two styles illustrate what Early Victorian Americans thought were symbolically appropriate for masculine and feminine environments. Mr. Wing is surrounded by furniture in the Grecian style. The cut of his clothing is trim and sleek like the machined sharp-edged profile of the furniture. Deep scrollwork in the furniture is played against flat and relatively unornamented surface; the style is severe and businesslike.

By contrast, Mrs. Wing sits on a sofa whose curvilinear lines relate to the rococo revival and femininity. Opposing C-scroll ornament and cabriole legs are features of this ornamental style. Her dress is elaborate; she wears a paisley shawl around her shoulders. Her hairstyle and lace headdress are fussy. Mr. Wing sits by a table with business papers. Mrs. Wing is also posed with the attributes of her

DAN FARBER, PHOTOGRAPHER

assigned role—a handkerchief, fan and nosegay. To emphasize the feminine qualities of the setting, a large basket of flowers blooms in the background. The rococo or "antique" style, as it was called, was considered especially appropriate for use in rooms intended for women—the boudoir, parlor or music room. To interchange the two figures in their opposite settings would have been unthinkable. Style played an important part not only in expressing but also in molding roles in society.

Pianoforte
Baltimore. 1830–1840.
By Joseph Hiskey, Pianoforte Maker. (b. in Vienna; d. in Baltimore, 1848). Mahogany with mahogany veneer and satinwood inlay; brass and gold-leaf decoration. H: 36″ W: 67″ D: 32½″.
Greenfield Village and the Henry Ford Museum, Dearborn, Michigan.

Joseph Hiskey's name first appeared in the Baltimore directory in 1819 as a pianoforte maker. His engraved label on paper was glued to the center of the pianoforte above the keyboard, colored and edged with gold leaf before the final shellac finish was applied to the whole surface of the case. The panel above the keyboard is actually an engraving showing a romantic pastoral landscape of trees and water, made by Medairy, Bannerman and Smith. The ornamental artist who decorated the case of this piece is unknown. Exuberance of form in the pedestal support of this instrument is only excelled by its brilliance of freehand gilt decoration. The upper part or case displays a rich contrast of broad dark panels against flamelike honey-colored veneer bands. Baltimorians seem to have favored this type of veneer treatment since the Federal Period.

Dressing Bureau
Baltimore, Maryland. 1830–1853.
Labeled by John Needles (1786–1878).
Mahogany on pine and tulip.
H: 79⅜" W: 46" D: 23⅜".
Winterthur Museum.

Few pieces of Early Victorian American furniture possess such design contrasts as this one. The upper section is alive with movement and richly carved ornament. By contrast, the lower or drawer section has smoothly shaped surfaces with only a few touches of carving at the wooden knobs and around the feet. The concept of contrasts was an important force in the imagination of nineteenth-century Americans. Good versus evil, fragile versus robust, light versus dark are but three of an infinite range of contrasts explored and exploited by all nineteenth-century arts including literature, music and architecture.

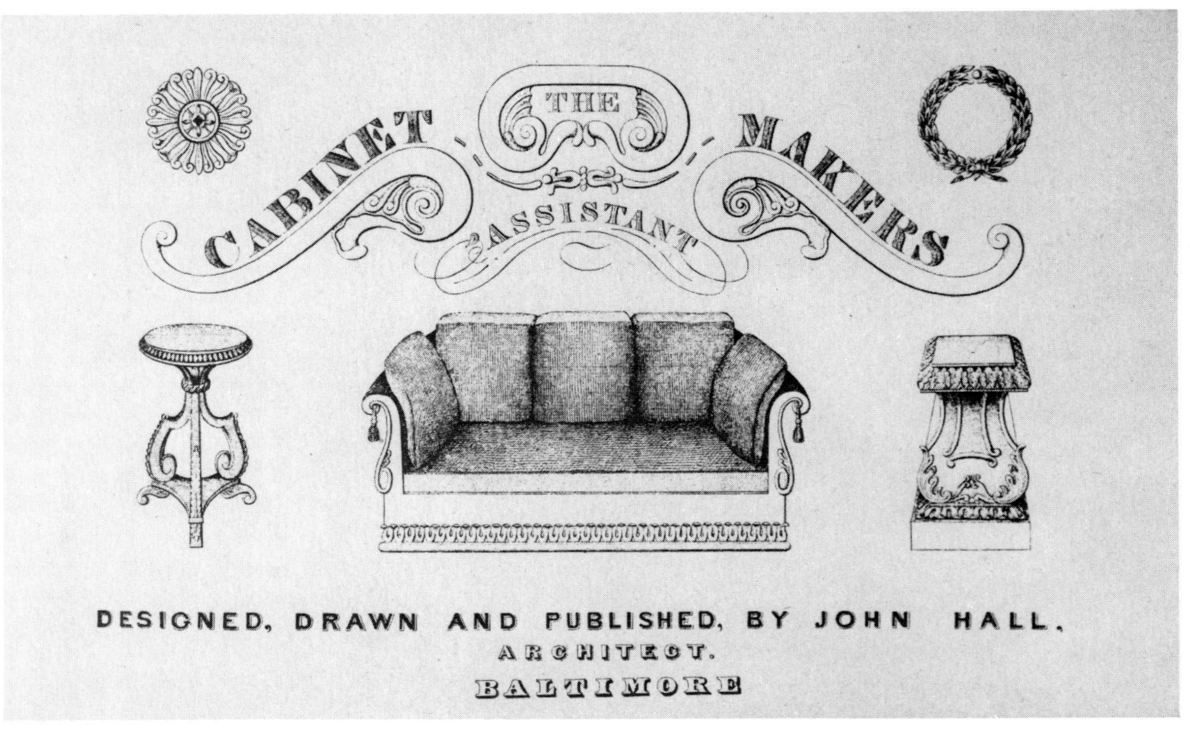

Title Page—The Cabinet Makers Assistant
By John Hall. Baltimore, Maryland. 1840.
H: 5½" L: 9⅜".

The first design book for cabinetmakers published in the United States was a modest work by draftsman John Hall, who identified himself as an architect.

Hall's book illustrates a style variously called pillar and scroll, Greco-Roman, ogee, or Early Victorian. This style has counterparts both in Early Victorian England and in the smooth lines of furniture made during the French restoration of the House of Bourbon (1814–1830). The visual effect of the furniture illustrated by Hall depends on the harmonizing of strong, sure, plain surfaces cut with steam-powered machinery from veneers of richly figured West Indian mahogany and satinwood.

Containing forty-four plates, this design book offered cabinetmakers patterns for work and instructions in perspective drawing. Earlier cabinetmakers' price books of the Federal Period were designed to serve as explanatory guides to pricing but not to assembling furniture patterns. They simply reflected the current standard prices for popular furniture forms.

RICHARD CHEEK, PHOTOGRAPHER

Center Table
Boston. 1830–1850.
Signed "S. Beal."
Pine and mahogany veneer, black and figured; marble top.
H: 30" W: 37¾" D: 30¾".
Private Collection.

In an advertisement in the *Daily Evening Transcript* for July 24, 1830, the Boston manufacturer Samuel Beal proclaimed a wide variety of furniture. His list included fancy chairs, wooden seated chairs (all colors), rocking chairs, desk stools, bureaus, dressing cases, secretaries, dressing Pembroke tables, Grecian and other tables, mahogany and birch Pembroke tables, workstands, toilet tables, washstands, couches, sofas, sofa bedsteads, looking glasses, bedsteads, fire sets, portable writing desks, timepieces, bellows and brushes, book racks, wardrobes, chairs, sinks, night cabinets, night chairs, cribs and cradles and chair cushions. Obviously he was more than a furniture manufacturer—he was a furniture and home furnishings dealer. Feathers and mattresses were also among his stock in trade.

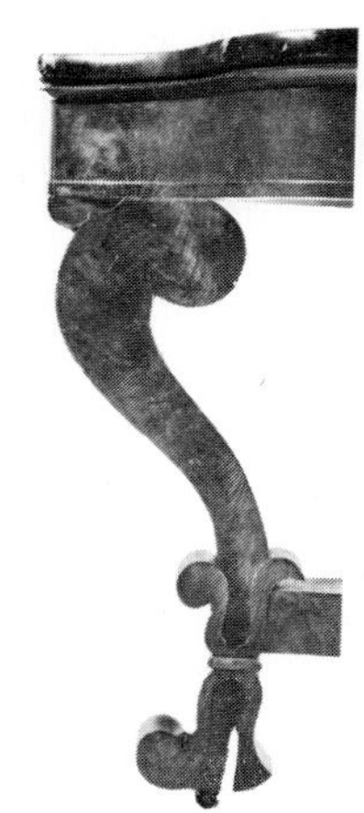

The fanciful scroll forms which comprise the supports to this table are representative of Early Victorian taste. The design is similar to others reproduced in John Hall's furniture pattern book, *The Cabinet Makers Assistant.* The table was probably termed "Grecian" in style. It was perfectly suited to the mixed Gothic and Greek revival house in Dorchester from which it came.

Secretary-Bookcase
Philadelphia. c. 1830.
Labeled by Anthony G. Quervelle (1789–1856).
Mahogany with maple, tulip and pine. H: 102″ W: 50″ D: 23½″.
Munson-Williams-Proctor Institute, Utica, New York.

Secretary-Bookcase
Philadelphia. c. 1827.
Labeled by Anthony G. Quervelle.
Mahogany, mahogany veneer, tulip, cedar, pine and burl ash.
H: 109½″ W: 66½″ D: 25½″.
The Philadelphia Museum of Art.

The Parisian émigré Anthony G. Quervelle moved to Philadelphia in 1817 and produced the finest cabinetry in town. Two of his most outstanding bookcases are compared. Both are monumental works of visually startling energy. Both are rigorously controlled exercises in geometric problems. Both use a distinctive large-scale, fan-shape relief in the lower section and present a prominent and richly carved foliate Classical cornice at the top. Other parallels and differences are obvious.

Desk and Bookcase
New York City. 1835–1840.
Possibly by Joseph Meeks and Sons.
Mahogany on pine. H: 91¾" W: 52⅜" D: 14³⁄₁₆".
The Metropolitan Museum of Art, New York.

Both Classical and Gothic details are combined here in a handsome mixture of pillar and scroll and Restoration styles. The Early Victorian Period in American furniture seemed to favor such admixtures of Romantic-Classicism.

Many hundreds of cabinetmaking firms throughout the larger cities of America produced furniture in this style.

DRAWING BY C. K. STELLWAGEN, 1864; WESTERN RESERVE HISTORICAL SOCIETY

Side Chair (One of a Pair)
New York City, New York. c. 1846.
Black walnut. H: 34" W: 17¼" D: 17".
Museum of Fine Arts, Boston.

M. DOUGLAS SCHMIDT, PHOTOGRAPHER

Victorian Americans were by no means adverse to mixing antique styles. Here, Gothic detail ornaments the classical form. This chair matches several which were made for President James K. Polk for the White House in 1846–1847.

During Abraham Lincoln's Presidency, twelve of these chairs were pictured in his Cabinet Room. Four chairs from this set are now in Lincoln's Bedroom; others are scattered in public and private collections. National Archives records show a White House order in 1846 for two groups of twelve "BW [black walnut?] Gothic Chairs" from J. and J. W. Meeks. This order may account for the chairs of Lincoln's Cabinet Room. The original upholstery which survives on some of the chairs is now a faded green plush. The chairs seem to correspond to those pictured in the 1864 sketch of the Cabinet Room by C. K. Stellwagen.

Attribution of these chairs to Meeks is complicated by an almost identical oak chair stenciled: "From A. & F. Roux/479 Broadway/ N.Y.," which can be dated from the address on the stencil to the year 1848. Other side chairs of this form are known in mahogany, walnut and oak.

Gaming Table
New York. 1829–1835.
Attributed to Joseph Meeks and Sons.
Mahogany. H: 30¼" W: 43½" D: 25½".
Collection of Lee B. Anderson.

In this table, Gothic and Classical form and detail are fancifully intermixed. A painted slate panel is inset on the top for gaming. Nineteenth-century Americans believed themselves the rightful heirs of artistic styles from all past civilizations. They believed it was their destiny to reshape past styles for new ends and to select handcrafted forms from antiquity that would suit the dawning era of large-scale factory production.

HELGA PHOTO STUDIO, INC.

HELGA PHOTO STUDIO, INC.

Serving Board
Boston, Massachusetts. c. 1837. Walnut, pink marble.
H: 35" W: 43½" D: 18½".
Collection of Lee B. Anderson.

Conservative in form, but advanced in ornamental detail, this sideboard or serving table was presented by a group of friends to the Boston Unitarian minister Theodore Parker (1810–1860) in 1837. The date is early for a piece of furniture with such an archaeologically correct approach to Gothic detail. But the overall form of the piece harkens backward to the Chippendale style of the eighteenth century.

Eighteen thirty-seven not only marks the year when Queen Victoria came to the throne, it also marks the moment when styles in American art took a clearly archaeological approach to reviewing past ornament and forms in architecture, furniture and other arts. The Gothic was only one of many styles that were reinterpreted with new knowledge and with more accurate vision than ever before.

PHOTOGRAPH BY WADHAMS/MAHAFFEY

Side or Hall Chair
Boston or New York. 1840–1850.
Mahogany, mahogany veneer, chestnut. H: 44½" W: 17½" D: 17½".
Museum of Fine Arts, Boston.

This chair is especially choice because it bears its original needlepoint seat and back.

The twisted rear posts and front legs are features found in many newspaper advertisements placed by Boston furniture makers. A. J. Downing called such twisted turnings "Elizabethan," but most Early Victorian Americans simply called the chair style "Gothic."

Small Side Chair
Boston, Massachusetts.
Labeled by Gilbert D. Whitmore (active c. 1843–1865).
Walnut; secondary wood: white pine.
H: 30¾" W: 13½" D: 14".
Collection of Lee B. Anderson.

A child's chair or a small and readily portable sample chair made for demonstration to obtain commissions, this chair in Gothic revival style has a charm that is missing in some of its larger counterparts. Its ornament is made simply with turning, saw work and carving.

HELGA PHOTO STUDIO, INC.

Gothic revival furniture made in nineteenth-century America is rare. Even rarer is furniture made in the Gothic style that was actually constructed from the designs of a major architect.

The small drawing shown on the opposite page, a unique document, is shown with pieces made after the drawings. The wheel-back chairs and pedestal table were made for William and Philip R. Paulding's grand Gothic-style villa "Lyndhurst" on the Hudson River near Tarrytown, New York. The group can be seen in the front hall of the house for which Andrew J. Davis designed the first section in

1838. Davis approached all of his work with vigor and a sensitivity to the picturesque effects of material and the qualities of light and shadow. He gathered ideas from a wide variety of sources. The most specific source of inspiration for Davis's furniture designs seems to have been the work of the English Gothic revivalist Augustus W. Pugin. Davis recomposed the ideas he selected and developed his own expressive "Gothic" solutions to modern furniture needs. His work is not as seriously archaeological as the designs of Pugin.

Richard Byrne (1805–1883) and Ambrose White (c. 1794–after 1866) were cabinetmakers on the Hudson who translated many of the Davis drawings into palpable reality. Davis's drawings and the pieces made after them represent some of the earliest and most important examples of Early Victorian Gothic revival furniture made in America.

Drawing
By Alexander J. Davis (1803–1892).
Drawing Probably Done in 1841.
Pencil on paper. H: 4 3/8" W: 6 5/8".
Avery Architectural Library, Columbia University.

Side Chair and Pedestal Table
Designed by Alexander J. Davis, 1841. Probably Made by Richard Byrne or Ambrose Wright, c. 1842.
Oak. Chair —H:37" W: 18 1/2" D: 17 1/2". Table—H: 29 1/4" Diameter of top: 34 1/2".
Lyndhurst, New York.

HELGA PHOTO STUDIO, INC.

STYLE ANTIQUE

DAN FARBER, PHOTOGRAPHER

New York Parlor View, 1854
From Gleason's Pictorial, *Boston, Saturday, November 11, 1854.*

A wealthy merchant's uptown parlor is illustrated with furniture made by Bembe and Kimmel of No. 56 Walker Street, New York. The taste for the French antique style is dominant. The editorial caption notes that: "A single glance at the furniture will satisfy the connoisseur that it is the production of a master hand. There is nothing obtrusive in the designs. The ornamentation is not vulgarly elaborate, but each single article is in keeping with the whole; hence the general effect is pleasing. A man of refinement would find the room suitable—a drawing room where a lady of elegant manners and educated taste might appropriately receive her guests." Despite what may seem an excess of elaborate, fussy, over-encumbered detail, the room does compose well as a whole. There is a spacious quality necessary and fitting for the generous dresses of the time, an aspect of room design which is often overlooked in modern re-creations of mid-nineteenth-century interiors.

The room is dominated by the étagère, the most elaborate piece of cabinetwork—an important symbol of status during the period. The center table and its adjacent sofa are the next most dominant elements. The tall pier glass expands the architectural character of the room. The flower stand at a window with a casually placed upholstered chair beside it introduces studied informality, as does the ottoman or small stool in the foreground.

The editorial identified Bembe and Kimmel as a "French house," for although the furniture was made in New York, the firm was, in fact, international. Bembe and Kimmel's European connections maintained their currency with fashions from abroad. As new models were introduced abroad, Bembe and Kimmel offered them in the United States.

Comparison: Étagères

Mid-Victorian Americans saw the flowering of the étagère as the most remarkable piece of furniture in the parlor. Two works are compared: one is from Philadelphia and the other (on overleaf), from Boston. The former is more gracefully curvilinear. Bostonians are not known to have ordered étagères of comparable complexity of line.

Étagère
Probably Philadelphia. c. 1850.
Rosewood. H: 9′ W: 6′.
Collection of Eileen Dubrow.

Victorian Americans most often lavished their greatest imaginative whimsy on what they called an *étagère*—a French term for a large whatnot. Its main function was to provide elaborate staging for trophies: China art objects and souvenirs of all sorts. The étagère was the focus of all available ornamental techniques—carving, turning, jigsaw work, and sometimes inlay and gold leaf. The resultant complexity was amplified by mirrors placed in the back and behind the side shelves.

Like an elaborate confection or dessert, this étagère was meant to be slowly examined section by section. It was a memory piece—a large trophy chamber upon which could be gathered a lifetime of experience associated with the objects collected.

Rococo revival furniture was expensive; it became the social index of success in a well-appointed parlor. Its complex carving and shaped form took skilled labor and much time. The suave urbanity of the work of Alexander Roux's shop in New York City is compared here with a lesser work—a rosewood cabinet étagère which was made by Elijah Galusha of Troy, New York. The urban craftsman clearly understood composition better. But even so, Galusha managed to create the necessary shimmering richness of surface in his version of the rococo style.

Étagère
Boston, Massachusetts. 1864.
Labeled "George Croome & Co., Upholsterers and Manufacturers of Fashionable Furniture."
Mahogany. H: 98" W: 68" D: 20½".
Museum of Fine Arts, Boston.

Bostonians were also attracted to the curved ornament of the rococo revival. While most of George Croome's advertisements seem to rely on Gothic-style furniture as a trademark, this piece shows that his shop catered to all tastes.

The top finial has been restored, but otherwise the piece is without flaw. By comparison with Philadelphia and New York étagères, this piece is relatively restrained. Yet it probably is not the most outlandishly rococo piece made in nineteenth-century Boston. Such furniture yet remains to be discovered.

Étagère
Troy, New York. c. 1850. Attributed to Elijah Galusha.
Rosewood, marble, glass.
H: 72½" W: 44" D: 22½".
Munson-Williams-Proctor Institute, Utica, New York.

An exuberant revival of the rococo style took place in most major cabinet shops of America between 1840 and 1860. The revival was far from a literal translation of the eighteenth-century rococo. Carved alternating, sweeping S-shaped scrolls often terminated in foliage or flowers as illusionistic as those of a nineteenth-century still life. Mid-nineteenth-century nature worship in America had pietistic overtones. Ornament was not just a matter of laborious, elaborate decoration.

The service the étagère performed was essentially a social one. As it was not a necessary piece of furniture, its richness implied that the owner had means to spend lavishly. Indeed, the more ornate the étagère the more effectively it served its social ends. The maker of this piece employed a power milling machine for molding detail to simulate the rippled surface of seventeenth-century Dutch framing. Machines were used to carve the gadrooned detail along the front edges of the cabinet top and shelves. While the general profile of much of the openwork might have been sawn with jig- or band saws, the finial work was accomplished by talented hand carving. Such a variety of skills were involved to produce a piece of this complexity that there is little doubt that many different craftsmen were involved.

Étagère
New York City. 1850–1857.
Labeled by Alexander Roux. Rosewood.
Metropolitan Museum of Art.

COURTESY OF PETER HILL

Alexander Roux (1837–1881) came closer to the eighteenth-century rococo style in this rosewood étagère and side table than did most of his contemporary cabinetmakers. Despite Roux's knowledge of the use of opposing C-scrolls and other principles of rococo design, he could not resist the nineteenth-century impulse to simulate nature in carved detail. The naturalism of the floral ornament is an astonishing accomplishment, reflecting the highest level of technical skill. Rosewood is not an easily worked material. Its grain is open and its resinous nature creates difficulties for finish and glue joinery. Challenge attracted the most able craftsmen in nineteenth-century America. The color of rosewood—varying from a dark red to orange veined with black in broad waving lines—held strong appeal. The beautifully variegated figure of the wood was obtained by sawing across the concentric rings of annular growth. This rich surface offered Roux the chance to heighten the illusion of movement within the wood itself even as the piece visually exploded with carving. Triumph after artistic triumph was achieved with garlands of flowers, bouquets and scrolls. At the focal point in the center of the apron was carved a portrait bust of a woman. Her hairstyle is distinctly eighteenth century. She probably was meant to represent the mistress of Louis XV, Madame de Pompadour.

End Table with Tilting Top
New York City. 1850–1860.
Stamped "A. Roux, New York."
Rosewood. H: 30" W: 19" L: 25½".
William Penn Memorial Museum.

This stylish table could be called "Bamboo Gothic." The turned uprights simulate bamboo and allude to the Orient. The treatment of the feet, by contrast, is angular with piercing vaguely reminiscent of the Middle Ages. Despite the strange synthesis of inspirations, the table has a vigor, quality and distinctive stance. Its proportions are harmonious and attractive. Its workmanship and overall quality speak well for the respected shop from which it came.

Card Table (One of a Pair)
New York City. 1852.
Labeled by Charles A. Baudouine (b. 1808, New York; d. 1895).
Rosewood. H: 29¾" L: 46" D: 16".
Munson-Williams-Proctor Institute, Utica, New York.

Certainly the most elegant of rococo revival tables made in mid-nineteenth-century America, this example does not rely on heavy bouquets of floral carving for its power. There is a fine balance between ornamented and plain surfaces, a good sense of proportion in the long and short scroll forms that oppose each other in alternating rhythms of movement. At the time this piece was made Charles A. Baudouine employed nearly seventy workers at his shop located at 335 Broadway. James Watson Williams ordered this table for his home, "Fountain Elms." It was meant to be used with its mate, pulled together as a "multi-form table." Each individual table could be opened with its top supported on pivoting legs.

End Table
Philadelphia. c. 1860.
Marked: "Regester Bell & Co., 526 Callowhill St., Phila. Pa."
Walnut with marble top. H: 28" W: 16" L: 21".
William Penn Memorial Museum.

A strong silhouette intrigued the designer of this table. The shapes are aggressive, angular and intimidating. The support to the marble top is imaginative and unusual. Although the top is not sound in terms of stress and joinery, that issue is irrelevant to Victorian taste. Much artistic criticism of the mid- to late nineteenth century was concerned with the use of silhouette or strong "sky blotch" effects. In this sense, the table succeeds admirably.

Coat Rack
Charleston, South Carolina. c. 1860. Mahogany; Cast-iron pan.
H: 85⅝" W: 31⅝" D: 13".
Privately Owned.

This splendid example of Mid-Victorian taste flutters with movement. It is richly inlaid with polished brass fleurs-de-lis, stringing and other ornament wherever the surface needs additional accents at points of transition.

The attribution to a South Carolina origin is simply an assumption, based on additional pieces which have survived together with this example in the same family ownership. Of all Eastern seaboard cities best noted for elegant brass inlay, Boston was paramount. But no known Boston furniture of this period excels this example in its richness of ornament or its effective silhouette.

Bedstead
New York. c. 1853.
Die stamped "J. H. Belter/Patent
Aug. 19, 1856/N.Y."
on head, foot and all four sides.
John Henry Belter (1804–1863). Laminated rosewood.
L: 86" H: (headboard) 64".
Mr. and Mrs. Richard Manney.

This piece represents Belter's greatest triumph as a designer and maker of furniture. Die-stamped in twelve places on the frame of this bedstead is Belter's notice of his patent dated August 19, 1856. The bedstead was made in two large pieces held together at the center with a notched frame rather than the usual stile and rail construction of the period. The technology made use of large sheets of beautifully figured laminated wood in much the same manner that plywood was shaped for molded chairs by Marcel Breuer and Charles Eames in the 1930s and 40s.

Belter's patent drawings for his molded bedstead showed clearly the nine layers of wood he preferred, laid at right angles, glued, and pressed between hot cauls for seven hours before the addition of more wood for carved ornament. The bedstead illustrated here conforms almost exactly to that of his patent illustration. However, this bedstead is less ornate than the drawing and shows to greater advantage the beauty of the sweeping lines of the bent wood than the patent drawing suggested.

Dressing Bureau
New York City. After 1856.
Laminated and carved rosewood; top, white marble.
H: 95" W: 49½" D: 25".
Brooklyn Museum.

The carving of the pediment on this bureau is heavier than that found on other Belter furniture. The bureau came as a gift to the Brooklyn Museum as a set with a laminated rosewood bedstead which bears a stamp, "J. H. Belter, Patent, August 15, 1856, N. Y." It seems possible that the bureau was from Belter's shop, but probably carved by a craftsman who might have done journeyman work in a number of other shops in town. Despite the concentration of florid rococo ornament at the crest and on the front of the bureau, the basic shape of the piece is remarkably simple.

HELGA PHOTO STUDIO, INC.

Dressing Bureau
New York. c. 1860.
Attributed to John Henry Belter (1804–1863).
Laminated rosewood. H: 94½" W: 47½" D: 23".
Mr. and Mrs. Richard Manney.

This is one of the few dressers that can be attributed to Belter with some confidence. The shape is very close to the patent drawing which Belter submitted for U.S. Patent No. 26,881, dated January 24, 1860. Like the patent, the serpentine front and sides of this cabinet are made of single pieces of laminated wood shaped in hot cauls and joined with a glued scarf at the back. It is a remarkable piece of construction, modern in its engineering methods, but overlaid with the customary rococo carving for drawer-pulls, ornamental crest and columnar corners. The advantage cited by Belter in his patent for working wood in this way was that the whole front and sides of the piece could be made of a single broad sheet and sawed apart for drawers. By making the face of the bureau out of a single laminated sheet he was able to report that the "whole front may be made to exhibit a degree of unity hardly practicable or possible where stretchers are required." Belter's patent also eliminated unnecessary dust boards and stretchers as space wasters between drawers.

Belter was a design functionalist concerned first with overall unity of design, economy and utility. For many people who see his works today, that message may be lost in the flurry of carved ornament.

HELGA PHOTO STUDIO, INC.

Center Table
New York. c. 1850–1860.
Attributed to John Henry Belter.
Laminated rosewood with rosewood top.
H: 28½" Diameter of top: 31¼".
Mr. and Mrs. Richard Manney.

A center table meant to dominate a parlor, this table was most probably accompanied by a suite of similarly carved furniture. The style was variously described by Victorians as "Antique," "the modern French style," "Louis Quatorze" or "Louis Quinze." None of these terms were accurate, for nineteenth-century revival styles treated forms very differently from their eighteenth-century models. The laminated and bentwood process utilized by Belter and his competitors allowed for an extravagance of deeply pierced arabesques and naturalistic ornament in natural wood not possible in eighteenth-century furniture. Roses, flower baskets, leafage and clusters of grapes were intertwined in this table in a manner compellingly nineteenth century in its imitation of nature.

Center Tables
New York. 1856–1861.
Labeled by John Henry Belter (1804–1863).

Circular Table—Laminated and carved rosewood; marble top (veined green and deep red). H: 28¼″ D: 38¼″.
Museum of the City of New York.

Born and trained in Germany, John Henry Belter came to America in the 1840s, quickly establishing himself as a master in his profession. By 1847 he had patented a machine for sawing "Arabesque Chairs," a jigsaw device to saw the intricate piercings of elaborately carved chair backs and aprons of tables. His most significant manufacturing innovations were methods to make deeply bent wood pieces and to multiply layered or laminated woods quickly. Belter did not claim to invent the laminating process nor to have exclusive rights to the use of cauls or molds to shape the wood. What he did claim in his patent dated February 23, 1858, was a special technique to manipulate the wood with staves, slots, cauls and sawing for more economical, efficient production. A table of this complexity could not have been produced by assembly-line methods or without highly technical and varied skills.

Belter's large factory employed German immigrant craftsmen who came to this country in large numbers during and after the European revolutions of 1848.

Oblong Table—Laminated and carved rosewood, white marble top.
H: 29″ W: 44″ D: 28″.
Mr. and Mrs. Richard Manney.

✶

HELGA PHOTO STUDIO, INC.

This table illustrates the enormous visual excitement made possible with new technology. Contrasting with the motion of the explosive ornament of the wood is the serenity of the simple, chalk-white marble top. The purity of white marble had a strong appeal for Victorians; it offered an effective opposition to the dark and tortured surface of the wood below. Such contrast was an essential part of Victorian aesthetic systems.

Couch
New York. c. 1850.
Belter School.
Laminated rosewood. H: 37¾" W: 39" D: 31".
Mr. and Mrs. Richard Manney.

HELGA PHOTO STUDIO, INC.

From the early nineteenth century to the present, the small-scale open-ended sofa has continued to enjoy popular appeal in this country. With each successive generation, its shape has changed. By the mid-nineteenth century, the head of the couch had acquired outscrolled wings or graceful arms shaped into the upholstered back panel. This form has been popularly called a *méridienne,* but most nineteenth-century Americans would have referred to it as a couch.

Buoyance for great physical comfort resulted from coil springs, tufting and an ample supply of down pillows. In a visual way the sinuous line of the back captures the essence of this idea. Such wavy form reflects the flexible nature and sensuousness of the upholstery.

HELGA PHOTO STUDIO, INC.

Pair of High-Backed Chairs
New York. c. 1850. Belter School. Laminated rosewood.
H: 43¾" W: 18" D: 21".
Mr. and Mrs. Richard Manney.

Victorians had a special affection for the high-backed chair. It could sustain a rich play of embellishment. Twined around the borders of these chair backs is writhing abstract form. The matrix of the back is a dense mass of grapes, roses, acorns and leaves. The carving certainly represents picturesque taste—where raw nature is controlled or domesticated for use by mankind. The carving manifests an era and culture in which nature was exploited in every way imaginable.

Armchair or Easy Chair
New York. c. 1850.
Probably by John Henry Belter.
Laminated rosewood.
H: 46" W: 25¾" D: 36¾".
Mr. and Mrs. Richard Manney.

John Henry Belter is reputed to have owned this armchair. Even if it were possible to prove that the chair came from his shop, that connection alone would not be sufficient evidence that Belter personally executed or supervised the carving. However, the delicacy of the chair's workmanship, the naturalism of the carving and the openness of its composition provide persuasive arguments for a Belter attribution. Belter's competitors did not handle their carved ornament with equal grace or ease. The strength of the laminated wood safe-guarded against the danger of splitting and allowed for sweeping, abstract lines never possible before.

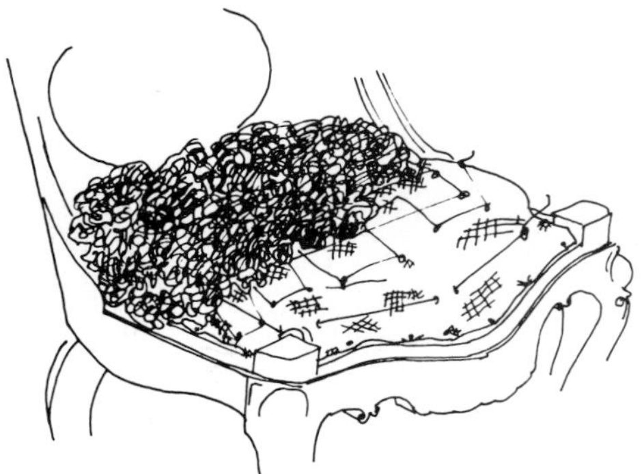

Horsehair and Stitching

Tying

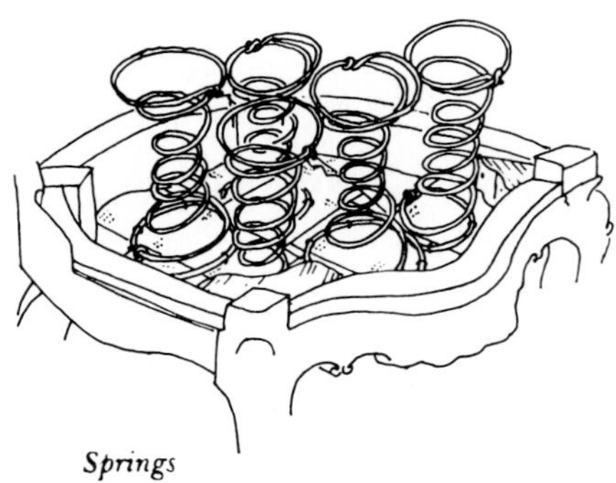

Springs

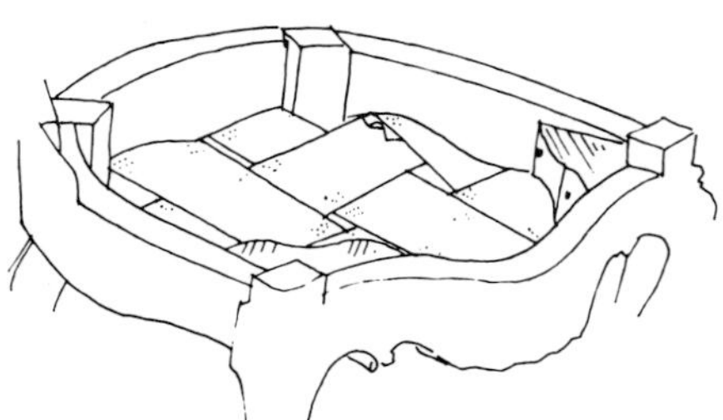

Webbing

RICHARD CHEEK, PHOTOGRAPHER

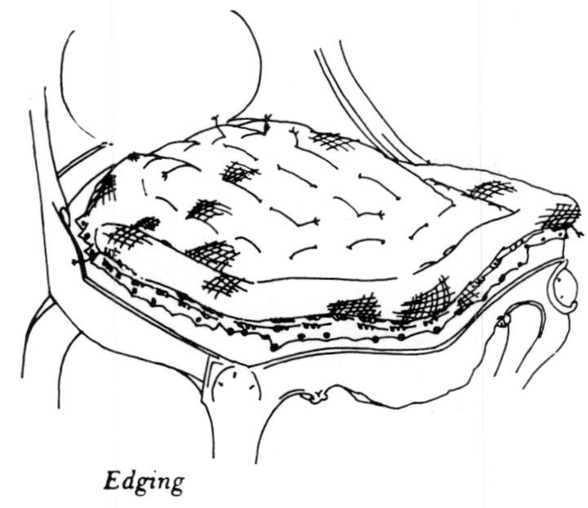

Edging

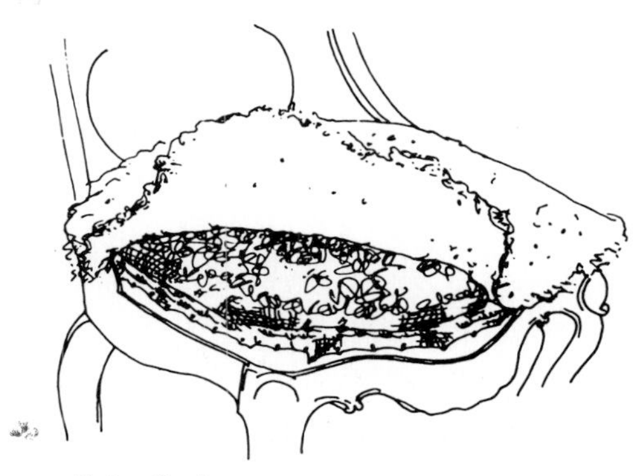

Cotton Batting

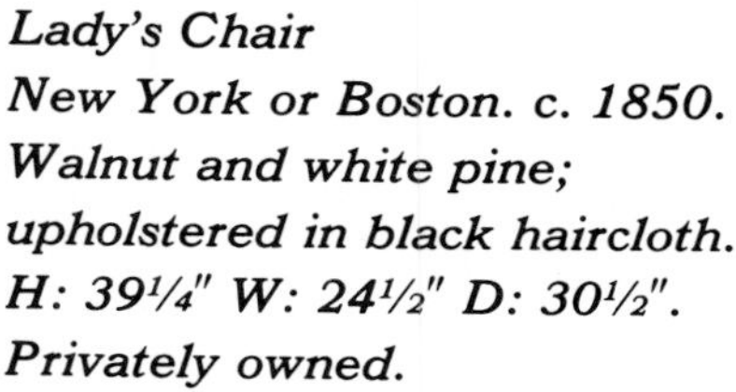

Lady's Chair
New York or Boston. c. 1850.
Walnut and white pine;
upholstered in black haircloth.
H: 39¼" W: 24½" D: 30½".
Privately owned.

The shaped figure of Victorian women is reflected in the outline of this chair. It has the sweeping silhouette and wasp waist formed by the artful manipulation of materials just like the whalebone corsetted figures of the mid-century. The seats of such Victorian chairs are spring supported and the backs are formed on a tightly sewn horsehair substructure.

Dramatic form was vital to Victorians even if it meant weakness to the basic structure of the work. As a result, chairs of this period were commonly doweled and glued together at joints where stress occurred (such as at the waist). When glue dried over several years, doweled joints came apart, leaving the owner with a problem of repair or replacement.

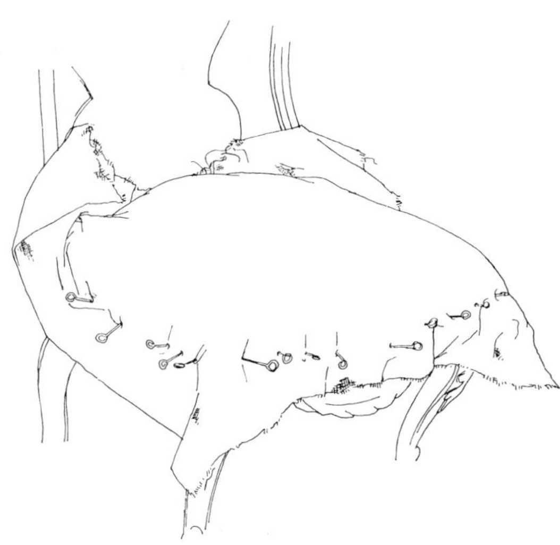

Muslin Cover Pinned for Tacking

DRAWINGS BY ALICE WEBBER

Looking Glass and Frame
Boston Area. c. 1860.
White pine with gesso, composition ornament, wire, gold leaf and distemper paint. H: 47" Diameter of glass: 23½".
Private Collection.

Virtuosity with molded putty or composition ornament makes this looking-glass frame exciting. To shape the swirling forms, the composition worker first prepared a wooden frame covered with a mixture of chalk and glue or gesso. Where ornament was to be placed on top and bottom, he nailed a support of wooden blocks and drove in nails part way to hold the molder's putty. This material, a complex mixture of oils, clay, sawdust and glues, gained its form through pressing in molds. It was held together with internal supporting wires. Several different sections were pressed and lifted gently out, carefully twisted into shape and attached to the frame and supporting blocks. After a few hours the putty hardened to its final form. The composition worker turned his work over to the gilder who sized, grounded, gold-leafed and burnished the ornament and frame. In order to conserve the gold leaf, the gilder finished the back and sides of the frame with golden ochre or earth-yellow pigment mixed in glue (a distemper binding). The convex mirror was inserted with a black-painted liner, and the whole was backed with pine boards.

Pier Looking-Glass Crest
Boston, Probably by Doe & Hazelton & Company.
1850–1860.
Pine with gesso, composition and gold leaf.
H: 16" W: 32".

The heights of rococo revival frenzy were seldom exceeded in New England furniture beyond that of this looking-glass frame. Burnished gold surfaces were contrasted with matt gilt to create a dazzling effect upon the viewer. The sweep of the S- and C-shaped ornament of the crest is as impressive as a wave of the sea.

Secretary-Bookcase
Made and Labeled by
Mitchell and Rammelsberg,
Cincinnati, Ohio. c. 1865.
Rosewood. H: 133" W: 60" D: 22".
The Newark Museum.

Furniture manufacturers in Midwestern cities from the 1860s on began to give serious competition to their Eastern counterparts. Major furniture factories prospered in Grand Rapids, in Cincinnati, and in other cities where rail, water and population growth and prosperity combined to make furniture production a profitable affair. The firm of Mitchell and Rammelsberg started in 1844 and grew in the 1860s to become the largest furniture business in the United States.

This desk or secretary-and-bookcase shows the solid sort of furniture that was desirable and harmonious with the Italianate and brownstone houses of the same period. Deep carving produced the effect of light and shadow desired by Americans who hoped to emulate European arts of the seventeenth and sixteenth centuries. While this cabinet must probably have been thought to represent Renaissance style, its use of ornament and overall form is characteristically Mid-Victorian.

Broad surfaces of richly carved ornament are distributed across the surface in a symmetrical but not very well integrated way. The lack of design integration reflects the separation of tasks inherent in factory production. It is unlikely that the man who did the case work also did the carved ornament, as this would not be an efficient production method. Production efficiency, however, frequently meant a loss in design integrity.

DAN FARBER, PHOTOGRAPHER

Watercolor
By A. Mayor, active 1850–1867 in Brooklyn, New York.
Dimensions: 5½″ × 6½″.
Museum of Fine Arts, Boston.

Not all mid-nineteenth-century rooms in urban America were furnished with the formal heavy mahogany or rosewood furniture of the rococo revival style. Upstairs rooms, which served informal needs, seem to have had a style of their own.

Painted cottage furniture, cheaply made but decorative and light in effect, gives this room its sprightly appearance. The linear effect of a spindly folding camp chair at the window is echoed in the table beside it. The hanging basket and wall lamp add other notes of easy adaptability that appeal to present-day taste. There is an appealing freshness and orderliness about the room that shows a Victorian-American appreciation for open space and restful surface at mid-century.

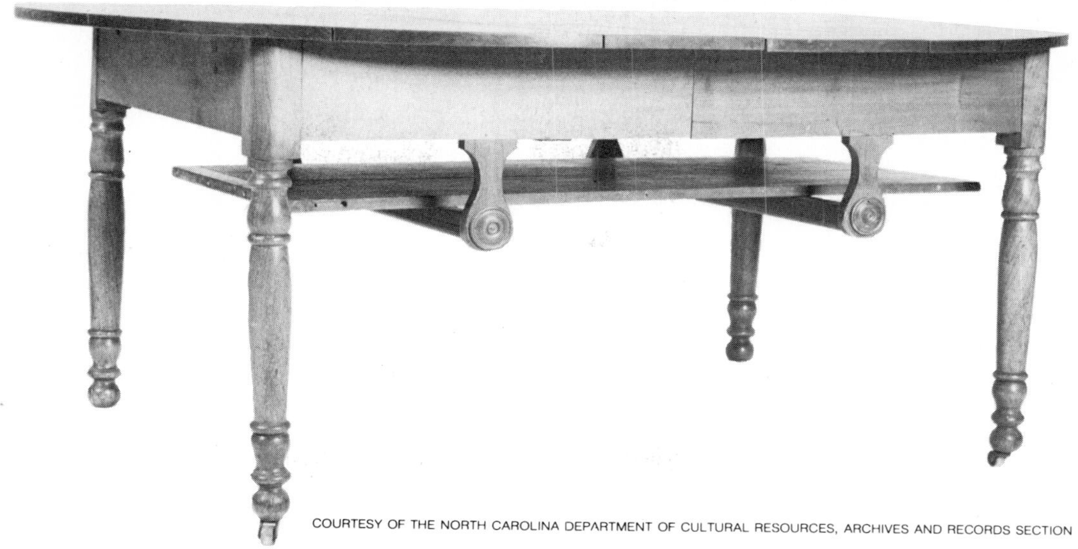

COURTESY OF THE NORTH CAROLINA DEPARTMENT OF CULTURAL RESOURCES, ARCHIVES AND RECORDS SECTION

Extension Table
Milton, North Carolina. c. 1855.
Made by Thomas Day (c. 1801–1861).
Walnut. H: 29" W: 49" L: 68".

Although this is a fairly ordinary piece of furniture, the story of its maker is extraordinary. A free black, Thomas Day, was so respected by his community of Milton, North Carolina, that in 1830 when he married a woman from Virginia, the inhabitants of his town petitioned the General Assembly of North Carolina to waive an immigration law (of 1826) which prevented blacks from moving from other slave states. The petition was successful and a bill was passed to allow his wife, Aquilla (Wilson) Day, to reside in North Carolina. This bill assured the Milton community that Day would not move his business and shop into Virginia.

By the 1850s Day employed eight other cabinetmakers, five of whom were white, a white laborer and six slaves. The 1850 census credited Mr. Day with about one-fourth of the capital investments for finish carpentry work and building in the state of North Carolina. His shop was powered with steam and his properties were among the finest in Caswell County.

With the financial panic of the late 1850s, Mr. Day's business began to fail. In 1858 he was forced into trusteeship and later declared insolvent. A year before he had won an "award premium" for a center table at the fifth annual North Carolina Fair.

Day followed closely the changing styles of Victorian furniture and adapted them to the tastes of prosperous persons of Piedmont, North Carolina, and nearby Virginia. A novel feature of this table is its suspended support brackets on which rest extra leaves; the leaves are stored underneath the table when it is not fully extended.

Dressing Chest
Boston Area. c. 1850.
Tulip and white pine painted and grained to simulate oak.
H: 78" W: 38¾" D: 19".
Privately Owned.

RICHARD CHEEK, PHOTOGRAPHER

Mass-produced or factory furniture of this sort was called "cottage furniture." Its use was in secondary or upstairs rooms such as bedrooms and servants' quarters, and for summer cottages. Cottage furniture was also recommended for and popular with working-class people. It was particularly suitable for the modest but artistic homes for which nineteenth-century architects published an astonishing variety of designs.

Construction of this chest was simple and economical. The drawer bottoms were made of single sheets of finely sawn tulipwood fitted into precision-cut grooves or rabbets on the lower sides of the drawers. Dovetail construction of the drawer sides was fairly large and simple. The power saws used in shaping the wood were mechanically true to the extent that little finishing was necessary. A few nails and screws fastened the case together, and the backside was painted an olive-ochre color. To offset the technical economy of the construction of this chest, its front was richly ornamented with grained decoration, bordered with painted rococo-like flourishes. A. J. Downing described such borders as "enriched with well-executed vignettes in the panels."

From the mid-nineteenth century to the end of Victoria's reign, painted furniture held great popular appeal in America. Most of it was cheap factory work, dressed up with painted ornament to please the eye while concealing shoddy structural details which resulted from its hasty assembly in the factories of the period. Although the interiors of such cottage furniture were usually left unfinished, the exterior surfaces were covered with graining, marbelizing and illusionistic natural detail of vines, leaves, flowers and fruit. Painting was necessarily confined to a series of stock scenes and motifs—the ornamentalist had to work quickly to make a living.

Painted Bedstead and Canopy
Gardner, Massachusetts. c. 1855.
Manufactured by Heywood Brothers & Company.

Painted Decoration Attributed to Thomas Hill (1829–1908) and Edward Hill (1843–1923).
Pine. H: 88½" W: 63½" L: 84½".
Museum of Fine Arts, Boston.

Two English brothers, Edward and Thomas Hill, who later became famous for mountain landscape paintings, started their artistic careers in Gardner, Massachusetts, as ornamental decorators for the Heywood furniture manufacturing company. Their most important piece was this unique bedstead painted as a special commission for the president of the Heywood Company.

This bedstead followed the conventional pattern of furniture for the period; it was made of relatively cheap wood but given a splendid appearance by being ebonized and embellished with romantic scenery and lush fruit still lifes, all enhanced with rococo revival borders of freehand-painted gilt work. The bedstead is the richest example of cottage furniture known. It is the mid-nineteenth-century equivalent in visual terms of eighteenth-century japanned furniture.

DAN FARBER, PHOTOGRAPHER

Tilt-top Table
Boston Area.
Signed: "J. Sharp." Dated 1869.
Probably chestnut and pine.
H: 43" (top down) 29" W: 21½" D: 28½".
Robert Treat Paine House, Waltham, Massachusetts.

This table is part of a set of painted chamber furniture. Representing the highest quality of workmanship for its time, not only in cabinetmaking but also in ornamental painting, the set was made for the Paine residence in Waltham when the earliest part of the house was completed.

Nothing is known about the painter "J. Sharp," who signed his name to the table and dated it 1869. Unlike most of his contemporary ornamentalists, he did not execute a simple decorative pattern of leafage, grain and foliage. Instead he created still-life paintings with convincing optical depth and represented fruit and flowers with such fidelity to light and shadow that the viewer is almost forced to believe in their actual presence.

DAN FARBER, PHOTOGRAPHER

E. IRVING BLOMSTRANN, PHOTOGRAPHER

Settee (One of a Pair)
Hartford, Connecticut. c. 1865.
Willow and pine. H: 42½" L: 55" D: 23".
The Wadsworth Athenaeum, Hartford, Connecticut,
Bequest of Elizabeth Hart Jarvis Colt.

In terms of design ingenuity few specimens of willow or wicker furniture made in America surpass this settee. It was made for "Armsmear," the home of Samuel Colt, manufacturer of firearms in Hartford, Connecticut. Most of the willow workers came from Bavaria, producing baskets as well as furniture. In 1873 the furniture factory where this piece was made was destroyed by fire; presumably the settee and its mate were made before that date.

The pattern of the back of the settee is hypnotic in its effect. Under the arms, the Gothic-style arches with their quadrafoil tracery create a stylistic fantasy in keeping with Victorian affection for things remote in time and space. Such willow furniture also recalls the China-trade rattan and India wares that were imported to this country throughout the nineteenth century.

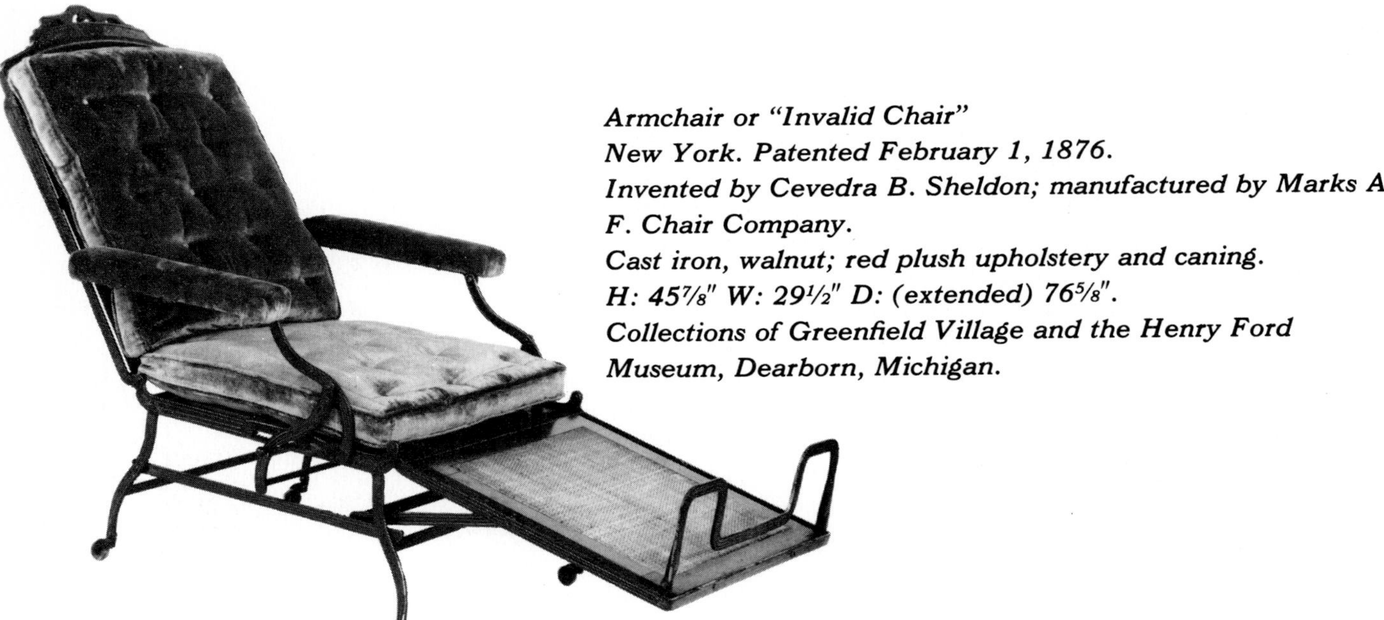

Armchair or "Invalid Chair"
New York. Patented February 1, 1876.
Invented by Cevedra B. Sheldon; manufactured by Marks A. F. Chair Company.
Cast iron, walnut; red plush upholstery and caning.
H: 45⅞" W: 29½" D: (extended) 76⅝".
Collections of Greenfield Village and the Henry Ford Museum, Dearborn, Michigan.

U.S. Patent office reports from the 1840s on carry notice of increasing numbers of inventions for patent furniture. Collapsible rockers, folding hide-a-bed cabinets, novel bedsprings, swivel chairs, baby walkers and jumpers, reclining chairs, and improvements in casters are but a few of the novel ideas that inventors and manufacturers submitted for patents. Improvement and reform were nineteenth-century bywords.

Invalid chairs were patented by the mid-nineteenth century. Augustus Eliaers of Boston advertised himself as a manufacturer of "patent Invalid chairs" (chairs with large wheels for ease of motion), the prototype of the wheelchair known today.

The novelty of the invalid chair illustrated here seems to be its cast-iron frame which is integrated into a rachet mechanism for raising and lowering the arms, back and footrest. It is a fairly simple contrivance not unlike mechanisms for later deck chairs for steamships. It is invitingly upholstered in what appears to be the original red plush cushions.

Folding Armchair
Boston, Massachusetts. c. 1880.
Made by the Boston Furniture Company.
Walnut, walnut burl and mahogany. H: 35½" W: 24½" D: 30¼".
Museum of Fine Arts, Boston.

A combination of novelty and economy created an extensive market for these popular and ingenious devices. This armchair bears the label of the Boston Furniture Company with patent dates for 1867, 1869 and 1879. It represents a specimen which was manufactured in different versions in many other cities.

The original tapestry upholstery of this chair has a broad central strip that was often used for such seating forms. Its carved detail is of a sort manageable for factory production, but handsome in effect. The popularity of such chairs suggests that they satisfied a public need to express good taste in furnishings without sacrificing economy or flexibility of function.

Reclining Armchair
New York. c. 1866 or Shortly Thereafter.
Marked: "Hunzinger/New York/Pat. Feb. 6/1866."
Walnut and other woods stained to look like walnut.
H: 38" W: 25½" D: 36½".
The Brooklyn Museum, Bequest of Elsie Patchen Halstead.

The popularity of patent furniture in the nineteenth century can be appreciated in the context of folding and reclining mechanisms exemplified by this chair. There is a relish that the designer took in the shape of the mechanism along with a fervent retention of ornamental and stylistic richness. Ornamental turnings, contrast of texture, fringe or pattern, were essential to almost every nineteenth-century furniture design. These elements gave furniture both authority and appeal. It is worth noting that this chair takes full advantage of an ingenious bracing system in the back to carry the thrust of the crossed legs and the weight of the sitter.

Wooton's Patent Desk
Indianapolis, Indiana. 1875–1884.
Black walnut with pine, poplar, maple and holly; bronze hinges and hardware.
H: 80" W: 48½" D: 31½".
Mr. and Mrs. Richard DuBrow.

As a symbol of taste, status and inventive genius, no piece of American furniture is more expressive of its time than the fabulous Wooton Patent Desk or Secretary. A Quaker with a family of seven children, William S. Wooton of Indianapolis invented, designed, patented and manufactured this marvel of ornament and gadgetry. It held enormous appeal for nineteenth-century businessmen who were managing large operations with an increasing complexity of

detail and paperwork. London dealers for the Wooton Desk advertized its merits in the following terms:

> One hundred and ten compartments, all under one lock and key. A place for everything and everything in its place. Order Reigns Supreme, Confusion Avoided. Time Saved. Vexation Spared. With This Desk one absolutely has no excuse for slovenly habits in the disposal of numerous papers, and a person of method may here realize that pleasure and comfort which is only to be attained in the verification of the maxim, a place for everything and everything in its place. Every portion of the desk is immediately before the eye. Nothing in its line can exceed it in usefulness or beauty, and purchasers everywhere express themselves delighted with its manifold convenience.
>
> *Graphic,* May 17, 1884.

What the desk provides is the formal orderliness and structured arrangement that is expressed in architectural and furniture design of the late nineteenth century. Complexity of detail in no way overshadowed the formal organization of the whole piece. Since Wooton himself was involved with a factory that employed as many as 150 workers, he understood the problems of the age, and capitalized on them. The Wooton factory made desks in four different grades and prices to suit the needs of every successful merchant or businessman—Ordinary Grade, Standard Grade, Extra-Grade and Superior-Grade desks. They ranged in price from $90 to $750. The photographs here show a Superior-Grade desk constructed of black walnut and French polished exotic veneers. Berlin bronze hardware was used on all grades of desks for heavy cast hinges, door handles and letter slots with escutcheon plates.

Drafting Table
Philadelphia. c. 1877.
G. Gates.
Cherry wood, iron and brass.
H: 31" W: (at widest part of base) 22½" D: 18".
William Penn Memorial Museum.

This adjustable drafting or folding table, patented June 19, 1877, was manufactured ready for shipping to customers together with a manufacturer's label containing directions for setting it up and operating it. While the main purpose of the table is functional and thoroughly modern in concept, the base betrays the Victorian love of ornament and concealment of what was considered "mere" utility. Four legs of angular and expressive form support the table pedestal with a thrust appropriate to the ponderous matters expected for the top. The stylistic note of the ornamental base is neo-Grec—an imaginative synthesis of Classic, Egyptian, Renaissance and Medieval ornament. Philadelphia, where this table was made, enjoyed a special flourishing of closely related architectural ornament in the 1870s.

Drawings of Augustus Eliaers' Patent Model for a Library Chair.
Museum of Fine Arts, Boston.

Augustus Eliaers was born and trained in France, where he came under the stylistic influence of the firm headed by Henri Fourdinois before coming to Boston in 1849. During the brief period before returning to his native country in 1860, he took out several patents for folding and invalid furniture. The most famous of his patent furniture was his mahogany folding library chair (1853). Full-size specimens of the chair survive and are stamped "Eliaers."

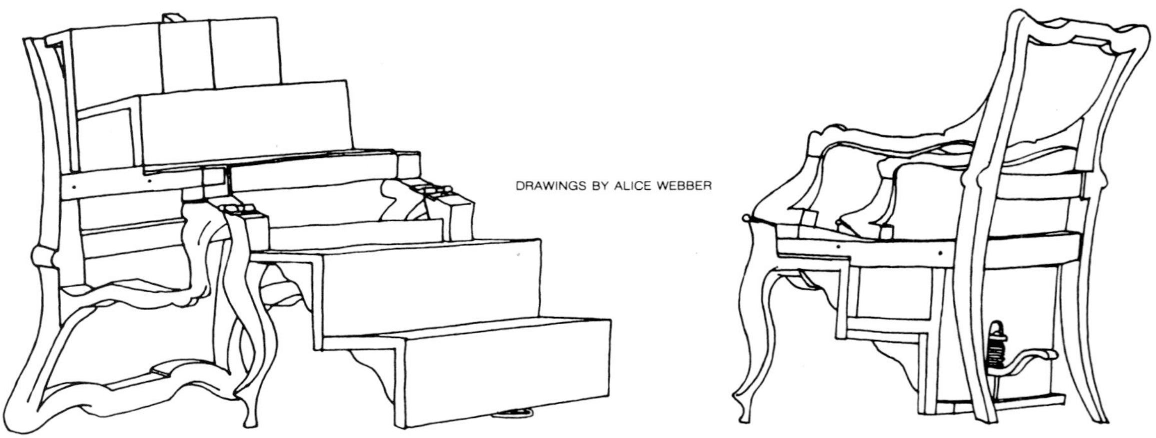

DRAWINGS BY ALICE WEBBER

Bookcase
Boston Area. c. 1880.
Walnut, elm burl veneer on white pine framing.
Composition drawer handle-pulls dated patent 1879.
H: 102" W: 48½" D: 17".
Private Collection.

Large-scale factory-made furniture of the Late Victorian Period was in demand in Boston as the population of the Back Bay area grew and the erection of large-scale residential structures occurred. While conservative in taste, still clinging to the Italianate formulae which appealed to New England gentry throughout the nineteenth century, this bookcase does exhibit some concessions to the neo-Grec taste in its simplicity of line and plainness of surface.

Cabinet
New York. c. 1875.
Made by Leon Marcotte.
Rosewood with kingwood, tulip and ebony inlays; secondary wood: mahogany; center panel: gilt bronze.
H: 5′ 7″ W: 5′.
The Newark Museum.

By the third decade of the nineteenth century, the finest cabinetmakers in this country were working in an eclectic style generally known as "Renaissance." This does not connote direct borrowings from sixteenth-century art as much as the spirit of the moment when designers, architects, sculptors and painters felt a resurgence of creative power. The major center of stylistic influence was the Academie des Beaux-Arts in Paris. In the hands of the best designers like Marcotte, who had been trained in France, furniture and its setting became highly organized in abstract patterns with vivid borders defining boundaries of panels and architectural elements. Optical tricks were played within inlays. Realistic sprays of flowers and ribbons were set into backgrounds as if they were paintings. Sculptural medallions like the one illustrated here on the center of the cabinet were used for pictorial purposes. The bronze panel shows a shepherd playing pipes for a maiden. It evokes the pastoral mood of eighteenth-century French art. Burled wood, ebonized bands and figured rosewood were all outlined with finely incised lines filled with gold leaf. Marcotte's geometric play upon varied and opulent surfaces suggests that the purpose of this cabinet was mainly ornamental. It was a showpiece rather than a cabinet for storage.

Cabinet
New York or Brooklyn. 1860–1880.
Signed "Gustafson."
Mahogany, rosewood, fruitwoods and
exotic woods. L: 74½" H: 60¾" D: 18¼".
Carl Crossman.

From the early 1870s the Renaissance revival was most expressively handled in America by highly trained European immigrant craftsmen who had mastered the complex art of using varied materials for ornament—porcelain plaques, ormolu mounts, gold leaf, ebony and exotic wood marquetry. Gustafson must belong to the group of craftsmen with extraordinary gifts in marquetry and design, but the international character of the craftsman's world during the second half of the nineteenth century may account for the wide diversity of styles and hearty mixture of stylistic motifs labeled under the general heading of "Renaissance." The projecting, rounded sides of the console brackets and vigorous volutes reflect a knowledge of Renaissance and Mannerist styles of the fifteenth and sixteenth centuries, but the incised gilt lines and fan-shaped classical touches are more properly identified as neo-Grec. The porcelain plaque with its cast brass frame and the metallic banding that dramatically outlines the piece are inspired by the style of Louis XVI.

This splendid work, so remarkably organized in the integration of its parts, must have had a monumental setting. It was customary to use such a piece in a drawing room, where it was likely to be called simply a "French cabinet."

Parlor Table
New Jersey. c. 1870.
Attributed to John Jelliff and Company.
Rosewood with exotic inlaid woods.
H: 29½" W: 31½" D: 22".
The Newark Museum.

The ingenious support structure for this tabletop was designed to steady the top and harmonize the foursquare pattern of the legs with the turnings of the center post. Flatness of surface and angular geometry were emphasized with shallow line-engraved ornament infilled with gold leaf. These features are typical of post-Civil War furniture made in the "Renaissance" style of the 1870s. The top is enriched with burled wooden borders and with floral and musical instrument pictorial inlay set into an ebonized field. This small specimen of highly individualistic taste expresses an era that celebrated individualism. Its structure reflects a modern approach to design in that the ornament is a direct product of the power machinery of its age.

Upholstered Armchair
Probably Boston. c. 1875.
Mahogany with burled walnut veneer.
H: 38" W: (across arms) 28" D: 32".
Private Collection.

An inviting shape to the back of this chair welcomes the sitter and is a suitable fit for the female dress of the Late Victorian Period. Despite the fact that the frame is solid mahogany, the construction method of dowel joinery used in holding together the parts of this chair proved inadequate in the hundred or so years of its use. Joints originally held with dowels and glue are now perceptibly open at the back of the right arm and at the juncture of the right back post and crest.

Despite faults in the joinery design, however, the chair serves its intended function—to provide an arresting profile or silhouette, to catch the viewer's fancy and to suggest in a visual way the idea of opulence and comfort. Richness of ornamental detail implied that the original owner of this chair was aware of and appreciated a noble period in European art.

Side Table
Probably Philadelphia. 1865–1880.
Oak with pink-and-white variegated marble top.
H: 30" L: 35½" D: 23⅜".
William Penn Memorial Museum.

"Renaissance" was the term most frequently used in the nineteenth century for the style of furniture represented by this table. The feature that suggests when this table was made is its incised line ornament. Ornament of this sort was cut by rotary-powered machine burrs or chisels. The peak of popularity for such ornament took place in the 1870s.

Pedestal
Probably New York City. c. 1870.
H: 46" W: 19" D: 15½".
Collection of the St. Louis Art Museum.

From the 1860s to the end of the nineteenth century the size of artistic pedestals paralleled the growth in the size of American domestic interiors. While not all pedestals were destined for sculptural figures, the ample dimensions and vigorous ornament of this one suggests that it must have been crowned with a stunning piece of sculpture.

The "Renaissance" style of this pedestal is very much in the French manner in which mounts and sculptural plaques are offset against ebonized and simulated exotic woods. The basic idea for this pedestal seems to come from the highly original designs of Vredeman de Vries or Crispin de Passe—fifteenth-century North European Mannerist designers who took perverse pleasure in inverting the tapered column and applying curious masks and bosses and other devices to furniture and architecture in an anti-academic manner.

M. DOUGLAS SCHMIDT PHOTOGRAPHY

DAN FARBER, PHOTOGRAPHER

Paine's Furniture Salesroom with Upright Folding Bed
Woodcut Illustration from Paine's Catalog, c. 1880.

Late Victorian furniture designers were obsessed with the desire to patent some unique invention that would forever secure their fortune. Among the most popular was the folding bed that turned into a false wardrobe changing the room from a bedroom to a parlor. Folding beds were not original to the Victorian era; they had been made in this country as early as the eighteenth century. However, nineteenth-century manufacturing ingenuity made it possible to add springs, precision hinges and other mechanical devices to these pieces so that even a small child could easily operate them.

Largeness of scale was an aesthetic necessity for furniture of the fashionable late nineteenth-century home. In Boston, the monumental residences that were being constructed in an area known as the Back Bay demanded furniture of generous size.

IX

1800–1850

The Frontier & Vernacular Traditions

BETWEEN 1800 AND 1850, the enterprising young American Republic claimed the land of this continent from coast to coast. With the Louisiana Purchase of 1803, the lands west of the Mississippi River to the Rocky Mountains were acquired from France by Thomas Jefferson for the United States. Few citizens, at this early date, grasped the meaning or the extent of the territories added to the United States. The lands beyond the Appalachian highlands were too vast in extent, too distant, and too different in environment and scale for most Easterners to comprehend fully. Through much of the first half of the nineteenth century, the great plains and the grasslands of the Louisiana Purchase were dubbed "the Great American Desert." Because few trees enhanced this flat landscape, the fertile prairie country was passed over by the earliest pioneers. They moved in search of woodlands which if not as fertile as the prairie, were a familiar environment to those who had recently departed from the East. The overland pioneer often was a descendant of wood craftsmen from the Eastern seaboard. He depended upon wood for daily needs and for shaping his habitat. Adaptation to new environments came about slowly and with difficulty. In the process the pioneer simplified craft production to the barest essentials, holding fast to traditional forms while paring away impractical ornament. In order to survive, settlers learned to share in the face of hardship. An aggressive back-country pride in survival and self-sufficiency developed among those who lived away from established manufacturing centers. Homemade and local products were often proclaimed superior to the "imported."

Hunger for new land, freedom from the constraint of the old social order and the hope to improve life were the main impulses for moving to the frontier. The idea of establishing new settlements and an improved social order in what was heralded as virgin wilderness held strong appeal. The thought of a free, adventurous and profitable life in woods or plains beyond the reaches of long-established settlements was an irresistible attraction to many persons both on the East coast and abroad.

By the nineteenth century, the Old Northwest Territory, which included the lands of Illinois, Indiana, Michigan, Ohio, Wisconsin and part of Minnesota, was already considered the old frontier. Opened for settlement by the last acts of the Continental Congress in an ordinance of 1787, the Old Northwest Territory developed rapidly. Partly because of its ready access to waterways, Ohio was settled early and became a state in 1803.

Even on the farthest frontier one could find pioneers clinging to cherished vestiges of what they left behind. As they cleared land for settlement they carried with them books by Lord Byron, Paine's *Age of Reason* and C. F. Volney's *Ruins* to insure that civilization would not be lost in the wilderness. For the same reason they recreated their material past as well as possible. Even though they were limited by available materials and tools, the shelter and furniture they built were familiar.

In spite of efforts to recreate the past, it was clear that something new and different occurred in the lives of all who settled on the frontier. Many developed a taste for the extravagant and theatrical. Unfettered by restrictive customs, by tradition-bound family connections and conservative, well-established businesses, the Westerner acquired such folk heroes as Mike Fink, Daniel Boone and David Crockett, who presented ordinary tastes and habits in extraordinary ways.

The frontier was far more an attitude than it was a geographical place. The American idea of the "frontier" was not the same as that held by Europeans. The term "frontier" in Europe connotes a static borderland between nations—a boundary of armed truce. In America, the term implied motion—an heroic thrust past the security of the known and the established. The excitement of a moving edge of settlement beyond the established and comfortable world was enhanced by expanding technology and a national belief in Manifest Destiny. The frontier was a state of mind accepted by those who chose (or were forced) to live somewhere between the remote wilderness of the trapper or scout and the well-established cities. This concept of the frontier is still with Americans—this longing for expansion and search for new opportunities and unexplored territories. Space is our current frontier.

Part of this attitude stretches back to the beginnings of European settlement on the Atlantic coast. Comparisons may be drawn between seventeenth- and nineteenth-century material culture and attitudes. Both were eras of radical change and population diffusion. Both were ages of discovery, rapid technological growth and adventure. On the frontier of the seventeenth century, American settlers held fast to craft traditions which became outmoded in urban areas abroad. The same held true on the nineteenth-century American frontier. While elaborate mechanization of the furniture industry on the Eastern seaboard made the rococo and Gothic revival furniture as ornamental as possible, in the far West settlers by necessity preserved the simple handcrafting traditions which had been the familiar vocabulary of furniture craftsmanship among the common man for generations.

Practical and unassuming, furniture of the frontier endures and enjoys a quiet integrity which is almost timeless. The basic structure of frontier furniture is rooted in the traditions that began in the late Middle Ages when movable furniture was first being developed in the Western world. Slat-back chairs, six-board chests, simple slab and trestle tables and plank stools persisted in the nineteenth-century forms of commonplace furniture.

The cultures of the nineteenth-century frontier were not homogeneous. Blending of cultures has never been as simple a matter as the melting-pot theory would imply. Natural resistance between Indian, Spanish, French, German and English cultures made the mix more analagous to that of a marbelized cake than to that of a melting pot. Fusion of craft practices and stylistic ideas was more often the exception than the rule. Since this country was composed of native inhabitants and settlers from many nations, the story of furniture production depends very much upon the dominant national vocabulary of the craftsman and his community. Yet certain common traits are found in the furniture of the frontier's many disparate communities and homesteads. In the early settlement, frontier craftsmen, whether German, Spanish, Dutch, Scandinavian or English, eliminated unnecessary detail or elaborate ornament in the serviceable furniture they made. Pioneers often brought richly ornamented pieces of furniture with them, but the earliest works made on the frontier were functional. The bare bones of utility (what we now call functionalism) dictated simple forms.

By the nineteenth century two basically different directions had evolved in American furniture making. First and best known were those craftsmen tied to land, property and business enterprise in major cities—the establishment of the furniture trade. They followed stylistic changes closely and maintained a standard of production to satisfy the moneyed class. By the mid-nineteenth century their furniture was richly upholstered, deeply tufted and made comfortable with the newly introduced coil-spring supports. This furniture was considered the ultimate triumph in style and comfort. By contrast, the second group of furniture craftsmen were more mobile. They sought a new life building towns at the edge of the wilderness. Some always moved on—chronic pioneers who pushed on as settlements grew and crowded them. Alert for new opportunities, they were often employed only part of the time in their furniture craft. Some were not fully trained; they developed woodworking skills from basic practical know-how. These fiercely self-sufficient pioneers raised cattle, mined, hunted, tended bees, surveyed, published newspapers, sold land—turning their hands to all the jobs necessary to found a new town or sustain life.

Both frontier settlement and furniture making went through a series of classic changes from primary settlement to urban growth. The speed with which this took place was remarkable; it was often accomplished within the life span of the first settler who staked claim to the land. The earliest phase after exploration was usually crude and temporary. The successful pioneer craftsman was usually an unspecialized worker who understood basic woodworking but did not have a sophisticated or high level of competence with advanced technology or precision tools. He used tools that had been fundamental since medieval times—the basic ax, adz, wedge, saw, hammer and auger. The more sophisticated pioneers smoothed edges of furniture with planes and chisels. Even those who possessed little refined experience in woodworking knew how to hew rough furniture from raw nature—splitting and bending green wood and binding it together with the hide, thong or gut of animals.

Most settlers brought some furniture with them. A chest, chair or table that could be stored in the wagon on the overland journey was an important luxury. It represented a significant emotional and cultural connection with the pioneer's past. It served immediate practical needs as the first phase of settlement took place. Whatever furniture was not carried had to be built. Bedsteads were frequently the first pieces rudely and quickly made. A typical pioneer bedstead consisted simply of a forked stick driven into the ground a few feet from the corner of the log cabin. Poles laid on the fork stretched to the openings in the logs and provided support or rails for clapboards which formed the bottom. On this platform, bedding was made of moss, grass or cornhusks, covered with a blanket. Such pioneer beds were found not only in Texas but in the cabins of the Southern frontier and of the Northern territories as well. Temporary shelters of the frontier—the lean-to, dugout, cave, tent or brush bower—rarely survive; neither do their contents. Written descriptions and a few rare sketches recall for us today the rough and simple structure of settlement furniture. Significantly, the first stage of frontier furniture and housing was not made to last.

Isolation brought on the second phase of frontier craftsmanship. As manufactured goods which had been brought to the frontier wore out (goods such as hinges, nails, locks and drawer-pulls), the pioneer craftsman adapted to circumstances. He "made do" with what he could fashion. Wooden pegs, leather thongs and wooden drawer-pulls were shaped and whittled as substitutes for manufactured parts. At this stage, pioneer crafts were made for individual needs or for family and friends. While parts of furniture and the whole pieces themselves were quickly and cheaply made, many surviving examples show a sense of style and careful thought. Neatness of finish and clever reuse of materials were common characteristics of pioneer furniture of the second phase of settlement.

Stick furniture made of bent willows, cottonwood or green ash lashed together with rawhide thongs continued a tradition of furniture making which had been practiced for generations throughout the Western world. The remarkable simplicity of furniture wrought in this manner during the second phase of pioneering settlement preserved old-fashioned furniture crafts even after such traditions were being superceded by factory-produced furniture in urban centers.

The most successful method of making furniture on the frontier was quick and direct. Some members of a pioneering community had special aptitudes for carpentry and excellence in woodworking skills. They took pride in their abilities and shared their work and knowledge with fellow pioneers in exchange for other skills such as tailoring, weaving or farming.

The third phase of furniture making on the frontier required specialization. It was possible to become successful as a frontier village specialist in cabinet- or chairmaking only after an adequate population base and local prosperity had come into being. When a whole community of pioneers settled a town, this base was established.

Refinement in workmanship often stood side by side with the rough-hewn and crude. Civilized and raw experience also blended in a variety of ways.

The third phase of frontier settlement and craft merged with the second in many ways. Small shops were organized as soon as they could be sustained. Hand- and foot-powered machinery brought to the frontier by craftsmen was soon superceded by water-powered saws and steam-driven engines. This marked a turning point for furniture production in the far West. As early as 1858 elaborate rococo revival furniture was being made in San Francisco.

The small shop craftsman first served local needs and then looked for a market and distribution beyond his immediate town. Successful craft centers were located where raw materials and the expanding marketplace converged. The site was often near rivers or rail depots, and close to stands of timber or at the crossing of major trails and transportation routes. Such advantageous locations encouraged the exportation of furniture. Towns such as St. Louis, St. Joseph, and Kansas City, Missouri, became known as outfitting or "jumping-off" points for the Westernbound pioneer. Such towns developed quickly as trade and barter centers as well as locations for craft shops.

Seasoning of timber for turning and cabinetwork required time and shelter, which in part explains why furniture production of any significant magnitude did not happen quickly. In the organized communities of the Mormon settlements in the Great Salt Lake Valley, Utah, the furniture industry came early. The Mormon spiritual and political leader, Brigham Young, was trained as a cabinetmaker and woodworker in upstate New York. In the early 1850s, soon after the initial settlement of Utah in 1847, Young established a woodworking shop which he used as a public works enterprise through which those who arrived at Salt Lake City looking for assistance were given goods or food as an exchange for service. The Great Salt Lake Public Works became known for the production of simple Empire-style painted chairs made of pine.

Frontier life ended in different parts of America at different times: when land was staked out and transportation and communication systems connected East and West; when wealth was sufficiently accumulated; and when technology and machine production replaced the handwork of the pioneer craftsman. For most parts of the country the frontier was at an end by 1904 when St. Louis celebrated the Louisiana Purchase and the exploration of Lewis and Clark with a world's fair. Yet the frontier attitude and memory of pioneering survived into the twentieth century. In some regions where craft traditions were strong, such as the German-Texas settlements between the Brazos and Colorado rivers and in the San Antonio region, hand-produced furniture persisted side by side with manufactured furniture.

With the end of the physical frontier in the late nineteenth century, some craftsmen had become aware that the romance of the frontier was special to consumers in the East. They began to make and export furniture which purposely evoked the spirit of early hunting and cattle days. As the frontier vanished, writers, artists and reporters searched eagerly for the picturesque in Western furniture as well as in the other arts. To meet this public interest, chairs and hat racks were made from the horns of Texas longhorn cattle. Today, horn furniture, like paintings by Frederick Remington, is associated with the rough life of the Western frontier; most was made for exhibitions, state fairs and for sale and distribution in the Eastern states. In fact, some of the horn furniture was not even made in the West at all. Some was manufactured in Austria for hunting lodges, libraries and gentlemen's billiard rooms and sold at Tiffany's in New York.

By the 1870s enthusiasm for rustic art, wilderness and the frontier promoted building of monumental Adirondack camps as retreats for the wealthy. The notion that America was a virgin country, unpolluted by previous generations of evil leaders, held enormous appeal. The romantic view of nature and landscape, evidenced by the Hudson River School of landscape painting and the belief that the good life was to be found away from urban congestion, contributed to the development of wilderness camps. It became an obsession of many New York businessmen to travel several hundred miles northward to the mountain regions where nature lay as unspoiled as they imagined it was in the far West. Large log "camp" buildings with huge stone fireplaces and massive interior exposed timbers were built to accommodate the desire for rustic seclusion in comfort: Camp Uncas, Camp Pine Knot and Kamp Kill Kare built in the 1890s were picturesque retreats for wealthy financiers. Furniture and furnishings in the grand camps were eclectic. Photographs of their interiors show a range from Far Eastern trophies and manufactured furniture to locally made tables and chairs. The most interesting furnishings made for the camps are rustic chairs, settles, bookcases and tables that displayed, patterned across surfaces, ingenious mosaics of wooden twigs that reflect the nature of the region. Like horn furniture, twig furniture was made to satisfy whim and fancy; both present a sense of self-conscious regionalism and a nostalgic view of American life implying rustic simplicity at the edge of wilderness. This highly romantic view had more to do with escape than it did with survival on the real frontier.

SPANISH

1846 Room
Palace of the Governors,
Santa Fe, New Mexico.

Seating furniture was rare in Spanish New Mexico, particularly prior to the nineteenth century. More typical than chairs were adobe *bancos* or wall benches. Both traditions of seating are seen in this room as well as two answers to storage needs. The painted chest on stand is supplemented by a niche, economically constructed—simply recessed into the wall and covered with carved planks pegged into the lintels of the opening. The room has been furnished to recreate the office of Governor Armijo (the last ruler of Spanish Colonial New Mexico) just prior to the arrival of Kearny's army of the West in Santa Fe in 1846.

The four distinctively different chairs grouped around the central table show a design source firmly rooted in peasant or folk furniture of seventeenth-century Spain, but they also exhibit an attempt to interpret the American Empire style. The Santa Fe Trail, which fostered the first communications between American traders and Spanish New Mexico, opened in 1821; therefore Empire designs were the earliest North American style from the East coast to which New Mexican carpenters were exposed. Regardless of design, the chairs have a common construction technique based on the use of oversized tenons with carved rather than turned spindles, and decorative motifs shallowly carved, incised or cut out. This construction was determined by the native material—soft yellow pine—that was worked almost exclusively by hand tools. Sawmills did not come to the Santa Fe area until the 1840s.

COURTESY OF THE MUSEUM OF NEW MEXICO

Several features of the room are products of the burgeoning American trade begun in the 1820s. Trade cloth, for instance, inspired the use of brightly colored calicoes as wainscoting, which served to keep the whitewash found on most interior and exterior adobe walls from rubbing off on people seated against the walls. The Anglo presence is also felt in the tin sconces, most early New Mexican examples of which were fashioned from imported food containers. The Saltillo blanket on the *banco* was imported from Mexico while the strips of *jerga* covering the hard-packed mud floor were woven locally.

RICHARD CHEEK, PHOTOGRAPHER

Storage Chest
New Mexico. c. 1800.
Pine. H: 17" W: 35½" D: 17".
The Colorado Springs
Fine Arts Center.

Original iron brackets, locks and fastening devices such as those shown here seldom survive in New Mexican furniture. Iron hardware was so rare and precious in New Mexico it was customarily removed and reused for other purposes. The handsome lock plate is richly shaped in its outline and punched with a pattern that relates to the incised scalloping along the border of the chest. The sunburst or floral-carved central ornament is especially well done, exerting a design focus to the severe geometry of the heavy board construction and dovetailing of the chest.

Storage Chest
New Mexico. 18th Century.
Pine. H: 17½" W: 52½" D: 16¼".
Collection of
Dr. and Mrs. Ward Alan Minge.

The large dovetailed corners and heavy rough-hewn pine boards of this chest create a solid appearance, which is enhanced by carved rosettes and scalloped, incised detailing around the edges. Found near Santa Cruz, New Mexico, it characterizes the work of a local carpenter, who perhaps made it to sell at a saint's day celebration.

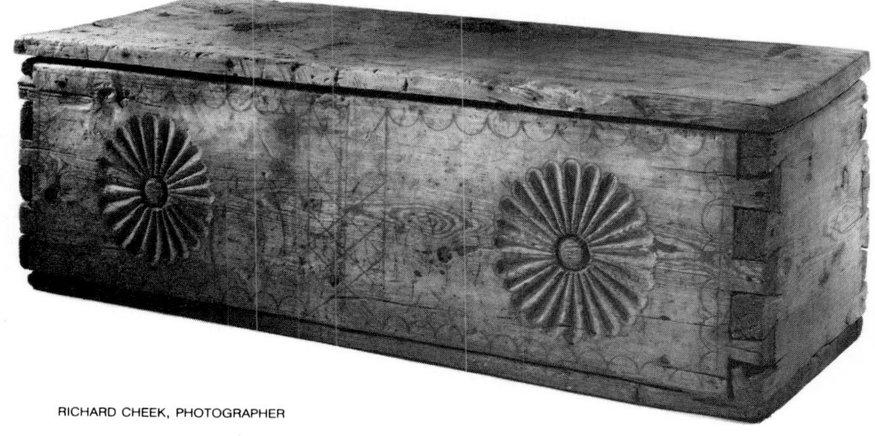

RICHARD CHEEK, PHOTOGRAPHER

Table with Single Drawer
New Mexico. Late 18th–Early 19th Century.
Pine. H: 28½" W: 28" D: 19⅝".
Collection of Dr. and Mrs. Ward Alan Minge.

Tables with deep drawers, such as this one, were first used in small churches and private chapels for storing vestments and other religious objects. Later, in the nineteenth century, they became a part of household furniture. This table made by a local craftsman, probably as a commission for his church, comes from the region of Tecolotita, New Mexico. The heavy, simple frame construction of the table reflects the New Mexican craftsman's limitations in terms of tools and materials. His working tools were primitive and unrefined, and the only wood available was pine. A leather thong is used here as a drawer-pull.

Side Chair
New Mexico. c. 1830–1850.
Pine. H: 39" W: 19½" D: 15¾".
Collection of Dr. and Mrs. Ward Alan Minge.

The simple architectonic form of this chair is indicative of local folk craftsmanship in a region where, for generations, few outside stylistic influences filtered through the isolation of frontier life. The form, construction and shallow chip carving of the chair derive from Spanish influence on Mexican and New Mexican craftsmanship. New Mexican furniture is characterized by its construction techniques. Chairs such as this were held together by large mortise-and-tenon joints, or the doweling of one part into another. Iron nails were not used because they were scarce, and fastening the thick, soft pine boards together with nails in the changeable New Mexican climate tended to split the wood.

Side Chair
Taos, New Mexico. c. 1850–1880.
Made by Manuel Archuleta.
Pine. H: 31¾" W: 16¼" D: 16¼".
The Colorado Springs Fine Arts Center.

RICHARD CHEEK, PHOTOGRAPHER

Stoutly and simply constructed with through-tenon joinery, the character of this chair recalls the seventeenth century more than the nineteenth century. Long after the Santa Fe trail brought Yankee settlers and their possessions from the East, New Mexican craftsmen continued to produce furniture along traditional lines, based on early Spanish models. This one is especially noteworthy because it can be traced to the name of its maker. The chair is rigid in its form and handsomely carved with shallow geometric gouged designs characteristic of earlier chairs from New Mexico. It represents a style that prevailed in Spain in the seventeenth century and persisted in the New World for a dozen generations thereafter.

RICHARD CHEEK, PHOTOGRAPHER

Chest
New Mexico. c. 1820–1850.
Pine. H: 26¾" W: 52½" D: 17½".
William Rockhill Nelson Gallery of Art, Kansas City, Missouri.

Highly unusual due to the asymmetry of the front panels, this chest has a personal character that is individualistic and appealing. The construction details of mortise-and-tenon joinery are clearly revealed in this photograph. So large are the tenons which pierce the legs that an intricate system of varied levels for tenons or interpenetration of tenons was devised. The board-and-frame joinery system of construction of this and other examples of Southwestern Spanish-style furniture shows the continuance well into the nineteenth century of an approach to furniture making that was two hundred years out of phase with what was current on the Eastern seaboard.

RICHARD CHEEK, PHOTOGRAPHER

Watercolor
Interior View: "My Cabin on Elk Creek, Montana Territory" by Peter Peterson Tofft (1825–1901). 1866. H: 8⅝" W: 10⅝". Museum of Fine Arts, Boston.

Interior views of frontier housing are so rare as to make this a major document. It shows a simple rough-hewn straight-leg table and dry sink on the right. The small window made use of precious glass. A barrel is under the table and a wooden trencher and a pan stand in the corner. An assortment of containers—tin, wood—and a carpet or quillwork pouch hang or stand at the fireplace wall. A large bag—hanging from the ceiling—probably contained meat. What seems to be a smoked leg of game hangs from a rafter. A coffee grinder is attached to the wall beneath a picture. Below is a pair of boots. A "squat seat" or box made of five boards with a rope-bail handle stands beside the boots. The handled box was a common container used in the West for picking and carrying wild fruits and berries. The artist sits on a folding chair of a form popular in the early West—a type often called a "miner's chair."

RICHARD CHEEK, PHOTOGRAPHER

Slat-Back Rocking Chair
Made in Pennsylvania c. 1850–1870; brought to Nebraska c. 1872.
Ash and tulip, painted; seat a later replacement.
H: 41½" W: 21" D: (seat) 15¼".
Nebraska State Historical Society, Lincoln, Nebraska.

This simple slat-back rocker, made in Pennsylvania, is typical of the furniture carried across the country in wagons and trains by pioneers in the West. Brought to serve immediate needs, such furniture held a special place in settlers' homes as a reminder of the East coast they had left. Early photographs of pioneers en route West almost invariably show furniture of this sort lashed to or sitting within wagons. At one time the seat was probably rushed. Modern factory-woven denim now is woven in strips to form the seat.

Bench
Aurora Colony, Oregon. c. 1860.
Maple and pine. H: 32" L: 123" W: 24".
Aurora Colony Historical Society, Aurora, Oregon.

Produced in the utopian community of Aurora, in Marion County, Oregon, this bench was once communal property. The Aurora Colony was founded in 1856 by Dr. William Keil, a German religious idealist, who led his group from Pennsylvania to Bethel Community in Missouri and finally to the Willamette Valley in Oregon. The spare, horizontal lines of this long bench harmonized with the simplicity and communitarian life espoused by Dr. Keil.

RICHARD CHEEK, PHOTOGRAPHER

Side Chair
Santa Fe, New Mexico. c. 1830–1850.
Pine and fruitwood. H: 34" W: 16" D: 16½".
Collection of Dr. and Mrs. Ward Alan Minge.

Representing an interesting combination of local construction techniques and outside design influences, this example of frontier neoclassicism suggests the mode of Duncan Phyfe and demonstrates vividly the influences of Yankee settlement in the Southwest. Undoubtedly copying a chair brought to New Mexico from the East, a local carpenter carved this chair in classical form. The large mortise-and-tenon joints and wooden pegs continue traditional New Mexican construction.

RICHARD CHEEK, PHOTOGRAPHER

RICHARD CHEEK, PHOTOGRAPHER

Side Chair
Mariposa, California. c. 1860.
Pine. H: 32" W: 15½" D: 16½".
The Oakland Museum, Oakland, California.

A California version of the Empire-style side chair, made of wood from Mariposa County, indicates the wide dispersion of a simple neoclassical style on the frontier during the second phase of settlement at mid-century.

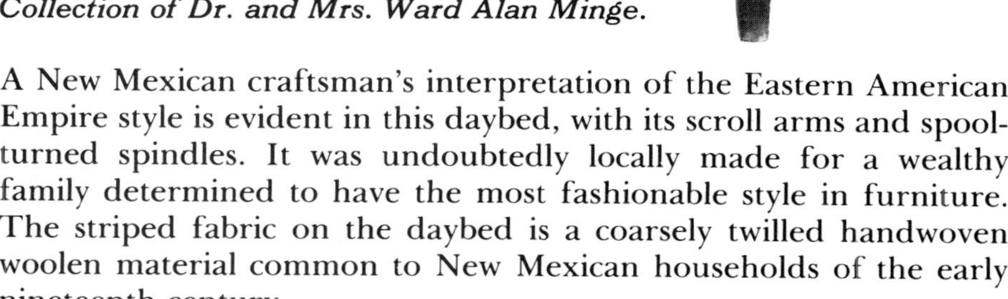

Daybed
New Mexico. c. 1830–1850.
Pine, painted blue.
H: 27″ L: 69″ W: 22½″.
Collection of Dr. and Mrs. Ward Alan Minge.

RICHARD CHEEK, PHOTOGRAPHER

A New Mexican craftsman's interpretation of the Eastern American Empire style is evident in this daybed, with its scroll arms and spool-turned spindles. It was undoubtedly locally made for a wealthy family determined to have the most fashionable style in furniture. The striped fabric on the daybed is a coarsely twilled handwoven woolen material common to New Mexican households of the early nineteenth century.

LLOYD W. RULE, PHOTOGRAPHER

Folding Table
Colorado, Probably Leadville. 1870–1880.
Walnut. H: 28⅝″ W: 22″ D: 16⅝″.
Molly Brown House, Historic Denver, Inc.

Margaret Tobin Brown, better known as the "unsinkable Molly Brown" (for her survival of the *Titanic* disaster), owned this whimsical little walnut table. The table illustrates a mania for jigsaw carpentry and is also a prime example of frontier ingenuity. Furthermore, it represents an effort to bring some semblance of the Renaissance revival style (if only in silhouette) to the remote mining town of Leadville.

In situ at the Molly Brown House in Denver, the table is somewhat overshadowed by the profuse ornament of the parlor, but it stands as a memento of Molly's Leadville days and as an example of her early aspirations to elegance, a dream that was finally fulfilled. The top of the table lifts off, allowing the four hinged legs to fold. A Leadville carpenter with an inventive flair for creating things both useful and visually stimulating probably made the table as part of a larger parlor suite. The fact that the table collapses surely accounts for its transportation to Denver and probably also for its eventual survival.

RICHARD CHEEK, PHOTOGRAPHER

Pie Safe
Southwestern Colorado. c. 1875.
Tulipwood, pine and tin.
H: 55⅛" W: 38½" D: 16½".
The State Historical Society of Colorado, Denver.

Throughout the West the punched-tin pie safe was a standard piece of kitchen furniture. Examples are found in Texas, California, Utah, the Oregon territory and elsewhere. This safe came from the Rourke Ranch on the Purgatory River in southeastern Colorado, where it was made by the ranch hands from discarded packing cases. The packing crates had originally contained factory-made parlor furniture that had been shipped from St. Louis to the Colorado ranching country, where it added elegance to an otherwise rough environment. The furniture crate came from the "J. H. Crane Furniture Warehouse," according to the stenciled label still visible on a back board of the pie safe.

Furniture Advertisement for J. T. Pidwell,
San Francisco Directory, *1858, p. 222.*

222 SAN FRANCISCO [P] DIRECTORY.

FURNITURE WAREROOMS,

NO. 140 WASHINGTON STREET.

J. T. PIDWELL

IMPORTER AND GENERAL DEALER IN

FURNITURE,

BEDDING, LOOKING GLASSES, &c.

Is constantly receiving fresh supplies, and is now prepared to sell at greatly reduced prices. Ladies and Gentlemen furnishing their Houses and Offices will find it to their advantage to call at 140 Washington Street.

He offers for sale that curiosity and "piece of economy," which was on exhibition at the Mechanic's Fair in this City,

PLYMTON'S PATENT SECRETARY BED.

Also, by late arrivals, a few of those justly celebrated

PIANOS!

Manufactured by JAMES W. VOSE, of Boston, and which are now taking precedence of all other Manufacturers, evidenced by the many Prize Medals awarded Mr. Vose. All Pianos warranted to give satisfaction.

ALSO,

CAHART & NEEDHAM'S PATENT AND AUSTIN'S MELODEONS,

Which will be sold cheap for cash, and a liberal discount given to Churches and Sabbath Schools, and to Music Teachers.

BUCKLEY'S FURNITURE POLISH,

Constantly on hand. This to Housekeepers and Furniture Dealers is invaluable. A small quantity of it produces effects truly astonishing.

No sooner were commodious homes built in the West than furniture of the most fashionable sort was imported. Victorian furniture in the rococo revival style, for example, was available in San Francisco in the 1850s. Imports came from the well-known Boston firm of James W. Vose. The H. R. and J. L. Plymton patent folding bed, also of Boston, provided style and economy of space. All such heavy and elaborate furniture had to be either hauled overland or carried by seagoing vessels. The transcontinental railroad did not near completion for another decade.

Oil on Canvas
"Brigham Young's Family" by William Warner Major (1804–1854).
Salt Lake City, Utah. c. 1840–1850. H: 25 W: 33" (unframed).
Church of Jesus Christ of the Latter-day Saints, Salt Lake City, Utah.

RICHARD CHEEK, PHOTOGRAPHER

This idealized portrait of the Brigham Young family was made by an English artist, William Warner Major, who joined the Mormon Church in Nauvoo, Illinois, in 1844. He sketched and painted during the journey across the continent to Utah from 1846–1848.

Although this work was painted on the frontier, the self-image of a proper Victorian middle-class family was so powerful that the artist shows us what Young and his family aspired to be rather than reflects objective reality. No furniture or architecture of the sort shown here was known in Utah in the 1850s.

Side Chair
Provo, Utah. c. 1851.
Willow with rawhide thong seat; painted green at a later date.
H: 32½" W: 17½" D: 13".
Lagoon Corporation.

According to a document taped to this slat-back chair it was "whittled and put together by the hands of Dominicus and Polly Miner Carter as they crossed the plains, reaching Provo in 1851. As they rode in their 'Prairie Schooner' the framework was whittled from willows, the back was fashioned from the rims of wagon wheels and the seat was woven of ox hide." Just how much truth there is in the particular details of this account is hard to prove, but the chair does represent a pioneering type light in weight and of the sort commonly found with similar histories. Such chairs seem not to have been made by specialists but by pioneers on the move.

Side Chair
Salt Lake City, Utah. c. 1860–1870.
Made by William Bell (1816–1886).
Pine, painted and stenciled. H: 32¼" W: 17½" D: 16½".
Lagoon Corporation.

As part of a public works program established in Salt Lake City by Brigham Young, a furniture workshop produced painted and grained Empire-style chairs of this type. Fashioned of soft pine with generous curves, these pioneer pieces were available to the expanding market of settlers who needed useful, rugged but stylish furniture. William Bell, who arrived in Salt Lake City in 1854, worked in Brigham Young's cabinetmaking shop for about fifteen years and is known to have produced chairs such as this.

RICHARD CHEEK, PHOTOGRAPHER

Rocking Armchair
Lehi, Utah. c. 1860–1880.
Made by Whipple and Kirkham.
Pine, painted red-brown and stenciled. H: 39" W: 20½" D: 18½".
Lagoon Corporation.

This is a frontier version of the so-called "Boston rocker"—but it is far beyond the shape of its original prototype. Missing scrolled ends to the arms would visually complete the astounding vigor of the overall form. One is tempted to call it an example of "frontier Baroque." The maker of this rocking chair was with the firm of Whipple and Kirkham, one of the earliest furniture manufacturers in the Rocky Mountains. This rocking chair represents the second stage of pioneering crafts, when adequate prosperity allowed for specialization of skills and the beginnings of mass manufacture. During initial settlement, most pioneers made things for their own use until sufficient numbers of others settled nearby and offered special skills in barter, trade or for cash. The transformation from primary settlement to this second stage came about rapidly in Mormon communities, since large numbers of highly organized pioneers built their towns in cooperative ventures of colonization literally overnight.

✶

Low Post Bedstead
Salt Lake City, Utah. c. 1860
Pine, grained to simulate rosewood. H: 48½" W: 50½" L: 83".
Private Collection.

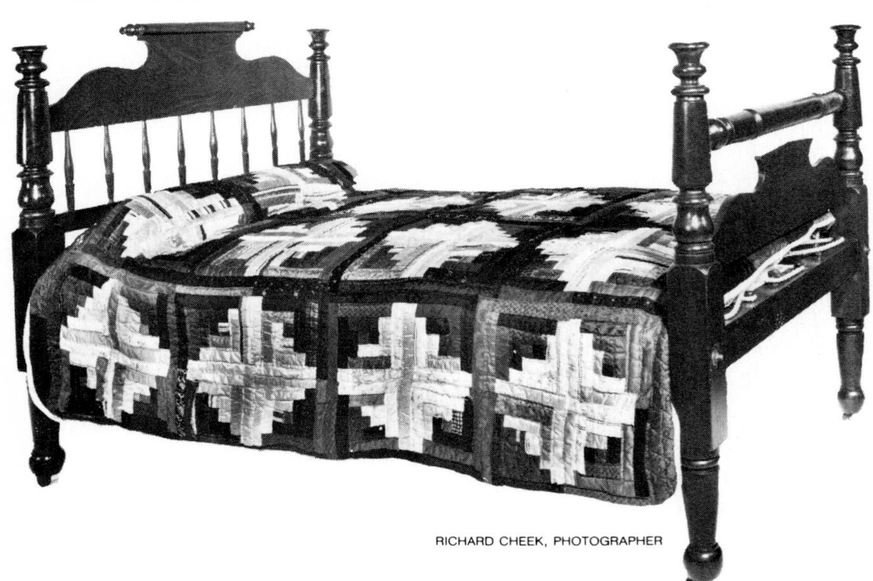

RICHARD CHEEK, PHOTOGRAPHER

A Mormon pioneer, Albert Perry Rockwood, owned this bed. Influential in the development of Salt Lake City, Rockwood became a legislator of the Utah Territory and participated in the protection of Mormon interests during the so-called "Utah War" of 1857.

The bed and the contemporary homemade silk patchwork coverlet represent the second phase of pioneering crafts—beyond the mere survival stage, yet prior to the era of rail importation. The bedstead was made locally in a small craft shop. It represents the persistence of classical taste in pioneer vernacular form.

RICHARD CHEEK, PHOTOGRAPHER

High Post Bed
Salt Lake City, Utah. c. 1860–1870.
Pine, grained to simulate oak. H: 78½" L: 68" W: 53¾".
Lagoon Corporation.

Counselor to Brigham Young, mayor of Salt Lake City, judge, general, peace commissioner, and a man of means, Daniel H. Wells, the original owner of this bed, was also appointed Superintendent of Public Works of Great Salt Lake City in 1848. It seems possible, therefore, that the bed was made by the furniture shop of the Public Works. Its simulated light oak graining is found elsewhere throughout the Salt Lake Valley in both furniture and architecture. In the cabinetmaker's price list published in the *Deseret News,* September 7, 1864, the agreed-upon price for an "eight square bedstead" was $16.00 in gold or its equivalent. As each post of this bed is divided into two square sections (the total being eight, combining head- and footposts), this bed would seem to meet that bill.

Around 1860, Walter Huish moved to Payson, Utah, bringing some of the earliest woodworking machinery to the area. The engine lathe and planing machinery that he imported allowed him to develop a planing mill, furniture factory and home furnishings store. He made chairs, washstands, dressers, bedsteads, cupboards, writing desks, bookcases, tables and coffins.

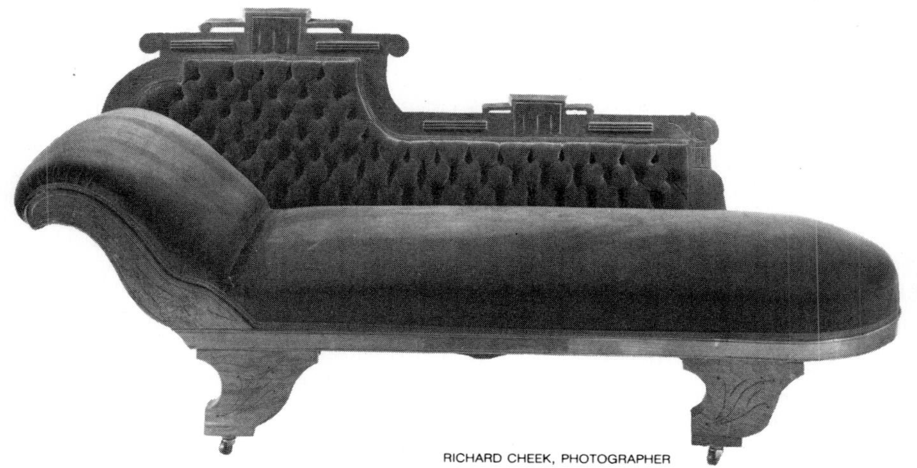

RICHARD CHEEK, PHOTOGRAPHER

Chaise Longue
Payson, Utah. 1870–1890.
Made by Walter H. Huish
(c. 1827–1898).
Walnut. H: 31½" L: 74" D: 29".
Lagoon Corporation.

Huish typifies the third phase of the pioneering experience—where modern technology and factory production bloomed in the far West, duplicating what was being done in Eastern and Midwestern cities. Huish, a pioneer cabinetmaker who moved from St. Louis to settle in Payson, was one of the first to manufacture furniture on a substantial scale in that region. Being a machinist by profession, his work has a production appearance about it—handwork minimized and unit costs kept low. This sofa is an early example of machine production in the pioneer West. Machine production quickly eclipsed handcraft shops.

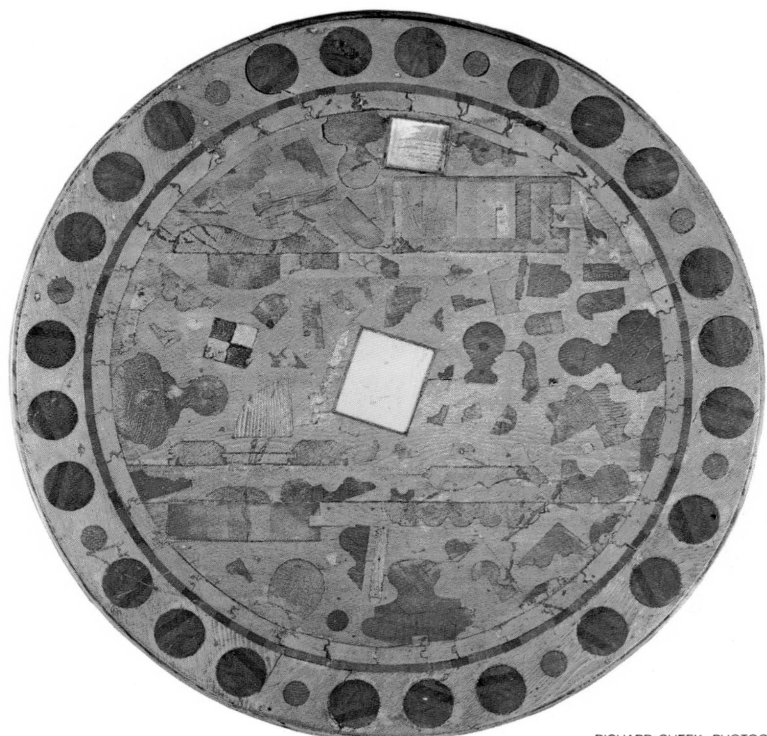

RICHARD CHEEK, PHOTOGRAPHER

Parlor Tabletop
Salt Lake City, Utah. 1889–1893.
Made by George Kirkham.
Pine and mixed wood inlay.
H: 29½" Diameter of top: 32½".
Lagoon Corporation.

During the period 1889–1893, while doing carpentry work in the Salt Lake Temple, George Kirkham collected scraps of moldings, banisters, door and floor trimmings and fashioned them into this tabletop. On it also appear small pieces of marble and granite used in the temple building. The largest piece in the tabletop is a trimming from the east front door of the temple. The glass covering the temple picture is a scrap of an accidentally broken plate-glass window. As a novelty piece, this table reveals the interest Mormons had in their own history, even as it was in the making.

Side Chair
Nacogdoches, Texas. c. 1830–1845.
Ash, elm; hickory bark seat.
H: 39" W: 18" D: 14½".
San Antonio Museum Association Collection,
Gift of Mr. and Mrs. C. D. Orchard.

The most unusual design of the back has vitality in its spacing. Contrasting with the sleek lines of the back and other smooth turned members is the rough texture of the woven bark seat. The craftsman who made this chair had a special design sensibility that made the most of simple elements.

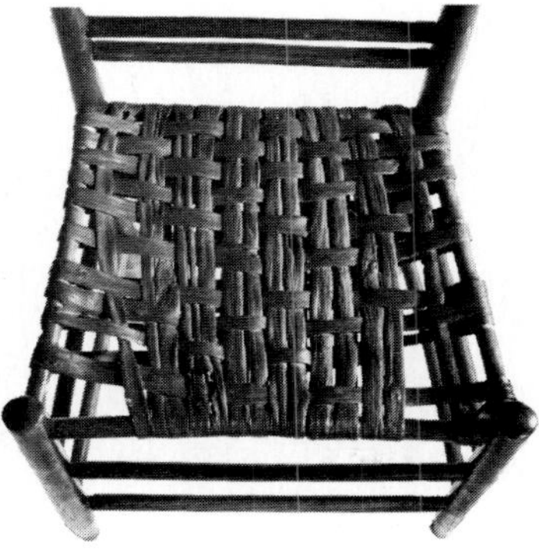

The most practical and popular piece of furniture made and used on the American frontier was the rawhide-seated slat-back side chair. Examples from the earliest days of European settlement are found in Oregon, Texas, California, Utah, Nebraska and Montana. In basic shape the chair differs by only a few stylistic features from those made by eighteenth-century and early nineteenth-century frontier settlers in Ohio, Louisiana and Missouri.

Spindle Bed
LaGrange, Texas. c. 1850.
Pine, stained red-brown. H: 35" L: 73½" W: 45½".
Collection of Walter Nold Mathis.

RICHARD CHEEK, PHOTOGRAPHER

The very essence of functional simplicity, this bed was made at a time when most fashionable furniture in the East was elaborate to the extreme. Western furniture design, as exemplified in this bed, developed organically out of the methods and materials that best solved the urgent needs of a mobile frontier society.

RICHARD CHEEK, PHOTOGRAPHER

Slant-Top Desk with Paneled Bookcase
Found in the Vicinity of Industry, Austin County, Texas. c. 1840.
Walnut. H: 67½" W: 43¾" D: 33".
Collection of Mrs. Charles L. Bybee.

This desk is a frontier version of the secretary form—an elegant piece of furniture familiar to immigrants from both the frontier of the South and the Appalachian East. Scalloped paneling on the single cupboard door suggests a close relationship of this piece in concept and design to Eastern and Southeastern furniture of the late eighteenth or early nineteenth century.

Three-Quarter High Post Bed
Tarrant County, Texas. c. 1850.
Elm and ash, stained black.
H: 52½" L: 73¾" W: 53".
Collection of Mrs. Charles L. Bybee.

RICHARD CHEEK, PHOTOGRAPHER

Wood turning in frontier furniture was generally coarse and bold. Few of the graceful curves of the furniture back East were remembered or used. But attempts were made to obtain graceful effects even in the most rudimentary way, as expressed in the posts of this roughly hewn bedstead. The apparent desire for cultural symbols on the frontier even in their most elementary state is what seems so poignant to those who admire and collect early Western furniture.

Jelly Cupboard
Austin County, Texas. c. 1850–1860.
Cedar. H: 65″ W: 44″ D: 19½″.
Collection of Mrs. Charles L. Bybee.

A food safe or cupboard, this piece of furniture was one of the essentials of frontier life. Continuing the tradition of fielded panel joinery a hundred years beyond the time of its popularity on the Eastern seaboard, it is a reminder that traditions persisted in the vernacular arts on the Southern and Western frontiers.

RICHARD CHEEK, PHOTOGRAPHER

Settee
Belleville, Texas. c. 1860.
Long-grained pine, oak.
H: 33½" W: 75" D: 25".
Collection of Mrs. Charles L. Bybee.

Parlor furniture was in demand soon after settlement. Local craftsmen supplied the needs with ingenious combinations of remembered forms.

The synthesis of stylistic influences in this case is typical of what happened in furniture making on the frontier. In this settee the arms follow the classical form of the Empire style common to side chairs; the back has the more fluid lines of the rococo revival. Intended as an important piece for the main room of the house, this settee expressed a degree of civilization. It also reflected the direct simplicity and charming inventiveness of frontier craftsmanship.

Daybed
Fayette County, Texas. c. 1870.
Oak, pine and ash;
traces of red-brown paint.
H: 32" L: 76" W: 28".
Collection of Mrs.
Charles L. Bybee.

Sleek, neatly designed and simply joined with through-tenon and dovetail construction, this daybed seems to have been inspired by the familiar shape of the frontier slat-back chair, and is reminiscent of neoclassical window and hall seats. Its basic form is simply an extension of a pair of slat-back chairs facing each other. The front and back seat rails are secured to the legs with large dovetails pinned to the frame. It is an admirable statement of functional simplicity. The daybed served an important function in frontier life. It was a substantial piece of parlor furniture that easily provided accommodation for an expanded household when travelers arrived unexpectedly.

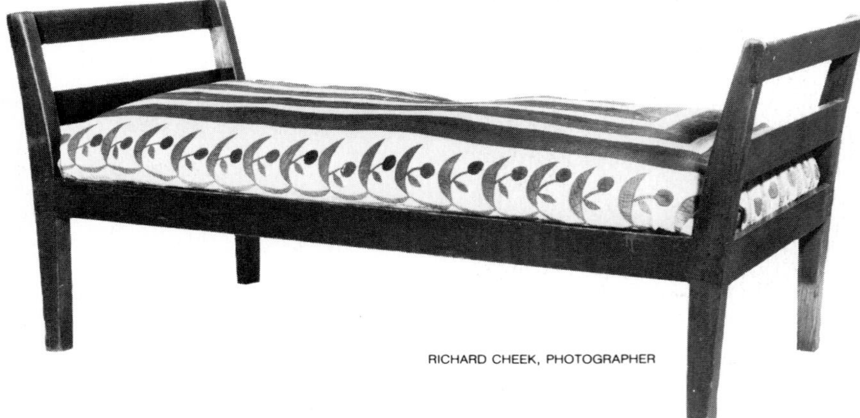

RICHARD CHEEK, PHOTOGRAPHER

Porch Bench
Washington County, Texas. c. 1860.
Pine, walnut, ash, cedar.
H: 31½" W: 83" D: 23¾".
Collection of Mrs. Charles L. Bybee.

Used outdoors on a porch, this bench is one of few such examples known today. It is a Texas version of an Empire-style scroll-arm sofa but adapted to the materials, skills and needs of the frontier. Repetition of its members sets up an appealing pattern which seems twentieth century in character.

The simple lines of this kitchen table, with its slightly tapering legs and top with curved ends, have an almost contemporary appearance. The table was made for Captain and Mrs. R. E. Stafford, who moved from Georgia to Colorado County in 1857. The tabletop, made of two broad planks joined underneath with a wooden spline, together with other details such as peg size and nail type, suggest a pre-1860 date for its construction. The glazed stoneware bowl and jar were made in Seguin, Texas, between 1857 and 1884.

Kitchen Table
Colorado County, Texas. c. 1857–1860.
Pine with limestone slab.
H: 30¾" L: 70" W: 35".
San Antonio Museum Association Collection,
Gift of Mrs. C. T. White.

RICHARD CHEEK, PHOTOGRAPHER

Food Safe
Bastrop, Texas. c. 1860.
Cypress, pine and tin. H: 75½" W: 39½" D: 21½".
Collection of Walter Nold Mathis.

The pierced tin panels of the food safe served both a decorative and a practical purpose. Pierced slits and holes, arranged in a variety of patterns in the tin, let air into the safe to ventilate its contents, which were protected from insects, mice and other pests.

Punched-tin cupboards were made throughout the East as well as the West during the nineteenth century. As soon as rolled iron sheeting coated with tin to prevent rust was available, a technological revolution in food preservation took place. Food was carried overland to the frontier in large tin containers. Pickled oysters, for example, were available in tin containers at most important outposts and trading stations in the far West. When the tin containers had served their purpose they were cut up and recycled by those who knew how to make the most of them. Some were used to ornament and ventilate food safes.

RICHARD CHEEK, PHOTOGRAPHER

Side Chair
Cat Springs, Texas. c. 1860.
Pine.
H: 33¼" W: 18" D: 14½".
Collection of Mrs. Charles L. Bybee.

Derived from a type of chair common throughout Northern European peasant cultures from the seventeenth century, this plank-seated chair was probably made by a German immigrant to Texas in whose vocabulary of style the traditions of centuries survived. In both rural Pennsylvania and Ohio, where Northern Europeans also settled, similar chairs are known to have been produced in the eighteenth and nineteenth centuries.

RICHARD CHEEK, PHOTOGRAPHER

Scroll-Back Armchair
Cat Springs, Texas. c. 1850.
Long-grained pine.
H: 30½" W: 20½" D: 18".
Collection of Mrs. Charles L. Bybee.

A rural Texas interpretation of the Empire style, the design of this armchair makes effective use of patterns in the wood. Had the chair been made in urban Eastern United States, it would have been made of mahogany, walnut or rosewood. Its stance and proportions also would have been more refined. The charm of this piece lies in its reference to neoclassicism, coupled with the evident struggle that its maker had to recall what he could of what was fashionable. In the process he developed some shapes that were peculiar to the frontier.

RICHARD CHEEK, PHOTOGRAPHER

Wardrobe
Fayette County, Texas. c. 1860–1870.
Marked "C.W." on back in chalk.
Cedar, painted and grained. H: 76½" W: 61" D: (at cornice) 23".
Collection of Mrs. Charles L. Bybee.

A traditional continental European form, this double-door wardrobe or *Schrank* reflects Germanic arts and skills in mid-nineteenth-century Texas. Made at a period of early prosperity in Texas history, the wardrobe must have once graced a substantial household. Its brilliantly decorated surface, with large panels painted to look like the cross section of a giant exotic tree, constituted a huge canvas for a nineteenth-century graining artist.

RICHARD CHEEK, PHOTOGRAPHER

Wardrobe
Columbus, Texas. c. 1880.
Cyprus and pine, painted. H: 93½" W: 56½" D: 29".
Collection of Mrs. Charles L. Bybee.

Colorfully contrasting paneling and applied turned balustrades and moldings create a vivid surface in this wardrobe, an example of Germanic Victorian Baroque on the frontier.

Side Table
Vicinity of Shulenberg, Texas.
c. 1880–1883.
Pine. H: 29" W: 33¾" D: 22¼".
Collection of Mrs. Charles L. Bybee.

Made at a time when ostentatious, ornamental furniture was popular in the East, this table with its simple lines and boldly figured wood is a delightful accommodation of a country craftsman's art to prevailing tastes. The table is an example of the handcrafted furniture still produced in rural Texas in the nineteenth century to meet the needs of a local market long after machine-made furniture, shipped by rail from other parts of the country, had become available.

RICHARD CHEEK, PHOTOGRAPHER

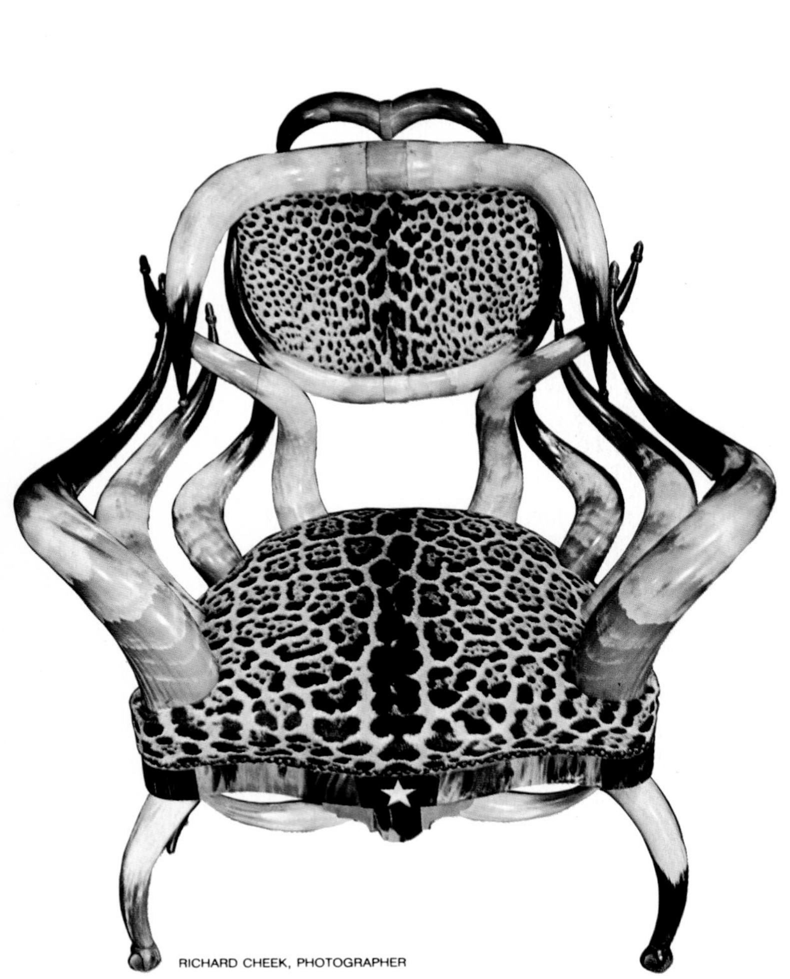

RICHARD CHEEK, PHOTOGRAPHER

Rocking Chair
San Antonio, Texas. c. 1880–1890.
Made by Wenzel Friedrich (1827–1902).
Steer horn and jaguar skin. H: 38½" W: 24"
D: (seat) 22". San Antonio Museum Association,
Gertrude and Richard Friedrich Collection.

By the end of the nineteenth century the frontier had been largely transformed by settlement and by transportation links with the East. As the frontier vanished, writers, artists and even craftsmen searched eagerly for the rustic image of the Old West. Furniture made from the horns of Texas longhorn cattle was but one item manufactured to meet public interest and demand. This chair was ingeniously cradled on iron springs for the ultimate in rocking comfort. Today, horn furniture is popularly associated with life on the Western frontier, yet much of it was made for exhibitions, state fairs and for sale in the East, where it was used in billiard rooms, libraries and summer camps.

X

1870–1930

Craft Revival, Reaction & Reform

Colonial Revival, Arts and Crafts, Art Nouveau

BY 1870 ACHIEVEMENT of industrial genius was measured by production, success by profit. Manufacturers, merchants and workers discovered a public eager to buy inexpensive, factory-made furniture. During the nineteenth century, small factories expanded to employ hundreds of workers who produced cheap furniture for a growing population.

At first such activity was viewed as progressive. It expressed an aesthetic of plenty. Furniture made for the working class was one goal of the social idealists of the nineteenth century who advocated the development of factory production.

But as specialization and advanced machine design improved, management's desire for profit led to methods which quickly eroded the initial benefits of factory production for the worker.

An examination of the catalogs of the International Centennial Exposition held in Philadelphia in 1876 reveals that progress and wealth were most frequently expressed in abundance of ornament. Partly because of the ease with which machines could multiply ornament, much of the furniture exhibited was garnished with frills that had little to do with its function. The complex technical processes applied to most of the fashionable furniture of this period sacrificed traditional handcraftsmanship for an abundance of machine-produced forms. Few Americans found anything objectionable in this substitution. However, some designers who understood the folly of resurrecting past historical styles searched for stylistic self-expression.

The desire for reform in the arts had been heralded by English designers as early as the 1830s when Augustus W. N. Pugin (1812–1852) championed the return to spiritual values in the arts and furniture. One of the major figures and propagandists of the Craft reform in England was William Morris (1834–1896). As a writer, social theorist, craftsman, designer and member of the group of artists known as the Pre-Raphaelites, Morris believed that the Medieval past offered inspiration for reform. He felt that the craftsmen of the Middle Ages, who had not been subject to the debilitating influence of the machine, were the ideal models. Simple imitation was not Morris's goal. He warned against the evils of slavish copying. Like John Ruskin, architect and art critic, and Thomas Carlyle, the historian, Morris hoped to solve the social and artistic problems of the industrialized society of the nineteenth century with a return to the spiritual qualities of handcraftsmanship of the Middle Ages. He felt that specialization in industry was a major problem in society: factory production denied the individual craftsman the kind of occupational satisfaction he had enjoyed for centuries. According to Morris's reasoning, both the maker and buyer were victimized as industrialization resulted in inferior objects and unsatisfied workers. Although Morris did concede that machines would probably remain a necessary evil and advised designers to use them wisely to develop products that would not imitate handwork, he felt that important benefits would be achieved by reorganizing the current system of industry. This reform gospel was simple and bold: workers could once again take pleasure in their daily productions, resulting in better-made products. If the profit motive were reduced, supply and demand could be balanced, overstockpiling eliminated, layoffs prevented. Working hours would be shorter and materials would not be misused or wasted as they were in factory production. The customer who would pay a higher price and receive a more durable piece of work would be less likely to discard it.

Bruce Talbert's *Gothic Forms Applied to Furniture* (London, 1867) championed the "honest" neo-Medieval or plank-construction furniture. It was followed by designer Christopher Dresser's *Principles of Decorative Design* in 1873, which stressed simplicity of form, respect for material and the importance of originality of design: "No past style is precisely suited to our wants," he advised. Dresser found what he called "gouty" forms of softly overstuffed rococo revival furniture most objectionable, and instead advocated the design of crisp, firmly upholstered, rectilinear neo-Medieval furniture, a style popularized to even a greater extent by Englishman Charles Lock Eastlake (1836–1906). Eastlake's popular *Hints on Household Taste* was first published in London in 1868 and in Boston in 1872. Eastlake considered solid wood furniture with rectangular joinery "honest." The ideal of furniture reformers of the 1870s and 1880s was expressed best in the solid workmanship of traditional oak joinery which stressed horizontal and vertical planes. These planes clearly defined the furniture without the confusion of curves. Rich use of material but simple construction was the advice that Eastlake dictated to makers of furniture in this vigorously angular style. He observed that unless honest workmanship was firmly established, no artistic furniture could be produced.

Two important American architects served as practitioners of the Eastlake reform style. Significantly, they believed that architecture was the "mother art" to which all other arts should be visually and harmoniously attuned. Henry Hobson Richardson (1836–1886) of Boston, and Frank Furness (1839–1912) of Philadelphia both insisted on architecturally designed furniture which they or their office staff determined would complement all other appointments for their buildings. They conceived the finished "whole" of their work as an organic unity of necessarily related parts. Their furniture designs consistently followed the individualistic character of their buildings. While both architects seem to have designed furniture in the "reformed" or "modern Gothic" taste of Eastlake and Talbert, each arrived at highly personal solutions to similar problems.

Artistic energy and talent moved westward, ready to rebuild Chicago after the disastrous fire of 1871. A sense of purpose and destiny was developed among Midwestern designers and architects Louis Henri Sullivan (1856–1924), Daniel H. Burnham (1846–1912), Dankmar Adler (1844–1900), William Holabird (1854–1923), Martin Roche (1853–1927) and John Wellborn Root (1850–1892). These innovative men played a major role in the rebuilding of Chicago in its boom years of the '80s and '90s.

By the turn of the century, arts and crafts societies had been established in major cities throughout America. In Deerfield, Massachusetts, members of the Arts and Crafts movement assumed a distinctly Early American crafts revival. Chests were made in the manner of seventeenth-century furniture from that area.

After the Sanitary Fairs of the Civil War and the Centennial Exposition in 1876, the nostalgia for American antiques had been formalized. The desire to collect and reproduce Early American furniture was part of the revolt against Victorian eclecticism and mass market ornament. Reformers looked to colonial America as a time of heroism, democracy and craft tradition. The appreciation of handiwork led to the search for a new, indigenous style using the design traditions of the colonial past.

Richardson and others adapted American colonial furniture forms for interiors of their new architecture. The "Colonial style" included design motifs and pieces of all periods from 1620–1830. The results of this search were often pleasing, occasionally preposterous. In 1884 *Cabinet-Making and Upholstery* reported, "there is little doubt but the manufacture of antiques had become a modern industry."

Interest in colonial relics produced serious studies of antiques as well as imitations. In the last decade of the nineteenth century a great variety of works on colonial furniture, architecture and arts and crafts were published: Dr. Irving Whitall Lyon's *The Colonial Furniture of New England,* published in 1891, a pioneering work in the field of decorative arts scholarship; Alvan Crocker Nye's *A Collection of Scale Drawings, Details and Sketches of What Is Commonly Known As Colonial Furniture, Measured and Drawn from Antique Examples* (1895); Newton W. Elwell's folio-sized volume of photographs, *Colonial Furniture and Interiors* (1896); and Alice Morse Earle's *Home Life in Colonial Days* (1898). Although advocates of the Colonial revival were interested in reviving and popularizing art forms that were traditionally American (and no doubt were appalled by the mass-produced Colonial curiosities pouring off the Midwestern furniture factory assembly lines), it was the honesty of the colonial cabinetmaker's materials and joinery techniques which appealed to their taste and sense of style.

The first phase of the Colonial revival was part of a general nationalistic pride, as well as a disdain for overstuffed Victorian furniture and a desire to return to times presumed to be simpler and more honest. In this latter sense, the Colonial revival was at first in harmony with the Arts and Crafts movement. Recognition of American furniture as worthy of serious display and study culminated in the Hudson Fulton Exhibition of 1909 in the Metropolitan Museum. Within a decade, by the First World War, the emphasis had changed from craftsmanship revival to a new, sleeker interpretation of the American past. By that time the major furniture-style trend was American Colonial. This second phase of the Colonial revival became such an all-pervasive movement that it finally suffocated popular taste for simple, rugged lines of mission oak furniture and the whiplash curves of the Art Nouveau.

The designers of the reform movement perceived in the Japanese crafts the same honesty, flatness, asymmetry and abstract ornamentation that they had found in Medieval furniture. They saw the persistence of handcraftsmanship lost in industrial society. With the exhibition of Japanese crafts at the 1876 Philadelphia Centennial and the publication of design books—such as Edward W. Godwin's *Art Furniture* (London, 1877)—Americans developed a craze for all things Japanese.

Ebonized, painted and inlaid art furniture and bamboo, rattan, willow and rustic stick chairs and tables were often used together (or made in sets) to suggest the stylish mode of Japanese art that inspired so many artists from the 1870s through the 1880s. The American landscape painter Frederick Church built his so-called Persian villa "Olana" on the Hudson. In his effort to synthesize the best from both Eastern and Western cultures, he combined ornament and form in an individualistic, dramatic manner. The expatriot American painter James McNeill Whistler (1834–1903) was also affected by Eastern civilization.

In contrast to the square, plain forms of the Arts and Crafts reform furniture and Japonica which had been popular for almost twenty years, a new sinuous style, the Art Nouveau, Jugendstil or *Nieuwe Kunst,* made its appearance in America from Continental Europe in the 1890s. This style derived its design inspiration from the rhythmic forms of plants. Art Nouveau was a reform movement that had its greatest force in France and other Continental countries. In America, the brilliant flowing forms of glass made by Louis Comfort Tiffany of New York and by Frederick Cardner of Corning, New York, represented the best translation of the Art Nouveau style. Large quantities of bentwood furniture, whose curving forms express the Art Nouveau style, were imported to this country not only from the Thonet Company of Vienna, Austria, but also from Jacob and Joseph Kohn of Vienna. The Kohn partners had sales outlets in New York City, Chicago and Toronto.

American-made Art Nouveau furniture is rare. The style seems to have had a greater impact on glass, fabric, books and other domestic crafts than upon furniture. An occasional furniture showpiece in the Art Nouveau style was made for special expositions, but this style was not easily adapted to the machine or to large-scale production. Therefore, it held limited appeal for American manufacturers. Though the curvilinear, animate lines of the Art Nouveau did not engage the attention of many American cabinetmakers, they added a dimension of design vitality to all the arts with ornamental touches and grace notes within domestic interiors.

The progressive trend taken by furniture designers at the end of the nineteenth and the beginning of the twentieth centuries toward severely plain and rugged work came to be called "mission." It was made to perform a specific function. Gustav Stickley (1858–1942), a leading proponent of the style, stated that this furniture was "simple, durable, comfortable and fitted for the place it was to occupy and the work it had to do." A reaction to the fragile, often insubstantial veneered furniture that was popular in the 1880s, it consisted of solid oak horizontal and vertical members.

Machine production was an essential part of life in the Craftsman Workshops, headed by Gustav Stickley in Eastwood, New York. Stickley was one of the most prolific writers and propagandists for the Arts and Crafts cause in his day. But unlike William Morris, Stickley advocated the use of modern tools and machines for his workshops. His furniture was simple and durable. Its form was based on vernacular plank construction, mortised and tenoned together with primitive vigor and mass. Stickley believed his furniture went beyond fashionable trends. The preferred wood was fumed oak, darkened to appear aged and waxed for a smooth finish. Seats were made of earth-toned leathers with large brass studding.

The fundamental character of this furniture was quickly imitated elsewhere throughout the United States. Elbert Hubbard of East Aurora, New York, produced mission-style furniture as well as lamps, bookends and hammered copper trays and candlestands in his Roycroft Shops, which opened in 1903. "Fra" Hubbard was not a designer or a craftsman, but directed by his personality, organization and sales ability, the East Aurora community became an enactment of the utopian ideals of William Morris, even though the Roycrofters' standards of craftsmanship often left much to be desired.

The Arts and Crafts movement was international. Trade schools and woodworking shops abroad produced furniture very similar to that made by Stickley, Hubbard and others. With an interested public receptive to principles of advanced functional design, Frank Lloyd Wright and the brothers Henry and Charles Sumner Greene of Pasadena, California, could advance their abilities and design ideas many steps further than they might otherwise have been able to do. The furniture that exhibited the greatest severity of line was the work of Will H. Bradley, whose designs illustrated in the *Ladies' Home Journal* of March 1902 seem to mark a transition from the intimate craftsman's point of view to a machine aesthetic which was to be more fully explored and exploited by later generations.

There is no single source of reform American furniture design. By the time the Beaux-Arts had been transplanted from Paris to the Chicago Exposition of 1893, Edison's perfected lights illumined a new revival of classicism. The Chicago School of innovation seemed for a time to have been eclipsed, as the Colonial revival style became a dominant trend for popular furniture manufacture. Separate analyses of Reform Eastlake, Neo-Gothic, Colonial, Oriental, Mission, Art Nouveau, Beaux-Arts and proto-modern fail to acknowledge their overlappings.

Bookcase
Designed by Isaac E. Scott (1845–1920).
Chicago. 1875.
Walnut, various other wooden inlays.
H: 86¼" W: 70¼" D: 14½".
Chicago School Architecture Foundation.

Made for the John J. Glessner house in Chicago, this bookcase represents an important example of eclectic medievalism as interpreted by a master designer-craftsman, Isaac E. Scott.

Scott in turn was influenced by Charles Eastlake whose book, *Hints on Household Taste* (London, 1868 and Boston, 1872), was so popular that both custom designers and furniture manufacturers copied the designs he illustrated. The bookcase resembles many of the plates in Eastlake's book. Both Eastlake and Scott combine flat, geometric ornament abstracted from nature and incised in shallow relief upon a generalized Gothic framework.

Another book which must have had a profound influence upon Scott's design sense was Bruce J. Talbert's *Gothic Forms Applied to Furniture, Metalwork and Decoration for Domestic Purposes* (London, 1867). This book illustrated a bookcase which was very similar to Scott's. A third influence was probably Christopher Dresser's *Principles of Decorative Design* (London, Paris, New York, 1873). In this book, Dresser instructs that furniture intended as art objects should incorporate these principles: Furniture should have a general overall form or mass with an effective silhouette or "sky blotch." The work should be divided into primary and secondary parts according to the laws of proportion. Enrichment of detail must be subordinated to the general mass. The material from which the furniture is fashioned should be worked in a natural and appropriate manner. Utility must precede beauty.

These five principles form the basis for reform in design in the late Victorian Period and were strictly followed by Scott in the work that he did for the Glessners. Scott apparently worked in Philadelphia between 1867 and 1869. By 1873 he was working in Chicago as a carver. In the 1880s he stylistically departed from Eastlake taste toward the more Oriental, aesthetic style of that decade.

Easel
Probably New York. 1870–1885.
Walnut. H: 82" W: 28".
The Brooklyn Museum.

The late nineteenth-century reformers sought to change designs lingering from the previous generation. Curved lines of the rococo revival and inflated forms of late Classical furniture were cited by Christopher Dresser (1834–1904) as examples of bad taste.

The rules cited in his *Principles of Design* are satisfied by this easel. It was made in order to display drawings and art prints. The hinged fall front of the easel was meant to enclose a folio of prints. The bar rest for the display of prints was attached above to the upper half of the easel.

Reform Gothic or "Eastlake" detail, inspired indirectly by the writings of John Ruskin, is highly geometric in its treatment on this easel. For the most part the walnut is exposed, but parts are ebonized in order to accent the restrained incised and gilt ornament typical of the 1870s.

Armchair
From the Winn Memorial Library, Woburn, Massachusetts.
c. 1879. Designed by H. H. Richardson and His Staff.
Probably Made by the Boston Furniture Company.
Oak. H: 33½" W: 29" D: 28".
Museum of Fine Arts, Boston.

This spare and intelligently structured chair is one of the strongest designs in the reform Gothic style in American furniture. The interpenetrating trussing of the front and back legs is braced by the thrust of the side rails. Legs are kept from splaying out by mortised, tenoned and pinned stretchers. The chair is broad, generous in its proportions and comfortable to sit on. Incorporating design principles that Charles Eastlake outlined in *Taste,* the chair's special combination of angularity with sweeping arches recalls the furniture designs suggested by Christopher Dresser, but this chair surpasses any chair illustrated by either.

Armchair
From the Crane Memorial Library,
Quincy, Massachusetts. 1880–1882.
Designed by H. H. Richardson (1836–1886) or Office.
Probably Made by
the A. H. Davenport Company, Boston.
Pine. H: 42" W: 32⅝" D: 21½".
Museum of Fine Arts, Boston.

Richardson and his office staff looked upon the architectural profession in terms of total design. Furniture, lighting, window and decorative glass design were all included in his concern to make his buildings complete and organic works of art. However, as he delegated work to trusted and talented artists, it is not known whether Richardson himself or a staff member designed this armchair. Clearly, the designer had a sense of humor, for he used the uprights of the front legs to create a rebus, the heads of cranes recalling the name of the library.

The design of the back with its sweeping bow-shaped uprights echoing the bow of the arms and front posts is a splendid note of harmony. The strong grain of the yellow pine wood provides a pattern that is repeated in the library's paneling and woodwork.

Bench
Boston Area. 1876–1879.
After Designs by H. H. Richardson.
Probably Made by the Boston Furniture Company.
Oak with leather seat. H: 37½" W: 72¼" D: 23¼".
Museum of Fine Arts, Boston.

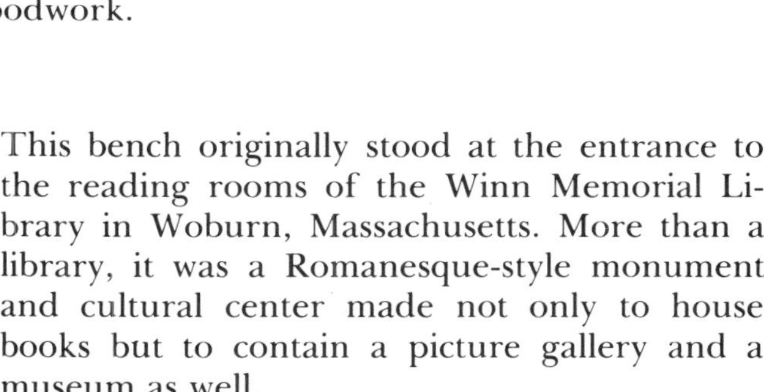

This bench originally stood at the entrance to the reading rooms of the Winn Memorial Library in Woburn, Massachusetts. More than a library, it was a Romanesque-style monument and cultural center made not only to house books but to contain a picture gallery and a museum as well.

The architect Henry Hobson Richardson developed a rich textural play of contrasting brickwork, ashlar stone and dressed stone throughout the building. Like the crisply accented windows and doorways of the library, the turnings of the bench carry a punctuated rhythm of textured outline. The turned spindles, chamfered legs and the fielded panel construction of the sides demonstrate a conscious return to the turner's and joiner's arts of a preindustrial age. The joints are mortised, tenoned and pegged in an attempt to simulate the "honest" craftsmanship of a bygone era. The work actually is all done with the most advanced machine technology of the day.

Tall Case Clock
In the Entrance Hall of the Billings Memorial Library.
Works by E. Howard & Co., Boston. Case Probably by A. H. Davenport Company, Boston. c. 1885. Oak.
H: 117″ W: 25″ D: (at base) 16″.
The Billings Memorial Library, now the Billings Student Center, the University of Vermont.

An early photograph of the tall case clock designed by architect H. H. Richardson or his staff shows it in exactly the same place that it stands today, to one side of a gigantic fireplace and between two card files. The clock design is one of the finest examples of its era, impressively proportioned and detailed with dazzling carving in Celtic or Byzantine-like intertwined labyrinths. The case resembles the more elaborate one made after Richardson's office designs for the New York State Capital, Court of Appeals Building, in 1880–1881. Because of the somewhat smaller scale of the Billings Library clock and its more compact arrangements of parts, it carries off the design with greater force than its larger prototype.

Armchair
c. 1885.
After Designs by H. H. Richardson's Office for the Billings Memorial Library.
Made by A. H. Davenport Company, Boston or Cambridge, Massachusetts.
Oak. H: 41" W: 20" D: 18½" H: (of seat) 17".
Robert Hull Fleming Museum, the University of Vermont.

COURTESY OF THE BILLINGS MEMORIAL LIBRARY

For this chair, Richardson and his office staff were inspired by early American Windsor chairs with bamboo turnings, and modified their design to suit the needs of nineteenth-century library seating. The Windsor chair designs which came from Richardson's office are as much a part of the ingenious, adaptive use of the Colonial revival as are their more famous architectural counterpart: the shingle-style housing which Richardson adapted from seventeenth-century New England architecture and applied to grand summer seaside housing for the wealthy leisured class.

At this point in the reform movement there seemed to be no sense of incongruity in placing Windsor-style furniture in massive stone Romanesque-style buildings as Richardson and his staff did first in the Winn Memorial Library, Woburn, Massachusetts. Exactly how much attention Richardson personally gave to the design of the furniture in many of his buildings remains an open question.

The wood in this chair was originally varnished to enhance the warm natural color of oak. This practice is contrary to the practice of early American Windsor chair manufacturers who used a variety of different woods for different structural reasons. Because this fundamental fact of Windsor chairmaking was not applied to the making of the Billings Memorial Library chairs, these chairs, long abused and neglected, show their wear. Pine rather than oak makes a more resilient and less vulnerable seat. Also, maple arms and ash spindles are less likely to fracture than oak. But in the late nineteenth century, oak was considered the noble wood for aesthetic reasons; durability and appearance of good craftsmanship seemed inherent in it. This chair has a dated appearance—not really like the Windsor work of the eighteenth or early nineteenth centuries. But it does speak eloquently for the best taste of its age.

Desk
Designed by Frank Furness. Philadelphia. c. 1875.
Walnut, white pine, tulip, mahogany.
H: 65" W: 62" D: 32½".
Philadelphia Museum of Art.

Drawing of Desk
By Frank Furness (1839–1912).
Philadelphia. c. 1875.
Pencil on paper. 7¹¹⁄₁₆" × 11⅛".
Philadelphia Museum of Art.

Side Chair
Philadelphia. 1875.
Walnut, ash, bald cypress; leather upholstery.
H: 30¾" W: 17⅜" D: 22¼".
Philadelphia Museum of Art.

Frank Furness, Philadelphia's most exciting and eccentric architect in the third quarter of the nineteenth century, effectively combined form and ornament to create visually arresting patterns and textures. His most famous building, the Pennsylvania Academy of Fine Arts at Broad and Cherry streets, has a forceful tripartite facade, covered with ornament in much the same way as this desk. The Moorish-inspired, dog-toothed arch of the desk front was a motif Furness often used in the 1870s and one he more fully developed in his 1869 interior of the Rodef Shalom Synagogue, which stood at Broad and Vernon streets, Philadelphia, until 1927.

This tambour-fronted desk was made for the house of Furness's brother, Horace Howard Furness, a Shakespearean scholar and professor at the University of Pennsylvania. As head of the building committee for the University Library, Horace Howard secured the commission for that impressive building for his architect brother, and in honor of the memory of H. H. Furness, the building bears his name. The desk, chair and drawing descended together in the Furness family.

The comparison of the design sketch with the finished work affords the rare opportunity of noting changes that occurred in the making of the desk. The metallic figures which support the gaslight globes and clock are much more delicate than the drawing indicates. This probably was a result of the purchase of the sculpture as stock items from an artistic supply house. By contrast, the ornamental cutwork in the wood faithfully follows the complexity of the original design. Such ornament seems to be inspired by books such as Christopher Dresser's *Principles of Decorative Design* (London, 1873) and Owen Jones's *Grammar of Ornament* (London, 1856) in which the importance of abstracting design from nature in flat geometric patterns is stressed. Since cabinetmaker Daniel Pabst (1827–1910) is known to have done other work for Furness, it seems reasonable to suspect that Pabst made these pieces.

Armchair
Designed by Frank Furness (1839–1912).
Philadelphia, Pennsylvania. c. 1871–1876.
Oak. Dimensions unknown.
Private Collection.

This chair and its companion pieces were designed to harmonize with the vigorous Medieval reform style of the Pennsylvania Academy of the Fine Arts, built at the same time that H. H. Richardson established his fame as a major American architect with his commission for the Trinity Church, Boston. Both Richardson and Furness were keenly interested in shaping all parts of their buildings, from overall site plan and space use, to the most minute details of furnishings and furniture.

Side Chair
Designed by William Price (1861–1916).
Rose Valley, Media, Pennsylvania. 1901–1909.
Oak; leather seat. H: 38″ W: 21″ D: 16¾″.
Mrs. Samuel S. Starr, Media, Pennsylvania.
The Philadelphia Museum of Art.

The Arts and Crafts community Rose Valley was founded in 1901 near Media, Pennsylvania. Like many American communities inspired by the writings and reform philosophy of William Morris, Rose Valley attempted to better a world that had been led astray by the Industrial Revolution. William Price, a Philadelphia architect, was the moving force behind Rose Valley. Its buildings were of rough-hewn stone with red-tiled roofs and walls of stucco inset with brightly colored decorative tiles. Furniture designed by Price and made at Rose Valley was stoutly framed in oak and was spare in ornament.

Library Table
Designed by Theophilus Parsons Chandler (1845–1928). Philadelphia Area. c. 1882.
Oak. H: 28" L: 44" D: 26".
Alfred D. Chandler.
The Philadelphia Museum of Art.

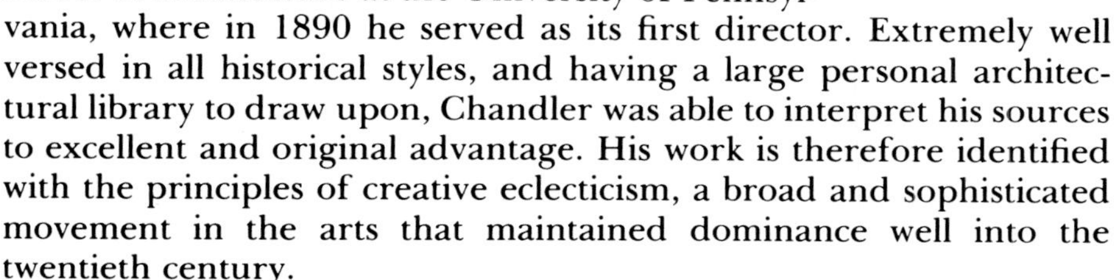

In its combination of Egyptian, Gothic and Classical details, this eclectic table is suggestive of the reform spirit of handcrafted oak furniture. The table was designed by Theophilus Chandler, a prominent Philadelphia architect whose most handsome building is the Swedenborgian Church at Chestnut and Twentieth streets in Philadelphia. Chandler is best known for having established the school of architecture at the University of Pennsylvania, where in 1890 he served as its first director. Extremely well versed in all historical styles, and having a large personal architectural library to draw upon, Chandler was able to interpret his sources to excellent and original advantage. His work is therefore identified with the principles of creative eclecticism, a broad and sophisticated movement in the arts that maintained dominance well into the twentieth century.

Drafting Table
Philadelphia, Pennsylvania. 1890–1900.
Designed by Wilson Eyre, Jr.
Oak. H: 33¼" W: 42¾" D: 29¾".
Dr. Edward Teitelman.
The Philadelphia Museum of Art.

Made for the studios of Philadelphia architect Wilson Eyre, Jr. (1858–1944), this drafting table is expressive of Eyre's design philosophy. He taught his students to be sparing with ornament and to let plain surface stand on its own. The purpose of ornament was to "describe" the design; "one of the great secrets," he said, is to "concentrate it."

The joinery of this drafting table represents the basic approach to design espoused by Arts and Crafts reformers—it was made of solid wood, mortised and tenoned with exposed pegs, and left with unadorned, spare surfaces. No glue, fancy veneer or unnecessary "frills" were added. It was structurally spare and "honest," built in a "craftsman-like" way.

New England Kitchen
Brooklyn and Long Island Fair, 1864.
The New York Historical Society.

The revival of American Colonial arts is customarily thought to begin with the Philadelphia Centennial of 1876. However, the Colonial revival started at an earlier date and was well enough established to ensure the popularity of a Colonial New England Kitchen at the Brooklyn and Long Island Fair of 1864.

Quaint furniture and appointments, relics of the past, were displayed in what was considered to be New England style. One of the chairs was one hundred and fifty years old and a table had once belonged to Governor Bradford. Trophies hung on the walls, including a rifle that belonged to Patrick Henry. Puritan Bibles and a canteen carried in the Revolutionary War helped to excite the visitors' imagination. Several ancient spinning wheels and a gigantic fireplace highlighted the room. Chowder, Indian pudding and Boston brown bread with pork and beans were served to visitors, and satisfied them that this was indeed an accurate and faithful restoration of the past. Even now and then an Indian, "hideous in horns and paint, would stalk solemnly through the crowd" to remind the visitors of the fear that nineteenth-century antiquarians were sure their forefathers had felt for the "wild men of the forest." The exhibit was an important precedent for another, more famous New England installation in the Philadelphia Centennial twelve years later.

PHOTOGRAPH BY WADHAMS/MAHAFFEY

Turned Armchair
Boston Area. c. 1875.
Oak, maple. H: 45¼" W: 24" D: 18".
Museum of Fine Arts, Boston.

This reproduction of the William Brewster chair at Pilgrim Hall in Plymouth was presented to Samuel Francis Smith, composer of "America," by the city of Boston in 1876, the year of America's centennial.

In an effort to be authentic, the maker of the chair faithfully reproduced the signs of age—omitting the bottom stretcher and top rail missing in the original Brewster chair, and turning the tops of the front posts with smooth nubs that recall the original battered ends. To make the importance of the chair clear, the reproduction was lettered "Elder Brewster 1620" at the top of both rear posts.

The chair documents the extraordinary power of the cult of old-time New England which took place by the third quarter of the nineteenth century. It forms an important component in the Arts and Crafts movement in the United States.

Side Chair
Designed by Shepley, Rutan and Coolidge or Perhaps Francis H. Bacon of the H. H. Richardson Office for the Converse Memorial Library, Malden, Massachusetts. 1886. Made by A. H. Davenport and Company. Oak. H: 37½" W: 17½" D: 19½".
The Converse Memorial Library.

Rather than looking to the Middle Ages for inspiration, the designer of this chair was inspired by the colonial or eighteenth-century past, yet it is in no way an imitation of a particular piece. The stretchers with their bulbous turnings recall similar forms found on Windsors. The urn-shaped splat of the back only vaguely recalls the splat of a Queen Anne-style chair. The freedom of movement in the crest and the carved leafage where it joins the splat show an interest in linear movement that became an obsession toward the end of the nineteenth century with Art Nouveau.

DAN FARBER, PHOTOGRAPHER

DAN FARBER, PHOTOGRAPHER

Windsor Armchair
Gardner, Massachusetts. c. 1900.
Branded "S. Bent & Bros., Inc. 1867, Gardner, Mass."
Maple, varnished dark brown. H: 38" W: 21" D: 24".
Museum of Fine Arts, Boston.

Responding to the popular taste for the Colonial revival in the early twentieth century, the Bent company produced thousands of maple, oak and ash Windsors of this sort which, because of their sturdy construction and practical utility, have served the public well. Unlike the early Windsor makers who used a variety of soft, hard and resilient woods for different parts of their chairs, the Bent factory machine-produced all parts from the same wood. Variations of different parts were therefore so slight that for a given model any part was interchangeable. Modern assembly-line methods were employed to produce a standard Windsor that has long enjoyed much popularity.

Side Chair
Boston Area. 1790–1805.
Reworked in the Middle and Late 19th Century.
Mahogany and maple. H: 37¾" W: 21½" D: 19⅜".
Museum of Fine Arts, Boston, Gift of Laura Huntington Smith.

This side chair, originally made in the Federal Period and now in the collection of the Museum of Fine Arts, illustrates several important points. The chair retains its original varnish that now, though black and crackled, is one of the rarest features to find on early American furniture.

During the course of the nineteenth century, three major additions or alterations were made, illustrating how interest in historical relics and antiques were first expressed by family members in the 1800s. Sometime between 1820 and 1860 about two inches were cut off the bottom of the chair legs in order to accommodate brass casters. An exposed seat rail was applied on the front and sides together with turned bosses at the corners at the top of each front leg. Bosses of this sort were popular in furniture and architecture of the Eastlake era, circa 1870–1880, so it seems reasonable to assume that this modification took place in the nineteenth century. At this time coil springs were added to the seat, and a remnant of early eighteenth-century needlework made in Norwich, Connecticut, was upholstered on top of the seat.

Eighteenth- and nineteenth-century furniture appears in this photograph of the parlor of the home of Mr. and Mrs. George Harding Smith, who lived in Norwood, Massachusetts, between 1899 and 1927. Inherited from ancestors and placed together in a sympathetic setting with Colonial revival woodwork of the late nineteenth century, the objects in the room reflect antiquarian interests and a sense of family roots.

The side chair on the right is a Federal Period example with a "Norwich school" needlework seat. The table and side chair on the left are Federal examples made in Boston or Salem. The other furniture was made in New England sometime between 1830 and 1860. The diverse styles represented were, at that time, labeled to be "Colonial," as was the late nineteenth-century brass chandelier. The melding of these old objects with newer pottery, porcelain and family mementos, needlework pictures and coats of arms was a favorite approach to interior decoration of late nineteenth-century New England homes.

Parlor at 193 Walpole Street, Norwood, Massachusetts. Photograph, circa 1900, Embossed "Norwood Photo Studio." Laura Huntington Smith.

Side Chair
Framingham, Massachusetts. 1917–1936.
Designed by Wallace Nutting (1861–1941). Branded on underside rear stretcher: "Wallace Nutting."
Maple and ash; rush seat. H: 46 7/8" W: 16 1/8" D: 16 1/2".
Yale University Art Gallery.

This "Pilgrim" chair was inspired by the slat-back, turned chairs of seventeenth- and early eighteenth-century New England with which Nutting was thoroughly familiar. The early furniture which most interested him captured the imagination of the pioneer collectors of the early twentieth century. Nutting's book, *A Furniture Treasury,* first printed in 1928 and reprinted in 1961, has remained a useful reference book not so much for its information, but for its 5,000 photographs and illustrations. Nutting's interpretation of an early slat-back chair reveals the common errors of reproduction furniture. Features which were considered especially desirable (such as heavy turnings and sturdy splats) are overemphasized here to such a degree that the chair is easily distinguished as twentieth- rather than seventeenth-century work.

"A Pointer from Grandpa"
Photograph by
Wallace Nutting (1861–1941).
Framington, Massachusetts. 1901.

This romantic view of the past was staged in an old New England house with old objects. Today, it symbolizes the common philosophy of reform in both the Arts and Crafts and Colonial revival movements—an attempt to revive the "honest simplicity" of the past.

COURTESY OF GENE CANTON

Curio Cabinet
Probably New York. c. 1880.
American cherry, ebonized; raised gilt gesso ornament and brass mounts.
H: 77" W: 51" D: 17½".
Museum of Fine Arts, Boston.

Craftsmen in the United States capitalized on American interest in Japanese culture by making furniture in this artistic, craft-oriented style. While this cabinet has the appearance of Japanese lacquerwork, no traditional Japanese craftsman would have recognized it as anything more than an amusing misunderstanding of Oriental detail superimposed on the form of a thoroughly Western cabinet. Nonetheless, this highly original adaptation made handsome use of delicately pierced brasses, pierced cloud-pattern carving on galleries and rails and effective low-relief gesso-work on the central panels. The gilded birds, trees, flowers and pomegranate motifs on these door panels were superbly executed. The overall proportions of the piece, its rectilinear shape and the prevalence of shallowly carved inset panels and trim show the influence of Edward W. Godwin's *Art Furniture* (London, 1877), the most influential design book published in the late nineteenth century on the subject of Anglo-Japanese-style furnishings.

Side Chair
Probably Philadelphia. c. 1885.
Mahogany. H: 36" W: 17¼" D: 17¼".
William Penn Memorial Museum.

The upholstery, which is original, consists of an intricate pattern of purple plush squares which complements the complexity of the back and other ornamental features. Incised carved lines which dress the small surfaces of exposed wood are filled with gold leaf. A rich tactile quality—the use of contrasting materials and textures—makes this chair especially fascinating. While some details make reference to historic styles, the overall approach to design cannot be identified with a specific period. It is a product of late nineteenth-century eclecticism.

The interpenetration of the crest rail by the side posts suggests that the maker of this chair was familiar with Eastlake's point of view: ". . . the first principles of decorative art, which require that the nature of construction, so far as is possible, should always be revealed, or at least indicated, by the ornament which it bears."

Slipper Chair
New York. c. 1880.
Labeled: "From John Helmsky & Son, New York."
Cherry and ash. H: 30" H: (seat) 14" W: 18" D: 18½".
Privately owned.

RICHARD CHEEK, PHOTOGRAPHER

This chair reflects the taste of the aesthetic movement that the English design reformer Edward W. Godwin called the "Anglo-Japanese style." Instead of copying Japanese furniture literally, the chair employs decorative motifs found in Japanese art and captures something of the precise, refined character found in Japanese woodworking. The sharp, flat, thin frame of the chair and the crisply turned rings on its legs demonstrate a concern for fine detail.

The horizontal and vertical members of the chair seem to interpenetrate in much the same fashion as the posts and rails of Japanese buildings. Except for the central panel, all ornament is abstract. The central panel is a separate piece placed into the back. The carving represents flowering branches and leaves, executed in a distinctly Japanese manner. Just below the urn finials, two carved details recall ornament popular in Federal furniture. At the juncture of legs and stretchers the structural character of the chair is defined with block-like sections revealing construction methods in "honest" terms.

Dressing Chest of Drawers
Brooklyn, New York. c. 1915.
Labeled "Nimura & Sato, Co.,
Japanese Bamboo Works . . . No. 707 Fulton Street, Brooklyn, N.Y."
Bamboo, cane white pine and tulip; cast brass pulls.
H: 78" W: 37½" D: 18".
The Brooklyn Museum, Gift of Herbert Hemphill.

Few examples of American-made furniture so successfully evoke the spirit of Japanese culture than this piece sold by a Japanese-American firm that dealt in Japanese goods and imported china. Significantly the only parts of this dresser that are genuinely Japanese are the imported bamboo, the woven cane and the two framed prints—both by Utagana Hiroshige (1797–1858), from the series "Hundred Views of Yedo." While the dressing chest may have been assembled by Japanese workmen in this country, the overall form of the piece is derived from Western furniture design, and has nothing to do with Japanese taste. Only the decorative bamboo ribbon-work, the scrolled bamboo of the sides, the bamboo fret of the crest and the bamboo of the margins of the chest recall the specialized bamboo craftsmanship for which the Japanese were famous.

Wardrobe
New York. c. 1880.
Marked by Herter Brothers.
Cherry ebonized and inlaid.
H: 78½" W: 49½" D: 26".
Metropolitan Museum of Art, New York.

Decorative ornament is masterfully inlaid on this wardrobe which stored the stage costumes and gowns of the actress Lillian Russell in the 1880s. The piece is distinguished by flatness of form and simplicity of outline. Shaped ornament is restricted to multiple reeding that emphasizes its box-like overall form. Inlaid into muted deep-brown panels are eight petaled flowers which cascade toward the drawers where they are collected. Compositionally, the design is similar to the Japanese wood-block prints that influenced European and American painting.

The back of the wardrobe is marked "Herter Bro's." This company was founded by Gustave Herter, who had been a silver designer for Louis Comfort Tiffany in the early 1860s. In 1868 Gustave sent his younger brother Christian to Paris to work for the prominent decorative artist Pierre Victor Galland. Upon his return to New York, Christian assumed the leadership of Herter Brothers, which dominated the fields of interior design, decorating and furniture making during the third quarter of the nineteenth century.

Christian Herter probably had no social reform notions in mind when he made this or similar pieces. If he did, his principles would undoubtedly not have been impressed on one of his clients, Jay Gould (1836–1892), the unscrupulous manipulator of railroad stock who attempted to corner the market on gold and nearly caused financial ruin to Wall Street on "Black Friday," 1869. Contrary to nineteenth-century belief, good art was not necessarily bought by good people, nor did it necessarily shape their lives in human terms.

Bentwood Side Chair
Vienna, Austria. c. 1880.
Made and Labeled by Jacob and Joseph Kohn.
Birch. H: 37" W: 16" D: 20".
Privately Owned.

Although this chair was not made in America, it was bought here. Bentwood chairs were very popular in the United States in the late nineteenth century. Such chairs were produced by the millions and sold around the world. Relatively cheap, lightweight and lively in design, imported bentwood chairs were used in private homes, public music halls, ballrooms and restaurants. Birch was the wood best suited to the elaborate steam process that made bending possible. Bentwood was a practical way to express the sweeping lines of the Art Nouveau style in furniture. Where members joined each other steel screws were countersunk and plugged with wooden dowels for ornamental effect. Construction of such chairs was sturdy. The caned seat was the only part that invariably gave way over the years. Since glue was not a major part of bentwood chair construction a mere turn of a screwdriver easily tightened the average bentwood chair that had loosened through use. The semiflexible but sturdy support of bentwood furniture has never lost popular appeal, and, in fact, is still being produced today. More common chairs made by the Kohn factory and by other bentwood factories in Vienna had much simpler legs and backs than the one illustrated here. Jacob Wirth's, an old Boston restaurant on Stewart Street, stands testament to the durability of the bentwood chair. Here bentwoods from Vienna dating from the last quarter of the nineteenth century are still in use.

JOSEPH SZASZFAI, PHOTOGRAPHER

Wicker Rocking Armchair
South Framingham, Massachusetts. c. 1893.
Made and Labeled by A. H. Ordway and Company.
Beechwood, iron and rattan.
H: 47" W: 27½" D: 18½".
Yale University Art Gallery.

Curved shapes of wicker furniture of the late nineteenth century hinted at the pleasure in visual movement of the Art Nouveau style. There is design movement in the shapes of the wicker and actual movement allowed by the rocking mechanism of the chair, which was patented by the Ordway Chair Company on April 22, 1890 and May 23, 1893. The label underneath the chair warns the public to beware of spurious imitations.

This is one of the most extraordinary examples of wicker furniture made in America to survive in such excellent condition. Its design and structure is pure fantasy—an imaginative product which evokes with exuberance the 1890s.

Tall-Backed Chair
Designed by Charles Rohlfs (b. 1853, retired mid-1920s). c. 1898. Oak.
H: 54″ W: 17½″ D: 16¼″.
Princeton Museum Collection.

This chair is one of the few examples of American-made furniture which adequately expresses the vigor of Art Nouveau ornament and design. Rohlfs' work was presented in the important Exhibition of Modern Decorative Arts in Turin in 1902, in the Buffalo Exposition of 1901, and in the St. Louis World's Fair in 1904. The turn of the century was a pivotal era—a time when modern designers were abandoning old, outmoded concepts and exploring a new, organic, plastic approach to art and nature. While Rohlfs designed this chair, he did not actually make it. He employed about eight workers to assist him in construction and ornamenting furniture. George Thiele was the carver of this chair, which was made for Rohlfs' living room.

Dressing Table and Stool
Providence, Rhode Island. 1899–1900.
Probably Designed by William Codman.
Made by the Gorham Silver Company.
Sterling silver.
Table—H: 58″ W: 38″ D: 19″.
Stool—H: 19″ W: 14″ D: 20″.
Privately Owned.

For the Paris exhibition that marked the close of the nineteenth century, the Gorham Silver Company produced this extraordinary work as a showpiece. Although rococo in form, these pieces of furniture with their flowing floral ornament were an American interpretation of the Art Nouveau style. They are somewhat naive in their approach. Their ornament is not integrated with the form as it would be in the most sophisticated Art Nouveau furniture.

The table contains 661 ounces of sterling silver and is recorded to have required 6,150 man hours to produce. The stool contains 99

RICHARD CHEEK, PHOTOGRAPHER

ounces of silver and required 23 hours to produce. Swans and vines, flowers and abstracted reflecting bosses intertwine in a delightful confusion of parts. When the Gorham Silver Company submitted its next masterworks to the St. Louis Fair in 1904, the pieces were distinctly more sculptural and involved broader surfaces with contrasting materials.

Americans seem to have failed to understand the importance of the free-flowing and tendril-like line of Continental design. The designer of these pieces, William Codman, had his own recognizable sense of style that did not even closely approximate the works of European master designers.

Side Chair
New York. c. 1905.
Designed by Louis Comfort Tiffany.
Oak; floral-printed velvet upholstery. H: 43" W: 19⅝" D: 23".
The Art Institute of Chicago.

This chair was part of a set commissioned for the Chicago home of William Wrigley. Aside from the muted tones and attractive pattern of the printed velvet upholstery, it is a fairly dull performance for Tiffany. But this chair characterizes what is lacking in so much American furniture of the Art Nouveau Period. It has none of the vitality, youthful movement or sensuality of the furniture made in France, Belgium and Austria. The problem with American furniture of this period seems closely connected to the rapid industrialization of the nation and the furniture industry in the third quarter of the nineteenth century. Up until the First World War, France and the Continent mechanized quite slowly and maintained a high degree of wood-crafting skills. In contrast, Americans eagerly embraced mechanization and lost much of the hand skill in woodworking present in the 1850s. For this reason the American furniture manufacturers were better prepared to accommodate the straight, clean lines of Arts and Crafts furniture than they were the sinuous three-dimensional movement of the Art Nouveau.

Side Chair (One of a Set of Two)
Nancy, France. 1900.
Made and Signed by Emile Gallé.
Various woods.
H: 35¾" W: 15½" D: 17¾".
Museum of Fine Arts, Boston.

Although made in France, these chairs were exported to the United States. One of them bears a brass label that identifies the import and sale company as Marshall Field of Chicago.

Pictorial inlays of poppies and water lilies in exotic woods decorate the backs of these chairs. Carving on the legs and sides adds movement and drama to the composition. At first glance the chairs seem to be the same in overall appearance, but each is quite different in detail. While these chairs are charming and original in their design, they do not move with the grace of the best of Art Nouveau furniture that came from the workshop of Gallé; therefore one can only surmise that these represent a restrained and fairly routine production made for export to the United States where the whiplash lines of the most exciting Art Nouveau designs were not received with great enthusiasm by the general public.

Curio Cabinet
New York. c. 1910.
Made and Labeled by George C. Flint & Co.
Mahogany and glass.
H: 58¾″ W: 36″ D: 16″.
The Metropolitan Museum of Art, New York.

Few examples of American-made furniture so closely follow the French Art Nouveau style as this cabinet. Indeed it is so imitative of a pair of cabinets by Louis Majorelle of Nancy, France, that it seems simply to be a modified copy. However, it is not as tall as the French pieces nor is it as asymmetrical. The poppy flower carved in the panel was a favorite motif of Majorelle as it was for many other Art Nouveau designers. The poppy's implications of exotic hedonism could not have escaped the notice of either designer or art patron.

Living-Room Interior, Home of R. M. Bond, De Land, Florida. From Title Page of Gustav Stickley's April 1912 Western Edition of The Craftsman *Furniture Catalog.*

Gustav Stickley selected this environment with its wood-beamed ceiling and toned-oak staircase to show how his furniture could be used in a harmonious setting. The rectangular surfaces of the architecture are echoed by those of the furniture—for example, the repeated verticals of the banister and the sides of the chair. Crisp and clean lines of the room and furniture intersect at right angles. Curves are not admitted, even at the fireplace where the light-colored bricks contrast with the dark woodwork. The sheer, light curtains at the windows are severe; the carpet has a restrained pattern executed in muted, deep color.

The room is planned for spaciousness without clutter. As a middle-class American interior dating before the First World War, the design is progressive although not out of keeping with the mainstream design principles of the time. The room represents one of many in its day which made the first important step toward modern design, a frank enjoyment of construction.

Furniture from Gustav Stickley's April 1912 Western Edition of The Craftsman *Furniture Catalog*

The diversity of Stickley's furniture is suggested by the following plates from his catalog. Missing is the sense of color, texture and subtle qualities of line.

Stickley's philosophy is symbolized in his trademark of a joiner's compass and the motto *"als ik kan"* (as I can). Stickley borrowed this motto from the fourteenth-century Flemish artist Jan van Eyck, who used it as a mixed expression of pride and modesty. Stickley stated that it was his aim "to express fundamental principles in both design and workmanship, to make furniture strong, durable and comfortable, and to base whatever beauty might be attained upon sound structural qualities and the natural interest of the materials used."

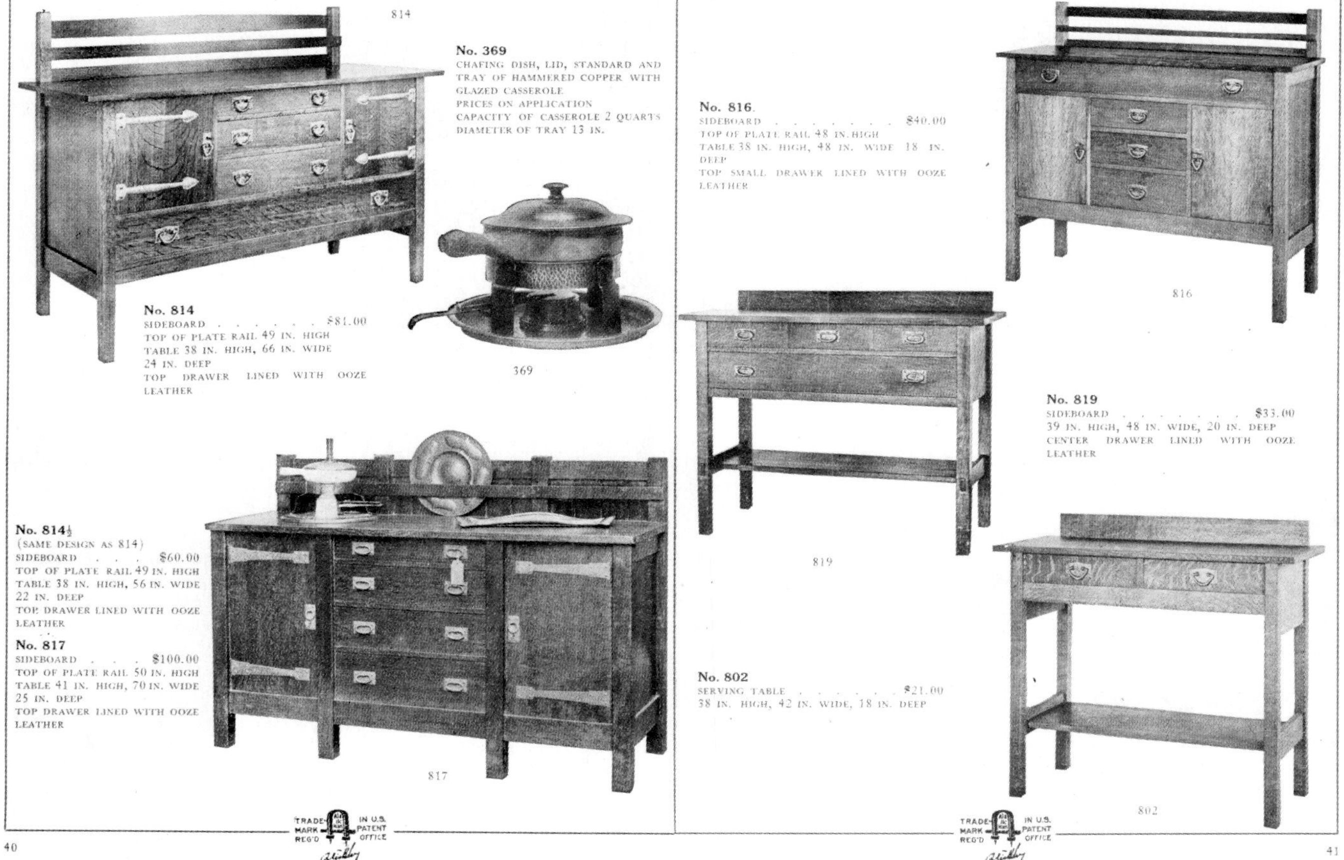
GUSTAV STICKLEY

814

No. 369
CHAFING DISH, LID, STANDARD AND TRAY OF HAMMERED COPPER WITH GLAZED CASSEROLE
PRICES ON APPLICATION
CAPACITY OF CASSEROLE 2 QUARTS
DIAMETER OF TRAY 13 IN.

No. 814
SIDEBOARD $81.00
TOP OF PLATE RAIL 49 IN. HIGH
TABLE 38 IN. HIGH, 66 IN. WIDE
24 IN. DEEP
TOP DRAWER LINED WITH OOZE LEATHER

369

No. 814½
(SAME DESIGN AS 814)
SIDEBOARD $60.00
TOP OF PLATE RAIL 49 IN. HIGH
TABLE 38 IN. HIGH, 56 IN. WIDE
22 IN. DEEP
TOP DRAWER LINED WITH OOZE LEATHER

No. 817
SIDEBOARD $100.00
TOP OF PLATE RAIL 50 IN. HIGH
TABLE 41 IN. HIGH, 70 IN. WIDE
25 IN. DEEP
TOP DRAWER LINED WITH OOZE LEATHER

817

TRADE MARK REG'D IN U.S. PATENT OFFICE

40

THE CRAFTSMAN

No. 816.
SIDEBOARD $40.00
TOP OF PLATE RAIL 48 IN. HIGH
TABLE 38 IN. HIGH, 48 IN. WIDE 18 IN. DEEP
TOP SMALL DRAWER LINED WITH OOZE LEATHER

816

No. 819
SIDEBOARD $33.00
39 IN. HIGH, 48 IN. WIDE, 20 IN. DEEP
CENTER DRAWER LINED WITH OOZE LEATHER

819

No. 802
SERVING TABLE $21.00
38 IN. HIGH, 42 IN. WIDE, 18 IN. DEEP

802

TRADE MARK REG'D IN U.S. PATENT OFFICE

41

RITA MCMAHON, PHOTOGRAPHER

Drop-Leaf Table
Made and Labeled by Leopold & J. George Stickley, Fayetteville, New York. c. 1908–1910.
Marked: "L. & J. G. Stickley Handcraft," red decal.
Oak. H: 30" Top: 42" × 42".
Jordan-Volpe Gallery.

Leopold and J. George Stickley, the makers of this table, were the less flamboyant brothers of the most famous member of the furniture-making family, Gustav Stickley. Their furniture, made in Fayetteville, New York, has long been considered of secondary importance to that of their brother. After Gustav's overextended business went bankrupt in 1915, they purchased his factory outside Syracuse in 1918, and continued producing craftsman furniture under the name of Stickley Manufacturing Company, Inc. The firm, still in operation, is best known today for cherry-wood reproductions of early American "Colonial" furniture.

The gateleg-trestle-base form of this table looks backward to seventeenth-century furniture of Puritan New England. The arrangement of the stretchers, however, suggests some inspiration from Japan. The table is highly practical and visually exciting. The effect of the rectangular openings between the legs is like an abstract painting by Piet Mondrian.

RICHARD CHEEK, PHOTOGRAPHER

Armchair Rocker
Made by Leopold and J. George Stickley,
Fayetteville, New York. 1900–1920.
Labeled: "The work of L. & J. G. Stickley."
Oak with white pine corner blocks and seat frame;
leather-covered seat cushion and
leather straps underneath rocker.
H: 33″ W: 28″ D: 32″.
Privately Owned.

Craftsman-Style Stool
Coastal United States. 1900–1915.
Oak with white pine seat blocks and leather cushion.
H: 16½″ W: 19¾″ D: 15½″.
Privately Owned.

The rocking chair's subtle design is expressed by the gentle arch of the front stretcher complementing the opposing arc on the crest of the back. Support brackets to the armrests are also shaped in a way that echoes the slight curvature of the back and the restrained arc of the rockers. The back posts are shaped to accommodate a canted angle for the slatted back. The spareness of design may be partly explained by economy suggested by machine technology. But that does not explain the whole effect, which is remarkably harmonious and satisfying—a tribute to the craftsman philosophy articulated by the best-known brother, Gustav Stickley, of Eastwood, New York. The craftsman furniture of the Stickley Brothers represents an important advance—it was well-designed furniture available at reasonable prices, it was not exclusively for the rich.

Side Chair
Made and Labeled by Gustav Stickley's Craftsman Workshops,
Eastwood, New York. c. 1908–1912.
Marked: "Als ik kan"; Stickley burned-in cypher on rear slat.
Oak with original "hard leather" upholstery and studs.
H: 37½″ W: 18″ D: 16½″.
Jordan-Volpe Gallery.

Almost primitive in its forthright simplicity, this Stickley chair design is stripped to essentials. Its original leather covering and brass studding recall seventeenth-century furniture made in America.

RITA MCMAHON, PHOTOGRAPHER

Trestle Table
Probably Made by United Crafts,
Syracuse, New York. c. 1903.
Designed by Harvey Ellis for Gustav Stickley.
Oak with inlay of various woods and metals.
H: 30" W: 35⅝" D: 20".
The Brooklyn Museum,
Gift of the Roebling Society.

The most gifted person to work for Gustav Stickley's United Crafts shops in Syracuse, New York, was the designer-artist Harvey Ellis, who probably produced the design for this table. Ellis started his career in Albany, New York, about 1873. He gained contact with the early phase of the Crafts movement through his work for H. H. Richardson designing the State Capitol Building. After working in the Midwest in the 1880s, he returned to Rochester. In 1903 he started publishing brilliant original designs in Gustav Stickley's magazine *The Craftsman,* and initiated the production of inlaid furniture for Stickley's United Crafts. After Ellis's death in 1904, Stickley's furniture no longer displayed inlaid ornament. Ellis's furniture design is characterized by the elegant elongated inlaid ornamental detail that graces the side of this table. It is an abstraction of motifs vaguely Icelandic in character, closely relating to the mature work of the British architect-designers M. H. Baillie Scott and Charles Rennie Mackintosh.

Desk
American. c. 1904.
Walnut. H: 49" W: 54½" D: 12".
The Brooklyn Museum,
Gift of the Roebling Society.

Few pieces of American furniture in the early twentieth century are more stylish than this desk. Its hammered copper hardware and inlaid pewter ornament are unusual details, closely related to the inlay by Harvey Ellis.

Reclining Chair
Made and Labeled by Gustav Stickley's
Craftsman Workshops, Eastwood, New York. c. 1905.
Marked: "Als ik kan"; Stickley red decal on rear slat.
Oak with leather upholstery (not original).
H: 40" W: 33" D: 37".
Jordan-Volpe Gallery.

RITA MCMAHON, PHOTOGRAPHER

Large, comfortable and masculine in its dimensions, this chair took inspiration from the design philosophy of William Morris, after whom such reclining chairs had been named. "Morris chairs" were made not just by Gustav and his brothers, Leopold and J. George, but by every enterprising furniture manufacturer of early twentieth-century America.

This example has unusually canted arms with broad surfaces. Comfort and convenience of the sitter are enhanced by a generous leather-covered pillow and a factory-made spring-supported seat. Although his products were machine produced by advanced manufacturing technology, Stickley and his fellow designers emphasized through-tenon construction and exposed pegs at the front of the chair as important symbols of hand craftsmanship.

Settle
Made and Labeled by Leopold and J. George Stickley,
Fayetteville, New York. c. 1908–1910.
Marked: "L. & J. G. Stickley Handcraft," red decal.
Oak with leather upholstery (not original).
H: 39" L: 60" D: 30".
Jordan-Volpe Gallery.

RITA MCMAHON, PHOTOGRAPHER

This handsome and durable piece of furniture satisfies needs for comfort, low upkeep, convenience and adaptability; but its sheer size demands a setting that is appropriate in scale. The bungalow house, popular among the middle class in the early twentieth century, offered an appropriate architectural setting.

Because of the architectural requirements of massive oak furniture of the craftsman era and because a piece of this size is not easily moved, packed or shipped, heavy oak furniture fell out of favor for almost fifty years.

MARVIN RAND, PHOTOGRAPHER

Writing Desk
Adelaide Tichenor House, Long Beach, California. 1904.
Designed by Charles S. Greene (1868–1957)
and Henry M. Greene (1870–1954), Long Beach, California.
Ash with oak doweling.
H: 50½" W: 31" D: 16".

The Greene brothers were influenced by works of Arts and Crafts designers both here and abroad. They had clipped and studied the highly schematic renderings of furniture Will Bradley illustrated in the *Ladies' Home Journal.* They had noted the work of Josef Hoffmann of Vienna whose Art Nouveau designs were published in 1901. Gustav Stickley was an even more important influence upon their work. But by 1904 their furniture had evolved into a highly personal style and became recognizably different from the work of the Stickleys.

This desk represents that important point of stylistic transition. Its freely shaped cleats were fastened with brass-headed screws arranged in a decorative pattern on the front. Beautifully mortised butterfly joinery holds the two-boarded sides together. Intricate structure revealed in a decorative way became the hallmark of Greene and Greene furniture, architecture and all their other designs. The Oriental "cloud" shape of the bracing suggests a further clue to their style. Profoundly influenced by the arts of Japan, the architecture and furniture of Greene and Greene represent a bridge between East and West, between the Arts and Crafts philosophy which revived medieval joinery and the aesthetic movement which advocated the Oriental approach to design.

Armchair
Designed by Charles and Henry Greene.
Pasadena, California. 1907.
Mahogany and ebony. H: 34" W: 24" D: 21¾".

The Greene Brothers and the craftsmen who executed their designs, Peter and John Hall, developed and refined the design ideas expressed in the furniture made for the Tichenor House. By 1907, when this chair was made for the Robert R. Blacker House, their architectural and furniture style was distinctively different from any other work being produced in America. Rudimentary cloud patterns which had been suggested in the strapwork bracing of the Tichenor desk assumed a more clearly Oriental character in the Greenes' work by this date. The characteristic use of dark pegging contrasting with the chair's lighter wood seems directly related to the patterns created by the screw details of the Tichenor desk.

By 1907, Greene and Greene furniture was suave and refined. The high quality of precise spline joinery, inlay work and carving which identifies Greene and Greene furniture can only be attributed to the personal attention of a master artist. Greene and Greene furniture follows all the design characteristics of Arts and Crafts furniture; its peculiar blend of Oriental design and Art Nouveau is so individualistic that it defies categorization.

Desk
Made by the Niedecken Walbridge Company, Milwaukee, Wisconsin. c. 1910.
Oak. H: 45⅛" W: 40 3/16" D: 23⅞".
The Art Institute of Chicago.

This desk is as exciting in its formal arrangement of parts as is Frank Lloyd Wright's architecture. Contrasts of ornamented and plain surfaces, voids versus solids and interpenetration of its members makes this desk one of the most vigorous examples of early twentieth-century furniture design. Its appearance of monumentality seems to be achieved through the severe geometry of its lines which take inspiration from classical antiquity and at the same time incorporate a sense of Oriental art. The design by George Niedecken for the Avery Coonley House of Riverside, Illinois, was probably made from a rough sketch by Wright.

This piece, far superior to the many routine examples of oak furniture of its age, speaks well for the genius of its design and the craftsman who made it.

Drawing by Will H. Bradley
For the Ladies' Home Journal, *February and March, 1902.*
Watercolor and ink on paper.
The Metropolitan Museum of Art, New York.

This drawing is deceptively advanced looking. Despite its mechanical precision and simplicity it is more closely related to the Art Nouveau movement than it is to the structuralism of machine-inspired art. Comparisons can be seen between Bradley's designs and pieces made after designs by Charles F. A. Voysey, Charles Mackintosh and M. H. Baillie Scott.

Cabinet with Drawers
Oakland, California. c. 1910.
Designed by Arthur F. and Lucia K. Mathews.
Made in The Mathews Furniture Shop, Oakland.
Carved, painted and inlaid woods; scarab hardware.
H: 46½" W: 81" D: 26½".
Collection of the Oakland Museum.

Artists Arthur and Lucia Mathews, husband and wife, collaborated with cabinetmaker Thomas A. McGlynn from about 1906 to 1920 to produce highly decorative art furniture. Their furniture shop in Oakland, California, employed about fifty craftsmen in the production of frames, boxes, jars, clock cases and other custom-made furniture. Shallow-relief carved ornament on this furniture was often enriched with original painted designs. Arthur generally designed the whole shape of a piece and Lucia painted its decorative surface. Both Arthur and Lucia were gifted painters and it is this talent that gives the furniture from their shop a distinctive personality, recognizable style and handsome quality. Even the frames which they produced to enhance their paintings were decorated with compositional devices designed to unify painting and frame. Rich and muted colors were preferred. The Mathews limited the intensity and tonal range of their colors in order to preserve the surface integrity of the furniture. Pattern and silhouette were emphasized rather than three-dimensional modeling. This deliberate selection is analogous to the way tonalist painters composed large decorative mural paintings in the late nineteenth and early twentieth centuries. One senses a keen awareness of nature modified by the artist's selective eye in the art of the Mathews painted furniture. The natural beauty of the Oakland area landscape had a profound influence upon their art. Japanese art, and the San Francisco Bay region school of simple, handcrafted architecture also served as additional sources of inspiration.

Mathews furniture is not easily identified stylistically but it certainly owes much to the Arts and Crafts movement. It includes elements of the Art Nouveau, and handsomely blends Oriental motifs with Beaux-Arts classicism. It is a decorative style more closely related to the tonalities and patterns of the work of James McNeill Whistler, or the decorative murals of the French painter Puvis de Chavannes, than to any other painted furniture made in America.

XI

1917–1980

Moderne to Contemporary

ACCEPTANCE OF THE MACHINE as a positive and creative aesthetic force marks the beginning of what we identify today as the modern era. Neither the Art Nouveau nor the Arts and Crafts movement offered real answers to the social ills that William Morris had foreseen. Nor did they address the aesthetic questions posed by new machines and materials. It took another generation to make effective use of the machine, to find new social meaning in its productive capacity, and to use its products in an artistically expressive way.

The American adventure with modern art began long before the upheaval of the First World War. Some of the more radical works of art displayed in the Armory Show in 1913 were evidence that painting and sculpture were well ahead of the "industrial arts," as furniture was classified at the time.

And far ahead of most American designers was the architect Frank Lloyd Wright, the first to proclaim that the machine was a "normal tool of civilization," and an early exponent of using its products imaginatively. Rooted in the Arts and Crafts movement, Wright's career anticipated and led the way into postwar modernism. As early as 1906 he designed metal office furniture for his innovative Larkin Building in Buffalo, New York, a model of efficiency and thoughtful planning which was demolished in 1949–1950.

In the Larkin Building, Wright introduced the vertically stacked steel filing cabinets which are commonplace office equipment today. Desks were designed with attached legless steel chairs to make office cleaning more efficient. Other chairs had casters on feet connected to a pedestal base. The frames were constructed of painted steel by the Van Dorn Iron Works Company of Cleveland, Ohio.

Accepting and adapting to the forward-looking aspects of machine production, Wright was one of the few designers to survive the cultural upheaval and disunity of the First World War. The war forged new relationships between government, business, manufacturing, design and labor. It stripped away old traditions and restraints, offering great opportunities to a new middle class of specialized technicians and working professionals with fresh vision. The war mobilization of 1917–1918 demanded new organizational skills, new solutions and new disciplines. This was true not only in America but in other countries of the Western hemisphere. Advanced planners in all fields questioned the old scheme of things and sought a new order to shape the world of the future.

Wright played an important part in the progressive movement. His thinking had a profound effect not only in America but abroad, where new ideas about design were fermenting. Wright had an enormous influence in the years 1914–1916 upon the first members of a group which published the international art journal *De Stijl.* Three architects, van t'Hoff, J. Wils and J. J. P. Oud, "abstracted" buildings into simple, geometric shapes in accordance with principles set forth in *De Stijl.* The precise geometry of their designs paralleled the abstract rectilinear paintings of Piet Mondrian. This new approach rebelled against historicism and sought a system of rational design.

The revolt was carried further by the second-generation de Stijl designer Gerrit Rietveld (1888–1964), who worked as a cabinetmaker before turning to architecture. He used only the most elementary planes and primary colors for furniture, and in 1918 designed his famous "red-blue" chair which was composed of light sheets of wood cantilevered on posts and rail. The chair was not particularly well constructed, but it was a radical design and conceived as a prototype of designs for the future. Although Rietveld claimed that the chair made no reference to earlier works, similar furniture had been made in the Adirondacks by the recluse Noah John Rondeau of Cold River, New York. Also, as early as 1915, William Laurel Harris published unpainted slab chairs of similar appearance. But while Harris constructed natural, simple and practical primitive works, Rietveld was self-consciously making a highly artificial, mechanistic and theoretical contribution to the history of design. He continued his experiments in primary form, and in 1920 designed a baby chair *(kinder stoel)* which was a lattice of lightweight overlapping framing. His 1923 Berlin chair reduced seating to skeletal simplicity, and in 1934 his *Zig Zag Stoel* was made of four simple slabs of wood angled at the seat. Rietveld's Schröder House in Utrecht (1924) was a structure of primary planes and simple spaces. He wrote:

> The design of this house was an attempt to break away from the routine ideas that still influenced architecture around 1920 after the honest styles of Berlage and other innovators. We used exclusively primary forms, spaces and colors, because they are so elementary as to be free of associations.

This approach reflected the intense desire of advanced designers to break with the past. It was more radical than anything then achieved in the United States.

A second important source of modern design theory came to the United States through a German art school, the Bauhaus. Founded in Weimar in 1919, the Bauhaus sought to unite the study of fine arts and craftsmanship, disciplines which had drifted apart over the years. Each student worked under a fine artist and a craftsman, aiming toward mastery of both the poetic and the practical. Students and faculty studied the machine and its implications; designs for assembly lines and the machine aesthetic were fundamental to Bauhaus philosophy.

Within this context, Marcel Breuer designed a chair of tubular steel and leather—the Wassily armchair, named for Kandinsky (1925). The chair has been the subject of considerable pedantic debate as to whether or not it was actually the first to be made of bent tubular steel; certainly it was among the earliest and most enduring examples, pointing the way for future experiments with factory-produced materials. In 1926, Mart Stam and Miës van der Rohe (1886–1969), the last director of the Bauhaus, designed a cantilevered chair in tubular steel. Miës van der Rohe's design of the German pavilion at the Barcelona International Exposition of 1929 translated into three dimensions the pure geometric qualities of a *De Stijl* painting. For the furniture he designed chairs with X-shaped, chrome-plated, strap-steel legs and upholstered cushions and back. The "Barcelona chair" is a classic of modern design and, along with the other two chairs described above, is still produced by Knoll International in New York.

The Bauhaus survived for only fourteen years and produced fewer than five hundred graduates before it was closed by the Nazis in 1933. But in time its influence was pervasive and dominant internationally; it expressed the needs of the twentieth-century designer through the integration of art and technology.

Thus, artists abroad were producing formal designs which stressed shapes natural to the machine and its products. Few Americans understood or benefited immediately from the formal, rational, almost mathematical precision of designs that came from de Stijl or the Bauhaus. A more direct influence on American furniture of the period was the 1925 Exposition Internationale des Arts Décoratifs et Industriels Modernes in Paris. The term Art Deco, now somewhat loosely used to describe design of the 1920s and 1930s in America, derives from it.

For most Americans, consciousness of modern art was stimulated by functional objects. "The most complete expression of the new art spirit," according to Léon Deshairs' introduction to *Modern French Decorative Arts,* was to be especially found in furniture design and construction allied to architecture: "To-day we stand before a decorative art that models itself on life as we are living it, that harmonizes with an architecture transformed by the progress of science and industry that, like fashion in dress, follows and obeys the spirit of the age." Illustrated were interiors and furniture by Francis Jourdain, Marcel Guillemard, Maurice Dufrène, J. Ruhlmann, Léon Jallot, René Joubert and others, who promoted a severity of plane and line which had not been popular in furniture before. Exactness of proportion and rich combinations of exotic woods such as amboyna, amaranth, palisander and ebony were suggested to combat the banality which threatened the work of designers favoring surfaces that were extremely flat and smooth. But in 1931 a second volume of *Decorative Arts* considered the critical question of using industrial products in furniture and concluded that today the problem of whether the home ought to reflect the factory or the street had lost its importance. By 1930 the decorator could be expected to borrow all the motifs and ideas he could from industry. Burnished metal was easy to maintain and lent itself to mass production; it was hard to imagine anything better than chromium steel "in an age which delights in impersonal art and simplified elegance." In five years furniture design had shifted from the use of mellow woods to polished chrome.

Soon after the Paris Exposition, major department stores in the United States staged their own popular exhibitions. In New York in 1927, R. H. Macy and Company introduced its customers to "Art Moderne." Lord & Taylor and B. Altman followed a year later with "French Decorative Arts." By the late 1920s, household furnishings began to reflect the world of modern technology—everyday objects could be considered an important part of the art world.

Preoccupation with surface decorative effects in the 1920s brought about the Zig Zag Moderne style, a new mode in architectural imagery. The style did not survive with vigor into the thirties. The most famous example of Zig Zag design is the stepped top of William Van Alen's Chrysler Building (1929–1930) on Forty-second Street in New York.

In 1929 the architect George Howe (1886–1955) with his partner William Lescaze started the design for the most advanced skyscraper of its day, the Philadelphia Savings Fund Society Building at the corner of Twelfth and Market streets in Philadelphia. Built between 1930 and 1932, the building was one of the first large office buildings in the country to be completely air-conditioned and to make use of stainless steel throughout. George Howe's concern for modern architecture and his contacts with Le Corbusier, Miës van der Rohe and Wright led him to creative and practical solutions.

Howe's building adhered to the basic tenets of the International style, defined by Henry-Russell Hitchcock and Philip Johnson in their publication for the architectural exhibition on the style held in

1932 at the new Museum of Modern Art in New York. Among the guiding principles of the International style were that architecture posed a problem of volume rather than mass, that it could be described as a skeleton covered with a skin. Functionalism was a prerequisite, and standardization or regularity of parts was implicit. Meaningless applied decoration was taboo. These principles also influenced the chrome-steel tubular furniture which Howe and his associates designed for the Philadelphia Savings Fund Society Building.

Yet before the International style found expression in the United States, important European designers had brought to America ideas which helped to pave the way. One of several talented immigrants from Austria and Germany at the time of the First World War was the Viennese architect Josef Urban (1872–1933) who worked in the Viennese Secessionist style. He designed stage sets for the Ziegfeld Follies, and in 1919 became the American manager for the Wiener Werkstätte of Austria. Ten years later he was one of a committee of architects whose designs for furniture were transformed into actual products by industrial artist-craftsmen and exhibited at the Metropolitan Museum of Art in New York. This exhibition, "The Architect and the Industrial Arts," was so popular that it stayed open for six months instead of the scheduled six weeks.

Paul T. Frankl (1887–1958), another immigrant from Vienna, arrived in 1914 but did not gain much attention until the Paris Exposition of 1925. His most famous designs were tall cabinets called "skyscraper furniture," which mirrored the stepped-back character of America's tall buildings. A writer as well as a designer, *New Dimensions* is his best-known work.

Gilbert Rhode (1894–1944) and Kem Weber (1889–1963) were two German designers who came to this country and stayed as a result of the war. Weber had worked with Bruno Paul at the Academy of Applied Arts in Berlin before coming to California in 1914 to design the German section of the Panama-Pacific Exposition in San Francisco. He remained in California and was one of three Americans who were invited to exhibit in Macy's 1928 Exposition of Arts and Trades. These designers are only a few of the many talented individuals from Austria and Germany who found themselves at work in the United States during the 1920s, when design began to change rapidly at the popular level.

When the Nazis closed the Bauhaus in 1933, a second migration from Germany began. Josef Albers, who taught drawing, furniture design and calligraphy at the Bauhaus, came to Black Mountain College in North Carolina. In 1950 he became chairman of the Design Department at Yale University. Walter Gropius accepted a professorship at Harvard University. Constructivist L. Moholy-Nagy moved to Chicago where he founded a school of design, the New Bauhaus, in 1937. Ernst Lichtblau of Vienna joined the faculty of the Rhode Island School of Design, and Miës van der Rohe moved to the United States in 1938 to become a professor of architecture at Illinois Institute of Technology.

In spite of the Depression of the 1930s and encroaching fascism in Europe, progressive ideas continued to be expressed forcibly and optimistically in American public buildings. Opening December 27, 1932, Radio City Music Hall made its visitors aware of the modern movement. Donald Deskey, who designed the interior, dealt with scale and decoration in an unusual and dramatic manner. From that time forward, designers gave special attention to theaters and movie houses, capturing the public fancy with arresting and sometimes outlandish combinations of materials, colors and shapes. Abstracted images of energy, power, motion, time, light and other agents of force and progress were popular motifs. Signs of the zodiac, the motion of waterfalls, lightning, clouds and leaf patterns and motifs from Mayan ruins were stylized into flat, schematic designs. The aggressive patterning was followed by the smoother rhythms and contours of streamlined architecture, furniture and industrial design of the mid-1930s.

Comparison of designs presented at two world fairs clarifies the basic change that took place. In 1933 the city of Chicago held a fair known as "The Century of Progress Exposition." Technical proficiency and scientific progress were expressed by model houses made of steel-frame boxes covered with enamel-coated metal plates. They were called Stran steel houses and they had sharp corners which gave them a boxy character. But by the 1939 New York World's Fair, streamlined rounded corners were the fashion and industrial designers—Norman Bel Geddes, Walter Teague, Raymond Loewy, Henry Dreyfuss—had come into the limelight. Bel Geddes was in charge of the Highways and Horizons Building for General Motors. Its rounded corners and sleek edges reflected the aerodynamic styling which gripped the imagination of American industrial designers and affected the shape of almost every kind of machine and man-made product well into the 1940s.

Hoping for progress, exhilarated with the speed of the transportation revolution and industrial advances, this new generation of designers concentrated their talents on shaping the interior and exterior surfaces of trains, automobiles and airplanes. Wind tunnel research had revealed that the teardrop shape, by decreasing wind resistance on moving objects, was the basic design form most suitable for machines for travel. This led to the discovery that motion could be suggested in a stationary object by giving it an overall teardrop form or shape.

Norman Bel Geddes contended that surface design could be shaped quite independently of the structural or functional forms within, that a smooth exterior could enhance a complex, irregular machine. Raymond Loewy's sleek shells for airplanes and locomotives became the most famous evidence of the impact of industrial design on the modern world—the term "streamliner" recalls the trains of the 1930s and 1940s.

The streamlined look found champions on all levels of furniture design. The exterior of Frank Lloyd Wright's S. C. Johnson Administration Building in Racine, Wisconsin (1936–1937), was a model of smooth-flowing organic plasticity. The desks and chairs within were rounded to conform with the overall shape of the building. At a more pedestrian level, Art Metal Company came out with the "Dynamic" office desk (1936), which featured the rounded corners and smooth sides of the new aesthetic in a very cautious way.

The streamline style was short-lived. But faith in technology and its potential for modern design did not die.

The designers who became prominent in the early 1940s owed much to the foundations laid by the pioneers of modern design, and particularly to the architects of the International style. That style was embodied in New York's Museum of Modern Art. The museum held an international design competition in 1941 and exhibited the winning furniture designs of architects Charles Eames (1907–1979) and Eero Saarinen (1910–1961). Both men were strongly influenced by the International style, but both departed from the rigors of its purest expression, finding fresh ways to express technological advances in the forms of mass-produced furniture. The catalog of the exhibition analyzed fundamental differences between the new furniture and the heavily upholstered furniture prevalent since the nineteenth century. The frame for suspending webbing and horsehair in traditional furniture was replaced by the armature of the new furniture, a form-fitted shell of bent plywood over which a new material, foam rubber, was molded and laminated with a tough skin of plastic. The new furniture was curved to suit the human body, its forms reflecting an affinity for the free-flowing shapes of contemporary sculpture.

Variations on the shell idea for furniture engaged the attention of both Eames and Saarinen for the rest of their design careers. Each went different ways with discoveries of the possibilities of new materials. Both benefited by having their designs produced by important manufacturing and sales firms. Charles Eames found sponsorship in the Zeeland, Michigan, based furniture manufacturing company, Herman Miller, through the encouragement and forethought of that company's designer, George Nelson. Saarinen affiliated with Knoll, a New York firm established by Hans Knoll, who came to the United States from Germany in 1937. The Knoll firm continues today and includes in its collections works of Harry Bertoia, a sculptor famous for his wire chairs; Warren Platner, an architect whose nickel-finish steel-rod-based furniture is an eloquent expression of constructivist style; and William Stephens, an industrial designer whose return to laminated wood furniture reflects a new direction.

Much furniture produced in the United States in the 1940s was banal and undistinguished. The Second World War dominated the decade of experimentation and uncertainty in public taste. Some firms, like the Dunbar Furniture Company of Berne, Indiana, maintained excellence by keeping a sensitive designer like Edward J. Wormley in charge. But many firms simply went on reproducing pallid replicas of Colonial furniture.

The impersonality of sleek furniture made automatically and frequently sold impersonally through a showroom or a decorator has been an important factor in the rise of the new craft movement. In many ways this movement directly challenges many of the basic tenets of faith of modernism. In the 1940s only isolated individuals were making one-of-a-kind pieces of furniture as artist-craftsmen. The senior figure of the movement was Wharton Esherick (1887–1970). His home and studio at Paoli, Pennsylvania, built by hand in the 1930s, is generally regarded as the mecca of the wood-craftsman movement in America today. His unconventional, free-form, sculptural furniture has been a source of inspiration to at least two generations of younger craftsmen. There is a certain amount of Art Nouveau influence in Esherick's work. Whether or not he was familiar with furniture made by the late nineteenth-century Catalán designer Antonio Gaudí is a moot point; they were at least spiritually related in their exploration of shaped form to create a sculptural environment.

The first generation of artist-craftsmen in America who followed Esherick includes George Nakashima, Sam Maloof and Arthur Carpenter. Developing personal styles and production practices quite independently, they all design, make and sell their own work, and represent the reintegration of craft, art and personal communication with the consumer.

New directions in sculptural furniture, fantasy and realism have been opened up by younger artists, such as Wendell Castle and Judy McKie. Individual involvement in furniture-making and buying is a sought-after remedy to the inner losses experienced through mechanization and depersonalization. The new craft movement is a healthy antidote to this and serves as a reminder that the individual craftsman working in a small shop remains a potent force.

Armchair
Designed by Frank Lloyd Wright (1869–1956).
Made for the Larkin Company Administration Building, Buffalo, New York. 1904.
Painted steel and oak. H: 37½" W: 24¹¹⁄₁₆" D: 21⅛".
Museum of Modern Art, New York.

Wright's drawing for this chair was even more advanced stylistically than the finished product. It indicated that the arms and legs were intended to form a continuous wraparound line from the upright of the back, down to the casters at the floor. This anticipated by more than two decades the bent-tubular-steel chairs of Marcel Breuer. The actual chairs made for the Larkin Building are more angular than the drawing; this angularity is harmonious with the overall cubistic character of the building.

The combination of industrial production with innovative artistic sensibilities was an unsurpassed achievement for its time.

Armchair ("Rood-Blauwe Stoel")
Designed by Gerrit Rietveld (1888–1964).
Holland. 1918.
Painted wood. H: 34" W: 26½" D: 26½".
Museum of Modern Art, New York, Gift of Philip C. Johnson.

In an attempt to break away from all routine ideas of the past, Gerrit Rietveld used the most basic system of frame and slab construction and painted his chair with primary colors: red, blue, yellow, and a neutral black. Rietveld discovered an affinity with a group of artists and designers in Leyden (van Doesburg, Mondrian and Oud) who had founded an international magazine of art, *De Stijl,* in 1917. Members of this group were influenced by the progressive work of Frank Lloyd Wright.

Barcelona Chair, in situ Barcelona, 1929.
Designed by Ludwig Miës van der Rohe, 1929.
Chrome-plated steel-bar frame; solid horsehair cushion, pigskin covering. H: 29⅞" W: 29⅝".
Miës Archives, Museum of Modern Art.

The designs by Miës van der Rohe for the German pavilion in the 1929 International Exposition in Barcelona marked a turning point in the development of architecture and furniture throughout the world. The pavilion is one of the most beautiful structures of its era; its furniture classic. Both stress elegance and opulence with simplicity and rich combinations of materials. The one-storey structure had a sweeping horizontal roof which hovered over vertical slab walls of richly figured onyx and travertine marble. Gray-tinted glass separated the interior from the exterior and black glass walls lined the reflecting pools. Complementing the building with elegance of their own were a few chairs, stools and glass-topped tables, formally arranged for the King and Queen of Spain.

The design of the Barcelona chair capitalizes on the properties of its materials. Elasticity of its steel legs carries through the arc of its back support. Tufted cushions are supported with leather straps with an economy of line and pattern. The detail and proportions of this furniture in its original setting represent the design philosophy of the architect—less is more.

Dining Chair with Arms
Designed by Ludwig Miës van der Rohe, 1926.
Manufactured by Knoll International, Inc., New York. 1977.
Tubular stainless steel, polished finish; saddle-leather sling-back and seat with nylon lacing.
H: 31" W: 21" D: 32½".

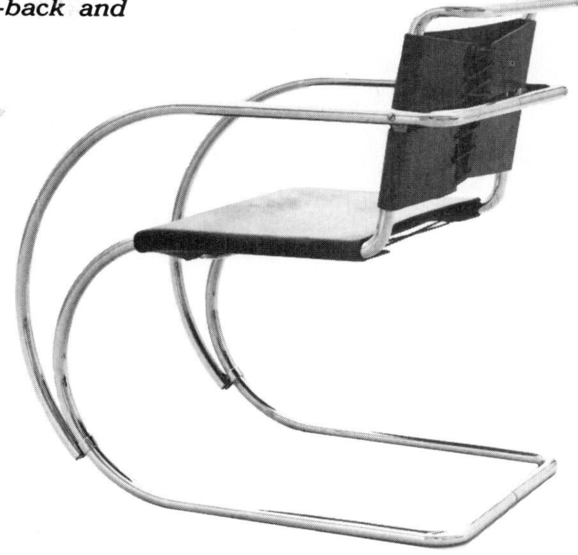

Elasticity of metal and the flexibility of a stretched material is exploited by Miës in his design for this classic in chair design. While Miës was not the first to use the cantilever principle in bent tubular furniture, he was among its earliest developers, together with Marcel Breuer of the Bauhaus and Mart Stam of Rotterdam. Design parallels between bentwood furniture and bent tubular steel are obvious, but the technology of fabrication and the final results are not comparable. The spring-like resiliance of bent-steel tubing offered a whole new prospect to contemporary furniture design that even today has not been exhausted in its possibilities.

This chair, handsome as it is with the sweeping continuous lines of its legs and back, fails in the awkward juncture of the arms to the front legs at this transition to the horizontal.

Lounge Chair
Designed by Ludwig Miës van der Rohe, 1931.
Manufactured by Knoll International, Inc., New York. 1977.
Polished stainless-steel frame; pleated foam-rubber upholstery with saddle-leather straps.
H: 37½" W: 23 9/16" D: 47 3/16".

Based on the same design as the famous dining chair with arms, this lounge chair is somewhat lower and broader in its proportions and is more satisfactory in that the arms are eliminated. There is a simple opulence to the piece, partly due to its proportions and partly to its detail and technically superb finish. While this and other furniture made from designs by Miës evokes the aesthetics of a machine age, these pieces are not mass produced. Hand craftsmanship is involved in the making of such furniture despite its seeming suitability to large-scale production.

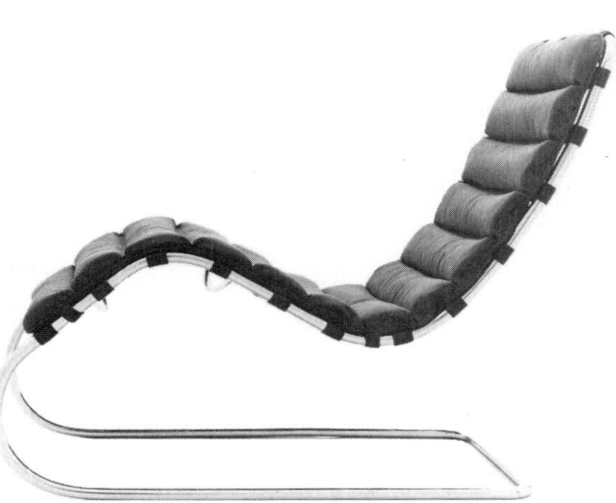

Side Chair
Designed by Marcel Breuer, 1928.
Made by Gebrüder Thonet, A.G., Germany.
Chrome-plated tube steel with caned-wood seat and back.

The Cesca chair is Breuer's most famous design, imitated throughout the world of contemporary furniture in many different variations. Its principle of cantilevered suspension in space is not unique in the history of furniture design but it most certainly was the most influential design to transform the concept of seating in the modern world. Cheap furniture made in the thirties and forties in America used this basic idea of a tube frame with a pressed-iron seat and back. Such inexpensive furniture was the standard choice of modern seating for restaurants and porches.

Among other designs in its Breuer collection, Knoll International in New York today produces a modified version of the Cesca chair, a matching armchair, and a related form, the Laccio table, with a U-shaped polished tubular-steel base and laminated plastic top.

Armchair (Lounge Chair)
Designed by Marcel Breuer, Germany. 1925.
Manufactured by Gebrüder Thonet, A.G., Germany.
Canvas and leather; chrome-plated steel tube frame.
H: 27¾" W: 30⅞" D: 25".
Museum of Modern Art.

The Wassily chair was the first bent-tubular-steel chair of consequence. Its designer, Marcel Breuer, was born in Hungary and studied painting and sculpture at the Art Academy of Vienna. Thereafter, he studied at the Bauhaus in Weimar, Germany, and in 1924 was put in charge of its furniture design department. In 1937 he came to the United States and formed a partnership in design and architecture with Walter Gropius.

An important exponent of design philosophy which integrated art and industry, Breuer organized the parts of this chair to serve more than the needs of seating. It offers the viewer a variety of interesting spaces with contrasts between complex and closed and simple and open parts. It presents an elegant suspension system. The novel problem of this system, however, was to carry the human body in a relaxed, informal manner. Breuer did not like the term "International style" and is reported to have said in 1948 that if it is considered identical with mechanical and impersonal rigorism then "down with International style." Anyway, the term is an unhappy one—just as unhappy as "functionalism."

Dining Room Furniture
Chrome-plated iron, glass, mirror; glazed-fabric upholstery.
Table—H: 28" W: 28" D: 28".
Armchairs—H: 29" W: 20" D: 20".
Made by the Howell Company, Geneva, Illinois.
Pottery pitcher—Franconia, New Hampshire: c. 1926.
Collection of James Kettlewell.

Americans were quick to seize upon the advanced ideas of the Paris Expositions of 1928 and 1929. Architects, designers and patrons grasped the essential features of the machine aesthetic adapting industrial materials for domestic uses with sleek "Deco" lines.

This furniture is neatly slip-jointed, bolted and welded together forming seamless, continuous contours, reducing fundamental design to basics.

Living-Dining Room
Designed by Florence Knoll.
Installation in the Detroit Institute of Arts Exhibition "For Modern Living," 1949.

An index of taste at the end of the 1940s was offered by the Detroit Institute of Arts exhibition "For Modern Living," which selected choice examples of furniture. The exhibition featured this installation designed by Florence Knoll.

Florence Knoll's installation in Detroit domesticated the design ideas of the Barcelona Pavilion. The area carpet was placed in the center of the room and the furniture was selected to emphasize the low, hovering qualities implicit in the fireplace wall. She changed the conventional focus on the fireplace by raising it onto a shelf. Upholstery was of washable or durable plastic, leather, jute or sailcloth. Furniture was scratch- and burn-resistant. A butcher-block top was used for the table, supported on four simple pipe-shaped legs.

The furniture used by Florence Knoll was designed by Pierre Jeanneret, Richard Stein, Franco Albini, Abel Sorensen, Eero Saarinen, Isamu Noguchi and Hardoy, Bonet and Kurchan. The familiar sling or lounge chair to the right of the fireplace is identical to one developed in 1938 by the team of Antonio Bonet, Juan Kurchan and Jorge Ferrari-Hardoy.

Sectional Sofa Designed by Saarinen and Eames. Bloomfield Hills, Michigan. 1940.

An important winning design in the Museum of Modern Art international competition and exhibition "Organic Design in Home Furnishings" was Charles Eames and Eero Saarinen's sectional sofa shown here in drawing and completed form. In 1940 it was highly innovative. Instead of using the normal coil spring of traditional furniture the designers chose to use a new sort of flat factory spring supported in a curved wooden shell. The form of that shell (a compound curve) was derived from a plaster model illustrated above the finished sofa in the exhibition.

Designs for Molded Seating
Museum of Modern Art, Modern Design Competition, 1940.

Charles Eames and Eero Saarinen were young architects and designers teaching together at Cranbrook, an art and prep school near Detroit, when the Museum of Modern Art design competition in 1940 awarded them special attention. Their new furniture employed the use of bent laminated wood used as a shell to form seating. Upon this shell, foam rubber and modern material was stretched to make the seating comfortable. The presentation in the Museum's catalog compared their new approach with the traditional upholstery methods—horsehair, webbing, springs, etcetera. The new approach was sleek looking and addressed the question of using new materials in efficient ways to lower costs. This new approach was rapidly imitated throughout the country. It is interesting to note that Miës van der Rohe's sketches in the early 1940s show that he too was grappling with the problems of conchoidal seat shells.

Both Eames and Saarinen became major figures in furniture design, concentrating upon new solutions.

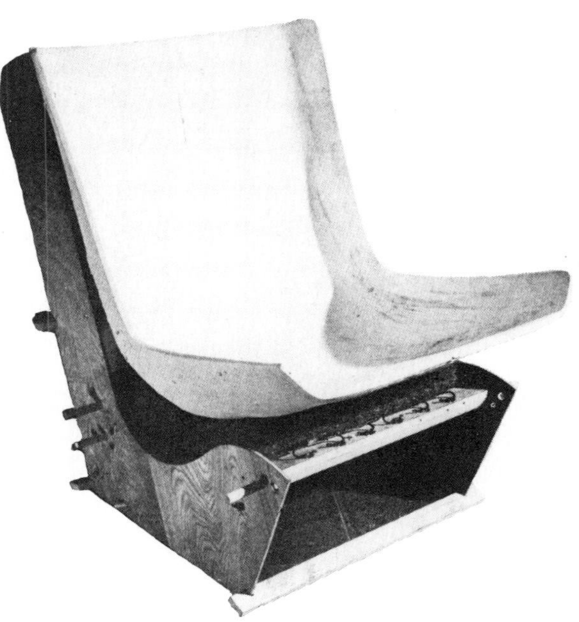

Side Chair, "DCW" (Dining Chair Wood)
Designed by Charles Eames (b. 1907). c. 1946.
Manufactured by Evans Products Co.
Ash, plywood with rubber and steel-bolt shock mounts.
H: 29½" W: 19½" D: 21".
Museum of Fine Arts, Boston.

This chair eloquently combines comfort and simplicity in such a way as to unite principles of fine arts with engineering genius. The chair was exhibited in the Museum of Modern Art in 1947.

The form of the chair parallels the ideals of abstract design in sculpture, architecture and other arts which underwent drastic simplification and abstraction during the 1940s. The basic ideas that made this chair possible had been known for almost a hundred years. Manufactured laminated parts of form-fitted furniture for large-scale production had a history of development for at least three generations. This particular chair combined what was already known with newly developed plywood processing and industrial fittings. What seems especially new is the way the five parts of the chair seem to hover in space—apparently independent, but obviously connected to each other. The expression of hovering parts evolved out of a design philosophy traceable to the International style in architecture.

Side Chair
Designed by Charles Eames, 1946.
Manufactured by the Herman Miller Furniture Company, 1947.
Labeled: "herman miller evans Charles Eames."
Molded five-ply wood seat and back with polished-steel rods and rubber shock mounts. H: 29⅜" W: 19¼" D: 20".
Museum of Fine Arts, Boston.

This chair was included in the Museum of Modern Art exhibition of 1947, designed by Ludwig Miës van der Rohe, entitled "One Hundred Useful Objects of Fine Design." After the exhibition closed, Charles Eames gave the chair to his friend, fellow designer Edward J. Wormley, who gave it to the Museum of Fine Arts in Boston in 1975.

Unlike the final production chair which has become known internationally as the "Eames chair," this example has its feet capped with rubber tips. Eames found that these caps tended to fall off and he substituted self-leveling nylon glides for feet. This minor change brought the chair to perfection.

The design appears deceptively simple. Eames has made the most effective use of the least amount of material—an approach to design which expresses a long-held American value, that of practical and economical functionalism. The seat is molded and fastened to its support like a metal tractor seat. Two different diameters of steel rods are used for support. For the legs a 5/8-inch rod is employed and for the seat and spine a more sturdy 7/16-inch rod is welded to the U-shaped legs. For the sake of balance and dynamic stability, the legs are welded to the spine at an angle that supports the weight of the sitter with much greater effect than if they were simply welded at right angles to the spine. The back is also inclined and forms a slightly obtuse angle with the seat. Rubber shock mounts are bonded to the wood and are bolted to the metal frame to make the chair supple and noise-free. The shape of the chair back has been described as a "rectangle about to turn into an oval, the transformation being arrested at a point midway between the two shapes." The shape of the seat is contoured in opposing directions on the side and front, which gives the whole an animated appearance. In 1969 Eames redesigned the chair by padding the surface of the plywood shell and increasing the comfort of the back and seat with urethane foam, fabric and a vinyl welt. The abstracted shapes of the plywood, balanced and connected to the legs and spine, are related aesthetically to the mobile sculpture of Alexander Calder and to the painted constellations of Joan Miró.

Armchair Rocker
Designed by Charles Eames, c. 1950.
Manufactured by the Herman Miller Furniture Company, 1950.
Labeled: "herman miller furniture company, Zeeland, Michigan"
"designed by Charles Eames"
"The shell is moulded by Zenith Plastic Co., Gardena, California."
Molded polyester, wire, birch runners, rubber shock mounts.
H: 27" W: 24 3/4" D: 23 1/2".
Museum of Fine Arts, Boston.

Molded polyester offered Eames a lightweight shell which he shaped to suit the human body. The shell was attached with rubber shock mounts to a sort of cat's cradle of wire which braced the legs and wooden rockers.

Even though this rocker looks somewhat dated, it represents an important step in the development of inexpensive durable furniture in this country. Eames adapted the polyester shell of this to another set of legs which were better integrated to the whole design. The new legs were made of zinc-coated U-shaped steel tubing. The new combination formed a four-legged stacking chair that has been popular and useful throughout the world. As recently as 1971 the molded polyester chair has evolved into a handsome aluminum-based swivel armchair with padded Naugahyde and vinyl binding of great technological sophistication and aesthetic appeal.

Side Chair
Designed by Frank Lloyd Wright (1867–1959) for the Imperial Hotel, Tokyo, Japan. 1921–1922.
Oak; yellow leatherette upholstery not original. H: 38" W: 16" D: 17".
Cooper-Hewitt Museum.

One of the wonders of the modern architectural world was Tokyo's Imperial Hotel, built after designs by Frank Lloyd Wright between 1916 and 1922. In this building Wright employed a strange mixture of ornament and structure seemingly inspired by Japanese and Mayan art. Partially because of Wright's unorthodox methods of design, and perhaps because of his non-rigid articulation of parts and his innovative floating concrete pier construction, the Hotel survived a mighty earthquake in 1924 which shook most other conventional buildings to the ground in Tokyo and Yokohama, only to be demolished in 1968.

The same design ingenuity was applied to the furniture within. This unusual chair was a part of the original furnishings. It is a striking design and one that arrests the eye with its bold geometry. The hexagonal back is divided in such a way as to represent either a diamond and chevron or a cube in perspective, depending upon the viewer's perception. The intricately structured support system of the seat seems overly braced and strangely articulated. Like the back, it has a zigzag quality which shows Wright's fertile imagination and ability to anticipate and adapt to design trends.

In a modest way, the chair represents highly individualistic qualities and the engaging personality of the designer who provided a listener or a viewer with the unexpected.

Dining Room—President's House, Cranbrook Academy of Art.
Designed by Eliel Saarinen.
Cranbrook, Michigan.

Table
Designed by Eliel Saarinen.
Made by the Company of Master Craftsmen. 1930.
Fir, ebony, hare, holly and box woods. H: 30″ D: 53″.

Chairs (Set of Eight)
Designed by Eliel Saarinen.
Made by the Company of Master Craftsmen. 1930.
Fir, ebony, painted stripes.
Reupholstered with velvet seat cushions, 1977. H: 37¼″.

Vase (Centerpiece)
Designed by Eliel Saarinen.
Made by the International Silver Company. c. 1935
Brass. H: 12½″.

Light Fixture
Designed by Eliel Saarinen.
Made by Edward F. Caldwell and Company. 1929–1930.
Brass. H: (with hangers) 40″ D: 21″.

Sculpture: "Head of a Dancing Girl" By Carl Milles.
c. 1912–1913.
Gilded bronze. H: 8″.

This room represents the apex of modern furniture design employing conventional materials for effect. Contrasts of surface and shape were held in elegant restraint by the Finnish-trained architect Eliel Saarinen (1873–1970).

A master of understated, intellectual design concepts in his own work, Saarinen influenced American design as president of the Cranbrook Academy of Art.

A significant style change followed quickly: design was simplified and industrial materials exploited. The machine aesthetic became a dominant force in design.

Side Table
Probably Designed by Dan Cooper (1901–1965) for James and Mary Louise Osborn.
New York City. c. 1930.
Formica, painted wood and iron.
H: 37″ W: 42″ D: 12½″.
Yale University Art Gallery.

JOSEPH SZASZFAI, PHOTOGRAPHER

The widespread acceptance of modern design principles which took place during the thirties had an impact that dramatically changed the appearance of cities and domestic interiors, both in this country and abroad. Streamlining was an essential ingredient of the new style, with the use of man-made or synthetic materials a natural component. This table illustrates both elements. It is sleek and it makes bold use of man-made products.

It is difficult in today's space age to recall the excitement caused by man-made synthetic products when they first came into existence in the 1930s and 1940s. As new products were discovered there was invariably a ready prophet to predict the end of the age of wooden furniture—that new furniture forms could be accepted only of plastics and other manufactured products. The spirit of such belief is embodied in furniture of this type.

Table
Probably Designed by Dan Cooper (1901–1965).
New York City. 1928–1940.
Made for James and Mary Louise Osborn.
Maple or birch veneer on mahogany; base painted black.
H: 30″ L: 68¼″ D: 38″.
Yale University Art Gallery.

The marked contrast of the light-colored figured veneer of this table's top and the dramatic black color of its base are in keeping with Dan Cooper's philosophy that "all good things go together." Geometry of form and elegant natural burl seem to represent the tensions of the era of the thirties when designers felt an intense desire to reconcile individualism with standardization. The table is severely architectural in its use of geometric shapes and makes use of the U-shaped supports fashionable in the 1930s. The designer of the table arrived at a geometric solution to its pattern in a way similar to the monumental symbol of the New York World's Fair of 1939—the Trylon and Perisphere conceived by Wallace K. Harrison and J. André Fouilhous. With a sense of new order in the modern world, advanced designers explored the use of basic geometric volumes to convey their understanding and attitudes toward the "Brave New World."

Furniture and Interiors
Radio City Music Hall, 1932.
Designed by Donald Deskey (b. 1894).

Sleek combinations of chrome, Bakelite, mirror, aluminum and neon lights captured the modern appearance that Donald Deskey sought throughout his furnishings of Radio City Music Hall in 1932. The foliate mural featuring over-scaled plants was painted by Yasuo Kuniyoshi (1893–1953). Exotic vegetation contrasted with the miracles of the machine world heightened the impact of the pure, machined surfaces upon the mind of the viewer. Mirrors reflected in mirrors caught the new neon light.

HELGA PHOTO STUDIO, INC.

Airfoam-cushioned chairs with chrome-plated steel legs surround a formica-topped table with tubular steel legs and metal circular base. With this declaration for the new machine age, Donald Deskey's design was a sensation.

HELGA PHOTO STUDIO, INC.

Womb Chair Group
Designed by Eero Saarinen (1910–1961).
Manufactured by Knoll Associates, New York. 1948.
Polished steel-rod wire frame and legs; upholstered shell.

This chair and its progeny evolved out of work in the 1940s when Saarinen collaborated with Charles Eames. They developed shell-constructed furniture with molded, form-fitting seats. By 1946 Saarinen found a sponsor for his ideas in the firm of Knoll. Eames pieces were produced by Evans Products, later by the Herman Miller Company. The world of contemporary furniture has not been the same since. The womb chair is one of the most comfortable and handsome designs of its day. It has not been eclipsed by new fashions.

Pedestal Table and Chair Group
Designed by Eero Saarinen (1910–1961).
Manufactured by Knoll Associates, New York. 1955–1956.
Cast aluminum, fused plastic, molded plastic.

Of all contemporary furniture designs the most eloquently simple and completely unified are the pedestal pieces which Saarinen began designing about 1953 by making full-scale models and trying them out with members of his family. His idea was to clear up the "slum of legs" beneath chairs and tables. By unifying the tops and bases with a simple, graceful column, Saarinen created a collection of classic pieces introduced in 1956.

Wire-Based Stools, Tables and Chairs
Designed by Warren Platner.
Manufactured by Knoll Associates, New York. 1961–1966.

Between 1963 and 1967 Warren Platner collaborated with the Knoll Design Development Group. What resulted from that collaboration is perhaps Platner's most widely admired furniture. His nickel-finished steel-rod-based chairs, stools and tables are subtly gathered at their centers. The optical results of this work give the viewer a sense of motion in the static object.

Platner's designs show his appreciation of the work which Russian-born constructivist Naum Gabo (b. 1890) had achieved in kinetic

sculpture, using plastic sheets upon which closely spaced nylon threads were strung to enclose varied spatial volumes. His sculpture and Platner's furniture allow the viewer to see through enclosed space but alter the perception of that space remarkably.

Designs for Seating
By Bill Stephens.
Manufactured by Knoll International, Inc., New York. 1967–1971.
Laminated oak veneer, handwoven wool upholstery.

Seating designed by Bill Stephens is expressive of humanistic rather than techno-centric values. It is comfortable, sleek and serviceable. It combines the recently revived public interest in light-colored laminated hardwood with an injected-molded shell for a continuous upholstered seat and back. The combination is superb, for although it is a highly technical achievement, it does not assert itself as such upon the viewer. There is an easy, inviting appearance to this furniture which is confirmed by its use. It is well-designed to support the human body and is pleasant to touch.

Stephens, who graduated in Industrial Arts from the Philadelphia College of Art in 1955, began working toward this product in 1964. At this time he was involved with tooling equipment to produce laminated chairs that prefigured his own. These chairs were designed for Knoll by Don Pettit, who, in turn, had worked both with Bertoia and Eero Saarinen. Stephens' work represents a handsome new hybrid of old and new methods and materials in furniture production. The Stephens chairs are lightweight, unostentatious and affordable—a happy combination.

Designs for Seating
By Harry Bertoia (1915–1978).
Manufactured by Knoll Associates, New York. 1951–1955.
Polished steel wire; cotton and/or Elastic Naugahyde upholstery.

Bertoia's designs for furniture reflect his background as a student and teacher of painting and metalcrafts at the Cranbrook Academy of Art and suggest his search for expressive form as a sculptor. His studies for furniture began in his workshop in Bally, Pennsylvania, in the late 1940s. Within a few years, in 1951, they had matured and were introduced by Knoll and have remained classic designs ever since. Bertoia explained his design process for this basic seating in disarmingly easy logic. Three factors were considered: space, form and the nature of the metal wire from which the frame was constructed. The form of the seating logically evolved by adding together many small units in geometric arrangement—rectangles, hexagons or triangles, welded together to produce a single large unit of the same basic shape. Like cellular structures, Bertoia explained, the design evolved naturally upon organic principles. Philosophically, his approach to design was "to make the environment more pleasant and varied by merging the efforts of technology and the creative arts."

Interior View
Designed by Wharton Esherick (1887–1970).
Wharton Esherick Museum, Paoli, Pennsylvania.
Spiral stair, oak, 1930.

Painter, sculptor, graphic artist and woodworker, Wharton Esherick's ideas serve as the springboard for recent developments in new handmade furniture. He explored impressionism in his painting; cubism, expressionism and fantasy in his prints and sculpture. He sifted through Art Nouveau, Art Deco and cubistic phases to finally find a personal expression in twisted, organic forms that seemed to grow naturally and evolve in space in a primitive, plastic way. He was familiar with the writings of anthroposophist Rudolph Steiner of Dornach, Switzerland, whose book *Ways to a New Style in Architecture* may have had an impact upon Esherick's designs. Steiner wrote that the interiors of buildings should reveal "a continuous relief sculpture . . . one plastic form." Esherick's interiors most certainly do present a harmonious sculptural plasticity.

The spine of the great staircase of his house was formed from a spiral-shaped trunk of oak with a Y fork at its top. Steps were hewn from oak slabs and pinned into the spine. The stairs were left freestanding without rail or support. Much of Esherick's furniture shows familiarity with the work of Munich painter and designer Richard Riemerschmid, whose furniture was exhibited in 1899 in the German Art Exhibition in Dresden. Esherick's works also show an affinity for painter, designer and architect Henry van de Velde whose home in Uccle near Brussels was designed in 1895 in a completely integrated, liberated aesthetic, expressed by a dynamic plasticity of form. Interest in unconventional shapes or asymmetry of composition persists in much of the new furniture being crafted by hand today.

Walnut Bench with Back
Made by George Nakashima (b. 1905), New Hope, Pennsylvania. 1979.
Walnut and ash. H: 31¼″ L: 85″ D: 36″.
Museum of Fine Arts, Boston.
Purchased Through Funds Provided by the National Endowment for the Arts and the Deborah M. Noonan Foundation.

George Nakashima, an American of Japanese ancestry, moved to New Hope, Pennsylvania, in 1943. His craftsmanship soon attracted wide attention and by 1949 his reputation as a designer and craftsman was well established. Today he is one of less than half a dozen senior craftsmen who make a livelihood through full-time work with handcrafted wooden furniture production. His approach to design reflects his Oriental view of art and nature but is also deeply rooted in historic American furniture traditions. He consciously rejects the values and the aesthetics of the machine age and space age.

The mighty slab seat of this walnut bench was formed from the trunk of a tree. Its natural fork at one end and its shaped sides are forms consciously adopted by Nakashima in designing the whole. Even a natural split at one end of the bench is given attention with a butterfly or double dovetail inlay to prevent further splitting. This play with nature and the use of natural forms for artistic advantage is characteristic of Nakashima's work.

Side Chair
Made by George Nakashima, New Hope, Pennsylvania. 1979.
Walnut and ash. H: 35½" W: 19½" D: 22".
Museum of Fine Arts, Boston.
Purchased Through Funds Provided by the National Endowment for the Arts and the Deborah M. Noonan Foundation.

Termed a "Conoid chair" by its maker, this trestle-based walnut frame with its cantilevered seat is one of the most comfortable examples of contemporary hardwood seating furniture. The resilient and contrasting ash spindles of its back are spoke-shaved in such a way as to offer the sitter an awareness of the handmade quality of the whole work. The seat is a single slab of figured walnut, handsomely sculptured and tapered toward the front edge.

Although the stance of the chair seems precarious, it is actually a beautiful study of the center of gravity and counterbalance—poised almost like a forward-leaning dancer of nogaku, Japanese drama.

Conoid Table and Conoid Chair
Made and Designed by George Nakashima (b. 1905), October, 1971; Design Introduced 1962.
Persian and English walnut.
Table—H: 28" W: 42" L: 80". Chair—H: 35" W: 20" D: 16".
New Hope, Pennsylvania.

COURTESY OF GEORGE NAKASHIMA; G. WILLIAM HOLLAND, PHOTOGRAPHER

Although Western seating furniture is not a part of traditional Japanese life, Nakashima has successfully blended ideas of West and East in all the works he produced. He does employ machine-powered tools to shape the form of furniture but he is diametrically opposed to the adoration of the machine in aesthetic terms. He feels a strong partnership with nature and composes his work in harmony with natural forms discovered in wood grain, extravagant burled figures of wood and in the textured outermost surfaces of the tree's growing edge. Evidence of such "discovery" is clear in the edge of the table in this composition. Allowing for "nature," the composition is still carefully controlled and artfully shaped.

Side Chair (One of a Set of Four)
Designed and Made by Tage Frid, Foster, Rhode Island. 1979.
Cherry with cowhide leather seat. H: 31¼" W: 19" D: 18".
Museum of Fine Arts, Boston.
Purchased Through Funds Provided by the National Endowment for the Arts and the Deborah M. Noonan Foundation.

The klismos form of ancient Classical furniture pictured on Grecian vases was the inspiration for this modern chair. The result is refreshing and beautiful. The chair is by no means an archaeologically correct copy; there is no mistake that it is a contemporary design. But the grace inherent in the ancient furniture is not lost in Frid's design.

Too subtle for photography is the fact that the elegantly tapered rear legs and posts are made up of multiple layers of cherry wood laminated together to offer great strength and resiliency to the back. A double chair-back settee based on this side chair was also made by Frid for the Museum of Fine Arts.

Frid came to America in 1948 from Denmark where he holds the distinguished title of master craftsman.

Three-Legged Stools
Designed and Made by Tage Frid. 1965.
Seat heights: 12", 16" and 21".
Large chair—H: 25¾" W: 17" D: 10¼".
Privately Owned.

The design of these stools overcomes the tipsy character of three-legged chairs which have a broad, full seat and only one leg in the back. Working out problems of balance and proportion, Frid developed a stable, comfortable three-legged stool that even looks good.

The process in designing the prototypes for these chairs began when Frid discovered that sitting on a six-inch-wide rail at a horse show was not uncomfortable. He then decided to determine the smallest comfortable seat he could design. A piece of wood six inches wide and 16 inches long with a ⅞-inch curve was the answer.

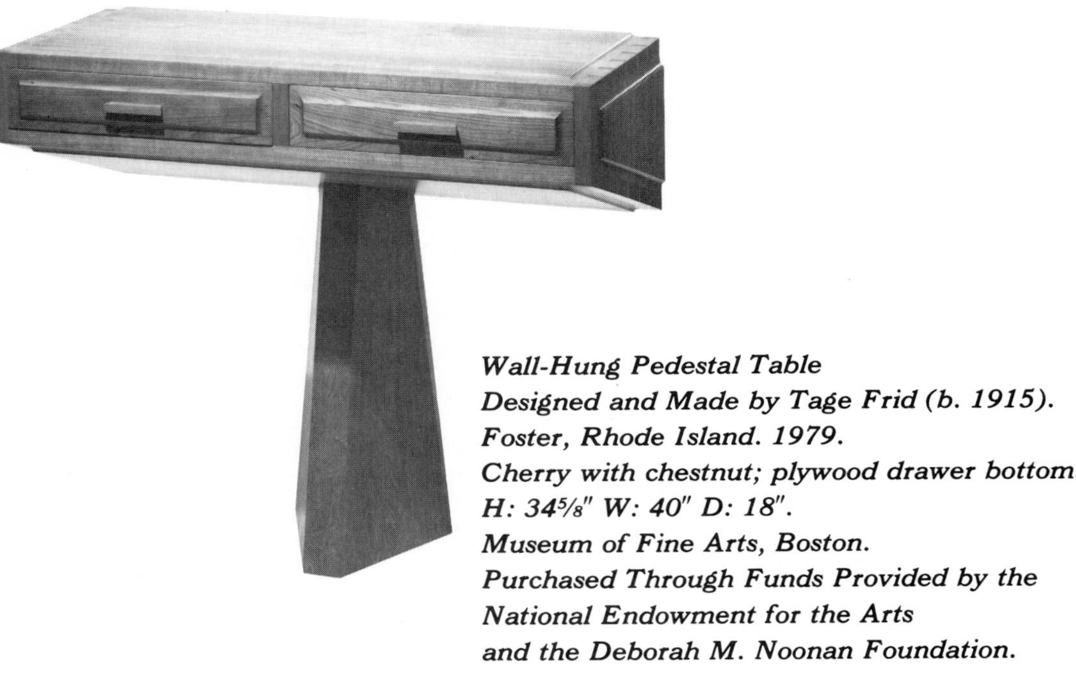

Wall-Hung Pedestal Table
Designed and Made by Tage Frid (b. 1915).
Foster, Rhode Island. 1979.
Cherry with chestnut; plywood drawer bottom.
H: 34⅝" W: 40" D: 18".
Museum of Fine Arts, Boston.
Purchased Through Funds Provided by the
National Endowment for the Arts
and the Deborah M. Noonan Foundation.

Precision workmanship is the hallmark of Frid's furniture. The drawers slide with such ease that the fit seems like the perfection of the ground surface of an optical instrument. The sleek architectural lines of the table conceal its two-part division. The upper half or drawer section is wall-mounted by an ingenious suspension system. A single slat of wood, which runs the length of the cabinet's back, is screwed to the wall. The upper border of the slat is beveled to fit into the rear edge of the tabletop like a giant horizontal dovetail. The cabinet merely hangs on a rail and the pedestal simply offers architectural logic and a sense of visual balance below.

The crispness of panel edges, graceful and generous dovetail details on the sides, and the rubbed oil finish give the table a distinguished quality and style.

RICHARD CHEEK, PHOTOGRAPHER

Bench with Rawhide Thong Seat
Designed and Made by Sam Maloof. Alta Loma, California.
Signed and Dated 1975.
Walnut, oiled and waxed. H: 17" W: 30½" D: 15½".
Museum of Fine Arts, Boston.

In 1949 when Maloof changed the course of his career from that of an architectural craftsman and graphics designer to a self-employed independent furniture designer-craftsman, one of the first forms that he developed was an elegant, adaptable and distinctive little bench that was easily moved and was beautifully crafted. The bench illustrated is a descendant of that early model. Although its details and structure have subtly improved over the years, the bench remains basically the same as the original model and forms an important part of Maloof's artistic repertoire.

Every year Maloof adds two or three new forms to his working program while he continues to produce earlier designs made over the past twenty years. This consistency of vision is unusual for a designer or a craftsman in the twentieth century. It represents a traditional approach to design that is not dependent on fashionable style trends.

✶

Rocking Chair
Designed and Made by Sam Maloof (b. 1916), Alta Loma, California.
Signed and Dated 1974. Walnut. H: 45" W: 27¾" D: 47".
Museum of Fine Arts, Boston.

COURTESY OF SAM MALOOF

A woman who had a bad back requested a chair to provide special support to her lumbar region. By shaping ribbed slats to satisfy her needs, Maloof found it useful to incorporate this discovery in the designs of other chairs, including this rocker. The support that these slats give the lower part of the back makes this rocking chair tremendously comfortable—even therapeutic.

A dozen laminated layers of walnut form the iron-hard structure of the rockers and their attachment to the frame. The lamination permits an exhilarating sweep of the rocker to balance the rest.

JONATHAN POLLOCK, PHOTOGRAPHER

Drop-Leaf Table with Chair
Designed and Made by Sam Maloof. Alta Loma, California.
Signed and Dated 1971;
Design Introduced 1968.
Walnut. H: 28" Greatest width: 48".

The legs of this table spread out near the floor almost like the roots of a tree; the pedestal forms the trunk. This living, organic design shows an affinity with nature that is a major part of Maloof's personal vision.

The natural pattern of wood grain is always revealed in Maloof furniture—especially emphasized where broad surfaces are sculptured. In this case, the leaves of the tabletop are made up of eleven boards joined together to carry through the pattern of the large-scale wooden hinges. Light-colored sapwood is left in a random way on some of the boards in order to emphasize the pattern. All surfaces are smoothed to an eggshell finish, oiled, waxed and polished to perfection.

Cradle
Designed and Made by Sam Maloof. Alta Loma, California.
Signed and Dated 1976.
Walnut. H: 42" W: 48" D: 24".
Owned by Mr. and Mrs. Herschel Roman, Seattle, Washington.

This suave piece of furniture evolved from a more complicated cradle hutch which Maloof made in 1968—a work now in the permanent collections of the Museum of Contemporary Crafts.

The boat-shaped cradle, one of five similar works, hangs like a swing suspended on trestle-based posts. Smooth articulation of parts with shaped transitions between joints and pegged tenons are all hallmarks of Maloof's style.

JONATHAN POLLOCK, PHOTOGRAPHER

Settee
Designed and Made by Sam Maloof. Alta Loma, California.
Signed and Dated 1975.
Walnut. H: 30½" W: 43" D: 25".
Museum of Fine Arts, Boston.

JONATHAN POLLOCK, PHOTOGRAPHER

This sculptural settee is among the half dozen most beautiful examples of seating made by a contemporary American craftsman. It is a classic form—a double chair-back settee with swept-back legs. The arms of the settee serve merely as guides to seating.

The broad expanse of the seat is made up of thick planks of sculptured walnut glued and doweled together. The span and strength of this seat is amazing. Undulations of the seat are complemented by the wave of the seat's back edge which is echoed in the crest rail. Rounded and sharp forms are contrasted throughout the piece in a fascinating interchange of hard and soft lines, recalling the anatomy of light and shadow as they play over wind-sculptured sand dunes or snowdrifts.

Two-Seater
Designed and Made by Wendell Castle (b. 1932).
Scottsville, New York.
Cherry. H: 58" W: 36" D: 24".
Museum of Fine Arts, Boston.

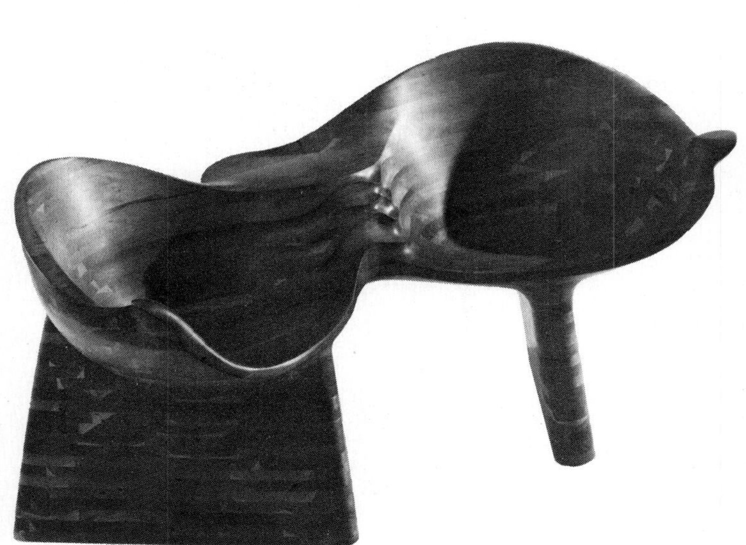

Hundreds of blocks of New York State cherry wood were cured and glued together before Castle shaped the sculptural form of this settee made for museum gallery seating. The effect is massive yet playful. The surface of the two-seater is smooth and polished. It invites the hand to explore its edges. Rounded forms contrast with crisp edges which are lost and found like the ripples of sand on a wave-washed beach. The sensory experience offered by this bench defies much conventional twentieth-century seating furniture which by comparison is dull. It is a work drenched with rich color and pattern and offers comfort with its playful fantasy.

Two vertical "rudders" set at right angles to each other support this unusual composition. While Castle's "two-seater" may not suit the decor of many homes, it is an impressive work which challenges routine design conventions of the twentieth century. A similar example is owned by the Metropolitan Museum of Art.

Double Chair-Back Settee
Designed and Made by Wendell Castle, 1979.
Oiled walnut. H: 28¾″ L: 47″ D: 17½″.

Side Chair
Designed and Made by Wendell Castle, 1979.
Oiled walnut. H: 28¾″ W: 25½″ D: 17¾″.
Museum of Fine Arts, Boston.

A graceful and playful interchange of solids and voids and round and crisp forms makes this settee a special piece of furniture. Its handsome double-yoke crest was the natural result of the juncture of two regular side chairs normally produced by Castle and craftsmen in his studio-shop. The extra length obtained by the settee gives it an exciting and decisive horizontal dimension and an unusual freedom of movement.

COURTESY OF WENDELL CASTLE; BRUCE MILLER, PHOTOGRAPHER

Using Wallace Nutting's *Furniture Treasury* as a source of design, Castle in this instance has created a spoof of early American Chippendale furniture. This similitude to a Philadelphia table (Nutting, Plate 1021) has brasses carved of wood and a hat and briefcase fixed solidly to the tabletop that does not fold open. The drawer slides open and in place of the usual pine bottom, Castle has added visual wit with a fancy striped zebrawood board.

Card Table with Hat and Briefcase
Made by Wendell Castle. Scottsville, New York. 1978.
Mahogany with zebrawood drawer bottom.
H: 38″ W: 24″ D: 22″.

Coffee Table
Designed and Made by William A. Keyser, Jr. (b. 1936). Rochester, New York. 1977.
Zebrawood vacuum formed and veneered on fiberboard core.
H: 18" L: 51" D: 25".

COURTESY OF WILLIAM A. KEYSER, JR.; DONALD L. SMITH, PHOTOGRAPHER

William A. Keyser, Jr., who teaches at the Rochester Institute of Technology, has the unusual ability to design for a specific problem and then execute the work with superb craftsmanship and originality. A single picture can only suggest the wide variety of his work.

This coffee table shows how Keyser solved a complex problem of geometry and balance. One side of the table is canted to allow comfortable footroom. The other side is sloped outwardly toward the floor to sustain balance. The conic ends echo this alternating rhythm, which gives the piece a dynamic but stable appearance. The table is light in weight, made of a fine vacuum-formed veneer over a framework core.

Practicality and fantasy are marvelously blended in the work of Judy McKie. A newcomer to the world of contemporary handmade furniture, she is no novice. For several years she practiced graphic design and made cloth wall hangings. Her recent furniture has captured national recognition.

The first drawings for this bench did not include wings on its sides. These evolved as the piece was constructed, as the necks of the horses became more elongated and the faces became more stylized, as if inspired by African masks. It would be tempting to call this a pegasus bench, but it draws from sources other than classical antiquity. The faces of this four-headed bench peer quizzically into space, provoking the imagination of the viewer. McKie's ability to combine fantasy and dream imagery with practical furniture is unusual and suggests exciting new possibilities.

Bench with Horses
Designed and Made by Judy Kensley McKie (b. 1944).
Somerville, Massachusetts. 1979.
Mahogany and leather.
H: 27¼" L: 60" D: 27".
Museum of Fine Arts, Boston.

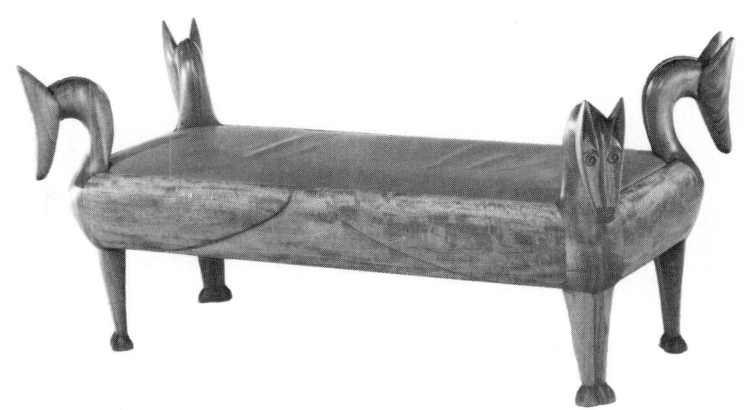

High-Tech White Plastic Furniture
Stack Tables
Designed by Giotto Stoppino, Kartell, Milano. 1975.
Made in U.S.A. by Beylerian, Limited; Sold by Bloomingdale's.
H: 17" Diameter of Tops: 18".

Stacking Storage Shelves
Designed by Anna Castelli, Kartell, Milano. 1975.
Made in U.S.A. by Beylerian, Limited; Sold by Bloomingdale's.
H: 15½" Diameter: 16½".

Chair Made by Herman Miller, 1972.
H: 32¾" W: 19¼" D: 23".
Museum of Fine Arts, Boston, Gift of Bloomingdale's, 1974.

Highly technical in their production, these resilient, slick, cast-plastic pieces of furniture exemplify a trend in Italian furniture design that was considered the most exciting development in the furniture industry evolving out of the taste of the late 1960s. Their production complexity is matched by the intricate connections that exist between designer, maker and marketing agencies. The final product is the result of many factors which transcend any single person's influence. It is against this type of impersonality that the new handmade furniture craftsmen rebel.

Interior Room Setting
By Tam Designs, New York City. 1977.

This room represents the environmental equivalent of minimal art in painting and sculpture. In fact, the design eliminates the traditional approach to furniture forms. Instead, a geometric system can be arranged into an infinite number of combinations for different uses. With rearrangement of cloth-covered foam-rubber wedges, the room can become a bedroom, living room, dining room—whatever is needed. Storage areas are concealed behind the upholstered wall panels.

This approach is the antithesis of the view that furniture should be a handcrafted work representing the aesthetics of the designer and maker.

Interior—Living Room. 1981.
Mr. and Mrs. Richard Klein, Massachusetts.

Coffee Table—Designed by George Nakashima (1905–). 1957. Walnut. H: 14¼″ W: 37″ L: 55″./Armchair—Designed by Wendell Castle (1932–). 1978. Signed and Dated "WC '78." Elm. H: 29¾″ W: 23″ D: 19″./Bench—Designed by Sam Maloof (1916–). 1975. Signed and Dated: "1975 No. 76." Walnut, leather thongs. H: 16½″ W: 15½″ L: 30½″./Rustic Armchair—Probably Upstate New York. c. 1890. Bent willow and ash, painted blue; brass tacks. H: 40″ W: 25″. D: 19″./Rustic Plant Stand—Probably Eastern Massachusetts. c. 1900. Pine and assorted woods, painted gold. H: 30″ W: 14″ D: 13″./Paper and Cloth Laminated Wall Hanging: "One Hundred and Forty-four Cows with Silken Tails." By Jody Klein (1931–). Waltham, Massachusetts. 1979. Paper, cotton fabric, silk. H: 44″ W: 44″.

Handmade hardwood furniture by three artist-craftsmen—George Nakashima, Wendell Castle and Sam Maloof—present a harmonious image despite their highly individualistic approaches. At the time when chrome, steel and plastic products were in their ascendancy, when crass commercialism in the popular furniture industry was rampant, each of these American artists had achieved professional maturity. Each has pioneered in the art and business of producing and marketing handmade wood furniture.

This collection represents part of artist Jody Klein's search for excellence and quality in her home. In addition to work by established artists, Klein has collected anonymous rustic furniture which complements and contrasts with the more formal pieces. This harmony reflects Klein's concern with craftsmanship both past and present.

Today's knowledgeable collectors will seek to unite comfort, function, form and beauty with personal meaning and taste.

RICHARD CHEEK, PHOTOGRAPHER

Glossary

Acanthus A conventionalized carved ornamentation patterned after acanthus leaves; the acanthus leaf was a decorative motif originally used on the ancient Corinthian capital.

Anthemion A carved ornamentation patterned after the Greek honeysuckle flower and leaf form.

Antique Vert Dark bronze-green paint highlighted with golden color to simulate an antique patina.

Appliqué Any ornamental detail made separately and then attached to the surface of a piece of furniture.

Apron A cross member or horizontal piece of wood below a tabletop, chair seat or underframing of a case piece. Also called a skirt.

Armoire A large, tall wardrobe, often with paneled doors, for the storage of clothing and linens. A French term for a furniture form which in seventeenth-century England was usually called a press or clothes press. Dutch and German equivalents were known respectively as a *Kas* or *Schrank* (p. 342).

Articulate To unite by means of a joint; to make a juncture between separate design elements.

Back Splat The upright, often center, support in a chair back (pp. 102–103).

Ball-and-Ring Lathe turning composed of alternating balls and narrow, sometimes raised, rings.

Ball Foot A large, round, turned foot (p. 18).

Balloon-back Chair A chair with an open back and usually a horizontal splat with the top or crest rail rounded and the stiles or uprights rounded to give an overall balloon shape to the back.

Baluster A turned vertical member or upright support (as a narrow upright column in the back of a chair or column on a cupboard) having a vaselike or urn-shaped outline. Also called a banister (pp. 8–9).

Bamboo-turned Turned with narrow rings to resemble the joints in a length of bamboo.

Banding A ribbon of contrasting inlay; a narrow edging or border of veneer.

Banister An upright support having a vaselike or turned outline. A corruption of the word baluster.

Banister-back Chair A chair with a back of vertically placed, turned banisters or balusters supported by a top cross rail and often with a lower cross rail several inches above the seat (pp. 298–299).

Banjo Clock A shelf or wall clock whose shape suggests a banjo; especially such a clock designed by Simon Willard of Roxbury, Massachusetts, patented in 1802; or a clock following his design.

Bargello A needlework pattern consisting of zigzag stripes. Also called "flame-stitch." During the 17th and 18th centuries, the pattern was called "Irish stitch" (p. 161).

Base The lower section of any two-part furniture form. The part of a piece of case furniture just above the feet and apron.

Bast A plaited woody fiber seat (splint seat).

Bauhaus School of architecture and industrial design founded in Vienna in 1919 by architect Walter Gropius, and influenced by the teaching of Henry van de Velde and the theories of the Werkbund. The Bauhaus advocated architectural functionalism as the form of expression of a radically changed society. The Nazis closed the Bauhaus in 1933, forcing its teachers into exile.

Beaded Molding Fine, convex, half-round molding, sometimes with a fillet on either side—like an astragal molding. Also a half-round molding carved to simulate beads along its length.

Beading Small, beadlike, semicircular projecting molding.

Bellflower Pendant An inlaid or painted ornament, resembling a string of bell-shaped flowers with buds of usually three or five pointed, narrow petals (p. 224).

Bentwood Furniture Wood furniture bent into elaborate curves by water, steam and pressure; patented in the United States by Samuel Gragg (*see* pp. 222–223) and later more fully developed by the German cabinetmaker Michael Thonet. First manufactured in Austria around 1840; then exported to the United States by Thonet and the Kohn Brothers; then copied and manufactured in America. (*Also see* p. 475.)

Bergère A French term for an upholstered chair with closed arms and a loose seat cushion, fashionable in late 18th-century America.

Biedermier Derived from the name of a political caricature appearing in a German newspaper which typified a well-to-do middle-class man without culture, this furniture style was simple in form and decorative detail. Popular between 1815 to around 1860, it incorporated a number of previous styles and was usually brightly finished with a high degree of surface polish.

Birdcage The double-block device with columns fitted between the top and the shaft of a tilt-top table that allows the top to tilt and rotate (p. 168).

Blanket Chest A low case piece with a hinged lid, a deep storage space, and sometimes one or two drawers below.

Block-front A desk or case piece that is divided into three vertical sections; the center section concave and the side sections convex. Most frequently found in 18th-century New England furniture—especially Boston and Newport; rarely made elsewhere in the colonies (p. 175).

Board Chest A simple chest constructed of six boards butted, lapped, nailed and hinged together. An economical alternative to joined chests, they continue to be made today. Also called a six-board chest (p. 12).

Bobeche A saucer-shaped disk to catch the drippings of a candle, set on the candle socket of a candlestick or sconce.

Bombé A modern term applied to an 18th-century furniture form with a base that has rounded, outward bulging or swelling sides and front. Also called a kettle base, this form in American furniture almost always was produced in or near Boston (p. 178).

Bonnet Top A pediment with a closed back forming the hood or top to a tall piece of case furniture; popular in America beginning around 1730 and throughout the 18th century (p. 302).

Boss A raised, applied ornament; usually circular or oval in shape (p. 18).

Bowfront The front of a case piece with a continuous convex or serpentine curve (p. 177).

Bracket A shaped support that braces the leg to the seat rail of a chair, or to a tabletop, or to the base of a case piece. Also a shelf, usually ornamental in character, with support from below.

Bracket Foot A simple case piece support shaped like a bracket with mitered corners. It can be plain, molded or scrolled.

Breakfront A large case piece with a projecting center section. Thomas Chippendale's *Director* illustrated such case furniture using the term "Library Bookcase."

Brettstuhl German term for a simple board chair with stick legs (p. 349).

Brewster Chair A type of chair styled after one that belonged to Elder William Brewster of the Plymouth Colony. It has boldly turned posts and decorative spindles in the chair back and below the seat and arms (p. 31).

Broken Pediment A triangular or curved architectural feature crowning case furniture whose lines are broken or interrupted at the apex where the crown is open.

Broken-Scroll Pediment *See* Scroll Pediment.

Buffet A cupboard or sideboard table. Also called a beaufet or beaufait. A term used loosely for a variety of serving cupboards or tables since the 16th century, now generally called "sideboard."

Bun Foot A large round foot slightly flattened at the top and bottom.

Bureau French term for a writing table. Variations on the form include *bureau plat* or flat-topped table. In America the slant-top desk and knee-hole dressing chest were also called bureaux.

Burled Having a distorted grain simulating the effect of tortoiseshell or other figured substances.

Burl Veneer An applied veneer consisting of the figured, mottled or speckled irregular wood cut from a diseased node or lump on a tree. Primarily used for decorative or ornamental effect.

Butterfly Hinge Usually a handwrought iron hinge with spreading wings, having its pivot at the center. Secured to a furniture piece with handwrought nails or screws (p. 6).

Cabriole Leg A curved leg with an outcurved knee and incurved ankle ending in an ornamented foot of various forms. The leg generally follows the shape of an inverted *S* (p. 93).

Cane Long, split strips of rattan bark used to weave chair backs and seats.

Canopy The framework atop a tall-posted bed. Also called a tester. The canopy or tester was usually draped with fabric (p. 261).

Cartouche A carved or inlaid ornament, usually in the form of an unrolled scroll, a shield, an oval or abstract form, with curled edges. A proper cartouche should bear or be able to bear an inscription.

Carver Chair A Pilgrim chair, similar to the Brewster chair, named after Governor John Carver. It has boldly turned posts and a rush seat, but unlike the Brewster chair, it has spindles only on the back (p. 30).

Case Piece A furniture form of boxlike or basic chest construction.

Cellarette A portable container designed in various forms, used for the storage of wine bottles in the dining room. The interior usually had a partitioned lead lining, and it was often fitted with side handles and a lock and key (p. 276).

Chair-back Settee A small sofa formed of two or three combined chair backs, the arms, back and legs similar to those of the open-back chairs of the particular period (p. 158).

Chair-Table An armchair with a back which when folded down forms a table (p. 27).

Chamber Chair *See* Commode Chair.

Chasing Ornamentation on a metal surface produced by hammering the metal with a chisel which has a rounded, polished edge rather than a cutting edge.

Cheney A popular imported wool textile used for upholstery in the 17th and 18th centuries.

Cheval Glass A full-length mirror that could be tilted in a frame. Also called a screen dressing glass in the 1800s. The base of a cheval glass is supported upon four legs—a horse (p. 244).

Chevron An inlaid or painted ornamentation having the shape of a *V* or an inverted *V*.

Claw-and-Ball Foot A carved foot representing a bird or animal claw grasping a ball. Most commonly used to terminate a cabriole leg (p. 105).

Club Foot A foot with a more assertive curve than that of the pad foot, with a sharply defined edge above the shoe. The typical club foot is found on much New England furniture of the Queen Anne Period.

Comb-back See Windsor Chairs.

Commode A low chest of drawers or low cabinet on legs. The term derives from France and therefore in the colonies its use suggests a form inspired by French taste. Made for display as well as storage, the commode form was normally ornate in decoration (p. 250).

Commode Chair A chair with a seat enclosing a chamber pot. Also called a chamber or necessary chair.

Compass Seat Rounded in the front and sometimes having incurving sides like the outline of a horseshoe, the compass seat was a term used in the 18th century to describe the form of chair seat which was most popular from around 1730 to the 1760s. In many areas the popularity of this chair seat persisted into the Federal Period.

Conoid Chair A chair with a basic cone shape or conoidal form.

Console Table *See* Pier Table.

Corner Block A reinforcing block glued and/or nailed or screwed into the corner of a chair or sofa frame to hold the leg and seat rail together (p. 147).

Corner Chair A chair with two backrests set at right

angles. It usually has one leg at the front, one in back, and one at each side. Also called a roundabout chair.

Cornice The horizontal crowning molding of case furniture equivalent to the top of an entablature in architecture. It varies with the order or style, but nearly always projects.

Cottage Furniture Factory-made, inexpensive furniture popular in the mid- to late 19th century. Usually painted with fruit, flower and vine motifs in light, cheerful colors (pp. 408–410).

Court Cupboard A 17th-century term for a large cupboard with an enclosed storage cabinet above and an open shelf or shelves below. Today, those with enclosed upper and lower sections are generally called press cupboards and those open below, court cupboards.

Craftsman Furniture Furniture in the Mission or oak style made and sold by Gustav Stickley and others from c. 1900 to c. 1920 (pp. 480–485).

Crest Rail The top rail of a chair back, settee or sofa. Also called a cresting rail.

Crewelwork Needlework decoration on a cotton and linen foundation embroidered with worsted wool or crewel yarn in floral and other designs. Used for bed hangings, spreads, chair backs, seats, clothing, framed pictures and tablecloths (p. 111).

Cross-Stretcher X-shaped horizontal braces or rails connecting and supporting the legs of chairs, tables and case pieces (pp. 67–68).

Crown Chairs Banister-back chairs so named for their pediment-like crests, some of which have heart-shaped cutouts (pp. 298–299).

C-Scroll A scroll carved in the basic form of the letter *C*.

Cup Turning A type of turning resembling an inverted cup.

Curule Chair A chair form designed after the ancient Roman chair of office, with a cross-base support and curved legs.

Cylinder-front or Fall-front Desk A desk with a front having a hinged one-piece lid or cover that resembles a section of a cylinder and rolls up into the desk top (p. 228).

Cyma Curve A double curve, one half of which is concave, the other convex. Also called an ogee.

Cypher Back Splat The back splat of a chair that has carved interwoven initials, usually surrounded by decorative scrollwork (p. 94).

Daybed In the William and Mary Period, a multilegged, horizontal piece of furniture, usually turned and carved. It was called a daybed in England, and in this country, a couch. It is similar to a chaise longue or long bench with a backed end, usually made to tilt; the seat and backrest made of cane or well padded and upholstered. Often it was supported on a stretchered frame with six to eight legs (pp. 80–81).

Deal Yellow-pine lumber; a term to distinguish English or European wood from American pine.

Dentil Decoration A series of small, toothlike, rectangular blocks; usually used under a cornice both in architecture and furniture.

Desk and Bookcase An 18th-century term for what today is often called a secretary. The upper section, or case with doors, usually has shelves for books or partitions. The lower case, sometimes with a recess for the sitter's knees, bears a writing surface, drawers and pigeonholes for papers (pp. 182–185).

Diapered Pattern An ornamental pattern consisting of one or more small connected, repeated diamond or geometric units of design.

Dished Top A tabletop with shallow, dishlike depressions around the edges or at the corners. Usually seen on tea tables.

Dovetail A right-angled joint formed by interlocking, flaring tenons which resemble a dove's tail.

Dowel A circular wooden pin or peg, driven into a hole to fasten two pieces of wood.

Dower Chest A hope chest for storing a young girl's accumulation of clothes, linens and other domestic articles in anticipation of marriage (pp. 322–324).

Drake Foot A three-toed foot. Also called a trifid foot (p. 127).

Draw Table A table whose top surface is enlarged by pulling or drawing out leaves from each end (p. 26).

Dresser A bureau or chest of drawers.

Drop An ornamented pendant, applied to the surface or free-hanging. Also the brass pulls often seen on furniture in the William and Mary style.

Dustboard The horizontal board between two drawers.

Églomisé Unfired painted glass panels, usually painted on the reverse side and sometimes protected with varnish, used as decorative inserts on mirrors and furniture pieces. French frame maker Jean-Baptiste Glomy (d. 1786) was the source of the term. Also called *verre églomisé* (p. 229).

Escritoire *See* Scrutoire.

Escutcheon A decorative brass plate around a keyhole.

Étagère An open, tiered stand of shelves with slender supports; the back often mirrored and with drawers below. Used for displaying curios or bric-a-brac and most popular during the Victorian Period. Also called a whatnot (pp. 389–392).

Fall-front Desk or Drop-front Desk Desk with a hinged cover that may be lowered to form a writing surface or table (p. 332).

Fauteuil French-style open-armed upholstered chair.

Festoon Decorative effect in the form of garlands or a series of loops or chain of flowers or leaves.

Fiddle-back The single back splat of a chair which resembles the outline of a violin. (A fiddle-backed chair.)

Fielded Panel A board shaped to a tapered edge set into a frame, and with a raised center section, field, or panel.

Figure To decorate with a pattern, as in "figured fabric" or "figured wallpaper."

Filigree Very delicate, intricate, lacelike ornamentation.

Finial A turned or carved decorative ornament, often used to crown the corners or center of the pediment on a large piece of case furniture. A pendant finial is a hanging or downward projecting finial, usually at the center of the apron or bottom of a piece of case furniture.

Fireback The back wall of a fireplace; early firebacks were usually made of cast-iron and often decorated with a crest and/or date or other ornamentation.

Flame-stitch *See* Bargello.

Fluting A series of rounded furrows or channels carved vertically into the wood surface (pp. 113, 115). The reverse of reeding.

Foliate Carving or Decoration Ornamentation done in leaflike forms.

Food Safe *See* Pie Safe.

Form An early term for a long bench or an extended version of a joint stool (p. 36). Also, the basic shape, body and structure of a furniture type, e.g., a chair, table, case piece are different furniture forms.

Fraktur Pennsylvania German hand-lettered, colored documents, frequently pasted underneath the lids of dower chests.

Fretwork An interlaced, often geometric ornamental design resembling latticework; either applied or carved in low relief.

Frieze The flat, central surface beneath a cornice molding; the central member of the entablature resting on the architrave.

Fustian A strong fabric with cotton weft and linen warp, usually having a pile face and twill weave, used as the ground cloth for needlework designs. Made in England throughout most of the 18th century.

Gadrooning Ornamental carving along borders of furniture consisting of fluting or reeding or both, often in a curved or spiral design (pp. 171, 174).

Gallery A balustrade or railing or raised fencelike structure of wood carving around the top of a table or other piece of furniture (p. 172).

Gallooning Narrow trimming or braided ribbon edging on upholstered furniture. Sometimes made of precious metallic thread or silk.

Gate-leg Table A drop-leaf table in which the legs, supported by stretchers, form swinging gates to support the leaves (p. 67).

Gesso A mixture of whiting, chalk or other substances, mixed with glue and water, applied to the surface of furniture to create a smooth base for painting, gilding or building up bas-reliefs. Also the ground surface, affixed to canvas, upon which the artist paints.

Girandole A circular wall mirror with a convex glass and scrolled candlebranches as part of the basic frame. From the French word *girandole,* a branched candlestick. Also called a girandole looking glass or girandole mirror (p. 245).

Girandole Clock A wall clock with a circular dial and pendulum door, usually elaborately decorated with gilt, as were the girandole mirrors of the Federal Period.

Glyph A carved channel or groove, usually vertical. Also, the pyramidal elements seen in the freize of the Doric order, usually in groups of three.

Gondola Chair A side chair with an open back and a wide, solid center back splat. The stiles or uprights are gently C-curved forward to join the seat rail.

Grecian Couch A term used during the era of Greek revival taste to describe the form of daybed which was popularly believed to represent a return to furniture designs of the ancient world (p. 279).

Guilloche An ornamental pattern consisting of a series of regularly intertwining, circular straps forming a continuous spiral decoration around a running line of bosses.

Highboy A tall case piece comprised of two sections of drawers; the lower section supported on legs. The term was not used in the 18th century—high chest, chest-on-frame or high chest of drawers are period terms used for this form (pp. 186–187).

High-Tech Furniture and interior design that uses utilitarian industrial equipment and materials, or imaginative, colorful simulations of them, incorporating the stark functionalism of such materials.

Hitchcock Chair A type of painted, open-back factory chair made from around 1826 to 1843, named after Lambert Hitchcock who first made a large number of these chairs in Connecticut. They were usually painted black with painted and stenciled decoration.

Horn Furniture Furniture made of steer, buffalo or elk horn; popular in America between 1860 and 1920. Horn furniture was also made abroad, particularly in Frankfurt and London (p. 452).

Huntboard Generally of Southern origin, a long, high sideboard table of shallow depth; in basic form simply a board or frame from which one served drinks to a group after the fox hunt. Also called a hunting table or hunting board. When fitted with drawers or cupboards, usually called a hunt sideboard (p. 238).

Incised Carving Carving cut into the surface to be ornamented by shallow knife work rather than deep chisel cuts.

Inlay Decoration, usually of a wood or layers of woods of a contrasting color or texture, set into the surface of a piece. Inlay decoration can be in floral, shell, geometric or other pictorial patterns, made not only by pattern of wood, but also by staining, scorching and incising. Metal, mineral, shell and materials other than wood are also used (p. 114).

Intaglio Designs or carving depressed, etched or cut slightly below the surrounding surface. Opposite of relief.

Japanning The process of covering a furniture piece with paint, gesso and varnish, gold powder and leaf to simulate Oriental lacquer, painting chinoiserie decoration in shallow relief (pp. 131–138).

Joiner A person who made furniture by mortise-and-tenon construction, framing members at right angles and fastening them together with pins or wooden dowels. A term for a furniture maker in common use in America before c. 1700.

Joint Stool An early seating form, the joint stool was a simple, backless seat of stout construction with turned legs joined together by stretchers (p. 36).

Kas A large press or wardrobe in the Dutch style, usually with heavy raised panels and a large overhanging cornice; often very decoratively painted (p. 21).

Kettle Base *See* Bombé.

Klismos A side chair derived from an ancient Greek form having a concavely curved back and incurved, saber legs (p. 257).

Knee The outcurved upper portion of a leg; especially of a cabriole leg.

Kneehole Desk or Kneehole Chest of Drawers A desk or chest with an open-spaced center in the front (for the sitter's legs), flanked by columns of drawers.

Ladder-back Chair *See* Slat-back Chair.

Latticework A crisscross design, either carved from a single piece of wood or separate, joined pieces. Most often seen on pediments of tall case pieces, but found on other furniture forms as well.

Lolling Chair The Federal Period term for an upholstered high-backed, open armchair which in the later 19th century was called a Martha Washington chair. Lolling chairs seem to have been a specialty of New England chairmakers as few, if any, are known to have been made in other regions of the United States (pp. 205–206).

Love Seat A 19th- to 20th-century term used for a small upholstered sofa or settee designed to seat two people. Not a term used in the 17th or 18th centuries.

Lowboy Modern term for a low case piece or table with drawers on mounted legs—dressing table or bureau dressing table were 18th-century terms. In America, often made en suite with a high chest, chest-on-frame or double chest of drawers.

Lunette A half-moon or semicircular ornament, usually inlaid, painted or carved (p. 251).

Marbleize To paint a wood or other surface to simulate marble.

Marlborough Leg A straight leg, often with a simple block foot, used on Chippendale chairs, tables and other forms of furniture (p. 162).

Marquetry Decorative and pictorial inlay work in which elaborate patterns are formed by the insertion of various woods or other materials (such as shell or ivory) into a wood veneer that is then applied to a ground surface.

Martha Washington Chair The term adopted in the Victorian Period to identify the lolling chair—the Federal Period nomenclature.

Medial Stretcher A center stretcher that connects two side stretchers.

Méridienne A French term for a sofa with a gently curved back, having one arm lower than the other (p. 399).

Molding Any narrow, continuous decorative surface, projecting or incised with shaped profile usually convex or concave or a combination of both.

Moquette A heavy wool fabric with a thick nap, often used in upholstery.

Moreen A coarse fabric of wool, wool and cotton, or cotton with a plain, glossy or moiré finish. Often with a zigzag watermark design or embossed.

Morris Chair An armchair with an adjustable back and cushions, first produced by William Morris, Philip Webb and the firm Morris, Marshall, Faulkner & Co., about 1866 in England. A wide variety of similar chairs made in America have become identified with this Morris prototype (p. 485).

Mortise and Tenon System of joinery basic to 17th-century wood-frame construction: a tenon or tongue of one piece of wood was inserted into the mortise or hole of another; a second, smaller hole was drilled for a peg that, once hammered into place, secured both pieces (p. 5).

Mounts Escutcheons, handle-pulls and other decorative as well as functional details applied to furniture pieces.

Muntin A molding or vertical wooden spacer between glass or panels.

Ogee *See* Cyma Curve.

Ormolu Gilded bronze used on ornamental mounts applied to furniture pieces. Usually cast, chased and colored by fire-gilt or mercury gilding. Both France and England produced ormolu mounts imported and used on furniture made in the United States from the 18th through the 19th centuries (p. 178).

Pad Foot A plain, oval-shaped, slightly carved foot (p. 120).

Palmette Ornamentation resembling the leaf of a palm.

Paterae Flat, circular or oval ornaments, carved in low relief or inlaid; cameo-like plaques.

Patina The quality of texture and color or finish that antique surfaces acquire with age. Sometimes artificially induced for artistic effect or to deceive.

Paw Foot A foot carved to represent an animal's paw, usually that of a lion; used on chairs, sofas and case pieces, especially during the revival styles of the 19th century.

Pedestal Table A table with a single column base.

Pediment The ornamental section surmounting a tall piece of case furniture. It may be arched, but more frequently is triangular in form, broken in profile at the top center and called a "broken" pediment or a "broken-scroll" pediment (p. 87).

Pembroke Table A drop-leaf table, usually with straight legs and with a long square or oval top. Its leaves fold down on opposite sides and small tray-like drawers are at each end (p. 173).

Piecrust Table A modern term for a tripod, often tilt-top, circular table whose top has a scalloped, molded rim resembling the edge of a piecrust. In the 18th century such tables were identified simply as tea tables or turn-up tables (p. 168).

Pierced Back Splat A chair back splat in which the carving is usually carved openwork, carved with a fret saw.

Pier Glass A narrow, tall mirror designed to be hung over a pier table on a wall filling space between two windows or doors. Usually carved and otherwise ornamented with burnished gold leaf and with ornate cresting. Popular in both the Chippendale and Federal periods (p. 164).

Pier Table A side table originally designed to stand against a pier or wall section between two windows or doors; usually a pier glass, a narrow, tall mirror and its ornate frame, was hung over the pier table (pp. 267–269).

Pie Safe A standard piece of kitchen furniture throughout the Old West as well as the East in the 1800s. Pierced tin front panels served both a decorative and practical purpose; the pierced slits and holes, arranged in a variety of patterns, let air in to ventilate the contents, which were protected from insects, mice and other pests. Sometimes the food was protected with screening or cloth rather than punched tin (p. 448).

Pilaster Detailed like a column and serving the decorative function of the same, the pilaster is merely a flattened version of a column projecting slightly from a building or piece of furniture.

Pin A slender dowel or whittled peg that secures or holds together a mortise-and-tenon joint (p. 5).

Pole Screen or Pole Fire Screen An adjustable oval or square frame attached and sliding on an upright pole supported by a base (most often tripod). Used to shield the face from the fire when seated near the hearth, the screen usually displayed the finest needlework of the mistress of the house (p. 193).

Press A simple upright closet or cabinet in which clothes, linen or other articles were kept. Not to be confused with a linen-press used to crease cloth with sharp folds for decorative table settings, especially in the 17th century.

Press Cupboard A large cupboard, similar to the court cupboard, but with both the upper and lower sections containing enclosed storage space for drawers (p. 19).

Quillwork Sconce Early sconce, made of seaweed, rocks, shells, mica flowers, wirework, wax figures of dolls, lamb and fruit—all coated with mica to shimmer in the candlelight. Rolled gilt paper, shaped like quills, was a major decorative feature of the sconce, suggesting the term (p. 83).

Rail A horizontal member of wood, usually joining vertical posts of furniture, as in stretchers of chair or table legs, or a crest rail or top rail of a chair.

Rake The slant or angle of a part of furniture away from the vertical mass of the piece.

Ratchet Candlestand A candlestand usually with a trestle base and a notched mechanism for raising or lowering a support for a candle (p. 319).

Rattan A type of climbing palm *(calamus)* whose stem is used to make furniture often of intricate design, as with caning.

Reeding Carving consisting of a series of rounded, convex, vertical lines, creating the effect of vertical reeds (p. 239). The reverse of fluting.

Relief Decoration or ornamentation that is convex or raised above the surface.

Reserve An area left the natural color of the background or original surface color.

Rococo A style of art and elaborate ornamentation

that is actively curvilinear with *S*-shaped motifs incorporating forms inspired by shells, rocks and foliage. A style having origins in France, spreading to England and the colonies as a decorative, ornamental style in the 18th century.

Roundabout Chair *See* Corner Chair.

Roycrofters A name for those who produced crafts under the direction of Elbert Hubbard (1856–1915) in East Aurora, New York.

Saber Leg Usually a front leg of a chair or sofa, curved inward in a gentle *S*-shaped profile.

Saddle Seat A chair seat shaped like the cup of a saddle with a slight center ridge at the front edge; most often used on Windsor chairs.

Saltire Stretcher An X-shaped, arched stretcher or two crossing horizontal supports (p. 172).

Screen Dressing Glass *See* Cheval Glass.

Scritoire *See* Scrutoire.

Scroll Pediment A pediment formed with symmetrically balanced swan-neck arches terminating in spirals and divided at the apex. Also called a broken-scroll pediment.

Scrollwork Curvilinear wood ornamentation often cut with a jigsaw.

Scrutoire An enclosed writing cabinet or writing table; old term for escritoire or writing desk.

Secretary A modern term for an 18th-century writing table and bookcase or desk and bookcase as the two-storied writing cabinets of the 18th century were called.

Settee A small sofa with arms and a back. The term sofa is more frequently encountered in 18th- and early 19th-century records (p. 158).

Settle Shaped from boards and popular from early colonization, the settle is a long bench with a high, solid back and arms, and an enclosed foundation which can be used for storage. It was usually used with cushions, pillows and blankets for warmth and comfort (p. 75).

Sewing Table *See* Worktable.

Shield-back Chair A chair with an open back carved in the shape of a shield (pp. 210–211).

Sideboard Generally a low, wide chest of drawers or case piece on legs with cupboard space; used against a side wall for storage and serving in the dining room (pp. 235–237). *See* Buffet.

Skirt *See* Apron.

Slat-back Chair A simple chair form with a back resembling a ladder, consisting of two upright posts connected by horizontal slats. Also called a ladder-back chair (p. 347).

Slipper Chair A high-backed, low-seated chair without arms (p. 107).

Slipper Foot An elongated, slim, pointed foot.

Slip-Seat A removable frame upholstered to conform to the inner borders of the chair seat frame. Usually webbed, padded and covered with fabric. Found on chairs from the Queen Anne Period to the present.

Sofa Table An oblong table with small drop-hinged leaves at the ends (p. 264).

Spade Foot A spade-shaped foot usually terminating a tapered, square-shaped leg. A common feature of Federal furniture.

Spanish Foot A slightly curved foot with vertical ribs and curled base. Sometimes called a paintbrush foot or Portuguese foot. A Baroque flourish most often seen on furniture of the William and Mary Period (p. 72).

Spindle A slender, turned member often used in chair backs (pp. 8–9). Also turned ornaments or columns on 17th-century case furniture.

S-Scroll A scroll carved in the basic form of the letter *S*.

Stiles The vertical side supports of a chair back.

Stopped Fluting Fluting in which the lower parts of the concave, carved channels are filled with reeding.

Stretcher A horizontal member supporting and bracing the legs of chairs, stools, tables or case pieces.

Stringing A very fine, thin band of wood or veneer inlaid in a contrasting wood ground for decorative effect. Similar to banding, but much finer.

Sugar Chest A specialized furniture form most popular in the South, the sugar chest frequently had a hinged lid on top covering a large divided storage chamber for brown and white sugar (p. 334).

Tambour A flexible sliding door made of thin strips of wood glued next to each other on a textile backing (as in tambour writing tables, secretary-bookcases or desks, p. 203).

Tavern Table A modern term for a small, low table, usually with turned legs and stretchers.

Sturdy and strong, these tables were designed originally for a variety of domestic uses, not necessarily exclusive to a tavern (p. 65).

Tester *See* Canopy.

Tilt-top Table A tripod table usually with a circular top which is hinged to tilt to a vertical position.

Trestle Table A long table with a board top supported by two or more cross braces and stretchers in place of legs (pp. 22–23).

Trifid Foot *See* Drake Foot.

Tripod Table A table with a pedestal base supported by three legs.

Trundle Bedstead A low, paneled frame set on wheels, designed to roll under a larger bed for storage during the day (p. 28).

Turkey Work A woven, knotted woolen pile upholstery material imitative of the textiles imported from the Middle East in the 17th century. Made by professional weavers in 17th-century England. Only rarely found surviving on early American furniture today (p. 40).

Turner One who forms turned furniture parts, such as balusters, spindles and bosses, with a lathe.

Turnings Balusters and spindles and other furniture parts that are shaped on a lathe.

Turret-top Modern term describing the scalloped top of some Boston tea tables, used to hold teacups (p. 297).

Valance Decorative scroll-like carving or shaping on the lower edge of a cross member; a conventionalized drapery.

Veneer A thin layer of wood glued onto a base wood for decorative effect.

Verdigris A blue-green color paint, from the Old French term *vert de Grice*—green of Greece; used to give an antique bronze-green effect of age or patina. Made of blue or green basic copper acetate.

Volute A spiral or scroll-shaped ornament.

Wainscot Chair A frame-and-panel joined chair with solid panels in the back and seat and sometimes with turned posts, shaped armrests and a carved back (p. 33).

Whatnot *See* Étagère.

Windsor Chairs Multiple-spindle-backed chairs made from the bending and shaping of green wood, they are constructed with a solid wood "saddle-like" seat and turned, splayed legs; the back may be shaped in various ways and is made of spindles joined to the back rail. Types of Windsors are: high-back, comb-, sack- or hoop-back, round-top, low-back, brace-back, writing and children's Windsors (pp. 286–295).

Wine Cooler or Wine Cistern *See* Cellarette.

Worktable A small table for storing sewing implements and materials for needlework; usually made with drawers and often with a suspended fabric workbag. Most popular in America in the Federal and Classical periods (p. 234).

Bibliography

By Wendell Garrett *and* Allison Eckardt

BOOKS AND CATALOGS

Amaya, Mario. *Art Nouveau.* London: Studio Vista, 1966. New York: E. P. Dutton, 1966.

Andrews, Edward Deming and Faith. *Religion in Wood: A Book of Shaker Furniture.* Bloomington and London: Indiana University Press, 1966.

Andrews, Edward D.; Malcolm, Janet; and Emerich, A. D. *Shaker Furniture and Objects of the Faith and Edward Deming Andrews Collections Commemorating the Bicentennial of the American Shakers.* Washington, D.C.: Renwick Gallery of the National Collection of Fine Arts, Smithsonian Institution Press, 1973.

Applegate, Judith. *Art Deco.* New York: Finch College Museum of Art, 1970.

Aslin, Elizabeth. *The Aesthetic Movement, Prelude to Art Nouveau.* New York: Frederick A. Praeger Publishers, 1969.

Bacot, H. Parrott. *Southern Furniture and Silver: The Federal Period, 1788–1830.* Baton Rouge: Louisiana State University Press, 1968.

Bailey, Chris H. *Two Hundred Years of American Clocks and Watches.* Englewood Cliffs, New Jersey: Prentice-Hall, 1975.

Baltimore Museum of Art. *Baltimore Furniture: The Work of Baltimore and Annapolis Cabinetmakers from 1760 to 1810.* Baltimore: The Baltimore Museum of Art, 1947.

Barbour, Frederick K. *Frederick K. and Margaret R. Barbour's Furniture Collection.* Hartford: The Connecticut Historical Society, 1963.

———. *A Supplement, Frederick K. and Margaret R. Barbour's Furniture Collection.* Hartford: The Connecticut Historical Society, 1970.

Bartlett, Lu, ed. *A Bit of Vanity: Furniture of Eighteenth-Century Boston.* Boston: Museum of Fine Arts, 1972.

Battersby, Martin. *The Decorative Thirties.* New York: Walker & Company, 1971.

———. *The Decorative Twenties.* New York: Walker & Company, 1969.

———. *The World of Art Nouveau.* New York: Funk & Wagnalls, 1968.

Belknap, Henry Wyckoff. *Artists and Craftsmen of Essex County, Massachusetts.* Salem, Massachusetts: Essex Institute, 1927.

Biddle, James. *American Art from the American Collections: Decorative Arts, Paintings, and Prints of the Colonial and Federal Periods from Private Collections in an Exhibition.* New York: The Metropolitan Museum of Art, 1963.

Bishop, Robert. *American Furniture, 1620–1720.* Dearborn: The Edison Institute, 1975.

———. *Centuries and Styles of the American Chair, 1640–1970.* New York: E. P. Dutton, 1972.

———. *How to Know American Antique Furniture.* New York: E. P. Dutton, 1973.

———, and Coblentz, Patricia. *The World of Antiques, Art, and Architecture in Victorian America.* New York: E. P. Dutton, 1979.

Bissell, Charles S. *Antique Furniture in Suffield, Connecticut, 1670–1835.* Hartford: The Connecticut Historical Society, 1956.

Bjerkoe, Ethel Hall. *The Cabinetmakers of America.* Garden City, New York: Doubleday & Co., 1957. Rev. ed. Exton, Pennsylvania: Schiffer Publishing Limited, 1978.

Black, Mary. *The New York Cabinetmaker and His Use of Space.* New York: New-York Historical Society, 1976.

Blackburn, Roderic H. *Cherry Hill: The History and Collections of a Van Rensselaer Family.* Albany: Historic Cherry Hill, 1976.

Boas, George, and Breckenridge, James D. *The Age of Elegance: The Rococo and Its Effect.* Baltimore: The Baltimore Museum of Art, 1959.

Bordes, Marilynn Johnson. *Baltimore Federal Furniture in the American Wing.* New York: The Metropolitan Museum of Art, 1972.

Boyd, E. *Popular Arts of Spanish New Mexico.* Santa Fe: Museum of New Mexico Press, 1974.

Brainard, Newton C. *Connecticut Chairs in the Collection of the Connecticut Historical Society.* Hartford: The Connecticut Historical Society, 1956.

Brandt, Frederick R. *Art Nouveau.* Richmond: Virginia Museum of Fine Arts, 1971.

Bridenbaugh, Carl. *The Colonial Craftsman.* New York: New York University Press, 1950.

Bridgeman, Harriet, and Drury, Elizabeth, eds. *The Encyclopedia of Victoriana.* New York: Macmillan, 1975.

Brunhammer, Yvonne, and others. *Art Nouveau Belgium/France.* Houston: Institute for the Arts, Rice University, 1976.

Buckley, Charles E., and others. *American Art of the Colonies and Early Republic: Furniture, Paintings and Silver from Private Collections in the Chicago Area.* Chicago: The Art Institute of Chicago, 1971.

Bulkeley, Houghton. *Contributions to Connecticut Cabinet Making.* Hartford: The Connecticut Historical Society, 1967.

Burroughs, Paul H. *Southern Antiques.* Richmond: Garrett & Massie, 1931.

Burton, E. Milby. *Charleston Furniture, 1700–1825.* Charleston: The Charleston Museum, 1955.

———. *Thomas Elfe, Charleston Cabinetmaker.* Charleston: The Charleston Museum, 1952.

Butler, Joseph T. *American Antiques, 1800–1900: A Collector's History and Guide.* New York: Odyssey Press, 1965.

Campbell, Christopher M. *American Chippendale Furniture, 1755–1790.* Dearborn: The Edison Institute, 1975.

Carpenter, Ralph E., Jr. *The Arts and Crafts of Newport, Rhode Island, 1640–1820.* Newport: Preservation Society of Newport County, 1954.

Cescinsky, Herbert. *English Furniture from Gothic to Sheraton.* 2nd ed., 1937. Reprint. New York: Dover Publications, 1968.

Chippendale, Thomas. *The Gentleman & Cabinet-Maker's Director.* 3rd ed. London: privately printed, 1762. Reprint. New York: Dover Publications, 1966.

Christiansen, E.O. *The Index of American Design.* New York: Macmillan, 1950.

Clark, Robert Judson, ed. *The Arts and Crafts Movement in America, 1876–1916.* Princeton: Princeton University Press, 1972.

Colby, Joy Hakanson, and others. *Arts and Crafts in Detroit, 1906–1976: The Movement, The Society, The School.* Detroit: Detroit Institute of Arts, 1976.

Comstock, Helen. *American Furniture, Seventeenth, Eighteenth, and Nineteenth Century Styles.* New York: Viking Press, 1962.

———. *The Looking Glass in America, 1700–1825.* New York: Viking Press, 1964.

———, **ed.** *The Concise Encyclopedia of American Antiques.* 2 vols. London: The Connoisseur, 1958.

Cooper, Wendy A. *In Praise of America: American Decorative Arts, 1650–1830/Fifty Years of Discovery Since the 1929 Girl Scouts Loan Exhibition.* New York: Alfred A. Knopf, 1980.

Corlette, Suzanne, and others. *From Lenape Territory to Royal Province, New Jersey, 1600–1750.* Trenton: New Jersey State Museum, 1971.

———. *The Pulse of the People: New Jersey, 1763–1789.* Trenton: New Jersey State Museum, 1976.

Cornelius, Charles Over. *Furniture Masterpieces of Duncan Phyfe.* Garden City, New York: Doubleday, Page & Co., 1922.

Craig, James H. *The Arts and Crafts in North Carolina, 1699–1840.* Winston-Salem: Museum of Early Southern Decorative Arts, Old Salem, Inc., 1965.

Crossman, Carl L. *The China Trade: Export Paintings, Furniture, Silver and Other Objects.* Princeton: Pyne Press, 1972.

Cummings, Abbott Lowell, ed. *Rural Household Inventories: Establishing the Names, Uses and Furnishings of Rooms in the Colonial New England Home, 1675–1775.* Boston: The Society for the Preservation of New England Antiquities, 1964.

Darmstadt, Jo, and others. *Craftsmen & Artists of Norwich—Furniture, Paintings, Clocks, Silver, Pewter, Pottery.* Stonington, Connecticut: Pequot Press, 1965.

Davidson, Marshall B. *The Bantam Illustrated Guide to Early American Furniture.* New York: Bantam Books, 1980.

———, **ed.** *Three Centuries of American Antiques.* Vol I: *The American Heritage History of Colonial Antiques.* Vol. II: *The American Heritage History of American Antiques from the Revolution to the Civil War.* Vol. III: *The American Heritage History of Antiques from the Civil War to World War I.* Reprint (3 vols. in 1). New York: Bonanza Books, 1979.

Detroit Institute of Arts. *American Decorative Arts from the Pilgrims to the Revolution.* Detroit: Detroit Institute of Arts, 1967.

Dow, George Francis. *The Arts & Crafts in New England, 1704–1775.* Topsfield, Massachusetts: Wayside Press, 1927. Reprint. New York: Da Capo Press, 1967.

Downs, Joseph. *American Chippendale Furniture, 1750-1780, A Picture Book.* Rev. ed. New York: The Metropolitan Museum of Art, 1949.

———. *American Furniture in the Henry Francis du Pont Winterthur Museum, Queen Anne and Chippendale Periods.* New York: Macmillan, 1952.

———. *The Greek Revival in the United States: A Special Loan Exhibition.* New York: The Metropolitan Museum of Art, 1943.

———. *Pennsylvania German Arts and Crafts: A Picture Book.* New York: The Metropolitan Museum of Art, 1949.

———, and Ralston, Ruth. *A Loan Exhibition of New York State Furniture with Contemporary Accessories.* New York: The Metropolitan Museum of Art, 1934.

Drexler, Arthur. *Charles Eames, Furniture from the Design Collection.* New York: The Museum of Modern Art, 1973.

Durant, Mary. *American Heritage Guide to Antiques.* New York: American Heritage Publishing Co., 1970.

Eastlake, Charles L. *Hints on Household Taste in Furniture, Upholstery, and Other Details.* London: Longmans, Green and Co., 1868. Reprint. New York: Dover Publications, 1969.

Elder, William Voss III. *Baltimore Painted Furniture, 1800–1840.* Baltimore: The Baltimore Museum of Art, 1972.

———. *Maryland Queen Anne and Chippendale Furniture of the Eighteenth Century.* Baltimore: The Baltimore Museum of Art, 1968.

Erving, Henry Wood. *The Hartford Chest.* New Haven: Yale University Press, 1934.

———. *Random Notes on Colonial Furniture: A Paper Read Before the Connecticut Historical Society in 1922 and Now Revised.* Hartford: privately printed, 1931.

Fabian, Monroe H. *The Pennsylvania-German Decorated Chest.* Clinton, New Jersey: Main Street Press, 1978.

Failey, Dean F., and others. *Long Island Is My Nation: The Decorative Arts & Craftsmen, 1640–1830.* Setauket, New York: Society for the Preservation of Long Island Antiquities, 1976.

Fairbanks, Jonathan; Sussman, Elisabeth; and others. *Frontier America: The Far West.* Boston: Museum of Fine Arts, 1975.

———**; Cooper, Wendy A.; and others.** *Paul Revere's Boston, 1735–1818.* Boston: Museum of Fine Arts, 1975.

Fales, Dean A., Jr. *American Painted Furniture, 1660–1880.* New York: E. P. Dutton, 1972.

———. "Boston Japanned Furniture." In *Boston Furniture of the Eighteenth Century,* edited by Walter Muir Whitehill, Brock Jobe, and Jonathan Fairbanks, pp. 49–70. Boston: Colonial Society of Massachusetts, 1974.

———. *Essex County Furniture: Documented Treasures from Local Collections, 1660–1860.* Salem, Massachusetts: Essex Institute, 1965.

———. *The Furniture of Historic Deerfield.* New York: E. P. Dutton, 1976.

Fales, Martha Lou Gandy. *Regional Characteristics of Empire Furniture.* Wilmington: Winterthur Museum, 1954.

Fede, Helen Maggs. *Washington Furniture at Mount Vernon.* Mount Vernon, Virginia: The Mount Vernon Ladies' Association of the Union, 1966.

Franklin, Linda Campbell. *Antiques and Collectibles: A Bibliography of Works in English 16th Century to 1976.* Metuchen, New Jersey, and London: Scarecrow Press, 1978.

Garrett, Wendell D., and others. *The Arts in America: The Nineteenth Century.* New York: Charles Scribner's Sons, 1969.

Giedion, Sigfried. *Mechanization Takes Command: A Contribution to Anonymous History.* New York: Oxford University Press, 1948.

Gilborn, Craig A. *American Furniture, 1660–1725.* London: The Hamlyn Publishing Group, Ltd., 1970.

Gloag, John. *Georgian Grace: A Social History of Design from 1660–1830.* London: Adams and Charles Black, 1956.

———. *A Short Dictionary of Furniture.* London: George Allen and Unwin, Ltd., 1952.

———. *A Social History of Furniture Design from B.C. 1300 to A.D. 1960.* New York: Crown Publishers, 1966.

Goodman, W. L. *The History of Woodworking Tools.* London: G. Bell and Sons, 1964.

Gottesman, Rita Susswein, comp. *The Arts and Crafts in New York, 1726–1776: Advertisements and News Items from New York City Newspapers.* New York: The New-York Historical Society, 1938.

———. *The Arts and Crafts in New York, 1777–1799: Advertisements and News Items from New York City Newspapers.* New York: The New-York Historical Society, 1954.

———. *The Arts and Crafts in New York, 1800–1804: Advertisements and News Items from New York City Newspapers.* New York: The New-York Historical Society, 1965.

Grand Rapids Museum. *Renaissance Revival Furniture.* Grand Rapids: The Grand Rapids Museum, 1976.

Greenlaw, Barry A. *New England Furniture at Williamsburg.* Williamsburg, Virginia: The Colonial Williamsburg Foundation, 1974.

Gruber, Frances. *The Art of Joinery: 17th-Century Case Furniture in the American Wing.* New York: The Metropolitan Museum of Art, 1972.

Hagler, Katharine Bryant. *American Queen Anne Furniture, 1720–1755.* Dearborn: The Edison Institute, 1976.

Hall, John. *The Cabinet Makers' Assistant.* Baltimore: John Murphy, 1840. Reprint. New York: National Superior, Inc., 1944.

Halsey, R.T.H.; Cornelius, Charles Over; and Downs, Joseph. *A Handbook of the American Wing.* New York: The Metropolitan Museum of Art, 1924.

Halsey, R.T.H., and Tower, Elizabeth. *The Homes of Our Ancestors: As Shown in the American Wing of The Metropolitan Museum of Art, From the Beginnings of New England Through the Early Days of the Republic.* Garden City, New York: Doubleday, Page and Co., 1925.

Hanks, David A. *The Decorative Designs of Frank Lloyd Wright.* New York: E. P. Dutton, 1979.

Hayward, Helena, ed. *World Furniture.* London and New York: The Hamlyn Publishing Group, Ltd., 1965.

Hayward, J. F. *English Desks and Bureaux.* London: Victoria and Albert Museum, 1968.

Heckscher, Morrison H. *In Quest of Comfort: The Easy Chair in America.* New York: The Metropolitan Museum of Art, 1971.

———, **and Miller, Elizabeth G.** *An Architect and His Client, Frank Lloyd Wright and Francis W. Little.* New York: The Metropolitan Museum of Art, 1973.

Hepplewhite, George. *The Cabinet-Maker & Upholsterer's Guide.* 3rd ed. London: I. & J. Taylor, 1794. Reprint. New York: Dover Publications, 1969.

Hillier, Bevis. *Art Deco of the 20's and 30's.* London: Studio Vista, 1968; New York: E. P. Dutton, 1968.

———. *The World of Art Deco.* New York: E. P. Dutton, 1971.

Hipkiss, Edwin J. *Eighteenth-Century American Arts: The M. and M. Karolik Collection of Paintings, Drawings, Engravings, Furniture, Silver, Needlework & Incidental Objects Gathered to Illustrate the Achievements of American Artists and Craftsmen of the Period from 1720 to 1820.* Boston and Cambridge, Massachusetts: Museum of Fine Arts and Harvard University Press, 1941.

Hitchings, Sinclair H. "Boston's Colonial Japanners: The Documentary Record." In *Boston Furniture of the Eighteenth Century,* edited by Walter Muir Whitehill, Brock Jobe, and Jonathan Fairbanks, pp. 71–75. Boston: Colonial Society of Massachusetts, 1974.

Hope, Thomas. *Household Furniture and Interior Decoration.* London: Longman, Hurst, Rees & Orme, 1807. Reprint. New York: Dover Publications, 1971.

Hopkins, Thomas Smith, and Cox, Walter Scott, comps. *Colonial Furniture of West New Jersey.* Haddonfield, New Jersey: Historical Society of Haddonfield, 1936.

Hornor, William Macpherson, Jr. *Blue Book Philadelphia Furniture, William Penn to George Washington.* Philadelphia: privately printed, 1935. Reprint. Washington, D.C.: Highland House Publishers, 1977.

Horton, Frank L. *The Museum of Early Southern Decorative Arts: A Collection of Southern Furniture, Paintings, Ceramics, Textiles, and Metalware.* Winston-Salem: Old Salem, Inc., 1979.

———, **and Weekley, Carolyn J.** *The Swisegood School of Cabinetmaking.* Winston-Salem: Museum of Early Southern Decorative Arts, 1973.

Howe, Katherine S., and Warren, David B. *The Gothic Revival Style in America, 1830–1870.* Houston: The Museum of Fine Arts, 1976.

Hummel, Charles F. *A Winterthur Guide to American Chippendale Furniture: Middle Atlantic and Southern Colonies.* New York: Crown Publishers, 1976.

———. *With Hammer in Hand: The Dominy Craftsmen of East Hampton, New York.* Charlottesville: The University Press of Virginia, 1968.

Jervis, Simon. *Victorian Furniture.* London: Sydney, Wardlock, 1968.

Jobe, Brock. "The Boston Furniture Industry 1720-1740." In *Boston Furniture of the Eighteenth Century,* edited by Walter Muir Whitehill, Brock Jobe, and Jonathan Fairbanks, pp. 3–48. Boston: Colonial Society of Massachusetts, 1974.

Kane, Patricia E. *Furniture of the New Haven Colony—The Seventeenth-Century Style.* New Haven: New Haven Colony Historical Society, 1973.

———. *300 Years of American Seating Furniture: Chairs and Beds from the Mabel Brady Garvan and Other Collections at Yale University.* Boston: New York Graphic Society, 1976.

Karpel, Bernard, ed. *Arts in America: A Bibliography.* 4 vols. Washington, D.C.: Smithsonian Institution Press, 1979.

Kauffman, Henry J. *Pennsylvania Dutch American Folk Art.* New York: American Studio Books, 1946.

Kaye, Myrna. "Eighteenth-Century Boston Furniture Craftsmen." In *Boston Furniture of the Eighteenth Century,* edited by Walter Muir Whitehill, Brock Jobe, and Jonathan Fairbanks, pp. 267–302. Boston: Colonial Society of Massachusetts, 1974.

Kebebian, Paul B., and Lipke, William C., eds. *Tools and Technologies: America's Wooden Age.* Burlington: Robert Hull Fleming Museum, University of Vermont, 1979.

Kenney, John Tarrant. *The Hitchcock Chair: The Story of a Connecticut Yankee—L. Hitchcock of Hitchcocks-ville—and an Account of the Restoration of This 19th Century Manufactory.* New York: Clarkson N. Potter, 1971.

Kettell, Russell Hawes. *The Pine Furniture of Early New England.* Garden City, New York: Doubleday, Doran and Co., 1929.

Kimball, Fiske. *The Creation of the Rococo Decorative Style.* Philadelphia: Philadelphia Museum of Art, 1943. Reprint. New York: Dover Publications, 1980.

———. *Mr. Samuel McIntire, Carver, the Architect of Salem.* Portland, Maine: Southworth-Anthoensen Press, 1940.

Kindig, Joseph K. III. *The Philadelphia Chair, 1685–1785.* York, Pennsylvania: Historical Society of York County, 1978.

Kirk, John T. *American Chairs: Queen Anne and Chippendale.* New York: Alfred A. Knopf, 1972.

———. *Connecticut Furniture, Seventeenth and Eighteenth Centuries.* Hartford: The Wadsworth Atheneum, 1967.

———. *Early American Furniture: How to Recognize, Evaluate, Buy & Care for the Most Beautiful Pieces—High Style, Country, Primitive & Rustic.* New York: Alfred A. Knopf, 1970.

Kouwenhoven, John, and Kaufmann, Edgar, Jr. *An Exhibition for Modern Living.* Detroit: Detroit Institute of Arts, 1949.

Labaree, Benjamin W., ed. *Samuel McIntire: A Bicentennial Symposium, 1757–1957.* Salem, Massachusetts: The Essex Institute, 1957.

Lea, Zilla Rider, ed. *The Ornamented Chair—Its Development in America (1700–1890).* Rutland, Vermont: Charles E. Tuttle, 1960.

Little, Nina Fletcher. *Country Arts in Early American Homes.* New York: E. P. Dutton, 1975.

———. *Neat and Tidy, Boxes and Their Contents Used in Early American Households.* New York: E. P. Dutton, 1980.

Lockwood, Luke Vincent. *Colonial Furniture in America.* 2 vols. New York: Charles Scribner's Sons, 1901. Rev eds., 1913, 1926 and 1951.

———. *The Furniture Collectors' Glossary.* New York: The Walpole Society, 1913. Reprint. New York: Da Capo Press, 1967.

———. *Three Centuries of Connecticut Furniture, 1635–1935.* Hartford: Tercentenary Commission of the State of Connecticut, 1935.

Loudon, John C. *An Encyclopaedia of Cottage, Farm and Villa Architecture and Furniture.* London: n. p., 1833.

Lovell, Margaretta Markle. "Boston Blockfront Furniture." In *Boston Furniture of the Eighteenth Century,* edited by Walter Muir Whitehill, Brock Jobe, and Jonathan Fairbanks, pp. 77–136. Boston: Colonial Society of Massachusetts, 1974.

Luther, Clair Franklin. *The Hadley Chest.* Hartford: Case, Lockwood & Brainard, 1935.

———. *Supplemental List of Hadley Chests Discovered Since Publication of the Book in 1935, Together with Changes in Ownership as Reported.* Hartford: Case, Lockwood & Brainard, 1938.

Lyle, Charles T. *New Jersey Arts and Crafts: The Colonial Expression.* Lincroft, New Jersey: Monmouth Museum, 1972.

Lyon, Irving Whitall, M.D. *The Colonial Furniture of New England: A Study of the Domestic Furniture in Use in the Seventeenth and Eighteenth Centuries.* Boston and New York: Houghton Mifflin and Co., 1891 and 1924. Reprint. New York: E. P. Dutton, 1977.

McClelland, Nancy. *Duncan Phyfe and the English Regency, 1795–1830.* New York: William R. Scott, 1939. Reprint. New York: Dover Publications, 1980.

McDermott, John Francis, ed. *Frenchmen and French Ways in the Mississippi Valley.* Urbana and Chicago: University of Illinois Press, 1969.

Madigan, Mary Jean Smith. *Eastlake-Influenced American Furniture, 1870–1890.* Yonkers, New York: The Hudson River Museum, 1973.

Mayhew, Edgar deN., and Myers, Minor, Jr. *A Documentary History of American Interiors: From the Colonial Era to 1915.* New York: Charles Scribner's Sons, 1980.

Meader, Robert F. W. *An Illustrated Guide to Shaker Furniture.* New York: Dover Publications, 1972.

Menten, Theodore, ed. *The Art Deco Style in Household Objects, Architecture, Sculpture, Graphics, Jewelry.* New York: Dover Publications, 1972.

Miller, Edgar G., Jr. *American Antique Furniture: A Book for Amateurs.* 2 vols. Baltimore: Lord Baltimore Press, 1937.

Miller, V. Isabelle. *Furniture by New York Cabinetmakers, 1650 to 1860.* New York: Museum of the City of New York, 1956.

Milley, John C., ed. *Treasures of Independence: Independence National Historical Park and Its Collections.* New York: Mayflower Books, 1980.

Montgomery, Charles F. *American Furniture: The Federal Period, in the Henry Francis du Pont Winterthur Museum.* New York: Viking Press, 1966.

———, **and Kane, Patricia E., eds.** *American Art: 1750–1800, Towards Independence.* Boston: New York Graphic Society, 1976.

Morse, John D., ed. *Country Cabinetwork and Simple City Furniture.* Charlottesville: The University Press of Virginia, 1970.

Myers, Minor, Jr., and Mayhew, Edgar deN. *New London County Furniture, 1640–1840.* New London, Connecticut: The Lyman Allyn Museum, 1974.

Naeve, Milo M. *The Classical Presence in American Art.* Chicago: The Art Institute of Chicago, 1978.

———. *The Way West: American Furniture in the Pikes Peak Region, 1872–1972.* Edited by Roberta McIntyre. Colorado Springs: Colorado Springs Fine Arts Center, 1972.

Nutting, Wallace. *Furniture of the Pilgrim Century (of American Origin), 1620–1720, with Maple and Pine to 1800, Including Colonial Utensils and Wrought-Iron House Hardware into the 19th Century.* Framingham, Massachusetts: Old America Company, Rev. ed., 1924.

———. *Furniture Treasury (Mostly of American Origin), All Periods of American Furniture with Some Foreign Examples in America, also American Hardware and Household Utensils.* 3 vols. Framingham, Massachusetts: Old America Company, 1928–33.

Ormond, Suzanne, and Irvine, Mary E. *Louisiana's Art Nouveau: The Crafts of the Newcomb Style.* Gretna, Louisiana: Pelican Publishing Co., 1976.

Ormsbee, Thomas H. *The Windsor Chair.* Great Neck, New York: Deerfield Books, 1962.

Ott, Joseph K., and others. *The John Brown House Loan Exhibition of Rhode Island Furniture, Including Some Notable Portraits, Chinese Export Porcelain & Other Items.* Providence: The Rhode Island Historical Society, 1965.

Otto, Celia Jackson. *American Furniture of the Nineteenth Century.* New York: Viking Press, 1965.

Page, John F. *The Decorative Arts of New Hampshire: A Sesquicentennial Exhibition.* Concord, New Hampshire: New Hampshire Historical Society, 1973.

———. *Litchfield County Furniture, 1730–1850.* Litchfield, Connecticut: Litchfield Historical Society, 1969.

———**, and Garvin, James L.** *Plain & Elegant, Rich & Common: Documented New Hampshire Furniture, 1750–1850.* Concord, New Hampshire: New Hampshire Historical Society, 1979.

Palmer, Brooks. *The Book of American Clocks.* New York: Macmillan, 1950.

Parsons, Charles S. *The Dunlaps and Their Furniture.* Manchester, New Hampshire: The Currier Gallery of Art, 1970.

Philadelphia Museum of Art. *Philadelphia: Three Centuries of American Art.* Philadelphia: Philadelphia Museum of Art, 1976.

Poesch, Jessie J. *Early Furniture of Louisiana, 1750–1830.* New Orleans: Louisiana State Museum, 1972.

Prime, Alfred Coxe. *The Arts & Crafts in Philadelphia, Maryland and South Carolina, 1721–1785.* Series 1, n.p.: The Walpole Society, 1929.

———. *The Arts & Crafts in Philadelphia, Maryland and South Carolina, 1786–1800.* Series 2, n.p.: The Walpole Society, 1932.

Quimby, Ian M.G., ed. *Arts of the Anglo-American Community in the Seventeenth Century.* Charlottesville: The University Press of Virginia, 1975.

———**, ed.** *Material Culture and the Study of American Life.* New York: W. W. Norton and Co., 1978.

———**, and Earl, Polly Anne, eds.** *Technological Innovation and the Decorative Arts.* Charlottesville: The University Press of Virginia, 1974.

Randall, Richard H., Jr. *American Furniture in the Museum of Fine Arts, Boston.* Boston: Museum of Fine Arts, 1965.

———. "Benjamin Frothingham." In *Boston Furniture of the Eighteenth Century,* edited by Walter Muir Whitehill, Brock Jobe, and Jonathan Fairbanks, pp. 223–250. Boston: Colonial Society of Massachusetts, 1974.

———. *The Decorative Arts of New Hampshire, 1725–1825.* Manchester, New Hampshire: The Currier Gallery of Art, 1964.

———. *The Furniture of H. H. Richardson.* Boston: Museum of Fine Arts, 1962.

Ray, Mary Lyn. *True Gospel Simplicity: Shaker Furniture in New Hampshire.* Concord, New Hampshire: New Hampshire Historical Society, 1974.

Rheims, Maurice. *The Flowering of Art Nouveau.* New York: Harry N. Abrams, 1966.

Rhode Island School of Design. *A Catalogue of an Exhibition of Paintings by Gilbert Stuart, Furniture by the Goddards and Townsends, and Silver by Rhode Island Silversmiths.* Providence: The Akerman-Standard Co., 1936.

Rice, Norman S. *New York Furniture Before 1840 in the Collection of the Albany Institute of History and Art.* Albany: Albany Institute of History and Art, 1962.

Rigby, Douglas and Elizabeth. *Lock, Stock and Barrel: The Story of Collecting.* Philadelphia, J. B. Lippincott, 1944.

Rovetti, Paul F., ed. *Simple Gifts: Hands to Work and Hearts to God.* Storrs, Connecticut: William Benton Museum of Art, 1978.

Sack, Albert. *Fine Points of Furniture, Early American.* New York: Crown Publishers, 1950.

[Sack, Harold; Albert M.; and Robert M.] *American Antiques from Israel Sack Collection.* 6 vols. Washington, D.C.; Highland House Publishers, n.d.–1979.

St. George, Robert Blair. *The Wrought Covenant: Source Material for the Study of Craftsmen and Community in Southeastern New England, 1620–1700.* Brockton, Massachusetts: Brockton Art Center, Fuller Memorial, 1979.

Saltar, Gordon. "New England Timbers. With an Annotated Bibliography." In *Boston Furniture of the Eighteenth Century,* edited by Walter Muir Whitehill, Brock Jobe, and Jonathan Fairbanks, pp. 251–264. Boston: Colonial Society of Massachusetts, 1974.

Saunders, Richard. *Collecting and Restoring Wicker Furniture.* New York: Crown Publishers, 1976.

Schiffer, Herbert F. and Peter B. *Miniature Antique Furniture.* Wynnewood, Pennsylvania: Livingston Publishing Co., 1973.

Schiffer, Margaret Berwind. *Chester County, Pennsylvania, Inventories, 1684–1850.* Exton, Pennsylvania: Schiffer Publishing, Ltd., 1975.

———. *Furniture and Its Makers of Chester County, Pennsylvania.* Philadelphia: University of Pennsylvania Press, 1966. 2nd rev. ed. Exton, Pennsylvania: Schiffer Publishing, Ltd., 1978.

Schiffer, Nancy and Herbert. *Woods We Live With: A Guide to the Identification of Wood in the Home.* Exton, Pennsylvania: Schiffer Publishing Ltd., 1977.

Schmutzler, Robert. *Art Nouveau.* Translated by Edouard Roditi. New York: Harry N. Abrams, 1962.

Schwartz, Marvin D. *American Interiors, 1675–1885: A Guide to the American Period Rooms in the Brooklyn Museum.* New York: The Brooklyn Museum, 1968.

———. *Victoriana: An Exhibition of the Arts of the Victorian Era in America.* New York: The Brooklyn Institute of Arts and Sciences, 1960.

———; **Stanek, Edward J.; and True, Douglas K.** *The Furniture of John Henry Belter and the Rococo Revival: An Inquiry into Nineteenth-Century Furniture Design Through a Study of the Gloria and Richard Manney Collection.* New York: E. P. Dutton, 1981.

Seale, William. *The Tasteful Interlude: American Interiors Through the Camera's Eye, 1860–1917.* New York: Praeger Publishers, 1975. 2nd rev. ed. Nashville: American Association for State and Local History, 1981.

Selz, Peter, ed. *Art Nouveau and Design at the Turn of the Century.* New York: The Museum of Modern Art, 1959.

Sembach, Klaus-Jurgen. *Style 1930.* Translated by Judith Filson. New York: Universe Books, 1971.

Shea, John G. *The American Shakers and Their Furniture, With Measured Drawings of Museum Classics.* New York: Van Nostrand Reinhold, 1971.

Sheraton, Thomas. *The Cabinet-Maker and Upholsterer's Drawing-Book.* 3rd rev. ed. London: T. Bensley, 1802. Reprint. Charles F. Montgomery and Wilfred P. Cole, eds. New York: Praeger Publishers, 1970.

Sikes, Jane E. *The Furniture Makers of Cincinnati, 1790–1849.* Cincinnati: privately printed, 1976.

Silvestro, Clement M.; Franco, Barbara; and others. *Masonic Symbols in American Decorative Arts.* Lexington, Massachusetts: Scottish Rite Masonic Museum of Our National Heritage, 1976.

Singleton, Esther. *The Furniture of Our Forefathers.* 2 vols. New York: Doubleday, Page and Co., 1900–1901.

Smith, George. *The Cabinet-Maker and Upholsterer's Guide: Being a Complete Drawing Book.* London: Jones and Co., 1826.

———. *Collection of Designs for Household Furniture and Interior Decoration.* London: J. Taylor, 1808. Reprint. Charles F. Montgomery and Benno M. Forman, eds. New York: Praeger Publishers, 1970.

Smith, Nancy A. *Old Furniture: Understanding the Craftsman's Art.* Indianapolis and New York: Bobbs-Merrill, 1975.

J. B. Speed Art Museum. *Kentucky Furniture.* Louisville: J. B. Speed Art Museum, 1974.

Spencer, Robin, and others. *The Aesthetic Movement and the Cult of Japan.* London: The Fine Arts Society, Ltd., 1972.

Sprigg, June. *By Shaker Hands: The Art and the World of the Shakers—The Furniture and Artifacts, and the Spirit and Precepts Embodied in Their Simplicity, Beauty, and Functional Practicality.* New York: Alfred A. Knopf, 1975.

Steinfeldt, Cecilia, and Stover, Donald Lewis. *Early Texas Furniture and Decorative Arts.* San Antonio: Trinity University Press, 1973.

Stillinger, Elizabeth. *The Antiquers: The Lives and Careers, the Deals, the Finds, the Collections of the Men and Women Who Were Responsible for the Changing Taste in American Antiques, 1850–1930.* New York: Alfred A. Knopf, 1980.

———. *The ANTIQUES Guide to Decorative Arts in America, 1600–1875.* New York: E. P. Dutton, 1972.

Stitt, Susan. *Museum of Early Southern Decorative Arts.* Winston-Salem, North Carolina: Museum of Early Southern Decorative Arts, Old Salem, Inc., 1972.

Stoneman, Vernon C. *John and Thomas Seymour, Cabinetmakers in Boston, 1794–1816.* Boston: Special Publications, 1959.

———. *A Supplement to John and Thomas Seymour, Cabinetmakers in Boston, 1794–1816.* Boston: Special Publications, 1965.

Stoudt, John Joseph. *Early Pennsylvania Arts and Crafts.* New York: A. S. Barnes, 1964. London: Thomas Yoseloff, Ltd., 1964.

Swan, Mabel Munson. *Samuel McIntire, Carver, and the Sandersons, Early Salem Cabinet Makers.* Salem, Massachusetts: Essex Institute, 1934.

Sweeney, John A. H. *Some Regional Characteristics in American Queen Anne Furniture.* Wilmington: Winterthur Museum, 1954.

———. *The Treasure House of Early American Rooms.* New York: Viking Press, 1963.

Taylor, Lonn, and Warren, David B. *Texas Furniture: The Cabinetmakers and Their Work, 1840–1880.* Austin: University of Texas Press, 1975.

Theus, Mrs. Charlton M. *How to Collect and Detect Antique Furniture, A Primer.* Savannah: privately printed, 1973.

———. *Savannah Furniture, 1735–1825.* Savannah: privately printed, 1967.

Tinkham, Sandra Shaffer, ed. *The Consolidated Catalog to the Index of American Design.* Teaneck, New Jersey: Somerset House, 1980.

Toller, Jane. *Papier-Mâché in Great Britain and America.* Newton, Massachusetts: Charles T. Branford, 1962.

Tracy, Berry B., and Gerdts, William H. *Classical America, 1815–1845.* Newark, New Jersey: The Newark Museum Association, 1963.

Tracy, Berry B.; Johnson, Marilynn; and others. *19th-Century America: Furniture and Other Decorative Arts, An Exhibition in Celebration of the Hundredth Anniversary of the Metropolitan Museum of Art.* New York: The Metropolitan Museum of Art, 1970.

Trent, Robert F. *Hearts and Crowns: Folk Chairs of the Connecticut Coast, 1720–1840, as Viewed in the Light of Henri*

Focillon's Introduction to Art Populaire. New Haven: New Haven Colony Historical Society, 1977.

Triggs, Oscar Lovell. *Chapters in the History of the Arts and Crafts Movement.* Chicago: The Bohemia Guild of the Industrial Art League, 1902.

University of Massachusetts Art Gallery. *The Connecticut Valley at Home: One Hundred Years of Domestic Art.* Amherst: University of Massachusetts Press, 1970.

van Ravenswaay, Charles. *The Anglo-American Cabinetmakers of Missouri, 1800–1850.* St. Louis: Missouri Historical Society, 1958.

———. *The Arts and Architecture of German Settlements in Missouri: A Survey of a Vanishing Culture.* Columbia, Missouri, and London: University of Missouri Press, 1977.

———. *The Creole Arts and Crafts of Upper Louisiana.* St. Louis: Missouri Historical Society, 1956.

Van Why, Joseph S., and MacFarland, Anne S. *A Selection of 19th-Century American Chairs.* Hartford: The Stowe-Day Foundation, 1973.

Vincent, Gilbert T. "The Bombé Furniture of Boston." In *Boston Furniture of the Eighteenth Century,* edited by Walter Muir Whitehill, Brock Jobe, and Jonathan Fairbanks, pp. 137–196. Boston: Colonial Society of Massachusetts, 1974.

Wainwright, Nicholas B. *Colonial Grandeur in Philadelphia: The House and Furniture of General John Cadwalader.* Philadephia: The Historical Society of Pennsylvania, 1964.

Walters, Betty Lawson. *Furniture Makers of Indiana, 1793 to 1850.* Indianapolis: Indiana Historical Society, 1972.

Ward, Gerald W. R., ed. *The Eye of the Beholder: Fakes, Replicas, and Alterations in American Art.* New Haven: Yale University Art Gallery, 1977.

Waring, Janet. *Early American Stencils on Walls and Furniture.* New York: William R. Scott, 1937.

Warren, David B. *Bayou Bend: American Furniture, Paintings and Silver from the Bayou Bend Collection.* Houston: The Museum of Fine Arts, 1975.

Welsch, Robert L.; Henning, Darrell; and Nelson, Marion J. *Norwegian-American Wood Carving of the Upper Midwest.* Decorah, Iowa: The Vesterheim, Norwegian-American Museum, 1978.

Wharton, Edith, and Codman, Ogden, Jr. *The Decoration of Houses.* 2nd ed. New York: Charles Scribner's Sons, 1902. Reprint. New York: W. W. Norton, 1978.

White, Margaret E. *The Decorative Arts of Early New Jersey.* Princeton: D. Van Nostrand Co., 1964.

———. *Early Furniture Made in New Jersey, 1690–1870.* Newark, New Jersey: The Newark Museum Association, 1958.

Whitley, Mrs. Wade Hampton (Edna Talbott). *A Checklist of Kentucky Cabinetmakers from 1775 to 1859.* Paris, Kentucky: privately printed, 1970.

Wilson, Richard Guy; Pilgrim, Dianne H.; and Murray, Richard N. *The American Renaissance, 1876–1917.* New York: The Brooklyn Museum, 1979.

Winchester, Alice. *How to Know American Antiques.* New York: Dodd, Mead & Co., 1951.

———, and the staff of *Antiques Magazine. The ANTIQUES Treasury of Furniture and Other Decorative Arts at Winterthur, Williamsburg, Sturbridge, Ford Museum, Cooperstown, Deerfield, Shelburne.* New York: E. P. Dutton, 1959.

———. *Collectors and Collections.* New York: *Antiques Magazine,* 1961.

———. *Living with Antiques.* New York: E. P. Dutton, 1963.

Winters, Robert E., Jr., ed. *North Carolina, 1700–1900.* Raleigh: North Carolina Museum of History, 1977.

Winterthur Museum. *Neoclassicism in the Decorative Arts: France, England and America.* Wilmington: Winterthur Museum, 1971.

Wright, Louis B., and others. *The Arts in America: The Colonial Period.* New York: Charles Scribner's Sons, 1966.

Yehia, Mary Ellen Hayward. "Ornamental Carving on Boston Furniture of the Chippendale Style." In *Boston Furniture of the Eighteenth Century,* edited by Walter Muir Whitehill, Brock Jobe, and Jonathan Fairbanks, pp. 197–222. Boston: Colonial Society of Massachusetts, 1974.

PERIODICALS

Ames, Kenneth L. "The Battle of the Sideboards." *Winterthur Portfolio 9* (1974): 1–27.

———. "Designed in France: Notes on the Transmission of French Style to America." *Winterthur Portfolio 12* (1977): 103–114.

———. "The Furniture of Fourdinois." *The Magazine Antiques* 110 (1976): 336–343.

———. "Grand Rapids Furniture at the Time of the Centennial." *Winterthur Portfolio 10* (1975): 23–50.

———. "The Rocking Chair in Nineteenth-Century America." *The Magazine Antiques* 103 (1973): 322–327.

Barbour, Frederick K. "Some Connecticut Case Furniture." *The Magazine Antiques* 83 (1963): 434–437.

Barnes, Jairus B. "Rococo Revival Furniture at the Western Reserve Historical Society." *The Magazine Antiques* 114 (1978): 788–793.

Bartlett, Lu. "John Shaw, Cabinetmaker of Annapolis." *The Magazine Antiques* 111 (1977): 362–377.

Beasley, Ellen. "Tennessee Cabinetmakers and Chairmakers Through 1840." *The Magazine Antiques* 100 (1971): 612–621.

Beckerdite, Luke. "City Meets the Country: The Work of Peter Eddleman, Cabinetmaker." *Journal of Early Southern Decorative Arts* 6 (1980): 59–73.

Berkeley, Henry J. "A Register of the Cabinetmakers and Allied Trades of Maryland as Shown by the Newspapers and Directories, 1746–1820." *Maryland Historical Magazine* 25 (1930): 1–29.

Bivins, John, Jr. "Baroque Elements in North Carolina Moravian Furniture." *Journal of Early Southern Decorative Arts* 2, no. 1 (1976): 38–63.

Blake, Channing. "Architects as Furniture Designers." *The Magazine Antiques* 109 (1976): 1042–1047.

———. "The Early Interiors of Carrère and Hastings." *The Magazine Antiques* 110 (1976): 344–351.

Bohdan, Carol Lorraine, and Volpe, Todd Mitchell. "The Furniture of Gustav Stickley. *The Magazine Antiques* 111 (1977): 984–989.

Bordes, Marilynn Johnson. "Reuben Swift, Cabinetmaker of New Bedford." *The Magazine Antiques* 112 (1977): 750–752.

Brazer, Esther Stevens. "The Early Boston Japanners." *The Magazine Antiques* 43 (1943): 208–211.

Brown, Michael K. "Scalloped-Top Furniture of the Connecticut River Valley." *The Magazine Antiques* 117 (1980): 1092–1099.

Buckley, Charles E. "Fine Federal Furniture Attributed to Portsmouth." *The Magazine Antiques* 83 (1963): 196–200.

———. "The Furniture of New Hampshire, A Bird's-Eye View from 1725 to 1825." *The Magazine Antiques* 86 (1964): 56–61.

Cantor, Jay. "When Wine Turns to Vinegar: The Critics' View of '19th-Century America.'" *Winterthur Portfolio 7* (1972): 1–28.

Carpenter, Ralph E., Jr. "Discoveries in Newport Furniture and Silver." *The Magazine Antiques* 68 (1955): 44–49.

———. "The Newport Exhibition." *The Magazine Antiques* 64 (1953): 38–45.

Carson, Marion S. "Henry Connelly and Ephraim Haines: Philadelphia Furniture Makers." *Philadelphia Museum Bulletin* 48 (1953): 35–47.

Catalano, Kathleen M. "Cabinetmaking in Philadelphia, 1820–1840: Transition from Craft to Industry." *Winterthur Portfolio 13* (1979): 81–138.

———, and Nylander, Richard C. "New Attributions to Adam Hains, Philadelphia Furniture Maker." *The Magazine Antiques* 117 (1980): 1112–1116.

Clunie, Margaret Burke. "Joseph True and the Piecework System in Salem." *The Magazine Antiques* 111 (1977): 1006–1013.

Comstock, Helen. "American Furniture in the Eighteenth Century." *The Connoisseur* 135 (1955): 63–71.

———. "The Bellflower in Furniture Design." *The Magazine Antiques* 68 (1955): 130–133.

———. "Cabinetmakers of the Norwich Area." *The Magazine Antiques* 87 (1965): 696–699.

———. "Frothingham and the Question of Attributions." *The Magazine Antiques* 63 (1953): 502–505.

———. "Furniture at the Forum, Regional Characteristics of American Furniture, II." *The Magazine Antiques* 55 (1949): 440.

———. "Furniture of Virginia, North Carolina, Georgia, and Kentucky." *The Magazine Antiques* 61 (1952): 58–100.

———. "An Ipswich Account Book, 1707–1762." *The Magazine Antiques* 66 (1954): 188–192.

———. "Rhode Island Block-Front Furniture." *The Connoisseur* 131 (1953): 91.

———."A Salem Secretary Attributed to William Appleton." *The Magazine Antiques* 89 (1966): 553–555.

———. "Southern Furniture Since 1952." *The Magazine Antiques* 91 (1967): 102–119.

Conger, Clement E. "Decorative Arts at the White House." *The Magazine Antiques* 116 (1979): 112–134.

———, **and Pool, Jane W.** "Some Eagle-Decorated Furniture at the Department of State." *The Magazine Antiques* 105 (1974): 1072–1081.

"Connecticut Cabinetmakers: Checklist up to 1820, Part I (A–L)." *Connecticut Historical Society Bulletin* 32 (1967): 97–144. "Part II (L–W)." 33 (1968): 1–40.

Cooper, Wendy A. "American Chairback Settees: Some Sources and Related Examples." *The American Art Journal* 9 (1977): 34–45.

———. "The Purchase of Furniture and Furnishings by John Brown, Providence Merchant, Part I, 1760–1788." *The Magazine Antiques* 103 (1973): 328–339. "Part II, 1788–1803." 103 (1973): 734–743.

"Country Furniture: A Symposium." *The Magazine Antiques* 93 (1968): 342–371.

Cromwell, Giles. "Andrew and Robert McKim: Windsor Chair Makers." *Journal of Early Southern Decorative Arts* 6, no. 1 (1980): 1–20.

Cummings, Abbott Lowell. "Notes on Furnishing the Seventeenth-Century House." *Old-Time New England* 46 (1956): 57–67.

Dahill, Betty. "The Sharrock Family: A Newly Discovered School of Cabinetmakers." *Journal of Early Southern Decorative Arts* 2, no. 2 (1976): 37–51.

Davidson, Ruth Bradbury. "American Gaming Tables." *The Magazine Antiques* 64 (1953): 294–296.

———. "Techniques of Furniture Decoration." *The Magazine Antiques* 93 (1968): 230–234.

Davies, Jane B. "Gothic Revival Furniture Designs of Alexander J. Davis." *The Magazine Antiques* 111 (1977): 1014–1027.

Deveikis, Peter M. "Hastings Warren: Vermont Cabinetmaker." *The Magazine Antiques* 101 (1972): 1037–1039.

DeVoe, Shirley Spaulding. "Candace Roberts, 1785–1806, Japanner and Ornamenter." *Connecticut Historical Society Bulletin* 27 (1962): 85–92.

Dorman, Charles G. "Delaware Cabinetmakers and Allied Artisans, 1655–1855." *Delaware History* 9 (1960): 111–217.

Downs, Joseph. "American Japanned Furniture." *Bulletin of the Metropolitan Museum of Art* 18 (1933): 42–48.

———. "American Japanned Furniture." *Bulletin of the Metropolitan Museum of Art* 25 (1940): 145–148.

———. "Derby and McIntire." *Metropolitan Museum of Art Bulletin* new series 6 (1947): 73–80.

———. "Furniture at the Forum, Regional Characteristics of American Furniture, I." *The Magazine Antiques* 55 (1949): 435–439.

———. "The Furniture of Goddard and Townsend." *The Magazine Antiques* 52 (1947): 427–431.

———. "John Cogswell, Cabinetmaker." *The Magazine Antiques* 61 (1952): 322–324.

Dulaney, William L. "Wallace Nutting: Collector and Entrepreneur." *Winterthur Portfolio 13* (1979): 47–60.

Elder, William Voss, III. "Maryland Furniture, 1760-1840." *The Magazine Antiques* 111 (1977): 354–361.

Erving, Henry Wood. "The Connecticut Chest." *Old-Time New England* 12 (1921): 14–18.

[Evans], Goyne, Nancy. "Francis Trumble of Philadelphia: Windsor Chair and Cabinetmaker." *Winterthur Portfolio One* (1964): 221–241.

Evans, Nancy Goyne. "The Genealogy of a Bookcase Desk." *Winterthur Portfolio 9* (1974): 213–222.

Fales, Martha Gandy. "Benjamin Ilsley, Cabinetmaker in Federal Portland." *The Magazine Antiques* 105 (1974): 1066-1067.

———. "The Shorts, Newburyport Cabinetmakers." *Essex Institute Historical Collections* 102 (1966): 220–240.

———, **and Fales, Dean A., Jr.** "Floral Carving on Early American Furniture." *The Magazine Antiques* 67 (1955): 316–320.

Farnam, Anne. "A.H. Davenport and Company, Boston Furniture Makers." *The Magazine Antiques* 109 (1976): 1048-1055.

———. "Essex County Furniture Carving: The Continuance of a Tradition." *Essex Institute Historical Collections* 116 (1980): 145–155.

———. "Furniture at the Essex Institute, Salem, Massachusetts." *The Magazine Antiques* 111 (1977): 958–973.

Faude, Wilson H. "Associate Artists and the American Renaissance in the Decorative Arts." *Winterthur Portfolio 10* (1975): 101–130.

Flannery, Margo C. "Richard Allison and the New York City Federal Style." *The Magazine Antiques* 103 (1973): 995–1001.

Forman, Benno M. "Continental Furniture Craftsmen in London: 1511–1625." *Furniture History* 7 (1971): 94–120.

———. "The Crown and York Chairs of Coastal Connecticut and the Work of the Durands of Milford." *The Magazine Antiques* 105 (1974): 1147–1154.

Franco, Barbara. "New York City Furniture Bought for Fountain Elms by James Watson Williams." *The Magazine Antiques* 104 (1973). 462–467.

Gaines, Edith. "The Robb Collection of American Furniture, Part I." *The Magazine Antiques* 92 (1967): 322–328. "Part II." 93 (1968): 484–489.

Garrett, Elisabeth Donaghy. "American Furniture in the DAR Museum." *The Magazine Antiques* 109 (1976): 750–759.

Garrett, Wendell D. "The Goddard and Townsend Joiners, Random Biographical Notes." *The Magazine Antiques* 94 (1968): 391–393.

———. "The Newport Cabinetmakers: A Corrected Check List." *The Magazine Antiques* 73 (1958): 558–561.

———. "Providence Cabinetmakers, Chairmakers, Upholsterers, and Allied Craftsmen, 1756–1838." *The Magazine Antiques* 90 (1966): 514–519.

Gilborn Craig. "Rustic Furniture in the Adirondacks, 1875–1925." *The Magazine Antiques* 109 (1976): 1212–1219.

Ginsburg, Benjamin. "Connecticut Cherry Furniture, With an Affinity for the Oriental." *The Magazine Antiques* 58 (1950): 274–276.

Golovin, Anne Castrodale. "Cabinetmakers and Chairmakers of Washington, D.C., 1791–1840." *The Magazine Antiques* 107 (1975): 898–922.

———. "Daniel Trotter: Eighteenth-Century Philadelphia Cabinetmaker." *Winterthur Portfolio 6* (1970): 151–184.

———. "William King, Jr., Georgetown Furniture Maker." *The Magazine Antiques* 111 (1977): 1032–1037.

Green, Henry D. "Furniture of the Georgia Piedmont Before 1830." *The Magazine Antiques* 110 (1976): 550–559.

Greene, Richard Lawrence. "Fertility Symbols on the Hadley Chests." *The Magazine Antiques* 112 (1977): 250–257.

Gusler, Wallace B. "The Arts of Shenandoah County, Virginia, 1770–1825." *Journal of Early Southern Decorative Arts* 5, no. 2 (1979): 6–35.

———. "Queen Anne Style Desks from the Virginia Piedmont." *The Magazine Antiques* 104 (1973): 665–673.

Hall, Elton W. "New Bedford Furniture: Check List of New Bedford Cabinetmakers and Related Craftsmen, 1792-1870." *The Magazine Antiques* 113 (1978): 1105–1127.

Hancock, Harold B. "Furniture Craftsmen in Delaware Records." *Winterthur Portfolio 9* (1974): 175–212.

Harlow, Henry J. "Decorated New England Furniture at Old Sturbridge Village." *The Magazine Antiques* 116 (1979): 860–871.

———. "Signed and Labeled New England Furniture at Old Sturbridge Village." *The Magazine Antiques* 116 (1979): 872–879.

Hauserman, Dianne D. "Alexander Roux and His 'Plain and Artistic Furniture.'" *The Magazine Antiques* 93 (1968): 210–217.

Hebb, Caroline. "A Distinctive Group of Early Vermont Painted Furniture." *The Magazine Antiques* 104 (1973): 458–461.

Heckscher, Morrison H. "The New York Serpentine Card Table." *The Magazine Antiques* 103 (1973): 974–983.

Held, Huyler. "Chests from Western Long Island." *The Magazine Antiques* 35 (1939): 14–15.

Hill, John H. "Furniture Designs of Henry W. Jenkins & Sons, Co." *Winterthur Portfolio 5* (1969): 154–187.

———. "The History and Technique of Japanning and the Restoration of the Pimm Highboy." *The American Art Journal* 8 (1976): 59–84.

Horton, Frank L. "Carved Furniture of the Albemarle: A Tie with Architecture." *Journal of Early Southern Decorative Arts* 1, no. 1 (1975): 14–20.

Hummel, Charles F. "Queen Anne and Chippendale Furniture in the Henry Francis du Pont Winterthur Museum, Part I." *The Magazine Antiques* 97 (1970): 896–903. "Part II." 98 (1970): 900–909. "Part III." 99 (1971): 98–107.

Johnston, Phillip. "Eighteenth- and Nineteenth-Century American Furniture at the Wadsworth Atheneum." *The Magazine Antiques* 115 (1979): 1016–1027.

Jones, Karen M. "American Furniture in the Milwaukee Art Center." *The Magazine Antiques* 111 (1977): 974–983.

Jones, N.D. "Norman Jones, Vermont Cabinetmaker." *The Magazine Antiques* 111 (1977): 1028–1031.

Kalec, Donald. "The Prairie School Furniture." *The Prairie School Review* 1 (1964): 5–21.

Kane, Patricia E. "American Furniture in the Yale University Art Gallery." *The Magazine Antiques* 117 (1980): 1314–1327.

———. "Furniture Owned by the Massachusetts Historical Society." *The Magazine Antiques* 109 (1976): 960–969.

———. "The Joiners of Seventeenth-Century Hartford County." *Connecticut Historical Society Bulletin* 35 (1970): 65–85.

Kaye, Myrna. "Marked Portsmouth Furniture." *The Magazine Antiques* 113 (1978): 1098–1104.

Kenney, Alice P., and Workman, Leslie J. "Ruins, Romance, and Reality, Medievalism in Anglo-American Imagination and Taste, 1750–1840." *Winterthur Portfolio 10* (1975): 131–164.

Keno, Leigh. "The Windsor-Chair Makers of Northampton, Massachusetts, 1790–1820." *The Magazine Antiques* 117 (1980): 1100–1107.

Keyes, Homes Eaton. "A Clue to New York Furniture." *The Magazine Antiques* 21 (1932): 122–123.

Kihn, Phyllis. "Ruggles and Dunbar, Looking Glass Manufacturers." *Connecticut Historical Society Bulletin* 25 (1960): 50–56.

Kimball, Fiske. "A Chest-on-Chest with Carving by Samuel McIntire." *Old-Time New England* 21 (1930): 87–89.

———. "The Estimate of McIntire." *The Magazine Antiques* 21 (1932): 23–25.

———. "Furniture Carvings by Samuel Field McIntire. I." *The Magazine Antiques* 18 (1930): 388–392. "II: Sofas." 18 (1930): 498–502. "III: Chairs." 19 (1931): 30–32. "IV: Other 'Carvers Pieces.'" 19 (1931): 117–119. "V: Case Pieces." 19 (1931): 207–210.

———. "Salem Furniture Makers. I: Nathaniel Appleton, Jr." *The Magazine Antiques* 24 (1933): 90–91. "II: Nehemiah Adams." 24 (1933): 218–220. "III: William Hook." 25 (1934): 144–146.

———. "Salem Secretaries and Their Makers." *The Magazine Antiques* 23 (1933): 168–170.

———. "The Sources of the 'Philadelphia Chippendale.'" *Pennsylvania Museum Bulletin* 21 (1926): 183–193.

———, **and Donnell, Edna.** "The Creators of the Chippendale Style." *Metropolitan Museum Studies* (1929).

Kirk, John T. "The Distinctive Character of Connecticut Furniture." *The Magazine Antiques* 92 (1967): 524–529.

Maga, Robert. "Elbert Hubbard's Roycrofters as Artist-Craftsmen." *Winterthur Portfolio 3* (1967): 67–82.

Landman, Hedy B. "The Pendleton House at the Museum of Art, Rhode Island School of Design." *The Magazine Antiques* 107 (1975): 923–938.

Lichten, Frances. "A Masterpiece of Pennsylvania-German Furniture." *The Magazine Antiques* 77 (1960): 176–178.

Little, Nina Fletcher. "Livery Cupboards in New England." *The Magazine Antiques* 84 (1963): 710–713.

Lockwood, Luke Vincent. "The Wesleyan Wainscot Chair." *The Magazine Antiques* 17 (1930): 519.

Lyon, Irving, Phillips, M.D. "The Cupboard of Ephraim and Hannah Foster of North Andover, Massachusetts." *Old-Time New England* 28 (1938): 123–125.

———. "The Oak Furniture of Ipswich, Massachusetts, Part I: Florid Type. Dennis-Family Furniture." *The Magazine Antiques* 32 (1937): 230–233. "Part II: Florid Type. Miscellaneous Examples." 32 (1937): 298–301. "Part III: Florid Type, Scroll Detail." 33 (1938): 73–75. "Part IV: The Small-Panel Type." 33 (1938): 198–203. "Part V: Small-Panel Type Affiliates." 33 (1938) 322–325. "Part VI: Other Affiliates: A Group Characterized by Geometrical Panels." 34 (1938): 79–81.

———. "A Pedigreed Cupboard Dated 1681 and Initialed ${}^{I}A^{E}$ for John and Elizabeth Appleton of Ipswich, Massachusetts." *Old-Time New England* 28 (1938): 119–122.

McElroy, Cathryn J. "Furniture in Philadelphia: The First Fifty Years." *Winterthur Portfolio 13* (1979): 61–80.

Madigan, Mary Jean Smith. "The Influence of Charles Locke Eastlake on American Furniture Manufacture, 1870–90." *Winterthur Portfolio 10* (1975): 1–22.

Mather, Christine. "The Arts of the Spanish in New Mexico." *The Magazine Antiques* 113 (1978): 422–431.

Monahon, Eleanore Bradford. "Providence Cabinetmakers." *Rhode Island History* 23 (1964): 1–22.

———. "Providence Cabinetmakers of the Eighteenth and Early Nineteenth Centuries." *The Magazine Antiques* 87 (1965): 573–579.

———. "The Rawson Family of Cabinetmakers in Providence, Rhode Island." *The Magazine Antiques* 118 (1980): 134–147.

———. "Thomas Howard, Jr., Providence Cabinetmaker." *The Magazine Antiques* 87 (1965): 702–704.

Montgomery, Charles F. "John Needles—Baltimore Cabinetmaker." *The Magazine Antiques* 65 (1954): 292–295.

———. "Tambour Desks and the Work of William Appleton of Salem." *The Walpole Society Note Book,* 1965. Reprint. Portland, Maine: Southworth-Anthoensen Press, 1967.

Mooney, James E. "Furniture at the Historical Society of Pennsylvania." *The Magazine Antiques* 113 (1978): 1034–1043.

Mooz, R. Peter. "The Origins of Newport Block-Front Furniture Design." *The Magazine Antiques* 99 (1971): 882–886.

———, **and Weekley, Carolyn J.** "American Furniture at the Virginia Museum of Fine Arts." *The Magazine Antiques* 113 (1978): 1052–1063.

Naeve, Milo M. "Daniel Trotter and his Ladder-Back Chairs." *The Magazine Antiques* 76 (1959): 442–445.

Nutting, Wallace. "A Sidelight on John Goddard." *The Magazine Antiques* 30 (1936): 120–121.

———. "Turnings on Early American Furniture, Part I." *The Magazine Antiques* 3 (1923): 212–215. "Part II." 3 (1923): 275–278.

[Nylander], Giffen, Jane C. "New Hampshire Cabinetmakers and Allied Craftsmen, 1790–1850: A Check List." *The Magazine Antiques* 94 (1968): 78–87.

Nylander, Jane. "Vose and Coats, Cabinetmakers." *Old-Time New England* 64 (1974): 87–91.

O'Donnell, Patricia Chapin. "Grisaille Decorated *Kasten* of New York." *The Magazine Antiques* 117 (1980): 1108–1111.

Ott, Joseph K. "Exports of Furniture, Chaises, and Other Wooden Forms from Providence and Newport, 1783–1795." *The Magazine Antiques* 107 (1975): 135–141.

———. "John Townsend, A Chair, Two Tables." *The Magazine Antiques* 94 (1968): 388–390.

———. "More Notes on Rhode Island Cabinetmakers and Their Work." *Rhode Island History* 28 (1969): 49–52.

———. "Notes on Rhode Island Cabinetmakers." *The Magazine Antiques* 87 (1965): 572.

———. "Recent Discoveries Among Rhode Island Cabinetmakers and Their Work." *Rhode Island History* 28 (1969): 3–25.

———. "Rhode Island Furniture Exports 1783–1800, Including Information on Chaises, Buildings, Other Woodenware, and Trade Practices." *Rhode Island History* 36 (1977): 3–14.

———. "Some Rhode Island Furniture." *The Magazine Antiques* 107 (1975): 940–951.

———. "Still More Notes on Rhode Island Cabinetmakers and Allied Craftsmen." *Rhode Island History* 28 (1969): 111–121.

Otto, Celia Jackson. "Pillar and Scroll: The Greek Revival Furniture of the 1830's." *The Magazine Antiques* 81 (1962): 504–507.

Page, John F. "Documented New Hampshire Furniture, 1750–1850." *The Magazine Antiques* 115 (1979): 1004–1015.

Park, Helen. "The Seventeenth-Century Furniture of Essex County and Its Makers." *The Magazine Antiques* 78 (1960): 350–355.

———. "Thomas Dennis, Ipswich Joiner: A Re-Examination." *The Magazine Antiques* 78 (1960): 40–44.

Pearce, John N., and Lorraine W. "More on the Meeks Cabinetmakers." *The Magazine Antiques* 90 (1966): 69–73.

———, **and Smith, Robert C.** "The Meeks Family of Cabinetmakers." *The Magazine Antiques* 85 (1964): 414–420.

Pearce, Lorraine Waxman. "The Distinctive Character of the Work of Lannuier." *The Magazine Antiques* 86 (1964): 712–717.

———. "Fine Federal Furniture at the White House." *The Magazine Antiques* 82 (1962): 273–277.

———. "The Work of Charles Honoré Lannuier, French Cabinetmaker in New York." *Maryland Historical Society Magazine* 55 (1960): 14–29.

Pierce, Donald C. "American Painted Furniture at the Brooklyn Museum, 1675–1875." *The Magazine Antiques* 110 (1976): 1292–1299.

———. "Mitchell and Rammelsberg, Cincinnati Furniture Manufacturers, 1847–1881." *Winterthur Portfolio 13* (1979): 209–230.

———. "New York Furniture at the Brooklyn Museum." *The Magazine Antiques* 115 (1979): 994–1003.

Poesch, Jessie J. "Early Louisiana *Armoires.*" *The Magazine Antiques* 94 (1968): 196–205.

———. "Furniture of the River Road Plantations in Louisiana." *The Magazine Antiques* 111 (1977): 1184–1193.

Powell, Lydia. "The Influence of English Design on American Furniture, Part I—The Earlier XVIIth Century." *Apollo* 67 (1958): 191–195. "Part II—The Late XVIIth and Early XVIIIth Century." 68 (1958): 35–38. "Part III—The Late XVIIIth Century." 68 (1958): 104–108. "Part IV—Philadelphia 'Chippendale.'" 68 (1958): 175–181. "Part V—'Chippendale' in New York and New England." 69 (1959): 38–43. "Part VI—The Early Federal Period." 70 (1959): 45–50.

Prown, Jules David. "Style as Evidence." *Winterthur Portfolio 15* (1980): 197–210.

Randall, Richard H., Jr. "'Boston Chairs.'" *Old-Time New England* 54 (1963): 12–20.

———. "An Eighteenth Century Partnership." *The Art Quarterly* 23 (1960): 152–161.

———. "George Bright, Cabinetmaker." *The Art Quarterly* 27 (1964): 134–149.

———. "Seymour Furniture Problems." *Boston Museum of Fine Arts Bulletin* 57 (1959): 103–113.

———. "Sources of the Empire Style." *The Magazine Antiques* 83 (1963): 452–453.

———. "William Randall, Boston Japanner." *The Magazine Antiques* 105 (1974): 1127–1131.

———. "Works of Boston Cabinetmakers, 1795–1825, Part I." *The Magazine Antiques* 81 (1962): 186–189. "Part II." 81 (1962): 412–415.

———, and McElman, Martha. "Ebenezer Hartshorne, Cabinetmaker." *The Magazine Antiques* 87 (1965): 78–79.

Rauschenberg, Bradford L. "The Royal Governor's Chair: Evidence of the Furnishing of South Carolina's First State House." *Journal of Early Southern Decorative Arts* 6, no. 2 (1980): 1–32.

———. "Two Outstanding Virginia Chairs." *Journal of Early Southern Decorative Arts* 2, no. 2 (1976): 1–23.

Ray, Mary Lyn. "A Reappraisal of Shaker Furniture and Society." *Winterthur Portfolio 8* (1973): 107–132.

Rhoades, Elizabeth, and Jobe, Brock. "Recent Discoveries in Boston Japanned Furniture." *The Magazine Antiques* 105 (1974): 1082–1091.

Richards, Nancy E. "Furniture of the Lower Connecticut River Valley: The Hartford Area, 1785–1810." *Winterthur Portfolio 4* (1968): 1–26.

Ring, Betty. "Peter Grinnell and Son: Merchant-Craftsmen of Providence, Rhode Island." *The Magazine Antiques* 117 (1980): 212–220.

Robinson, Olive Crittendon. "The Decorated Chairs of the 1800's." *The Antiques Journal* 18 (1963): 8–9.

———. "Signed Stenciled Chairs of W.P. Eaton." *The Magazine Antiques* 56 (1949): 112–113.

Rogers, M.R. "David Poignand, Cabinet Maker." *Bulletin of the City Art Museum, St. Louis* 1 (1957): 5–9.

Roth, Rodris. "American Art, the Colonial Revival and 'Centennial Furniture.'" *The Art Quarterly* 27 (1964): 57–81.

———. "A Patent Model by John Henry Belter." *The Magazine Antiques* 111 (1977): 1038–1040.

Sack, Harold."Authenticity in American Furniture." *Art in America* 48 (1960): 72–75.

———. "Restorations in American Furniture—What Is Acceptable?" *The Magazine Antiques* 89 (1966): 116–121.

St. George, Robert Blair. "Style and Structure in the Joinery of Dedham and Medfield, Massachusetts, 1635–1685." *Winterthur Portfolio 13* (1979): 1–46.

Saunders, Richard H. "Collecting American Decorative Arts in New England, Part I, 1793–1876." *The Magazine Antiques* 109 (1976): 996–1003. "Part II, 1876–1910." 110 (1976): 754–763.

Schopfer, Jean. "L'Art Nouveau: An Argument and Defense." Translated by Irene Sargent. *The Craftsman* 4 (1903): 229–238.

Schwartz, Marvin D. "American Painted Furniture Before the Classical Revival." *The Magazine Antiques* 69 (1956): 342–345.

Scott, G.W., Jr. "Lancaster and Other Pennsylvania Furniture." *The Magazine Antiques* 115 (1979): 984–993.

Scott, Kenneth, and Kettell, Russell H. "Joseph Hosmer, Cabinetmaker, His Life, His Work." *The Magazine Antiques* 73 (1958): 356–359.

Scotti, N. David. "Notes on Rhode Island Cabinetmakers." *The Magazine Antiques* 87 (1965): 572.

Shettleworth, Earle G., Jr. "The Radford Brothers: Portland Cabinetmakers of the Federal Period." *The Magazine Antiques* 106 (1974): 285–289.

Smith, Michael O. "North Carolina Furniture, 1700-1900." *The Magazine Antiques* 115 (1979): 1266–1277.

Smith, Robert C. "Architecture and Sculpture in Nineteenth-Century Mirror Frames." *The Magazine Antiques* 109 (1976): 350–359.

———. "Finial Busts on Eighteenth-Century Philadelphia Furniture." *The Magazine Antiques* 100 (1971): 900–905.

———. "The Furniture of Anthony G. Quervelle, Part I: The Pier Tables." *The Magazine Antiques* 103 (1973): 984–994. "Part II: The Pedestal Tables." 104 (1973): 90–99. "Part III: The Worktables." 104 (1973): 260–268. "Part IV: Some Case Pieces." 105 (1974): 180–193. "Part V: Sofas, Chairs, and Beds." 105 (1974): 512–521.

———. "Furniture of the Eclectic Decades, 1870–1900." *The Magazine Antiques* 76 (1959): 50–53.

———. "'Good Taste' in Nineteenth-Century Furniture." *The Magazine Antiques* 76 (1959): 342–345.

———. "Gothic and Elizabethan Revival Furniture, 1800–1850." *The Magazine Antiques* 75 (1959): 272–276.

———. "Key Pieces of Federal Furniture." *The Magazine Antiques* 72 (1957): 240–243.

———. "Late Classical Furniture in the United States, 1820–1850." *The Magazine Antiques* 74 (1958): 519–523.

———. "A Philadelphia Desk-and-Bookcase from Chippendale's *Director*." *The Magazine Antiques* 103 (1973): 128–135.

———. "Philadelphia Empire Furniture by Antoine Gabriel Quervelle." *The Magazine Antiques* 86 (1964): 304–309.

———. "Rococo Revival Furniture, 1850–1870." *The Magazine Antiques* 75 (1959): 470–475.

Snow, Julia D. Sophronia. "Daniel Clay, Cabinetmaker of Greenfield." *The Magazine Antiques* 25 (1934): 138–139.

Snyder, John J., Jr. "The Bachman Attributions: A Reconsideration." *The Magazine Antiques* 105 (1974): 1056–1065.

———. "John Shearer, Joiner of Martinsburgh." *Journal of Early Southern Decorative Arts* 5, no. 1 (1979): 1–25.

Somerville, Romaine S. "Furniture at the Maryland Historical Society." *The Magazine Antiques* 109 (1976): 970–989.

Sommer, Frank. "John F. Watson: First Historian of American Decorative Arts." *The Magazine Antiques* 83 (1963): 300–303.

Sprigg, June. "Marked Shaker Furnishings." *The Magazine Antiques* 115 (1979): 1048–1058.

Stickley, Gustav. "The Structural Style in Cabinet-Making." *The House Beautiful* 15 (1903): 19–23.

Stockwell, David. "Aesop's Fables on Philadelphia Furniture." *The Magazine Antiques* 60 (1951): 522–525.

———. "Irish Influence in Pennsylvania Queen Anne Furniture." *The Magazine Antiques* 79 (1961): 269–271.

———. "Notes on the Construction of Philadelphia Cabriole Chairs." *The Magazine Antiques* 58 (1950): 286–288.

Stone, Stanley. "Documented Newport Furniture: A John Goddard Desk and John Townsend Document Cabinet in the Collection of Mr. and Mrs. Stanley Stone." *The Magazine Antiques* 103 (1973): 319–321.

———. "Rhode Island Furniture at Chipstone, Part I." *The Magazine Antiques* 91 (1967): 207–213. "Part II." 91 (1967): 508–513.

Stoneman, Vernon C. "The Pedimented Tambour Desks of the Seymours." *The Magazine Antiques* 74 (1958): 222–225.

Streifthau, Donna. "Cincinnati Cabinet- and Chairmakers, 1819–1830." *The Magazine Antiques* 99 (1971): 896–905.

Strickland, Peter L.L. "Documented Philadelphia Looking Glasses, 1800–1850." *The Magazine Antiques* 109 (1976): 784–794.

———. "Furniture by the Lejambre Family of Philadelphia." *The Magazine Antiques* 113 (1978): 600–613.

Swan, Mabel Munson. "Boston's Carvers and Joiners, Part I: Pre-Revolutionary." *The Magazine Antiques* 53 (1948): 198–201. "Part II: Post-Revolutionary." 53 (1948): 281–285.

———. "Elijah and Jacob Sanderson, Early Salem Cabinetmakers." *Essex Institute Historical Collections* 70 (1934): 323–364.

———. "Furniture of the Boston Tories." *The Magazine Antiques* 41 (1942): 186–189.

———. "Furnituremakers of Charlestown." *The Magazine Antiques* 46 (1944): 203–206.

———. "The Goddard and Townsend Joiners, Part I." *The Magazine Antiques* 49 (1946): 228–231. "Part II." 49 (1946): 292–295.

———. "John Goddard's Sons." *The Magazine Antiques* 57 (1950): 448–449.

———. "John Ritto Penniman." *The Magazine Antiques* 39 (1941): 246–248.

———. "The Johnstons and the Reas—Japanners." *The Magazine Antiques* 43 (1943): 211–213.

———. "McIntire: Check and Countercheck." *The Magazine Antiques* 21 (1932): 86–87.

———. "McIntire Vindicated: Fresh Evidence of the Furniture Carvers of Salem." *The Magazine Antiques* 26 (1934): 130–132.

———. "Newburyport Furnituremakers." *The Magazine Antiques* 47 (1945): 222–225.

———. "A Revised Estimate of McIntire." *The Magazine Antiques* 20 (1931): 338–343.

———. "Some Men from Medway." *The Magazine Antiques* 17 (1930): 417–421.

Symonds, R.W. "English Furniture and Colonial American Furniture—A Contrast." *The Burlington Magazine* 78 (1941): 182–187.

Talbott, Page. "Boston Empire Furniture. Part I." *The Magazine Antiques* 107 (1975): 878–887. "Part II." 109 (1976): 1004–1013.

Trent, Robert Francis. "The Endicott Chairs." *Essex Institute Historical Collections* 114 (1978): 103–119.

———. "A History for the Essex Institute Turkey-Work Couch." *Essex Institute Historical Collections* 113 (1977): 29–37.

van Ravenswaay, Charles. "The Forgotten Arts and Crafts of Colonial Louisiana." *The Magazine Antiques* 64 (1953): 192–195.

———. "Missouri River German Settlements, Part II: The Decorative Arts, 1831–1900." *The Magazine Antiques* 113 (1978): 394–409.

Walters, Betty Lawson. "The King of Desks, Wooten's Patent Secretary." *Smithsonian Institution Studies in History and Technology* 3 (1969).

Warren, William L. "Were the Guilford Chests Made in Saybrook? Part I." *Connecticut Historical Society Bulletin* 23 (1958): 1–10. "Part II: More About Painted Chests." 23 (1958): 50–60.

Waters, Deborah Dependahl. "Wares and Chairs: A Reappraisal of the Documents." *Winterthur Portfolio 13* (1979): 161–174.

Weil, Martin Eli. "A Cabinetmaker's Price Book." *Winterthur Portfolio 13* (1979): 175–192.

Whallon, Arthur. "Indiana Cabinetmakers and Allied Craftsmen, 1815–1860." *The Magazine Antiques* 98 (1970): 118–125.

Winchester, Alice, and others. "Southern Furniture, 1640–1820." *The Magazine Antiques* 61 (1952): 38–100.

Wright, Edward, ed. "John Needles (1786–1878): An Autobiography." *Quaker History* 58 (1969): 3–21.

Wright, R. Lewis. "The Johnsons: Chairmaking in Mecklenburg County, Virginia." *The Journal of Early Southern Decorative Arts* 6, no. 2 (1980): 33–47.

Yehia, Mary Ellen. "Chairs of the Masses: A Brief History of the L. White Chair Company, Boston, Massachusetts." *Old-Time New England* 63 (1972): 33–44.

Young, M. Ada. "Five Secretaries and the Cogswells." *The Magazine Antiques* 88 (1965): 478–485.

Zimmerman, Philip D. "A Methodological Study in the Identification of Some Important Philadelphia Chippendale Furniture." *Winterthur Portfolio 13* (1979): 193–208.

Index

D

E